COGNITIVE PSYCHOLOGY
A Student's Handbook

Michael W. Eysenck
Royal Holloway and Bedford New College
London University

Mark T. Keane
University of Wales College of Cardiff

 LAWRENCE ERLBAUM ASSOCIATES, PUBLISHERS
Hove and London (UK)   Hillsdale (USA)

Copyright © 1990 by Lawrence Erlbaum Associates Ltd.
   All rights reserved. No part of this book may be reproduced in any
   form, by photostat, microform, retrieval system, or any other
   means without the prior written permission of the publisher.

Reprinted 1990, 1991

Lawrence Erlbaum Associates Ltd., Publishers
27 Palmeira Mansions
Church Road
Hove
East Sussex, BN3 2FA
United Kingdom

British Library Cataloguing in Publication Data

Eysenck, Michael W.
   Cognitive psychology : a student's handbook
   1. Cognitive psychology
   I. Title   II. Keane, Mark T.
   153

   ISBN 0-86377-153-X
   ISBN 0-86377-154-8 (Pbk)

Typeset by Litho Link Ltd., Welshpool, Powys
Printed by BPCC Wheatons, Exeter

To my son Willie with love
(M.W.E)

To those of my generation
who have spread the grey wing upon every tide
(M.T.K)

Everything should be made as simple as possible, but not simpler.

Albert Einstein

CONTENTS

PREFACE

This book had its origins in a very pleasant lunch at Frederick's, which is a stylish restaurant in Islington, North London. Mike Forster, the supremo of Erlbaum U.K., gently suggested to the first author that a second edition of *A handbook of cognitive psychology* would be a good idea. The first author politely declined because of the work that would be involved. However, he softened in his attitude when Mike Forster suggested that the book might be co-authored. Some time later, the first author, the second author, and Mike Forster all had a very pleasant lunch at Frederick's, and the project came alive.

The Preface of *A handbook of cognitive psychology* made it clear why it is difficult to write a textbook of cognitive psychology: "One of the more intractable problems that any author has to face up to when attempting to chart the progress of cognitive psychology is the extremely diverse and sprawling nature of the current scene. What we may loosely term the 'cognitive approach' is to be found increasingly in such disparate areas as neuropsychology, artificial intelligence, applied and 'real-life' research, developmental psychology, and social psychology." During the six years intervening between the writing of *A handbook of cognitive psychology* and the writing of this book, that problem has become even more intractable. Indeed, we are both firmly of the opinion that the proliferation of cognitive psychology has been so great that it is now impossible to provide a comprehensive coverage of cognitive psychology within the covers of a single book.

How have the authors of this book responded to the challenge of writing about the mushrooming area of cognitive psychology? In essence, the approach we have taken is to focus on three major approaches within cognitive psychology: mainstream cognitive psychology; cognitive science; and cognitive neuropsychology. By so doing, we hope that we have been able to impose some order on what might otherwise appear somewhat chaotic.

In doing this we have been guided by the philosophy adopted in the first handbook. That is, the aim has been to provide an introduction to cognitive psychology that is comprehensible to undergraduates and, at the same time, to make the work sufficiently deep for those who want to go further into the subject. It is this philosophy that we have tried to capture in the subtitle of the book; the book should act as a source book or handbook for students.

We are very grateful to several people for reading an entire draft of this book and offering valuable advice on how it might be improved. They include Gillian Cohen, Andy Ellis, Al Parkin, Trevor Hartley, R.Q. Goodwin, and Ann Colley. Their expertise has helped us to fill some of the lacunae that they spotted in the first draft. We would also like to thank all those who commented on various chapters: Chris Barry, Martin Braine, Mike Brayshaw, Ruth Byrne, Patricia Cheng, Peter Cheng, Martin Conway, John Domingue, Marc Eisenstadt, Dedre Gentner, Ken Gilhooly, Richard Griggs, Pete Hampson, James Hampton, Nigel Harvey, Tony Hasemer, Hank Kahney, George Kiss, Nick McDonald, Carol McGuinness, Enrico Motta, Tim Rajan, John Richardson, Yvonne Rogers, David Shanks, Bob Sternberg, and Arthur Stutt.

The first author would like to express profound gratitude to his wife Christine and to his three children (Fleur, Willie, and Juliet) for the tolerance and understanding they all showed while he was locked away working on the Macintosh word processor in his study at home. However, there were occasions when Fleur and Willie made it clear that they regarded playing MacGames on the word processor as even more important than allowing Daddy to get on with writing this book.

The second author would like to thank Ruth Byrne for her constant friendship and his parents Joe Keane and Maureen Keane for putting up with him. He would also like to thank the Human Cognition Research Laboratory at The Open University for funding him in a Post-Doctoral Fellowship while he was writing the book. Thanks should also go to the motorised fan which helped him survive a hot summer's writing.

Mike Eysenck & Mark Keane   November, 1989

Chapter One

INTRODUCTION

COGNITIVE PSYCHOLOGY AS A SCIENCE

As our understanding of the world and space has advanced in the latter part of the 20th century, we have turned (somewhat belatedly) towards attempting to understand each other and our mental space. In scientific circles, this has been marked by a rapid increase in research in cognitive psychology and by the emergence of cognitive science as a unifying programme for studying the mind. In the popular media, there are numerous books, films, and television programmes on the more accessible aspects of cognitive research. However, cognitive psychology's coming out has not been easy. Like a self-conscious adolescent under the watchful eye of disapproving parents, it has had problems finding its identity, especially its identity as a scientific enterprise.

If the health of an academic discipline can be judged by the number of its adherents, then cognitive psychology is certainly thriving. In a fairly recent survey of academic psychologists in America, it was found that over three-quarters of them claimed to be cognitive psychologists! The size of this army marching under the cognitive psychology banner may be due, in large part, to the increasing breadth with which the term is used. Virtually all of those interested in perception, learning, memory, language, concept formation, problem solving, or thinking call themselves cognitive psychologists, despite the great diversity of experimental and theoretical approaches to be found in these areas.

One way of understanding contemporary cognitive psychology is to consider it in its historical context. There have been substantial changes within psychology during this century, and these changes are related to changing conceptualisations of science. The traditional view of science, which parallels the views of the man in the street, has three central tenets:

- it maintains that whatever science is, it is *objective*;
- this objectivity is considered to be exemplified by cool-headed scientists who record the facts about nature through *observation* and *experimentation*;
- it sees scientific knowledge as the result of the amalgamation of these facts into law-like *generalisations*.

According to this perspective, the scientist's task is no more complicated than measuring the temperature of boiling water repeatedly until enough "facts" have been amassed to form the generalisation, "All water boils at 100° centigrade." However, whereas this approach may seem applicable to the physical sciences such as chemistry and physics, it leaves many other sciences like psychology and sociology out in the cold. At least it did until Behaviourism, one of the parents of cognitive psychology, made psychology fit this view of science.

Behaviourism was influenced by an extreme version of this traditional view of science called *logical positivism*. Logical positivists (e.g. Ayer; Carnap) maintained that theories were only to be justified by an appeal to observed facts, and that theoretical constructs were meaningful only to the extent that they could be observed. This view was implemented by some Behaviourists such as Watson and Skinner, who formed a "scientific psychology" by admitting only observable entities and rejecting the use of hypothetical mental constructs. In this approach, the emphasis was on the relationship between observable stimuli (i.e. aspects of the situation) and observable responses (i.e. aspects of the organism's behaviour).

What this meant in practice can be seen if we consider classical conditioning as studied by Pavlov. For example, dogs naturally salivate (a response) when they see food (a stimulus). If a tone (a stimulus) is presented several times shortly before food, then it acquires the power to produce salivation. This can be explained by assuming that one stimulus (the tone) can substitute for another (the food), without really considering what is happening between stimulus and response.

Skinner (1971) was one Behaviourist who was strongly influenced by the logical positivist view of science. He drew an analogy between early physics and 20th-century psychology to illustrate his views, pointing out that the early Greeks knew a little about physics and psychology. He noted that Aristotle talked of physical forces as hypothetical, anthropomorphic states (anthropomorphism involves attributing human characteristics to nonhuman entities). For example, Aristotle suggested that a falling body accelerates because it becomes more jubilant at finding itself nearer home. According to Skinner (1971), physics has progressed beyond these early views, whereas psychology has not. Why is there this difference? Physics progressed because it replaced its unobservable anthropomorphisms with mathematical relationships and because it has increasingly relied on observation and experimentation. Psychology has failed to progress because it has not adopted the same strategy.

Cognitive psychology arose out of this historical context primarily because of two major developments. Firstly, at a very general level, the traditional view of science was undermined in a manner which liberated cognitive psychology to form its own scientific identity. Secondly, Behaviourism simply failed to measure up to the job of being a satisfactory science of human cognition, and so fresh ideas started to spring up on both sides of the Atlantic.

Many of the limitations of Behaviourism spring from its reliance on observable stimuli and responses. For example, suppose we present someone with a difficult problem (the stimulus) and wait patiently for 20 minutes until they produce the solution (the response). It is blatantly obvious here that an exclusive focus on observable stimuli and responses is totally uninformative about what is really of interest (i.e. the thought processes and strategies involved in problem solution).

However, the emphasis which Behaviourists placed on observable phenomena is still detectable in contemporary cognitive psychology. As the cognitive psychologist George Miller humorously remarked, "Some of my friends—and I won't name names—would not believe that people had two arms and two legs unless you could do an experiment proving it" (Baars, 1986, p. 217).

Changing Views of Science

Nearly all of the fundamental tenets of the traditional view of science have been savaged by 20th-century philosophers of science (mainly Karl Popper, Thomas Kuhn, Imre Lakatos, and Paul Feyerabend). Karl Popper (1968; 1969; 1972; see also Magee, 1973) undercut the traditional view of the objectivity of scientific observation. He argued that observation was not as objective as it seemed, but was actually rather theory driven. His famous lecture demonstration was to tell people in the audience: "Observe!", to which the obvious and immediate retort was, "Observe what?" This demonstration makes the point that no one ever observes without some idea of what it is they are looking for. In other words, scientific observation is always driven by hypotheses and theories, and what you observe depends in part on what you expect to see.

Karl Popper also made the important point (as Hume had done before him) that theories based on generalisations from instances (i.e. induction) could never be justified logically as being true. As the philosopher Bertrand Russell pointed out, a scientist turkey might form the generalisation "Each day I am fed" because for all of his life this had been the case. However, this generalisation provides no certainty that the turkey will be fed tomorrow, and if tomorrow is Christmas Eve it is likely to be proved false. Popper concluded that the hallmark of science is not generalisation but falsification. Scientists attempt to form theories and hypotheses which could potentially be shown to be untrue by experimental tests. According to Popper, falsification is what separates science from religions and pseudo-sciences such as psycho-analysis and Marxism.

There is obvious sense in Popper's argument. However, it should be pointed out that many examples of good science involve both confirmation and falsification. In addition, most scientists and other people have a tendency to seek confirmatory rather than disconfirmatory evidence (see Evans, 1989; Mitroff, 1974; Mynatt, Doherty, & Tweney, 1977). It is certainly true that established theories should be falsifiable, but it will often be more beneficial to a scientist to seek confirmatory evidence during the development of a new theory (Chalmers, 1982).

Several other philosophers of science have examined the development of the physical sciences, and argued that the enterprise has important social and subjective aspects to it. Thomas Kuhn (1970; 1977) argued that science has two modes (normal and revolutionary science), and that the transition from one mode to the other involves an intellectual crisis in a discipline. During periods of normal science, a discipline is dominated by a particular theoretical orientation which Kuhn called a *paradigm*. This paradigm is generally accepted by scientists in the field, even though it may not account for all of the available evidence brought to light by experimentation. Indeed, disconfirmatory evidence may be ignored or dismissed as an anomaly produced by some fault in the experimental apparatus. However, the paradigm does account for the phenomena which scientists regard as being central to the field. The major activity of normal science is to perform experiments which test and elaborate the details of the paradigm. A classic example is the use of Newtonian mechanics by physicists up until the emergence of relativity theory.

Just like old gunfighters, paradigms do not last forever. Periods of "revolutionary science" occur during which the old paradigm is overthrown as a consequence of the build-up of failed predictions and of gaps in its explanatory completeness. What is interesting about such crisis points is that adherents of the old paradigm resist change as long as possible until they can no longer hold out against the onslaught. When the change occurs and revolution takes place, most of the evidence accounted for by the old paradigm is re-interpreted and integrated into the new paradigm. At that point, peace breaks out and normal science resumes. Examples of this are the Copernican revolution, where the old Ptolemaic view that the planets and the sun revolved around the earth was replaced by our present view that the earth and the other planets revolve around the sun. In a similar fashion, Einstein's relativity theory involved a re-interpretation of Newtonian mechanics, which had been the dominant view for several centuries.

Kuhn's (1970; 1977) view that social and other subjective pressures lead scientists to adhere to paradigms that are manifestly inadequate has been taken to extremes by Paul Feyerabend (1975). He argued reasonably convincingly that the methodologies of science have failed to provide rules which are adequate to guide the activities of scientists. The only rule that appears to be generally applicable is that "anything goes." Furthermore, he maintained that science progresses by a sort of "who-shouts-the-loudest" strategy, in which publicity and visibility count for more than quality of research. If that is the case, then science may have practically no special features which elevate it above ancient myths or voodoo.

Of course, Feyerabend's (1975) arguments are well over the top. However, his views and those of other 20th-century philosophers of science have established the point that the division between science and nonscience is by no means as clear cut as used to be believed. This is a very liberating idea for cognitive psychology. It means that psychology need not attempt to model itself on the lines of any of the physical sciences: instead, it paves the way for the discipline to form its own scientific identity. Such a course is more reasonable than aping the physical sciences. Cognitive psychology faces very special problems because of its subject matter, namely, the mind. In fact, many of the developments of the last 30 years in cognitive psychology and in the cognitive sciences can be viewed as the creative organisation of a particular brand of science designed to solve a special set of problems. Before turning to these developments, let us first consider the historical antecedents of cognitive psychology.

Antecedents of Cognitive Psychology

It is notoriously difficult to pin-point the precise moment at which any major academic discipline started, and cognitive psychology is no exception. However, the ideas of William James (1890) and Tolman (1932) form important landmarks. William James was a theorist rather than an experimentalist, but his contributions to attention and memory have a very contemporary feel about them even a century later. For example, James drew a distinction between *primary memory* (or the psychological present) and *secondary memory* (or the psychological past). Almost exactly this distinction was resurrected 70 years later when cognitive psychologists began to study short-term and long-term memory systematically (see Chapter 5).

In spite of the historical importance of William James, the influence of Edward Tolman on cognitive psychology is in some ways even more interesting. Tolman (1932) always regarded himself as a Behaviourist, and he demonstrated his adherence to Behaviourism by carrying out most of his research on the humble rat. Given his background, it is striking that he found himself becoming a kind of cognitive psychologist. In essence, Hull and other Behaviourists had argued that the ability of rats to run rapidly through mazes could be accounted for by assuming that they learned to associate the stimuli of the maze with particular responses (e.g. muscle movements). Tolman and his associates discovered that rats who had learned to run through a maze were well able thereafter to swim through it when it was flooded. This indicated that the rats had not really been learning certain specific motor responses at all. Instead, according to Tolman, the rats formed a "cognitive map," or internal representation of the maze, and this cognitive map made it easy for them to run or to swim through the maze. This recognition by a leading Behaviourist that learning, even in rats, can be understood only by focusing on *internal* structures and processes rather than on motor responses was a major step on the road to cognitive psychology.

Another major influence on contemporary cognitive psychology is the research which was carried out by neuropsychologists in the 19th century (Morton, 1984). In essence, they attempted to explain the various kinds of language impairment exhibited by brain-damaged patients in terms of damage to specific language-processing components. They also attempted to identify the parts of the brain in which these components were located. Most of the theoretical efforts of these neuropsychologists look rather primitive nowadays, but it is noteworthy that they were struggling with issues which are still regarded as important by today's cognitive psychologists.

Despite the important early work of James, Tolman, the 19th-century neuropsychologists, and others, it was only during the 1950s that cognitive psychology properly got off the ground. Several different strands of thinking all conspired to overthrow the prevailing orthodoxies at about the same point in time, and cognitive psychology emerged as a result. For example, Noam Chomsky (1957; 1959) of the Massachusetts Institute of Technology made it very clear how hard-pressed Behaviourism was to explain the acquisition and nature of a central human ability, language. Chomsky himself is a linguist rather than a psychologist, but his transformational grammar theory of language inspired cognitive psychologists such as George Miller to test his ideas in the laboratory.

From another perspective, the advance of telecommunications technology led to theories of communication systems (e.g. Shannon & Weaver, 1949), which were later extended to human beings. As a consequence, ideas about coding information, limited-channel capacity, and the distinction between serial (i.e one process at a time) and parallel (i.e. more than one process at a time) processing all found their way into psychological theories. Many of these ideas were also to be found in the work on human factors carried out during World War II. The synthesis of these lines of work, and their application to distinctly psychological issues, led directly to the highly influential theorising of Donald Broadbent (1958) at the Applied Psychology Unit in Cambridge. He had the major insight that one could begin to understand phenomena such as perception, attention, and short-term memory by constructing an information-processing theory in which information flowed through a cognitive system. In other words, instead of looking at perception, attention, and short-term memory separately, Broadbent (1958) considered them all as interdependent ingredients in a single cognitive system.

The advent of the digital computer was another major influence on the formation of cognitive psychology. Psychologists and philosophers have always had a fondness for using the most advanced technological developments as metaphors for aspects of human functioning. Well-known examples are Descartes' use of hydraulically operated automata in St. Germain and Sigmund Freud's use of Vienna's extensive water-works system (see Fancher, 1979). Not surprisingly, many theorists responded to the invention of the digital computer with attempts to compare the human mind to the functioning of a computer. Like the computer, man was viewed as an *information processor*. At the same time, with the growing influence of the discipline of artificial intelligence, the relationship between the mind and the computer became close. Now psychologists could use computer ideas as metaphors for human thinking, and they could also implement their theories physically on the same machines in the form of computational models. In fact, the influences between artificial intelligence and cognitive psychology were not entirely one way, since attempts to understand cognition also led to new discoveries in computation. Indeed, two of today's leading cognitive psychologists (Allen Newell and Herb Simon) are considered to be among the founders of artificial intelligence.

Everyone has a birthday, and cognitive psychology is no exception. There is some consensus that many of the influences described here coalesced in the critical year of 1956. Several important meetings took place in that year, and crucial papers were published. For example, at one meeting at the Massachusetts Institute of Technology, Chomsky gave a preliminary paper on his theory of language, George Miller presented his paper on the magic number seven in short-term memory (Miller, 1956), and Newell and Simon discussed their very influential computational model called the General Problem Solver (discussed in Newell, Shaw, & Simon, 1958; 1960). The first systematic attempt to consider concept formation from a cognitive psychological perspective was also reported in 1956 (Bruner, Goodnow, & Austin, 1956).

It is also of historical note that 1956 is generally regarded as the year in which artificial intelligence was founded. This occurred at the famous Dartmouth Conference, which was attended by Chomsky, McCarthy, Minsky, Newell, Simon, and Miller (see Gardner, 1985). With the benefit of hindsight, we can see that 1956 witnessed the birth of both cognitive psychology and cognitive science as major disciplines. Books devoted to certain aspects of cognitive psychology began to appear (e.g. Broadbent, 1958; Bruner et al., 1956). However, it took several years before the entire information-processing viewpoint reached undergraduate courses, since the first general textbook of cognitive psychology was that of Ulrich Neisser (1967).

Information Processing: Consensus

For a period of several years, covering the 1960s and most of the 1970s, it was the fashion to follow Broadbent (1958) in regarding much of cognition as consisting of a sequential series of processing stages. When a stimulus is presented (so the reasoning went), basic perceptual processes occur, followed by attentional processes that transfer some of the products of the initial perceptual processing to a short-term memory store. Thereafter, rehearsal serves to maintain information in the short-term memory store, and some of that information is transferred to a long-term memory store. One of the most sophisticated theories of this type was put forward by Atkinson and Shiffrin (1968; see Chapter 5).

This kind of theoretical orientation, in which information processing involves an invariant sequence of stages, provided a simple and coherent framework for writers of textbooks. It was possible to follow the stimulus input from the sense organs to its ultimate storage in long-term memory by means of successive chapters on perception, attention, short-term memory, and long-term memory.

One slight problem with this theoretical approach is that it cannot readily accommodate some fundamental cognitive activities such as thinking and problem solving, but many textbook writers dealt with this in a robust manner by simply omitting such topics. A far more significant difficulty is that the sequential stage model is a gross over-simplification and is demonstrably wrong in several respects. In particular, the model appears to make the erroneous assumption that stimuli impinge on an inactive and unprepared organism. In fact, while processing is substantially affected by the nature of presented stimuli, it is also affected crucially by the individual's past experience, expectations, and so on.

Matters can be clarified by reference to a distinction that is often made between *bottom-up* or *stimulus-driven processing* and *top-down* or *conceptually driven processing*. Bottom-up processing refers to processing directly affected by stimulus input, whereas top-down processing refers to processing affected by what an individual brings to a stimulus situation (e.g. expectations determined by context and past experience). As an example of top-down processing, it is easier to read the word "well" when poorly written if it is presented in the context of the sentence, "I hope you are quite _ _ _ _," than when it is presented on its own. The evidence discussed in this book demonstrates conclusively that most cognitive activity involves these two kinds of processing in combination. The sequential stage model deals almost exclusively with bottom-up or stimulus-driven processing, and its failure to consider top-down processing is its single greatest inadequacy.

Towards the end of the 1970s, theorists (e.g. Neisser, 1976) started to argue that cognitive activity consists of interactive bottom-up and top-down processes occurring at the same time. This appears to be the case for virtually all cognitive processes. On the face of it, perception and remembering might seem to be exceptions, because perception obviously depends heavily on the precise stimuli presented (and thus on bottom-up processing) and remembering depends crucially on stored information (and thus on top-down processing). In fact, however, perception is also much affected by the perceiver's expectations about to-be-presented stimuli (see Chapters 2 and 3), and remembering depends far more on the exact nature of the environmental cues provided to facilitate recollection than was thought at one time (see Chapter 5).

Despite arguments about the relative importance of bottom-up and top-down processes, cognitive psychologists at the end of the 1970s were in general agreement that the information-processing paradigm was the appropriate way to study human cognition. This state of affairs was well described by Lachman, Lachman, and Butterfield (1979). Information processing did not really provide a grand theory about the nature of cognition. Instead, it provided a loose set of ideas which could be used to construct theories of cognition, and so it can best be regarded as a framework.

The information-processing framework has several basic characteristics:

- people are viewed as autonomous, intentional beings who interact with the external world;
- the mind through which they interact with the world is a general-purpose, symbol-processing system;
- symbols are acted on by various processes which manipulate and transform them into other symbols which ultimately relate to things in the external world;
- the aim of psychological research is to specify the symbolic processes and representations which underlie performance on all cognitive tasks;
- cognitive processes take time, so that predictions about reaction times can be made if one assumes that certain processes occur in sequence and/or have some specifiable complexity;
- the mind is a limited-capacity processor having both structural and resource limitations;
- this symbol system depends on a neurological substrate, but is not wholly constrained by it.

Many of these ideas stemmed from the view that human cognition can be understood by comparison with the functioning of computers. As Herb Simon (1980, p.45), a psychologist who won the Nobel Prize for economics, expressed it, "It might have been necessary a decade ago to argue for the commonality of the information processes that are employed by such disparate systems as computers and human nervous systems. The evidence for that commonality is now overwhelming." However, as we shall see shortly, many cognitive psychologists are by no means as convinced as Simon that computer and human functioning are very similar.

Most of the theories we examine in this book either assume the basic tenets of the information-processing framework or else attempt to clarify more precisely what they involve (e.g. the exact nature of the resource limitations or the processes involved in a given task). However, there are theorists who have explicitly rejected some of the ideas underlying the information-processing approach (e.g. see the later section on connectionist modelling methods).

One of the reasons why it is difficult to identify the core ideas in the information-processing framework is the open-ended nature of the computational metaphor. When scientists construct theories on the basis of metaphors or analogies to other mechanisms, the comparisons are clear and bounded. For example, in characterising light in terms of waves, the nature of waves is clear-cut, and their relevant aspects can be used directly to understand light. In the case of the computational metaphor, however, new extensions of it become possible as computer technology develops. For example, in the 1950s and 1960s, researchers mainly used the general properties of the computer to understand the mind (e.g. that it had a central processor and memory registers). Many different programming languages had been developed by the 1970s, and this led to various aspects of computer software and languages being used (e.g. Johnson-Laird, 1977, on analogies to language understanding).

Readers may very well be asking themselves whether the information-processing framework provides an adequate basis for theories in cognitive psychology. This issue is discussed in more detail in Chapter 14, but the gist of that subsequent discussion can be anticipated here. In essence, the information-processing approach tends to be rather limited because the cognitive system is considered in isolation from motivational and emotional influences (but see Chapter 13). It is also limited in that individual differences in cognitive functioning are often ignored. In a nutshell, the assumptions incorporated into the information-processing approach may be reasonable as far as they go, but they do not go far enough.

Information Processing: Diversity

Most researchers in cognitive psychology still adhere to the general principles of the information-processing framework. Despite this, the contemporary picture is one of considerable diversity in terms of aims and approaches. At the risk of over-simplification, it is possible to identify at least three major groupings of cognitive psychologists:

- experimental cognitive psychologists, who follow the experimental tradition of cognitive psychology, but do no computational modelling;
- cognitive scientists, who construct computational models and who take the computer metaphor very seriously. They differ among themselves as to the value of rigorous experimentation; and
- cognitive neuropsychologists, who argue that investigation of the patterns of cognitive impairment shown by brain-damaged patients can provide valuable information concerning normal human cognition.

It is important to note that basically we are dealing with stereotypes. Many researchers vacillate among the various categories, and so the distinctions are by no means absolute. Nevertheless, the fact that there are numerous researchers who fall squarely into one or other of the categories suggests that the proposed three categories possess some validity. It is a matter of current debate in cognitive psychology whether experimental cognitive psychologists are an endangered species, and whether cognitive scientists who still carry out proper experiments are at a pupa stage on the way to becoming fully-fledged cognitive scientists (see Gardner, 1985). This tension owes something to philosophical perspectives on the best route to the truth; these can be divided into empiricist and rationalist perspectives. Empiricists (e.g. experimental cognitive psychologists) assume that the truth about the world is to be gained through observation and experimentation. In contrast, rationalists (e.g. hard-nosed cognitive scientists) assume that truth is to be found through the construction of formal systems such as those in mathematics and logic.

Our view is that empiricism and rationalism are both dangerous if taken to extremes. Empiricism can lead to unproductive and atheoretical experimentation, and rationalism can lead to an elegant formal system which bears little or no relationship to any external reality. Furthermore, we believe that cognitive psychologists face very difficult problems, and that it is desirable for them to make use of all of the kinds of relevant information which are available. In other words, we will be doing our best to provide a synthesis of the insights which have emerged from the different approaches adopted by experimental cognitive psychologists, cognitive scientists, and cognitive neuropsychologists.

It could be argued that applied cognitive psychologists form a fourth grouping within cognitive psychology. It is, indeed, the case that some cognitive psychologists are engaged in "pure" research under laboratory conditions, whereas other cognitive psychologists carry out "applied" research out in the real world. However, the differences between them are more in terms of *what* they study and the methods used rather than in terms of *theoretical preconceptions*.

Since experimental cognitive psychologists are simply following in the historical tradition which was discussed earlier, there is no need to describe the general characteristics of what they do in any greater detail here. In the case of cognitive scientists and cognitive neuropsychologists, however, it will be useful to consider more closely how they tackle the task of understanding human cognition. Accordingly, the following sections of this chapter address these issues.

Summary

Cognitive psychology as an approach based on the information-processing framework emerged in the 1950s. The time was ripe for change because of changing views of the nature of science and because the prevailing Behaviourism had failed to provide an adequate account of human cognition. Among the other factors involved in the emergence of cognitive psychology was the advent of the digital computer, which seemed to many psychologists to provide a useful metaphor for human cognitive functioning.

Contemporary cognitive psychology sometimes seems to resemble the messenger in "Alice in Wonderland" who went in all directions at once. However, some broad themes can be identified. Many cognitive psychologists continue to carry out traditional laboratory-based research on normal individuals, whereas others prefer to investigate brain-damaged patients in the hope that their cognitive impairments will shed light on normal human cognition. Still others (sometimes called cognitive scientists) prefer to focus on computer programs as the way to increase our understanding of cognition.

COGNITIVE SCIENCE

As we have seen, cognitive scientists are fond of constructing computational models in order to enhance their knowledge of human cognition. In order to understand the role of modelling, it is useful to consider how models are used in engineering. Imagine that an engineer is employed to construct a suspension bridge which is the first of its kind. Rather than building and re-building the bridge until it stays up, the engineer decides to test the plan by building a scale model. Therefore, using bits of plaster for the concrete parts and copper wire for the steel hawsers, the engineer constructs a model which has the same dimensions, strengths, and weaknesses as the proposed bridge.

Two important things emerge from this exercise. First, the engineer learns that the on-paper plan of the bridge can be physically realised, i.e. that the cross-spars and the distance the suspension towers are apart are sufficient to hold the bridge up. Of course, the attempt to build the model may lead to a modification of the plans if the structure does not seem to be stable or the plans are ill-specified. Second, the engineer can use the model to test predictions about what might happen to the bridge under various conditions. For example, the effects of high winds and traffic on the bridge could be simulated by adding weights along the length of the model and placing it in a wind tunnel.

Models of psychological processes can be used in similar ways to test and validate theories. *Computational models* provide important information about whether the concepts used in a theory can be specified in detail and they allow one to simulate the effects of different conditions. *Mathematical models* are particularly useful for determining the variables which underlie a phenomenon and the relative importance of these variables to the phenomenon. We will concentrate on the former in this part of the chapter, because they are the hallmark of the cognitive science approach.

Computational Modelling: From Flowcharts to Simulations

Computer scientists have been scathing about the approach to theory adopted by many experimental cognitive psychologists. The reason is that cognitive psychologists often specify their theory simply in verbal form (e.g. "There is a short-term memory store and a long-term memory store, and rehearsal is the main process involved in information moving from the former to the latter store"). Such verbal statements tend to be extremely vague from a scientific perspective, and this can make it very difficult to decide whether or not the evidence fits the theory. In contrast, cognitive scientists produce computer programs that are meant to represent cognitive theories with all of the details made explicit. When they are constructing large computer programs, they often plan them in advance by using flowcharts in order to be clear about what the program is to do and how it will do it. An example of a very hairy flowchart is shown in Fig. 1.1. This is a flowchart of a bad theory about how we understand sentences. It assumes that a sentence is encoded in some form and then stored. After that, a decision process (indicated by a diamond) determines if the sentence is too long. If it is too long, then it is broken up and we return to the encode stage to re-encode the sentence. If it is not too long, then another decision process decides if the sentence is ambiguous. If it is ambiguous, then its two senses are distinguished and we return to the encode stage. If it is not ambiguous, then it is stored in long-term memory. After one sentence is stored, we return to the encode stage to consider the next sentence.

Sometimes researchers and students make sarcastic comments about flowcharts, asking questions such as "What happens in the boxes?" or "What goes down the arrows?" Such comments do point to genuine criticisms. We really need to know what is meant by "encode sentence," how long is "too long," and how sentence ambiguity is tested. For example, after deciding that only a certain length of sentence is acceptable, it may turn out that it is impossible to decide whether the sentence portions are ambiguous without considering the entire sentence. In other words, the boxes may look all right at a superficial glance, but real contradictions may appear when their contents are specified.

In similar fashion, exactly what goes down the arrows is critical. If one examines all of the arrows converging on the "encode sentence" box, it is clear that a lot more needs to be specified. There are four different kinds of thing entering this box: an encoded sentence from the environment; a sentence which has been broken up into bits by the "split-sentence" box; a sentence which has been broken up into several senses; and a command to consider the next sentence. This means that the "encode" box has to do several different specific operations. In addition, it may have to record the fact that an item is either a sentence or a possible meaning of a sentence, or that an item may be part of another sentence. Thus, several other complex processes have to be

*A flowchart of a
bad theory about
how we
understand
sentences.*

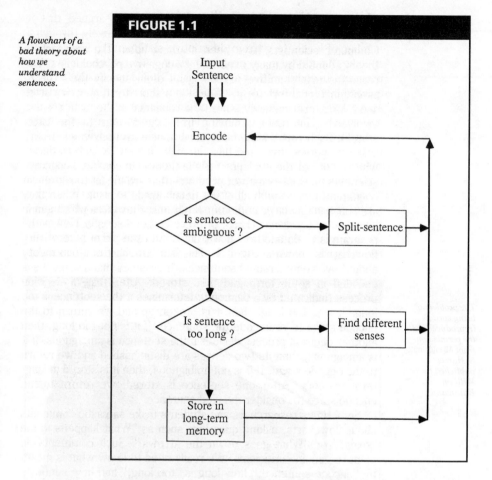

FIGURE 1.1

Input
Sentence

Encode

Is sentence
ambiguous ?

Split-sentence

Is sentence
too long ?

Find different
senses

Store in
long-term
memory

specified within the "encode" box to handle these tasks, but the flowchart sadly fails to address these issues. The gaps in the flowchart show some similarities with those in the formula shown in Fig. 1.2.

Of course, not all theories expressed as flowcharts possess the deficiencies of the one we have just considered. However, it is generally true that implementing a theory as a program is a good method for checking that it really does make sense, and that it contains no hidden assumptions or vague terms. In the previous example, this would involve specifying the form of the input sentences, the nature of the storage mechanisms, and the various decision processes (e.g. those about sentence length and ambiguity). Typically, cognitive scientists use one of the artificial intelligence programming languages such as LISP or PROLOG to write such programs (Clocksin & Mellish, 1981; Eisenstadt, 1988; Hasemer & Domingue, 1989; Winston & Horn, 1988).

There are many issues surrounding the use of computer simulations and the ways in which they do and do not simulate cognitive processes. Palmer and Kimchi (1986) argued that it should be possible to decompose a theory successively through a number of levels (e.g. from descriptive statement to flowchart to specific functions in a program) until one reaches a written program. In addition, they argued that it should be possible to draw a line at some level of decomposition, and say that everything above that line is psychologically plausible and everything below the line is not. This issue of separating psychological aspects of the program from other aspects arises because there will always be parts of the program which have little to do with the psychological theory, but which are there simply because of the particular programming language being used and the machine the program is running on. For example, in order to see what the program is doing it is necessary to have print commands in the program which show the outputs of various stages on the computer's screen. However, no one would argue that such print commands form part of the psychological model. Other issues arise about the relationship

FIGURE 1.2

The problem of being specific (reproduced with the permission from All ends up *by S. Harris, published by William Kaufmann).*

between the performance of the program and the performance of human subjects. For example, it is seldom meaningful to relate the speed of the program doing a simulated task directly to the reaction time taken by human subjects, because the processing times of programs are affected by psychologically irrelevant features. Programs run faster on more powerful computers, or if the program's code is interpreted rather than compiled. Despite these problems, the various materials which are presented to the program should result in differences in program operation time that are correlated closely with differences in subjects' reaction times with the same materials. At the very least, the program should be able to reproduce the same outputs as subjects when given corresponding inputs.

The computer programs or models we have been discussing can be used in the ways indicated by the engineer example. First, they are very useful tools for theorists since they both force and allow them to conceive of cognitive processes and representations in a concrete fashion. Second, the model can be used to run different materials in order to see if any unexpected consequences arise. It is very easy for the theorist to assume that a theory is a general one and, therefore, that the model can handle many different sorts of materials. However, it often transpires that this assumption is false, and that the theory requires revision.

Computational Modelling Techniques

The general characteristics of computational models of cognition have been discussed at some length. It is now time to deal with some of the main types of computational model which have been used in recent years. This will reveal the great variety of approaches to computational modelling which can be adopted. Three main types are outlined briefly here: semantic networks; production systems; and connectionist networks.

Semantic Networks

Consider the problem of modelling what we know about the world (see Chapter 7 for further details). There is a long tradition from Aristotle and the British empiricist school of philosophers (Locke, Hume, Mill, Hartley, Bain) of arguing that all knowledge is in the form of associations. Three main principles of association have been proposed: (1) contiguity: Two things become associated because they occurred together in time; (2) similarity: Two things become associated because they are alike; and (3) contrast: Two things become associated because they are opposites. There is a whole class of cognitive models which owe their origins to these ideas; they are called *associative* or *semantic* or *declarative networks*.

Semantic networks have the following general characteristics:

- Concepts (e.g. "chair"; "cow") are represented by linked nodes to form a network.

- These links can be of various kinds; they can represent simple relations like *is–a* (e.g. John *is–a* policeman) or more complex relations like *play, hit, kick.*
- The nodes themselves and the links among nodes can have various activation strengths which represent the similarity of one concept to another. Thus, for example, a dog and a cat node may be connected by a link with an activation of 0.5, whereas a dog and a pencil may be connected by a link with a strength of 0.1.
- Most processes occurring in the network serve to change the activation values of the links between nodes. For example, in learning that two concepts are similar, the activation of a link between them may be increased.
- The way in which activation spreads through a network can be determined by a variety of factors. It can be affected by the representation of the initial activation, by the proximity of a node to the point of activation, or by the amount of time that has passed since the onset of activation.

Part of a very simple network model is shown in Fig. 1.3. It corresponds closely to the one proposed by Collins and Loftus (1975). Several variations on this basic theme exist (e.g. Anderson, 1983). In spite of the fact that most networks are based

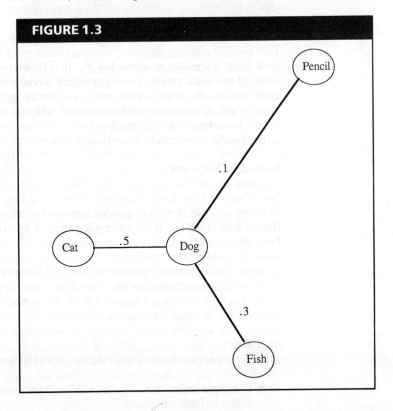

FIGURE 1.3

A schematic diagram of a simple semantic network with nodes for various concepts (i.e. dog, cat) and links between these nodes indicating the differential similarity of these concepts to each other.

on rather simple ideas, semantic network models have been successful in accounting for a variety of findings. For example, the word "dog" is recognised more readily if it is preceded by the word "cat" This semantic priming effect (Meyer & Schvaneveldt, 1971) is easily modelled using such networks.

At their best, semantic networks are both flexible and elegant modelling schemes. A good example is Anderson's (1983) theory of cognition. This theory makes use of a semantic network (or declarative network as he calls it) as well as a production system (see following).

Production Systems

Another popular approach to modelling cognition involves production systems. Production systems are made up of productions, and a production is an "IF . . . THEN" rule. These rules can take many forms, but an example we might want children to have is, "If someone smiles at you, then smile back." In a typical production system model there is a long-term memory that contains a large set of these IF . . . THEN rules. There is also a working memory (i.e. a system holding information that is currently being processed). So, if the information arrives from the environment to working memory that "someone is smiling at you," it will match the IF-part of the rule in long-term memory, and trigger the THEN-part of the rule (i.e. smile back). As a consequence, the world will be full of smiling children!

Production systems have the following general characteristics:

- They have a large number of IF . . . THEN rules.
- They have a working memory which contains information.
- The production system operates by matching the contents of working memory against the IF-parts of the rules and executing the THEN-parts.
- If some information in working memory matches the IF-part of many rules, there may be other *conflict-resolution rules* that select one of these matches as being better than the others.

Consider a very simple production system which operates on lists of letters involving As and Bs (see Fig. 1.4). The system has two rules:

1) IF a list in working memory has an A at the end
   THEN replace the A with AB
2) IF a list in working memory has a B at the end
   THEN replace the B with an A

If we give this system different lists, then different things will happen. If we give it CCC, this will be stored in working memory but will remain unchanged because it does not match any of the IF-parts of the two rules. If we give it A, then it will be modified by the

A schematic diagram of a simple production system.

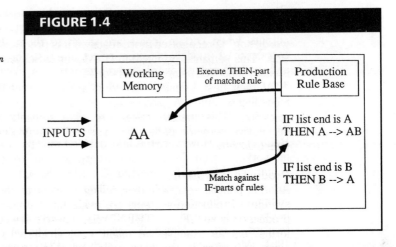

FIGURE 1.4

Working Memory

Execute THEN-part of matched rule

Production Rule Base

INPUTS   AA

IF list end is A
THEN A --> AB

IF list end is B
THEN B --> A

Match against
IF-parts of rules

rules after the A is stored in working memory. This A is a list of one item and as such it matches rule 1. Rule 1 has the effect of replacing the A with AB, so that when the THEN-part is executed working memory will contain an AB. On the next cycle, AB does not match rule 1 but it does match rule 2. As a consequence, the B is replaced by an A, leaving an AA in working memory. The system will then continue in the same fashion, producing AAB, then AAA, then AAAB, and so on.

Production systems are useful as psychological models because many aspects of cognition can be specified as sets of IF . . . THEN rules. For example, chess knowledge can readily be represented as a set of productions based on rules such as "If the Queen is threatened, then move the Queen to a safe square." In this way, people's basic knowledge of chess can be modelled as a collection of productions and gaps in this knowledge as the absence of some productions. Allen Newell and Herb Simon (1972) were the first psychologists to establish the usefulness of production system models in the characterisation of higher-level cognitive processes like problem solving and reasoning (see Chapters 11 and 12). However, it should be noted that these models are not only useful in these areas. As Holland, Holyoak, Nisbett, and Thagard (1986) have shown, more elaborate versions of such systems can be used to model many diverse aspects of cognition, from reinforcement behaviour in rats to memory phenomena and learning.

Connectionist Networks
Connectionist networks, neural networks, or *parallel distributed processing models* as they are variously called are relative newcomers among computational models of cognition. These connectionist networks differ from other computational modelling techniques in several respects. All previous techniques were marked by the need to program explicitly all aspects of the model, and by their use of explicit symbols to represent concepts.

Connectionist networks, on the other hand, can to some extent program themselves in that they can "learn" to produce specific outputs when certain inputs are given to them. Furthermore, connectionist modellers often reject the use of explicit rules and symbols and use distributed representations, in which concepts are characterised as patterns of activation in the network (see Chapter 7).

Early theoretical proposals about the possibility of learning in neural-like networks were made by McCulloch and Pitts (1943) and Hebb (1949). However, the first detailed models of simple neural networks, called Perceptrons, were shown to have several limitations (Minsky & Papert, 1969; 1988; Rosenblatt, 1959). By the late 1970s, hardware and software developments in parallel computing offered the possibility of constructing multi-layered networks that could overcome many of these original limitations (Ballard, 1986; Feldman & Ballard, 1982; Hinton & Anderson, 1981; McClelland, Rumelhart, and the PDP Research Group, 1986; Rumelhart, McClelland, and the PDP Reseearch Group, 1986).

Connectionist networks typically have the following characteristics:

- The network consists of elementary or neuron-like *units* or *nodes*, which are connected together so that a single unit has many links to other units.
- Units affect other units by exciting or inhibiting them.
- The unit usually takes the weighted sum of all input links and produces a single output to another unit if the weighted sum exceeds some threshold value.
- The network as a whole is characterised by the properties of the units which make it up, by the way they are connected together, and by the algorithms or rules used to change the strength of connections among units.
- Networks can have different structures or layers; they can have a layer of input units, intermediate layers (of so-called "hidden units"), and a layer of output units.
- A representation of a concept can be stored in a distributed manner by a pattern of activation throughout the network.
- The same network can store many different patterns in this way without them necessarily interfering with each other if they are sufficiently distinct.
- One algorithm or rule used in networks to permit learning to occur is known as *backward propagation of errors* (BackProp).

You probably noticed that there appear to be some similarities between connectionist networks and semantic networks. It is certainly true that some of the terms used (e.g. node, activation) are the same, but there are a number of major differences. For example, each concept (e.g. chair) is represented by a single node in a particular location within semantic network models, whereas each concept is distributed over numerous nodes within connectionist models.

In order to understand connectionist networks more fully, let us consider how individual units act when activation impinges on them. Any given unit can be connected to several other units (see Fig. 1.5). Each of these other units can send an excitatory or an inhibitory signal to the first unit. This unit generally takes a weighted sum of all of these inputs. If this sum exceeds some threshold it produces an output. This output may feed into another unit which does the same.

FIGURE 1.5

A multi-layered connectionist network with a layer of input units, a layer of internal representation units or hidden units, and a layer of output units. Input patterns can be encoded, if there are enough hidden units, in a form that allows the appropriate output pattern to be generated from a given input pattern (reproduced with the permission of David E. Rumelhart & James L. McClelland from Parallel distributed processing: Explorations in the microstructure of cognition, Vol. 1, *published by the M.I.T. Press, 1986 by The Massachusetts Institute of Technology).*

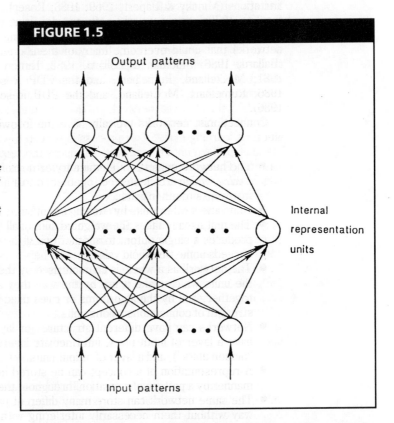

Output patterns

Internal representation units

Input patterns

These networks can model cognitive behaviour without recourse to the kinds of explicit rules found in production systems. They do this by associating various inputs with certain outputs, and by storing patterns of activation in the network. The models typically make use of several layers to deal with any complex behaviour. One layer consists of input units which encode a stimulus as a pattern of activation in those units. Another layer is an output layer, which produces some response as a pattern of activation. When the network has learned to produce a particular response at the output layer following the presentation of a particular stimulus at the input layer, it can exhibit behaviour which looks like a rule being applied. In other words, the pattern of activation which exists across the units in the network will produce a certain response pattern to a certain stimulus pattern, as if it had learned a rule of the form IF such-and-such is the case THEN do so-and-so. However, no such rule exists in the model.

One of the most critical aspects of connectionist networks is the learning rule or algorithm used to form patterns of activation in the network. One algorithm that has been used to permit connectionist networks to learn is called backward propagation or BackProp. BackProp allows a network to learn to associate a particular input pattern with a particular output pattern. At the beginning of the learning period, the network is set up with random connections among the units. During the early stages of learning, after the input pattern has been presented, the output units often produce a response that is not the required output pattern. What BackProp does is to compare this imperfect pattern with the known required response, noting the errors that occur. It then back-propagates activation through the network so that the units are adjusted in such a way that they will tend to produce the required pattern on the next learning cycle. This process is repeated with a particular stimulus pattern until the network produces the required response pattern. Thus, the model can be made to learn the behaviour with which the cognitive scientist is concerned, rather than being explicitly programmed to produce it.

Networks have been used in this and in other ways to produce very interesting results. Several examples will be discussed throughout the text (see, for example, Chapters 7 and 8), but one concrete example may be mentioned here. Sejnowski and Rosenberg (1987) produced a connectionist network called NETtalk which takes an English text as its input and produces reasonable English speech as its output. Even though the network is trained on a limited set of words, it can pronounce the words from new text with approximately 90% accuracy. Thus, the network appears to have learned the "rules of English pronunciation," but it has done so without having explicit rules that combine and encode sounds in various ways.

Connectionist models such as NETtalk have great "gee whiz" value, and are currently attracting the attention of a whole army of researchers. Many of the members of this army might object to our classification of connectionist networks as merely one among a number of modelling techniques. Some have argued that connectionism is a new paradigm in Kuhn's sense. If one examines the fundamental tenets of the information-processing framework, then connectionist schemes seem to violate one or two of them. For example, symbol manipulation of the sort found in production systems does not seem to occur in connectionist networks. The complex issues raised by connectionist theories will be returned to later in the book.

Summary

Cognitive scientists often specify their theoretical proposals using computational modelling techniques. Modelling allows theorists: (i) to determine if their theory can be specified in particular situations; (ii) to test the theory under different conditions and circumstances; and (iii) to make specific predictions about quantitative outcomes in behaviour. Theories can be stated in terms of flowcharts, but flowcharts are often imprecise. It is preferable to validate these theoretical treatments by constructing precise programs. The three main computational modelling techniques used by cognitive scientists are semantic networks, production systems, and connectionist networks.

A more detailed evaluation of the cognitive science approach will be held over until several concrete examples of the approach have been considered. This evaluation is to be found in Chapter 14.

COGNITIVE NEUROPSYCHOLOGY

An approach to cognitive psychology which has become increasingly influential in recent years is cognitive neuropsychology. In essence, cognitive neuropsychology is concerned with the patterns of cognitive performance in brain-damaged patients, and involves identifying those aspects of cognition which are intact or impaired. Such information can be extremely useful for a number of different reasons, two of which are of particular importance. The first reason is that the cognitive performance of brain-damaged patients can be explained by theories within cognitive psychology. Such theories specify the processes or mechanisms involved in normal cognitive functioning, and it should in principle be possible to account for many of the cognitive impairments of brain-damaged patients in terms of selective damage to some of those mechanisms.

The second reason is that it may be possible to use information from brain-damaged patients to reject theories proposed by cognitive psychologists, and to propose new theories of normal cognitive functioning. This objective of cognitive neuropsychology was expressed very well by Ellis and Young (1988, p.4): "The second aim of cognitive neuropsychology is largely responsible for the recent upsurge of interest in the approach. It is to draw conclusions about normal, intact cognitive processes from the patterns of impaired and intact capabilities seen in brain-injured patients. In pursuing this second aim, the cognitive neuro-psychologist wishes to be in a position to assert that observed patterns of symptoms could not occur if the normal, intact cognitive system were not organised in a certain way." In other words, the intention is that there should be bi-directional influences of cognitive psychology on cognitive neuropsychology and of cognitive neuropsychology on cognitive psychology. Historically, the former influence has been the greater one until comparatively recently, but the latter is becoming relatively more important year by year.

Before discussing the cognitive neuropsychological approach in more detail, it may be useful to discuss a concrete example of cognitive neuropsychology in operation. Atkinson and Shiffrin (1968) argued that there is an important distinction between a short-term memory store (i.e. a store containing information which is currently being processed) and a long-term memory store (i.e. a store containing information which has left consciousness), and that information enters into the long-term store as a result of rehearsal and other processing activities in the short-term store. Relevant evidence from the cognitive neuropsychological perspective was obtained by Shallice and Warrington (1970). They investigated a patient KF, who had suffered damage to a part of the brain specialized for speech perception and production. KF appeared to have severely impaired short-term memory, but essentially intact long-term memory.

The investigation of this patient served two important purposes. First, it provided an entirely new kind of evidence to support the theoretical distinction between two memory systems. Second, and perhaps more importantly, it pointed to a real deficiency in the theoretical model of Atkinson and Shiffrin (1968). If, as this model suggests, long-term learning and memory depend upon the short-term memory system, then it is very surprising that someone with a grossly deficient short-term memory system also has normal long-term memory. The appropriate interpretation of the findings from KF is discussed further in Chapter 5.

The case of KF illustrates very clearly the potential power of cognitive neuropsychology. The study of this one patient provided strong indications that the dominant theory of memory at the end of the 1960s was seriously inadequate. This is no mean achievement for a study based on one subject!

Cognitive Neuropsychological Evidence

How do cognitive neuropsychologists set about the task of understanding how the cognitive system functions? A crucial goal is the discovery of *dissociations*, which occur when a patient performs normally on one task but is impaired on his or her performance of a second task. In the case of KF, a dissociation was found between performance on short-term memory tasks and on long-term memory tasks. As we have seen, such evidence can be used to argue that normal individuals possess at least two separate memory systems.

There is a potential problem with drawing sweeping conclusions from single dissociations, however. A patient may perform poorly on one task and reasonably well on a second task because the first task is more complicated and difficult than the second. In other words, the brain damage suffered by the patient may not have impaired *specific* aspects of cognitive functioning, but may instead have had the *general* effect of reducing the ability to cope with difficult tasks of all kinds. It is generally agreed that the solution to this problem is to look for *double dissociations*. A double dissociation between two tasks (1 and 2) is shown when one patient performs normally on task 1 and at an impaired level on task 2, and another patient performs normally on task 2 and at an impaired level on task 1. If a double dissociation can be demonstrated, then the results cannot be explained in terms of one task being intrinsically more difficult than the other.

In the case of short-term and long-term memory, such a double dissociation has been demonstrated. While KF had impaired short-term memory but intact long-term memory, most amnesic patients (see Chapter 6 for a review) actually have severely deficient long-term memory but intact short-term memory. It is rather difficult to account for this double dissociation without assuming that there are two distinct memory systems which can suffer damage separately from each other.

An alternative approach is based upon associations, i.e. the tendency of different patients to exhibit impaired performance on the same set of tasks. If such an association across tasks is shown, it is tempting to assume that there is a common cognitive process or mechanism underlying performance on all of the tasks showing impairment. However, damage is very often not limited to highly specific areas of the brain. Therefore, the tasks in question may require different cognitive processes, but the processes they require may be very close together anatomically, so that damage to one cognitive process is usually accompanied by damage to all of the others. As Ellis and Young (1988) pointed out, the clearest indication that an association has occurred simply because of the accident of anatomical closeness in cognitive processes is finding a patient who does not show impaired performance across all of the tasks on which most patients are impaired.

This discussion of the way in which cognitive neuropsychologists proceed may have made it sound reasonably straightforward to use data from brain-damaged patients to understand human cognition. However, reality is much more complex than that. If brain damage were usually very limited in scope and affected only a single cognitive process or mechanism, then cognitive neuropsychology would be a relatively simple enterprise. In fact, brain damage is often rather extensive, so that several different cognitive systems are all impaired to a greater or a lesser extent. This means that considerable ingenuity is often needed to make sense of the tantalising glimpses of human cognition provided by brain-damaged patients.

Theoretical Assumptions

Cognitive neuropsychologists differ among themselves in the theoretical assumptions they are willing to make when trying to make sense of their data. However, most cognitive neuro-psychologists subscribe to the following assumptions (with the exception of the first one):

- Most patients can be categorised in terms of *syndromes*, which are based on co-occurring sets of symptoms.
- The cognitive system exhibits *modularity*, i.e. there are several relatively independent cognitive processors or modules. Brain damage will typically impair only some of these modules, leaving the others intact.
- There is a meaningful relationship between the organisation of the physical brain and that of the mind; this assumption is known as *isomorphism*.
- Investigation of cognition in brain-damaged patients can tell us much about cognitive processes in normal individuals; this important assumption is closely bound up with the other assumptions.

Syndromes
The traditional approach within neuropsychology made considerable use of *syndromes*. In essence, it was claimed that certain sets of symptoms or impairments were usually found together, and each set of co-occurring symptoms was used to define a separate syndrome. Thus, for example, patients with intact short-term memory but severely impaired long-term memory were said to be suffering from "the amnesic syndrome."

This syndrome-based approach has some things to recommend it. In particular, it allows one to impose some order on the numerous cases of brain-damaged patients who have been studied by assigning them to a relatively modest number of categories. It is also of use in identifying those areas of the brain primarily responsible for cognitive functions such as language, because one can look for those parts of the brain which are damaged in all those patients having a particular syndrome. However, a syndrome-based approach suffers from a number of disadvantages. It leads researchers to exaggerate the similarities among different patients all allegedly suffering from the same syndrome. It also suffers from the problem that those symptoms or impairments said to form a syndrome may be found in the same patients because the underlying cognitive processes are anatomically adjacent rather than because there are any underlying common cognitive processes.

In recent years, there have been attempts to suggest more specific syndromes or categories based on our theoretical understanding of cognition (e.g. Shallice, 1979). One of the problems here is that the discovery of new patients with unusual patterns of deficits and the occurrence of theoretical advances mean that the categorisation system is in a constant state of flux. As a consequence, Ellis (1987) has argued convincingly that attempts at categorisation should largely be abandoned. Instead, cognitive neuropsychology should proceed on the basis of intensive single-case studies in which individual patients are studied on a wide variety of tasks. According to the logic of this approach, an adequate theory of cognition should be as applicable to the individual case as to groups of individuals, and so single-case studies provide a perfectly satisfactory test of cognitive theories. The great advantage of this approach is that there is no need to make simplifying assumptions about which patients do and do not belong to the same diagnostic categories.

While we are generally sympathetic to Ellis's (1987) position, he has probably over-stated the value of single-case studies. If our theoretical understanding of an area (e.g. memory) is rather limited, then it may be extremely difficult to make sense of the findings from individual patients. In such circumstances, it may make sense to adopt the syndrome-based approach until the major theoretical issues have been clarified. Furthermore, many experimental cognitive psychologists are somewhat uneasy at the idea of attaching great general theoretical significance to the findings from individuals who may be quite unrepresentative even of brain-damaged patients. Experimental cognitive psychologists have always favoured comparisons between groups of subjects, an approach which tends to avoid the potential problems of building sweeping conclusions on the basis of atypical individuals. This issue is discussed further in Chapter 14.

Modularity
The whole enterprise of cognitive neuropsychology is based upon the assumption that there are numerous *modules* or cognitive processors within the brain. These modules are relatively independent of each other in their functioning, so that damage to one module does not directly affect the functioning of other modules. Modules are anatomically distinct, so that brain damage will often affect some modules while leaving others intact.

According to this modularity view, cognitive neuropsychology offers the exciting prospect that it may facilitate the task of discovering the nature of the major building blocks of cognition. Thus, for example, a double dissociation indicates that two tasks make use of different modules or cognitive processors, and so a series of double dissociations can be used to provide a sketch-map of our modular cognitive system.

The notion of modularity is closely associated with Fodor (1983), who published a book entitled *The modularity of mind*. He tried to identify the main distinguishing features of modules, and came up with the following suggestions: informational encapsulation; domain specificity; mandatory operation; and innateness. Informational encapsulation means that a module functions independently from the functioning of other modules. Domain specificity means that each module can process only one kind of input (e.g. words, faces). Mandatory operation simply means that the functioning of a module is not under any form of voluntary control (mandatory = compulsory). Finally, the notion that modules are innate means that they are inborn.

Fodor's (1983) ideas are important because they represent one of the first serious attempts to define what we mean by a module or cognitive processor. However, many psychologists have criticised the inclusion of mandatory operation and innateness as two of the criteria for modularity. Some modules may operate in a rather automatic fashion, but there is little evidence to suggest that they all do. So far as innateness is concerned, it is implausible to suppose that the modules underlying language skills such as reading and writing are innate, since these are skills which the human race has possessed only in comparatively recent times.

From the perspective of cognitive neuropsychology, these criticisms do not pose any special problems. If the assumptions of informational encapsulation and domain specificity remain tenable, then data from brain-damaged patients can continue to be used in the hunt for cognitive modules. This would still be true even if it turned out that several modules or cognitive processors were neither mandatory nor innate.

It should be noted here that it is not only cognitive neuropsychologists who subscribe to the notion of modularity. The great majority of experimental cognitive psychologists and cognitive scientists also believe in modularity. On this particular issue, the three groups differ primarily in terms of the preferred methods for demonstrating modularity. However, limitations of the modular approach adopted by cognitive neuropsychologists are discussed in Chapter 14.

Isomorphism

If cognitive neuropsychology is to prove a fruitful approach to the understanding of human cognition, then it has to be assumed that there is some meaningful relationship between the way in which the brain is organised at a physical level and the way in which the mind and its cognitive modules are organised. This assumption has sometimes been called *isomorphism*, which means that two things (e.g. brain and mind) have the same shape or form. Thus, for example, it is expected on the modularity view that each module will have a somewhat different physical location within the brain, and that all of the physical representations of any given module will be in adjacent areas of cortex. These expectations may or may not be confirmed by empirical evidence. If they are not, then cognitive neuropsychology will become a more complicated enterprise than it appears to be at present.

An assumption which is related to isomorphism is that there is localisation of function. This means that any specific function or process occurs in a particular location within the brain. It is interesting to note that the notion of localisation of function appears to be in conflict with the connectionist account, according to which a process (e.g. activation of a concept) can be distributed over a wide area of the brain. There is, as yet, no definitive evidence to support one view over the other.

Evaluation

It is natural for the reader to want to know whether the various theoretical assumptions underlying cognitive neuropsychology are right or wrong. However, this may not be a very fruitful question to ask. In some sense, modules do not "really" exist; rather, they are convenient theoretical devices used to clarify our understanding. Therefore, the issue of whether the theoretical assumptions discussed here are valuable or not is probably best resolved by considering the extent to which cognitive neuropsychology is successful in increasing our knowledge of cognition. In other words, the proof of the pudding is in the eating. It is still too early to be certain that cognitive neuropsychology, relying as it does on largely untested assumptions, will prove successful. However, as is shown by the research of cognitive neuropsychologists discussed in later chapters (especially Chapters 6, 9, and 10), the omens are basically favourable.

The reader may have formed the impression that cognitive neuropsychology is the greatest invention since sliced bread, but it is only fair to mention some of its problematical aspects. It tends to be assumed by cognitive neuropsychologists that brain-damaged patients are just like the rest of us, except that one or more of the modules underlying human cognition are severely impaired or destroyed. This assumption is particularly important when it comes to using data from patients to draw conclusions about cognitive functioning in normal individuals. The problem is that the assumption is very often false. As Caramazza (1984) has pointed out, brain-damaged patients will frequently respond to their cognitive impairments by making use of "compensatory operations." In other words, they will attempt to minimise the disruption of their everyday lives by using what remains of their cognitive system in new and different ways.

Although he was not strictly speaking about brain-damaged patients, von Senden's (1932) discussion of cataract patients who have gained their sight after an operation is relevant at this point. These patients were very slow to acquire even the rudiments of visual perception, and a major reason for this was that they had developed skills using the other sense modalities to compensate for the lack of vision. They found it very difficult to abandon these skills in order to derive full benefit from the gift of sight. In other words, their cataracts led them to perceive the world in ways which were quite different from those used by normal individuals.

Ellis and Young (1988) have attempted to minimise the force of this objection to cognitive neuropsychology by arguing that the compensatory operations used by brain-damaged patients are usually relatively modest in scope. More specifically, they claimed that brain-damaged patients may make use of different strategies, but that (Ellis & Young, 1988, p.19): "the mature brain is not capable of sprouting new modules after brain injury." That is a reasonable point, but they seem to under-estimate the problems posed by strategic changes. If we are trying to understand how a particular module normally functions, then it may be extremely difficult to do this if that module is simply not functioning in a normal way in brain-damaged patients. The notion that damage can lead to new ways of functioning can be seen by analogy if we consider that damaging a radio by taking out one of its transistors can cause it to start howling.

There are other significant problems with the cognitive neuropsychological approach, but these are dealt with later in the book after the relevant research has been considered. The interested reader should refer to Chapter 14.

Summary

Cognitive neuropsychologists investigate cognitive functioning in brain-damaged patients. The single most important theoretical assumption made by cognitive neuropsychologists is that the cognitive system is basically modular, i.e. it consists of numerous relatively independent cognitive processors. Brain damage typically impairs the functioning of some (but not all) of these modules, and so it should ultimately be possible to use patient data to specify the number and nature of cognitive modules. In practice, brain damage is often rather extensive, and this complicates the enterprise. In addition, brain-damaged patients may resort to various strategies to allow them to cope with their problems, and these strategies also complicate the task of interpreting cognitive neuropsychological evidence. In spite of these complexities, cognitive neuropsychology has proved to be a useful test-bed for theories of normal cognitive functioning, and it has also led directly to theoretical developments.

ORGANISING AND STRATIFYING COGNITIVE PSYCHOLOGY

There are two general theoretical issues which are worth considering at this point. The first issue concerns terms such as "framework," "theory," and "model." Many students (and even some professional cognitive psychologists!) are confused about the relationships between these terms, and it seems desirable to clarify matters. The second issue concerns the relationship between the various disciplines which have an impact on cognitive psychology. For example, how are we to integrate computational models, brain neuropsychology and neurophysiology, and evidence from psychological experiments?

The second issue resembles that confronted much earlier by physicists, chemists, and biologists. While biology deals with the gross functioning of bodily organs, chemistry can deal with the same subject matter at a finer level in terms of molecular changes. At the most detailed level, quantum physics can characterise the activity of the sub-atomic particles that form atoms, which in turn make up the molecules. In some cases, different levels of description are appropriate for different levels of analysis. For instance, most of molecular chemistry could be characterised in terms of quantum physics, but the resultant theory would be too detailed and complicated to be of much use. Since the disciplines relevant to cognitive psychology are still being developed, there is no consensus on how they might relate to each other. However, one possible view of how it might be done was proposed by David Marr (1982), and will be discussed shortly.

Frameworks, Theories, Models, and Architectures

It is important at this point to distinguish between a number of terms which differ in their degree of specificity: *framework, theory, model,* and *architecture*. A framework is a general set of ideas which is drawn upon by theorists within a particular discipline (see Anderson, 1983). Other terms which are essentially synonymous with "framework" are *approach, paradigm,* and *metatheory* (see Baars, 1986; Kuhn, 1970; Lachman, Lachman, & Butterfield, 1979). The general framework which is most commonly used by cognitive psychologists is the information-processing framework. The important thing about frameworks is that they should be regarded as useful or not useful rather than correct or incorrect. The reason for this is that they consist of high-level assumptions which cannot be tested directly at an experimental level.

In contrast, *theories* should be stated in terms which permit researchers to determine whether they are correct or incorrect. Theories are more constrained than frameworks, and often provide precise accounts of the underlying mechanisms and influences which give rise to a set of phenomena. Theories differ considerably from each other in terms of their scope, i.e. the range of phenomena with which they are concerned.

Theories are typically too general to make predictions about specific situations. However, a model is a particular instantiation of a theory which relates that theory to a specific situation. This then makes it possible to make relatively detailed predictions. For example, suppose we have a theory which states that all problem solving simply involves trial and error. If we wanted to apply this theory to problem solving in chess, then we would have to construct a model of how we would expect trial and error to manifest itself in the chess situation.

One of the problems with cognitive psychology is that there has been a proliferation of theories, but it is often not clear how these theories relate to each other. In other words, theories in cognitive psychology do not coalesce to form a unified theory of human cognition. This state of affairs contrasts with the early days of psychology, when there were several grand theories (proposed by giants such as James, Freud, and Wundt), but relatively few specific theories of cognitive performance. A *cognitive architecture* is intended to provide the missing theoretical integration, and is thus far broader in its scope than most theories. According to Anderson (1983, p. ix), cognitive architectures are designed to "capture the basic principles of operation built into the cognitive system." There are only a few theoretical formulations which lay claim to be cognitive architectures. These include Anderson's (1983) ACT* (pronounced ACT-star for Adaptive Control of Thought) and Newell's SOAR system (standing for State, Operator, And Result), which is discussed by Laird, Newell, and Rosenbloom (1987; Newell, 1989).

A Framework for Theories in Cognitive Psychology

A very important issue for cognitive psychology concerns the marriage of psychological theory with computational modelling and with the neurosciences. One of the hopes behind connectionism was that one could relate psychological functioning to brain functioning rather directly because of the neuron-like properties of connectionist networks. However, connectionist networks actually differ substantially from brain neurons and synapses (Crick, 1989; Crick & Asanuma, 1986), and some have argued (e.g. Smolensky, 1988) that connectionist models should be thought of as operating above the neuronal level.

David Marr (1982) proposed a very interesting framework for organising theories of mental processes. While the general applicability of his framework has been questioned (Anderson, 1987b; Newell, 1982), it does nevertheless present a tantalising glimpse of how one might co-ordinate the different levels of theory within cognitive psychology. Marr's (1982) research was mainly concerned with visual processes, and a more detailed treatment of his framework as applied to vision is to be found in Chapter 2.

Marr (1982) outlined three levels at which an information-processing theory should be characterised (see Table 1.1). The top level, which he called the *computational level*, contains a specification of what needs to be computed in order for a particular

TABLE 1.1

Marr's (1982) Framework for Theories

Computational Theory	The goal of the computation, why it is appropriate, what the logic of the strategy carried out might be.
Algorithmic Level	How can the computational theory be implemented, the representation for the input, and the algorithm for the transformation.
Hardware Level	How can the representation and the algorithm be realised physically.

task to be carried out. This level constitutes a formal statement of the various outputs resulting from different inputs. Some people find the term "computational level" unhelpful, preferring the term "functional level", because (Arbib, 1987, p.478): "it is far from indicating the steps—serial or parallel—whereby computation is to be undertaken; rather, it corresponds to what in computer program synthesis would be a specification of the program in input/output terms, plus perhaps a top-down sketch of program design."

The computational level is also concerned with specifying *why* the stated strategy and computations are appropriate. In other words, it is concerned with the *purpose* of the computation. In the case of visual perception, for example, the purpose is to transform input in the form of the pattern of light produced by the external environment into output in the form of information about environmental objects which can then be used to plan action.

At the intermediate, or *algorithmic level*, the exact nature of the computation is specified. At this level, the representations one is using and the algorithms or rules operating on those represent-ations should be indicated. This level should capture the detailed processing steps which intervene between the inputs and outputs, and it should do so in a fashion which takes account of the human mechanisms involved in processing. Chomsky (1957) produced a computational level theory which was designed to generate all of the legal sentences in human language, but he deliberately paid no attention to human limitations in terms of processing capacity or distractibility from the task in hand.

The final level, the *hardware level*, is the brain. The brain obviously imposes limitations on the kinds of representations and algorithms which can actually be used. In practice, we usually know so little of brain functioning that such knowledge hardly constrains theorising at the algorithmic level. However, there are exceptions. As we will see in Chapter 2, the discovery of cells within the brain's visual system which are especially sensitive to certain kinds of stimulus has had a definite impact on theories of vision.

It is important to note that these three levels are quite distinct from each other. While there are some interdependencies among them, the different levels do not simply decompose into each other. In other words, there will be concepts at one level which have no corresponding entities at another level. It is also worth bearing in mind that Marr (1982) was proposing a framework. As such, it is neither right nor wrong, but stands or falls on the basis of its usefulness in research.

Summary

There are some important issues surrounding the organisation and stratification of theory in cognitive psychology. First, four distinct theoretical constructs can be distinguished: frameworks; theories; models; and cognitive architectures. A framework is a broad pool of ideas and techniques which can be used to construct theories. A theory is an abstract statement which accounts for the underlying mechanisms and influences on a set of cognitive phenomena. A model is a specification or instantiation of a theory in a particular situation. A cognitive architecture is a general theoretical edifice that unites a number of more specific theories.

Second, there is the issue of how to deal at a theoretical level with the inter-relationships of the various disciplines contributing to cognitive psychology. Marr (1982) proposed a three-levelled framework for organising multi-disciplinary theories. It has a computational level, an algorithmic level, and a hardware level.

EMPIRICAL METHODS IN COGNITIVE PSYCHOLOGY

We have seen that cognitive psychologists differ widely in their approaches and in their theoretical orientations. However, all of those cognitive psychologists who carry out experiments are faced by the same problem of deciding what measures to take in order to understand human cognition. For example, there are various ways of attempting to identify the nature and duration of the component processes involved in the performance of a cognitive task. One of the most useful is the subtraction method.

Subtraction Method

The subtraction method was originally proposed by Donders (1868). Its basic logic is that the duration of a processing stage can be measured by comparing the time taken to solve a version of a task including that processing stage with a second version of the task that differs from the first version only by the omission of that processing stage. The difference in solution time for the two versions of the task represents the time spent on the processing stage of interest. In principle, successive deletions can be used in order to obtain an estimate of the duration of each processing stage. In terms of an analogy, one could calculate the length of time taken to eat a meal on the motorway by comparing the time to drive from A to B including a meal on the way with the time taken to drive the same route without stopping for refreshment.

There are several cases in which the subtraction method has been used successfully. For example, consider research carried out by Clark and Chase (1972) on the sentence-picture verification task. A sentence such as, "Star isn't below plus,' is followed by a picture such as *, and the task is to decide as rapidly as possible whether the sentence is a true description of the picture. The sentence can take one of eight forms: the preposition can be either "above" or "below"; the subject of the sentence can be "star" or "plus"; and the statement can be positive ("is") or negative ("isn't").

When the sentence precedes the picture, Clark and Chase (1972) assumed that the first step involves representing the sentence in terms of its underlying propositional structure (proposition = assertion which is true or false). They argued that the preposition "below" takes longer to process than the preposition "above" (parameter a), and that negative sentences take longer to process than positive sentences (parameter b). The second step is to encode the picture into propositional form with the same preposition ("above" or "below") as used in the sentence. The next step is to compare the sentence and picture representations. It takes less time to perform the comparison when the first noun in the two propositional representations is the same than when it is different (parameter c), and the comparison time is less when neither representation contains a negative than when one of them does (parameter d). The fourth, and final, step is the production of a response, and it was assumed that the time taken for this is a constant (parameter t_0).

The subtraction method can be applied to the sentence-picture verification task by comparing response times as a function of the exact sentence and picture presented. Thus, for example, the sentence "A is below B" has parameters a and t_0 assigned to it when it is true, whereas the sentence "A is above B" has only parameter t_0 assigned to it if it is true. Thus, the difference in solution time should reflect the duration of parameter a. The theoretical model based on this approach to estimating parameter times was found to account for over 99% of the variation in response time from one condition to another.

One of the problems with the subtraction method is that the experimenter must have a precise conceptualisation of the component processes involved in the performance of a task before the subtraction method can be used. More importantly, the subtraction method is based on the assumption that processing is *discrete* or *serial*, meaning that all of the processing at one stage of processing is completed before the next processing stage begins. If that assumption is correct, then it should be possible to insert or delete processing stages from a cognitive task without affecting the other processing stages in any way. In fact, it is very likely that the assumption that processing is *discrete* or *serial* is often incorrect, and this limits the usefulness of the subtraction method. Processing at later stages can sometimes start before the completion of previous processing stages (e.g. McClelland & Rumelhart, 1981; Chapter 9), and theories incorporating that notion are called *cascade models*. In a nutshell, the subtraction method works well with relatively simple tasks involving discrete or serial processing, but many tasks are probably better considered from the more complex perspective of the cascade-model approach.

Introspection

In spite of the doubts about the subtraction method and other techniques, there is no dispute that measures of *behaviour* (e.g. speed of performance; accuracy of performance) can provide vital evidence about cognitive functioning. However, what is much less clear is the status that should be accorded to *introspection* (defined in the Oxford English Dictionary as "examination or observation of one's own mental processes").

Historically, views about the value of introspection have varied enormously over the centuries. Over 2000 years ago, Aristotle argued that introspection was the only method available to study thinking, and concluded that the content of the mind consisted mainly of images organised on the basis of association by contiguity. This associationistic approach was developed by the British empiricists such as Hobbes, Locke, and Mill. In contrast, Sir Francis Galton, the brilliant Victorian polymath, argued that the position of consciousness "appears to be that of a helpless spectator of but a minute fraction of automatic brain work."

The Würzburg school, working in Germany around the end of the 19th Century, agreed broadly with Galton's position on the basis of their various experiments. The Würzburg psychologists gave people simple tasks, such as producing word associations, and then immediately asked them to introspect. They discovered that trained subjects often provided peculiarly formless reports, which they regarded as evidence for "imageless thought."

With the advent of Behaviourism, introspection was discarded as a technique, and theorists such as John Watson attempted to explain away thinking as merely sub-vocal speech. The ludicrous nature of this view was made clear by the philosopher Herbert Feigl, who commented wittily that Watson "made up his windpipe that he had no mind." In contemporary cognitive psychology, the prevalent view is that introspection provides valuable evidence about some mental processes, but not about others. In general terms, it is assumed that relatively slow processes or the products of those processes (e.g. those involved in much problem-solving) may be amenable to introspection, whereas very rapid processes (e.g. those usually involved in retrieving knowledge from long-term memory) are not. However, until quite recently there were only sporadic attempts to provide criteria for deciding when introspection is of use.

The middle-of-the-road consensus that introspection is often a useful technique was rudely disrupted in a well-known article by Nisbett and Wilson (1977). They argued that introspection is practically worthless, and illustrated their argument with a number of examples. One of these examples was the work of Ghiseli (1952). He discussed the ways in which the creative process operated in a number of distinguished people and concluded (Ghiseli, 1952, p.15) that: "Production by a process of purely conscious calculation seems never to occur." Indeed, several creative workers indicated that they were sometimes unaware that any process was occurring until the time at which the solution to a problem appeared in consciousness. Ghiseli (1952, p.26) quoted the words of Henry James, the author and brother of the psychologist William James, who deliberately consigned an idea to the unconscious:

I was charmed with my idea, which would take, however, much working out; and because it had so much to give, I think, must I have dropped it for the time into the deep well of unconscious cerebration: not without the hope, doubtless, that it might eventually emerge from that reservoir, as one had already known the buried treasure to come to light, with a firm iridescent surface and a notable increase in weight.

At a more experimental level, Nisbett and Wilson (1977) referred to several studies in which the participants seemed entirely oblivious of the processes involved in determining their behaviour. For example, in one study subjects were presented with five essentially identical pairs of stockings arrayed horizontally in front of them, and they were asked to decide which pair was the best. After they had made their choice, they were asked to indicate why they had chosen that particular pair. Most of the subjects chose the right-most pair, and so their decisions were actually affected by relative spatial position. However, the subjects did not offer spatial position as a reason for making their choice. Indeed, they vehemently denied that it had played any part at all in their decision. Instead, they referred to slight differences in colour, texture, and so on among the pairs of stockings as having been important.

According to Nisbett and Wilson (1977), such failure to be aware of the processes instrumental in affecting one's own behaviour is the rule rather than the exception. How, then, can one account for the fact that people are often fairly accurate in their introspective reports about their own mental processes? Nisbett and Wilson (1977, p.248) argued that this can be explained in terms of a priori theories: "We propose that when people are asked to report how a particular stimulus influenced a particular response, they do so not by consulting a memory of the mediating process, but by applying or generating causal theories about the effects of that type of stimulus on that type of response." This view was supported by discovering that an individual's introspections about what is determining his or her behaviour are often no more accurate than the guesses about those determinants made by other people. This suggests that introspection does not provide any "magical access" to valuable information not possessed by other people.

If the conclusions of Nisbett and Wilson (1977) are correct, then cognitive psychology is in big trouble. Research on human memory relies very heavily on introspection, since most measures of retention depend on conscious awareness that certain information was presented at an earlier time. It would also be extremely difficult to conduct experiments on visual illusions if introspection is useless, and the same is true of many other perceptual phenomena (e.g. after-images).

Striking evidence that introspective evidence can be very misleading and uninformative has been obtained in recent research by cognitive neuropsychologists. For example, Weiskrantz (1986) investigated a patient, DB, who had a brain operation because of his severe and frequent migraine attacks. After the operation, DB had an area of subjective blindness within the visual field in which he claimed to be able to see nothing. Despite this lack of introspective evidence, DB was able to locate stimuli in the "blind" part of his visual field, to distinguish between moving and stationary visual stimuli, and to decide whether a light was present or absent. DB felt that he was simply guessing on these tasks, and was very surprised to learn how accurate his "guesses" had been. Weiskrantz (1986) used the term "blindsight" to refer to this phenomenon of a discrepancy between objective measures of responding to visual stimuli and introspective evidence (see Chapter 3 for more details).

There are numerous examples of a related phenomenon in amnesic patients (see Chapter 6 for a review). They frequently learn new skills as well as normal individuals, but have little or no introspective awareness of having performed the task previously. Here again there is a discrepancy between the behavioural and the introspective evidence.

The arguments of Nisbett and Wilson (1977) and the evidence from cognitive neuropsychology indicated the importance of re-thinking the value of introspective evidence in cognitive psychology. Ericsson and Simon (1980; 1984) responded to the challenge by proposing criteria for distinguishing between valid and invalid uses of introspection, including the following:

- It is preferable to obtain introspective reports during the performance of a task rather than retrospectively. In view of the fallibility of human memory, retrospective reports may be incomplete due to failures of retrieval from long-term memory.
- Subjects are more likely to produce accurate introspections when asked to describe what they are attending to, or thinking about, than when required to interpret a situation or to speculate about their thought processes.
- It is clear that people cannot usefully introspect about several kinds of processes (e.g. neuronal events; recognition processes).

According to Ericsson and Simon (1980, p.23), the degree of involvement of attention is of crucial importance: "Our model assumes that *only information in focal attention* can be verbalised . . . With increase in experience with a task, the same process may move from cognitively controlled to automatic status, so that what is available for verbalisation to the novice may be unavailable to the expert."

Careful consideration of the studies which Nisbett and Wilson (1977) regarded as striking evidence of the worthlessness of introspection reveals that, in virtually every case, subjects provided retrospective interpretations about information which had probably never been fully attended to. In other words, none of the criteria for valid introspective evidence was fulfilled in most of those studies.

At a rather more theoretical level, Ericsson and Simon (1980) argued persuasively that accurate introspection or verbalisation concerning cognitive processes has to be based on information contained in either short-term or long-term memory. As a consequence, introspections may be incomplete if the appropriate information never enters the short-term store (e.g. due to lack of focal attention); or if information previously available in the short-term store is not stored in long-term memory; or if information is stored in long-term memory but cannot be retrieved. Since introspection depends to such an extent on the short-term store, the limitations of that store (e.g. small capacity; detailed information not normally stored) directly affect the process of introspection.

Even if introspective reports can frequently be accepted as valid, there is the further methodological problem that requiring people to provide such reports while performing a task may change the nature of the cognitive processes that are under study. However, common sense suggests that the extent of any disruption of ongoing cognitive processes depends on the kinds of information that subjects are asked to provide in their introspective reports. Disruption should be minimal if subjects are simply asked to "think aloud"; in contrast, disruption should be maximal if subjects are asked to provide complex interpretations concerning information which would not normally be in focal attention. Probably the most crucial factor is whether or not the information required in introspective reports is accessible without changing the focus of attention.

There are many cases in which thinking aloud has been found to have no systematic effect on the structure and course of the processes involved in performing a task. For example, Newell and Simon (1972) compared the performance of subjects who were not asked to provide introspective reports with that of subjects told to think aloud on tasks involving the discovery of proofs in propositional logic. Detailed analysis of the correct and incorrect steps taken by the two groups of subjects revealed no important differences. Furthermore, the two groups did not differ in the number of correct solutions.

In sum, while there are various limitations on introspection as a method for identifying cognitive processes, it can be a valid and extremely useful technique under some circumstances. Ericsson and Simon (1980) have made the important point that the limitations of introspection correspond closely to the limitations of the memory system.

Summary

Cognitive psychologists have an impressive range of techniques available for assessing cognitive processes (e.g. the subtraction method). Most of these techniques involve behavioural measurement, and it is clear that behavioural measures can be very informative about underlying processes. What is more controversial is whether introspection is a useful tool. It is probably true that introspection is valuable under certain conditions, and Ericsson and Simon (1980) have attempted to spell out those conditions. In essence, introspection which involves descriptive reporting of the current contents of focal attention is likely to be valid, whereas interpretative accounts of past events are usually of little value.

OUTLINE OF THE BOOK

One of the problems with writing a textbook of cognitive psychology is that virtually all of the processes and structures of the cognitive system are interdependent. Consider, for example, the case of a student reading a book in order to prepare for a forthcoming examination. Hopefully the student is *learning* something, but there are several other processes going on as well. *Visual perception* is involved in the intake of information from the printed page, and presumably there is *attention* to the content of the book (although attention may be captured by extraneous stimuli). In order to profit from the book, the student must possess considerable *language skills*, and must also have rich *knowledge representations* which are relevant to the material in the book. There may be an element of *problem solving* in the student's attempts to relate what is in the book to the possibly somewhat conflicting information which has been learned elsewhere. Furthermore, what is learned now will depend on the students *emotional state* at the time of learning. Finally, the acid test of whether the learning has been effective comes during the examination itself, when the material contained in the book must be *remembered*.

The words italicised in the previous paragraph indicate some of the major ingredients of human cognition, and they form the basis of our coverage of cognitive psychology. However, whereas all of these ingredients actually interact with each other, we are constrained by the serial nature of books to discuss some aspects of cognition before others. The organisation of the book is broadly to start with the initial stages of stimulus processing (e.g. perception; attention), followed by analysis of the later stages of processing (e.g. memory; problem solving). In view of its central significance in human cognition, there is detailed discussion of language in its various forms (reading; listening; speaking; and writing). All of these processes depend on stored knowledge, and the representation and organisation of knowledge received are dealt with at length as a separate topic and in conjunction with the other topic areas.

In view of the interdependent functioning of all aspects of the cognitive system, there is great emphasis in this book on the ways in which each process (e.g. perception) depends on other processes and on structures (e.g. attention; long-term memory; stored representations). This should facilitate the task of making sense of the complexities of the human cognitive system.

However, in order to achieve a complete grasp of perception, attention, or whatever, it is necessary to read the whole book. Once you have digested that unwelcome piece of news, we hope very much that you will find cognitive psychology to be of interest, and that you will come to share the authors' enthusiasm for the challenge of understanding the complexities of the human mind in action.

SUMMARY

The rise of cognitive psychology has occurred for several different reasons. Views of science have changed dramatically during the course of the 20th Century. In the early years of this century it was still possible to believe that science was a simple matter of collecting objective facts and trying to make sense of them. The Behaviourists tried to make psychology conform to this view of science, but the attempt failed. Cognitive psychology came into being in part because of the growing recognition that science is a considerably more complex activity than used to be thought, and so a more complex approach to human cognition was appropriate.

A major factor in the emergence of cognitive psychology was the development of computers. It was initially argued that there were some interesting similarities between human and computer functioning, but more recently there have been serious efforts to exploit the computer metaphor much more fully.

The displacement of Behaviourism by cognitive psychology can be regarded as a paradigm shift, in the sense that an entirely different approach to human cognition was being proposed. Cognitive psychologists espoused the information-processing framework which bore little resemblance to what had happened before. Although it is nearly always difficult to put a date on such matters, there are reasons for arguing that 1956 marked the true beginnings of cognitive psychology more than any other year.

If we look at the contemporary scene, it is possible to identify at least three major branches of cognitive psychology. First, there are experimental cognitive psychologists, who are primarily involved in empirical research on normal subjects. Second, there are cognitive scientists, who combine experimentation and the computational modelling of human cognition. Third, there are cognitive neuro-psychologists, who investigate the patterns of cognitive impairments shown by brain-damaged patients, and relate them to normal functioning.

Theorising within cognitive psychology can occur at several different levels. A framework is very broad and consists of assumptions which cannot be submitted to experimental test. A theory is more precise; it makes various predictions which can be tested. A model is still more precise; it typically consists of a theory applied to a particular situation. A cognitive architecture consists of an ambitious attempt to identify the crucial processes and mechanisms involved in all of cognition.

At the empirical level, cognitive psychologists have made use of numerous behavioural measures in order to understand cognition. There has been much controversy on the issue of whether introspection can shed light on cognitive processes. Probably the most convincing argument is that it can sometimes, especially when subjects are asked to introspect about events in focal attention, and when they are asked to describe their thoughts rather than to interpret experience.

FURTHER READING

Baars, B.J. (1986). *The cognitive revolution in psychology*. New York: Guilford Press. This provides an excellent account of the move from Behaviourism to information-processing psychology. What makes the book really interesting is that a large part of it is given over to interviews with key figures in the science and with their personal views of how the changes took place.

Crick, F. (1989). *What mad pursuit?* New York: Basic Books. Francis Crick, who was one of the discoverers of the structure of D.N.A., was also a member of the PDP group. His discussion of the findings of the connectionists focuses on the neurological implications.

Ellis, A.W. & Young, A.W. (1988). *Human cognitive neuropsychology*.London: Lawrence Erlbaum Associates Ltd. Everything you ever wanted to know about cognitive neuropsychology is contained within the pages of this comprehensive book.

Gardner, H. (1985). *The mind's new science*. New York: Basic Books. This is a readable account of the emergence of cognitive science in its various forms.

Chapter Two

PATTERN RECOGNITION

INTRODUCTION

This chapter and the following one deal with perception. We can perhaps most appropriately begin with a consideration of the concept of "perception". Definitions have changed over the years as the study of perception has become increasingly dominated by the cognitive perspective. This can be illustrated by comparing the definitions offered by Bartley (1969) and by Roth (1986). According to Bartley (1969, pp. 11–12), "*Perception* is the immediate discriminatory response of the organism to energy-activating sense organs . . . To discriminate is to make a choice reaction in which contextual conditions play a deciding role." In contrast, Roth (1986, p. 81) provides a much more cognitive and contemporary definition: "The term *perception* refers to the means by which information acquired from the environment via the sense organs is transformed into experiences of objects, events, sounds, tastes, etc."

This process of transforming and interpreting sensory information is a complex one, and involves a considerable variety of processing mechanisms. At the very least, perception depends upon basic physiological systems associated with each sensory modality, together with central brain processes which integrate and interpret the output from these physiological systems. Not surprisingly, major contributions to our knowledge of perception have come from advances in both physiology and psychology. There is also increasing interest within the field of artificial intelligence (see Roth, 1986) in the possibility of computer simulation of certain key aspects of perception.

The enormous volume of research on perception means that it is totally out of the question to provide comprehensive coverage of perception from the physiological, psychological, and artificial intelligence perspectives within the confines of two chapters. What has been attempted is rather more limited. One major limitation is that our major focus is on the visual modality rather than any other. There are basically two reasons for this. First, more is known about visual perception than about perception in the other sensory modalities. Second, the visual modality is probably the most important sense modality for sighted individuals, with visual information influencing cognition more than information in any other modality. However, those working in speech recognition might well want to disagree with us!

A very important area of research within perception is concerned with the perception of language in both its written and spoken forms. The somewhat specialised area of language perception is dealt with in Chapter 9.

This chapter deals with some of the most central issues in visual perception, namely, those relating to pattern recognition. Pattern recognition involves identifying or recognising two-dimensional and three-dimensional stimuli in the environment. It is possible to sub-divide pattern recognition into word recognition, face recognition, object recognition, and so on. Pattern recognition may seem like a rather straightforward matter, but as we will see shortly, it is actually rather complicated in terms of the processes involved.

One of the major problems for theorists interested in pattern recognition is to account for the amazing flexibility of the human perceptual system as it copes with a multitude of different stimuli. An example of this flexibility which has been much favoured by textbook writers is our ability to recognise different visual presentations of the letter "A." In spite of the considerable variations in orientation, in typeface, in size, and in writing style of the letter "A" which we encounter, we generally recognise it rapidly and accurately.

Even though it is not known in detail how pattern recognition occurs, it is clear at a very general level that it involves matching information extracted from the visual stimulus with information stored within the memory system. When the stimulus information has been compared with stored information, a decision is made as to which information in long-term memory provides the best match to the stimulus. In order to understand pattern recognition fully, the reader should refer to Chapter 8, where theoretical approaches to the storage of concepts in memory are discussed. Of particular relevance is the work of Rosch (e.g. Rosch, Mervis, Gray, Johnson, & Boyes-Braem, 1976).

Various kinds of pattern-recognition theory have been advanced in order to explain the processes involved in the matching of stimulus information to stored information. Most of them are template theories, prototype theories, or feature theories. Accordingly, we consider each of these three theoretical approaches in turn. Other aspects of pattern recognition were addressed by the Gestalt psychologists, and their approach is also considered.

TRADITIONAL THEORETICAL APPROACHES

Template Theories

The basic idea behind template theories is that stimulus information is compared directly to various miniature copies (or templates) of previously presented stored patterns, which are stored in long-term memory. A stimulus is identified or recognised on the basis of that template producing the closest match to the stimulus input.

This kind of theory is beguilingly simple, but matters become more complicated when we consider how template theories attempt to explain the ease with which patterns are recognised in the face of changes in size, orientation, colour, and so on. It could be argued, of course, that there is a separate template for every conceivable instance of a pattern. However, this would be tremendously uneconomical in storage terms, and thus is quite implausible. The problem could be alleviated if it were assumed that the match between the internal representation of the stimulus input and the stored template need not be perfect. Alternatively, the number of templates required for pattern recognition could be reduced to a more realistic level if the stimulus input underwent a normalisation process (i.e. producing an internal representation in a standard position, size, and so on) before the search for a matching template began. However, the advantages of postulating such a normalisation process may be illusory. The reason is that the normalisation process itself must be supplemented by some additional processing mechanisms that are able to recognise the appropriate size and orientation of each visual pattern. Against this, it could be argued that normalisation is often facilitated by the fact that visual patterns are typically presented in some larger context, and this context provides useful indications as to the proper size and orientation of the pattern.

All in all, template-matching theories tend to be rather unwieldy and ill-equipped to account for the versatility of perceptual processing. These inadequacies are especially obvious when the stimulus belongs to an ill-defined category, i.e. a category for which no single template could possibly suffice (e.g. a building or a book).

Prototype Theories

Whereas most template theories treat each stimulus as a separate entity, prototype theories claim that similarities among related stimuli play an important role in pattern recognition. More specifically, prototype theories argue that each stimulus is a member of a class of stimuli, and that it shares key attributes of that class. Pattern recognition involves comparing stimuli to prototypes, which are abstract forms representing the basic or most crucial elements of a set of stimuli. Thus, for example, a prototypical aeroplane might consist of a long tube with two wings attached. Some theorists prefer the term "schemata" (schema = organised package of knowledge) or "structural descriptions" instead of "prototypes." There is additional coverage of prototype theories in Chapter 8.

One obvious advantage of prototype theories over template theories is that the information stored in long-term memory consists of a manageable number of prototypes rather than a virtually infinite number of templates. At the empirical level, some of the strongest evidence in favour of the prototype approach was obtained by Franks and Bransford (1971). They started by constructing prototypes. This was done by combining geometric forms such as circles, stars, and triangles into structured groupings. Several distortions of these prototypes were then formed by applying one or more transformations to them. Subjects were then shown some of these distorted patterns (but not the prototypes themselves), followed by a recognition test.

The results were quite striking (see Fig. 2.1). The subjects were most confident that they had seen the prototype, in spite of the fact that the prototypes had not been shown to them at all! In contrast, they had seen examples of the other kinds of patterns, although not the exact stimuli presented on the recognition test. Those patterns differing from a prototype by a single transformation were next most confidently recognised, and there was a straightforward relationship between the degree of similarity of a pattern to its prototype and recognition confidence. In another similar experiment, reported by Franks and Bransford (1971), a stimulus that the subjects had seen before was rated as no more familiar than a stimulus they had not seen before, provided that the two stimuli contained the same number of transformations from the prototype.

What do these findings mean? The simplest explanation is that the subjects used information from the various patterns presented initially in order to construct prototypes that were then stored in

Recognition memory for geometric forms varying in their similarity to the prototype defined by the number of transformations from the prototype. None of the forms had actually been presented before. Data from Franks & Bransford (1971).

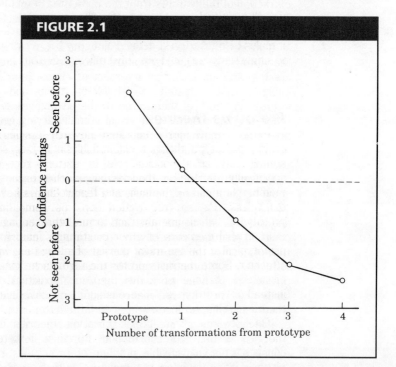

FIGURE 2.1

long-term memory. This prototype knowledge was then used to classify and identify new stimuli, with recognition being simply a function of the extent to which any given pattern matched the stored prototype.

Prototype theories are quite promising, but they possess certain limitations. Most of them are not very explicit about the details of the matching process between the internal representation of a stimulus and a prototype. For example, the comparisons involved in the matching process may occur either serially (one at a time) or in parallel (two or more at a time). Since the matching process could take a very long time to achieve pattern recognition if it operated serially, it is likely that comparisons between internal representations of stimuli and prototypes are made in parallel. Prototype theories also typically fail to explain how pattern recognition is affected by the context in which a stimulus is presented as well as by the stimulus itself.

Feature Theories

The various difficulties that have beset template and prototype theories have led to the development of feature theories, in which it is assumed that a pattern consists of a set of specific attributes or features. For example, a face could be said to possess various different features: a nose, two eyes, a mouth, a chin, and so on. The process of pattern recognition is assumed to begin with the extraction of the features from the presented stimulus. This set of features is then combined, and compared against information stored in memory.

If we return to the question of how the letter "A" is recognised, then it might be argued by feature theorists that its crucial features are two straight lines that intersect or almost intersect, with an angle of approximately 45° between them and a cross-bar intersecting both of them. One of the advantages of this kind of theoretical approach is that visual stimuli varying greatly in size, orientation, and minor details may nevertheless share the same defining features and thus be identifiable as instances of the same pattern.

Gibson (1969) indicated one way in which letters of the alphabet could be identified on the basis of a feature analysis. She identified 12 features of letters (e.g. closed loops; horizontal line segments; and vertical line segments), and argued that any stimulus letter could be identified correctly by comparing its feature content with that of each of the letters of the alphabet. For example, only the letter "O" is symmetrical and has a closed curve. One of the most obvious predictions from this theoretical position concerns the kinds of errors that are made when a letter is identified: Those letters sharing the most features with the letter actually presented should have the greatest probability of being confused with it. There is some empirical support for this prediction, but the evidence is not very strong.

A slightly different experimental approach was taken by Gibson, Shapiro, and Yonas (1968). They measured the length of time it took to decide whether two-letter stimuli were the same or different. Their key finding was that response latencies on trials where two different letters were presented were directly related to the number of features the letters shared. Thus, for example, it took longer to decide that "P" and "R" were different than to decide that "G" and "W" were different.

The feature-theory approach to letters has also received support from the visual search task, in which a target letter has to be detected as rapidly as possible in a block of letters. The nontarget, or distractor, letters may be either similar or dissimilar to the target letter in their features. Neisser (1964) used lists like those shown in Fig. 2.2, and instructed his subjects to search for the letter "Z". He discovered that the target letter was detected much faster on average when the distractor letters shared few features with it (e.g. List 2) than when they shared a number of features (e.g. List 1), indicating the important role played by features on this task.

FIGURE 2.2

Illustrative lists to study word search. The distractors in List 2 share fewer features with the target letter Z than do the distractors in List 1.

LIST 1	LIST 2
IMVXEW	ODUGQR
WVMEIX	GRODUQ
VXWIEM	DUROQG
MIEWVX	RGOUDQ
WEIMXV	RQGOUD
IWVXEM	UGQDRO
IXEIVW	GUQZOR
VWEMXI	ODGRUQ
MIVEWX	DRUQGO
WXEIMV	UQGORD

While Neisser's classic research suggested the importance of feature analysis to letter perception, there is evidence from other studies that it is not only the specific features which are of importance. For example, Lupker (1979) found that rapidly presented letters were confused on the basis of their overall shape as well as on their features. The implication is that letters are processed in terms of both their overall shape and their specific features.

Stabilised Retinal Images

The importance of features in perception has also been shown in research on stabilised retinal images. A stabilised retinal image is one that remains in the same position on the retina regardless of any eye movements. Stabilised retinal images can be achieved in many ways. For example, a visual stimulus can be projected on to the retina by means of a miniature projector positioned on a contact lens worn by the individual. When the eye moves, so does the contact lens (and thus the projector and the retinal image), but the visual image does not move relative to the retina. The stabilised retinal image fades within a minute or so, but the entire image does not disappear all at once. What generally happens is that features disappear and then reappear as meaningful units. Thus, the visual stimulus "BEER" may come to be perceived as "PEEP", "PEER", "BEE", or "BE" (Pritchard, 1961).

Evaluation

Feature theories are appealing because they replace the countless templates required by template theories with a much smaller number of features that can be combined and recombined to permit pattern recognition. They also possess the merit (as we have just seen) that they are in accord with some of the evidence. However, everything in the garden is not lovely. Feature theories are clearly over-simplified in a number of ways which are considered next.

The first major limitation of feature theories is that they de-emphasise the role played by contextual effects and by expectations in pattern recognition. The importance of contextual effects was demonstrated convincingly by Weisstein and Harris (1974). Subjects attempted to detect a line which was embedded either in a briefly flashed three-dimensional form or in a briefly flashed less coherent form. According to feature theories, the target line should always activate the same feature detectors irrespective of the visual context, and so the coherence of the form in which it is embedded should not affect detection. In fact, target detection was greatest when the target line was part of a three-dimensional form, and deteriorated as this form became flatter and more incoherent. Weisstein and Harris (1974) called this "the object-superiority effect", and it shows that some kind of modification of feature theories is needed. Perhaps the notion that the features of a pattern are extracted prior to the construction of the form and structure of that pattern is incorrect.

A much simpler demonstration of the effect of context on pattern recognition is shown in Fig. 2.3. The middle letter is precisely the same in both words, but despite the fact that the features and their arrangement are identical it is interpreted differently as a function of the word context.

The second major limitation of features theories concerns the extent to which such theories are applicable to all types of visual stimuli. You may have noticed that many of the experimental studies of the role of features in pattern recognition have used letters as the visual stimuli. This has been done because letters are relatively simple stimuli possessing readily identifiable features. It

The effect of context on pattern recognition. The middle letter is seen as an "H" in one word but as an "A" in the other.

FIGURE 2.3

SAE

BAT

would be extremely difficult to apply a feature analysis to some of the complex stimuli (e.g. faces; buildings) which we encounter in our everyday lives. The third major limitation of feature theories is that pattern recognition does not depend solely on listing the features of a stimulus. For example, the letter "A" consists of two oblique uprights and a dash, but these three features can be presented in such a way that they are not perceived as an "A": \ /-. In other words, in order to understand pattern perception we need to consider the relationships among features as well as simply the features themselves. It is also likely that some features are more important than others in pattern recognition. Complex feature theories that take such considerations into account resemble prototype theories in many ways.

The fourth major limitation of the feature-theory approach is that its assumption that pattern recognition begins with an analysis of the specific features of visual stimuli is not always correct. It appears to be the case that pattern recognition is often based on the overall shape of a visual stimulus rather than on the characteristics of its component features. The issues are dealt with more fully in the next section of the chapter, where there is a discussion of the alternative Gestalt viewpoint.

At a rather superficial level of analysis, it might appear that advances in the neurophysiology of vision provide strong evidence in favour of the feature-theory approach. As a result of research initiated by Hubel and Wiesel (1962), simple cells, complex cells, and hyper-complex cells have been identified within the brain's visual system. The simple cells differ from each other in the kind of stimulus to which they are maximally responsive, leading them to be divided into edge detectors, slit detectors, and line detectors. These simple cells have often (rather misleadingly) been called feature detectors. Complex cells resemble simple cells in that the optimal stimulus is still a line, slit, or edge, but the two kinds of cells differ in that the location of the stimulus within the cell's receptive field is much more critical in determining the response of simple cells. Hyper-complex cells resemble complex cells, but their responsiveness is much affected by the length of the visual stimulus.

Since these various cells in the brain are maximally responsive to certain specific aspects or features of visual stimuli, it might seem that they constitute the feature detectors postulated by feature theorists. The function of a feature detector is to indicate the presence of a particular stimulus feature regardless of the presence of other stimulus features. However, the responsiveness of visual cortical cells is typically not independent of other stimulus features. Instead, it is affected by additional features such as length and stimulus location. In essence, these cells simply fail to provide definitive evidence about stimulus features, a point which is discussed in more detail later in the chapter.

These considerations lead us to the fifth major limitation of the feature-theory approach. In essence, feature analysis is often a far more complicated business than is allowed for by most feature theories. The neurophysiological evidence indicates that the information about features provided by visual stimuli is often incomplete or ambiguous, and that it is by no means straightforward to produce an accurate feature analysis from the visual input. The subsequent discussion of Marr's (1982) theory will reveal more clearly the true complexities of feature analysis.

The sixth limitation of feature theories is that they tend to treat all features or attributes of stimuli in the same way. That this is an over-simplification was argued by Garner (1974). He proposed a distinction between *separable* and *integral* attribute combinations. Attribute combinations are said to be separable if they are perceived in terms of their separate attributes (e.g. form and size), whereas they are regarded as integral if they are not perceived separately (e.g. hue and brightness of a coloured form). As a consequence, a change in just one attribute with integral attribute combinations produces a difference in the appearance of the whole stimulus rather than simply in the changed attribute. More specifically, Garner (1974) suggested that there are two types of integral combinations: those for which such global or holistic perception is necessary, and those which people prefer to process holistically, but which can be processed attribute by attribute when such processing is advantageous.

One way of testing Garner's (1974) views is by means of a restricted classification task (see Spoehr & Lehmkuhle, 1982, for a review). Subjects are shown three stimuli varying along two dimensions. Each set of stimuli consists of two stimuli which are the same with respect to one dimension, but differ substantially on the other dimension; the third stimulus is similar to, but not identical to, one of the other stimuli on both dimensions. The subjects' task is to decide which two stimuli are most similar to each other. The expectation is that the two stimuli which are the same on one dimension should be grouped together (i.e. dimensional classification) when stimuli with separable dimensions are used, because it is obvious that they are identical on that dimension. In contrast, the prediction is that overall similarity should determine grouping with integral stimuli, so that the two stimuli that are similar but not identical on both dimensions should be grouped together.

Both of these predictions have been confirmed. Shepp, Burns, and McDonough (1980) discovered that 90% of groupings involving the integral dimensions of rectangle length and width were based on overall similarity. On the other hand, dimensional classifications were made 78% of the time when stimuli varying in the separable dimensions of circle size and angle of radius were used (Burns, Shepp, McDonough, & Wiener-Ehrlich, 1978).

Our discussion of separable and integral dimensions has implied that any dimensional combination is either integral or separable.

In fact, it is probably more realistic to regard integrality and separability as the end points of a continuum. In sum, the notion that pattern recognition involves feature analysis is a reasonable one. However, the importance of feature analysis depends greatly on the nature of the stimulus and on the extent to which relevant top-down processes are available. Even when feature analysis plays a major role in pattern recognition, there are complexities associated with extracting the appropriate features from the visual input and with taking account of the inter-relationships of features which have generally been ignored by feature theorists.

The Gestalt Approach

According to the feature-theory approach, pattern recognition is based on the individual features or elements of a visual pattern. An alternative viewpoint was put forward by the Gestaltists in the 1920s. They were a group of German psychologists (including Koffka, Kohler, and Wertheimer) who emigrated to the United States between the two World Wars. In direct contrast to feature theorists, they argued that pattern recognition is based on the overall shape of a visual stimulus rather than on its component features. In line with this, the Gestaltists proposed the concept of the "gestalt" (meaning "whole" or "configuration") as the major unit of analysis within perception, and proclaimed that "the whole is more than the sum of its parts." This basic aspect of the Gestaltist position was expressed in the following way by Wertheimer (1958, p. 135): "The way in which parts are seen, in which subwholes emerge, in which grouping occurs, is not an arbitrary piecemeal . . . summation of elements, but is a process in which character-istics of the whole play a major determining role."

This may sound like mumbo-jumbo, but there are actually various ways of testing it. For example, it follows from the Gestalt perspective that it should be possible to replace the original parts of a stimulus with other parts while still managing to retain the quality of the whole or the gestalt. This is known as "transposition." A simple example is the way in which a melody remains the same when it is transposed into a key in which all of the notes are changed.

One of the implications of the Gestalt approach is that the overall gestalt or whole may be perceived before the parts comprising the gestalt. The idea may sound far-fetched, but it was put to the test in an important series of experiments carried out by Navon (1977). He drew a conceptual distinction between local and global features. Local features are more specific than global features and are consequently "part-like," whereas global features are more "whole-like." The distinction can be clarified by means of an example based on the kind of stimuli used by Navon (1977). In this example (see Fig. 2.4), the "H" is the global feature and the several small "s"s are the local features.

FIGURE 2.4

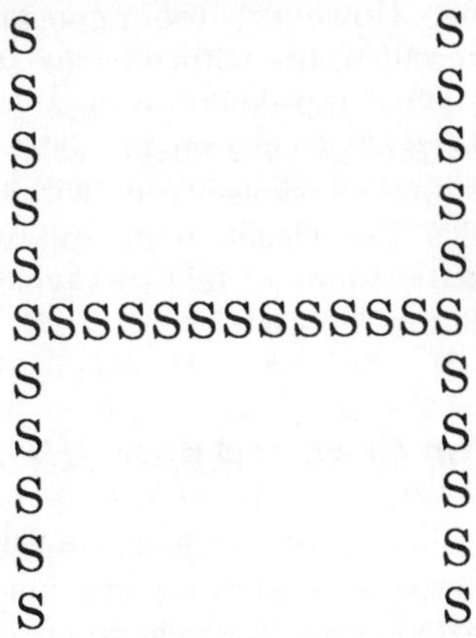

The kind of stimulus used by Navon (1977) to demonstrate the importance of global features in perception.

```
   S                S
   S                S
   S                S
   S                S
   S                S
   SSSSSSSSSSSSS
   S                S
   S                S
   S                S
   S                S
   S                S
```

In one of Navon's (1977) experiments, subjects looked briefly at a large letter made up of many small letters while deciding as rapidly as possible whether an "H" or an "S" had been presented auditorily. When the global letter was the same as the auditory letter, speed of auditory discrimination was increased, whereas there was an interference effect when it was different. More surprisingly, performance on the auditory task was totally unaffected by the nature of the local letters, and most of the subjects even failed to notice that the large letters were constructed out of small letters.

These findings suggest that global features are perceived more readily than local features, as the Gestaltists would have expected. Why should this be so? Perhaps when there is only sufficient time for a partial perceptual analysis, it is usually more valuable to obtain information about the general structure of a perceptual scene than about a few isolated details.

The experiment that we have just discussed shows that the whole can be perceived before its parts, but it is not clear how much control people have over their perceptual processes. If, for example, someone wanted to perceive the local features while ignoring the global features, would this be possible? Navon (1977) attempted to answer this question in a further study in which the stimuli were again large letters made out of small letters. The task was to decide as rapidly as possible whether the global letter was an "H" or an "S," or alternatively whether the small letters were "H"s or "S"s. Decision speed with the large or global letter was unaffected by the nature of the local or small letters. In contrast, performance speed with the local letters was greatly slowed when the global letter conflicted with the local letters. This latter finding suggests that it is difficult, or even impossible, to avoid perceiving the whole, and that global processing necessarily occurs before any more detailed perceptual analysis.

Navon's (1977) work implies that the notion that perceptual analysis involves building up a representation of a visual scene from its individual elements may be misguided. Instead, initial global structuring is often fleshed out by progressively more and more fine-grained analyses. There is obvious sense in having the perceptual system operate in this fashion, because it enables important objects in the visual scene to be identified and perceived with minimal delay. However, it is clear that the perceptual system does not invariably work like this. The large letters in Navon's (1977) studies were not all that large, never exceeding 5.5° of visual angle (visual angle = the angle formed at the eye by rays from the extremities of an object). Kinchla and Wolf (1979) used similar stimuli to those of Navon (1977), but with sizes ranging up to 22.1° of visual angle. They discovered that the local letters were easier to respond to than the global one when the global letter exceeded 8° of visual angle. They concluded reasonably enough that those forms in the visual field having an optimal size are processed first.

In sum, the Gestalt notion that pattern recognition often depends on the overall shape of a visual stimulus rather than on its individual features has received some support. However, there are clearly cases in which it does not apply. Factors such as the sizes of the local and global features, the viewing conditions, and the nature of the observer's task are all likely to play a part in determining the role played by individual features in pattern recognition. The Gestalt approach to visual perception involved more theoretical assumptions than we have considered here; some of those additional assumptions are discussed a little later in the chapter.

Summary

Several theoretical approaches to pattern recognition have been discussed. Template theories are based on the assumption that there are templates in long-term memory which are matched with presented stimuli. Such theories tend to be unwieldy, and have great difficulty in accounting for the flexibility of human perception. Prototype theorists argue that there is a manageable number of prototypes or structural descriptions stored in memory rather than an excessively large number of templates. Prototype theories often fail to take proper account of the influence of context on perception. They are also usually somewhat vague about the details of how stimuli are matched against prototypes.

Feature theorists emphasise the point that each visual stimulus can be regarded as consisting of a number of features. They claim that pattern recognition is based on an analysis of the features of presented stimuli. There are various problems with this approach: the importance of the inter-relationships among features is de-emphasised; contextual factors are ignored; and the notion that pattern recognition is based entirely on feature analysis is clearly over-simplified. The Gestaltists proposed the strongly contrasting view that the whole stimulus is perceived before its parts. This does appear to happen under some circumstances, but much less frequently than the Gestaltists would have expected.

OBJECT RECOGNITION

Throughout the waking day we are bombarded with information from the visual environment. Most of the time we are able to make sense of that information, and this usually involves identifying or recognising the objects which surround us. Object perception or recognition generally occurs in such an effortless fashion that it is difficult to believe that it is actually a rather complex achievement.

The complexities of object recognition can be grasped if we consider some of the processes which are involved. First, there are usually numerous different overlapping objects in the visual environment, and we must somehow decide where one object ends and the adjacent object starts. This almost certainly requires a substantial amount of information processing, as can be seen if we consider the visual environment of the first author as he is writing these words. According to a rapid count, there are well over 100 objects visible in the room in front of him and in the garden outside, and over 90% of these objects overlap, and are overlapped by, other objects. Second, objects can be recognised accurately over a wide range of viewing distances and orientations. For example, there is a small table directly in front of the first author. He is confident that this table is round, although there is an elliptical shape in the retinal image (i.e. the image formed on the light-sensitive cells at the back of the eye). The term "constancy" is used to refer to the fact that the apparent size and shape of an object do not change in spite of large variations in the size and shape of the retinal image.

Third, we recognise that an object is, say, a chair without any apparent difficulty. However, chairs vary enormously in their visual properties (e.g. colour, size, shape, texture). It is not immediately obvious how we manage to allocate such heterogeneous visual stimuli to the same category (e.g. chairs), but considerable learning is presumably involved. The discussion of the representation of concepts (e.g. Rosch et al. 1976) in Chapter 8 is relevant here.

Marr's Computational Theory

The Basic Theory

We have seen during the course of this chapter that there are various different approaches to the study of perception, of which the psychological and the physiological have been the most important historically. There are increasing signs that the approach based on artificial intelligence will ultimately prove important as well, especially if it becomes possible to produce a computer program that enables a machine to recognise objects in the real world. The reader may feel that what is needed is some kind of integration of information from the psychological, physiological, and artificial intelligence viewpoints, and this is exactly what the late David Marr and his colleagues have attempted to do for visual perception. Their computational theory is discussed at length in various places (e.g. Frisby, 1986; Marr, 1982).

Marr's (1982) starting point was that there are a number of different levels of explanation. Consider, for example, the kinds of explanation which could be proposed for a car and its functioning. At one level, a car consists of an engine, four wheels, a chassis, gears, and numerous other bits and pieces. At another level, we could describe the role of the battery in supplying electricity, the engine-cooling characteristics of the radiator, the operations of the carburettor, and so on. Finally, we could explain a car in terms of its function, which is of course to transport people and their belongings from one place to another along the road system.

As we saw in Chapter 1, Marr (1982) identified three levels of explanation for visual perception. The top level is the computational level, which relates to the purpose of perception, and the bottom level is the hardware level (i.e. the brain). At an intermediate level, there is the algorithmic level which is concerned with the detailed processes involved in perception.

While all of these levels of explanation are important in their own right, the computational theory level may well be of particular significance. An indication of why this is so can be obtained by referring back to the car example. It would be possible to have a thorough understanding of how each of the various components of a car works, but without knowing what a car is for there would be little grasp of *why* a car has those particular components interconnected in the way they are. Once we realise that a car is essentially a means of transport, it then follows that it needs a source of energy, aerodynamically sound shape, ways in which its movements can be controlled, and so on, and it becomes clear why cars are designed in the way they are.

We have dealt with some of the general characteristics of Marr's (1982) theoretical approach, and it is now time to consider in more detail his theory of visual perception. In essence, he proposed that the processes involved in vision produce a series of *representations* (i.e. descriptions) which provide increasingly detailed information about the visual environment. According to Marr

(1982), there are three major kinds of representation which need to be distinguished:

- The *primal sketch*, which provides a two-dimensional description of the main light-intensity changes in the visual input, including information about edges, contours, and blobs. This representation is observer-centred, which means that the visual input is described only from the observer's viewpoint.
- The *2.5-D sketch*, which incorporates a description of the depth and orientation of visible surfaces, making use of information provided by shading, texture, motion, binocular disparity, and so on. Like the primal sketch, it is observer-centred.
- The *3-D model representation*, which describes three-dimensionally the shapes of objects and their relative positions in a way which is independent of the observer's viewpoint.

The Primal Sketch

According to Marr (1982), it is possible to identify two versions of the primal sketch. These are the raw primal sketch and the full primal sketch. In essence, the raw primal sketch contains information about light-intensity changes in the visual scene, and the full primal sketch is formed as a result of making use of this information to identify the number and outline shapes of visual objects. Perhaps the most interesting theoretical problem involved in constructing the primal sketch stems from the fact that light-intensity changes often provide ambiguous information about the appropriate way of organising the visual field. Consider, for example, Fig. 2.5. In 2.5 (a) and 2.5 (b), the dots could be grouped either horizontally or vertically; the lines in 2.5(c) could be seen as either two crossing lines or a V-shaped line and an inverted V-shaped line; and the figure in 2.5 (d) could be seen as either a circle or as an incomplete circle.

Before proceeding with our account of Marr's (1982) views on the primal sketch, it is worth spending a little time to consider some of the relevant ideas of the Gestaltists. One of their main interests was in the organisation of the visual field. Their fundamental principle of perceptual organisation was the law of Prägnanz, which Koffka (1935, p. 110) expressed as follows: "Psychological organisation will always be as 'good' as the prevailing conditions allow. In this definition the term 'good' is undefined." In practice, the Gestaltists regarded a good form as the simplest or the most uniform of the available alternatives.

While the law of Pragnanz was their key organisational principle, the Gestaltists also proposed several other laws, most of which can be subsumed under the law of Pragnanz. Some of these laws are illustrated in Fig. 2.5. The fact that three horizontal arrays of dots

Examples of some of the Gestalt laws of perceptual organisation: (a) the law of proximity; (b) the law of similarity; (c) the law of good continuation; and (d) the law of closure.

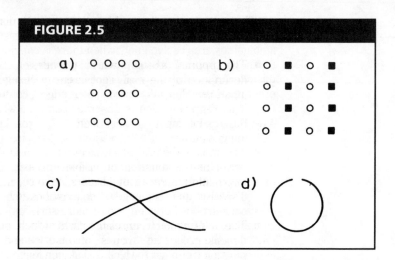

FIGURE 2.5

rather than vertical arrays are perceived in 2.5 (a) indicates that visual elements tend to be grouped together if they are close to each other (the law of proximity). Figure 2.5 (b) illustrates the law of similarity, according to which elements will be grouped together perceptually if they are similar to each other. Vertical columns rather than horizontal rows are seen because the elements in the vertical columns are the same, whereas those in the horizontal rows are not. We see two crossing lines in Fig. 2.5 (c), because according to the law of good continuation we group together those elements requiring the fewest changes or interruptions in straight or smoothly curving lines or contours. Figure 2.5 (d) illustrates the law of closure, according to which missing parts of a figure are filled in to complete the figure. Thus, a circle is seen in spite of the fact that it is incomplete.

These, and other, Gestalt laws of perceptual organisation make reasonable intuitive sense, but they are obviously descriptive statements possessing little or no explanatory power. The Gestaltists appear to have believed that their laws reflected basic organisational processes within the brain, but it is much more plausible to assume that the laws arise as a result of experience. It tends to be the case that visual elements which are close together, similar, and so on, belong to the same object, and presumably this is something which we learn.

Marr (1976) made use of the insights of the Gestalt psychologists when he attempted to design a computer program to proceed from the raw primal sketch to the full primal sketch. It is not possible here to go into the details of how this was accomplished. However, he discovered that it was useful to make use of two rather general principles when designing the program: the *principle of explicit naming* and the *principle of least commitment*. According to the principle of explicit naming, it is useful to give a name or symbol to a set of grouped elements. The reason is that the name or symbol can be used over and over again to describe other sets of grouped elements, all of which can then form a much larger grouping. According to the principle of least commitment, ambiguities are resolved only when there is convincing evidence as to the appropriate resolution. This principle is useful because mistakes at an early stage of processing can then lead on to several other mistakes.

The 2.5-D Sketch

According to Marr (1982), various stages are involved in the transformation of the primal sketch into the 2.5-D sketch. The first stage involves the construction of a *range map* ("local point-by-point depth information about surfaces in the scene," Frisby, 1986, p. 164). After this, higher-level descriptions (e.g. of convex and concave junctions between two or more surfaces) are produced by combining information from related parts of the range map. More is known of the processes involved in constructing a range map than in proceeding from that to the 2.5-D sketch itself, and our coverage will reflect that fact.

What kinds of information are used in changing the primal sketch into the 2.5-D sketch? Those used include shading, motion, texture, shape, and binocular disparity. Since Marr (1982) made a number of contributions to our understanding of the ways in which binocular disparity is used in depth perception, we will focus on that source of information.

"Binocular disparity" refers to the fact that the visual information presented to the two eyes is not precisely the same. That can be observed very clearly if you hold a finger up close to your nose and then look at it with one eye at a time. The further away from you an object is, the smaller the binocular disparity becomes; binocular disparity could thus be used in order to work out the relative distances of different objects.

According to Marr and Poggio (1976) and Marr (1982), the task of using the information available from binocular disparity in order to construct a range map involves rather complex processes. Among the problems which need to be resolved is how to ensure that the information from the two eyes is matched up appropriately (the so-called "correspondence problem"). Marr and Poggio (1976) proposed three rules that might be useful in handling the correspondence problem:

- Binocular combination rule 1: Elements in the primal sketches formed from the input to each eye are matched with each other only if they are compatible (e.g. having the same colour; edges having the same orientation).
- Binocular combination rule 2: Each element is only allowed to match with one element in the other primal sketch. If it were not for this rule, then it would be possible for an element to appear in more than one place at the same time.
- Binocular combination rule 3: Prefer matches between two points or elements where the disparities between the two

primal sketches are similar to the disparities between nearby matches on the same surface. This rule makes sense because nearby points on a surface are likely to be approximately the same distance away from the observer, and the disparity information takes distance into account.

Frisby (1986) pointed out that the third rule of those listed seems the least adequate. For example, if an object slants steeply away from the observer, then nearby points will not have very similar disparities. As a consequence, there may be a failure to match corresponding points with each other.

The 3-D Model Representation

The 2.5-D sketch suffers from a number of limitations. For example, it does not contain information about those surfaces of objects in the visual field which are hidden from view. In addition, it is observer-centred, which means that the representation of an object will vary considerably depending upon the angle from which it is observed. This enormous variety of representations obviously provides a poor basis for identifying the object by matching it up with stored object information in long-term memory. These are some of the reasons why it is important for viewers to go on to compute the 3-D model representation, which does not have these limitations.

Marr and Nishihara (1978) identified three desirable criteria for a 3-D model representation:

- *Accessibility*, which refers to the ease with which the representation can be constructed.
- *Scope* and *uniqueness*, with "scope" referring to the extent to which the representation is applicable to all of the shapes in a given category, and "uniqueness" meaning that all the different views of an object produce the same standard representation. Frisby (1986, p. 168) cites the following description of a tin of beans as an example of uniqueness: "Two flat round surface patches joined to the edges of a cylindrical surface." The enormous advantage of a unique description or representation is that it much easier to match it with the appropriate object knowledge in memory.
- *Stability* and *sensitivity*, with "stability" indicating that a representation incorporates the similarities among objects, and "sensitivity" indicating that it incorporates the salient differences.

Marr and Nishihara (1978) made only limited progress in their attempt to describe what is involved in 3-D model representations. However, they did propose that the primitive units for describing objects should be cylinders. They also proposed that these primitive units should be hierarchically organised, with high-level units providing information about object shape and low-level units providing more detailed information. The flavour of this theoretical approach can be seen in the description by Marr and Nishihara (1978) of the human form:

> First the overall form of the "body" is given an axis. This yields an object-centred coordinate system which can then be used to specify the arrangement of the "arms," "legs," "torso," and "head". The position of each of these is specified by an axis of its own, which in turn serves to define a coordinate system for specifying the arrangement of further subsidiary parts. This gives us a hierarchy of 3D models. . . The shapes . . . are drawn as if they were cylindrical, but that is purely for . . . convenience: It is the axes alone that stand for the volumetric qualities of the shape, much as pipecleaner models can serve to describe various animals.

This account of the hierarchical organisation of the human form is illustrated in Fig. 2.6. This Figure shows how the human form can be decomposed into a series of cylinders at different levels of generality.

FIGURE 2.6

The hierarchical organisation of the human figure (Marr & Nishihara, 1978) at various levels: (a) axis of the whole body; (b) axes at the level of arms, legs and head; (c) arm divided into upper and lower arm; (d) a lower arm with separate hand; and (e) the palm and fingers of a hand.

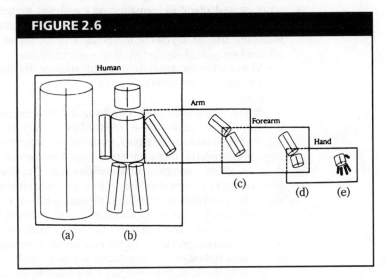

Evaluation

One of Marr's greatest successes was to make it clear that object recognition is a much greater achievement than had generally been realised. The information received by the eyes is typically ambiguous and constantly changing, and the visual information provided by an object may differ radically as a function of the viewing angle. As a consequence, rather complex theories are probably going to be needed to account for object recognition. Marr's (1982) theoretical approach represented a good first approximation to the level of theoretical complexity that will be needed.

One of the reasons why Marr (1982) came to believe that object recognition involves very complex processes was because of the problems he and others experienced when they tried to develop computer programs that could handle very simple visual environments. The fact that it is extremely difficult to simulate even basic perceptual processes suggests that human perception is considerably more involved than one might imagine.

The notion that perceivers construct a series of progressively more complex representations appears to have much to recommend it. The fact that this theoretical approach evolved from an attempt to integrate information from the psychological, physiological, and artificial intelligence viewpoints strengthens the belief that it is on the right lines. As we will see in the next section, much of the relevant cognitive neuropsychological evidence is consistent with the assumption that object recognition requires a series of stages of processing. On the negative side, Marr's computational approach has focused mainly on the early stages of object recognition. While the theory has proved reasonably successful at accounting for the formation of the primal sketch and the 2.5-D sketch, we do not as yet have a detailed understanding of the processes involved in transforming the 2.5-D sketch into the 3-D model representation. Another limitation is that Marr (1982) had relatively little to say about the ways in which visual processes are affected by prior knowledge of the objects in the visual scene. It would not be true to claim that he ignored the impact of prior knowledge, but it is probably correct that he de-emphasised its influence.

A final limitation was pointed out by Tenebaum, Witkin, and Wandell (1983). They noted that Marr (1982) often seemed to regard the existence of a computational theory that could achieve certain perceptual goals as proof that the computational theory described how that aspect of perception actually operates in human perceivers. For example, Marr (1982) discovered by computational methods that depth and surface orientation can be inferred without making use of knowledge about the object, and this led him to conclude that the representation of depth and orientation always precedes object recognition. Of course, the conclusion does not necessarily follow.

Cognitive Neuropsychology

As we will see shortly, cognitive neuropsychologists have discovered that brain-damaged patients differ in the specific impairments to object recognition from which they suffer. Marr's (1982) theoretical approach provides a useful framework for considering many of these impairments. Of particular relevance is Marr's (1982) assumption that three successive representations (i.e. the primal sketch, the 2.5-D sketch, and the 3-D model representation) are formed when a visual stimulus is presented. Brain damage might impair the ability to form any of these representations, with the precise nature of the perceptual deficit depending on which kind of representation was adversely affected. It also follows from Marr's (1982) theoretical position that impaired ability to form either the primal sketch or the 2.5-D sketch would seriously reduce (or even eliminate) the ability to form the 3-D model representation.

The natural starting point for a consideration of the cognitive neuropsychological evidence relevant to Marr's (1982) theory would appear to be those brain-damaged patients who are unable to form even primal sketches. However, they have such general impairments of visual perception that their perceptual deficits would tell us little about the organisation of perceptual abilities. Of greater theoretical interest are those patients who have a mixture of intact and impaired perceptual abilities, and such patients will be the focus of subsequent discussion.

Problems with 2.5-D Sketches

If a patient found it difficult to form 2.5-D sketches, but could form primal sketches and had access to semantic knowledge about objects, what would one expect of his or her perceptual perform-ance? On the positive side, some basic processes of visual perception would be intact, including those involved in the initial analysis of light-intensity changes. In addition, objects would be identifiable from information provided by sense modalities other than the visual. On the negative side, such a patient would have severe shape-processing impairments, and would be unable to copy presented objects. He or she would also be unable to identify objects solely on the basis of visual information.

As the review by Ellis and Young (1988) makes clear, there are some brain-damaged patients whose perceptual abilities and deficits resemble those just described. For example, there is a patient, S, who was studied by Benson and Greenberg (1969). He retained some perceptual skills in the visual modality, as was shown by his ability to distinguish between relatively small differences in brightness and to find his way safely around the hospital in which he was living. He could also identify objects provided that appropriate nonvisual (e.g. auditory or tactile) cues were available. In marked contrast, however, S was extremely poor at identifying objects on the basis of vision alone. His problems with shape and object perception were so great that he could not copy simple figures, and he was even unable to decide which out of an array of four figures was the same as a sample figure.

S's perceptual performance apparently indicated that he could no longer make use of form-and shape-processing abilities underlying the formation of 2.5-D sketches. However, his residual visual abilities suggested that he might well be able to form at least an approximation to the primal sketch representation. The notion that patients such as S have relatively intact basic perceptual abilities has not commanded universal approval. Campion and Latto (1985) investigated a patient, RC, who resembled S in a number of ways. Both patients had suffered from accidental carbon monoxide poisoning, showed poor object recognition in the visual modality but not in other modalities, and demonstrated some basic visual abilities. It was discovered that RC had numerous small areas of blindness within his field of vision, and these blind areas may well have played a part in impairing his object perception.

In sum, there are two schools of thought concerning the appropriate explanation of the perceptual deficits shown by patients such as S and RC One possibility is that their perceptual problems are mainly at the level of form-and shape-processing, and another possibility is that difficulties in forming 2.5-D sketches stem from perceptual impairments at a more basic level. It is highly probable that basic perceptual impairments (e.g. RC's blind areas) sometimes disrupt object perception. However, the fact that the extent of such impairments does not correlate highly with problems of object perception (e.g. Young & Ellis, 1988) indicates that impaired object perception cannot be entirely accounted for in terms of sensory deficits.

Problems with 3-D Model Representations

According to the model put forward by Marr (1982), it is theoretically possible for brain-damaged patients to have problems with object perception revolving around the task of turning the 2.5-D sketch into the 3-D model representation. What pattern of perceptual performance would one expect to find in such patients? They might be able to draw visually presented objects reasonably accurately, since this ability requires only an adequate 2.5-D sketch. However, they would experience great difficulty in recognising objects presented from unusual angles, because they would lack the ability to transform the observer-centred 2.5-D sketch into the object-centred 3-D model representation. Finally, if semantic knowledge about objects were intact, then such patients might be able to recognise objects which were viewed from the most typical angle. In those circumstances, the 2.5-D sketch would most closely resemble the 3-D model representation, and so the problems stemming from difficulties with transforming one representation into the other would be minimised.

Patients who at least approximate to this description were studied by Warrington and Taylor (1978). These patients had posterior injuries of the right cerebral hemisphere. Warrington and Taylor (1978) made use of pairs of photographs of objects, in which the same object had been taken from usual and unusual views. The distinction between "usual" and "unusual" was not defined very precisely by Warrington and Taylor (1978). However, the crucial point is that unusual or unconventional views of objects require greater transformation than do usual views to produce a 3-D model representation. For example, their usual view of a flat-iron was photographed from above, whereas the unusual view was photographed so that only the base of the iron and part of the handle were visible.

In one test the photographs were shown individually. The brain-damaged patients were reasonably good at identifying the objects when they were shown in a usual or conventional view, but they were very poor at identifying the same objects when shown in an unusual view. More dramatic evidence of the problems that these patients have was obtained in another test. Pairs of photographs (one usual view and one unusual view) were presented together, and the patients had to decide whether the two photographs showed the same object. The patients did poorly on this task. This indicates that they found it difficult to identify the object shown from an unusual view even when they knew what it might be on the basis of their identification of the accompanying usual view.

The fact that the patients in the study by Warrington and Taylor (1978) performed well with the photographs showing usual views suggests that most of the processes involved in object perception and recognition were intact. Their considerably poorer performance with unusual than with usual views is most plausibly explained in terms of difficulties in changing 2.5-D sketches into 3-D model representations.

Humphreys and Riddoch (1984, 1985) pointed out that the view of an object can be unusual in at least two different ways. It can be unusual because a distinctive feature of the object is hidden from view or because the object is foreshortened, thus making it difficult to determine its principal axis of elongation. Accordingly, they used photographs in which some of the unusual views were based on obscuring a distinctive feature, whereas others were based on foreshortening. There were two tasks: object naming and matching, in which two photographs of the same object were presented along with a third photograph showing a visually similar distractor.

Humphreys and Riddoch (1984; 1985) obtained data on the naming and matching tasks from four patients with right posterior cerebral lesions. In essence, these patients performed poorly with the foreshortened photographs but not with those in which a distinctive feature was not visible. How do these findings relate to Marr's (1982) theoretical model of object perception and recognition? According to Marr and Nishihara (1978), foreshortening makes it especially difficult to attain a 3-D model representation, and this would appear to be the most appropriate explanation of the data.

More Complex Perceptual Problems

We have so far considered patients who have very clear impairments to some of the processes necessary for object recognition. There are other patients whose perceptual deficits are rather more difficult to account for on Marr's (1982) theory. Some patients have poor object recognition in spite of the fact that most of the component processes involved are largely intact. For example, Humphreys and Riddoch (1987) investigated a patient,

HJA, who experienced problems with object recognition after suffering a stroke. Even when he was able to identify an object, it typically took him 20–30 seconds to do so. However, his ability to form 2.5-D sketch representations appeared to be intact, as was demonstrated by his ability to copy drawings of objects. He showed a good ability to construct 3-D model representations, in that he was able to match foreshortened views to typical views of the same objects. In addition, his semantic knowledge of objects appeared to be intact. He could provide good definitions of objects (even those he could not recognise), and he could draw objects accurately from memory.

How can we account for HJA's problems with naming objects, given that many of his basic perceptual skills and his semantic system were essentially intact? Part of the answer is probably that the perceptual representations he constructed often failed to access the relevant information about objects stored in the semantic system. However, Humphreys and Riddoch (1987) proposed that HJA's problems revolved around difficulties with the *integration* of visual information. They argued that the reason why he took so long to identify those objects he was finally able to name was because he was struggling to relate the stimulus features to each other.

In sum, the case of HJA is of considerable theoretical significance. It suggests that the integration of information from visually presented objects may play a greater role in object recognition than has usually been realised. This has direct implications for theories of object recognition.

As Ellis and Young (1988) pointed out, a condition known as *optic aphasia* is also of theoretical interest. Optic aphasics can name objects which they have touched, and they can indicate by mime the use of objects which they have seen. However, they have great difficulty in naming objects purely on the basis of having seen them.

In order to understand what is involved in optic aphasia, it is useful to consider the theoretical framework provided by Ellis and Young (1988). They suggested that there are three different kinds of stored object information which play a part in object recognition:

- *Object recognition units*: There is an object recognition unit corresponding to each known object, containing information about its structural characteristics.
- *Semantic system*: This contains information about object meaning.
- *Speech output lexicon*: This contains information about the names of objects.
- According to Ellis and Young (1988), stored information about visually presented objects is accessed serially in the order just described. Therefore, for example, the name of an object can be retrieved only after the appropriate object recognition unit and relevant semantic information have been accessed.

Riddoch and Humphreys (1987) investigated a patient, JB, who had the classic symptoms of optic aphasia. In addition, they discovered that he performed at about the normal level on a task of deciding whether line drawings represented real or meaningless objects. This suggests that he was able to gain access to the relevant object recognition units when drawings of real objects were presented. Why, then, did he experience such difficulties in identifying or naming objects? According to Ellis and Young (1988), the links between the object recognition units and the semantic system may have been impaired. This notion receives support from another finding reported by Riddoch and Humphreys (1987). They discovered that JB was very poor at drawing objects from memory, even when he could remember relevant semantic information about the objects concerned. This suggests that he could not readily access object recognition units from the semantic system, which is consistent with the hypothesis that the links between the two systems were impaired.

How was JB able to mime the use of visually presented objects if he had such difficulty in accessing the semantic system and speech output lexicon? It is possible (cf. Ellis & Young, 1988) that there are links between object recognition units and the system responsible for miming object use, so that it is possible to mime the use of a seen object without necessitating the use of the semantic system at all.

As Ellis and Young (1988, p. 56) pointed out: "Optic aphasia forces us to think more carefully about the different types of information we can access from seen objects." The fact that optic aphasics find it relatively easy to access some kinds of information about objects (e.g. miming of use) but very difficult to access other kinds of information (e.g. object naming) suggests that there are a number of different storage systems containing information about objects. These complexities will need to be incorporated into theories of object recognition.

Summary

The most influential theory of object recognition is the one proposed by the late David Marr. He attempted in an ambitious way to integrate psychological and neurophysiological data within a computational approach. His research demonstrated that object recognition is a considerably more complex business than most psychologists had assumed it to be. According to Marr (1982), three successive representations are formed during the perceptual process: the primal sketch; the 2.5-D sketch; and the 3-D model representation. Much is known of the characteristics of the primal sketch, but the details of the other representations are still unclear.

Cognitive neuropsychology has amply confirmed the view that there are several different components or processes involved in object recognition. Marr's (1982) contention that observers construct a series of progressively more complete perceptual representations receives broad support from the cognitive neuropsychological evidence. However, some brain-damaged patients have patterns of object-recognition impairment which suggest that more attention needs to be paid to the kinds of stored information about objects which are used in object recognition. This might not have become apparent from studies of normal individuals, who typically access all of the relevant information about objects very rapidly and very accurately.

Finally, it should be noted that much of the research on object recognition is somewhat limited, in that the focus is typically on the recognition of single objects presented in isolation. Under naturalistic conditions, of course, an object is usually encountered as only part of a visual scene. The rest of the visual scene provides contextual information, which, as we have seen, can systematically influence object recognition.

FACE RECOGNITION

There are various reasons for devoting a separate section of this chapter to face recognition. First, since face recognition is the most common way of identifying people we know, the ability to recognise faces is of tremendous significance in our everyday lives. Second, while face recognition shares some similarities with other forms of object recognition, it also differs in some respects. Therefore, one cannot simply assume that what has been found to be the case with object recognition generally will apply to face recognition. Third, there has been a substantial amount of impressive research and theorising on face recognition in recent years. As a result, we know more about the processes involved in face recognition than about those involved in most other forms of object recognition.

Some of the most interesting evidence that face processing may differ in major ways from the processing of objects has emerged from the study of a face-processing disorder known as *prosopagnosia*. Prosopagnosic patients are unable to recognise familiar faces, and this can even extend to their own faces seen in a mirror. However, they have some ability to recognise familiar objects. This inability to recognise faces does not occur because they have forgotten the people concerned, because they can still recognise familiar people from their voices and their names. There have been different opinions as to how to interpret the findings from prosopagnostic patients. It has been suggested that these patients have problems in recognising faces simply because more precise discriminations are required to distinguish between one face and another than to distinguish between different objects (e.g. a chair and a table). An alternative position is that there are specific processing mechanisms involved in face recognition.

Evidence supporting the notion of face-specific processes was obtained by DeRenzi (1986). The prosopagnostic patient studied by DeRenzi was very good at making fine discriminations (e.g. between Italian coins and others; between his own handwriting and that of others), but he was unable to recognise friends and relatives by sight. These findings, and others discussed by Ellis and Young (1988), suggest that there are face-specific processes, even if the details of such processes are not known as yet.

Bruce and Young's Model

The most developed model of face recognition was proposed by Bruce and Young (1986). They argued that there are several different types of information which can be obtained from faces, and which correspond to the eight components of their model (see Fig. 2.7). All of these components will be described shortly, but it is worth noting here and now that it is not assumed that all of these components are involved in face recognition for every face. According to Bruce and Young (1986), there are major differences in the processing of familiar and unfamiliar faces. The recognition of familiar faces primarily depends upon structural encoding, face recognition units, person identity nodes, and name generation, whereas the processing of unfamiliar faces involves structural encoding, expression analysis, facial speech analysis, and directed visual processing.

The face-recognition model put forward by Bruce and Young (1986) consists of the following components:

- *Structural encoding*: This produces various representations or descriptions corresponding approximately to those identified within Marr's (1982) model.
- *Expression analysis*: An individual's emotional state can be inferred from an analysis of information about their facial features.
- *Facial speech analysis*: Speech perception can be facilitated by detailed observation of a speaker's lip movements (McGurk & MacDonald, 1976).
- *Directed visual processing*: For certain purposes (e.g. to decide whether most psychologists have beards), specific facial information may be processed selectively.
- *Face recognition units*: Each face recognition unit contains structural information about one of the faces known to the viewer.
- *Person identity nodes*: These provide information about the person concerned (e.g. their occupation, interests, friends, contexts in which encountered, etc.).
- *Name generation*: A person's name is stored separately from other information about them.
- *Cognitive system*: The cognitive system contains additional information (e.g. that actors and actresses tend to have attractive faces) that is sometimes of use in face recognition; it also plays an important part in determining which component or components of the system receive attention.

The model of face recognition proposed by Bruce and Young (1986).

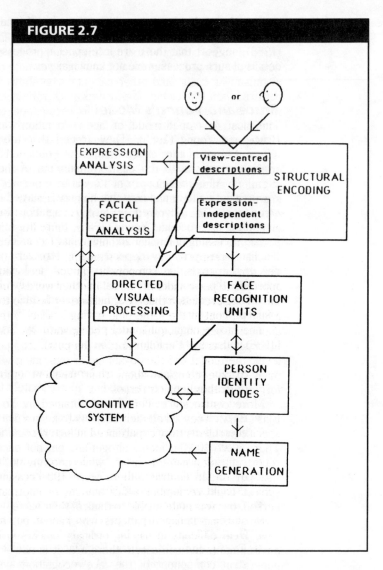

FIGURE 2.7

Experimental evidence

There are numerous studies which provide evidence relevant to an evaluation of the above model, and the interested reader is referred to Bruce (1988) for a detailed analysis. This evidence includes laboratory studies on normal individuals, cognitive neuropsychological investigations of brain-damaged patients, and diary studies. What we will do here is to consider fairly briefly some of the most important studies based on each of these approaches.

One of the major theoretical assumptions made by Bruce and Young (1986) is that familiar and unfamiliar faces are processed in different ways. For example, it is obvious that several components of the face recognition model (i.e. face recognition units, person identity nodes, name generation) cannot be used with unfamiliar faces. This theoretical analysis has interesting implications for the study of brain-damaged patients. If it were possible to find patients who showed good recognition of familiar faces but poor recognition of unfamiliar faces, and other patients who showed the opposite pattern, then this would obviously provide rather strong evidence that the processes involved in the recognition of familiar and unfamiliar faces are different.

Malone, Morris, Kay, and Levin (1982) obtained evidence which is exactly in line with these theoretical predictions. They tested one patient who showed reasonable ability to recognise photographs of famous statesmen (14 out of 17 correct), but who was severely impaired in a task involving matching unfamiliar faces. A second patient was quite different, performing at a normal level on matching unfamiliar faces, but having great difficulties in recognising photographs of famous people (only 5 out of 22 correct).

Let us return to the model shown in Fig. 2.7. It indicates that the name generation component can be accessed only via the appropriate person identity node. In other words, the model makes the strong prediction that we should never be able to put a name to a face without at the same time having available other information about that person (e.g. his or her occupation, the contexts in which he or she has been encountered in the past). At a purely anecdotal level, the model has the advantage of explaining why it is that so many people complain about their frequent embarrassment at forgetting other people's names.

More convincing evidence was obtained by Young, Hay, and Ellis (1985). They asked their subjects to keep a diary record of the specific problems they experienced in face recognition day by day. There were 1008 incidents altogether, but not once did a subject report putting a name to a face while knowing nothing else about that person. In contrast, there were 190 occasions on which a subject could remember a fair amount of information about the person, but was quite unable to think of their name.

Most brain-damaged patients who cannot put names to faces have great difficulty in naming ordinary objects in their everyday environment. In such cases, therefore, it is not simply the name generation component of the face-recognition system which is impaired. However, McKenna and Warrington (1980) reported the case of a patient, GBL, whose naming problems seemed to be fairly specific to faces. GBL was able to supply accurate information about 90% of famous people whose photographs she saw, but could name only 15% of them. In contrast, she named 80% of European cities and 100% of English towns that she was asked to identify on the basis of their locations on a map.

According to the model, another kind of problem should be fairly common. If the appropriate face recognition unit is activated, but the person identity node is not, then there should be a feeling of familiarity coupled with the inability to think of any relevant information about them (e.g. where they have been seen before, what they do for a living, their name). In the set of incidents collected by Young et al. (1985), there were 233 occasions on which this was reported.

Reference back to Fig. 2.7 suggests further predictions about familiar faces that follow from the Bruce and Young (1986) model. When we look at a familiar face, familiarity information from the face recognition unit should be accessed first, followed by information about that person (e.g. occupation) from the person identity node, followed by that person's name from the name generation component. It follows that familiarity decisions about a face should be made faster than decisions based on person identity nodes. As predicted, Young, McWeeny, Hay, and Ellis (1986b) discovered that subjects decided whether or not a face was familiar more rapidly than they decided whether or not a face was that of a politician.

It also follows from Bruce and Young's (1986) theoretical position that decisions based on person identity nodes should be made faster than those based on the word generation component. Young, McWeeny, Ellis, and Hay (1986a) found that subjects were much faster to decide whether a face belonged to a politician than they were to produce the person's name.

Evaluation

There is convincing evidence that several different components are involved in face processing, and that familiar and unfamiliar faces are typically processed quite differently. It thus appears that the model proposed by Bruce and Young (1986) is on the right lines. This is particularly the case so far as familiar faces are concerned. It seems reasonably well established that information about familiar faces is accessed sequentially, as the model assumes, and that the order in which different kinds of information are accessed also corresponds to theoretical assumptions.

The main inadequacies of the model relate to insufficient specification of some of the components and processes involved in face recognition. Perhaps the clearest example of this is the cognitive system. As Bruce and Young (1986, p.321) admit, the cognitive system "serves to catch all those aspects of processing not reflected in other components of our model." Another example concerns the account given of the processing of unfamiliar faces, which is much less detailed than the one offered of familiar faces.

The difference in the adequacy of the interpretations of face recognition with familiar and unfamiliar faces can be seen if we consider context effects. It has been found with both familiar and unfamiliar faces that the speed and accuracy of recognition are much affected by the context in which a face is presented. In the case of familiar faces, advance contextual information about the individual's occupation or where they have previously been encountered activates the person identity node, and this in turn can activate the appropriate face recognition unit and thus facilitate recognising a face as familiar (note the arrow running from the person identity node to the face recognition unit in Fig. 2.7). In the case of unfamiliar faces, context effects have also been found. For example, unfamiliar faces are recognised better if they are shown for a second time against the same background context as at the first showing (Beales & Parkin, 1984). This kind of finding is rather difficult to incorporate within the model shown in Fig. 2.7.

Summary

Face recognition is an aspect of object recognition which is of particular significance in our everyday lives. Face recognition shares many of the processes typically involved in object recognition, but none of the general theories of object recognition provides a satisfactory account of face recognition. Bruce and Young (1986) attempted to fill this gap by proposing a theory of face recognition. This theory appears to be on the right lines as indicated by diary studies, by laboratory research, and by the investigation of brain-damaged patients. In particular, it seems reasonably well established that the various components they have identified are, indeed, involved in face recognition. However, the details of how these processing components or systems work still need to be fleshed out, especially so far as the processing of unfamiliar faces is concerned.

SUMMARY

Pattern recognition, which is concerned with assigning meaning to visual stimuli, is a complex business. The appearance of objects changes constantly as we move through the environment, but this rarely produces any apparent difficulty in identifying objects or in making sense of our environment. Even when confronted by a visual stimulus we have never seen before (e.g. a new type of bird or plane), we are usually confident that we know the category to which it belongs.

There have been numerous theoretical attempts to understand the processes involved in pattern recognition, but most of them are demonstrably inadequate. Template theorists argue that stimuli are matched against miniature copies or templates of previously presented patterns. Unless the implausible assumption is made that there is an almost infinite number of templates to handle all eventualities, template theories are generally inadequate to account for the versatility of perceptual processing. Prototype theories have some advantages over template theories, in that the number of prototypes (i.e. abstract forms representing the basic elements of the stimuli belonging to a given category) needed for pattern recognition is much smaller than the number of templates. However, prototype theorists tend to be imprecise about the details of how pattern recognition occurs, and it is by no means clear that all categories of stimuli can plausibly be represented by a single prototype.

Feature theorists emphasise that any stimulus can be regarded as consisting of a number of specific features, and that feature analysis plays a crucial role in pattern recognition. It is probable that feature analysis is generally involved in pattern recognition, but most feature theories suffer from several deficiencies. For example, the role of top-down or conceptually driven processes in perception is de-emphasised, and insufficient attention is paid to the importance of considering the inter-relationships among features as well as the features per se. In addition, it is usually assumed (quite erroneously) that the processes involved in extracting features from visual stimuli are very straightforward.

David Marr proposed a computational approach which faced up to the complexities of pattern recognition to a much greater extent than had previous approaches. His basic idea was that perceivers construct a series of representations during the course of pattern recognition: the primal sketch; the 2.5-D sketch; and the 3-D model representation. Marr's general approach has received support from much of the evidence, including that obtained from brain-damaged patients by cognitive neuropsychologists. In general terms, Marr focused primarily on the early stages of object recognition, and so relatively little is known of how the 3-D model representation is constructed from the 2.5-D sketch. Recent cognitive neuropsychological evidence suggests that there are greater complexities associated with stored information about objects than was appreciated by Marr (1982).

One of the most important and complex visual objects is the human face. Several different processing components need to be postulated in order to account for face recognition, as is illustrated by the eight-component model proposed by Bruce and Young (1986). Their model provides a convincing account of many of the phenomena of face recognition, but some of the components involved (e.g. the cognitive system) are clearly under-specified. In addition, their description of the processing of familiar faces is more convincing than that of the processing of unfamiliar faces.

FURTHER READING

Bruce, V. (1988). *Recognising faces*. London: Lawrence Erlbaum Associates Ltd. This is an up-to-date and comprehensive account of our understanding of the processes involved in face recognition.

Ellis, A.W. & Young, A.W. (1988). *Human cognitive neuropsychology*. There are three chapters in this book devoted to an analysis of perception from the perspective of cognitive neuropsychology. They consider perception in brain-damaged patients in considerably more detail than we have been able to do here.

Frisby, J.P. (1986). *The computational approach to vision*. In I. Roth & J.P. Frisby, *Perception and representation: A cognitive approach*. Milton Keynes: Open University Press. This provides one of the more readable introductions to David Marr's important contribution. However, you should be alerted to the fact that it is quite heavy going in places!

Humphreys, G.W. & Riddoch, M.J. (Eds.) (1987). *Visual object processing*. London: Lawrence Erlbaum Associates Ltd. Several major contemporary approaches to object recognition are presented, with both normal and clinical populations being considered.

Pinker, S. (1984). Visual cognition: An introduction. *Cognition*, *18*, 1–63. Theoretical positions on pattern recognition are discussed very thoroughly.

Chapter Three

THEORETICAL ISSUES IN PERCEPTION

INTRODUCTION

Pattern recognition, which was discussed in the previous chapter, is a key topic within perception. However, there are some very general theoretical issues in perception which received no more than a cursory mention in that chapter, but which deserve greater coverage. One of these issues concerns the possibility of perception or perceptual processes occurring in the absence of conscious awareness, and is the focus of the first part of this chapter. The second part of this chapter is concerned with the fact that perception depends in complex ways on the perceiver's expectations and previous knowledge as well as on the information available in the stimulus itself. There has been much theoretical controversy about the relative contributions of the perceiver and of the stimulus to perception, and this controversy is discussed at some length.

PERCEPTION WITHOUT AWARENESS

It is natural for us to regard perception as a processing activity of which the individual is consciously aware, and this orientation has been shared by most psychologists interested in perception. In line with this, it is worth noting that most perception research relies heavily on individual subjects' reports of what he or she is perceiving. This practice of relying on introspective evidence would appear to make little or no sense unless there is conscious awareness of perceptual activity.

This popular view of perception appears to rule out the possibility of subliminal perception, i.e. perception occurring even though the stimulus input is presented so briefly or at such low intensity as to be below the threshold of conscious awareness.

Popular interest in the possibility of subliminal perception arose approximately 30 years ago in the United States of America. Allegedly subliminal messages exhorting people to buy a particular brand of drink were shown to cinema audiences. It was claimed that these messages generated an enormous increase in the sales of the drink in question during the intermission, because conscious defences against advertising were being bypassed.

All these years later, there is still controversy about the existence or otherwise of subliminal perception. This is due in part to deficiencies in much of the research in this area, and in part to serious disagreements about what would constitute acceptable evidence of subliminal perception. However, some of the more convincing research evidence will be presented shortly.

The question of whether it is possible to have perception without conscious awareness has also been addressed by cognitive neuropsychologists. Some brain-damaged patients are apparently able to respond appropriately to visual stimuli which they report being unable to see. Weiskrantz (1986) has used the term "blindsight" to refer to this paradoxical state of affairs, and it is obviously a fascinating phenomenon. The evidence on blindsight is dealt with later in this section.

In sum, we will be concerned with the theoretically important issue of the extent to which perceptual processing can occur without conscious awareness. Studies of subliminal perception in normal individuals and of blindsight in brain-damaged patients have suggested that much perceptual processing is possible in the absence of conscious awareness, but there are some die-hard traditionalists who refuse to accept the evidence at face value.

Subliminal Perception

Much of the evidence on subliminal perception was discussed by Dixon (1981, p. 262). He arrived at the following challenging conclusions:

> The brain responds to external stimuli which, for one reason or another, are not consciously perceived. The effects of such stimuli may be almost as varied as those of sensory inflow which *does* enter consciousness. They include the evoking and determination of cortical potentials, changes in the E.E.G., the production of electrodermal responses, and changes in sensory threshold. They also include effects on memory, the influencing of lexical decisions, and such subjective manifestations as changes in conscious perceptual experience, dreams, and the evoking of appropriate affects.

Subliminal perception has been investigated using several different paradigms. A number of studies have used the lexical decision task, in which subjects have to decide as rapidly as possible whether or not a string of letters forms a word. The decision time for a word stimulus (e.g. "DOCTOR") is shorter when the preceding stimulus or prime is a word related in meaning (e.g. "NURSE") than when it is unrelated in meaning (e.g. "LIBRARY"). This is known as the "semantic priming effect". Marcel (1983) was able to obtain a semantic priming effect even when the subjects apparently had no conscious awareness of the initial word. This was accomplished by presenting it very briefly and following it by a pattern mask. Before the main series of trials, there was an adjustment of the time interval between the initial word and the pattern until the subjects detected the presence of the word on under 60% of occasions when they were asked to guess whether or not a word had been presented.

In another experiment, Marcel (1983) investigated a modified version of the Stroop effect. In the standard task (Stroop, 1935), subjects have to name the colours in which words are printed. Naming speed is slowed when the words are conflicting colour names (e.g. the word RED printed in green), and this is known as the Stroop effect. Marcel (1983) presented his subjects with colour patches, each of which had a colour word superimposed in the centre. When the word is visible, the typical Stroop effect is obtained. However, Marcel's (1983) key finding was that a Stroop effect of comparable magnitude could be obtained even when a pattern mask was used so that the subjects could apparently not detect the presence of the colour word. As in the other experiment, the time interval between the word and the pattern mask was adjusted so that the presence of a colour word was detected less than 60% of the time when the subjects were asked to guess.

This evidence may seem convincing, but there are some problems with it. In particular, it should be noted that discrimination performance (i.e. masked word present or absent?) at 60% was above the chance level of 50%. Cheesman and Merikle (1984; 1985) used the same modified Stroop task, but they reduced detection or discrimination performance to chance level. When they did so, they discovered that there was no longer any Stroop interference effect. While you may feel that this finding indicates that the meaning of words cannot be accessed in the absence of conscious awareness, matters are actually rather more complex than that. As Cheesman and Merikle (1984; 1985) discovered, it is perfectly possible for subjects to report that they are unaware that a word has just been presented in spite of their ability to perform at above chance level on the detection or discrimination task (i.e. guessing whether the masked word was a colour name).

Cheesman and Merikle (1984; 1985) argued that it was important to distinguish between the *objective* threshold of conscious awareness (based on detection or discrimination guessing performance) and the *subjective* threshold (based on subjective reports as to whether or not there was conscious awareness). The objective threshold is lower than the subjective threshold. When the modified Stroop task was used with the colour words below the subjective threshold but above the objective threshold, Cheesman and Merikle (1984; 1985) obtained significant evidence of Stroop interference. Since the Stroop effect involves the processing of the meaning of the colour words, it appears that they were able to demonstrate that the meaning of words can be accessed in the absence of conscious awareness. This is, of course, on the assumption that the subjective threshold provides a reasonable assessment of the threshold of conscious awareness.

How can we account for the existence of subliminal perception? One reasonable possibility is that the physiological threshold for a stimulus is usually lower than its subjective awareness threshold. As a consequence, a modest level of stimulus energy may suffice to activate peripheral sensory organs and relevant cortical areas without being intense enough to produce conscious perception. Libet (1973) recorded cortical evoked potentials (i.e. patterns of activity within the brain in response to stimulation) from fully conscious subjects, and found that a weak tactile stimulus did not lead to conscious perception, but did elicit the early components of the evoked response. An increase in stimulus strength was associated with reported awareness of the stimulus, and the later components of the evoked response were elicited.

Perceptual Defence
Some of the major theoretical controversies raised by research on subliminal perception apply equally strongly to the phenomenon of perceptual defence, in which emotionally charged stimuli are perceived less readily than relatively neutral stimuli. There is a Freudian feel about perceptual defence. Freud's notion that the ego can be protected by refusing to acknowledge threatening environmental stimuli is entirely consistent with the phenomenon.

It has sometimes been argued that the elevated recognition threshold for emotive stimuli such as taboo or obscene words is due to some kind of response bias. For example, subjects may sometimes recognise an embarrassing stimulus but be reluctant to report it. One way of reducing or eliminating this problem of response bias is to arrange matters so that subjects do not actually have to say or write down the emotionally charged stimuli. Hardy and Legge (1968) achieved this by asking their subjects to detect the presence of a faint auditory stimulus while watching a screen upon which emotional or neutral words were presented subliminally. Nearly all of the subjects failed to notice that any words had been presented, but the auditory threshold was higher when emotional words were being presented. In other words, the auditory stimulus needed to be louder in order to be detected when an emotional rather than a neutral word was presented subliminally on the screen.

One popular way of explaining perceptual defence has been by means of the fragmentation or partial cue hypothesis. The basic idea is that conscious perception of part of a visually presented word (e.g. "sh*t") may inhibit further perceptual processing if it is suspected that the word may be rude or obscene. There may be a grain of truth in this hypothesis, but it does not seem relevant to the study by Hardy and Legge (1968), since their subjects were not even aware that any words had been presented. Furthermore, it is not altogether clear how inhibition of visual perceptual processing would lead to elevation of the auditory threshold.

Perceptual defence poses a problem for many theories of perception, largely because of the difficulty of deciding how it is that the perceiver can selectively defend himself or herself against an emotional stimulus unless he or she has already perceived the stimulus and identified it. The essence of this paradox was expressed clearly by Howie (1952, p. 311): "To speak of perceptual defence is to use a mode of discourse which must make any precise or even intelligible meaning of perceptual defence impossible, for it is to speak of perceptual process as somehow being both a process of knowing and a process of avoiding knowing."

How can we explain this apparently logical paradox? The most straightforward answer (Dixon, 1981; Erdelyi, 1974) is to reject the notion of perception as a unitary event, and to replace it with a conceptualisation in which perception involves multiple processing stages or mechanisms, with consciousness perhaps representing the final level of processing. It is thus possible for a stimulus input to receive considerable perceptual processing without conscious awareness of the products of that processing, and this may well be the case with perceptual defence. The conclusions apply with much more force if one is willing to accept the subjective threshold of conscious awareness rather than the objective threshold.

Blindsight

Some brain-damaged patients suffer from an impairment of visual perception in which they are blind in part of the visual field, in the sense that there is no conscious awareness of stimuli presented to it. Despite this, they are able to make some accurate judgements and discriminations about visual stimuli presented to this blind area. Patients with this strange combination of characteristics are said to exhibit "blindsight" (Weiskrantz, 1986).

The most thoroughly investigated patient with blindsight is DB, who has been examined by Weiskrantz (1986). DB's perceptual problems stemmed from an operation which was designed to reduce the number of severe migraines from which he suffered. Following the operation, DB was left with an area of subjective blindness in the lower left quadrant of the visual field. He was able to detect whether or not a visual stimulus had been presented to the blind area, and he could also identify its location. However, he appeared to possess only rudimentary ability to discriminate shapes, and this may well depend on little more than the ability to discriminate the orientations of lines.

Weiskrantz (1990) has described the range of preserved abilities in the blind area which have been found in patients suffering from blindsight, although most patients do not exhibit the entire range. The location of objects in space has been revealed either by reaching towards them or by appropriate eye movements. Discrimination performance has indicated that there can be processing of the presence and direction of movement in the blind area. Patients have been able to show above chance performance in deciding whether two stimuli (one presented to the blind area and one to another part of the visual field) match or mismatch. A further preserved ability in some patients is colour discrimination in the blind area.

The phenomenon of "blindsight" would seem to provide very strong evidence that extensive perceptual processing can occur despite an absence of conscious awareness. However, there are some legitimate doubts about the strength of that evidence. Consider, for example, some of the comments made by patients with blindsight. DB claimed that he had a sense that "something was there", although he also said that he did not "see" anything (Weiskrantz, 1980). The patient EY "sensed a definite pinpoint of light", although "it does not actually look like a light. It looks like nothing at all" (Weiskrantz, 1980). These comments suggest that some of the patients sometimes found themselves in an intermediate state of awareness in which they had a "gut feeling" that there was something in the blind region (Weiskrantz, 1990). The fact that the patients often could not verbalise exactly what they did experience makes it difficult to know exactly what was going on.

Evaluation and Summary

There is a great variety of evidence which appears to indicate reasonably clearly that perception of the meaning of stimuli can occur in the absence of conscious awareness. This evidence is based on several different perceptual tasks and covers normal and patient populations. However, as we will see shortly, not everyone is willing to accept the findings at face value.

Holender (1986) is one of those who is sceptical of many of the claims that have been made for perception of meaning without awareness. He evaluated evidence that stimulus meaning can be accessed outside of awareness from three kinds of study: dichotic listening; parafoveal vision; and visual pattern masking. The dichotic listening task (discussed further in Chapter 4) involves presenting two auditory messages at the same time, one to each ear, with the subject instructed to attend to and repeat back (or shadow) only one of the messages. Subjects usually report little or no conscious awareness of the meaning of the unattended or ignored message, but its meaning does sometimes affect performance (e.g. Von Wright, Anderson, & Stenman, 1975).

Studies of parafoveal vision are conceptually similar to those involving dichotic listening. Subjects typically focus on a visual stimulus presented to the centre of the visual field (foveal vision) and visual stimuli are occasionally presented outside of that area (parafoveal vision). The meaning of visual stimuli presented to the parafoveal area will sometimes influence performance despite the fact that subjects indicate that they were not consciously aware that such stimuli had been presented.

Studies of visual pattern masking typically involve presenting a visual stimulus, then a visual mask containing patterned information, and finally a second visual stimulus requiring a response. The response to the second visual stimulus has been found to be influenced by the meaning of the first stimulus. This has been found even when the presentation time of the first stimulus is so rapid that subjects cannot say what it was or even whether or not a stimulus was presented (e.g. Marcel, 1983).

Holender (1986, p. 1) summarised his views on the extent to which these different kinds of studies have established the phenomenon of access to stimulus meaning outside of conscious awareness as follows:

> (1) Dichotic listening cannot provide the conditions needed to demonstrate the phenomenon. These conditions are better fulfilled in parafoveal vision and are realised ideally in pattern masking. (2) Evidence for the phenomenon is very scanty for parafoveal vision, but several tentative demonstrations have been reported for pattern masking. It can be shown, however, that none of these studies has included the requisite controls. (3) On the basis of current evidence it is most likely that these stimuli were indeed consciously identified.

Our view is that there are various reasons why his conclusions should not be accepted. First, Holender (1986) defined lack of awareness in visual pattern masking studies as the inability to make a voluntary discriminative response (e.g. was it a word or not a word?) to the first stimulus. In other words, he argued that one should use the objective threshold rather than the subjective threshold to assess conscious awareness. As we saw earlier, according to this criterion, subjects often demonstrate "awareness" of a stimulus even when they totally deny seeing it (see Cheesman & Merikle, 1984; 1985)! This suggests that accurate discriminative responses can sometimes be produced as a result of active perceptual processing below the level of conscious awareness.

Second, Holender (1986) adopted a "head-counting" approach to evaluating the evidence, arguing in effect that most of the studies had failed to provide acceptable evidence of semantic activation without conscious awareness. As Marcel (1986, p.40) pertinently pointed out, "This is equivalent to seeking evidence of black swans in ten samples of swans, finding them in two of the samples, and then concluding that the bulk of the evidence goes against their existence!"

Third, Holender (1986) ignored several areas of research which have provided powerful evidence of extensive perceptual processing in the absence of awareness. For example, he failed to discuss the phenomenon of "blindsight", which as we have seen provides reasonably strong evidence for perception without conscious awareness.

In sum, the fundamental issue in this area is the reliance that should be placed on subjects' reports of their conscious experience (i.e. the subjective threshold). It seems to us that one should rely on these reports if one is to examine perception without awareness, even though various other measures can also usefully be recorded. If we do that, then it is highly probable that perception without awareness is possible. In contrast, Holender (1986) and others are unwilling to accept what subjects say about their conscious awareness. Their reliance on more stringent criteria (e.g. the objective threshold) makes it more difficult to demonstrate perception without awareness.

PERCEPTION: CONSTRUCTED OR DIRECT?

In an extremely general sense, there are clearly two main sources of information that can be used in order to perceive the external world in an accurate fashion. One consists of the currently available sensory input, and the other consists of relevant past knowledge and experience stored in the brain. The term *bottom-up* or *data-driven processing* has been used to refer to those processes influenced solely by the sensory input, whereas the term *top-down* or *conceptually driven processing* has been used to describe those processes which depend upon past knowledge and experience, or upon contextual information.

The distinction between bottom-up and top-down processing is of relevance to the theories discussed in the previous chapter. For example, feature theories tend to emphasise the bottom-up or data-driven processing of stimulus features while relatively ignoring any top-down influences on perception. Marr's (1982) theory also focuses on bottom-up processing, but the influence of top-down processes is recognised.

Since common sense indicates that perception depends on both bottom-up and top-down processes, the theoretically interesting issues are: (i) to consider *how* these processes influence perception; and (ii) to evaluate the relative importance of the two kinds of processes on perception. These issues can perhaps most adequately be addressed by looking in some detail at theories which focus predominantly on top-down or bottom-up processes. Bruner (1957), Neisser (1967), and Gregory (1972; 1980) proposed constructive or hypothesis-testing theories of perception emphasising the role of top-down processes in perception, and Gibson (1966; 1979) argued in favour of direct perception based squarely on bottom-up processes. These respective theoretical positions are examined next.

Constructive Theories

While there are some differences of opinion among Bruner (1957), Neisser (1967), and Gregory (1972; 1980), they all agree on the following assumptions:

- Perception is an active and constructive process.
- Perception is not directly given by the stimulus input, but occurs as the end-product of the interactive influences of the presented stimulus and internal hypotheses, expectations, and knowledge. In other words, sensory information is used as the basis for making *inferences* about the presented stimulus.
- Since it is influenced by hypotheses and expectations which will sometimes be incorrect, perception is prone to error.

The flavour of this theoretical approach was captured by Gregory (1972), who claimed that perceptions are constructions "from floating fragmentary scraps of data signalled by the senses and drawn from the brain memory banks, themselves constructions from the snippets of the past." More specifically, the frequently inadequate information supplied to the sense organs is used as the basis for making inferences or forming hypotheses about the nature of the external environment.

Contextual information is one kind of information which might be used to make inferences about the nature of a visual stimulus. Examples of how context can influence the identification of letters and lines were given in the previous chapter, and contextual influences on object recognition have also been demonstrated. For example, Palmer (1975) presented a scene (e.g. a kitchen) in pictorial form, followed by the very brief presentation of the picture of an object. This object could be appropriate to the context (e.g. loaf), or it could be inappropriate (e.g. mailbox or drum). There was also a further condition in which no contextual scene was presented. The context had a systematic effect on the probability of identifying the object correctly: that probability was greatest when the object was appropriate to the context, intermediate when there was no context, and lowest when the object was inappropriate to the context.

According to the constructive theorists, perception basically involves using inferential processes (e.g. hypotheses, expectations) to make sense of the information presented to the sense organs. It follows from this theoretical position that the formation of incorrect hypotheses or expectations will lead to errors of perception. An interesting illustration of how perceptual errors can occur was provided by Ittelson and Cantril (1954). They argued that, if the current situation appears familiar but is actually novel, then the perceptual hypotheses formed may be well wide of the mark. An example of this is the well-known Ames distorted room. The room is actually of a most peculiar shape, but when viewed from a particular point it gives rise to the same retinal image as a conventional rectangular room.

It is perhaps not surprising in the circumstances that observers decide that the room is like a normal one. However, what is somewhat surprising is that they maintain this belief even when someone inside the room walks backwards and forwards along the rear wall, apparently growing and shrinking as he or she proceeds! The reason for the apparent size changes is that the rear wall is not perpendicular to the viewing point: one corner is actually much further away from the observer than the other corner. As might be expected by constructive theorists, there is a greater likelihood of the room being perceived as having an odd shape and the person walking inside it remaining the same size when that person is the spouse or close relative of the observer.

Another illustration of the possible pitfalls involved in relying too heavily on expectations or hypotheses comes in a classic study by Bruner and Postman (1949). Their subjects expected to see conventional playing cards, but some of the cards used were incongruous (e.g. black hearts). When these incongruous cards were presented briefly, subjects sometimes reported that they saw brown or purple hearts. In this case we have an almost literal blending of stimulus information (bottom-up processing) and stored information (top-down processing).

Probably the best known inaccuracies in perception occur with the various visual illusions. According to Gregory (1970; 1980), many of the classic visual illusions can be explained in a general way by assuming that previous knowledge derived from the perception of three-dimensional objects in space is applied inappropriately to the perception of two-dimensional figures. For example, people typically see a given object as having a constant size despite variations in the retinal image by taking account of its apparent distance. Size constancy means that an object is perceived as having the same size whether it is looked at from a short or a long distance away. This constancy contrasts with the size of the retinal image, which becomes progressively smaller as an object recedes into the distance. Gregory's (1970; 1980) misapplied size-constancy theory argues that this kind of perceptual processing is applied wrongly to produce several visual illusions.

In the Müller-Lyer illusion (see Fig. 3.1), the vertical line in the

FIGURE 3.1

The Müller–Lyer illusion.

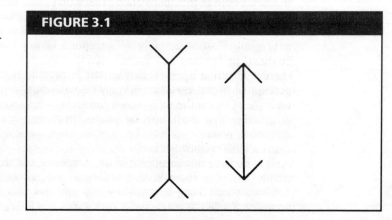

figure on the left appears longer than the vertical line in the figure on the right, although they are in fact of the same length. The Müller-Lyer figures can be regarded as simple perspective drawings of aspects of three-dimensional objects. Thus, the figure on the left can be thought of as the inside corner of a room, and the figure on the right as the outside corner of a building. In other words, the outgoing fins represent lines approaching us, whereas the ingoing fins stand for lines receding into the distance. Thus, the vertical line on the left is in some sense further away from us than the vertical line on the right. Since the retinal images of the two vertical lines are the same size, the implication of size-constancy scaling is that a more distant line of the same retinal size as a less distant line must actually be longer, and that, of course, is the Müller-Lyer illusion.

In essence, then, the misapplied size-constancy theory claims that the internal processes that use apparent distance to gauge apparent size are misapplied to illusion figures, such as those of the Müller-Lyer. But, you may very well argue, why is it that the figures appear flat and two-dimensional if they are treated in many ways as three-dimensional objects? According to Gregory (1970; 1980), cues to depth are used in a relatively automatic way to trigger constancy scaling whether or not the figures are seen to be lying on a flat surface. The fact that the Müller-Lyer figures do, indeed, take on a three-dimensional appearance when they are presented in the dark as luminous two-dimensional outlines tends to support this point of view.

This theory is ingenious, but it has by no means gained universal acceptance. Gregory's claim that luminous Müller-Lyer figures are seen three-dimensionally by everyone is incorrect, and it is not clear theoretically why there should be these individual differences. It is particularly puzzling from the perspective of Gregory's theory that the Müller-Lyer illusion can still be obtained when the fins on the two figures are replaced by other attachments such as circles or squares. This suggests that the vertical line may appear longer or shorter than its actual length simply because it is part of a large or a small object. It is likely (Day, 1980) that more than one factor contributes to the Müller-Lyer illusion.

Evaluation
The whole thrust of the constructivist position is that perception involves applying various inferential processes to the "floating fragmentary scraps of data signalled by the senses" (Gregory, 1972). This appears to lead to the prediction that perception will often be in error. As a consequence, the greatest criticism of the constructivist theory is that it does not naturally account for the fact that perception is typically accurate. If we are constantly using hypotheses and expectations to interpret sensory data, why is it that these hypotheses and expectations are correct nearly all of the time? Presumably the answer is that sensory data usually provide

sufficient information to identify objects and people in the environment. However, if bottom-up or data-driven processes are of major importance in perception (and they certainly are), then one must conclude that the constructivist theorists have attached undue significance to hypotheses and expectations.

Constructivist theorists have probably had their greatest success in explaining visual illusions. The misapplied size-constancy theory has generated numerous specific predictions about the nature and extent of illusory effects, and most of these predictions have been confirmed. The constructivist approach is also supported by several studies looking at the effects of context on perception (e.g. Palmer, 1975). However, it should be noted that context is most likely to influence perception when a stimulus is presented very briefly. Brief presentation reduces the impact of bottom-up processes, and allows more scope for top-down processes (e.g. hypotheses, expectations) to operate.

In other cases, the predictive power of the constructivist approach is considerably less because it is not obvious what hypotheses or expectations would be formed. For example, let us return to the study (Ittelson & Cantril, 1954) in which someone walks backwards and forwards along the rear wall of the Ames distorted room. Subjects can interpret what they are seeing by hypothesising that the room is distorted and the person remains the same size, or by assuming that the room is normal but the person grows and shrinks. It seems to the authors of this book that the former hypothesis is more plausible than the latter one, but for some reason subjects tend to make the latter hypothesis.

In sum, there is no doubt that hypotheses and expectations do sometimes play a role in perception in the way suggested by constructivist theorists. However, the influence of such top-down processes is generally only substantial when stimuli are presented very briefly or in a degraded form. Since these conditions probably obtain only relatively infrequently in everyday life, constructivist theories may have less relevance to normal situations than to artificial laboratory situations.

Direct Perception

A theoretical approach which seems in many ways almost diametrically opposed to that of the constructivist theorists was proposed by Gibson (1966; 1979). His theory is basically a bottom-up theory, in that he claimed that there is much more information potentially available in sensory stimulation than is generally realised. More specifically, here are some of his main theoretical assumptions:

- The pattern of light reaching the eye can be thought of as an *optic array*; this contains all of the visual information from the environment striking the eye.
- This optic array provides unambiguous or invariant information

about the layout of objects in space. This information comes in many forms, including texture gradients, optic flow patterns, and affordances (all of which are described next).

• Perception involves "picking up" the rich information provided by the optic array in a direct fashion which involves little or no information processing.

In order to understand Gibson's theoretical position, it is probably useful to consider how his interest in perceptual phenomena developed. He was given the task in the 2nd World War of preparing training films which would describe the problems which pilots experience when taking off and landing. This led him to wonder exactly what information pilots have available to them while performing these manoeuvres. He discovered what he termed *optic flow patterns*, which can be illustrated by considering a pilot approaching the landing strip. The point towards which the pilot is moving appears motionless, with the rest of the visual environment apparently moving away from that point. The further any part of the landing strip is from that point, the greater is its apparent speed of movement.

According to Gibson (1966; 1979), such optic flow patterns can provide pilots with unambiguous information about their direction, speed, and altitude. Gibson was so impressed by the wealth of sensory information available to pilots in optic flow patterns that he subsequently devoted himself to an analysis of the kinds of information available in sensory data under other conditions. For example, he argued that *texture gradients* provide very useful information. If you were unwise enough to stand between the rails of a railway track and look along the track, the details would become less clear as you looked into the distance. In addition, the distance apart of the connections would appear to reduce. The resultant texture gradient is shown in Fig. 3.2.

We have seen that objects slanting away from you have an increased gradient, or rate of change, of texture density as you look from the near edge to the far edge. Gibson (1966; 1979) claimed that observers "picked up" this information about the gradient of texture density from the optic array. As a consequence, at least some aspects of depth are perceived directly.

The gradient of texture density and optic flow pattern illustrate some of the information inherent in the optic array which can be used to provide an observer with an unambiguous spatial layout of the environment. In more general terms, Gibson (1966; 1979) argued that certain higher-order characteristics of the visual array change whereas others remain unaltered when observers move around their environment. These transpositions and invariants supply crucial evidence that is "picked up" in a direct fashion by the perceiver. Thus, for example, the lack of apparent movement of the point towards which we are moving forms one of the invariant features of the optic array.

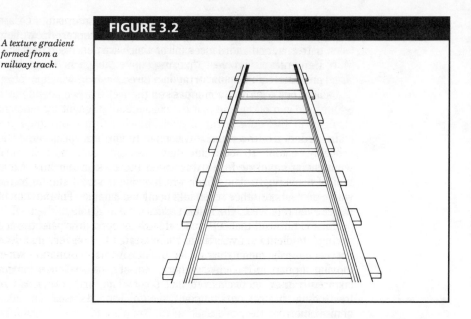

FIGURE 3.2

A texture gradient formed from a railway track.

How can the Gibsonian approach handle the problem of meaning? Gibson (1979) rejected the conventional view that we perceive a meaningful environment because of the involvement of relevant knowledge stored in long-term memory. Instead, he claimed that all of the potential uses of objects (or what he referred to as their *affordances*) are directly perceivable. For example, a ladder "affords" ascent or descent, and a chair "affords" sitting. Those particular affordances of an object which are detected depend on the perceiver's species and on his or her current psychological state. Thus, a hungry person will perceive the affordance of edibility when presented with an orange, whereas an angry wife may detect the affordance of projectile and throw the orange at her bemused husband.

The notion of affordances is very important to Gibson (1979). It forms part of his attempt to demonstrate that all of the information needed to make sense of the visual environment is directly present in the visual input. If he had not proposed the notion of affordances, or something very similar, then he would have been forced to admit that the meaning of objects is stored in long-term memory rather than being directly perceivable.

Evaluation

Gibson's (1966; 1979) contribution has proved to be a valuable one in many ways. He made a serious attempt to grapple with the issue of how it is that the constantly changing information presented to the eyes generally leads to very fast and very accurate perception of the environment. Of particular importance is his successful demonstration that visual stimuli provide considerably more information than had been thought previously. In some ways,

Gibson's pioneering efforts anticipated the later theorising of Marr (1982), which was discussed in the previous chapter. However, Gibson was very much less explicit than Marr in his theorising. Marr's algorithmic level of theorising (see Chapters 1 and 2) is largely absent from Gibsonian theory.

Gibson quite correctly emphasised the fact that we spend much of our time in motion, and that the consequent moment-by-moment changes in the optic array provide much information about the characteristics of the visual environment. This emphasis should be seen in the context of research into visual perception at the time when he was putting forward his theoretical ideas. Such research typically involved static observers looking at visual stimuli, often with chin rests or other restraints being used to prevent movement of the eyes relative to the visual stimuli.

Gibson showed that information such as optic flow patterns and texture gradients is available to the observer. However, that does not necessarily mean that we actually use this information when moving around in the environment. So far, the evidence on this issue is rather inconclusive. Even if we do use the kinds of information in the optic array which Gibson focused on, it is improbable that they are used in the simple and direct fashion he envisaged. Marr's theoretical approach indicates some of the complexities associated with extracting information from visual stimuli, and makes it appear altogether improbable that Gibson was right to claim that perception does not require information processing.

Gibson's theoretical approach provides an explanation of how it is that we are able to perceive the environment in an accurate fashion. As a consequence, his theory often has no plausible explanation of the inaccuracies and distortions which are found in perception. According to Gibson, most of the laboratory demonstrations of inaccurate perception occur in circumstances which are very different from those prevailing in the natural environment. For example, distortions of visual perception are often produced by presenting stimuli very briefly or in a two-dimensional form (e.g. visual illusions), whereas normal visual perception involves three-dimensional objects which are visible over relatively long periods of time.

Gibson is correct in arguing that inaccurate perception often depends on the use of very artificial situations. However, the notion that visual illusions are merely unusual trick figures dreamt up by psychologists to baffle ordinary decent folk does not apply to all of them. There are at least some visual illusions which produce effects similar to those to be found in normal perception. Consider, for example, the vertical-horizontal illusion shown in Fig. 3.3. The two lines are actually the same length, but the vertical line appears to be longer than the horizontal line. This tendency to over-estimate vertical extents relative to horizontal ones can readily be shown with real objects by taking a teacup, saucer, and two similar spoons. Place one spoon horizontally in the saucer and the other

*The vertical–
horizontal
illusion.*

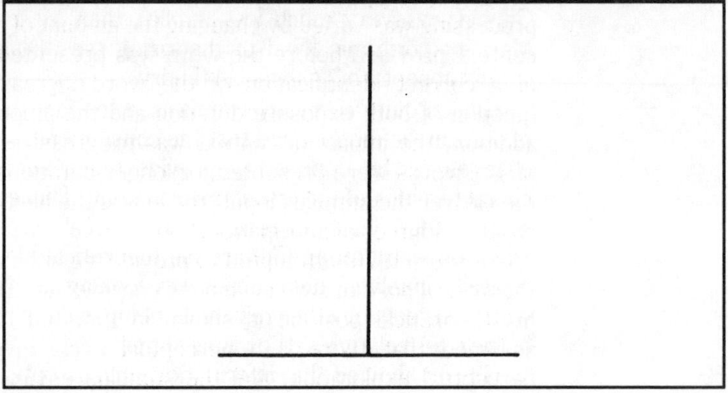

FIGURE 3.3

spoon vertically in the cup, and you should find that the vertical spoon looks much longer than the horizontal spoon.

A final weakness of Gibson's approach is his treatment of meaning in perception. Despite Gibson's (1979) arguments, it is fairly obvious that stored knowledge often plays a part in object recognition and perception. For example, the first author has a sofa bed in his study. When he looks at it, it may provide the affordance of sitting. However, it is also an article of furniture which used to belong to his mother-in-law, and it has been used as a space rocket by his children. The Gibsonian notion of affordances simply fails to do justice to the wealth of meaning which we frequently perceive in objects and people.

Theoretical Synthesis

A good starting point for deciding whether perception depends more on bottom-up or on top-down processes is the realisation that the relative importance of these two kinds of processes is affected by a variety of factors. As was mentioned earlier in the chapter, visual perception may well be very largely determined by bottom-up processes when the viewing conditions are good, but may increasingly involve top-down processes as the viewing conditions deteriorate because of very brief presentation times or lack of stimulus clarity. In line with this analysis, Gibson concentrated on visual perception occurring under optimal viewing conditions, whereas constructivist theorists emphasising top-down processes in perception have tended to use very sub-optimal viewing conditions (e.g. brief tachistoscopic presentations).

In most circumstances, perception undoubtedly involves the combined influence of bottom-up and top-down processes. Total reliance on bottom-up processes would be unwise because of the ambiguous and imprecise nature of much visual stimulation, and we would very often be hallucinating if we used only top-down processing. The contribution of both kinds of processing to word perception was demonstrated by Tulving, Mandler, and Baumal

(1964). The role of bottom-up processing was manipulated by altering the exposure duration, and the involvement of top-down processing was varied by changing the amount of relevant sentence context provided before the word was presented. The probability of a correct identification of the word increased directly as a function of both exposure duration and the amount of context. In addition, the impact of context was progressively reduced as the target words were presented for longer durations, suggesting that the clearer the stimulus input, the less is the necessity to make use of other sources of information.

Neisser (1976) attempted to provide a synthesis of the different theoretical positions we have been considering. The basic outline of his theoretical position is shown in Fig. 3.4. In essence, it is assumed that there is a perceptual cycle involving schemata, perceptual exploration, and the stimulus environment. Schemata contain collections of knowledge derived from past experience which serve the function of directing perceptual exploration towards relevant environmental stimuli. Such exploration often involves movement around the environment. Perceptual exploration leads the perceiver to sample some of the available stimulus information. If the information obtained from the environment fails to match information in the relevant schema, then the information in the schema is modified appropriately.

In the terms we have been using, the perceptual cycle described by Neisser incorporates elements of bottom-up and of top-down

FIGURE 3.4

The perceptual cycle as proposed by Neisser (1976).

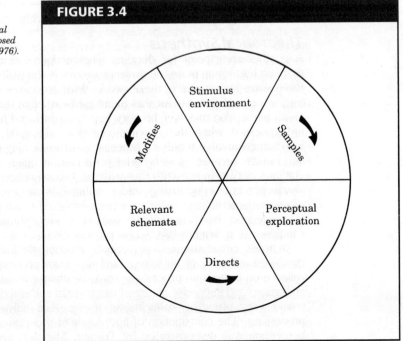

Stimulus environment

Modifies

Samples

Relevant schemata

Perceptual exploration

Directs

processing. Bottom-up processing is represented by the sampling of available environmental information which can modify the current schema. Top-down processing is represented by the notion that schemata influence the course of the information processing involved in perception. Of course, Neisser's theory is rather sketchy. However, it appears to be on the right lines. Specific examples of theories assuming an interaction between bottom-up and top-down processing are discussed later in the book (e.g. the theory of spoken language comprehension proposed by Marslen-Wilson and Tyler, 1980, dealt with in Chapter 9).

Summary

Constructive theories emphasise the role of inferential processes in perception. The existence of visual and auditory illusions, and the perceptual errors which occur in everyday life, provide some support for such theories. However, the information provided by the stimulus itself is obviously of major significance. Gibson and others have been successful in demonstrating that stimuli contain much more potentially available information than used to be thought. It is thus possible that inferential processes are necessary only relatively rarely. As Neisser (1976) pointed out, it is likely that perception typically depends on bottom-up and top-down processes interacting with each other in complex ways.

SUMMARY

Most studies of perception have relied on subjects' reports to ascertain what they have perceived. This can be regarded as adequate only if perception necessarily involves conscious awareness. However, there is evidence from within both cognitive psychology and cognitive neuropsychology to indicate that this is an unduly restrictive view of perception. With normal individuals, there are numerous demonstrations of subliminal perception (i.e. perception in the absence of conscious awareness). There are methodological problems with many of the studies, but overall there is little doubt that subliminal perception exists. This conclusion is strengthened by studies of brain-damaged patients exhibiting "blindsight", which involves accurate performance on perceptual tasks in the absence of any acknowledged awareness of seeing anything.

A major theoretical controversy concerns the relative importance of bottom-up or data-driven processes and of top-down or conceptually driven processes in perception. Constructivist theorists, who emphasise the contribution of top-down processes, argue that errors in perception (e.g. visual illusions) indicate that many phenomena cannot be explained in terms of bottom-up processes. However, it is not altogether clear on that theoretical position why perceptual errors are not much more prevalent than they actually are.

In contrast, Gibson argued that perception can be understood in terms of bottom-up processes. According to him, there is far more information available in the stimulus input than has generally been appreciated, and this is especially true when the observer is moving through the visual environment. Despite the successes of the Gibsonian approach, it is by no means clear that a bottom-up approach can provide an adequate account of the role of meaning in perception.

The most reasonable position is that the relative importance of bottom-up and top-down processing depends on the particular circumstances in which perception occurs. Most of the time, both kinds of processing will jointly determine perceptual experience and performance. As a consequence, what is needed is more of a theoretical understanding of the ways in which bottom-up and top-down processing interact. The theory proposed by Neisser (1976) represents a step in that direction.

FURTHER READING

Bruce, V. & Green, P. (1985). *Visual perception: physiology, psychology, and ecology*. London: Lawrence Erlbaum Associates Ltd. This is an excellent book, which includes a very readable account of the controversy between the Gibsonian and constructivist positions. A revised edition of this book was published in 1990.

Dixon, N.F. (1981). *Preconscious processing*. Chichester: Wiley. This book provides a thorough discussion of the evidence in favour of subliminal perception by an acknowledged expert in the area.

Ullman, S. (1980). Against direct perception. *Behaviourial and Brain Sciences, 3*, 373–415. This reference gives detailed arguments against the Gibsonian approach to perception.

Weiskrantz, L. (1986). *Blindsight: A case study and implications*. Oxford: Oxford University Press. There is very detailed coverage of the patient DB, including a clear indication of the difficulties of establishing the phenomenon of blindsight.

Chapter Four

ATTENTION AND PERFORMANCE LIMITATIONS

INTRODUCTION

The concept of "attention" has had a rather fluctuating history during the past century. It was regarded as an important concept by many philosophers and psychologists in the late 19th century the early Behaviourists, who regarded all internal processes or hypothetical constructs such as attention with the greatest suspicion. Attention became fashionable again following the publication of Broadbent's book *Perception and communication* in 1958, but more recently the prevalent view has been that it is too amorphous to be of much value. Moray (1969) pointed out that attention is sometimes used to refer to the ability to select part of the incoming stimulation for further processing, but it has also been regarded as synonymous with concentration or with mental set. It has also been applied to search processes in which a specified target is looked for, and it has been suggested that attention co-varies with arousal (e.g. the drowsy individual is in a state of low arousal and attends little to his environment).

There is an obvious danger that a concept that is used to explain everything will turn out to explain nothing. However, attention is most commonly used to refer to selectivity of processing, and this was the sense emphasised by William James (1890, pp. 403–404):

> Everyone knows what attention is. It is the taking possession of the mind, in clear and vivid form, of one out of what seem several simultaneously possible objects or trains of thought. Focalisation, concentration, of consciousness are of its essence. It implies withdrawal from some things in order to deal effectively with others.

Within the general area of attention research there are several important issues that need to be considered. If we ask what makes us attend to some things rather than others, then the usual answer is that we choose to attend to sources of information that are relevant in the context of our present activities and intentions. That is true as far as it goes, but it also has to be recognised that some stimuli draw attention to themselves. Berlyne (1960) argued that such stimuli are typically those that conflict with expectation; they tend to be novel, surprising, incongruous, complex, or intense. The main evidence for this position is that such stimuli tend to elicit the orientation or "what is it?" reaction, which is thought to reflect attention. Stimuli that are novel, incongruous, or surprising also tend to be well remembered (Eysenck, 1972; Von Restorff, 1933), which suggests that they are thoroughly processed. It is disappointing that there has been little recent interest in the determinants of "involuntary" attention in view of its general significance.

There is an important distinction between *focused* attention and *divided* attention. Focused attention is studied by presenting people with two or more concurrent stimulus inputs and instructing them to process and respond to only one. Work on focused attention can tell us how effectively people can select certain inputs rather than others, and it enables us to investigate the nature of the selection process and the fate of unattended stimuli. Divided attention is also studied by presenting at least two concurrent stimulus inputs, but with instructions indicating that all stimulus inputs must be attended to and responded to. Studies of divided attention provide useful information about an individual's processing limitations, and may tell us something about attentional mechanisms and their capacity.

Before proceeding to a discussion of focused and divided attention, it should be noted that there is a major limitation in most of the research on attention. We know very well that we can attend either to the *external* environment or to the *internal* environment (i.e. our own thoughts and information in long-term memory). While no one denies this, most of the work on attention has been concerned only with attention to the external environment. Why should this be so? By far the most important reason is that experimenters can identify and control the stimuli presented in the external environment in a way which is simply not possible with internal determinants of attention.

In sum, the scope of research and theory on attention is rather broad, and only some aspects of it will be considered in this chapter. An indication of how different topics within attention are related to each other is provided in Fig. 4.1.

FOCUSED AUDITORY ATTENTION

In principle, attention could be focused on stimuli in any of the various sensory modalities. However, in practice, nearly all of the research on focused attention has involved either the visual or the auditory modality. It is a historical curiosity that there were literally dozens of studies on focused auditory attention before serious work on focused visual attention started. In deference to this

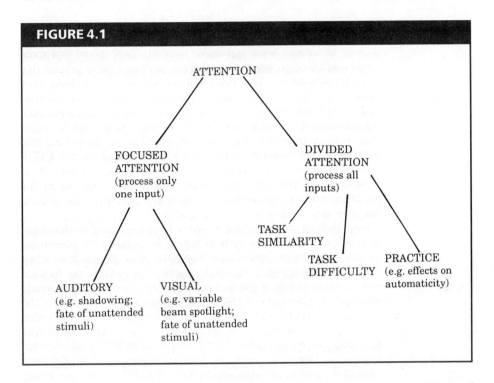

FIGURE 4.1

Topics relating to attention.

historical state of affairs, we will start our coverage of focused attention by considering the auditory modality. Research here has been concerned mainly with the so-called shadowing technique, and that forms the basis of the next section.

The Shadowing Technique

Systematic research on focused attention was initiated by Colin Cherry (1953). He was working in an electronics research laboratory at the Massachusetts Institute of Technology, but somehow managed to find himself involved in psychological research. What fascinated Cherry was the so-called "cocktail party" problem. Of course, cocktail parties can pose a number of problems, but the one that interested Cherry was our ability to follow just one conversation even when several different people are talking at the same time. Cherry discovered that this ability involves making use of physical differences among the auditory messages in order to select the one of interest; these physical differences can include differences in the sex of the speaker, in voice intensity, and in the location of the speaker. When Cherry presented two messages in the same voice to both ears at once (thus eliminating these physical differences), listeners found it remarkably difficult to separate out the two messages on the basis of meaning alone.

Cherry also carried out experiments in which one auditory message had to be shadowed (i.e. repeated back out loud) at the same time as the second auditory message was played to the other ear. Very little information seemed to be extracted from the second or nonattended message, and listeners seldom noticed when that message was spoken in a foreign language or in reversed speech. In contrast, physical changes such as the insertion of a pure tone were almost always detected. The conclusion that unattended auditory information receives practically no processing was supported by other evidence. It was discovered, for example, that there is practically no memory for words on the unattended message, even when they are presented 35 times each (Moray, 1959).

Broadbent (1958) felt that these findings from the shadowing paradigm were important. He was also impressed by data from a memory task in which three pairs of digits were presented to a subject dichotically, i.e. three digits were heard one after the other at one ear, at the same time as three different digits were presented to the other ear. Subjects demonstrated a clear preference for recalling the digits ear by ear rather than pair by pair. In other words, if 496 was presented to one ear and 852 to the other ear, recall would be 496852 rather than 489562.

Broadbent's Theory

Broadbent (1958) accounted for these, and other, findings by making the following assumptions:

- Two stimuli or messages presented at the same time gain access in parallel (i.e. together) to a sensory buffer.
- One of the inputs is then allowed through a filter on the basis of its physical characteristics, with the other input remaining in the buffer for later processing.
- This filter is necessary in order to prevent overloading of the limited-capacity mechanism beyond the filter; this processes the input thoroughly.

This theory handles Cherry's basic finding rather neatly. The unattended message is rejected by the filter and thus receives minimal processing. It also accounts for performance on Broadbent's dichotic task because the filter selects one input at a time on the basis of the most salient physical characteristic distinguishing the two inputs (i.e. the ear of arrival). In spite of the theory's successes, however, it fails to explain other findings. It assumes that the unattended message is always rejected at an early stage of processing, but this is not correct. The original shadowing experiments made use of subjects who had little or no previous experience of shadowing messages, so that nearly all of their available processing resources had to be allocated to the shadowing task. The importance of this fact was demonstrated by Underwood (1974), in an experiment in which subjects attempted to detect a single digit appearing on either the shadowed or the nonshadowed message. Naive subjects detected only 8% of the digits on the nonshadowed message, suggesting very limited processing of that message. However, when the same task was performed by Neville Moray, a prominent researcher in this area who has great experience of shadowing, he detected 67% of the nonshadowed digits.

The early work on shadowing was also somewhat limited in that the attended and unattended inputs were usually rather similar (i.e. they were both auditorily presented verbal messages). Allport, Antonis, and Reynolds (1972) found that combining shadowing of passages from George Orwell's *Selected essays* with the learning of auditorily presented words led to minimal learning of the words, a finding to be expected on the basis of Broadbent's (1958) filter theory. However, when the same shadowing task was combined with picture learning, subsequent memory for the pictorial information was reasonably good. The implication is that the limitations on the processing of two concurrent (i.e. presented at the same time) inputs are less rigid than was implied by Broadbent. More specifically, if the two inputs are dissimilar from each other, then it is often possible to process both of them in a more thorough fashion than was allowed for on Broadbent's filter theory.

In the initial studies on shadowing, it was usually reported that none of the meaning of the unattended message was processed. This was in line with Broadbent's theory, according to which inputs rejected by the filter would be processed only in terms of their physical characteristics. However, these early studies suffered from a potentially serious limitation. It was concluded that there was no processing of the meaning of unattended messages because of the subjects' lack of conscious awareness of their meaning. It is at least possible that meaning can be processed without any awareness, and this possibility needed to be investigated.

The issue of processing of meaning without awareness was looked at by Von Wright et al. (1975). In the first stage of the experiment, subjects attended to a long list of words, and sometimes received an electric shock when the Finnish word meaning "suitable" was presented. In the second stage of the study, subjects shadowed one auditory list of words and ignored a second concurrent list. When the previously shocked word (or a word very similar in sound or meaning) was presented on the nonattended list, there was a noticeable galvanic skin response. This suggests that information on the unattended message was processed in terms of both sound and meaning, in spite of the fact that the subjects were not consciously aware that the previously shocked word had been presented. However, it should be noted that in this and other similar experiments, galvanic skin responses were detected on only a fraction of the trials. Therefore, thorough processing of unattended information presumably occurred only some of the time.

There is quite a lot of evidence that there is less processing of meaning on the unattended message than on the attended one. In particular, words on the unattended message do not seem to be integrated into larger meaning units such as phrases or sentences. It has been found (Underwood, 1977) that the shadowing response to a word on the attended message is speeded up if it is preceded by information related in meaning presented in either the shadowed or the unattended message. However, increasing the amount of such relevant context from one word to an entire sentence increases speed of shadowing only when the context is present in the shadowed message.

In sum, there can be far more thorough processing of the nonshadowed message than would have been expected from Broadbent's (1958) theory. He proposed a relatively rigid system of selective attention that cannot account for the great variability in the amount of analysis of the nonshadowed message that is actually observed. The same rigidity of the filter theory is also shown in its assumption that the filter selects information on the basis of physical features. This assumption is supported by the tendency of subjects to recall dichotically presented digits ear by ear, but a small change in the basic experiment can alter the order of recall considerably. Gray and Wedderburn (1960) made use of a version of the dichotic task in which "Who 6 there" might be presented to one ear at the same time as "4 goes 1" was presented to the other ear. The preferred order of report from subjects in this experiment was not ear by ear; instead, it was determined by meaning (e.g. "Who goes there" followed by "4 6 1"). The implication is that selection can occur either before the processing of information from both inputs or afterwards. The fact that selection can be based on the meaning of presented information is inconsistent with filter theory.

Alternative Theories: Treisman and Deutsch and Deutsch

How can the various findings on focused attention be explained theoretically? Treisman (1964) favoured a modified version of Broadbent's (1958) theory in which the analysis of unattended information is merely *attenuated* or reduced. Whereas Broadbent had claimed that the bottle-neck occurred early in processing, Treisman suggested that the location of the bottle-neck was more flexible. In essence, she proposed that stimulus analysis proceeds in a systematic fashion through a hierarchy starting with analyses based on physical cues, syllabic pattern, and specific words, and moving on to analyses based on individual words, grammatical structure, and meaning. If there is insufficient capacity to permit full stimulus analysis, then tests towards the top of the hierarchy are omitted. In addition, expected stimuli are treated differently to other stimuli, with the analysing systems being pre-biased towards them.

Treisman's theory clearly accounts for the extensive processing of unattended sources of information that proved embarrassing for

Broadbent. However, the same facts can also be explained by a rather different theory put forward by Deutsch and Deutsch (1963). They argued that all incoming stimuli are fully analysed, with one input determining the response on the basis of its importance or relevance in the situation. Their theory is similar to those of Broadbent and of Treisman in postulating the existence of a bottle-neck in information processing, but it is quite different in placing the bottle-neck much nearer the response end of the processing system. A number of subsequent theories follow similar lines (e.g. Shiffrin & Schneider, 1977).

On the face of it, Treisman's theory is more plausible than that of Deutsch and Deutsch. In particular, it seems very uneconomical for all inputs to be analysed completely, and then to have most of the analysed information forgotten almost at once in the way proposed by Deutsch and Deutsch. However, it is much better to adjudicate between theories on the basis of empirical evidence rather than vague notions of plausibility, and Treisman and Geffen (1967) attempted to do just that. Their subjects shadowed one of two concurrent auditory messages, and at the same time monitored both messages in order to detect target words. The detection of a target word was indicated by a simple tapping response.

The crucial findings related to the tapping rates on the two messages. According to Treisman's theory, there should be attenuated analysis of the nonshadowed message, and so fewer targets should be detected on that message than on the shadowed one. In contrast, the assumption made by Deutsch and Deutsch, namely, that there is complete perceptual analysis of all inputs, leads to the prediction that there should be no difference in detection rates between the two messages. In fact, the shadowed or attended message showed a very large advantage in detection rates over the nonshadowed message, with the detection rates being 87% and 8%, respectively.

Deutsch and Deutsch (1967) naturally enough argued the toss over this apparent refutation of their theoretical position. They pointed out that their theory assumed that only important inputs led to responses. Since the task used by Treisman and Geffen (1967) required their subjects to make two responses to target words appearing in the shadowed message (i.e. shadow and tap) but only one response to targets in the nonshadowed message (i.e. tap), there is clearly a sense in which the shadowed targets were more important than the non shadowed ones.

Treisman and Riley (1969) attempted to resolve matters by ensuring that exactly the same response was made to targets occurring in either message. They did this by telling their subjects to stop shadowing and to tap as soon as they detected a target in either message. The findings were less dramatic than in the earlier study by Treisman and Geffen, but it was still the case that many more target words were detected on the shadowed message than on the nonshadowed message.

Johnston and Heinz's Theory

Deutsch and Deutsch (1963) assumed that selection always occurs after full analysis of all inputs has taken place, an assumption which suggests that selective attention occurs in a rather rigid and fixed way. In contrast, Johnston and Heinz (1978) proposed a more flexible model in which selection is possible at several different stages of processing. According to them:

- The more stages of processing that take place prior to selection, the greater are the demands on some processing capacity.
- Because of this, selection occurs as early in processing as is possible in view of the prevailing circumstances and task demands.

Some of these ideas were tested by Johnston and Heinz (1979). Target words which had to be shadowed were presented to both ears at the same time as nontarget words. In a low sensory discriminability condition, both sets of words were spoken in the same male voice, whereas in a high sensory discriminability condition the targets were spoken in a male voice and the nontargets in a female voice. According to Johnston and Heinz (1979), selection based on sensory information can be used in the high sensory discriminability condition, but selection at a later stage of processing for meaning is necessary in the low sensory discriminability condition.

In other words, Johnston and Heinz predicted that non-targets would be more thoroughly processed in the low sensory discriminability condition. In contrast, theories of the kind proposed by Deutsch and Deutsch make the assumption that there is essentially complete analysis of the nontarget words irrespective of the amount of sensory discriminability between the target and nontarget words. In fact, more processing resources were used with low sensory discriminability, and recall of nontarget words was higher in the low sensory discriminability condition. It thus appears that the amount of processing of nonshadowed stimuli varies as a function of task demands in a way more consistent with Treisman's approach than with that of Deutsch and Deutsch.

Further evidence of processing flexibility was obtained by Johnston and Wilson (1980). Pairs of words were presented together dichotically (i.e. one word to each ear), and the task was to identify target items consisting of members of a designated category. The targets were ambiguous words having at least two distinct meanings. For example, if the category was "articles of clothing", then "socks" would be a possible target word. Each target word was accompanied by a nontarget word biasing the appropriate meaning of the target (e.g. "smelly"), or a nontarget word biasing the inappropriate meaning (e.g. "punches"), or by a neutral nontarget word (e.g. "Tuesday"). When subjects did not know which ear targets would arrive at (divided attention), appropriate nontargets facilitated the detection of targets and inappropriate nontargets impaired target detection (see Fig. 4.2).

Thus, when attention needed to be divided between the two ears, there was clear evidence that the nontarget words were processed for meaning. On the other hand, when subjects knew that all of the targets would be presented to the left ear, the type of nontarget word presented at the same time *had no effect on target detection*. This suggests that nontargets were not processed for meaning in this focused attention condition, and that the amount of processing received by nontarget stimuli is often only as much as is necessary to perform the experimental task.

Summary

In sum, evidence has accumulated over the years to indicate that the analysis of unattended auditory inputs can be more extensive than was originally thought. This may be due in part to the fact that the shadowing requirement does not always "capture" attention, so that so-called unattended inputs may actually receive some attention, but this is hardly the whole story. The most reasonable account of focused attention is along the lines suggested by Treisman (1964) and by Broadbent (1971), with reduced or attenuated processing of sources of information outside of focal attention. However, the extreme notion that all inputs are fully analysed (Deutsch & Deutsch, 1963) remains fairly popular in spite of its inflexibility.

What can be concluded about the controversy concerning the amount of processing of unattended auditory stimuli? In view of the data from the shadowing paradigm obtained by Treisman and Geffen (1967), Treisman and Riley (1969), and Johnston and Heinz

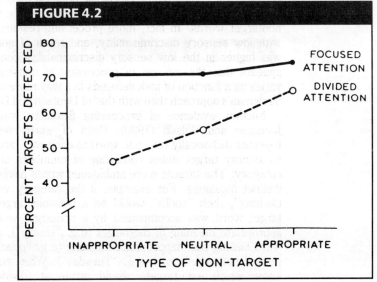

FIGURE 4.2

Effects of attention condition (divided versus focused) and of type of non-target on target detection. Data from Johnston and Wilson (1980).

(1979), the full analysis theory seems rather dubious. In contrast, attenuation theories of the type subscribed to by Treisman (1964) and by Broadbent (1971) account satisfactorily for most of the findings.

FOCUSED VISUAL ATTENTION

We have so far considered focused attention almost entirely from the perspective of auditory attention. However, there has also been a substantial amount of research on visual attention. In general terms, there are important similarities between focused attention in the auditory and visual modalities. Nevertheless, it seems desirable to consider in some detail the characteristics of focused visual attention.

It has often been argued that focused visual attention is rather like a spotlight. That is, everything within a relatively small area can be seen very clearly, but it is much harder (or impossible) to see anything not falling within the beam of the spotlight. Furthermore, most spotlights have adjustable beams, so that the area covered by the beam can be enlarged or decreased. It has been claimed that visual attention has the same characteristics.

Reasonably convincing evidence that visual attention does resemble a variable beam was obtained by LaBerge (1983). In his study, five-letter words were presented. A probe requiring a rapid response was occasionally presented instead of, or immediately after, the word. The probe could appear in the spatial position of any of the five letters of the word. In one condition an attempt was made to focus the subjects' attention on the middle letter of the five-letter word by asking them to categorise that letter. In another condition, the subjects were required to categorise the entire word. It was hoped that this would lead the subjects to adopt a broader attentional beam.

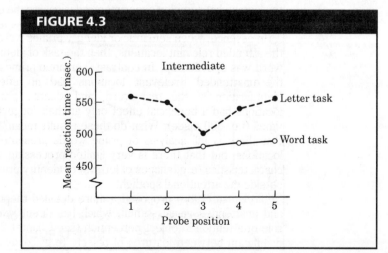

FIGURE 4.3

Mean reaction time to the probe stimulus as a function of probe position. The probe was presented at the time that a letter string would have been presented. Data from LaBerge (1983).

The main findings are shown in Fig. 4.3. In order to interpret them, we need to make the reasonable assumption that the probe was responded to faster when it fell within the central attentional beam than when it did not. On this assumption, the results indicate that the attentional spotlight can be either very narrow or rather broad, depending on the precise requirements of the task.

Various attempts have been made to work out the minimum width of the attentional spotlight. This has often been done by discovering how far an irrelevant stimulus has to be moved away from an attended stimulus in order for it to have no disruptive effect on performance with the attended stimulus. According to Humphreys (1981), the minimum width of the spotlight is less than 0.5° when attention is focused on the centre of the fovea (the part of the retina associated with clearest vision), but it increases to more than 1° when attention is moved 1° away from the centre of the fovea.

Unattended Visual Stimuli

We saw earlier in our consideration of the shadowing task that there is, generally, rather limited processing of unattended auditory stimuli. What happens to unattended visual stimuli? According to evidence collected by Johnston and Dark (1985), the answer appears to be "Not very much". They used a task in which subjects were asked to attend to relevant locations within a visual display in order to detect occasional target words. From time to time a *prime* word was presented in a relevant or an irrelevant (i.e. nonrelevant) location. This prime word was presented for between 60 and 500 msec, and was followed by a *test* word. This test word was presented initially in an unreadable form, but it was gradually clarified until it could be identified. The prime word was sometimes related in meaning to the test word (i.e. it was a semantic prime), and at other times it was the same as the test word (i.e. it was an identity prime). What was of major interest with this somewhat complex experimental design was the extent to which the prime word facilitated the task of identifying the test word.

In essence, when semantic or identity primes were presented to the attended relevant locations, then the task of identifying the test word was speeded up. In contrast, semantic primes presented to the unattended irrelevant locations had no effect at all on identification of the test word, and identity primes in these locations had a beneficial effect only at their longest presentation times (i.e. 500 msec). What do these results mean? They indicate that there is full analysis of prime words presented to attended locations, but that there is very limited processing of the physical characteristics (e.g. shapes of letters) of identity primes presented outside the attentional spotlight.

Treisman (1988) proposed a more detailed theory of attended and unattended visual stimuli, which has direct relevance to the role of attention in object perception (see Chapter 2). She drew a distinction between features of objects (e.g. colour, size, lines of particular orientation) and the objects themselves, and argued for the following theoretical position:

- There is a rapid initial parallel process involving the visual features of objects in the environment; this is not dependent upon attention.
- There is a second, serial process in which features are combined to form objects (e.g. a large, red chair).
- Features can be combined by focused attending to the location of the object, in which case focused attention provides the "glue" which constructs unitary objects from the available features.
- Feature combination can also be influenced by stored knowledge (e.g. bananas are usually yellow).
- In the absence of focused attention or relevant stored knowledge, features will be combined in a random fashion; this random combination will often produce incorrect combinations known as "illusory conjunctions".

Treisman and Gelade (1980) obtained strong support for this feature integration theory. In one of their experiments, subjects searched for a target in a visual display containing between 1 and 30 items. The target was either an object (a green letter "T"), or it consisted of a single feature (either a blue letter or an "S"). It was predicted that focused attention would be needed to detect the former target (because it was defined by a combination of features), but that the latter target could be detected in the absence of focused attention because it was defined by a single feature.

The results on trials when a target was presented were exactly as predicted. The number of items in the visual display substantially affected detection speed when the target was defined by a conjunction of features (i.e. a green letter "T") because focused attention was required, but there was practically no effect of display size when the target was defined by a single feature (a blue letter or an "S").

According to the feature integration theory, lack of focused attention should produce a state of affairs in which the features of different objects are processed but remain "unglued". This should lead to the random combination of features and illusory conjunctions just referred to. This prediction was confirmed by Treisman and Schmidt (1982). They obtained numerous illusory conjunctions when attention was widely distributed, but not when the stimuli were presented to focal attention. The notion that accurate detection of feature conjunctions or objects requires focused attention, whereas that of simple features does not, was confirmed by Vaughn (1984). He discovered that accurate processing of features was possible at greater distances from the fixation point than was possible for feature conjunctions.

In spite of the empirical support for feature integration theory, there are increasing signs that it is over-simplified (see Humphreys & Bruce, 1989, for a detailed evaluation). For example, the evidence of LaBerge (1983) indicates that subjects can attend to all of the letters in a word; this suggests that it is not necessary for serial attention to combine the features of each letter before the letters can be combined to form a word. It could be argued that this happens because much relevant learning has facilitated the perceptual processes. However, it should be noted that Treisman and Gelade (1980) failed to obtain parallel processing with their conjunctive target (i.e. a green letter "T") even after the subjects were given lengthy practice.

Even more convincing evidence that object features do not always have to be combined via slow serial attentional processing was obtained by Humphreys, Riddoch, and Quinlan (1985). They used a task resembling that used by Treisman and Gelade (1980), except that subjects were asked to detect a target of an inverted T against a background of Ts the right way up. They discovered that the time taken to detect the target was scarcely affected by the number of distractors. This suggests that the features of the target (i.e. a vertical line and a horizontal line) were combined without the benefit of focused attention. Feature combination by serial attention may be needed only when there are particular problems in discriminating between target and distractor stimuli; in the study by Humphreys et al. (1985) the discrimination was a simple one, and serial attention was not required.

There are obviously a number of complexities associated with the various findings we have considered in this section. However, most of the findings are consistent with the following generalisation (Johnston & Dark, 1986, p. 56): "Stimulus processing outside the attentional spotlight is restricted mainly to simple physical features."

Summary and Evaluation

The simple analogy between visual attention and a spotlight with an adjustable beam has proved remarkably accurate. There appears to be considerably more processing of visual stimuli falling within the beam of the spotlight than of those falling outside it, and the spatial area encompassed by the beam varies widely as a function of the nature of the task. The evidence is by no means conclusive, but it suggests that there is little or no processing of the meaning of visual stimuli falling outside of the attentional spotlight. Moreover, such stimuli receive no more than very limited processing of their physical characteristics. Despite the general value of comparing visual attention to a spotlight, there are some indications in the literature that visual attention may be rather more complex than that comparison would suggest. For example, Egly and Homa (1984) used a visual display in which there were three rings (inner, middle, and outer). Sometimes the subjects anticipated that a crucial stimulus would appear in the middle ring, but it actually appeared in the inner or the outer ring. According to the spotlight analogy, the anticipation that the middle ring would be important should have caused the attentional spotlight to expand to cover the middle and inner rings. The prediction is, therefore, that performance should have been better when the crucial stimulus appeared in the inner ring than in the outer ring, but performance was actually equally poor in both cases. Presumably the attentional beam is more flexible than the beam of an ordinary spotlight.

There is evidence that the features of objects can be processed rapidly and in parallel, but that combining features to form objects requires focused attention. However, it is sometimes the case that features can be combined without the involvement of focused attention.

DIVIDED ATTENTION

What happens when people endeavour to do two things at once? The answer obviously depends on what "things" we are referring to. Sometimes the attempt is successful, as when an experienced motorist drives a car and holds a conversation at the same time, or a tennis player notes the position of his opponent while running at speed and preparing to make a stroke. At other times, as when someone tries to rub his stomach with one hand while patting his head with the other, or a learner driver tries to control a car while talking, there can be a complete disruption of performance. In this section of the chapter, we will be concerned with some of the factors that determine how well two tasks can be performed concurrently (i.e. at the same time).

Hampson (1989) made the important point that focused and divided attention are more similar in some ways that one might have imagined. Factors (e.g. use of different modalities) which facilitate focused or selective attention generally also make divided attention easier. The reason for this, according to Hampson (op. cit., p. 267), is that: "anything which minimises interference between processes, or keeps them 'further apart' will allow them to be dealt with more readily either selectively or together." It will be useful to bear this generalisation in mind throughout the subsequent coverage of research on divided attention.

At a more theoretical level, the breakdowns of performance often found when two tasks are combined shed light on the limitations of the human information-processing system. It has been assumed by many theorists that such breakdowns reflect the limited capacity of a single multi-purpose central processor or executive that is sometimes simply referred to as "attention". Other theorists are more impressed by our apparent ability to perform two relatively complex tasks at the same time without disruption or interference. Such theorists tend to favour the notion of several specific processing resources, arguing that there will be no interference between two tasks provided that they make use of different processing resources.

It is probably true to say that there has been more progress at the empirical level than at the theoretical level. It is now possible to predict reasonably accurately whether or not two tasks can be combined successfully, but the accounts offered of many of the findings by different theorists are very diverse. Accordingly, we will make a start by discussing the factual evidence before moving on to the murkier issue of how the data are to be explained.

Task Similarity

When we think of pairs of activities that are performed well together in everyday life, the examples that come to mind usually involve two rather dissimilar activities (e.g. driving and talking; reading and listening to music). There is plenty of evidence that the degree of similarity between two tasks is of great importance. As we saw earlier in the chapter, when people attempted to shadow or repeat back prose passages while learning auditorily presented words, their subsequent recognition-memory performance for the words was at chance level (Allport et al., 1972). However, the same authors found that memory was much better when shadowing was combined with visually presented words to learn, and it was excellent (90% correct) when the to-be-remembered material consisted of pictures.

Any adequate analysis of the effects of similarity on dual-task performance must recognise that there are a number of different kinds of similarity that need to be distinguished. Wickens (1984) reviewed the relevant evidence. He concluded that two tasks interfere to the extent that they have the same stimulus modality (visual or auditory), make use of the same stages of processing (input, internal processing, and output), and rely on related memory codes (verbal or visual). It should also be added that response similarity is important. For example, McLeod (1977) required subjects to perform a continuous tracking task with manual responding at the same time as a tone-identification task. Some of the subjects responded vocally to the tones, whereas others responded with the hand not involved in the tracking task. There were very few errors on the tone-identification task, but performance on the tracking task was worse under high response similarity (manual responses on both tasks) than under low response similarity (manual responses on one task and vocal ones on the other).

Similarity of stimulus modality has probably been more thoroughly explored than the other kinds of similarity. We have already seen that it is difficult to handle two concurrent auditory inputs, and the same is true of two visual inputs presented together. Kolers (1972) invented a headgear with a half-silvered mirror. When he wore it, the visual world in front of him and the visual world behind him were both available in the binocular field of view. He discovered that he could attend either forwards or backwards at will, with the unattended scene simply "disappearing".

However, it was not possible to attend to both visual inputs at the same time.

More direct evidence concerning the importance of stimulus modality was obtained by Treisman and Davies (1973). They found that two monitoring tasks interfered with each other much more when the stimuli on both tasks were presented in the same sense modality (visual or auditory) than when they were presented in different modalities.

It is clear in a general sense that the extent to which two tasks interfere with each other is a function of their similarity. However, what is singularly lacking is any satisfactory measure of similarity: How similar are piano playing and poetry writing, or driving a car and watching a football match? Only when there is a better understanding of the processes involved in the performance of such tasks will sensible answers be forthcoming.

Practice

Common sense suggests that the old saying, "Practice makes perfect," is especially applicable to dual-task performance. For example, people who have just learned touch-typing would undoubtedly find their typing performance greatly disrupted by holding a conversation or listening to the radio, but expert typists do not. While there is still little theoretical understanding of exactly what is happening, recent research provides overwhelming support for common sense. In a celebrated study by Spelke, Hirst, and Neisser (1976), two students called Diane and John received five hours' training every week for four months on a variety of tasks. Their first task was to read short stories for comprehension at the same time as they wrote down words to dictation. They found this very difficult initially, and their reading speed and handwriting both suffered considerably. After six weeks of training, however, they were able to read as rapidly and with as much comprehension when taking dictation as when only reading, and the quality of their handwriting had also improved.

In spite of this impressive dual-task performance, Spelke et al. were still not satisfied. They discovered, for example, that Diane and John could recall only 35 out of the thousands of words they had written down at dictation. Even when 20 successive dictated words formed a sentence or came from a single semantic category, the 2 subjects were unaware of the fact. With further training, however, they learned to write down the names of the categories to which the dictated words belonged while maintaining normal reading speed and comprehension.

Spelke et al. (1976, p. 229) wondered whether the popular notion of man's limited processing capacity was accurate, basing themselves on the dramatic findings of John and Diane:

They understood both the text they were reading and the words they were copying. In at least this limited sense, they achieved a true division of attention: They were able to extract meaning simultaneously from what they read and from what they heard . . . People's ability to develop skills in specialised situations is so great that it may never be possible to define general limits on cognitive capacity.

There are alternative ways of interpreting these findings. Perhaps the dictation task was performed rather automatically, and so placed few demands on cognitive capacity, or there might have been a rapid alternation of attention between reading and writing. Hirst, Spelke, Reaves, Caharack, and Neisser (1980) attempted to refute these alternative interpretations. They claimed that writing to dictation was not done automatically because the subjects understood what they were writing. They also claimed that reading and dictation could only be performed together with success by the strategy of alternation of attention provided that the reading material was simple and highly redundant, but they discovered that most subjects were still able to read and take dictation effectively when less redundant reading matter was used.

The studies by Spelke et al. (1976) and by Hirst et al. (1980) are often thought to demonstrate that two relatively complex tasks can be performed together without disruption provided that sufficient practice is given. This is not the case. One of the subjects used by Hirst et al. was tested at dictation without reading, and made fewer than half the number of errors that occurred when reading at the same time. Another reason for doubting the sweeping conclusions usually drawn from these studies is the fact that the reading task gave the subjects tremendous flexibility in terms of when they attended to the reading matter. Such flexibility makes the strategy of alternation of attention much more workable than it would be with tasks where there is moment-by-moment control of the subject's processing activities.

There are other cases of apparently successful performance of two complex tasks, but the requisite skills were always highly practised. In a study by Allport et al. (1972), expert pianists were able to play from seen music while at the same time repeating back or shadowing heard speech, while Shaffer (1975) found that an expert typist could type and shadow at the same time. While these studies are usually regarded as evidence of completely successful task combination, there are some signs of interference when the data are inspected closely (Broadbent, 1982).

There are several reasons why practice might facilitate the concurrent performance of two tasks. In the first place, subjects may develop new strategies for performing each of the tasks so as to minimise any task interference. Secondly, the demands that a task makes on attentional or other central resources may be reduced as a function of practice. Thirdly, while a task may initially require the use of several specific processing resources, practice may permit a more economical mode of functioning that relies on fewer such specific resources. These various possibilities will be considered in more detail a little later in the chapter.

Task Difficulty

It seems fairly obvious that the ability to perform two tasks together in an adequate fashion depends in some sense on the difficulty of the two tasks. However, the notion of "task difficulty" is rather vague, and there are undoubtedly several ways in which one task can be more difficult than another. In spite of problems with the assessment of task difficulty, there are several studies showing the expected pattern of results. Sullivan (1976) gave her subjects the two tasks of shadowing an auditory message and detecting target words on a nonshadowed message. When the shadowing task was made more difficult by using a less redundant message, fewer targets were detected on the nonshadowed message.

The effects of task difficulty on the performance of two concurrent tasks are by no means always as expected. One reason for this was suggested by Norman and Bobrow (1975), who distinguished between *data-limited* and *resource-limited* processes. If performance is resource-limited, then an increase in the amount of resources invested in the task would improve performance. This is not the case when performance is data-limited; here the problem is one of poor quality of the task stimuli or inadequate information in memory.

Increasing the difficulty of one task will impair performance on a second, concurrent task only if extra resources are allocated to the first task. If data limitation is involved, then quite different results may be obtained. Consider an extreme example of someone reading and listening at the same time. Turning out all of the lights certainly makes the reading task more difficult, but this does not lead to impaired performance on the listening task.

It has sometimes been assumed that the demands for resources of two tasks when performed together are equal to the sum of the demands of the same tasks when performed separately. This assumption of additivity of demands is often inaccurate, because the necessity to perform two tasks together often introduces fresh demands of co-ordination and avoidance of interference. Such fresh demands were observed by Duncan (1979) in an experiment in which subjects had to respond as rapidly as possible to closely successive stimuli, one requiring a left-hand response while the other called for a right-hand response. The relationship between each stimulus and response was either corresponding (i.e. rightmost stimulus calling for response of the rightmost finger, and leftmost stimulus requiring response of the leftmost finger) or crossed (e.g. leftmost stimulus requiring response of the rightmost finger). Overall performance was surprisingly poor when the relationship between *one* stimulus and its response was corresponding, whereas the relationship between the *other* stimulus and its response was crossed. Under these conditions, the subjects may sometimes have been confused, as was suggested by the fact that the errors were largely those expected if the inappropriate stimulus-response relationship had been selected. In this case, the uncertainty and confusion caused by mixing two different stimulus-response relationships added a completely new complexity to performance that did not exist when only one of the tasks was performed on its own.

Theoretical Accounts: Central Capacity vs. Modularity

A straightforward way of accounting for many of the dual-task findings is to assume that there is some central capacity which can be deployed flexibly across a wide range of activities. This central processor possesses strictly limited resources (and is sometimes referred to as attention or effort). The extent to which two concurrent tasks can be performed successfully depends upon the demands which each task makes on those resources. If the combined demands of the two tasks do not exceed the total resources of the central capacity, then the two tasks will not interfere with each other. When the resources are insufficient to meet the demands placed on them by the two tasks, then disruption of performance is inevitable. The amount of disruption suffered by either task will be affected by the ways in which the available resources are allocated. More specifically, performance levels will be determined by the principle of complementarity (Norman & Bobrow, 1975), according to which an increase in the use of resources by one task produces a commensurate decrease in the resources available for the other task. In addition to Norman and Bobrow, theories of this basic kind have been put forward by various other theorists (e.g. Johnston & Heinz, 1978).

According to all central capacity theories, the crucial determinant of dual-task performance is the difficulty level of each of the tasks, defining difficulty in terms of the demands placed on the resources of the central capacity. We saw earlier that manipulations of task difficulty often produce the expected results, but there are numerous exceptions. In particular, any effects of task difficulty are sometimes swamped by those of the degree of similarity between tasks. The basic problem for central capacity theories occurs in situations where we consider four tasks (e.g. A, B, C, and D). If we pair A with C, and B with C, and discover that A interferes more with the performance of C than B does, then central capacity theories argue that A requires more of the resources of the central capacity than B. That conclusion leads to the prediction that A will also interfere more with the performance of D than B will. If it turns out that the performance of D is less disrupted by A than by B, then no simple central capacity theory can account for the data.

This rather abstract account can be rendered more concrete by considering an example of this kind of interactive effect. Segal and Fusella (1970) combined image construction (visual or auditory) with signal detection (visual or auditory). The findings are shown in Fig. 4.4. The auditory image task impaired detection of auditory signals more than the visual image task did, suggesting to central capacity theorists that the auditory image task is more difficult and requires more resources than the visual image task. This interpretation seems rather suspect, however, since the auditory image task was *less* disruptive than the visual image task when each task was combined with a task requiring detection of visual signals. In this case, task similarity was clearly of paramount importance, and an account based on some general capacity is unwarranted.

Some theorists have become so disenchanted with the notion of a central capacity or attentional system that they have argued that no such capacity or system actually exists. For example, Allport (1980) claimed that the term "attention" is often used as a synonym for the less acceptable term "consciousness", and that there is no proper specification of how it is supposed to operate. Perhaps his main argument against continuing to postulate the existence of attention or central capacity is that it has not proved fruitful in terms of deepening our understanding. For example, it is very easy to "explain" dual-task interference by claiming that the resources of some central capacity have been exceeded, and to account for a lack of dual-task interference by proposing that the two tasks did not exceed those resources. However, such reasoning singularly fails to provoke any further, and more searching, examination of what is happening.

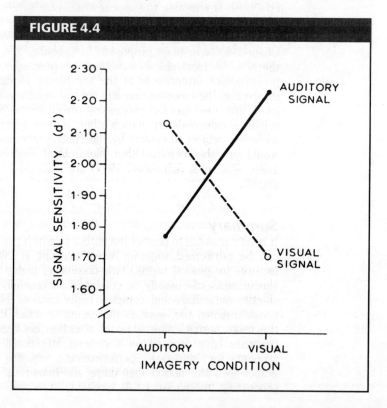

Sensitivity (d') to auditory and visual signals as a function of concurrent imagery modality (auditory versus visual). Adapted from Segal & Fusella (1970).

FIGURE 4.4

SIGNAL SENSITIVITY (d')

2·30
2·20
2·10
2·00
1·90
1·80
1·70
1·60

AUDITORY SIGNAL

VISUAL SIGNAL

AUDITORY   VISUAL
IMAGERY CONDITION

It is instructive at this point to compare the views of central capacity theorists with those of cognitive neuropsychologists. It may be remembered from Chapter 1 that cognitive neuropsychologists assume that the processing system is modular, i.e. it consists of numerous relatively independent processors or modules. Some of the most convincing evidence for modularity comes from the study of language in brain-damaged patients (see Chapters 9 and 10). This has revealed, for example, that reading is a complex skill which involves several rather separate processing mechanisms. If the processing system consists of a large number of specific processing mechanisms, then it is clear why the degree of similarity between two tasks is so important: Similar tasks compete for the same specific processing mechanisms or modules, and thus produce mutual interference, whereas dissimilar tasks involve different mechanisms, and may thus not interfere with each other at all.

There are obviously substantial differences between central capacity theorists, with their emphasis on a very *general* processing mechanism, and cognitive neuropsychologists, with their assumption that there are numerous *specific* processing mechanisms. However, since central capacity theories provide a straightforward account of the effects of task difficulty on dual-task performance and modular theories can explain task similarity effects, it is tempting to suppose that some synthesis of the two theoretical approaches might be valuable. Various theories of this type (e.g. Baddeley, 1986; Norman & Shallice, 1980, discussed in Chapter 5) have been proposed. In essence, it is assumed that there is a hierarchical structure of processes. The central processor or attention is at the top of the hierarchy, and it is involved in the co-ordination and control of behaviour. Below this level are the specific processing mechanisms which operate relatively independently of each other. If these specific mechanisms were not subject to control by the central processor, then chaos would probably result. Other hierarchical models (e.g. Logan, 1988; Shiffrin & Schneider, 1977) are discussed in the following section.

Summary

It is only possible to predict the extent to which two different tasks can be performed together when account is taken of several factors. In general terms, two dissimilar, highly practised, and simple tasks can usually be combined successfully, whereas two similar, unfamiliar, and complex tasks cannot. There are other considerations, too, such as the extent to which the structure of the tasks permits alternation of attention between them. Some theorists have focused on a general attentional mechanism to account for dual-task performance, whereas others have emphasised the notion that there are numerous rather specific processing mechanisms. At present, it would appear that a synthesis of these theoretical viewpoints, incorporating both a general and several specific mechanisms, probably provides the most adequate basis for explaining dual-task interference effects.

AUTOMATIC PROCESSING

One of the key phenomena within the dual-task paradigm is the dramatic improvement that practice often has on performance (e.g. Spelke et al., 1976). There are several possible explanations of this phenomenon. However, the commonest view is that some processing activities cease to make any demands on central capacity or attention as a result of prolonged practice; in other words, they become automatic. Numerous definitions of "automaticity" have been offered, but there is fairly good general agreement on some of the main criteria (Jonides, Naveh-Benjamin, & Palmer, 1985; Logan, 1988; Shiffrin, Dumais, & Schneider, 1981):

- automatic processes are fast;
- automatic processes do not reduce the capacity for performing other tasks (i.e. they demand zero attention);
- automatic processes are unavailable to consciousness; and
- automatic processes are unavoidable (i.e. they always occur when an appropriate stimulus is presented, even if that stimulus is outside the field of attention).

As Hampson (1989, p.264) pointed out: "Criteria for automatic processes are easy to find, but hard to satisfy empirically." For example, the requirement that automatic processes should require no attention at all means that they should have no influence on the concurrent performance of an attention-demanding task. In practice, this is rarely the case (see Hampson, 1989, for a review). There are also problems with the unavoidability criterion. The Stroop effect, in which the naming of the colours in which words are printed is slowed down by using colour words (e.g. the word "GREEN" printed in red), has usually been regarded as involving unavoidable and automatic processing of the colour words. However, Kahneman and Henik (1979) discovered that the Stroop effect was much larger when the distracting information (i.e. the colour name) was in the same location as the to-be-named colour rather than in an adjacent location within the central fixation area. This means that the processes producing the Stroop effect are not entirely unavoidable, and thus that they are not completely automatic in the strict sense of the term.

What appears to be the case is that there are a relatively small number of processes which are fully automatic in the sense of conforming to the criteria described here, and a much larger number of processes which are only partially automatic. Later in this section we consider a theoretical approach (that of Norman & Shallice, 1980) which distinguishes between fully automatic and partially automatic processes.

Shiffrin and Schneider's (1977) Theory

One of the most influential theories in this area was proposed by Schneider and Shiffrin (1977) and Shiffrin and Schneider (1977). They argued for a theoretical distinction between controlled and automatic processes. According to them:

- Controlled processes are of limited capacity, require attention, and can be used flexibly in changing circumstances.
- Automatic processes suffer no capacity limitations, do not require attention, and are very difficult to modify once they have been learned.

Schneider and Shiffrin tested these ideas in a series of experiments. They made use of a task in which subjects memorised one, two, three, or four letters (the memory set), were then shown a visual display containing one, two, three, or four letters, and finally decided as rapidly as possible whether any one of the items in the visual display was the same as any one of the items in the memory set. In many of their experiments, the crucial manipulation was the kind of mapping used: Consistent versus varied. In a consistent mapping condition, only consonants were used as members of the memory set, and only numbers were used as distractors in the visual display (or vice versa). In other words, if a subject was given only consonants to memorise, then he or she would know that any consonant detected in the visual display must be an item from the memory set. In contrast, the varied mapping condition involved using a mixture of numbers and consonants to form the memory set and to provide distractors in the visual display.

The results revealed striking effects for the mapping manipulation (see Fig. 4.5). The numbers of items in the memory set and visual display both greatly affected decision speed under varied mapping conditions, with the effects being approximately as large on negative trials (i.e. when the visual display did not contain any of the memorised items). With consistent mapping conditions, decision speed was almost unaffected by the sizes of the memory set and visual display.

According to Schneider and Shiffrin, a controlled search process was used with varied mapping; this involves serial comparisons between each item in the memory set and each item in the visual display until a match is achieved or until all of the possible comparisons have been made. On the other hand, performance with consistent mapping reflects the use of automatic processes operating in parallel and independently. According to Schneider and Shiffrin (1977), these automatic processes evolve as a result of years of practice in distinguishing between letters and numbers.

The notion that automatic processes develop through practice was investigated in a direct fashion by Shiffrin and Schneider (1977). They used consistent mapping with the consonants B to L comprising one set and the consonants Q to Z forming the other set. As before, items from only one set were always used in the

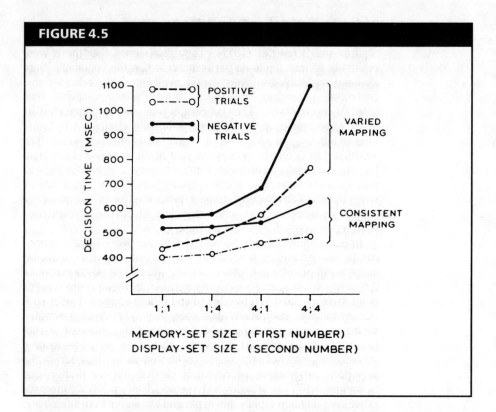

FIGURE 4.5

Response latency on a decision task as a function of memory-set size, display-set size, and consistent versus varied mapping. Data from Schneider & Shiffrin (1977).

construction of the memory set, and the distractors in the visual display were all selected from the other set. There was a substantial improvement in performance over a total of 2100 trials, and it appeared to reflect the growth of automatic processes.

The evidence discussed so far has suggested that automatic processes operate more rapidly and efficiently than controlled processes, but for a complete picture we must consider the potential disadvantages of automatic processing. The most obvious problem with automatic processes is their lack of flexibility, which is likely to disrupt performance when there is a change in the prevailing circumstances. This was confirmed in the second part of the study just described. The initial 2100 trials with one consistent mapping were followed by a further 2400 trials with the reverse consistent mapping. For example, if the memory-set letters were always taken from the second half of the alphabet during the first part of the experiment, then they were drawn from the first half of the alphabet during the second part. This reversal of the mapping conditions had a markedly adverse effect on performance; indeed, it took nearly 1000 trials under the new conditions before performance recovered to its level at the very start of the experiment!

Of course, it could be argued that performance normally suffers when the way in which a task has been carried out in the past is no longer appropriate, and thus that an explanation in terms of automaticity is not required. This possibility was explored by Shiffrin and Schneider (1977). They discovered that there were relatively minor effects on performance when the conditions were changed for subjects given varied mapping. This indicates that controlled processes are much more easily modifiable than automatic processes. This conclusion was further supported by other experiments in which subjects initially attempted to locate target letters anywhere in a visual display, but were then instructed to detect targets in one part of the display and to ignore targets that appeared elsewhere in the display. The key finding was that subjects were less able to ignore part of the visual display when they had developed automatic processes as a consequence of consistent mapping than when they had made use of controlled search processes due to varied mapping.

In sum, Shiffrin and Schneider (1977) discovered that attention can be divided among several information sources with reasonable success when automatic processes are used. The position is quite different with respect to focused attention, in which some sources of information must be attended to and others ignored. Under such circumstances, controlled processes largely prevent unwanted processing from occurring, whereas automatic processes disrupt performance because of automatic responses to to-be-ignored stimuli. In a nutshell, the major conclusion to be drawn from the important programme of research carried out by Shiffrin and Schneider (1977) is as follows (Eysenck, 1982, p.22): "Automatic processes function rapidly and in parallel but suffer from inflexibility; controlled processes are flexible and versatile but operate relatively slowly and in a serial fashion."

Of course, Shiffrin and Schneider only examined controlled and automatic processes in the context of visual tasks. It is possible that different results might be obtained in other sensory modalities. However, Poltrock, Lansman, and Hunt (1982) investigated the effects of consistent and varied mapping on auditory target detection, and obtained very similar results to those of Shiffrin and Schneider (1977).

Evaluation of Shiffrin and Schneider

The theoretical approach of Shiffrin and Schneider (1977) is important. However, there are various criticisms that can be made of it. There is a puzzling discrepancy between theory and data with respect to the identification of automaticity. The theoretical assumption that automatic processes operate in parallel and place no demands on capacity means that there should be a slope of zero (i.e. a horizontal line) in the function relating decision speed to the number of items in the memory set and/or in the visual display when automatic processes are used. In fact, while Shiffrin and Schneider argued that their consistent mapping conditions produced automaticity, they typically found that decision speed was slower when the memory set and the visual display both contained several items (e.g. see Fig. 4.5).

The greatest weakness of Shiffrin and Schneider's approach is that it is in many ways descriptive rather than explanatory. If one argues that some processes become automatic as a result of practice, that tells us rather little about what is actually happening. Practice may simply lead to a speeding up of the processes involved in performing a task, or it may lead to a dramatic change in the nature of the processes themselves. Cheng (1985) has used the term "restructuring" to refer to the latter state of affairs. For example, if you are asked to add ten twos, you could do this in a rather laborious way by adding two and two, and then two to four, and so on. Alternatively, you could short-circuit the whole process by simply performing the multiplication ten times two. The crucial point is that simply discovering that practice leads to automaticity does not make it clear whether the same processes are being performed more efficiently or whether entirely new processes are being used.

Cheng argued that most of Shiffrin and Schneider's findings of automaticity were actually based on restructuring. More specifically, she claimed that subjects in the consistent mapping conditions did not really search systematically through the memory set and the visual display looking for a match. If, for example, they knew that any consonant in the visual display had to be an item from the memory set, then they could simply scan the visual display looking for a consonant without regard to which consonants were actually in the memory set.

Schneider and Shiffrin (1985) admitted that some of their earlier findings could be accounted for by assuming that subjects in consistent mapping conditions made use of knowledge about the categories being used. However, they also pointed out that most of the dramatic differences between consistent and varied mapping (e.g. rejection of to-be-ignored stimuli) could not be explained in terms of restructuring. They also referred to other research which strengthened the case for automatic processing, based on the assumption that two tasks can be performed together efficiently provided that at least one of the tasks involves automatic processing. The reason for this is that automatic processes allegedly place no demands on capacity. In a study on visual search, Schneider and Fisk (1982) discovered that one controlled (varied mapping) and one automatic (consistent mapping) task could be performed as well together as separately after extensive practice, whereas two controlled processing tasks could not be combined successfully. These findings provide striking confirmation of the notion that automatic processes can sometimes be performed without any measurable cost.

Less impressive evidence was reported by Schneider and Fisk (1984). They compared subjects on a main task that was either performed on its own or at the same time as a consistent mapping task allegedly performed automatically. There was a decrement of

11% in performance of the main task when the consistent mapping task was carried out at the same time. Schneider and Shiffrin (1985, p.427) argued that this finding did not necessarily throw doubt on the use of automatic processes on the consistent mapping task, because "lack of interference between two processes implies that at least one is automatic, but interference does not imply the converse." They are correct in arguing that there are various reasons why two tasks might interfere with each other, such as difficulties in co-ordinating them. However, it is not clear how great an interference effect there can be before one must conclude that neither task uses automatic processes.

Norman and Shallice's (1980) Theory

Norman and Shallice (1980) and Shallice (1982) proposed a theory which took account of the distinction between fully automatic and partially automatic processes. They argued that instead of the usual distinction between automatic and attentional or controlled processes, it was preferable to identify three different levels of functioning:

- Fully automatic processing controlled by schemata (i.e. organised plans).
- Partially automatic processing involving contention scheduling without deliberate direction or conscious control; contention scheduling is used to resolve conflicts among schemata.
- Deliberate control by a supervisory attentional system.

According to Norman and Shallice (1980), fully automatic processes occur with very little conscious awareness of the processes involved. Such automatic processes would frequently disrupt behaviour if left entirely to their own devices. As a consequence, there is an automatic conflict resolution process known as contention scheduling, which selects one of the available schemata on the basis of environmental information and current priorities. There is generally more conscious awareness of the partially automatic processes involving contention scheduling than of fully automatic processes. Finally, there is a higher level control mechanism known as the supervisory attentional system. This system is involved in decision making and trouble-shooting, and it permits flexible responding in novel situations. The supervisory attentional system and the neuropsychological evidence in its support are discussed more fully in Chapter 5.

In sum, the theoretical approach of Norman and Shallice (1980) and Shallice (1982) incorporates the interesting notion that there are two separate control systems: contention scheduling and the supervisory attentional system. This contrasts with the views of Shiffrin and Schneider (1977) (and of many other theorists) that there is a single control system. The approach of Norman and Shallice appears preferable, because it provides a more natural explanation for the fact that some processes are fully automatic whereas others are only partially automatic.

Logan's (1988) Theory of Automaticity

What exactly happens as automaticity develops through prolonged practice? We have seen that Shiffrin and Schneider failed to provide an adequate answer, and it is generally true that this key issue has not received the thorough consideration which it deserves. Shiffrin and Schneider (1977) suggested only that practice allows a task to be performed with progressively fewer processing resources, and that this reduction in the number of processing resources needed leads to automaticity.

As Logan (1988) pointed out, their account suffers from the severe limitation that it does not spell out in any detail exactly *why* practice has this effect. Accordingly, he attempted to fill this gap by making the following assumptions:

- Separate memory traces are stored away every time a stimulus is encountered and processed.
- Practice with the same stimulus leads to the storage of more and more information about the stimulus, and about what to do with it.
- This increase in the knowledge base with practice permits rapid retrieval of relevant information as soon as the appropriate stimulus is presented.
- "Automaticity is memory retrieval: Performance is automatic when it is based on a single-step direct-access retrieval of past solutions from memory" (Logan, 1988, p. 493).
- In the absence of practice, the task of responding appropriately to a stimulus requires thought and the application of rules; after prolonged practice, the appropriate response is stored in memory and can be accessed very rapidly.

These theoretical views allow us to make coherent sense of many of the characteristics of automaticity. Automaticity is found with consistent but not with varied mapping (Shiffrin & Schneider, 1977), because it is only with consistent mapping that there is an accumulation of highly similar memory traces in which any given stimulus is always associated with the same response. Automatic processes are fast because they require only the retrieval of "past solutions" from long-term memory. Automatic processes have little or no effect on the processing capacity available to perform other tasks because the retrieval of heavily over-learned information is relatively effortless. Finally, there is no conscious awareness of automatic processes because no significant processes intervene between the presentation of a stimulus and the retrieval of the appropriate response.

In sum, Logan (1988, p.519) encapsulated his theoretical position in the following way: "Novice performance is limited by a lack of knowledge rather than by a lack of resources . . . Only the knowledge base changes with practice." It is premature to attempt an evaluation of this approach, but it seems probable that Logan is right in his basic assumption that an understanding of automatic, expert performance will require detailed consideration of the knowledge acquired with practice, rather than simply the changes in processing which occur.

Summary

It has often been claimed that there is a valid distinction between attentional or controlled processes and automatic processes. In contrast to attentional processes, automatic processes are fast, they do not reduce the capacity for performing other tasks, and they are unavailable to conscious awareness. There is general agreement that prolonged practice is of fundamental importance to the development of automaticity, but it is much less clear how practice produces automaticity. According to Logan (1988), what happens is that practice leads to an increase in the knowledge base, and this in turn permits rapid retrieval of relevant information and fast action.

ACTION SLIPS AND ABSENT-MINDEDNESS

Some of the theoretical notions considered in this chapter are relevant to an understanding of the commonplace phenomenon of absent-mindedness. Psychologists often refer to this phenomenon by the term "action slip", meaning the performance of an action that was not intended. At the most general level, it seems obvious that attentional failures usually underlie action slips. However, it may well be that there are several different kinds of action slips, each of which requires its own detailed explanation.

Diary Studies

Since it is extremely difficult to study action slips under laboratory conditions, the first prerequisite is to collect numerous examples of action slips and attempt to assign them to a manageable number of categories. This was done by Reason (1979) and by Reason and Mycielska (1982). Reason asked 35 people to keep diaries of their action slips over a 2-week period. Over 400 action errors were reported altogether, most of which belonged to 5 major categories. Forty percent of the action slips involved *storage failures* in which intentions and actions were either forgotten or recalled incorrectly. Reason (1979, p.74) quoted the following example of a storage failure: "I started to pour a second kettle of boiling water into a teapot full of freshly made tea. I had no recollection of having just made it."

A further 20% of the errors were *test failures* in which the progress of a planned sequence was not monitored sufficiently thoroughly at crucial junctures. An illustrative test failure from one person's diary went as follows (Reason, 1979, p.73): "I meant to get my car out, but as I passed through the back porch on my way to the garage I stopped to put on my wellington boots and gardening jacket as if to work in the garden." *Subroutine failures* accounted for a further 18% of the errors; these involved insertions, omissions, or re-orderings of the component stages in an action sequence. Reason (1979, p.73) gave the following example of this type of error: "I sat down to do some work and before starting to write I put my hand up to my face to take my glasses off, but my fingers snapped together rather abruptly because I hadn't been wearing them in the first place." There were relatively few examples of action slips belonging to the two remaining categories of *discrimination failures* (11%) and *programme assembly failures* (5%). The former category consisted of failures to discriminate appropriately between stimulus objects (e.g. mistaking shaving cream for toothpaste), and the latter category consisted of inappropriate combinations of actions (e.g. Reason, 1979, p.72): "I unwrapped a sweet, put the paper in my mouth, and threw the sweet into the waste bucket." Reason and Mycielska (1982) made use of more data than Reason (1979). They had access to a total of 625 errors from 98 people, but arrived at very similar categories to those previously used by Reason (1979).

Theories of Action Slips: Norman and Reason

Reason (1979) has proposed a theoretical account of action slips. However, before considering that, we will consider the theoretical views of Norman (1981), who has also examined action slips in detail. He assumed that actions are determined by the activation of appropriate schemata or organised plans, and that these schemas are hierarchically organised. According to Norman, the highest level schema represents the overall intention or goal (e.g. buying a present), and the lower level schemata correspond to the actions that are involved in accomplishing that goal (e.g. taking money out of the bank, taking the train to the nearest shopping centre). All of these schemata come into play when their level of activation is sufficiently high and the appropriate triggering conditions exist (e.g. getting into the train when it arrives at the station). Their activation level is determined by current intentions and by the immediate environmental situation.

According to Norman's (1981) schema model, there are three major reasons why slips of action occur:

- there may be errors in the formation of the intention to do something;
- there may be faulty activation of a schema, leading to activation of the wrong schema or loss of activation of the right schema;

- there may be faulty triggering of active schemata, leading to the wrong schema determining action.

Many of the action slips recorded by Reason (1979) can be related to this theoretical framework. For example, discrimination failures can lead to errors in the formation of the intention, and storage failures for intentions can produce faulty activation of schemata. Finally, programme assembly failures often produce faulty triggering of active schemata.

Before considering Reason's alternative theoretical views on action slips, it is worth considering the value of diary studies. It would clearly be unwise to attach much significance to the percentages for the various kinds of action slips. In the first place, the figures are based solely on those action slips that were noticed, and we do not know how many cases of each kind of slip went completely undetected. Secondly, the number of occurrences of any particular kind of action slip is meaningful only when we have some idea of the number of occasions on which that kind of slip might have happened but did not. For example, the small number of discrimination failures may reflect either good discrimination on the part of the diary keepers, or the relative lack of situations requiring anything approaching a fine discrimination.

When we look in detail at slips of action, it is of interest that they nearly all occur during the performance of highly practised and over-learned activities. This is in some ways rather surprising and paradoxical, because errors generally decrease as skills are acquired. Reason (1979) accounted for this apparent paradox by distinguishing between two modes of control over motor performance:

- A *closed-loop* or *feedback mode of control*, in which visual and other feedback is used by some central processor or attentional system to provide moment-by-moment control of behaviour, is used extensively during the early stages of skill acquisition.
- As a result of extensive practice, this closed-loop mode is increasingly replaced by an *open-loop mode of control* in which motor performance is controlled by motor programmes or by pre-arranged instruction sequences. A crucial aspect of the open-loop mode is that it frees the resources of the central processor to engage in processing activities that may have little relevance to the current motor performance.

The advantages of the open-loop mode are obvious in that attentional resources are not committed exclusively to the ongoing task and can thus be flexibly deployed. However, there are some disadvantages. In particular, an individual who is operating in the open-loop mode and attending to nontask information may fail to return to the closed-loop mode as and when appropriate. As a consequence, slips of action occur. This theoretical position was spelled out by Reason (1979, p. 85):

- "the performance of a highly practised and largely automatised job liberates the central processor from moment-to-moment control"
- "since, like Nature, focal attention abhors a vacuum it tends to be 'captured' by some pressing but parallel mental activity so that, on occasion, it fails to switch back to the task in hand at a 'critical decision point'"
- "and thus permits the guidance of action to fall by default under the control of 'strong' motor programmes"

How well does this hypothesis account for action slips? This question can only be answered by considering the various types of action slips separately. One common type of action slip involves repeating an action unnecessarily because the first action has been forgotten. Common examples are attempting to start a car that has already been started, or brushing one's teeth twice in quick succession. We know, from studies in which listeners attend to one message and repeat it back (i.e. shadow it) while ignoring a second concurrent message, that unattended information is held very briefly and then forgotten. When the initial starting of a car or brushing one's teeth occurs "automatically" in the open-loop mode, it would be predicted that subsequent retention of the information that the action has been performed should be extremely poor.

Many action slips can be accounted for when it is appreciated that most action sequences consist of a number of distinct motor programmes. While each individual motor programme can be carried out without close control by the central processor, a switch to the closed-loop mode of control is essential at certain points in the sequence of actions, especially when a given situation is common to two or more motor programmes, and the strongest available motor programme is inappropriate. The person who put on his gardening clothes instead of getting the car out exemplifies the way in which strong but unplanned actions can occur in the absence of attentional control.

William James (1890, p.115) gave an example of attentional failure leading to use of a strong but inappropriate motor programme: "Very absent-minded persons in going to their bedroom to dress for dinner have been known to take off one garment after another and finally to get into bed, merely because that was the habitual issue of the first few movements when performed at a later hour." In other words, one of the consequences of relatively automatic functioning is an inflexible sequence of motor activities based on the relative strengths of the various motor programmes. Most situations call for some flexibility in the nature and ordering of the components of an action sequence, and such flexibility can only occur with the closed-loop model of control.

On the basis of the discussion so far, it might be argued that people would function more efficiently if they placed less reliance on automatic processes and more on the central processor. However, such an argument is suspect because automated

activities can sometimes be disrupted if too much attention is paid
to the details of task performance. For example, it can become
more difficult to walk down a deep spiral staircase if attention is
paid to the leg movements involved. Moreover, Reason's diarists
produced an average of only one action slip per day, which is by no
means an indication that their usual processing strategies were
ineffective. All in all, most people seem to use the closed-loop and
open-loop modes of control very efficiently. The optimal strategy
involves very frequent shifts from one mode of control to the other,
and it is noteworthy that these shifts are performed with great
success for the most part. Action slips are the consequences of a
failure to shift from open-loop to closed-loop control at the right
moment. While they are theoretically important, action slips usually
have a minimally disruptive effect in everyday life. Of course, there
may be important individual differences. The tendency of academics
to attend to their own profound inner thoughts may mean that there
is a grain of truth in the stereotype of the absent-minded professor!

Summary

Action slips (i.e. the performance of actions that were not
intended) have been investigated by means of diary studies, in
which subjects keep daily records of any slips which they make.
Various categories of action slip have been identified, but they all
tend to involve highly practised activities. Highly practised skills
typically do not require detailed attentional monitoring except at
critical decision points. Failures of attention at such decision points
cause many action slips. Failure to remember what was done a few
seconds previously is responsible for many other action slips.
Action slips are of theoretical interest because they tell us about
the functioning of attention. They are also of practical relevance
because many disasters (e.g. the Chernobyl nuclear accident)
occur as a result of action slips.

SUMMARY

The concept of "attention" has been used in several different ways.
However, the two most common meanings relate to selective
processing and to mental effort or concentration. Paradigms
involving focused attention have typically been used in order to
investigate selective attention. The essence of such paradigms is
that two (or more) stimuli are presented at the same time, and the
subject's task is to respond to one stimulus (i.e. the attended
stimulus) and to ignore the other stimulus (i.e. the unattended
stimulus).

Researchers investigating focused attention in the auditory
modality have been very concerned with the issue of how the
process of attentional selectivity works. A closely related issue
concerns the fate of the unattended stimulus. One extreme
possibility is that the attended stimulus is distinguished from the

unattended stimulus at a very early stage of processing, so that the unattended stimulus receives minimal processing. The other extreme possibility is that both the attended and unattended stimuli are processed thoroughly, but that only the attended stimulus affects the subsequent response. Neither extreme possibility appears to be correct. In fact, there is typically some processing of unattended stimuli, with the amount of such processing varying flexibly as a function of how easy it is to discriminate between the attended and unattended stimuli.

Similar findings have been obtained when focused attention in the visual modality has been investigated. Visual attention has been compared to a spotlight with an adjustable beam. Stimuli which are presented outside of the attentional beam generally receive very little processing, especially of their meaning.

There have been numerous studies using the divided attention paradigm. In this paradigm, subjects are presented with two tasks at the same time with instructions to attempt to perform both of them as well as possible. In other words, the divided attention paradigm differs from the focused attention paradigm in terms of whether the instructions require both or only one of two concurrent tasks to be performed. At an empirical level, the main issue is to identify those factors which determine whether two tasks can be performed successfully at the same time. Three of the major factors are task similarity; task difficulty; and practice. The best conditions for performing two tasks together are when the two tasks are dissimilar from each other, when they are relatively easy tasks, and when they are well-practised tasks. In contrast, the worst conditions occur when the tasks are highly similar, rather difficult, and have been practised very little.

Several theorists have considered the effects of practice in detail. Most of them have argued that at least some processes become automatic with practice. Opinions differ as to the criteria for automaticity, but it has been assumed that automatic processes are fast, that they do not reduce the capacity available for other tasks, and that there is no conscious awareness of them. There is no doubt that there are often enormous changes in performance as a result of practice, but relatively little progress has been made in understanding exactly how practice leads to automaticity. However, Logan (1988) has made the interesting suggestion that increased knowledge about what to do with different stimuli is stored away with practice, and that automaticity occurs when this information can be retrieved very rapidly.

The phenomenon of absent-mindedness can be see as due, at least in part, to attentional failure. What often happens is that an individual runs off a sequence of highly practised and over-learned motor programmes. Attentional control is not required during the time that each programme is running, but is needed when there is a switch from one programme to another. Failure to attend at these choice points can lead to the wrong motor programme being activated, especially if it is stronger than the appropriate programme. Since optimal performance requires very frequent shifts between the presence and absence of attentional control, it is perhaps surprising that absent-mindedness is not more prevalent than it actually is.

FURTHER READING

Broadbent, D.E. (1982). Task combination and selective intake of information. *Acta Psychologica, 50,* 253–290. This includes a good analysis of the findings from studies of divided attention.

Hampson, P.J. (1989). Aspects of attention and cognitive science. *The Irish Journal of Psychology, 10,* 261–275. As the title suggests, this article demonstrates how cognitive science is of potential relevance to an understanding of the phenomena of attention. As such, it provides a number of interesting insights into the relationship between two areas which have generally been treated separately.

Johnston, W.A. & Dark, V.J. (1986). Selective attention. *Annual Review of Psychology, 37,* 43–75. This paper is very good on the empirical findings of research on attention, and it provides a useful and readable review of contemporary theories of selective attention.

Kahneman, D. & Treisman, A. (1984). Changing views of attention and automaticity. In R. Parasuraman & D.R. Davies (Eds.), *Varieties of attention.* London: Academic Press. A penetrating critique of many views on attention and automaticity is offered.

Reason, J.T. & Mycielska, K. (1982). *Absent minded? The psychology of mental lapses and everyday errors.* Englewood Cliffs, N.J.: Prentice-Hall. The phenomenon of absent-mindedness is discussed in detail, and a theory to account for it is proposed.

Chapter Five

MEMORY: STRUCTURE AND PROCESSES

INTRODUCTION

*T*his chapter is concerned with normal human memory. Any adequate analysis of human memory must probably consider both the *structure* of the memory system and the *processes* operating within that structure. *Structure* refers to the way in which the memory system is organised, and *processes* refer to the activities occurring within the memory system. Accordingly, there are major sections in this chapter dealing with structure and processes.

There are also important distinctions between *encoding*, *storage* and *retrieval*. "Encoding" refers to those events occurring during the presentation of to-be-remembered information. Encoding processes determine what is stored within the memory system, and the conditions at the time of a retention test determine what information can subsequently be retrieved or recovered. The next two major sections of this chapter deal primarily with the ways in which information is encoded and stored in memory, and the following major section deals with the issue of how information is then retrieved from the memory system. The final major section deals with some important contemporary views on human memory.

Despite the importance of the distinctions between structure and process and among encoding, storage, and retrieval, it is worth emphasising that one cannot have structure without process or retrieval without prior encoding and storage. It is only when processes operate on the essentially passive structures of the memory system that the system becomes active and of use. So far as storage and retrieval are concerned, Tulving and Thomson (1973, p. 359) pointed out that, "Only that can be retrieved that has been stored, and . . . how it can be retrieved depends on how it was stored."

THE STRUCTURE OF MEMORY

The Spatial Metaphor

When people think about the mind, they often liken it to a physical space, with memories and ideas as objects contained within that space. Thus, we speak of ideas being in the dark corners or dim recesses of our minds, and of holding ideas in mind. Ideas may be in the front or the back of our minds, or they may be difficult to grasp. With respect to the processes involved in memory, we talk about storing memories, searching or looking for lost memories, and sometimes of finding them. An examination of our usual way of talking about memory, therefore, suggests that there is general adherence to what might be called the spatial metaphor. According to advocates of the spatial metaphor:

- memories are treated as objects stored in specific locations within the mind;
- the retrieval process involves a search through the mind in order to find specific memories.

Plato (the Greek philosopher) made an early use of the spatial metaphor as a guide to understanding memory phenomena. He compared the mind to an aviary, in which the specific memories were represented by birds. As with most spatial metaphors of memory, remembering information was assumed to involve a search process. Information was remembered when the appropriate bird was caught, whereas an error in recall occurred when the wrong bird was seized.

Plato's bird-brain analogy is somewhat embarrassing for contemporary cognitive psychologists because even some fairly recent theories of memory show clear resemblances to it. However, while the spatial metaphor has shown extraordinary longevity, there have been some interesting changes over time in the precise form of analogy used. In particular, technological advances have influenced theoretical conceptualisations (Roediger, 1980). The original Greek analogies were based on wax tablets and aviaries; these were superseded by analogies involving switchboards, gramophones, tape recorders, libraries, conveyor belts, and underground maps. Most recently, the workings of human memory have been compared to computer functioning (e.g. Atkinson & Shiffrin, 1968), and it has been proposed that the various memory stores found in computers have their counterparts in the human memory system.

Cognitive psychologists have tended to take the spatial metaphor for granted. However, one common criticism of it concerns its apparent inability to explain the fact that we can often decide very rapidly that we do *not* know something. The most obvious assumption based on the spatial metaphor is that there would be a thorough memory search in order to ascertain that some piece of information was not present. In fact, people can decide very quickly that letter strings such as MANTINESS are not English words. They are also sometimes able to make negative decisions about issues such as whether they know certain words well enough to be able to use them in a sentence, or whether they have visited certain cities, faster than they can make positive decisions (Kolers & Palef, 1976).

A further substantial problem with the spatial metaphor is that it implies that the storage system is rather inflexible. If everything we know is stored within a three-dimensional space, then some kinds of information must be stored closer together than others. It has been suggested (e.g. Broadbent, 1971) that the organisation of information within the memory system resembles a library, with semantically related items of information being stored together. However, the cataloguing system used in most libraries would break down completely if a novel category of books were requested (e.g. books with red covers or with more than 700 pages), and this illustrates clearly the potential inflexibility of a memory system based on the spatial metaphor.

Most versions of the spatial metaphor imply that search and retrieval processes can be used successfully only when the nature of the requested information is compatible with whatever classification system is used to organise the contents of memory. In fact, retrieval demonstrates much greater flexibility than this. In essence, reliance on the spatial metaphor leads to an over-emphasis on the ways in which information is represented in the memory system, and an under-emphasis on the processes operating on those memorial representations.

There are various alternatives to the spatial metaphor. One alternative which is becoming increasingly popular is based on the notion of parallel distributed processing. According to parallel distributed processing theorists, information about an individual or an event is stored in the form of numerous connections among units and is not stored in a single place as the spatial metaphor assumes. Some of the advantages of this approach to human memory will be considered later in this chapter.

Memory Stores

Several memory theorists (e.g. Atkinson & Shiffrin, 1968; Waugh & Norman, 1965) attempted to describe the basic architecture of the memory system in terms of a number of stores. Their theories overlapped considerably, so that it is possible to discuss the multi-store approach on the basis of the common features of the various theories. According to the multi-store theorists, there are three types of memory store:

- sensory stores, which are modality-specific and hold information very briefly;
- a short-term store of rather limited capacity;
- a long-term store of essentially unlimited capacity which can hold information over extremely long periods of time.

The basic ingredients of the multi-store model are shown in Fig. 5.1. It was assumed that information from the environment is initially received by the sensory stores. These stores are modality-specific, with a separate sensory store corresponding to each of the sensory modalities (e.g. vision, hearing). Information is held very briefly in the sensory stores, with some of it being attended to and processed further by the short-term store. In turn, some of the information processed in the short-term store is transferred to the long-term store. According to Atkinson and Shiffrin (1968; 1971), long-term storage of information often depends on rote rehearsal, with a direct relationship between the amount of rehearsal in the short-term store and the strength of the stored memory trace.

FIGURE 5.1

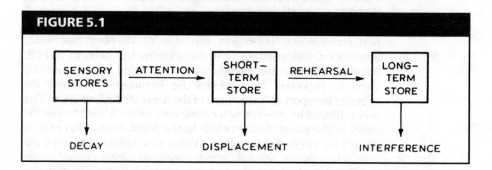

The multi-store model of memory.

It is worth noting at this point that there is considerable overlap between the areas of attention and memory. As a consequence, much of the coverage of attention earlier in the book is relevant here. For example, Broadbent's (1958) theory of attention was in many ways the main precursor of the multi-store approach to memory, and there is a definite resemblance between the notion of a sensory store and his "buffer" store.

Inspection of Fig. 5.1 indicates that the multi-store approach incorporated a number of structural and processing assumptions. The memory stores themselves form the basic structure, and processes such as attention and rehearsal control the flow of information between the memory stores. However, the emphasis within this approach to memory was on structure rather than on the processes operating within that structure.

Sensory Stores
At any given moment, our senses are bombarded with an enormous amount of information, most of which does not receive any attention. For example, if you are sitting down in a chair as you read this, then tactile information from that part of your body in contact with the chair is probably available. However, if you have any interest in what you are reading, then you have probably been unaware of that tactile information until now. Is such information lost immediately, or does it remain in the processing system for a brief period of time? As we shall see, information in most, if not all,

of the sense modalities persists for some time after the end of stimulation. The value of this persistence of sensory information is that it facilitates the task of extracting its most important aspects for further analysis.

Nearly all of the work on the sensory stores has concentrated on the visual and auditory modalities, which are the most important ones in our everyday lives. So far as the visual or iconic store is concerned, the classic demonstration of its existence was provided by Sperling (1960). When he presented his subjects with a visual array containing 3 rows of 4 letters each for 50msec, and asked them to recall as many letters as possible, he discovered that they could usually report only 4 or 5 of them. However, most of the subjects claimed that they had actually seen many more letters than they had been able to report.

Sperling wondered whether this puzzling discrepancy between performance and self-report was due to the fact that visual information was available after the stimulus had been turned off, but so transiently that the information had faded before most of it could be reported. He explored this hypothesis by asking the subjects to report only one-third of the presented information. This was achieved by presenting a cueing tone either 0.1sec before the onset of the visual display (which lasted 50msec) or at intervals of up to 1sec after stimulus offset. A high tone indicated that the top row of letters was to be reported, a medium tone was used to cue recall of the middle row, and a low tone meant that the bottom row of letters was to be recalled. Since the three rows were tested at random, it was possible to estimate the total amount of information available to each subject by multiplying the number of letters recalled by three.

The results with this partial report procedure were quite striking. When the tone was presented immediately before or after the onset of the display, approximately 9 letters appeared to be available, but this dropped to 6 letters when the tone was heard 0.3sec after the presentation of the display, and it fell to 4.5 letters with an interval of 1sec. On the basis of such findings, it is now generally accepted that information in visual or iconic storage decays within approximately 0.5sec. It has often been assumed in addition that information in iconic storage is held in a relatively raw and uninterpreted form corresponding fairly directly to the physical stimulus. However, subjects do better on Sperling's task when the letters in noncued rows resemble English words than when they do not (Butler, 1974), which suggests that iconic information is not necessarily in an unanalysed form.

How useful is iconic storage? A trenchant attack on its usefulness was mounted by Haber (1983). He claimed that the iconic store is irrelevant to normal perception, except possibly when attempting to read in a lightning storm! He argued that "frozen iconic storage of information" may be valuable in the laboratory when you are confronted with very brief presentations of single stimuli, but similar conditions practically never occur normally. In the real world, the icon formed from one visual fixation would be rapidly masked (or covered over) by the next fixation, and so could not assist perception.

In fact, Haber is quite mistaken. As Coltheart (1983a) pertinently noted, Haber assumed that the icon is created at the *offset* of a visual stimulus, whereas it is actually created at its *onset*. Thus, even with a continuously changing visual world, there is plenty of opportunity for iconic information to be used. Indeed, the mechanisms responsible for visual perception invariably operate upon the icon, rather than directly upon the visual environment itself. Thus, the iconic store is an integral part of visual perception rather than a laboratory curiosity.

There is considerable evidence for a transient store in the auditory modality. It is often known as the "echoic store", and is usually assumed to consist of relatively unprocessed auditory input. For example, suppose that someone who is reading a newspaper or book is asked a question. The person addressed will sometimes ask, "What did you say?", and at the same time realise that he does know what has been said. This "playback" facility depends on the workings of echoic memory.

A related phenomenon was explored by Treisman (1964), who asked people to repeat back aloud (i.e. shadow) the message presented to one ear while ignoring a conconcurrent message presented to the other ear. She presented the same message to both ears, but in such a way that the shadowed message either preceded or followed the nonshadowed message. When the non-shadowed message preceded the shadowed message, the two messages were only recognised as being the same when they were within 2sec of each other. This suggests that the temporal duration of unattended auditory information in echoic storage is approximately 2sec, although other estimates are slightly longer (e.g. Darwin, Turvey, & Crowder, 1972).

Short-term and Long-term Stores

The distinction that multi-store theorists have drawn between a short-term and a long-term store resembles that proposed by William James (1890) between primary memory and secondary memory. Primary memory relates to information that remains in consciousness after it has been perceived, and that forms part of the psychological present, whereas secondary memory contains information about events that have left consciousness, and are therefore part of the psychological past.

Attempting to remember a telephone number for a few seconds is an everyday example of the use of the *short-term store* or *primary memory*. It illustrates two key characteristics that are usually attributed to this store: (1) extremely limited capacity (we cannot remember a sequence of more than about eight digits); and (2) fragility of storage, since the slightest distraction usually causes us to forget the number.

It is difficult to provide an accurate estimate of the capacity of short-term memory. As we will see in Chapter 6, the assumption that there is a *single* capacity is incorrect. Instead of a unitary short-term store there are actually various different components of short-term memory, each of which has its own capacity. Despite this major problem, there have historically been two popular ways of assessing the capacity of short-term memory: span measures and the recency effect in free recall. An example of a span measure is digit span, in which subjects have to repeat back a list of random digits in the correct order as soon as they have been spoken. Miller (1956), in a classic article, pointed out that the span of immediate memory is generally "seven, plus or minus two" whether the units are numbers, letters or words. More specifically, he claimed that approximately seven *chunks* of information could be held in short-term memory at one time (chunk = a familiar unit of information based upon previous learning and experience). However, Simon (1974) discovered that the number of chunks in the span was less with larger chunks (e.g. eight-word phrases) than with smaller chunks (e.g. one-syllable words).

A problem with span measures of short-term storage capacity is that long-term memory may play a part in determining the span. For example, when digit strings are presented for immediate serial recall, and one digit string is surreptitiously repeated several times, performance on the repeated string becomes progressively superior to that on the non-repeated strings (Bower & Winzenz, 1969). This suggests that some information about the repeated digit string is stored in long-term memory.

The recency effect in free recall (free recall = producing the to-be-remembered information in any order) refers to the fact that the last few items in a list are usually much better remembered in immediate recall than are the items from the middle of the list. Counting backwards for only 10sec between the end of presentation and the start of recall virtually eliminates the recency effect, but has essentially no effect on recall of the other list words (Glanzer & Cunitz, 1966). The findings from this study are shown in Fig. 5.2. It has often been assumed that the two or three words in the recency effect are in the short-term store at the end of the list presentation, and it is for this reason that they are so vulnerable to the interpolated task of counting backwards.

Despite the complexities associated with assessing the capacity of the short-term store, there is general agreement that its capacity is strictly limited. This is a major difference between it and the long-term store, for which there are no known limits. How do we know that long-term memory has enormous storage capacity? Those who learn most efficiently are generally those who already have the greatest amount of information stored in long-term memory. This is exactly the opposite of what would be expected if the long-term memory store had a relatively modest capacity.

What appeared at the time to be strong evidence for the multi-store approach came from neuropsychological research into brain-

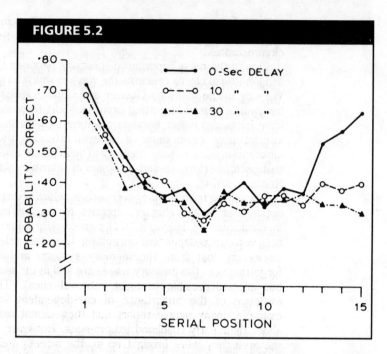

FIGURE 5.2

Free recall as a function of serial position and duration of the interpolated task. Adapted from Glanzer & Cunitz (1966).

damaged patients. As was discussed in Chapter 1, rather convincing evidence that two tasks involve different processing mechanisms can be obtained if there is a double dissociation, i.e. some patients perform normally on task A but very poorly on task B, whereas other patients perform normally on task B but very poorly on task A. A double dissociation involving short-term and long-term memory has been demonstrated using amnesic patients.

Many amnesic patients suffer from Korsakoff syndrome, and have become amnesic as a result of alcoholism. One of the most striking characteristics of these patients is how normal they can appear on superficial acquaintance. For example, they are well able to hold a conversation. This suggests very strongly that their short-term memory is reasonably good, because it is essential to remember what the other person has just said in order to have a sensible conversation. More formal investigations (e.g. Baddeley & Warrington, 1970; Butters & Cermak, 1980) have revealed that Korsakoff amnesic patients have normal digit span and an unimpaired recency effect. In contrast to their good short-term memory, these patients have extremely poor long-term memory for much information, and it is this severe impairment of long-term memory which basically defines the so-called amnesic syndrome (see Chapter 6 for details).

The reverse problem of very poor short-term memory combined with normal long-term memory is relatively rare, but a few such cases have been reported. These cases include KF, a patient who had suffered damage in the left parieto-occipital region following a motor-cycle accident. KF had no difficulty with long-term learning and recall, but his digit span was grossly impaired (a ceiling of two items) and he had a recency effect in free recall of only one item (Shallice & Warrington, 1970) under some circumstances.

One of the most important distinctions between the short-term and long-term stores concerns the ways in which forgetting occurs. We saw in the study by Glanzer and Cunitz (1966) that counting backwards caused forgetting from the short-term store. This may have happened either because counting backwards is a source of interference, or because it diverts attention away from the information in short-term memory. The available evidence suggests that both interference and diversion of attention play a part (e.g. Reitman, 1974).

Forgetting from the long-term store, which is discussed in more detail later in the chapter, appears to involve rather different mechanisms. As Tulving (1974) pointed out, we must distinguish between trace-dependent forgetting (i.e. the relevant memory traces are lost from the memory system) and cue-dependent forgetting (i.e. the memory traces are still in the memory system, but are inaccessible to most retrieval cues). There is much evidence of the importance of cue-dependent forgetting. For example, many people report that they cannot remember much about their early childhood experiences. However, if they revisit the area they were brought up in, the streets and houses often serve as powerful retrieval cues that enable them to reconstruct many childhood events.

Evaluation

The multi-store model served an important function historically. It was perhaps the first theory of memory which provided a systematic account of the structures and processes comprising the memory system. In addition, the conceptual distinction between three different kinds of memory stores (sensory stores, short-term store, and long-term store) still makes sense. In order to justify the notion that there are three qualitatively different types of memory store, it is obviously necessary to demonstrate that there are important differences among them. The available evidence has done precisely that. The memory stores have been shown to differ from each other in at least the following ways: temporal duration, storage capacity, forgetting mechanism, and effects of brain damage.

We will see shortly that there are serious limitations with the multi-store model. However, it is of interest that many contemporary memory theorists have used the multi-store model as the starting point of their theories. For example, much theoretical effort in the last ten years or so has gone into the attempt to provide a more refined account of the long-term store than that offered by Atkinson and Shiffrin (1968). Such attempts constitute a refinement rather than a rejection of the multi-store approach.

The greatest problem with the multi-store model is that it is very over-simplified. The multi-store theorists assumed that both the short-term and long-term stores were unitary, i.e. that each store always operated in a single, uniform fashion. Evidence that the short-term store is not unitary was obtained by Warrington and Shallice (1972). They carried out further investigations on the patient KF, who you may remember was found to have an impaired short-term store but an intact long-term store. Warrington and Shallice discovered that KF's short-term forgetting of auditory letters and digits was considerably greater than his forgetting of visual stimuli. Shallice and Warrington (1974) then found that KF's short-term memory deficit was limited to verbal materials such as letters, words, and digits, and did not extend to meaningful sounds such as cats mewing or telephones ringing. In other words, we cannot simply argue that KF had impaired short-term memory. Instead, according to Shallice and Warrington (1974), his problems centred on the "auditory-verbal short-term store." Thus, their evidence compelled them to abandon the simple-minded view of the short-term memory store put forward by the multi-store theorists.

The multi-store model is similarly over-simplified when it comes to long-term memory. There is an amazing wealth of information stored in our long-term memory, including knowledge that Elizabeth Taylor is a film star, that $2 + 2 = 4$, that we had eggs and bacon for breakfast, and perhaps information about how to ride a bicycle and to play the piano. It seems intuitively unreasonable that all of these various forms of information are all stored in precisely the same form within a single long-term memory store. As we shall see in the following chapter, research on amnesic patients has provided powerful evidence that there are two or more rather separate long-term memory systems. However, these important theoretical distinctions are missing from the multi-store approach.

A final weakness of the multi-store theory approach which will be discussed here concerns the role of rehearsal. The theory assumes that the major way in which information is stored in long-term memory is via rehearsal in the short-term store. In fact, while the amount of rehearsal is often relevant to long-term memory in studies of free recall of words lists (e.g. Rundus & Atkinson, 1970), the role played by rehearsal becomes markedly less important if we consider other learning situations. For example, when people read newspapers or novels, they usually retain some information in long-term memory, but it seems intuitively unreasonable to assume that active rehearsal is usually involved. Even if rehearsal is involved extensively in learning tasks, necessitating the verbatim recall of unrelated words presented rapidly, there is no good reason to extrapolate from such findings to more normal memorial functioning. These deficiencies of the theory are symptomatic of the general lack of attention paid to processes by Atkinson and Shiffrin (1968).

Working Memory

We have seen that the multi-store model fell into disfavour because its accounts of short-term and of long-term memory were clearly over-simplified. Contemporary views on short-term memory will be discussed here, reserving detailed consideration of modern views on long-term memory for Chapter 6.

Baddeley and Hitch (1974) responded to the mounting criticisms of the existing theories of short-term memory by arguing that the concept of the short-term store should be replaced with that of working memory. According to them,
the working memory system consists of three components:

- a modality-free central executive resembling attention;
- an articulatory loop which holds information in a phonological (i.e. speech-based) form;
- a visuo-spatial scratch pad (now known as sketch pad) which is specialised for spatial and/or visual coding.

The most important component of working memory is the central executive. It has limited capacity, and is used when dealing with most cognitively demanding tasks. The articulatory loop and the visual-spatial sketch pad are slave systems that can be used by the central executive for specific purposes. The articulatory loop is organised in a temporal and serial fashion.

Information about the articulatory loop was obtained in a word-span study by Baddeley, Thomson, and Buchanan (1975). They discovered that their subjects could provide immediate serial recall of approximately as many words as they could read out loud in two seconds. This suggested that the capacity of the articulatory loop is determined by temporal duration in the same way as a tape loop.

The characteristics of the visuo-spatial sketch pad are less clear than those of the articulatory loop. However, Baddeley (1986, p. 109) has defined it as: "a system especially well adapted to the storage of spatial information, much as a pad of paper might be used by someone trying for example to work out a geometric puzzle." The emphasis in the definition on spatial information probably stems at least in part from the work of Baddeley and Lieberman (1980). They drew a distinction between spatial and visual coding, and found that spatial coding was more important than visual coding in a variety of tasks. Accordingly, they tentatively concluded that the visuo-spatial sketch pad relies primarily on spatial rather than on visual coding.

There are a number of obvious advantages of the working memory model proposed by Baddeley and Hitch (1974) over the earlier formulation of Atkinson and Shiffrin (1968). First, the working memory system is concerned with both active processing and transient storage of information, and so is of relevance to activities such as mental arithmetic (Hitch, 1978), verbal reasoning (Hitch & Baddeley, 1976), and comprehension (Baddeley & Hitch, 1974), as well as to traditional memory tasks. Second, the working memory model is better placed to provide an explanation of the partial deficits of short-term memory that have been observed. If brain damage affects only one of the three components of working memory, then selective deficits on short-term memory tasks would be expected. Third, the working memory model incorporates verbal rehearsal as an optional process that occurs within only one component of working memory (i.e. the articulatory loop). This seems more realistic than the enormous significance given to verbal rehearsal within the multi-store model of Atkinson and Shiffrin (1968).

Inner Speech
The working memory model has been applied to various practical issues, one of which concerns the role of "inner speech" in reading. According to Huey (1908):

> The carrying range of inner speech is considerably larger than that of vision . . . The initial subvocalisation seems to help hold the word in consciousness until enough others are given to combine with it in touching off the unitary utterance of the sentence which they form . . . It is of the greatest service to the reader or listener that at each moment a considerable amount of what is being read should hang suspended in the primary memory of the inner speech.

On the assumption that inner speech is essentially synonymous with articulation within the articulatory loop, it is possible to test Huey's (1908) hypothesis in a relatively direct fashion. Subjects can be asked to carry out a reading task either on its own or at the same time as performing an articulatory suppression task (e.g. repeatedly saying something simple like "hi-ya" or "the"). The basic assumption is that the articulatory suppression task effectively prevents use of inner speech on the reading task.

Articulatory suppression often has surprisingly little effect on reading performance. Baddeley (1979) discovered that articulatory suppression produced no increase in either processing time or errors on the task of deciding on the truth of simple sentences such as "Canaries have wings" and "Canaries have gills." Levy (1978) asked subjects to decide whether test sentences conveyed the same meaning as sentences which had been presented previously. Thus, the original sentence, "The solemn physician distressed the anxious mother," might be followed by a correct paraphrase (e.g. "The solemn doctor upset the anxious mother") or by an incorrect paraphrase (e.g. "The solemn officer helped the anxious mother"). Performance was not affected by articulatory suppression.

Evidence that inner speech may be used on at least certain reading tasks was obtained by Baddeley and Lewis (1981). They presented sentences that were meaningful or anomalous because two words in a meaningful sentence were switched around (syntactic anomaly) or because a totally inappropriate word replaced one of the words in the sentence (semantic anomaly). Speed to decide whether each sentence was meaningful was unaffected by articulatory suppression, but suppression increased errors on the syntactic anomaly sentences from 15.9% to 35.6%, while also having a modest effect on the semantic anomaly sentences. In other words, it looks as if the articulatory loop is particularly useful in retaining information about the order of words, and so order information (as in the syntactic anomaly sentences) is very vulnerable to suppression.

Neuropsychological Evidence

According to the working memory model put forward by Baddeley and Hitch (1974), the articulatory loop plays a crucial role in most short-term memory tasks involving verbal material. It would be expected, therefore, that brain-damaged patients with poor short-term memory would have impaired functioning of the articulatory loop. However, Shallice and Warrington (1974) and Shallice and Butterworth (1977) obtained neuropsychological evidence that was difficult to reconcile with that expectation.

Shallice and Warrington (1974) found that the brain-damaged patient KF had impaired immediate span (relative to normal controls) for auditorily presented words, but not for meaningful sounds. These findings could be explained by assuming that he had a severely deficient articulatory loop, except for the fact that all of the subjects in this study performed an articulatory suppression task. Since articulatory suppression is supposed to prevent the articulatory loop from being used for any other purpose, a deficient articulatory loop could not be used to explain the results.

Shallice and Butterworth (1977) investigated a patient JB, who had grossly impaired immediate memory performance with auditory but not with visual presentation. These findings suggest that she had damage to the articulatory loop, but a complicating factor is that the pattern of her pausing during continuous speech indicated essentially normal fluency.

Another patient, PV, was studied by Basso, Spinnler, Vallar, and Zanobio (1982). She had relatively intact articulatory processes as indicated by her ability to recite the alphabet and numbers in sequence. However, she did not appear to use this ability when tested on memory span. Her memory span for visually presented letters remained the same whether or not articulation was prevented by an articulatory suppression task, and there was also evidence that she did not use articulation with spoken letters. Despite this, her memory span for spoken letters was worse when the letters were phonologically similar (i.e. they sounded alike) than when they were phonologically dissimilar (i.e. they sounded different). Thus, PV seemed to be processing phonologically (in a speech-based manner), but without making use of articulation.

The Updated Working Memory Model

Baddeley (1986) reacted to the neuropsychological evidence discussed earlier, as well as to other problematical aspects of the original working memory model, by proposing a revised version of the model. He drew a distinction between a phonological (speech-based) store and an articulatory control process (see Vallar and Baddeley, 1984, for details). According to Baddeley the articulatory loop consists of:

- a passive phonological store which is directly concerned with speech perception; and
- an articulatory process that is linked to speech production.

Phonological (speech-based) information about words can be entered into the phonological store in three different ways:

- directly through auditory presentation;
- indirectly through subvocal articulation; or
- indirectly via phonological information stored in long-term memory.

The findings from the patients KF, JB, and PV can be accounted for by assuming that they all have a deficient phonological store. This explains why these patients have particular problems with auditory rather than visual presentation: auditory presentation of verbal stimuli necessarily involves the phonological store, whereas visual presentation does not.

Evidence from cognitive neuropsychology can also be used to shed light on other characteristics of the articulatory loop. For example, does subvocal articulatory activity within the articulatory loop require use of the speech musculature, or does it operate at a more central level? Suggestive evidence was obtained by Baddeley and Wilson (1985). They studied an Oxford University student, GB, who was completely unable to speak apart from a single meaningless sound, together with five further similar cases. These patients suffered from anarthria, i.e. their general language abilities were intact, but damage to the system controlling the speech musculature prevented them from speaking. Despite the fact that they had essentially no use of their speech musculature, they appeared to be able to engage in subvocal rehearsal or articulation.

Baddeley discussed these cases in some detail. His final conclusion was as follows (1986, p. 107): "The loop and its rehearsal processes are operating at a much deeper level than might at first seem likely, apparently relying on central speech control codes which appear to be able to function in the absence of peripheral feedback."

The role of inner speech or the articulatory process in reading was referred to earlier. It will be remembered that the evidence from normal subjects suggests that inner speech is most useful when it is important to take account of the exact order of the words in sentences. Some confirmatory evidence from within cognitive neuropsychology was obtained by Bub, Black, Howell, and Kertesz (1987). They investigated a patient, MV, with very deficient inner speech. However, when written sentences were presented she had problems with syntactically anomalous sentences in which the word order had been altered, but not with semantically anomalous sentences in which an inappropriate word replaced the correct word. This confirms the view that inner speech serves to preserve word order, and that is one of its major contributions to the reading process.

There are some intriguing suggestions that cognitive neuro-psychology may be of value in understanding the nature of the central executive component of the working memory system. Baddeley (1986) has developed the notion of the central executive by suggesting that it may resemble the supervisory attentional system described by Norman and Shallice (1980) and by Shallice (1982) (see discussion of Norman and Shallice's theory in Chapter 4). According to Shallice (1982), the supervisory attentional system has limited capacity, and is used for a variety of purposes. These include trouble-shooting when lower processing systems seem inadequate; tasks requiring planning or decision making; and situations where poorly mastered response sequences are involved.

Shallice (1982) and Baddeley (1986) both suggest that extensive damage to the frontal lobes may cause impairments to the supervisory attentional system or central executive. Patients with frontal lobe damage present a wide variety of symptoms, but Rylander (1939, p. 20) described the classical frontal syndrome as involving: "disturbed attention, increased distractibility, a difficulty in grasping the whole of a complicated state of affairs . . . well able to work along old routines lines . . . cannot learn to master new types of task, in new situations."

In other words, patients with the frontal syndrome behave as if they lacked a control system that allowed them to direct, and to re-direct, their processing resources flexibly and appropriately. Most of their processing resources appear to be intact, but there is no overall direction of the kind that in most people is provided by the central executive or supervisory attentional system.

Evaluation

The revised working memory model proposed by Baddeley (1986) illustrates how valuable research in cognitive neuropsychology can be. Investigations of brain-damaged patients revealed that the initial version of the model (Baddeley & Hitch, 1974) was over-simplified. They also pinpointed the deficiencies in that original version. As a consequence, a more complex (but more realistic) account of the articulatory loop component of the working memory system has now been put forward.

On the negative side, it is unfortunate that there has been so little clarification of the role played by the key component of the working memory system, the central executive. It is claimed that the central executive is of limited capacity, but no one has been able to measure that capacity. It is also claimed that the central processor is "modality-free" and used in numerous processing operations, but the precise constraints on its functioning are unclear.

Summary

According to the multi-store model approach, there are three different kinds of memory store: sensory stores; short-term memory store; and long-term memory store. The evidence fully supports the notion that there are three qualitatively different kinds of memory store, which differ from each other in terms of temporal duration, storage capacity, forgetting mechanism, and effects of brain damage. However, it is indisputable that the multi-store model is very over-simplified. It assumes that the short-term and long-term memory stores are unitary, i.e. that each store functions in a uniform fashion. In fact, it appears that short-term memory consists of various different components, and that different kinds of long-term memory system can be identified (see Chapter 6 for details). In other words, the multi-store theorists provide a reasonable framework within which to consider human memory, but they fail to produce detailed accounts of the functioning of the different memory stores.

The working memory model was proposed in an attempt to eliminate some of the deficiencies of the multi-store model. In essence, the unitary short-term store was replaced by a multi-component working memory system consisting of a central executive, an articulatory loop, and a visuo-spatial sketch pad. The working memory model is supported by evidence from both normal and brain-damaged patients. This is especially the case so far as the articulatory loop is concerned, since that is easily the most investigated component of the working memory system. The precise functioning of the central executive still remains obscure.

MEMORY PROCESSES

Suppose that you were interested in looking at the effects of the *processes* occurring at the time of learning on subsequent long-term memory. How would you set about exploring this issue experimentally? One reasonable method which has been used very frequently is to present several groups of subjects with the same list of nouns, and to ask each group to perform a different activity or orienting task with the list. The tasks used can range from counting the number of letters in each word to thinking of an appropriate adjective for each word.

If subjects were told that their memory was going to be tested, they would presumably realise that a task such as simply counting the number of letters in each word would not enable them to remember very much. There would thus be a natural temptation for them to process the words more thoroughly. Therefore, in order to control the subjects' processing activities as much as possible, the experimenter does not tell them that there is going to be a memory test. Finally, all of the subjects are unexpectedly asked to recall as many of the words as they can. Since the various groups are all presented with exactly the same words, any differences in recall must reflect the influence of the processing tasks rather than the characteristics of the stimulus words (e.g. word frequency or word length).

Hyde and Jenkins (1973) carried out a typical experiment using the approach just described. They used words that were either associatively related or unrelated (in terms of meaning), and different groups of subjects performed each of the following five orienting tasks: (1) rating the words for pleasantness; (2) estimating the frequency with which each word is used in the English language; (3) detecting the occurrence of the letters "e" and "g" in the list words; (4) deciding the part of speech appropriate to each word; and (5) deciding whether the list words fitted sentence frames.

Five groups of subjects performed the orienting tasks with no instructions to learn the material (orienting task plus incidental learning), and an additional five groups carried out the tasks, but were also asked to try to remember the words (orienting task plus intentional learning). Finally, there were control subjects who received intentional learning instructions but no orienting task. All of the groups were given a test of free recall shortly after the completion of the orienting task.

The results are shown in Fig. 5.3. They can be interpreted most simply in the light of the assumptions made by Hyde and Jenkins (1973) that rating pleasantness and rating frequency of usage both involve semantic processing (i.e. processing of meaning), whereas the other three orienting tasks do not. If we are willing to make that somewhat dubious assumption, then retention was 51% higher

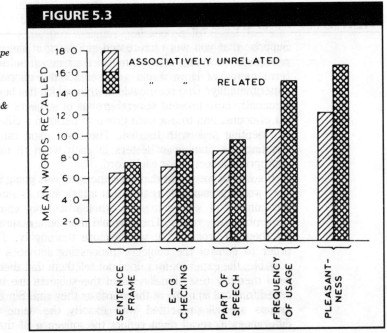

Mean words recalled as a function of list type (associatively related or unrelated) and orienting task. Data from Hyde & Jenkins (1973).

FIGURE 5.3

ASSOCIATIVELY UNRELATED

"   "   RELATED

MEAN WORDS RECALLED

18·0
16·0
14·0
12·0
10·0
8·0
6·0
4·0
2·0

SENTENCE FRAME

E–G CHECKING

PART OF SPEECH

FREQUENCY OF USAGE

PLEASANT-NESS

after the semantic tasks than the nonsemantic tasks on the list of associatively unrelated words; with the list of associatively related words, there was an 83% superiority for the semantic tasks.

Incidental learners performing a semantic orienting task recalled as many words as intentional learners in the control groups. The implication is that intent to learn is not of crucial importance; rather, it is the nature of the processing activity that determines how much is remembered subsequently. Finally, and rather surprisingly, there were practically no recall differences between intentional and incidental learners who performed the same orienting task. It might have been expected that intentional learners performing a nonsemantic task would engage in additional processing of the meaning of the list words and so increase their recall, but this was apparently not the case.

This study by Hyde and Jenkins (1973) has been discussed in detail because it is representative of work in this area. Indeed, all of their major findings have been repeated many times. As we will see in the next section, Craik and Lockhart (1972) made use of earlier findings, resembling those of Hyde and Jenkins, in proposing an influential theory.

Levels-of-processing Theory

Craik and Lockhart (1972) put forward a levels-of-processing theory that attempted to provide a broad framework within which memory phenomena could be understood. They assumed that the attentional and perceptual processes operating at the time of learning determine what information is stored in long-term memory. More specifically, they argued that there are a number of different levels of processing, ranging from shallow or physical analysis of a stimulus (e.g. processing of the lines, angles, and brightness of visual stimuli) to deep or semantic analysis. The crucial notion of depth of processing was further explained by Craik (1973, p. 48): " 'Depth' is defined in terms of the meaningfulness extracted from the stimulus rather than in terms of the number of analyses performed upon it."

The most important theoretical assumptions made by Craik and Lockhart (1972) were as follows:

- the level or depth of processing received by a stimulus has a substantial effect on its memorability;
- deeper levels of analysis produce more elaborate, longer lasting, and stronger memory traces than do shallow levels of analysis.

The findings of Hyde and Jenkins (1973), as well as those of numerous other researchers, are very much in line with the predictions of the levels-of-processing approach. However, it became apparent that the approach was over-simplified, and so various modifications and additions were proposed.

Elaboration

Craik and Tulving (1975) obtained evidence that the depth of processing is not the only factor determining long-term memory. They discovered that elaboration of processing (i.e. the amount of processing of a particular kind) is also important. In one of their experiments, subjects were presented on each trial with a sentence containing a blank as well as a word, and were asked to decide whether the word fitted appropriately into the blank space. Elaboration was manipulated by varying the complexity of the sentence frame between the simple (e.g. "She cooked the _") and the complex (e.g. "The great bird swooped down and carried off the struggling _"). Finally, there was an unexpected cued recall test, in which the subject was given the sentence frame and asked to recall the word that had been presented with it.

For those words that were compatible with the sentence frame, cued recall was twice as high for words accompanying complex sentences as for words paired with simple sentences. Since the same deep or semantic level of analysis was involved in both conditions, the obvious conclusion is that some factor in addition to processing depth must be important. Craik and Tulving identified this additional factor as elaboration.

Those theorists who have favoured an elaboration theory of memory have often assumed that there is a direct relationship between the sheer number of elaborations and the probability of recall. However, it is probable that the kind of elaboration is also important. Bransford, Franks, Morris, and Stein (1979) presented either minimally elaborated similes (e.g. "A mosquito is like a doctor because they both draw blood") or multiply elaborated similes (e.g. "A mosquito is like a raccoon because they both have heads, legs, jaws"). Recall of the simile with the first noun used as a cue (e.g. "mosquito,") was much better for the minimally elaborated similes than for the multiply elaborated ones, indicating that the nature and degree of precision of semantic elaborations are relevant when predicting the effects of elaboration on retention.

Distinctiveness

Eysenck (1979a) argued that long-term memory is affected by distinctiveness of processing as well as by the depth and elaboration of processing. In other words, memory traces which are distinctive or unique in some way will be more readily retrieved than memory traces which closely resemble a number of other memory traces. This distinctiveness theory was investigated by Eysenck and Eysenck (1980), who made use of nouns having irregular grapheme-phoneme correspondence. What that means is that the nouns are not pronounced in conformity with normal pronunciation rules (e.g. "glove" would rhyme with "cove" if it had regular grapheme-phoneme correspondence, and the "b" in "comb" would be sounded). Subjects were asked to perform the shallow or nonsemantic orienting task of pronouncing such nouns as if they had regular grapheme-phoneme correspondence, which presumably produced distinctive and unique memory traces (nonsemantic, distinctive condition). Other nouns were simply pronounced in their normal fashion (nonsemantic, nondistinctive condition), and still others were processed in terms of their meaning (semantic condition).

On a subsequent unexpected recognition-memory test, words in the nonsemantic, distinctive condition were much better remembered than those in the nonsemantic, nondistinctive condition (see Fig. 5.4). Indeed, they were remembered almost as well as the words in the semantic conditions. Similar, although less striking, findings were obtained on a test of free recall. These results demonstrate the importance of distinctiveness to long-term memory.

Recognition-memory performance as a function of the depth and distinctiveness of processing. Data from Eysenck & Eysenck (1980).

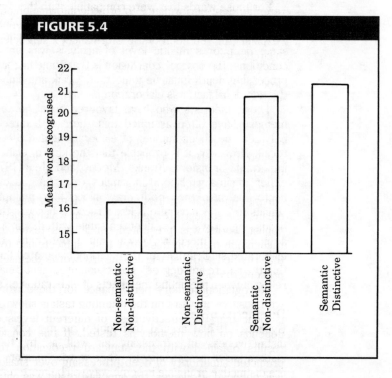

FIGURE 5.4

Evaluation of Levels-of-processing Theory

Craik and Lockhart (1972) and Craik and Tulving (1975) were obviously correct in assuming that the processes which take place at the time of learning have a major impact on subsequent long-term memory. That may sound obvious, but surprisingly little research prior to 1972 involved an investigation of learning processes and their effects on memory. It is also a contribution of this theoretical approach to have identified the depth and elaboration of processing as factors which need to be considered when comparing the effectiveness of different learning processes.

On the negative side, there are several major criticisms of levels-of-processing theory which need to be made. It is often difficult with many of the orienting tasks used to be sure what the level of processing actually is. For example, in the study by Hyde and Jenkins (1973) discussed earlier, they assumed that judging a word's frequency involved thinking of its meaning, but it is not altogether clear why this should be so. They also argued that the task of deciding the part of speech to which a word belongs is a shallow processing task, but other researchers claim that the task involves deep or semantic processing.

In essence, the problem is caused by the lack of any independent measure of processing depth. This can lead to the unfortunate state of affairs described by Eysenck (1978, p. 159): "In view of the vagueness with which depth is defined, there is danger of using retention-test performance to provide information about the depth of processing, and then using the putative depth of processing to "explain" the retention-test performance, a self-defeating exercise in circularity."

Craik and Lockhart (1972) argued that deep or semantic processing will always lead to superior long-term memory over shallow or nonsemantic processing. However, it has become increasingly apparent that the effects of different processing tasks on memory depend heavily on the nature of the memory test which is used. For example, Morris, Bransford, and Franks (1977) argued that stored information (whether deep or shallow) is remembered only to the extent that it is of relevance to the memory test. Their subjects had to answer semantic or shallow (rhyme) questions for lists of words. Memory was tested either by means of a standard recognition test, in which a mixture of list and nonlist words was presented, or it was tested by a rhyming recognition test. On this latter test, subjects had to select words that rhymed with list words; the list words themselves were not presented.

Recognition-memory performance for those words associated with positive answers on the orienting task is shown in Fig. 5.5. It is clear that the effectiveness of different levels of processing depends on how memory is tested. If one considers only the results obtained with the standard recognition test, then the predicted superiority of deep processing over shallow processing was obtained. However, the opposite result was obtained with the rhyme test, and this represents an experimental disproof of the notion that deep processing always enhances long-term memory.

How can one interpret the findings of Morris et al. (1977)? They argued that their findings supported a *transfer-appropriate processing* view of memory. This view assumes that different kinds of processing lead learners to acquire different kinds of information about a stimulus. Whether the information stored as a result of performing a given processing task leads to subsequent retention depends upon the relevance of that information to the kind of memory test that is used. For example, storing semantic

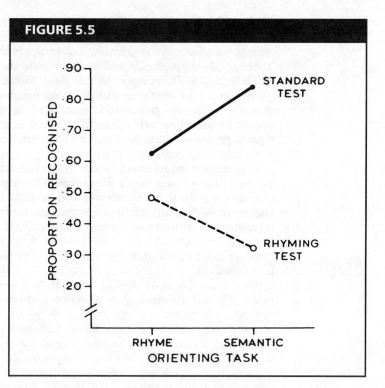

Mean proportion of words recognised as a function of orienting task (semantic or rhyme) and of the type of recognition test (standard or rhyming). Data are from Morris et al. (1977), and are from positive trials only.

information is essentially irrelevant when the memory test requires the identification of words rhyming with list words. What is required for this kind of test is shallow rhyme information.

A fundamental assumption of the levels-of-processing theory is that deep processing produces memory traces which are more durable and longer lasting than the memory traces produced by shallow processing. In other words, the rate of forgetting over time is assumed to be inversely related to the depth of processing. This prediction can be tested only when the amount of learning at different levels of processing is equated, a requirement that has not usually been fulfilled. When the number of learning trials was manipulated in order to produce comparable acquisition at deep and shallow levels of processing, the rate of forgetting was not affected by processing depth (Nelson & Vining, 1978). It may well be that variations in depth of processing affect the speed of learning rather than the rate of forgetting.

A final problem with the levels-of-processing approach is that it seems in many ways to describe rather than to explain what is happening. Craik and Lockhart (1972) argued that deep processing leads to better long-term memory than does shallow processing, but they failed to provide any detailed account of exactly *why* it is that deep processing is so effective.

Summary

According to levels-of-processing theory, long-term memory is mainly determined by the processing which occurs at the time of learning. More specifically, deep or semantic processing leads to much better long-term retention than does shallow or nonsemantic processing. This prediction has been confirmed numerous times. However, levels-of-processing theory is inadequate because it tends to ignore the role of the retrieval environment in determining long-term retention. In essence, it is the *relevance* of what has been learned to the demands of the memory test which determines whether or not retention will occur. The processing which occurs at the time of learning is important, as levels-of-processing theorists have indicated. However, elaboration or extensiveness of processing and distinctiveness of processing need to be considered as well as the depth of processing.

REMEMBERING AND FORGETTING

Everyone is fairly knowledgeable about their own memory abilities. We know that it tends to become progressively more difficult to remember an event with the passage of time, and that there are many things that we can recognise but cannot recall (e.g. an acquaintance's name). Of particular interest is the tip-of-the-tongue phenomenon, in which we often seem to be sure that we know something even when we cannot call the desired information to mind. For example, Brown and McNeill (1966) discovered that students who read out dictionary definitions of rare words, and were asked to identify the words defined, were often unable to do so in spite of feeling that the answer was on their tip of their tongue. Related to this phenomenon are those cases in which we cannot immediately recall the answer to a question, and are almost certain that the answer would not occur to us even with a great deal of thought (e.g. "What is the name of the sixth President of the United States of America?" for English people).

Memory theorists have put forward numerous theories of retrieval and forgetting designed to elucidate these, and other, phenomena. They have been especially concerned with the ways in which the probability of retrieval is affected by the precise form of retention test that is used. While it is true that there is usually less evidence of forgetting on tests of recognition memory than of recall, there are a number of exceptions. It has been common to assume that any particular kind of retention test always leads subjects to use an invariant set of processing operations, but it is probable that the true state of affairs is actually much more complex. The point was well expressed by Reitman (1970, p. 485):

> To what extent can we lump together what goes on when you try to recall: (1) your name; (2) how to kick a football; and (3) the present location of your car keys? If we use introspective evidence as a guide, the first seems an immediate automatic response. The

second may require constructive internal replay prior to our being able to produce a verbal description. The third . . . quite likely involves complex operational responses under the control of some general strategy system. Is any unitary search process, with a single set of characteristics and input-output relations, likely to cover all these cases?

As will become clear, no entirely satisfactory theory of forgetting has been put forward. However, it has been established that several different factors play a part in determining forgetting. We now have a reasonable understanding of phenomena such as the typical superiority of recognition memory over recall, and of the requisite conditions for producing the reverse effect. Such progress is encouraging given that systematic research into retrieval processes started only 25 years ago.

Permanent Memory

A fundamental issue is whether forgotten information is permanently stored but inaccessible, or whether it has simply been lost from the memory system. Sometimes, it is relatively easy to demonstrate that forgotten information is still stored, as when a failure to recall some item of information is followed by successful recognition memory. However, if information is neither recalled nor re- cognised, and other retention tests also fail to produce memory for the information, then matters are much more difficult to interpret. Complete forgetting is logically consistent with both loss of information and inaccessibility of permanently stored information. In spite of these uncertainties, many prominent psychologists from Freud to Tulving have favoured the hypothesis of permanent storage. This hypothesis can be expressed in the following fashion (Loftus & Loftus, 1980):

"Everything we learn is permanently stored in the mind, although sometimes particular details are not accessible (p.410)."

Loftus and Loftus (1980) conducted an opinion poll among psychologists, and discovered that 84% of them endorsed this statement. If it were possible to settle scientific issues in the same way as political elections are decided, then the permanent memory hypothesis would be the clear winner. In fact, of course, we really should pay some attention to the relevant evidence, and it is to this that we now turn.

Electrical Stimulation

Psychologists who believe in permanent memory frequently cite the work of Wilder Penfield. He operated on numerous epileptic patients, and he often stimulated the surface of the brain with a weak electric current in an attempt to identify the area of the brain involved in producing epileptic attacks. He discovered that the stimulating electrode sometimes appeared to cause the patient to re-experience events from his or her past with great vividness. Penfield (1969, p. 165) argued that his findings indicated permanent storage of information:

> It is clear that the neuronal action that accompanies each succeeding state of consciousness leaves its permanent imprint on the brain. The imprint, or record, is a trail of facilitation of neuronal connections that can be followed again by an electric current many years later with no loss of detail, as though a tape recorder had been receiving it all.

Close examination of Penfield's data indicates that his conclusions cannot be accepted. Only 7.7% of his patients showed any evidence of recovery of long-lost memories, and many of these apparent memories were probably reconstructions rather than genuine recollections. For example, one patient claimed that she saw herself as she had appeared in childhood, and that she felt as if she were actually reliving the experience. Penfield emphasised the vividness and the detail of the patients' remembered experiences, but in most cases the recollections were rather vague and limited to a single sense modality (visual or auditory). From a scientific point of view, it is especially unfortunate that Penfield did not have any independent verification of the events which his patients claimed to remember during electrical stimulation.

Hypnosis
The media have reported numerous cases where it appeared that hypnosis was remarkably effective in bringing forgotten memories to light. For example, the Israeli National Police Force and many other police forces have used hypnosis in their attempts to collect relevant evidence from eyewitnesses about matters such as car number plates and the physical characteristics of wanted criminals. However, it is by no means clear that the hypnotic method is actually anything like as effective as has been claimed. What seems to happen is that the hypnotised individual is less cautious than normal in his or her reported memories. As a consequence, he or she produces numerous recollections, many of which are entirely inaccurate. For example, it has been found that people under hypnosis confidently "recall" events from the future!

In an interesting attempt to discover the ability of hypnosis to improve memory, Putnam (1979) showed people a videotape of an accident involving a car and a bicycle. They were then asked a series of questions, some of which contained misleading information. Some of the subjects were asked these questions while in a hypnotised state, having been told that they would be able to see the entire accident very clearly under hypnosis. In fact, the hypnotised subjects made *more* errors in their answers than did the nonhypnotised subjects, and this was particularly true with the misleading questions. These findings led Putnam (1979, p.444) to conclude that subjects are "more suggestible in the hypnotic state and are, therefore, more easily influenced by the leading questions."

Evaluation

In sum, an examination of the evidence indicates that the widespread acceptance of the permanent memory hypothesis is unwarranted. Part of the reason for its popularity is probably that it is unfalsifiable: Information may be stored somewhere in long-term memory even if there is no evidence at all that it can be retrieved. This point must be conceded, but it is important to note that no compelling evidence in support of permanent memory has ever been obtained. This fact, together with its unfalsifiability, indicates that the permanent memory hypothesis should be rejected. However, common sense would suggest that the better the original learning (e.g. in terms of depth of elaborativeness), the more likely it is that the resultant memory will be permanent.

Two-process Theory

One of the most obvious facts about memory is that it is usually much easier to remember previous events or experiences when memory is tested by recognition rather than by recall. In tests of recall, the subject has to produce the to-be-remembered information. In tests of recognition memory, in contrast, the to-be-remembered information is presented along with irrelevant information, and the subject has to decide whether each piece of information has been presented before. Over the years there have been numerous attempts to account for the phenomenon of recognition being generally superior to recall, with one of the most influential being the two-stage or two-process theory (see Watkins and Gardiner, 1979, for a review). Several slightly different versions of this theory have been proposed, but what they have in common is the following:

- recall involves a search or retrieval process, which is followed by a decision or recognition process based on the apparent appropriateness of the retrieved information;
- recognition involves only the second of these two processes.

Two-process theory therefore claims that recall involves two fallible stages, whereas recognition involves only a single fallible stage. It is for this reason that recognition is superior to recall. According to this theory, recall occurs only when an item is both retrieved and then recognised. The notion that the probability of recall is determined by the probability of retrieval multiplied by the probability of recognition was tested by Bahrick (1970) in a test of cued recall (words were presented as cues to to-be-remembered list words). He used the probability of the cue producing the to-be-remembered word in free association as an estimate of the retrievability of the to-be-remembered word, and he ascertained the probability of recognition by means of a standard recognition test. The level of cued recall was predicted reasonably well by multiplying together those two probabilities.

Further evidence that people can recall information by making extensive use of the retrieval process and then deciding which of the items produced by the retrieval process are appropriate was obtained by Rabinowitz, Mandler, and Patterson (1977). They compared recall of a categorised word list (a list containing words belonging to several different semantic categories) under standard instructions, and under instructions to generate as many words as possible from the categories represented in the list, saying aloud only those they thought had actually been presented in the list.

When there was a short retention interval, subjects given the latter generation-recognition instructions recalled 23% more words than those given standard recall instructions. However, the generation-recognition instructions had very little effect on recall when recall was tested one week after learning. It appears that the generate-recognise strategy described by the two-process theory can be useful in increasing recall, at least at relatively short retention intervals.

Evaluation

Despite the success of two-process theory, it has attracted a lot of criticism. For example, there are circumstances in which recall is considerably superior to recognition memory. Watkins (1973) presented subjects with pairs of items such as "EXPLO–RE" and "SPANI–EL." They were then given tests either of cued recall (e.g. "EXPLO–?" and "SPANI–?" or of recognition (e.g. "RE" and "EL"). Recall was dramatically higher than recognition for the second member of each pair (67% recall to 9% recognition).

A related phenomenon which also poses considerable problems for two-process theory is known as *recognition failure of recallable words*, or *recognition failure*. This occurs when learning is followed by a recognition-memory test and then a test of recall, and some of the items which are not recognised are nevertheless subsequently recalled (e.g. Tulving & Thomson, 1973). According to two-process theory, recognition failure should practically never happen. This is because recall requires retrieval and recognition of the to-be-remembered item.

How can we account for the findings of Watkins (1973) and those of other researchers who have shown that recall can be better than recognition? In essence, the argument is that people normally store in long-term memory not only to-be-remembered information (e.g. "RE" and "EL"), but also contextual information which was presented at the same time (e.g. "EXPLO" and "SPANI". Both recall and recognition tend to be best when the contextual information present at the time of learning is also present at the time of the memory test. Therefore, the rule of thumb is that the way to make recall better than recognition is to ensure that the contextual information available on the recall test is the same as that available at learning, whereas the contextual information available on the recognition test is quite different to that available at learning. This is exactly what Watkins (1973) did. The cues used in cued recall (e.g. "EXPLO" and "SPANI") re-presented the contextual information available at the time of learning, whereas this contextual information was absent during the recognition test.

A related problem with the two-process theory concerns the assumption that there is no retrieval problem in recognition memory, because the retrieval process is not involved at all. This assumption has been tested by using two groups of subjects who study the to-be-remembered words under the same conditions. Both groups are then tested for recognition memory, one group with the test context matching the study context, and the other group with different study and test contexts. Context is usually in the form of additional words presented along with the to-be-remembered words. Recognition memory is typically higher when the study and test contexts are the same than when they are different (e.g. Tulving & Thomson, 1971). The fact that recognition memory is susceptible to context effects suggests that there can be a retrieval problem in recognition memory, which is manifestly contrary to the spirit of two-process theory.

Encoding Specificity

A theoretical approach differing considerably from that of two-process theory has been put forward by Endel Tulving (1982; 1983). He assumes that there are basic similarities between recall and recognition, although he has increasingly admitted that there are some major differences. He also assumes that contextual factors are important, and that what is stored in memory represents a combination of information from the to-be-remembered material and from the context.

Tulving has incorporated these ideas into his encoding specificity principle, which was expressed in the following terms by Wiseman and Tulving (1976, p. 349): "A to-be-remembered (TBR) item is encoded with respect to the context in which it is studied, producing a unique trace which incorporates information from both target and context. For the TBR item to be retrieved, the cue information must appropriately match the trace of the item-in-context." A few years later, Tulving (1979, p. 408) put forward a somewhat simpler and more precise formulation of the encoding specificity principle:

> The probability of successful retrieval of the target item is a monotonically increasing function of informational overlap between the information present at retrieval and the information stored in memory.

For the benefit of any reader wondering what "monotonically increasing function" means, it refers to a generally rising function which does not decrease at any point. In other words, the greater the similarity is between the information in memory and the information available at retrieval, the better memory will be.

It will be noticed that the encoding specificity principle does not refer explicitly to either recall or recognition. The reason is that it is intended to apply equally to both forms of retention test. There have been numerous attempts to test the notion of encoding specificity, but what is common to virtually all of them is that there are at least two learning conditions and at least two retrieval conditions. The basic idea is that this allows the experimenter to demonstrate (as the encoding specificity principle claims) that memory depends on both the information in the memory trace stemming from the learning experience and the information available in the retrieval environment.

A concrete example of this research strategy in action comes in a study by Thomson and Tulving (1970). They presented pairs of words in which the first word was the cue and the second word was the to-be-remembered word. The cues were either weakly associated to the list words (e.g. "Train–BLACK") or were strongly associated (e.g. "White–BLACK"). On the subsequent recall test, some of the to-be-remembered items were tested by weak cues (e.g. "Train–?"), whereas others were tested by strong cues (e.g. "White–?"). The results are shown in Fig. 5.6. As would be expected on the encoding specificity principle, recall performance was best when the cues provided at recall were the same as those provided at input. Any change in the cues lowered recall,

FIGURE 5.6

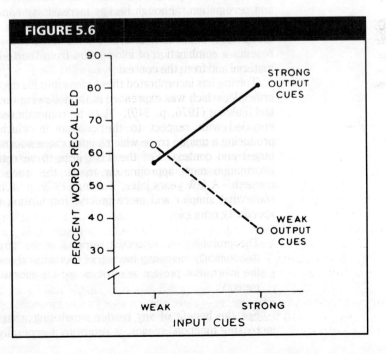

Mean word recall as a function of input cues (strong or weak) and output cues (strong or weak). Data from Thomson & Tulving (1970).

even when the shift was from weak cues at input to strong cues at recall.

Tulving (1982; 1983) argued that there are some differences in the processes involved in recall and recognition. In essence, while the amount of informational overlap between information in the memory trace and in the retrieval environment is crucial to both recall and recognition, a greater amount of informational overlap is required for successful recall than for successful recognition. The reason is that recall involves naming a previous event whereas recognition involves only a judgement of familiarity. Tulving's argument is a reasonable one, but there is relatively little evidence for or against it at present.

Evaluation

What is the importance of Tulving's contribution? One of the valuable features of his theoretical approach is the emphasis placed on the notion that memory depends jointly on the nature of the memory trace and on the information available in the retrieval environment. Another valuable aspect is the notion that contextual information plays an important role in retrieval. Contextual influences had usually been ignored or de-emphasised prior to Tulving's encoding specificity principle, and yet there is now strong evidence that both recall and recognition memory are affected greatly by the similarity of context at learning and at test.

On the more critical side, Solso (1974, p. 28) identified a genuine difficulty with Tulving's encoding specificity principle:

> If a cue was effective in memory retrieval, then one could infer it was encoded; if a cue was not effective, then it was not encoded. The logic of this theorisation is "heads I win, tails you lose" and is of dubious worth in the history of psychology. We might ask how long scientists will puzzle over questions with no answers.

It is certainly true that there is a danger of circularity in applying the encoding specificity principle. Memory is said to depend on "informational overlap" and, in the absence of any direct measure of that overlap, it is tempting to infer the amount of informational overlap on the basis of retention-test performance. However, we can manipulate the encoding conditions at the time of learning so as to produce systematic and predictable effects on the memory trace. In this way we are not totally reliant on information about the success or otherwise of differential retrieval cues to infer the nature of the memory trace. As a result, it is possible to escape some of the dangers of circularity of reasoning.

Another serious problem associated with Tulving's theoretical position is his view that the information available at the time of retrieval is compared in a very simple and direct fashion with the information stored in memory to ascertain the amount of informational overlap. This seems very unlikely if one considers what happens if memory is tested by asking the question, "What did you do six days ago?" Most people answer a question like that by engaging in a rather complex problem-solving strategy which takes some time to reconstruct the relevant events. Tulving's approach has very little to say about how retrieval operates under such circumstances.

Interesting evidence that recall is more complex than is allowed for in Tulving's approach has been obtained by Jones (1982a). Subjects were shown a list of apparently unrelated cue-target word pairs (e.g. "regal–BEER"), followed by a test of cued recall (e.g. "regal–?"). Some of the subjects were told before recall that reversing the letters of each cue word would produce a new word that was related to the target word (e.g. "regal" produces "lager", which suggests "BEER"). Informed subjects recalled more than twice as many words as uninformed subjects.

According to Jones (1982a), there are two different ways in which recall can occur:

- the direct route, in which the cue permits direct accessing of the to-be-remembered information;
- the indirect route, in which the cue leads to recall via the making of inferences and the generation of possible responses.

The encoding specificity principle appears to envisage that recall will occur via the direct fashion. In contrast, the indirect route closely resembles the recall process as described by the two-process theorists. This route, which was not properly considered by Tulving, was available to the informed subjects in the study by Jones, and explains their recall superiority.

A final limitation of Tulving's approach that will be discussed here concerns context effects in memory. Tulving (1982; 1983) assumed that context affects recall and recognition in the same ways, but that is not entirely true. Baddeley (1982) has proposed a distinction between intrinsic context and extrinsic context. Intrinsic context has a direct impact on the meaning or significance of a to-be-remembered item (e.g. strawberry versus traffic as intrinsic context for the word "jam"), whereas extrinsic context (e.g. the room in which learning takes place) does not.

According to Baddeley, recall is affected by both intrinsic and extrinsic context, whereas recognition memory is affected only by intrinsic context. Convincing evidence that extrinsic context has quite different effects on recall and recognition was obtained by Godden and Baddeley (1975; 1980). In the study by Godden and Baddeley (1975), subjects learned a list of words either on land or 20ft underwater, and were then given a test of free recall either on land or underwater. Those who learned on land recalled more on land than underwater, and those who learned underwater did better when tested underwater. Retention was approximately 50% higher when learning and recall took place in the same extrinsic context (see Fig. 5.7). Godden and Baddeley (1980) carried out a very similar study, but testing memory by means of a recognition test instead of by recall. They discovered that recognition memory was not affected by whether or not the extrinsic context at the time of the recognition test was the same as at the time of learning (see Fig. 5.7).

Recent Views on Recall and Recognition

One of the features of most approaches to recall and recognition, including the two-process and encoding specificity theories, is the notion that there is only one way in which recall occurs and only one way in which recognition occurs. However, there is a growing awareness that there are probably several different strategies which can be used in order to produce recall and recognition. We

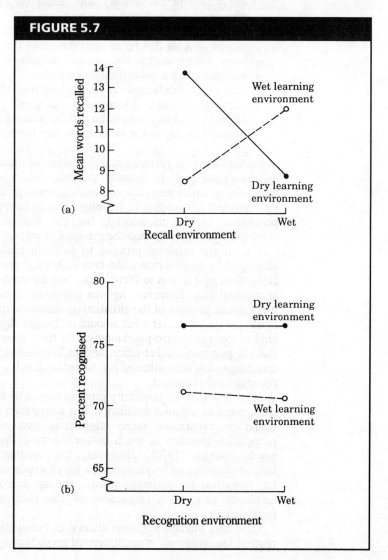

FIGURE 5.7

(a) Recall in the same vs. different contexts, data from Godden & Baddeley (1975). (b) Recognition in the same vs. different contexts, data from Godden & Baddeley (1980).

have already seen an example of this more modern approach in the work of Jones (1982a; see also Jones, 1987). Similar attempts have been made to identify the various strategies used in tests of recognition memory, one of which is now discussed in some detail.

Mandler's Theory of Recognition Memory

Mandler (1980) argued that recognition memory can involve two distinct mechanisms:

- One mechanism is based on the *familiarity* of the stimulus; familiarity is determined by the amount of intra-item organisation, which in turn depends on the degree of integration of the sensory and perceptual elements of the stimulus.
- If the level of stimulus familiarity is high, then the subject rapidly decides that he or she recognises the stimulus; if the level of familiarity is low, a rapid decision is made that the stimulus is not a to-be-remembered item.
- The other mechanism is *identification*, which involves a retrieval process. Identification is used if the level of familiarity is intermediate, so that an accurate decision cannot be made simply on the basis of stimulus familiarity.

Identification via retrieval makes use of the organised nature of long-term memory to recover relevant contextual information about the stimulus (e.g. the contexts in which it has usually been encountered). According to Mandler, the familiarity and retrieval processes operate in parallel, but the familiarity process is completed more rapidly than the retrieval process.

Use of the retrieval process to facilitate recognition can be illustrated by an experience the first author had several years ago. He walked past a man in Wimbledon, and felt immediately that he recognised him. However, he was somewhat puzzled because it was difficult to think of the situation or situations that he had seen him in previously. After a fair amount of thought about it (this is the kind of thing academic psychologists do think about!), he realised that the man was a ticket-office clerk at Wimbledon railway station, and this greatly strengthened his conviction that the initial feeling of recognition was correct.

It is clear that the familiarity process cannot be based simply on the amount of stimulus familiarity. If it were, then common words would be recognised more often than rare words. In fact, recognition memory is much better for rare than for common words (Gregg, 1976). However, the relative increment in familiarity produced by presenting a list of words would be greater for rare than for common words, and so it may be that the familiarity process is responsive to this relative increment in familiarity.

How can Mandler's (1980) theory of recognition memory be tested? One relatively straightforward prediction is possible on the basis of Mandler's further assumption that familiarity decays more rapidly over time than do the organisational or structural effects involved in the retrieval process. As a consequence, recognition-memory decisions at long retention intervals should be more likely to involve the retrieval process than those at short retention intervals. This prediction can be tested by using a task devised by Mandler (1967). He asked people to sort a fairly long list of unrelated words into categories (two was the minimum permitted and seven the maximum). On a subsequent unexpected test of free recall, there was a remarkably strong relationship between the number of categories used in sorting and the number of words recalled, with each additional category adding approximately four words to the total words recalled. Presumably the information was organised more efficiently in long-term memory with the larger number of categories, and this facilitated retrieval.

Mandler, Pearlstone, and Koopmans (1969) used the same sorting task used by Mandler (1967), and tested recall and recognition immediately, after two weeks, and after five weeks. Organisation in terms of the number of categories used in sorting became an increasingly important determinant of recognition-test performance.

Recognition performance following a sorting task was explored further by Mandler and Boeck (1974). They argued that relatively fast recognition decisions reflect mainly the familiarity process, whereas relatively slow decisions are based to a greater extent on the retrieval process. As a consequence, the organisational factor of the number of categories used in sorting should affect slower responses to a greater extent than faster responses. This prediction was supported by the evidence.

What are the problems with Mandler's (1980) two-process theory of recognition memory? Firstly, the familiarity and retrieval processes are specified in a very imprecise and incomplete fashion. Secondly, there is considerable uncertainty about the relative roles played by the two processes in most situations. There is, for example, very little evidence to indicate that the familiarity and retrieval processes actually operate at the same time rather than the familiarity process preceding the retrieval process.

Current Views on Recall

So far as recall is concerned, the views of Jones (1978; 1982a; 1987) represent contemporary thinking. In approximate terms, he proposed that recall is sometimes a rather laborious process, requiring the generation of possible items followed by decisions about their appropriateness. As was pointed out earlier, this is very much in the spirit of the two-process theory. In addition, however, he argued that recall sometimes works by making a direct match between the information available at the time of recall and the information stored in long-term memory. This is very similar to Tulving's encoding specificity principle. In other words, rather than attempting to decide whether the two-process theory or the encoding specificity principle provides the superior account of recall, it may well be preferable to conclude that both theories are applicable in certain circumstances.

These views on recall and recognition make it clear that there is no simple answer to the question of the similarity between the processes involved in recall and in recognition. If there are at least two recall processes and two recognition processes, then the degree of similarity manifestly depends on which recall process is compared with which recognition process. One of the issues which needs further consideration is to identify more precisely the circumstances in which each particular process is used.

Limitations of Recall and Recognition

If you want to decide whether information which someone learned previously has been forgotten, then the obvious thing to do is see whether they can recall or recognise that information. However, there is increasing evidence (discussed in detail in Chapter 6) that these tests of memory can be very inadequate. For example, brain-damaged patients suffering from amnesia can be taught reasonably complex skills if they are given sufficient practice. However, they often do not recognise the apparatus used in the skill training, even though they have seen it numerous times before!

What is going on here? It appears to be of crucial importance that recall and recognition both depend to some extent on conscious awareness of information stored in long-term memory. In contrast, performing a skill at a high level clearly involves memory for previous learning, but there does not need to be any conscious awareness of that previous learning. In other words, conscious awareness of what has been learned is not always necessary for good levels of long-term memory. The obvious implication is that memory measures (such as recall and recognition) which depend in part on conscious awareness can provide no more than partial information about the accessibility of knowledge stored in long-term memory (see the discussion on implicit and explicit memory in Chapter 6).

Tulving (1989) has provided an interesting analysis of some of the theoretical issues involved. He argued that most cognitive psychologists have adopted a rather limited view on ways of measuring human memory because they subscribe to the *doctrine of concordance of cognition, behaviour, and experience* (hereafter shortened to the *doctrine of concordance*). According to this doctrine (Tulving, 1989, p. 8):

> . . . there exists a close and general, even if not perfect, agreement between what people know, how they behave, and what they experience. Thus, conscious awareness is required for, and therefore accompanies, the acquisition of knowledge, or its retrieval from the memory store; retrieved knowledge guides behaviour, and when this happens, people are aware of the relation between the knowledge and the behaviour.

According to the doctrine of concordance, there are close links between behaviour, knowledge, and experience. As a consequence, assessing a subject's behaviour on a recall or recognition test tells us something about his or her knowledge and experience as well. It follows that we do not need to bother with separate assessments of knowledge and experience. However, the problem is that the doctrine of concordance is probably wrong. For example, the fact that amnesic patients sometimes demonstrate memory for past learning in their behaviour but not at all in their conscious experience or recollection indicates that concordance is not always found.

Gardiner (1988) demonstrated a failure of concordance in recognition memory. In essence, he used a levels-of-processing situation in which subjects were required to pay attention to either the sound or the meaning of each word in a list. This was followed by a recognition test. For each word that was recognised, the subject was asked to indicate whether he or she *remembered* (i.e. had conscious awareness of) the word's appearance in the list, or whether he or she merely knew in some other way that it was a list word. As expected, processing of meaning led to better recognition memory than processing of sound. However, this was found only with words which were remembered. Performance was essentially the same in the two processing conditions for words which the subjects knew had been in the list.

Gardiner's findings indicate that subjects do not necessarily have conscious recollective experience for words which are recognised on a memory test. In other words, memory performance or behaviour cannot be equated with conscious experience. What we have here are findings which appear to be incompatible with the doctrine of concordance.

In a nutshell, adherence to the doctrine of concordance made it sensible to limit the assessment of memory to measures of recall and recognition. Increasing evidence that the doctrine of concordance is wrong means that we need to assess memory in a variety of different ways in order to achieve a full understanding of human memory and its functioning.

Summary

In spite of its popularity, the notion that there is permanent memory for everything which has previously been learned has very little empirical support. It is certainly true that much stored information is difficult to gain access to on standard memory tests, but it does therefore not follow that the only reason for forgetting is an access problem.

Several theories of recall and recognition have been proposed. It is becoming increasingly clear that both recall and recognition involve a more complicated range of strategies than was previously believed. More specifically, retrieval can occur in a relatively direct or "automatic" fashion, or it can occur in a more indirect or "problem-solving" fashion. This multi-strategy approach is fine as far as it goes, but it is necessary to spell out in more detail the circumstances in which each strategy is used.

As is discussed in some detail in Chapter 6, the conventional measures of memory performance (i.e. recall and recognition) provide only partial evidence about the functioning of the memory system. Alternative behavioural measures of retention which do not depend on conscious awareness or recollection of past events sometimes produce findings which are very different to those obtained from conventional tests. The implication is that tests of recall and recognition are less revealing about human memory than cognitive psychologists used to think.

PARALLEL DISTRIBUTED PROCESSING

Parallel distributed processing (P.D.P.) models or connectionist networks provide an increasingly influential way of considering human learning and memory (parallel = more than one process occurring at a time; distributed processing = processing occurring in a number of different locations). The basic characteristics of this approach were considered in Chapter 1, and should perhaps be re-read by any reader who has forgotten what was said there. Several different P.D.P. models have been proposed. However, the focus in this chapter will be on those assumptions which are common to most of these models.

It is assumed in most of the theories discussed earlier in this chapter that there are huge numbers of memory traces stored in long-term memory, and that retrieval involves gaining access to the information in a particular memory trace. The assumptions incorporated into parallel distributed processing models are very different. In essence, it is assumed within such models that the information about a person, object, or event is stored in several inter-connected units rather than in a single place. Thus, for example, you may have a friend called Simon who is a psychologist, 45 years old, married, with two children. According to the P.D.P. model put forward by McClelland (1981), each of these pieces of information about Simon is stored in a separate unit. Learning involves increasing the connection strengths among these units. Retrieval involves gaining access to one or more of these units, which then activate the other units and re-create our knowledge of Simon. It is also assumed that each unit is involved in the representation of several different individuals or objects.

What are the advantages of the P.D.P. approach? The notion that knowledge about a person or object is distributed across several units rather than being concentrated in a single memory trace means that the system can often function reasonably well even if a unit is damaged or imperfect information is supplied to it. Consider, for example, the task of deciding which prime minister was male, very domineering, and won the Falklands War. In all probability you thought of the answer almost immediately in spite of being misled by the first piece of information or cue (i.e. maleness). This is readily explained by P.D.P. models. All three cues activate their respective units, and these units then activate other units associated with them. As a consequence, there is more activation of the name "Thatcher" than of any other name.

In contrast, consider a theory according to which retrieval works in a serial fashion in which only one cue at a time is considered. The cue "male" restricts the search to the names of male prime ministers, and then an attempt is made to think of domineering male prime ministers. From that smaller list, there is no one who also won the Falklands War, and so retrieval fails.

Another virtue of the P.D.P. approach to learning and memory is that it permits what McClelland, Rumelhart, and Hinton (1986) refer to as "spontaneous generalisations". Spontaneous generalis-ations involve "remembering" general information that was not learned in the first place. For example, if someone asks you whether right-wing people tend to be older or younger than left-wing people, you might happen to know the answer because it is part of your stock of knowledge. According to P.D.P. theorists, however, you might be able to come up with the right answer simply on the basis of specific information about individuals. The cue "right-wing" would activate information about all of the right-wing people you know, including information about their ages, and the same thing would happen for the cue "left-wing". In other words, novel and spontaneous generalisations can be produced readily even though the sought-for information is not directly stored in memory.

McClelland et al. (1986) pointed out that P.D.P. models allow for what they term "default assignment," in which missing information about an individual or an object is filled in on the basis of information about similar individuals or objects. Suppose, for example, that you forget how old your friend Simon is. When Simon's characteristics (e.g. a friend; psychologist; married; two children) are activated, they will activate units containing inform-ation about other individuals resembling Simon. If (as in the case of the first author), most of the married psychologists you know who have two children are in their forties, then that information will be activated. In other words, Simon's age becomes "mid-fortyish" by means of a default assignment, and you may not be aware that your assessment of his age was not based on direct knowledge.

There is plenty of experimental evidence of default assignment (see Chapter 9 for a fuller account). For example, Bower, Black, and Turner (1979) presented stories involving everyday events such as going to a restaurant. On a subsequent recognition memory test, subjects claimed that information which would naturally form part of such an event (but which had not been stated explicitly) had actually been presented. The reason for this is presumably because subjects filled in the missing information by means of default assignment.

More potential advantages of the P.D.P. approach to memory are discussed by McClelland and Rumelhart (1986a; 1986b), but there is space here to discuss only two more. People typically behave as if they had both general and specific information stored in long-term memory, and an issue which has to be faced by memory theorists is how to account for the relationship between these two kinds of information. For example, we have stored information about specific dogs we have encountered, but we also have more general and abstract information about what a "dog" is. The P.D.P. approach provides a reasonably convincing account of how general information can emerge from specific information (see McClelland & Rumelhart, 1986a; 1986b, for details). In essence, presentation of the word "dog" leads to the activation of numerous units relating to specific dogs we know. This leads via an averaging process to a set of attributes (e.g. number of legs, size, colour, etc.) corresponding in some sense to a "typical" dog.

The final advantage of the P.D.P. approach to memory concerns its treatment of amnesia (see McClelland & Rumelhart, 1986b). While the memory impairments of amnesic patients are varied and complex (see Chapter 6), it tends to be the case that they are better able to learn and to remember the *common* features of situations than the *idiosyncratic* features found in only one situation. Some understanding of this pattern of impairment can be gained if we make the simple assumption that learning experiences produce a smaller increase in the connection strengths among the relevant units for amnesic patients than for other people. This slower rate of learning means that amnesics should show very poor memory for the nonrepeated, idiosyncratic features of situations, because connection strengths remain low. This prediction is certainly in accord with the evidence. On the other hand, amnesic patients should eventually show learning for repeated information as the relevant connection strengths slowly but surely increase, and this is also supported by the evidence. The fact that amnesic patients can learn some things (e.g. many motor skills) as rapidly as normals is accounted for by arguing that the kinds of learning involved are those which are not facilitated by large increases in the strengths of connections among units. However, McClelland & Rumelhart (1986b) do not provide a detailed or convincing account of what is actually involved.

It is rather difficult at present to provide a proper evaluation of the P.D.P. or connectionist approach to learning and memory, because the approach is still in its infancy. However, the reason for the great interest in the P.D.P. approach is that it appears to offer a powerful conceptual framework within which to consider the functioning of human memory. In particular, a memory system in which processing is parallel is potentially more powerful and flexible than one in which processing does not occur in parallel. Psychophysiological assessment of brain activity is entirely consistent with the view that processing typically occurs in a parallel rather than in a serial fashion. However, as Johnson-Laird (1988a, p. 193) pointed out, "Whatever sort of computations brain cells carry out—and little is known of their nature—they are not satisfactorily idealised by network units. The brain is not wired up in a way that resembles any of the current connectionist proposals."

One of the characteristics of P.D.P. theories which makes evaluation difficult is the fact that the issues addressed by P.D.P. theorists overlap only partially with those of the other theorists considered in this chapter. However, there must be some doubt as to whether the complexities of memory processes and structures identified by cognitive psychologists can be captured adequately by the P.D.P. emphasis on strengths of connections of units.

SUMMARY

This chapter has been concerned with major theories of learning and memory. These theories differ in terms of whether they are concerned mainly with the structures or processes involved in memory. They also differ in terms of whether they focus on the storage of information or its subsequent retrieval.

Many theories of memory make use of the spatial metaphor. In other words, it is assumed that memories are stored in specific locations within the mind, from which they may be retrieved. Perhaps the best known theoretical approach of this type is the multi-store theory, according to which there are separate sensory, short-term, and long-term stores. There is reasonably strong evidence to support the notion of a number of qualitatively different memory stores. However, the multi-store approach provides a very over-simplified view of the memory system. For example, multi-store theorists assumed that there are unitary short-term and long-term stores, whereas the reality seems to be considerably more complex.

Some theorists have criticised the multi-store and other related theoretical approaches for focusing too much on the *structure* of memory. They have argued that we should pay more attention to the *processes* involved. The most celebrated theory emphasising memory processes was the levels-of-processing theory of Craik and Lockhart (1972). They (and their followers) have identified depth of processing (i.e. extent to which meaning is processed), elaboration of processing, and distinctiveness or uniqueness of processing as key factors in determining subsequent long-term memory.

The main problem with the levels-of-processing theory, as with the multi-store theory, is that it is over-simplified. It is probably true that depth, elaboration, and distinctiveness of processing generally enhance long-term memory, but it is certainly not true that these three factors are the only ones which influence it. For example, the relevance of the information stored at the time of learning to the memory test used is an extremely important determinant of long-term memory.

Many psychologists believe in permanent memory. However, research has provided little support for the notion that everything we have ever learned is still stored somewhere in long-term memory, even though it may be almost totally inaccessible.

Theory and research on retrieval have concentrated almost exclusively on recall and recognition. Several theories of recall and recognition have been proposed, and there has been much controversy as to whether the processes involved in recall and recognition are basically similar or not. Nearly all of the earlier theories assumed that the processes involved in recall are always the same regardless of what was being recalled, and the same was assumed of recognition memory. However, there is a growing awareness that recall sometimes occurs in a relatively fast and direct fashion, whereas at other times it occurs in an indirect fashion which can resemble problem solving. In similar fashion, recognition sometimes occurs straightforwardly on the basis of stimulus familiarity, and sometimes it requires the retrieval of relevant contextual information. One of the implications of this view is that the processes involved in recall and recognition are sometimes similar and sometimes not, depending upon the particular requirements of the respective recall and recognition tests.

Recent research and theory are making the complexities of human memory increasingly apparent. Adherence to the doctrine of concordance made it reasonable to rely solely on tests of recall and recognition to study retrieval. However, growing dissatisfaction with that doctrine has led to an increased emphasis on alternative measures (see Chapter 6). The traditional notion of specific memory traces containing all of the information we possess about objects and people has also been challenged recently by parallel distributed processing theorists. They claim that information is distributed across numerous inter-connected units, and preliminary evidence suggests that this may be a valuable way of conceptualising human memory.

FURTHER READING

Baddeley, A.D. (1982). Domains of recollection. *Psychological Review*, *89*, 708–729. This article provides a good discussion of several of the theories dealt with in this chapter.

Cohen, G., Eysenck, M.W., & LeVoi, M.E. (1986). *Memory: A cognitive approach*. Milton Keynes: Open University Press. This book contains a section by Eysenck on working memory and the levels-of-processing approach, and a section by LeVoi on retrieval from long-term memory.

Horton, D.L. & Mills, C.B. (1984). Human learning and memory. *Annual Review of Psychology*, *35*, 361–394. This provides a useful overview of recent theory and research.

McClelland, J.L. & Rumelhart, D.E. (1986a). A distributed model of human learning and memory. In D.E. Rumelhart, J.L. McClelland, & the PDP Research Group (Eds.), *Parallel* distributed processing: *Explorations in the microstructure of cognition, Vol. 1: Foundations.* Cambridge, Mass.: M.I.T. Press. Many of the key ideas underlying the PDP approach to memory are spelled out in this chapter.

Parkin, A.J. (1987). *Memory and amnesia.* Oxford: Blackwell. This book provides a readable introduction to the area of memory.

Chapter Six

MEMORY THEORIES AND AMNESIA

INTRODUCTION

There is an old (and somewhat tasteless) joke which goes like this: "What do you call someone who can't remember things?" "It doesn't matter what you call them, they won't remember anyway!" The correct answer, of course, is that someone with a severe memory impairment is suffering from amnesia. Instead of making jokes about amnesic patients, we should rather be concerned about the very disruptive effects that amnesia has on their everyday lives.

Over the last ten years or so, there has been increasing interest in the study of brain-damaged patients suffering from amnesia. Indeed, it is probably true to say that a majority of the most important research on human memory in recent years has been on amnesic patients. As a consequence, it is well worth devoting a chapter to the insights which have come from cognitive neuro-psychologists studying amnesic patients.

Why exactly are amnesic patients of interest to cognitive psychologists? One major reason is that the study of amnesic patients provides a good *test-bed* for existing theories of normal memory. As we saw in the previous chapter, the notion that there is a valid distinction between short-term and long-term memory stores has been tested by investigating amnesic patients. The discovery that some patients have severely impaired long-term memory but intact short-term memory, whereas a few patients show the opposite pattern, is rather strong evidence that there are separate short-term and long-term stores.

The second major reason is that amnesia research is increasingly leading to new theoretical developments. That is to say, studies of amnesia have suggested theoretical distinctions which then prove to be of relevance to an understanding of memory in normal individuals. Relevant examples are discussed during the course of this chapter.

The major concern of this chapter is with theories of memory, and with the theoretical implications of amnesia research. However, in order to make sense of the findings from amnesic patients, it is clearly necessary to have some background understanding of the amnesic condition. The first point that needs to be emphasised is that the reasons why patients have become amnesic are very varied. Closed head injury is the most common factor responsible for amnesia, but the fact that patients with closed head injury tend to be difficult to work with means that most experimental work has focused on patients who have become amnesic because of chronic alcohol abuse (Korsakoff's syndrome). Bilateral stroke is another factor causing amnesia. It is a matter of some controversy whether there are sufficient similarities in the nature of the memory impairment among these various groups to justify considering them together.

Those who favour considering most amnesic patients as a homogeneous group often refer to the "amnesic syndrome". The main characteristics of this syndrome are as follows:

- There is a very marked impairment of the ability to remember new information which was learned after the onset of the amnesia; this is known as *anterograde amnesia*.
- There is often great difficulty in remembering events which occurred prior to amnesia; this is known as *retrograde amnesia*, and is especially pronounced in patients with Korsakoff's syndrome.
- Despite these severe memory problems, amnesic patients typically have a normal level of intelligence. This indicates that their cognitive problems are mainly limited to the memory system.
- Patients suffering from the amnesic syndrome generally have a relatively intact immediate or short-term memory as indexed by measures such as digit span (i.e. the ability to repeat back a random string of digits immediately after presentation). This is shown at an informal level by the fact that it is possible to have a normal conversation with an amnesic patient, something that would be impossible unless amnesic patients were able to remember what has just been said.
- It has been known for a long time that patients with the amnesic syndrome usually have some remaining learning ability after the onset of the amnesia, in spite of their generally poor long-term memory for new information.

It has been established that many amnesic patients conform reasonably well to these characteristics of the "amnesic syndrome". However, some theorists (e.g. Parkin, 1990) have argued that there are actually a number of somewhat distinct syndromes, and others (e.g. Ellis & Young, 1988) have rejected the syndrome approach altogether. Some of the major issues here are discussed in the next section.

THE AMNESIC SYNDROME OR SYNDROMES?

As Parkin (1984; 1987) pointed out, the amnesic syndrome can be produced by damage to a number of brain structures. These structures are to be found in two separate areas of the brain: a subcortical region called the diencephalon, and a cortical region known as the medial temporal lobe.

Chronic alcoholics who develop Korsakoff's syndrome have brain damage in the diencephalon, but typically the frontal cortex is also damaged (Wilkinson & Carlen, 1982). In contrast, herpes simplex encephalitis (which involves inflammation of the brain) has been found to cause widespread damage to the medial temporal lobe. There are also a number of cases in which some of the temporal lobe was removed from epileptic patients in an attempt to reduce the incidence of epileptic seizures. As a consequence, many of these patients (including the much studied HM) became severely amnesic (Scoville & Milner, 1957).

Diencephalon Vs. Temporal Lobe Damage

We have seen that amnesia can result from damage to either the diencephalon (plus frontal cortex) or to the medial temporal lobe. It is natural to ask whether the nature of the memory impairments varies as a function of which brain structure has been damaged. Parkin (1984; 1990) has provided a provisional answer to that question. In general terms, Korsakoff patients with damage to the diencephalon (and generally to the frontal lobes) have rather more extensive memory problems than patients with damage to the medial temporal lobe. For example, Korsakoff patients virtually always have severe retrograde amnesia, whereas temporal lobe patients vary enormously in terms of the amount of retrograde amnesia they exhibit. In addition, Korsakoff patients typically exhibit a lack of insight into the seriousness of their deficient memory system, and they are more susceptible to interference in short-term memory tasks.

Another way in which Korsakoff patients are more impaired than other amnesics was discovered by Shinamura and Squire (1986). They initially asked their subjects to recall the answers to general information questions. Then the subjects indicated the extent to which they felt they knew the answers they had been unable to recall and would be able to recognise them. Finally, they were given a recognition-memory test for the items. The Korsakoff patients' feeling-of-knowing predictions were much less accurate than those of other amnesic patients, with the other amnesics performing at the same level as normal controls. As Shinamura and Squire (1986, p. 459) concluded, "Presumably Korsakoff's syndrome typically produces a more widespread cognitive deficit than is observed in other forms of amnesia."

In spite of the accumulating evidence that Korsakoff patients are impaired in more ways than temporal lobe patients, there is an extremely important exception which suggests that they may actually be less severely impaired overall. It appears that temporal lobe patients have a fast forgetting rate for information learned after the onset of amnesia, whereas Korsakoff patients sometimes have the same forgetting rate as normals provided that sufficient learning trials are given in the first place. Lhermitte and Signoret (1972) presented pictures of nine common objects in a three-by-three display, and then re-presented them in a different order. The patients' task was to indicate where the pictures had been presented initially. It took the Korsakoff patients 13 trials on average to learn the location, whereas 2 out of 3 of the temporal lobe patients did not achieve complete learning in 20 trials. The remaining temporal lobe patient then forgot almost everything about the display in 3 minutes, whereas the Korsakoff patients showed reasonable memory even 4 days later.

Evidence consistent with that of Lhermitte and Signoret was obtained by Parkin and Leng (1987). They compared recognition memory for pictures in Korsakoff patients and in patients with medial temporal lobe damage. Learning was equated by ensuring that all of the subjects could recall the pictures immediately and also recognise them all one minute later. The Korsakoff patients forget the pictures considerably more slowly than the temporal lobe patients.

Theorists differ in the conclusions which they have drawn from this evidence. This is partly due to the fact that only relatively few studies have directly compared amnesic patients with damage in different parts of the brain. Weiskrantz (1985) has argued that the evidence is not sufficient to warrant distinguishing among different groups of amnesic patients. He pointed out that the precise location of the lesion (i.e. the damage) is usually not known, and that many so-called temporal lobe patients may also have damage to the diencephalon. Weiskrantz explained the slower forgetting rate shown by Korsakoff patients than by temporal lobe patients by claiming that it is due to the lesser severity of the memory impairment. However, since Korsakoff patients tend to have a greater variety of memory problems than other amnesic patients, it is not clear that an alleged difference in amnesic severity can account for the data.

Parkin's Theory

A more promising theoretical approach was proposed by Parkin (1990). He argued that damage to the temporal lobes, to the diencephalon, and to the frontal cortex has different effects, and that account must be taken of these different effects when attempting to understand amnesia. According to Parkin:

- damage to the temporal lobes causes rapid forgetting of information;
- damage to the diencephalon causes problems with discrimination of contextual information (e.g. the time and place at which an event happened).

- damage to the frontal lobes causes susceptibility to interference, poor feeling-of-knowing, and problems with temporal discrimination (i.e. when events occurred).

It is difficult to evaluate Parkin's theory on the basis of the available evidence. However, there do appear to be genuine differences in the nature of the memory problems experienced by amnesic patients with damage in different areas of the brain. This means that there are great dangers of over-simplification associated with using the term "amnesic syndrome" rather than specifying more precisely which part of the brain is damaged. Parkin's theoretical approach also makes it clear that the findings from Korsakoff patients will often be somewhat difficult to interpret. This is because most Korsakoff patients have suffered damage to two different parts of the brain, i.e. the diencephalon and the frontal lobes, and damage to each of these areas produces a rather different pattern of impairment.

Korsakoff Patients

It is important to note that most investigations of amnesia have made use almost exclusively of Korsakoff patients. This means that the majority of statements about the characteristics of the amnesic syndrome are actually based on findings obtained from Korsakoff patients. Since that is the case, it is worth considering in more detail how suitable such patients are from the point of view of understanding the processes underlying amnesia. Unfortunately, there are two major difficulties posed by Korsakoff patients. The first is that the amnesia usually has a gradual onset, being caused by an increasing deficiency of the vitamin thiamine which is associated with chronic alcoholism. This means that it is often difficult to know whether past events occurred before or after the onset of amnesia, and thus poor memory for such events may reflect either retrograde or anterograde amnesia.

The second difficulty, as we have already seen, is that brain damage in many Korsakoff patients is rather widespread. Structures within the diencephalon such as the hippocampus and the amygdala are usually damaged, and these structures appear to be of vital significance to memory. In addition, of course, there is very often damage to the frontal lobes. This may produce a range of cognitive deficits which are not specific to the memory system, but which have indirect effects on memory performance. In other words, cognitive neuropsychologists would find it easier to make coherent sense of findings from Korsakoff patients if brain damage were limited to the diencephalon, but this is rarely the case.

Summary

The notion that there is a single identifiable amnesic syndrome seems less plausible in the light of recent evidence. In approximate terms, the nature of the memory impairments in amnesia depends on which parts of the brain are damaged. More specifically, the temporal lobes, the diencephalon, and the frontal lobes all make different contributions to memory functioning. Most investigations of amnesia have focused on Korsakoff patients. These patients often have damage to the diencephalon and to the frontal lobes, which complicates the task of understanding their memory problems.

RESIDUAL LEARNING CAPACITY

If we are to understand amnesia, then it is extremely important to consider which aspects of learning and memory remain relatively intact in amnesic patients. These aspects are commonly referred to as the "residual learning ability." We would like to be in a position to draw up lists of those memory abilities impaired and not impaired in amnesia. By comparing the two lists, it should in principle be possible to identify those processes and/or memory structures which are primarily affected by amnesia. Theoretical accounts of the amnesic syndrome can then proceed based on a solid foundation of knowledge. In this section of the chapter we consider residual learning capability, and in the next section there is a discussion of theoretical distinctions involving categorisation of intact and impaired memory skills.

Short-term Memory

We saw in the last chapter that many amnesic patients have a reasonably intact short-term memory system but a severely deficient long-term memory system, although a few amnesic patients show the opposite pattern. More specifically, it has been found (e.g. Butters & Cermak, 1980) that Korsakoff patients perform as well as normals on the digit-span task, in which random digits must be repeated back immediately in the correct order. It is especially noteworthy that similar results have also been reported in non-Korsakoff patients, details of which are now given.

NA became amnesic as a result of having a fencing foil forced up his nostril and into his brain, probably causing damage to the diencephalon. Teuber, Milner, and Vaughan (1968) discovered that he performed at the normal level on span measures. HM had an operation which damaged the temporal lobes, together with partial removal of the hippocampus and amygdala. He also turned out to have a normal level of short-term memory performance as indexed by immediate span (Wickelgren, 1968).

As Ellis and Young (1988, pp. 291–292) argued in their discussion of short-term memory in amnesics: "It would be interesting even if only some amnesics showed normal immediate recall in the context of deficient long-term recall; the fact that the great majority do is particularly impressive." The one qualification that might be put on that statement is that span measures are by no means the only way in which short-term memory can be assessed.

However, Baddeley and Warrington (1970) observed normal performance by amnesic patients on a number of different tasks allegedly measuring short-term memory.

While most amnesic patients have reasonably intact short-term memory, the few patients who have been found to have memory problems mainly involving short-term memory are of great theoretical interest. As we will see a little later, the development of theories of short-term memory has been much influenced by evidence obtained from brain-damaged patients with partial deficits in short-term memory.

Skills

Most of the evidence of residual learning capability in amnesics has been obtained from tasks involving motor or other skills. The tasks on which amnesics have been shown to acquire skills are very varied (see Parkin, 1987, for a review). These tasks include the following: dressmaking; billiards; finger mazes; tracking a moving target on a pursuit rotor; jigsaw completions; reading mirror-reversed script; mirror drawing; and the Tower of Hanoi. In addition, there is good evidence that skills acquired before the onset of amnesia tend to be retained. For example, Schachter (1983) described an amnesic patient whose golfing skills remained intact.

There are two issues which are important in considering the learning of skills by amnesics. One is whether this strange mixture of skills all reflect the same underlying mechanisms, and the other is whether amnesics' ability to acquire these skills is as good as that of normals. On the first issue, it is still not clear whether the range of preserved skills identified so far makes any psychological sense, but there is a suspicion that it may not. On the second issue, there are some cases in which amnesics learn skills as rapidly as normals, and other skills where their rate of learning is significantly slower. It is to some of these apparent inconsistencies in the literature that we now turn.

Speed of Skill Acquisition

Corkin (1968) reported that the amnesic patient HM was able to learn the pursuit rotor, which involves manual tracking of a moving target, and mirror drawing. His rate of learning was slower than that of normals on the pursuit rotor, but was approximately normal on the mirror-drawing task. In contrast, Cermak, Lewis, Butters, and Goodglass (1973) found that Korsakoff patients learned the pursuit rotor as fast as normals. However, the amnesic patients were slower than the normals at learning a finger maze.

There have been a number of studies of reading mirror-reversed script. In these studies it is possible to distinguish between general improvement in speed of reading produced by practice and more specific improvement produced by re-reading the same groups of words or sentences. Cohen and Squire (1980) reported that amnesics demonstrated general and specific improvement in reading mirror-reversed script, and there was still evidence of improvement after a delay of three months. Martone, Butters, Payne, Becker, and Sax (1984) also obtained general and specific improvement in amnesics. However, while the general practice effect was as great in amnesics as in normals, the specific practice effect was not. It may be that normals (but not amnesics) are able to use speed-reading strategies to facilitate reading of repeated groups of words.

One of the most dramatic examples of preserved skill in amnesic patients was reported by Cohen (1984) based on a task known as the Tower of Hanoi. This is a problem-solving task which requires the subject to move five rings from peg to peg, but with the restrictions that only one ring can be moved at a time, and that a larger ring must never be placed on top of a small one (see Chapter 11). Despite the fact that this is a rather complex task, Cohen discovered that amnesics found the optimal solution as quickly as normal controls. The two groups did differ, however, when they were given a recognition-memory test in which positions of the rings which are or are not encountered en route to the optimal solution were presented. The control subjects were reasonably good at recognising those configurations of the rings encountered at intermediate stages of solution, whereas the performance of the amnesic subjects was near to chance level.

The findings reported by Cohen were so dramatic that various other researchers have attempted to replicate them, but unfortunately without success. For example, Beatty, Salmon, Bernstein, Martone, Lyon, and Butters (1987) compared the performance of an amnesic patient with normal controls on the Tower of Hanoi puzzle, and found that the patient's rate of learning was much slower.

What Skills Are Preserved?

It is clear that amnesic patients show good, or even normal, rates of learning for several tasks involving different skills. What is much more difficult to do is to describe what (if anything) these tasks have in common. However, a start has been made by Moscovitch (1984). He argued that amnesics typically perform well on tasks which possess three characteristics:

- it is obvious to the patient what is required;
- the necessary responses are already in the patient's repertoire; and
- there is no need to refer to any specific past events in order to solve the task.

Moscovitch has provided a useful description of some of the main features of those tasks on which amnesics show good skill learning. However, the next step is the difficult one of explaining why it is that amnesic patients can handle such tasks better than others.

Perceptual Learning: Priming

If people are shown the same stimulus on two separate occasions, then they are usually faster to identify the stimulus on the second occasion. This so-called repetition-priming effect can occur even if there is no conscious awareness that the stimulus was presented previously. Priming effects have been demonstrated in amnesics, but it is not yet clear whether the various priming effects all depend on the same processes.

Crovitz, Harvey, and McClanahan (1981) presented "picture puzzles" that were difficult to identify on two successive days. They discovered that the time taken by amnesic patients to identify these pictures was much less on the second day than it had been on the first one. This indicates that a considerable amount of perceptual learning had occurred. Despite the improvement in performance, however, the amnesics were very poor in terms of recognition memory for repeated pictures.

A related phenomenon was obtained by Cermak, Talbot, Chandler, and Wolbarst (1985). They presented a list of words, followed by two tasks for the subjects to perform. One task was perceptual identification, and involved presenting the words at the minimal exposure time needed to identify them correctly. The other task was a straightforward test of recognition memory. The findings are shown in Fig. 6.1. Korsakoff patients performed much worse than nonamnesic alcoholics on the recognition-memory test, but the two groups of subjects had a comparable level of performance on the perceptual identification test.

Moscovitch (1985) made use of a lexical decision task, in which subjects have to decide as rapidly as possible whether a string of letters is or is not a word. Response speed is usually faster for repeated words, i.e. there is a repetition-priming effect. Amnesic patients had a normal repetition-priming effect, but they showed extremely poor recognition-memory performance for the repeated words.

The fact that amnesics show priming effects has been used to facilitate their learning, using a technique known as the *method of vanishing cues* (Glisky, Schachter, & Tulving, 1986). Amnesic patients were given a definition from computer terminology together with the name of the relevant command (e.g. "to store a program" linked with "SAVE"). Learning was tested by re-presenting the definition along with the first letter of the command. If the patient could not think of the name of the command, further letters were supplied until the correct answer was forthcoming. All of the amnesic patients were eventually able to produce the appropriate commands for each of 15 different definitions in the absence of any cues.

In sum, amnesics exhibit a variety of repetition-priming effects. Their performance is greatly improved by the prior presentation of stimuli despite an absence of conscious awareness that these stimuli have previously been presented. There has been some controversy as to whether this disparity between performance and conscious awareness is unique to amnesic patients. Some evidence

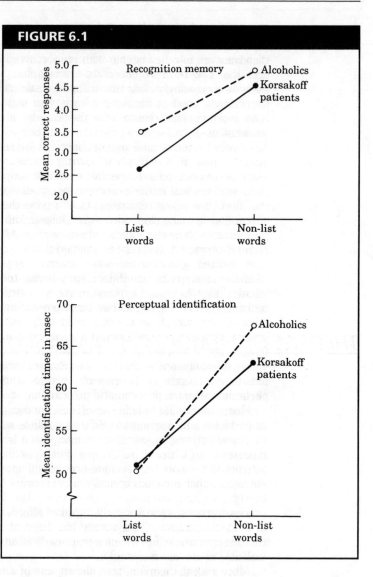

FIGURE 6.1

Recognition memory and perceptual identification of Korsakoff patients and nonamnesic alcoholics; delayed conditions only. Data from Cermak, Talbot, Chandler, & Wolbarst (1985).

that it is not was obtained by Meudell and Mayes (1981). They used a task in which cartoons had to be searched for specified objects. When amnesics repeated the task seven weeks later, they found the objects faster than the first time in spite of very poor recognition memory for the cartoons. When normals were tested at the much longer interval of 17 months, they showed exactly the same pattern. This suggests that repetition-priming effects in the absence of conscious awareness of having seen the stimuli before may be a general characteristic of poor memories rather than being specific to amnesic patients.

Summary

It used to be thought that amnesic patients were at a severe disadvantage to other people with respect to all forms of learning and the long-term retention of information. However, it has become increasingly clear that many amnesic patients are actually surprisingly good at acquiring a variety of skills and knowledge. The most obvious reason why the learning abilities of amnesic patients used to be under-estimated is because amnesics often have very limited or nonexistent conscious awareness of what they have learned. It is only when learning is assessed in ways which place no reliance on introspective evidence that the true extent of amnesics' residual learning capability becomes clear.

One of the major requirements of a good theory of amnesia is that it should make clear why some skills and abilities are more or less intact in amnesic patients, whereas other skills and abilities are severely impaired. It cannot be claimed that any current theory has achieved that goal, but there are several theories that represent useful first steps to understanding. Ideally, theories of amnesia should also help to explain memory functioning in normal individuals. It is to such theories that we now turn.

THEORIES OF MEMORY AND AMNESIA

As was mentioned earlier in the chapter, there has been an interesting change in theories of amnesia. Until recently, most theorists attempted to apply pre-existing theories of normal memory functioning to amnesics. Thus, for example, the evidence of Baddeley and Warrington (1970) and others seemed at one time to provide strong support for the multi-store approach which was discussed in Chapter 5. A few years later, Cermak (1979) attempted to apply the levels-of-processing approach to amnesia. He argued that amnesics typically fail to process the meaning of to-be-remembered information, and that this lack of semantic processing causes the severely impaired long-term memory found in amnesic patients. This theory has been abandoned, because there is overwhelming evidence that nearly all amnesic patients are well able to process meaning.

More recent theorists have shown less of a tendency to adopt the approach of attempting to make previously existing theories fit the facts of amnesia. Instead, they have started by considering the pattern of deficits exhibited by amnesic patients, and then constructed new theories designed to accommodate that pattern. This is especially true of the approach proposed by Schachter (1987), which is discussed later in the chapter. His theoretical distinction between implicit and explicit memory is one which arose largely in the context of amnesia research, but which has had a profound impact on thinking about normal human memory functioning.

Some of the major theories which are of relevance to both amnesia and normal human memory are discussed in this chapter.

An important point which is worth emphasising is that many of these theories overlap with each other. This fact, coupled with the imprecision of many of the theoretical constructs used, means that it is very difficult to decide which theoretical approaches are more promising than others.

Episodic Versus Semantic Memory
The Theoretical Distinction

As was discussed in Chapter 5, our long-term memories contain an amazing variety of different kinds of information. There is as a consequence a natural temptation to assume that there are a number of different long-term memory systems, each of which is specialised for certain types of information. One of the most influential of such distinctions among long-term memory systems was proposed by Tulving (1972), and is discussed at greater length in Chapter 8. He distinguished between episodic and semantic memory. Episodic memory has an autobiographical flavour about it, referring to the storage of specific events or episodes which occurred in a particular place at a particular time. Thus, memory for what you had for breakfast this morning or for what happened last Christmas Day are examples of episodic memory.

In contrast, semantic memory contains information about our stock of knowledge about the world. Tulving (1972, p. 386) defined semantic memory in the following way:

> It is a mental thesaurus, organised knowledge a person possesses about words and other verbal symbols, their meanings and referents, about relations among them, and about rules, formulas, and algorithms for the manipulation of these symbols, concepts, and relations. Semantic memory does not register perceptible properties of inputs, but rather cognitive referents of input signals.

There has been some controversy about the usefulness of the distinction between episodic and semantic memory. There is a clear difference in *content* between the information in episodic and in semantic memory, but it is far less obvious that there is a difference in the *processes* involved. One of the reasons for doubting that there are two separate memory systems is the fact that episodic and semantic memory are strongly interdependent in their functioning. Consider, for example, memory for what you had for breakfast this morning. While this is basically stored in episodic memory, semantic memory is also involved in that your knowledge of the world allowed you to identify what was on your plate as bacon, eggs, sausages, toast, or whatever. Thus, episodic and semantic memory usually work in tandem.

Relevance to Amnesia

It has been argued by a number of theorists (e.g. Parkin, 1982; Tulving, 1983) that amnesic patients provide the strongest available evidence for the distinction between episodic and semantic memory. The essence of their theoretical position can be indicated very briefly:

- Amnesic patients have a severe deficit in the ability to store new information in episodic memory.
- Semantic memory in amnesic patients is essentially intact.

This view has an immediate appeal. There is little doubt that amnesic patients have a severely deficient episodic memory, as this description by Korsakoff (1889) of a typical amnesic patient reveals: "He does not remember whether he had his dinner, whether he was out of bed. On occasion the patient forgets what happened to him just an instant ago: you came in, conversed with him, and stepped out for one minute; then you come in again and the patient has absolutely no recollection that you had already been with him." There is also little doubt that major parts of semantic memory are generally intact in amnesic patients. The most obvious examples of this are their largely unimpaired language skills, including vocabulary and grammar, and their essentially normal performance on intelligence tests.

Despite the superficial attractiveness of explaining amnesia in terms of intact semantic memory but impaired episodic memory, there is a general acceptance nowadays that this view is seriously flawed. In a nutshell, the problem is that one is not comparing like with like. Language and the abilities required to perform well on intelligence tests are nearly always acquired before the onset of amnesia, whereas conventional tests of episodic memory are based on information acquired *after* the onset of amnesia. Thus, the findings described so far are consistent with the simple notion that amnesia impairs the ability to learn new information, but has relatively little effect on the ability to remember information learned prior to the onset of amnesia. What is needed is to consider amnesics' ability to acquire new semantic memories in the amnesic state, and their ability to recall episodic memories dating back to the period prior to amnesia. This will allow us to decide whether it is the nature of the memory (episodic or semantic) or the time of acquisition which is crucial.

The available evidence indicates quite clearly that amnesic patients have problems adding to the information in semantic memory. Gabrieli, Cohen, and Corkin (1983) gave the amnesic patient HM extensive training in the task of learning the meanings of unfamiliar words which had come into popular use after the operation causing his amnesia. HM showed very little ability to acquire the meanings of these words, in spite of receiving extensive practice every day for a ten-day period.

Most other amnesics similarly fail to update their semantic memories to take account of changes in the world that have happened since the onset of their amnesia. As Baddeley (1984) has pointed out, many amnesics do not know the name of the current prime minister or president, and have very poor recognition memory for the faces of people who have become famous only comparatively recently. All of this evidence strongly indicates that it is only semantic memories acquired prior to the onset of amnesia which are unaffected in amnesics.

There is evidence indicating that amnesics have some ability to recall episodic memories which antedate amnesia onset. Zola-Morgan, Cohen, and Squire (1983) presented a list of ten words (e.g. flag, bird, window) to Korsakoff patients and to normals one at a time, and instructed them to recall a specific event suggested by each word. The Korsakoff patients were able to do this almost as readily as the normal controls. This suggests that episodic memories of distant events (the average age of the memories was 30 years) are still accessible. However, it is not certain that the memories recalled by the amnesic patients actually possessed the immediacy and autobiographical flavour of genuine episodic memories.

In sum, the distinction between episodic and semantic memory has proved less useful than was once believed in describing what is intact and what is impaired in the memory systems of amnesic patients. The available evidence suggests the pattern shown in Table 6.1. Most amnesic patients have a reasonably good recollection of semantic and episodic memories established before the onset of amnesia, but rather poor memory for semantic and episodic information encountered afterwards.

This should come as no surprise in view of the strong links between episodic and semantic memory. Hintzman (1983; 1986) suggested that semantic memories are formed out of episodic memories. For example, the information that two plus two equals four is stored in most adults' semantic memory. In young children, however, there will usually be several episodic memories corresponding to the occasions on which their parents or teachers have told them that two plus two makes four. As time goes by, what is common to all of those episodic memories (i.e. the fact that two plus two equals four) will form a semantic memory, whereas the unique information about time and place in each episodic memory will fade. If that speculative account is approximately

---

TABLE 6.1

Effects of Amnesia on Old and New Episodic and Semantic Memories

Memory System	Time of Learning	Amnesics' Memory	Evidence
Semantic	Before amnesia	Good	Intact language & intelligence
Semantic	After amnesia	Very poor	Gabrieli et al. (1983)
Episodic	Before amnesia	Fair	Zola-Morgan et al. (1983)
Episodic	After amnesia	Very poor	Dozens of laboratory studies

correct, then it would be unrealistic to expect episodic memory to be impaired with no adverse effects on semantic memory.

Context Processing Deficit Theory

We saw in the Chapter 5 that context plays an important part in memory. Long-term memory is generally better when the context at the time of the memory test is the same as the context at the time of learning than when it differs. Contextual information is also important in allowing us to distinguish between otherwise similar memories.

Several theorists (e.g. Huppert & Piercy, 1976; Mayes, Meudell, & Pickering, 1985) have proposed the following hypothesis:

amnesic patients can store information about the to-be-remembered information, but have great difficulty in storing contextual information in long-term memory.

Since contextual information about time and place is found with episodic but not with semantic memories, it is clear that this theory overlaps with theories emphasising a deficit in episodic memory in amnesic patients.

Some of the most convincing evidence in favour of the context processing deficit theory was obtained by Huppert and Piercy (1976). They presented some pictures on day 1 of the experiment, and some pictures on day 2. Some of the pictures presented on day 2 had been presented on day 1 and some had not. Ten minutes after the day 2 presentation, there was a test for recognition memory, on which subjects were asked which pictures had been presented on day 2. As can be seen in Fig. 6.2, the control subjects had no problem, correctly identifying nearly all of the pictures that had been presented on day 2, and incorrectly identifying very few of the pictures that had been presented only on day 1. The Korsakoff patients did much worse, correctly identifying only 70% of the day 2 pictures, and incorrectly identifying 51% of the pictures presented only on day 1. A subsequent study by Huppert and Piercy (1978) indicated that this modest recognition-memory ability was entirely due to the fact that the day 2 pictures tended to be slightly higher in familiarity than the day 1 pictures, rather than to specific memory for time of learning. In other words, Korsakoff patients showed practically no memory for temporal context.

Since poor long-term memory in amnesic patients has been shown many times, the study by Huppert and Piercy (1976) may not seem to be of any great interest. However, they then asked their subjects whether they had ever seen the pictures before. With this test, it was not necessary to have stored contextual information in order to demonstrate recognition memory. Accordingly, both the Korsakoff patients and the normal controls performed at a very high level, and hardly differed in their performance (see Fig. 6.2). Thus, information about the pictures

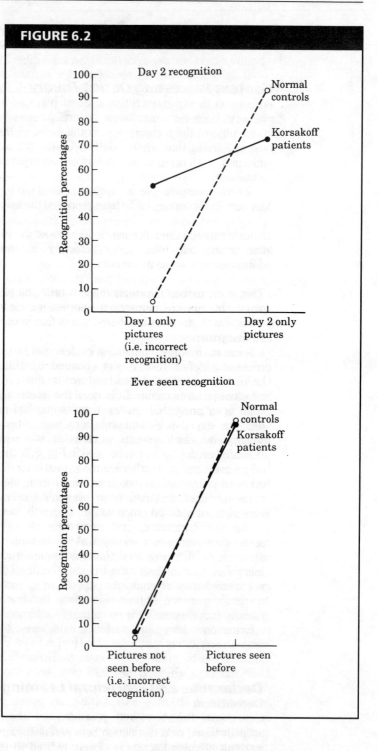

Recognition memory for pictures in Korsakoff patients and normal controls. Data from Huppert & Piercy (1976).

themselves was definitely stored in long-term memory, but very little (if any) information about the circumstances in which the pictures had been seen previously was available.

It may make sense to relate the results of the studies by Huppert and Piercy (1976; 1978) to the theory of recognition proposed by Mandler (1980), discussed in Chapter 5. In essence, Mandler argued that there are two mechanisms by which recognition memory can occur: stimulus familiarity, and identification, which involves the retrieval of relevant contextual information. The first mechanism appears to be almost intact in amnesic patients, but the second mechanism is severely impaired.

More evidence of a contextual processing problem in amnesic patients was obtained by Schachter, Harbluk, and McLachlan (1984). Fictitious statements about famous people (e.g. "Bob Hope's father was a fireman") were read to amnesic patients by two different experimenters. The fictitious statements were often remembered subsequently by the patients, but without any recollection of who had told them the information in the first place. This phenomenon has been called "source amnesia," and reflects an inability to store and/or remember contextual information.

Evaluation
It is not clear within context processing deficit theory exactly *why* amnesic patients are able to store information about the target, to-be-remembered, stimulus, but cannot store relevant contextual information. After all, what is regarded as the target stimulus and what is regarded as the context is often largely arbitrary and depends on the experimenter's whim. Mayes et al. (1985) suggested that amnesic patients have reduced processing resources, and so are only able to process to-be-remembered information adequately by ignoring contextual information. There may be some mileage in this suggestion, but it is obviously necessary to obtain independent evidence that amnesic patients do, indeed, have reduced processing resources.

At the empirical level, the context processing deficit theory has some problems in accounting for the fact that amnesic patients show poor learning of semantic memories. Since semantic memories by definition do not contain contextual information, it is not immediately obvious why a problem in processing contextual information would impair the ability to acquire new semantic memories. However, it is entirely possible that contextual information plays some part in the acquisition of semantic memories.

Declarative and Procedural Learning
Definitions
Cohen and Squire (1980) proposed an alternative theoretical account based on a distinction between declarative and procedural learning. This distinction is closely related to that made by Ryle

(1949) between *knowing that* and *knowing how*. Declarative learning corresponds to knowing that, and covers both episodic and semantic memory. Thus, for example, we know that we had porridge for breakfast this morning, and we know that Paris is the capital of France. In contrast, procedural learning corresponds to knowing how, and refers to the ability to perform skilled actions (e.g. riding a bicycle, playing the piano) without the involvement of conscious recollection.

Cohen (1984, p. 96) provided more formal definitions of declarative and procedural knowledge. According to him, procedural knowledge is involved when: "experience serves to influence the organisation of processes that *guide* performance without access to the knowledge that underlies the performance." Cohen claimed that declarative knowledge is represented: "in a system quite compatible with the traditional memory metaphor of experimental psychology, in which information is said to be first processed or encoded, then stored in some explicitly accessible form for later use, and then ultimately retrieved upon demand." The distinction between declarative and procedural knowledge is discussed further in Chapter 8.

Theory
According to Cohen and Squire (1980) and Squire and Cohen (1984):

- amnesic patients have a severe impairment of the system involved in declarative learning; and
- amnesic patients have a relatively intact procedural learning system.

The notion that amnesics find it difficult to acquire new declarative knowledge is consistent with the evidence reviewed in the previous section. We saw there that amnesics cannot readily form new episodic or semantic memories, and declarative knowledge consists, by definition, of episodic and semantic memories. On the other hand, amnesics often acquire motor skills as rapidly as normals do, which is in line with the notion that their procedural learning skills are unimpaired. An anecdote involving Clarapede (1911) also fits well with the theoretical position of Cohen and Squire (1980) and of Cohen (1984). He hid a pin in his hand before shaking hands with one of his amnesic patients. After that, she was reluctant to shake hands with him, but she could not explain why. Thus, her motor performance (procedural knowledge) indicated that learning had occurred, but her conscious recollection (declarative knowledge) did not.

Evaluation
The declarative-procedural distinction has proved to be of use in accounting for normal memory performance as well as the nature of the memory deficit in amnesia. However, the theoretical account of

amnesia proposed by Cohen and Squire (1980) is not without difficulties. Firstly, it is by no means clear that the theory really explains what is involved in amnesia. Instead, what it does is to describe a way of categorising those memory skills which are and are not impaired in amnesic patients. Secondly, the distinction between declarative and procedural knowledge is not a very precise one. Part of the problem is that many skills involve a combination of both kinds of knowledge. For example, the ability to play golf would appear to be largely procedural, because it involves motor skills of which there is no conscious awareness. However, many golfers possess relevant declarative knowledge (e.g. "Keep your left arm straight"; "Keep your head still") that also influences their performance on the golf course.

Thirdly, it is difficult to argue that all of the memory abilities which remain essentially intact in amnesics involve procedural learning. Those aspects of short-term memory unaffected by amnesia cannot plausibly be regarded as procedural, and it is also doubtful whether repetition priming is genuinely procedural.

Fourthly, there is evidence that many amnesics are able to acquire declarative information. Cermak and O'Connor (1983) discovered that an amnesic patient (SS) was able to learn several specific instructions and facts. Schachter et al. (1984) found that amnesics were able to learn numerous fictitious statements about famous people, even though they were unable to remember the circumstances in which they learned the information.

Explicit and Implicit Memory
Definitions
Graf and Schachter (1985) and Schachter (1987) have drawn a theoretical distinction between explicit memory and implicit memory. These terms were defined by Graf and Schachter (1985, p. 501) in the following way: "Implicit memory is revealed when performance on a task is facilitated in the absence of conscious recollection; explicit memory is revealed when performance on a task requires conscious recollection of previous experiences." Thus, traditional measures of memory such as free recall, cued recall, and recognition all involve use of direct instructions to retrieve information about specific experiences, and are therefore measures of explicit memory.

Evidence
How can we show that the distinction between explicit and implicit memory is actually of importance? One way is to demonstrate that certain manipulations (e.g. learning instructions) have quite different effects on the performance of explicit and implicit memory tasks. This strategy has been used frequently with normals (see Schachter, 1987, for a review). For example, Jacoby and Dallas (1981) used recognition memory as their measure of explicit memory and word identification as their measure of implicit

memory (on a word-identification task a word is presented extremely rapidly, and the subject tries to decide which word it is). Before these tasks were given, subjects were presented with a list of words and had to answer questions about them. Some of the questions related to the meaning of the words (semantic questions), whereas others were concerned with whether the word rhymed with another word (rhyme questions), or contained a particular letter (physical questions). For each type of question, either a "yes" or a "no" response was appropriate. Explicit memory on the recognition test was higher for those words whose meaning had been processed. The type of question had no effect on implicit memory in the form of the word-identification task (see Fig. 6.3), but performance in all conditions was much higher than for words which had not been seen before (perceptual recognition = 65%). The differential effect of question type on explicit and implicit memory suggests that different processes are involved in the two kinds of memory.

The distinction between explicit and implicit memory has proved particularly useful when considering the nature of the memory impairment in amnesic patients. According to a number of theorists including Schachter (1987):

- amnesic patients are at a severe disadvantage when tests of explicit memory are used;
- amnesics often perform at normal levels on tests of implicit memory.

Recognition memory and perceptual recognition as a function of type of question and of the appropriate response (yes or no). Data from Jacoby & Dallas (1981).

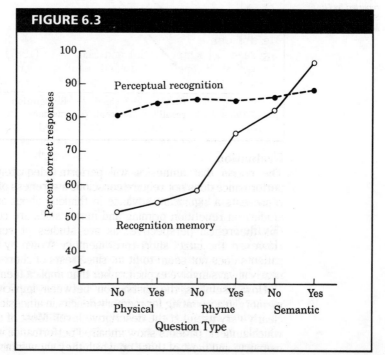

FIGURE 6.3

The value of the distinction between explicit and implicit memory for an understanding of amnesia was shown clearly in an experiment by Graf, Squire, and Mandler (1984). Word lists were presented, with the subjects deciding how much they liked each word. The lists were followed by one of four memory tests. Three of the tests (free recall; cued recall; recognition) involved explicit memory, and the fourth test (word completion) involved implicit memory. On the word completion test, subjects were given three-letter word fragments (e.g. BAR–) and simply had to write down the first word they thought of which started with those letters (e.g. BARTER; BARGAIN). Implicit memory was assessed by the extent to which the word completions corresponded to words on the list previously presented. Amnesic patients did much worse than controls on all of the tests of explicit memory, but there was no difference between the two groups in their performance on the test of implicit memory (see Fig. 6.4).

FIGURE 6.4

Free recall, cued recall, recognition memory, and word completion in amnesic patients and controls given the liking task. Data from different experiments reported by Graf, Squire, & Mandler (1984).

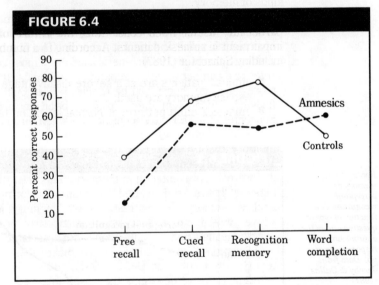

Evaluation

The notion that amnesics will perform adequately when their performance does not require conscious awareness of remembering represents a significant advance in thinking about amnesia. Most studies on repetition priming and motor skills are consistent with this theoretical perspective, as are studies of verbal memory. However, the intact short-term memory shown by most amnesic patients does not seem to fit in, since tests of short-term memory nearly always involve explicit rather than implicit memory.

How useful is the distinction between implicit and explicit memory in accounting for memory deficits in amnesic patients? It is clearly very useful at the descriptive level. Most of those tasks on which amnesic patients show impaired performance involve explicit memory, and most of those on which they show intact performance

involve implicit memory. The intact short-term memory performance of most amnesics is the only major exception, and may well
require a very different kind of explanation. However, the notion
that amnesic patients have deficient explicit memory does not in
and of itself constitute an explanation. As Schachter (1987, p. 501)
pointed out, implicit and explicit memory "are *descriptive*
concepts that are primarily concerned with a person's psychological
experience at the time of retrieval."

The nonexplanatory nature of the explicit-implicit distinction can
be seen if we consider why it is that amnesic patients typically have
impaired explicit memory but intact implicit memory. It is possible
that the impairment in explicit memory occurs because of problems
at the time of learning, as is proposed by advocates of the context
processing deficit theory. On the other hand, the problem could be
primarily one of retrieval, in which amnesic patients have great
difficulty with gaining conscious access to stored information.

Theoretical Considerations

How can we make theoretical headway in understanding what is
involved in explicit and implicit memory? The first step is to realise
that both terms are very general, and are almost certainly used to
refer to a number of rather separate phenomena. It is probable that
more than one theory will be required to account for the various
findings. The present state of play has been discussed very well by
Schachter (1987). He distinguished between three broad categories
of theory: activation theory; processing theory; and multiple-
memory theory. According to activation theory (e.g. Graf et al.
1984), the presentation of a word leads to *automatic* activation of
its internal representation in memory. This activation may last for
minutes, hours, or days, and it facilitates performance on tests of
implicit memory. In contrast, explicit memory is enhanced by
active or elaborative processing, particularly processing of the
word's meaning and its connections with associated words.

Activation theory allows one to make sense of the findings
reported by Jacoby and Dallas (1981), and shown in Fig. 6.3. The
different types of questions they used involved a manipulation of
elaborative processing, and this manipulation affected explicit
memory as assessed by recognition memory. In contrast,
automatic activation occurs regardless of the presence or absence
of elaborative processing, and so the type of question used had no
effect on implicit memory in the form of the word-identification
task.

Some processing theorists (e.g. Roediger & Blaxton, 1987)
have tried to shed light on explicit and implicit memory by making
use of the distinction between data-driven and conceptually driven
processes. In essence, data-driven processes are those triggered
off directly by external stimuli, whereas conceptually driven
processes are those initiated by the subject. They include
expectations about the nature of the presented stimuli and
elaborative processing of stimuli. The crucial assumption is that

data-driven processes generally underlie performance on tests of implicit memory, whereas conceptually driven processes generally sustain performance on tests of explicit memory.

An apparently crucial difference between activation theory and processing theory concerns the issue of whether amnesic patients have implicit memory for novel information (e.g. unrelated pairs of words or nonwords). According to activation theorists, only words with pre-existing representations in memory can be activated. As a consequence, novel information should not receive activation, and therefore there should be no implicit memory for such information. In contrast, processing theorists argue that implicit memory depends on data-driven processes. Since such processes can presumably be used with novel information, the prediction from processing theory is that there should be implicit memory for novel information.

The relevant evidence is discussed by Schachter (1987). It is, unfortunately, rather inconclusive (e.g. McAndrews, Glisky, & Schachter, 1987). Novel and complex sentences (e.g. "The haystack was important because the cloth ripped") were presented once, together with cues designed to make them easier to understand (e.g. "parachute"). Even though their amnesic patients had no explicit memory for the sentences and cues, they showed implicit memory by generating the appropriate cues when given the sentences on their own and asked to produce cues that made the sentences understandable. In contrast, Schachter and Graf discovered that severely amnesic patients failed to reveal implicit memory for new associations. The implication is that neither activation theory nor processing theory is entirely adequate; however, it has proved difficult to replicate the findings of Schachter and Graf (1986), at least with Korsakoff patients.

It will be remembered that Schachter (1987) also discussed multiple-memory system theory approaches, of which there are several. However, the best known of these approaches is none other than the theory proposed by Cohen and Squire (1980), and based on the distinction between procedural and declarative knowledge. This theoretical approach has already been discussed in some detail, and its strengths and weaknesses identified.

In sum, examination of the activation, processing, and multiple memory system approaches reveals that none of the approaches is decisively superior to the others. Each approach accounts for some of the data more comfortably than do the other approaches, but has problems in accounting for all of the data. The processing and multiple memory system approaches suffer from a further problem. The processing theory of Roediger and Blaxton (1987) assumes that data-driven processes are not associated with conscious recollection, and the multiple memory system theory of Cohen and Squire (1980) assumes the same for procedural knowledge. However, in neither case is it made clear why this should be the case.

Summary

There has been considerable theoretical progress in the past 10 or 15 years, and much of this progress has stemmed from research with amnesic patients. The multi-store model, the levels-of-processing approach, and the theoretical distinction between semantic and episodic memory have all encountered problems when it comes to explaining amnesia. This has led to a re-evaluation of their usefulness as theoretical approaches to normal human memory. More recent theories, such as those based on the distinction between procedural and declarative knowledge or that between explicit and implicit memory, are more promising. These theories have described the characteristics of amnesia with reasonable success, and have altered thinking about normal memory functioning. It remains unclear whether amnesia is better regarded as involving impairment to one or more memory systems (e.g. declarative knowledge system), or whether the form of testing (e.g. explicit versus implicit) is the more crucial factor. At present, a number of different theories can account for most of the available findings. What is required is for researchers to make the existing theories more precise and detailed, and then to devise more informative experiments in which the predictions of these theories are different.

SUMMARY

Many of the most important theoretical advances during the 1980s arose out of the substantially increased amount of research on amnesia. While that research has proved fruitful, it has also proved to be complex. The first complication is whether there really is an "amnesic syndrome", in the sense of a high degree of similarity of memory problems in most sufferers from amnesia. The evidence increasingly suggests that the notion of an amnesic syndrome is an over-simplified one, and that damage to the temporal lobes, or to the diencephalon, or to the frontal cortex causes somewhat different patterns of impairment. This diversity may prove helpful to theoretical development in the future, but so far it has been regarded largely as adding unwelcome confusion.

One of the reasons why the study of amnesic patients has been so rewarding is that it has provided a different way of evaluating theories of normal memory. For example, the multi-store model is based on the view that there is a single short-term store and a single long-term memory store. This view appears woefully limited when one considers those amnesic patients who have a complex pattern of intact and impaired aspects of long-term or of short-term memory functioning. In similar fashion, it is somewhat disconcerting for advocates of the levels-of-processing approach to discover that most amnesic patients can process information in terms of its meaning, but that this deep processing has practically no beneficial effect on long-term memory. Finally, the distinction between episodic (autobiographical) and semantic (knowledge) memory has been very influential. However, the fact that the memory deficits in amnesia cannot really be accounted for in terms of the distinction has reduced its theoretical significance.

The most exciting upshot of investigating amnesic patients has been the way in which new theoretical distinctions have been introduced or developed. For example, the distinction between procedural (knowing how) and declarative (knowing that) knowledge is one that was originally put forward many years ago. However, the distinction has assumed an entirely new importance because the notion that amnesics have intact procedural learning but impaired declarative learning provides a reasonably accurate summary of the evidence. Even more strikingly, the distinction between implicit and explicit memory is one that has received its strongest support from the study of amnesic patients, and the distinction is now generally felt to be of major significance.

Why is the distinction between implicit and explicit memory so important? One of the main reasons is that it indicates some of the limits of traditional methods for assessing memory. Tests of free recall, cued recall, and recognition memory are all based squarely on explicit memory, in that the subjects are instructed that they should attempt to remember as much as possible of the previous list, prose passage, or whatever. While this may appear to be an entirely reasonable way of proceeding, the evidence from amnesic patients indicates that much information that cannot be accessed on direct tests of explicit memory is available on indirect tests of implicit memory. The implication that memory can be demonstrated by performance (implicit memory) in the absence of any conscious awareness of memory (explicit memory) means that conscious awareness is of much less importance to memory than had been thought previously.

FURTHER READING

Ellis, A.W. & Young, A.W. (1988). *Human cognitive neuro-psychology*. London: Lawrence Erlbaum Associates Ltd. (Chapter 10). They provide a detailed analysis of recent research on amnesia, and a critical evaluation of the major theories.

Parkin, A.J. (1987). *Memory and amnesia*. Oxford: Blackwell. This book provides a readable account of recent theories of memory, and of their relevance to amnesia research. It is particularly good in its demolition of the view that there is a homogeneous "amnesic syndrome".

Schachter, D.L. (1987). Implicit memory: History and current status. *Journal of Experimental Psychology: Learning, Memory, and Cognition, 13*, 501–518. The theoretical distinction between implicit and explicit memory is discussed thoroughly in relationship to evidence from both normal and amnesic populations.

Squire, L.R. (1987). *Memory and brain*. Oxford: Oxford University Press. A very detailed discussion of amnesia by one of the leading researchers in the area.

Chapter Seven

MENTAL REPRESENTATION

INTRODUCTION

Any chapter entitled "Mental Representation" needs to be subtitled with the comforting words "Don't Panic!," like Douglas Adams' (1984) inter-galactic hitch-hiker's guide. Exactly how we represent the world "inside our heads" has been one of *the* big questions in philosophy, psychology, and linguistics for centuries. Paivio (1986) has proposed that it is, perhaps, the most difficult problem in all of the sciences to solve. Of course, the expert's irritant is the student's horror. Ideas which are uncertain or controversial become transformed into monsters in textbooks, since their underpinnings are often unclear.

The importance of this chapter to the understanding of subsequent chapters cannot be understated. For example, in Chapter 8, when we talk about the organisation of knowledge, we will essentially be concerned with the way in which mental representations are structured or organised in long-term memory; in Chapters 9, 10, 11, and 12 we will be looking at the use of mental representations in language comprehension and thinking.

Figure 7.1 gives a rough idea of the main concerns of this chapter by showing the different distinctions that can be made between representations. At the highest level we can make a broad distinction between the external representations we use in everyday life and internal, mental representations. We will begin by considering the different categories into which external represent-ations can be split (e.g. pictures and words). This should give us a feel for some of the distinctions which are made between mental representations. Mental representations can be considered from two main perspectives: as symbolic representations and as distributed representations (the names are not well chosen because both involve symbols). We use the term perspective rather than distinction for this division because several theorists have argued that distributed representations are merely symbolic representations at a more detailed level. For most of the chapter we will concentrate on the more fully-elaborated and traditional symbolic view.

Outline of the different types of representations discussed in this chapter and the distinctions that can be made between them.

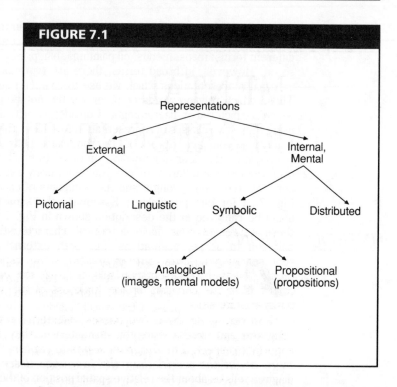

FIGURE 7.1

Symbolic mental representations can be divided into analogical and propositional representations. The prime example of an analogue representation is a visual image, although analogue representations come in several different forms (e.g. auditory images, mental models). Propositional representations are more abstract, language-like representations. A propositional represent-ation captures the concepts underlying a situation; for example, the concepts underlying the situation of a book being on a desk—this being notated as ON(BOOK, DESK). Initially, it is important to be clear that propositional representations are only *language-like*; they are *not* words but rather capture abstract, ideational content. The analogue–propositional distinction is controversial, as some theorists argue that images are not really a separate or special category of representation but can be reduced to propositional representations. This so-called imagery–propositional debate forms the backbone of the chapter, since it has been a major issue in modern cognitive psychology. But let us now turn to an expansion of what we mean by all of these terms: representation, mental representation, analogical, propositional, symbolic, and distributed.

What is an External Representation?

A representation is any notation or sign or set of symbols which "re-presents" something to us. That is, it stands for some thing in the absence of that thing; typically, that thing is an aspect of the external world or our imagination (i.e. our own internal world). What we have called an external representation comes in many different forms: maps, menus, oil paintings, blueprints, stories, and so on. However, in broad terms, there are two main classes of external representations which we use to characterise our world: Those which rely on words or other written notations and those which are pictorial or diagrammatic. Consider a practical example of using these two classes of representation to achieve the same end.

Imagine you have to work out the room allocations for a number of people on the floor of a building. In order to be clear about the occupancy of the different offices you might draw a diagram of the corridor, the rooms along it and the occupants of each room (see Fig. 7.2a for one possibility). Essentially the same information could be captured in the description shown in Fig. 7.2b. Both of these representations have a critical characteristic which is common to all representations (i.e. both external and mental representations). *They only represent some aspects of the world.* Neither representation tells us what the colour of the carpet is in the corridor, or the thickness of the walls or the position of fire exits.

However, while these two classes of external representation (diagrams and words) share this characteristic they differ in one important respect. *The diagram seems to capture "naturally" more about the world than the language description.* The diagram tells us about the relative spatial position of the rooms. For example, we know that Hank's room faces Kerry's room and that

FIGURE 7.2

An example of the two main types of external representations: (a) a pictorial representation of the occupants of several rooms along a corridor and (b) a linguistic description of the same information.

Mark 118	Kerry 119	Judith 120	Illona 121
Corridor			
Marc 125	Hank 124	Ingrid 123	No one 122

Mark is in Room 118 No one is in Room 122
Kerry is in Room 119 Ingrid is in Room 123
Judith is in Room 120 Hank is in Room 124
Illona is in Room 121 Marc is in Room 125

Ilona's room is at the opposite end of the corridor to Marc's room. The linguistic description would have to include more sentences to represent this information.

In respect of this characteristic, pictures and diagrams are said to be analogical. When two things have the same structure, but differ in other respects, we usually call them analogous. Pictures and diagrams are called analogical because their structure resembles that of the world; in this case, the spatial configuration of the rooms is the same as that of the actual rooms. In general, linguistic descriptions do not have this analogical property because, as the linguist Ferdinand de Saussure (1960) pointed out, the relationship between a linguistic sign and that which it represents is arbitrary. There is no inherent reason why small, furry, household pets should be labelled by the letters "c-a-t-s." If the English language had developed along other lines they could just as well have been called "sprogdorfs." Even onomatopoeic words (like "miaow") which seem to mimic the sound they represent are really arbitrary; as evidenced by their failure to be used in every language. In Irish, for example, the word for "miaow" is "meamhlach."

These, then, are the primary characteristics of external representations. As we shall see later, some of these characteristics are shared with internal, mental representations. However, before we move on to internal representations, consider several more detailed distinctions which can be made between these two classes of external representations.

Properties of Linguistic and Pictorial Representations

We have already seen that, unlike linguistic representations, pictorial representations tend to be analogical. This essential difference can be elaborated further in terms of the detailed properties manifested by both classes of external representation. Consider two representations, one which is in English and another which is pictorial, of the same thing: A book on a desk (see Fig. 7.3).

There are several ways in which these two representations differ (see Kosslyn, 1980; 1983). First, the linguistic representation is made up of discrete symbols. The words can be broken down into letters but these are the smallest units one can use. A quarter of the letter "B" is not a symbol that can be used in the language. However, a pictorial representation has no obvious smallest unit. It can be broken up in arbitrary ways and these parts can still be used as symbols (e.g. the corner of the table, half the spine of the book, or even just a single dot from the picture).

Second, a linguistic representation has explicit symbols to stand for the things it represents (e.g. words for the "book" and the "desk" and the relation between them, "on"). The picture does not

FIGURE 7.3

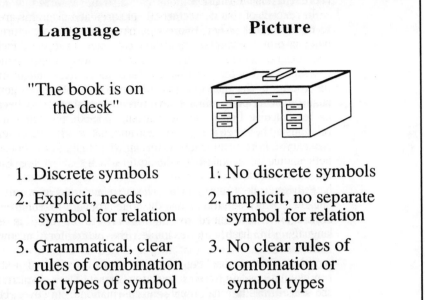

Language	Picture
"The book is on the desk"	
1. Discrete symbols	1. No discrete symbols
2. Explicit, needs symbol for relation	2. Implicit, no separate symbol for relation
3. Grammatical, clear rules of combination for types of symbol	3. No clear rules of combination or symbol types
4. Abstract	4. Concrete

Some of the major differences in the properties of two external representations of the same situation.

have distinct symbols for everything it represents. In particular, there is no explicit symbol for the relation between the book and the desk. "On-ness" is shown implicitly by the way the book and the desk are placed; that is, "on" cannot be represented by itself but only in a given context.

Third, in the linguistic representation the symbols are organised according to a set of rules (i.e. a grammar). One cannot say "on is table the book" and have a meaningful combination. These rules of combination exploit the fact that there are different classes of symbols (e.g. nouns and verbs). Pictures do not seem to have grammars of the same sort in that: (1) they do not have different distinct classes of symbol; and (2) if there are rules of combination they are much looser than those in a linguistic representation.

Fourth, the linguistic representation is *abstract* in that the information which it characterises could have been acquired from any form of perception (e.g. by touch, by vision) and bears no direct relationship to a given modality. In contrast, the picture is more concrete in the sense that, while the information it represents could have been acquired from a variety of perceptual sources, it is strongly associated with the visual modality.

From External to Internal, Mental Representations

Many of the characteristics and distinctions which we have made about external representations can also be asserted of mental representations. First, all mental representations only represent some aspect of the environment (whether that environment be the external world or our own imagined world). Second, the distinction between the two broad classes of representation (i.e. pictorial and linguistic representations) is paralleled by two classes of mental representations, the distinction between analogical and propositional representations. *Analogical representations* tend to be images which may be either visual, auditory, olfactory, tactile, or kinetic. *Propositional representations* are language-like representations which capture the ideational content of the mind, irrespective of the original modality in which that information was encountered.

Furthermore, the properties which we asserted of pictorial and linguistic representations can also be applied to their mental correlates. Analogical representations are nondiscrete, can represent things implicitly, have loose rules of combination and are concrete in the sense that they are tied to a particular sense modality. Propositional representations are discrete, explicit, are combined according to rules, and are abstract. They are abstract in the sense that they can represent information from any modality; but it should also be stressed that, unlike the words of a language, they usually refer to distinct and unambiguous entities. That is, the propositions for the example in Fig. 7.3—represented as ON(BOOK, DESK) to distinguish it from the linguistic representation—refers to a specific book and a specific desk and to a specific relationship of ON between them (see the section on "Mental Models", page 235, for an alternative conception of propositions).

In conclusion, the distinctions between external representations give some idea of those that can be made between analogical and propositional representations. In later sections, we will go into further detail about these differences and some of the debates which have surrounded these ideas. It should be pointed out that most of the discussion of analogical representations will concentrate on the most widely examined type of analogical representation; namely, visual images. To finish on a counterpoint, those readers who found some of the properties which distinguish the two forms of mental representation a shade unconvincing should be aware that some commentators have argued that it is next to impossible to distinguish totally between the two forms of representation (for good discussions see Boden, 1988, and P.J. Hayes, 1985).

Summary

Representations can be divided into external representations and internal, mental representations. External representations divide into two broad classes: those that are pictorial and those that are based on language. Both types of representation re-present some aspect of the world but they differ in the extent to which they parallel the structure of the world. Mental representations can be divided along similar lines; into analogical and propositional representations. Mental representations that are analogical (like visual images) are nondiscrete, organised by loose rules of combination, concrete, and modality-specific. Propositional representations are discrete, organised by strict rules, abstract, and uniquely referential.

IMAGERY AS ANALOGICAL REPRESENTATION

Historically, imagery has been "researched" for a long time. Over 2000 years ago, Aristotle regarded imagery as the main medium of thought. Furthermore, orators in ancient Greece used imagery-based, mnemonic techniques to memorise speeches (see Yates, 1966); a technique which is still sold today as an aid to improving one's memory. This interest in imagery carries through in a continuous line via Locke and Berkeley to the 19th-Century research of Galton (see Mandler & Mandler, 1964). Galton (1883) distributed a questionnaire among his eminent scientific colleagues, asking them to imagine their breakfast table that morning. Surprisingly enough, several reported no conscious mental imagery at all.

As in Galton's studies, much of this early research relied on the use of introspective evidence. During the behaviourist era, when introspection fell into disrepute and mental representations were in a sense "banned," research on imagery lay fallow for a number of years. However, with the advent of the information processing approach in cognitive psychology and the emergence of cognitive science, the study of mental representations once again became respectable. The motivation for this was that, for reasons of clarity and specificity, it was necessary to be representationally precise about the possible mechanisms which underlie human cognition. For example, Newell and Simon's (1972) pioneering work was wholly predicated on representing the basic mechanisms which underlay problem-solving behaviour. However, no sooner had researchers returned to examining imagery using new and more rigorous experimental methods, than further controversy arose.

The debate which emerged can be summarised in terms of two basic questions. First, exactly what is imagery? Commonsensically, it is easy to answer this: "It is what I have in my head when I imagine something." However, from the point of view of the scientific study of imagery this is not enough; we need to know about the exact nature of images, what basic mechanisms underlie their operation, and whether they differ in any significant fashion from propositional representations. Researchers have taken up one of two basic positions on the latter issue. Stated crudely, the first position maintains that images are picture-like representations which operate in their own special medium and are quite distinct from propositional representations. The opposing view maintains that ultimately images are not really a different form of represent-ation at all but are merely a superficially different way of rendering propositional information. In the next sub-section, we will consider some of the experimental evidence for the first of these views, before dealing with the controversy itself.

The second question is related to the first but is subtly different. It is concerned with whether imagery has any *functional significance*. That is, some have argued that imagery is a mere epiphenomenon; for example, that even though imagery may accompany thinking it is not necessary for it to occur; it does not play a causal role in thought. Consider another example of an epiphenomenon. The lights blinking on the outside of a computer indicate something about its internal operations but are not causally necessary for this activity to occur. If some of the bulbs were broken, the machine's internal computations would go on regard-less. Thus, the bulbs are epiphenomenal to the system's processing. In the same way, those who argue that imagery is epiphenomenal would say that if conscious images were suppressed cognition would go on operating as normal.

Paivio's Dual-Coding Theory

One of the catalytic contributions to the reawakening of research on imagery was the formulation by Allan Paivio of his dual-coding theory (see Paivio, 1971; 1979; 1983; 1986). The basic proposals of the theory are as follows:

- Two basic independent but interconnected coding or symbolic systems underlie human cognition: a nonverbal system and a verbal system.
- Both systems are specialised for encoding, organising, storing and retrieving distinct types of information.
- The nonverbal (or imagery) system is specialised for processing nonverbal objects and events (i.e. processing spatial and synchronous information) and thus enters into tasks such as the analysis of scenes and the generation of mental images.
- The verbal system is specialised for dealing with linguistic information and is largely implicated in the processing of language; because of the serial nature of language it is specialised for sequential processing.
- Both systems are further sub-divided into several sensori-motor sub-systems (visual, auditory, and haptic) (see Table 7.1).
- Both systems have basic representational units: *logogens* for the verbal system and *imagens* for the nonverbal system, which come in modality-specific versions in each of the sensorimotor sub-systems.
- The two symbolic systems are interconnected by referential links between logogens and imagens.

TABLE 7.1

The Relationship Between Symbolic and Sensorimotor Systems and Examples of the Types of Information Represented in Each Sub-system in Paivio's Dual-coding Theory

	Symbolic Systems	
Sensorimotor	*Verbal*	*Nonverbal*
Visual	Visual Words	Visual Objects
Auditory	Auditory Words	Environmental Sounds
Haptic	Writing Patterns	"Feel" of Objects
Taste	–	Taste Memories
Smell	–	Olfactory Memories

FIGURE 7.4

A schematic outline of the major components of dual-coding theory. The two main symbolic systems—the verbal and nonverbal systems—are connected to distinct input and output systems. Within the two systems are associative structures (involving logogens and imagens) that are linked to one another by referential connections. (Adapted with permission from Mental representations: A dual coding approach *by Allan Paivio, 1986, published by the Oxford University Press.)*

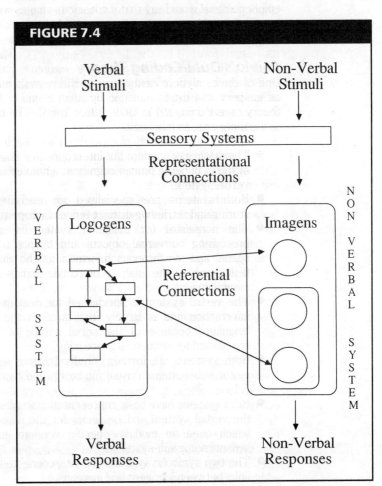

Stated in a simpler fashion, the essence of dual-coding theory is that there are two distinct systems for the representation and processing of information. A verbal system deals with linguistic information and stores it in an appropriate verbal form. A separate nonverbal system carries out image-based processing and representation (see Fig. 7.4). Each of these systems is further divided into sub-systems which process either verbal or nonverbal information in the different modalities (i.e. vision, audition, haptic, taste, smell). However, it should be noted that there are no corresponding representations for taste and smell in the verbal system (see Table 7.1).

Within a particular sub-system when a spoken word is processed, for example, it is identified by a logogen for the auditory sound of the word. The concept of a logogen comes from Morton's (1969; 1979) theories of word recognition. Paivio (1986, p. 66) characterises a *logogen* as a modality-specific unit that "can function as an integrated, informational structure or as a response generator": For example, there may be logogens for the word "snow." Logogens are modality-specific, in the sense that there are separate logogens for identifying the spoken sound "snow" and its visual form (i.e. the letters "s-n-o-w"). The corollary of logogens in the nonverbal system are *imagens*. Imagens are basic units which identify and represent images, in the different sensorimotor modalities. The important point to note about logogens and imagens is that they allow the theorist to posit a processing unit which identifies or represents a particular item (i.e. an image of a dog or a particular word) without having to specify the internal workings of this processing unit or the detailed representation of the item being processed. As we shall see later, this is one criticism of Paivio's work.

The verbal and nonverbal systems communicate in a functional fashion via relations between imagens and logogens. The simplest case of such a relation is the referential link between an object and its name. That is, if you see a visual object (e.g. a dog runs by) it would be recognised by an imagen and a link between this imagen and an auditory logogen for the word "dog" may bring the word "dog" to mind. Thus, the links between these basic units constitute the fundamental ways in which the sub-parts of the two symbolic systems are interconnected.

Predictions and Evidence from Dual-coding Theory

Evidence for dual-coding theory has been provided in a number of distinct task areas: for instance, in semantic memory tasks and episodic memory tasks (see Chapters 6 and 8 for definitions), neuropsychological studies, and problem solving situations. These experiments typically try to test two main predictions: (1) that the two symbolic systems operate in an independent fashion in some circumstances; and (2) that the two symbolic systems produce additive effects in other circumstances.

For example, consider an experiment where subjects are given different types of materials to memorise (e.g. words versus pictures) and we measure the amount they recall at a later stage. When memory processes are predicted to involve one symbolic system *or* the other, the effects found should reflect the operation of a single system; in the sense that a specific effect found for one system should differ markedly from that found in the other. That is, the systems should appear to be independent. Alternatively, where a memory task is predicted to involve both systems, there should be an additive effect on subjects' ability to remember the materials. That is, because both systems are, in some sense, working together, their performance should be better than when a single system is involved. Consider three classic cases from memory experiments designed to test the theory: the differences between recalling pictures and words, the effects of word imaging and concreteness, and repetition effects.

Effects of Dual Codes on Free Recall

Consider the experimental situation where subjects are given either a set of pictures or a list of words to memorise. If the pictures were of common objects then subjects would be likely to name them spontaneously during the memorising part of the experiment (see Paivio, 1971). Thus, both systems are brought into play. In contrast, the words would be likely to be memorised in a purely verbal fashion (assuming that subjects would not spontaneously image the objects referred to by the words). Hence, there should be additive effects in recall performance for pictures, which should be absent for words, because they would be memorised in terms of two codes rather than just one. This is typically what is found, with pictures being remembered in both free-recall and recognition tasks more readily than words (Paivio, 1971). In fact, pictures are recalled so much more easily than words that Paivio has proposed that the image code is mnemonically superior to the verbal code, although exactly why this should be so is not clear.

These additive effects are not only found between pictures and words. Initial results suggested that they could also be found between different classes of words. Some words are more concrete and evoke images more readily than other words. If words are concrete (in the sense of denoting things which can be perceived by one of the sense modalities) rather than abstract, they appear to be retrieved more easily (see Paivio, Yuille & Madigan, 1968, for evidence of this). As in the case of the picture-word differences, words which are rated as being high in their image-evoking value or concreteness (or both) are likely to be encoded using two codes rather than just one (for reviews of the results of item-memory tasks see Cornoldi & Paivio, 1982; Richardson, 1980). So again there seems to be an additive contribution to performance when both systems are involved in the task.

It should be noted that there has been some controversy over this dual-code explanation of recall differences for concrete and abstract words. Part of the problem is that the results are of a correlational nature; they merely show that the imagibility/concreteness of words correlates with good recall performance. They do not show a causal connection between concreteness and recall. We can test for such a causal connection by varying the instructions given to subjects when they are memorising the words. If one uses interactive-imagery instructions (e.g. form images depicting objects interacting in some way), then it is typically found that performance is improved for concrete materials but not for abstract materials (see Richardson, 1980). This is perfectly consistent with dual-code theory because the imagery instructions should invoke the use of both encoding systems for the concrete words but not for the abstract words.

Unfortunately, similar instructions which do not involve imaging have the same effect; verbal mediation instructions (e.g. form short phrases including the list of items) result in concrete materials being recalled more readily than abstract materials. On the basis of these results, Bower (1970; 1972) proposed that interactive imagery and verbal mediation instructions were both effective in that they increased the organisation and cohesion of the to-be-remembered information. To test this hypothesis, Bower presented subjects with pairs of concrete words using three different types of instructions for different groups: interactive-imagery instructions, separation-imagery instructions (i.e. construct an image of two objects separated in space), or instructions to memorise by rote. On a subsequent cued-recall task, the interactive-imagery subjects performed much better than the separation-imagery subjects, who in turn performed no better than subjects instructed to use rote memorisation. In other words, interactive-imagery instructions are effective because they enhance relational organisation. So, in terms of the recall differences between concrete and abstract words, there are some difficulties for Paivio's theory. However, we should point out that Paivio has gone some way towards accounting for these results by including organisational assumptions within each of his symbolic systems, which account for differences between interactive-imagery and separation-imagery instructions (see Paivio, 1986, Chapters 4 and 8). However, in general, the debate on the role of imagery in the recall of concrete and abstract words is not yet fully resolved. Recently, Marschark, Richman, Yuille, and Hunt (1987) have proposed an account which rejects the proposal that imaginal codes are stored in long-term memory, but rather argues that verbal and imaginal processing systems operate on a more generic, conceptual memory.

Further evidence for the additivity and functional independence of the two systems comes from other studies on free recall (Paivio, 1975; Paivio & Csapo, 1973). In these experiments, subjects were shown a series of concrete nouns and were asked to either image to the presented noun or to pronounce it. In the five-second interval between the presentation of items they were asked to rate the difficulty of imaging or pronouncing the word. In one experimental manipulation, subjects were repeatedly presented with a given word. In some cases, the repetition encouraged dual coding, in that subjects had to image it on one occurrence and pronounce it on the next. In other cases, the repetition was predicted to lead to continued encoding in a single code, as subjects had to either image the word again or pronounce it again. After subjects had carried out this stage of the experiment they were, without prior warning, asked to recall the presented words.

Several interesting results were found which supported dual-coding theory. First, the probability of imaged words being recalled was twice as high as that for pronounced words, indicating the superiority of nonverbal codes in recall. Second, the imagery-instructions raised the level of recall to the same high level which is normally seen for the encoding of pictures under comparable conditions. Third, in the conditions which predicted dual coding, there was an additive effect on recall relative to recall levels calculated for once-presented items that had been imaged or pronounced. Fourth, in contrast to these results, when a repeated word was encoded in the same way on each presentation, the massed repetitions did not produce similar additive effects (see Fig. 7.5).

The relative proportions of correct responses when subjects repeatedly pronounced or imaged pictures or words in a free recall task (adapted from Paivio & Csapo, 1973).

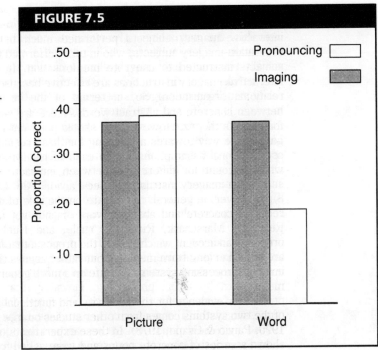

FIGURE 7.5

Interference Within a Single System

Paivio's theory sees the routes which perception and imagery follow to be basically the same. For example, in talking about the nonverbal system he says that it is responsible both for the cognitive task of forming visual images and the perceptual task of scene-analysis. Therefore, any findings which demonstrate interference between perceptual and imagery tasks are a further source of evidence for the theory. That is, if performance on a perceptual task is disrupted by carrying out an imagery task, and vice versa, it seems likely that both tasks are making use of the same resources or processing components. Such interference has been found on a regular basis. For example, Segal and Fusella (1970) asked subjects to form both visual and auditory images and then asked them to perform a visual or auditory detection task. They found that auditory images interfered more with the detection of auditory signals and visual images interfered more with visual detection. Since there was some interference in all conditions it seems reasonable to conclude that there is a generalised effect of mental imagery upon perceptual sensitivity in addition to a large modality-specific effect.

However, it is not enough simply to demonstrate interference. One needs to pin-point the specific processes which are responsible for the interference and also, if possible, to show where perceptual and image-based processing diverge into their own distinct processes. More detailed evidence of this sort has been found in a task used by Baddeley, Grant, Wight, and Thomson (1975). In this experiment, subjects were played an auditory message describing the locations of digits within a matrix with a view to trying to reproduce the matrix later. The message was either hard or easy to visualise. The interfering task involved a pursuit rotor (i.e. visually tracking a light moving along a circular track). While this task results in a distinct type of interference—performance on easily-visualised messages is retarded, while the nonvisualisable message is unaffected—the interference is not due specifically to the perceptual processes involved in vision. Rather, Baddeley and Lieberman (1980) have shown that if the concurrent task is specifically visual (e.g. the judgement of brightness) rather than visual and spatial (as the pursuit rotor seems to be), then the interference effects disappear. Similarly, when the concurrent task is purely spatial (i.e. when blindfolded subjects were asked to point at a moving pendulum on the basis of auditory feedback), the pattern of interference found reproduces the effects found in the original Baddeley et al. experiment. In summary, it appears that the recall of visualisable (or easily-imagined) messages of the kind used in these experiments is interfered with by spatial processing rather than by visual processing, indicating that these spatial processes are somehow shared by perceptual and image-based processing within the nonverbal system (see Logie & Baddeley, 1990, for a review of more recent research on this topic).

In a sense, this issue of interference belies a deeper assumption; namely that visual imagery involves visual rather than spatial representations. It is argued that if visual imagery involves visual representations then these representations will be shared with the visual system and hence interference will occur. However, recently Farah, Hammond, Levine, and Calvanio (1988) have said that it is a mistake to argue that imagery is either visual *or* spatial. Rather they have shown, using neuropsychological evidence, that imagery is both visual and spatial and taps into distinct visual and spatial representations.

Neuropsychological Evidence

Paivio also makes some claims about the localisation of the two symbolic systems within the brain which find support from the neuropsychological evidence. For instance, for most people the left hemisphere is implicated in tasks which involve the processing of verbal material. In contrast, the right hemisphere tends to be used in tasks which are of a nonverbal nature (e.g. face identification, memory for faces, and recognising nonverbal sounds). Furthermore, within each hemisphere there seems to be some localisation for the sensorimotor sub-systems: visual, auditory, and tactile (see Cohen, 1983). Although dual-coding theory posits distinct symbolic systems, Paivio does not maintain that these distinct systems reside in distinct hemispheres, although the systems are localised to some extent.

There is some evidence for localisation differences on concrete and abstract words, which disrupt a simple left-right division. Word recognition studies, using tachistoscopes, have shown that there are hemispheric differences in the processing of concrete and abstract words (see Paivio, 1986, Chapter 12). Typically, abstract words which are presented to the right visual field, and hence are processed by the left hemisphere, are recognised more often than those presented to the left visual field (i.e. processed by the right hemisphere). However, concrete words are recognised equally well irrespective of the visual field (and hence the hemisphere) to which they are presented. It should be pointed out that the findings have not been consistent (Boles, 1983), although there is a tendency for the performance asymmetries to be less consistent for concrete than for abstract words. Converging evidence also comes from so-called deep-dyslexic patients, who have widespread lesions in the left hemisphere. Generally, they have greater difficulty reading abstract low-imagery words than concrete high-imagery words (see Coltheart, Patterson, & Marshall, 1980; Paivio & te Linde, 1982). We shall see later, in the presentation of Kosslyn's theory, that some more recent evidence presents a clearer picture for what might be happening in both hemispheres (see Farah, 1984).

Intermediate Summary

In conclusion, several sources of evidence support Paivio's proposals that there are two separate but interdependent symbolic systems. First, the theory accounts for the picture–word and concrete–abstract word differences in free recall studies, although it is not the only possible explanation of some of the latter results. The interference which dual-coding theory predicts between perceptual and image-based processes within the nonverbal system has been found, although its locus in the visual modality seems to lie in spatial processing. Finally, there is some evidence for the localisation of different symbolic systems within different parts of the cerebral hemispheres. So, on the issue of the broad distinctions between verbal and nonverbal processing in the brain, dual-coding theory is moderately successful. However, in later sections we will see that the picture can be construed in a more complicated fashion. More immediately, in the next sub-section we will look at further evidence which approaches imagery from a slightly different but equally informative angle.

The Structure of Images: Evidence

If we stand back from the details of Paivio's theory it is immediately clear that it lacks something which the ordinary person in the street would want to know about imagery: Namely, what are images? More precisely, "What are the special properties of images which distinguish them from other modes of conscious thought?," "How are images represented before the mind's eye?," and "What sorts of operations can one do with images?" Other researchers, who are concerned with the structure of imagery per se, have attempted to answer some of these questions. Two sets of experiments are particularly famous. First, experiments on *mental rotation* in which people are given tasks which seem to demand the dynamic transformation of visual images. Second, experiments on *image scanning* in which people have to scan an image moving across an imaged map.

Mental Rotation

In a series of experiments the mental rotation of a variety of imaged objects has been examined (e.g. Cooper, 1975; Cooper & Podgorny, 1976; Cooper & Shepard, 1973; Shepard, 1978 for a review; Shepard & Metzler, 1971). For example, Cooper and Shepard presented subjects with alphanumeric items in either their normal form or in reversed, mirror-image form (see Fig. 7.6). In the experiment subjects were asked to judge whether a test figure was the normal or reversed version of the standard figure. The test figures were presented in a number of different orientations (see Fig. 7.6). In general, it was found that the farther the test figure was rotated from the upright standard figure, the more time subjects took to make their decisions (see Fig. 7.7). These experiments have been carried out on a variety of different objects, indicating that there was some generality to the findings (e.g. digits, letters, or block-like forms have been used).

The impression we get from these experiments is that visual images have all the attributes of actual objects in the world. That is, that they take up some form of mental space in the same way that

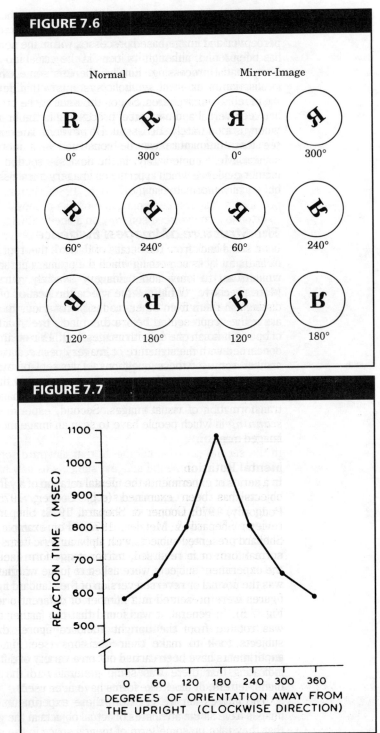

FIGURE 7.6

The different degrees of rotation performed on the materials in Cooper & Shepard (1973) for normal letters (on the left) and mirror-imaged letters (on the right).

Normal   Mirror-Image

0°   300°   0°   300°

60°   240°   60°   240°

120°   180°   120°   180°

FIGURE 7.7

The mean time to decide whether a visual stimulus was in the normal or mirror-image version as a function of orientation. Data from Cooper & Shepard (1973).

REACTION TIME (MSEC)

1100
1000
900
800
700
600
500

0   60   120   180   240   300   360

DEGREES OF ORIENTATION AWAY FROM THE UPRIGHT (CLOCKWISE DIRECTION) physical objects take up physical space in the world, and that these objects are mentally moved or rotated in the same way that objects in the world are manipulated. In short, the image seems to be some "quasi-spatial simulacrum of the 3-D object" (see Boden, 1988). This view, however, is not wholly justified as there are some conditions under which mental rotation effects differ from physical rotation. If the imagined object becomes more complex subjects are less able to make correct judgements about its appearance when rotated (Rock, 1973). Such a problem would not arise in the physical rotation of a physical object.

Similarly, people's capacity to imagine rotated objects (even simple cubes) depends crucially on the structural description of the object they adopt implicitly (Boden, 1988; Hinton, 1979). Hinton provides a practical demonstration of this proposal. You are asked to imagine a cube placed squarely on a shelf with its base level with your eyes. Imagine taking hold of the bottom corner that is nearest your left hand with your left hand, and the top corner that is furthest away from your left hand with your right hand, taking the cube from the shelf and holding it so that your right hand is vertically above your left. What will be the location of the remaining corners? Most subjects tend to reply that they will form a square along the "equator" of the cube. In fact, the middle edge of the cube is not horizontal but forms a zig zag. This occurs because one does not take the image of the cube (as it is in reality) and rotate it, rather one is working off some less elaborated, structural description. Inconsistencies like this have fuelled the controversy which has arisen between propositional and imagery theorists, which we will consider in a later section.

Image Scanning
In the second set of experiments that illustrate something of the possible nature of mental images, subjects usually have to scan an imaged map mentally (e.g. Kosslyn, Ball, & Reiser, 1978). Typically, in these experiments subjects are given a fictitious map of an island with landmarks indicated by Xs (see Fig. 7.8 for an example). Initially, subjects spend some time memorising the map, until they can reproduce it accurately as a drawing. In the crucial stage of the experiment, they are then given the name of an object, and are asked to image the map and focus on that object. Five seconds later, a second object is named and subjects are instructed to scan from the first object to the second object by imaging a flying black dot. Since the objects on the map have been placed at different distances from one another, it is possible to determine whether the time taken to scan from one object on the map to another is related to the actual distance on the map between these two points. Using experimental procedures of this type, it has been found repeatedly that the scanning time is related linearly to the actual distance between points on the map; that is, the scanning time increases proportionately with the actual distance between

two points. This result lends support to the view that images have special, spatial properties which are analogous to those of objects and activities in the world.

However, there is a worry about these results; we will elaborate in detail later. It is expressed succinctly by Baddeley (1986, p. 130) when he says that: "I have a nagging concern that, implicitly, much of the experimental work in this field consists of instructing the subject to behave as if he were seeing something in the outside world . . . Whether such results tell us how the system works, or indeed tell us much about the phenomenology, I am as yet uncertain."

FIGURE 7.8

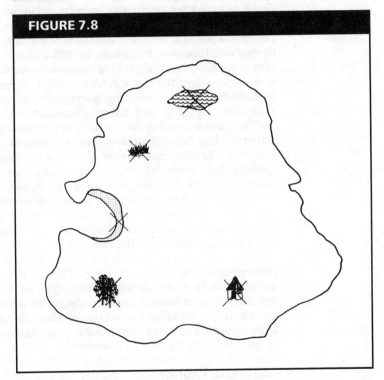

An example of the materials used in mental scanning experiments. Subjects had to image a black dot moving from one point on the map (indicated by the x-ed features) to another. (Adapted from Ghosts in the mind's machine; Creating and using images in the brain *by Stephen Kosslyn, by permission of the author and the publisher, W.W. Norton & Company Inc. Copyright 1983 by Stephen M. Kosslyn.)*

Summary

Images are one form of analogical, mental representation. In the main, most of the research and theory on imagery has focused on visual imagery rather than on, for example, auditory or olfactory imagery. Allan Paivio has maintained, in his dual-coding theory, that there are two distinct symbolic systems; a verbal, linguistically based system and a nonverbal, image-based system. There is considerable evidence from a variety of task domains for the view that the two systems are separate (e.g. memory and interference studies). Other research, on mental rotation and mental scanning, has concentrated more on the exact nature of images rather than on distinguishing between image and linguistic codes. This research has provided evidence which supports the view that visual images have special, analogue properties. However, this proposal has been questioned by some researchers.

PROPOSITIONAL REPRESENTATIONS

As we saw earlier, in cognitive psychology, propositional representations are considered to be explicit, discrete, abstract entities which represent the ideational content of the mind. They represent conceptual objects and relations in a form which is not specific to any language (whether it be Russian, Serbo-Croatian, or Urdu) or to any modality (whether it be vision, audition, olfaction, or touch). Thus, they constitute a universal, amodal, *mentalese*, the basic code in which all cognitive activities are proposed to be carried out. However, this leaves us with a puzzle. If propositional representations are abstract, language-non-specific, and amodal, how do we characterise them? Well, when theorists want to be explicit about the use of propositional representations they use aspects of a logical system called the *predicate calculus*.

One can imagine that the contents of the mind might be object-like entities that are related together in various ways by conceptual relations. The predicate calculus provides a convenient notation for realising these intuitions; the links or relations are represented as *predicates* and the object-entities as *arguments* of these predicates. By definition, a predicate here is anything which takes an argument or a number of arguments. The terminology sounds daunting but the idea is relatively simple. If I want to express the idea that "the book is on the table"; then the link or relationship between the book and the table is represented by the predicate ON (where the capitals represent the notion that we are dealing with the mental content of ON and not the word "on"). The arguments that the ON predicate links are the conceptual entities, the BOOK and the TABLE. In order to indicate that ON takes these two arguments, the objects are usually bracketed in the following manner:

ON (BOOK, TABLE)

Predicates can take any number of arguments; so, the sentence "Mary hit John with the stick and the stick was hard" can be notated as follows:

HIT(MARY, JOHN, STICK) & HARD(STICK)

The predicates HIT and HARD are first-order predicates; that is, they take object constants as their arguments. Whenever one has a predicate and a number of arguments combined in this fashion the whole form is called a proposition, as is the combination of a number of such forms (i.e. the whole of the expression just discussed is also a proposition).

There are also second-order predicates that take propositions as their arguments. So, in characterising the sentence "Mary hit John with the stick and he was hurt" we can use the second-order predicate CAUSE to link the two other propositions:

CAUSE [HIT(MARY, JOHN, STICK),
        HURT (MARY, JOHN)]

Cognitive psychologists have used these notations to express *mental, propositional representations*. However, psychologists do not use all the strictures employed by logicians using the predicate calculus. In logic, a proposition can be either true or false and this has important consequences for logical systems. Most psychologists are not overly concerned with the formal properties of propositions (one important exception is the work on deductive reasoning in Chapter 12). In short, typically, theorists merely use the notion that ideational content can be stated in terms of predicates taking one or more arguments.

In an empirical context, the basic properties of propositions are rarely tested directly but are simply assumed. Their characteristics are, however, tested at a more gross level when they are combined to represent knowledge. In Chapter 8, on the organisation of knowledge, we shall look at a variety of the uses to which propositional representations are put; in semantic networks and schemata (see e.g. Collins & Quillian, 1969; Rumelhart & Ortony, 1977). Finally, in practical terms propositional representations are very useful for computational modelling. The predicate calculus can be implemented very easily in modern artificial intelligence computing languages like LISP (Steele, 1984; Winston & Horn, 1988) or PROLOG (Clocksin & Mellish, 1981; Eisenstadt, 1988). This has allowed researchers to be very precise about theories based on propositional representations and to construct and run computer models of cognitive processes.

Summary
Propositional representations are an abstract mentalese which can represent ideational content irrespective of its original source in any language or any of the senses. Empirically, propositional representations are usually only examined when they are supposed to underlie complex knowledge structures in cognition. These representations are typically expressed using aspects of the predicate calculus. The predicate calculus is a logical system which is a specialisation of another logical system called the propositional calculus.

THE IMAGERY–PROPOSITIONAL DEBATE I

Thus far we have attempted to consider images and propositions in an equal light. However, in the last two decades one of the major issues in cognitive psychology has been whether there is any need to postulate images at all; therefore, some have proposed that cognition should only be analysed in terms of propositions. The main exponent of this position, Zenon Pylyshyn, has argued his point in two distinct waves. In this section we look at his first wave of criticisms made in the early 1970s, before considering how they were answered by imagery theorists. Later we will deal with his more recent criticisms.

Pylyshyn's First Wave of Criticisms

Pylyshyn's (1973; 1979) first wave of arguments were a mixture of a mild attack on the vagueness of the concept of imagery and the more trenchant criticism that images are epiphenomenal. In his 1973 paper, entitled *What the mind's eye tells the mind's brain*, he pointed out that imagery researchers assumed that images were picture-like entities without realising the inappropriateness of this metaphor. For instance, he argued, when we forget parts of an image, we forget meaningful parts, not random parts as would be the case if an image was like a picture (e.g. a corner of a picture which does not represent a meaningful part can be torn off). Furthermore, if images were like pictures then one needs a "mind's eye" to perceive them and this introduces an infinite regress. If one asks "What does this mind's eye see?" the most obvious answer is "Another image", but this raises the question we started out with again "What sees this image?", and so on. In short, these criticisms indicate that, although the proposal that images are picture-like is intuitively plausible, as a theory of imagery it is seriously flawed and under-specified.

More deeply, Pylyshyn also attempted to argue that one could not escape positing a propositional code in which all processing, be it verbal or nonverbal, was carried out. He pointed out that since verbal and nonverbal codes are in different formats one has to specify how one code can be related to the other. Pylyshyn argued that one required a third code which intervened between the other two and that this common code or interlingua should be propositional. This echoes the general argument that since we can process information in different forms and can usually pass from one form of information to another, there must be a basic mentalese which underlies all cognitive activity.

Even the strongest evidence from mental rotation studies can be re-interpreted within this propositional framework. For example, a propositional representation could represent the same object in several different orientations. A letter in its upright orientation could be represented propositionally by predicates which specify the features of the letter that are at the top, bottom, left, and right; for the letter "A" one could have the proposition TOP(35°-VERTEX, LETTER-A) to indicate that the pointed feature is the top of the letter A. So when one has to rotate the object by 180° a set of processes switch the top to be the bottom and the bottom to be the top. It could be argued that this would not lead to the predicted differences in rotation times since the simple processes which change the orientation predicates (i.e. top, bottom, 5° tilt) will carry out any rotation (whether it be of 180° or 30°) in the same number of simple steps. But an extra assumption can be added to handle this objection. A propositional theorist could argue that while rotation could be done in one step by a propositional system, it is often important to simulate how the object would actually rotate in space; e.g. one might simulate, step by step, the arc of a bouncing ball to see if it will clear an object in its path. Similarly, the propositional operators might change the orientation predicates in a step-by-step fashion (e.g. from top to 30° tilt, from 30° tilt to 60° tilt and so on until 150° is changed to bottom), thus leading to the same predictions as the imagery account.

This is an instance of the general argument (made by Anderson, 1978, p.263) that it is impossible to determine unequivocally the format of a representation used in any cognitive task, because any theory which proposes a certain representation in combination with a certain set of processes can be mimicked by another theory using a different representation and a different set of processes.

Counter-arguments to the First Wave

Several counter-arguments to Pylyshyn's initial criticisms were put forward (see e.g. Kosslyn, 1980; 1981). The nub of these counter-arguments was that the picture metaphor of imagery was made of straw and that few researchers subscribed to it. Images are not pictures but are quasi-spatial entities generated from some store of perceptual experience in long-term memory.

The proposal that an interlingua was needed to move from one code to another was countered by the argument that this leads to an infinite regress. That is, if one needs a propositional code to intervene between a verbal and nonverbal code then surely one also needs another code to come between the verbal code and the propositional code, and so on (see Anderson, 1978).

The argument that all imagery phenomena can be accounted for by propositional accounts is perhaps the hardest to answer. This places the onus of proof on imagery theorists to specify how images could operate without recourse to mental eyes and to specify the distinctive or special properties of imagery. This, as we shall see in the next section, is exactly what Stephen Kosslyn attempted to do in his theory. However, a meta-theoretical point can also be made about the nature of this reduction-to-propositions argument. Theories are not only to be evaluated in terms of the amount of evidence they can take into account. They must also be evaluated in terms of their *suggestiveness* or *generativity*; that is, the extent to which they appear "naturally" to suggest a set of novel, untested phenomena. For instance, the tortuous explanation of the rotation studies in propositional terms accounts for the data but it has a very *ad hoc* ring to it. The propositional theory, unlike the imagery theory, does not *suggest* that people might carry out mental rotation but it can explain it after the fact. So, it should be noted that even poorly developed imagery theories can be more *generative* than propositional theories.

Summary

In the 1970s several arguments were advanced (mainly by Zenon Pylyshyn), which maintained that the concept of "imagery as pictures" was fundamentally flawed and that all the phenomena attributed to imagery were best accounted for within a purely propositional framework. Many of these initial arguments were ill-formed but they did spur investigators of imagery to be more specific about the terms and theories they proposed.

KOSSLYN'S THEORY AND COMPUTATIONAL MODEL OF IMAGERY

Throughout the 1970s and early 1980s Stephen Kosslyn and his associates tested and developed a theory which can be viewed as a response to the sorts of criticisms raised by Pylyshyn. The basic position taken by Kosslyn was that imagery is worth examining as a separate construct because, although it may partly be based on propositional representations, it has its own privileged properties which deserve investigation.

The Theory and Model

Kosslyn's (Kosslyn, 1980; 1981; 1983; Kosslyn & Shwartz, 1977) theory, which has been specified in a computational model, can be summarised roughly as follows (see Fig. 7.9):

- Visual images are represented in a special, spatial medium.
- The spatial medium has four essential properties: (i) it functions as a space, with limited extent, it has a specified shape and a capacity to depict spatial relations; (ii) its area of highest resolution is at its centre; (iii) the medium has a grain that obscures details on "small" images; (iv) once the image is generated in the medium it begins to fade.
- Long-term memory contains two forms of data structures: image files and propositional files. Image files contain stored information about how images are represented in the spatial medium and have an analogical format. Propositional files contain information about the parts of objects, how these parts are related to one another and are in a propositional format. Propositional files and image files are often linked together.
- A variety of processes use image files, propositional files and the spatial medium in order to generate, interpret, and transform images.

Consider the basic task of generating an image of a duck. The theory maintains that several structures and processes are involved: the spatial medium in which the duck is to be represented, the propositional and image files which store the knowledge about the duck, and the processes which generate the image in the medium from these files.

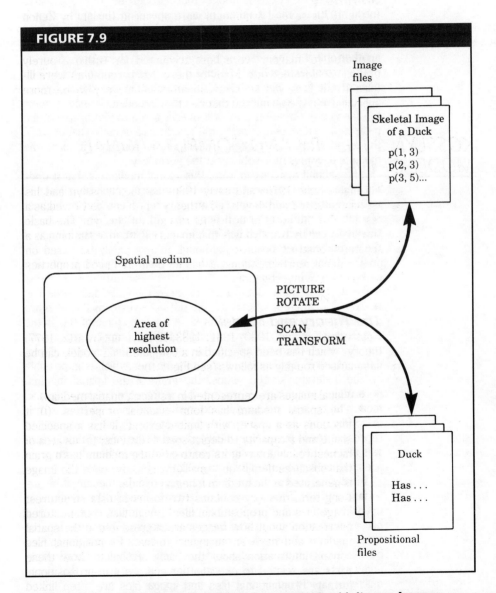

FIGURE 7.9

Image files

Skeletal Image of a Duck

p(1, 3)
p(2, 3)
p(3, 5)...

Spatial medium

Area of highest resolution

PICTURE ROTATE

SCAN TRANSFORM

Duck

Has . . .
Has . . .

Propositional files

A schematic diagram of Kosslyn's computational model of imagery. Images are constructed and manipulated (using the PICTURE ROTATE, SCAN, and TRANSFORM processes) in the highest area of resolution in the spatial medium using the information stored in image files and propositional files in long-term memory.

The Spatial Medium

The spatial medium in which the duck is to be represented is modelled as a cathode-ray tube in Kosslyn's computational model (see Kosslyn & Shwartz, 1977). That is, the medium has a surface that can be divided up into dots or pixels, each of which can be characterised by co-ordinates indicating where a dot is on the screen. The theory mentions four properties of this spatial medium. First, that it functions as a space, in the sense that it preserves the spatial relations of the objects it represents. So if I represent an object in the extreme top left of this space and another object in the extreme bottom left, then the relative position of the two objects will be preserved (i.e. the second object will be beneath the first object). The spatial medium is also like a physical space in that it has a limited extent and is bounded. If images move too far in any direction they will overflow the medium, like a film projected on a screen. Finally, the space has a definite shape; while the central area of highest resolution is roughly circular, the medium becomes more oblong at the periphery.

The second main attribute of this spatial medium is that it does not necessarily represent images at a uniform resolution. Rather, at the centre of the medium, an image is represented at its highest resolution. From there out it begins to get fuzzier. This is akin to the visual field which also has its highest resolution at the centre of the scene being viewed.

Third, the medium has a grain. The grain of a photograph or a cathode-ray tube refers to the size of the basic dots of colour that make it up. If these dots are very large then the detail one can represent is limited, whereas if the dots are very small a lot more detailed images can be represented. A good example of this is the comparison between a conventional Teletype computer screen and the Apple Macintosh screen. The latter has the grain to depict different letter fonts and pictures in a manner which is impossible on the Teletype screen. Thus, the grain of the spatial medium determines what can and cannot be represented clearly. It also means that when an image is reduced in size then parts of it may disappear, because the grain may not be detailed enough to represent these parts. Specifically, a part of the larger image which was represented by a configuration of dots may, when the image is reduced, be represented by a single dot.

Finally, as soon as an image is generated in the medium it begins to fade and so, if the image is to be maintained in the medium, it needs to be regenerated or refreshed. A similar type of fading occurs with after-images in the visual system. When we look at bright lights and then close our eyes, we see after-images caused by the over-stimulation of our retinal cells. Although these after-images are not the same as visual images, they have this same quality of rapidly fading after they first appear.

Image and Propositional Files

Returning to our duck, we have a fair idea of where she is represented but not how we come to represent her. In Kosslyn's computational model it is assumed that we have image files which represent the co-ordinates of dot-like points in the spatial medium. These image files can represent a whole object or various parts of an object. Specifically, some image files characterise a *skeletal image* which depicts the basic shape of the object, but lacks many of its details. These detailed parts of images may be represented in other image files, for reasons which will become apparent later. In terms of our example, the image in Fig. 7.10a is a rough, skeletal image of the duck, and Fig. 7.10b shows the addition of one of her parts (i.e. the wings).

The propositional files list the properties of ducks (e.g. HAS–WINGS, HAS–FEET) and the relationships between these properties and a "foundation part" of the duck (i.e. its body). The *foundation part* is that part which is central to the representation of the object and will be linked to the skeletal image file for the object. The propositional file for the duck might, thus, contain entries which relate the wing parts of the duck to the foundation part: For example, WINGS LOCATION ON–EITHER–SIDE BODY, indicating that the wings are on either side of the body. Each of these parts would have a corresponding image file which contains the basic material for constructing the image of a given part in the spatial medium. Propositional files also contain more information about the rough size category of the object (e.g. very small, small, large, enormous) and information about superordinate categories of the objects (e.g. in the case of the duck, bird would be the most likely superordinate; see Kosslyn, 1980; 1983, for details; and Chapter 8).

The information in the propositional files is connected to the image files. So, for example, the foundation part in the propositional file has a link or pointer to the image file which contains the skeletal image of the object. Similarly, the detailed parts of the object have links to image files containing images of these parts. For example, the wings-part is linked to an image file containing co-ordinate information for the construction of an image of a wing.

Imaging Processes

Finally, when one is asked to image a duck, several processes go to work using various propositional and image files to generate an image of the duck in the spatial medium. In the model, the main process is called IMAGE and it breaks down into three sub-processes: PICTURE, FIND, and PUT. When asked to image, the IMAGE process first checks to see whether the object (i.e. the duck) mentioned in the instructions has, in its propositional-file definition, a reference to a skeletal-image file. If such a file is present then the PICTURE process takes the information about the co-ordinates of the image and represents it in the spatial medium (see Fig. 7.10). Unless the location or size of the image is specified (e.g. image a giant duck) the image is generated in that part of the spatial medium which has the highest resolution and at a size which fills the region of highest resolution. The PUT process directs the PICTURE process to place the remaining image-parts at the appropriate locations on the skeletal image. For example, PUT might use the propositional information about the location of the wings to add them to the side of the skeletal image of the body. PUT, however, must use FIND to locate the objects or parts already in the image to which the new, to-be-imaged parts can be related. When the appropriate size and location of the wings are known they are added to the image (see Fig. 7.10b).

In cases where more specific instructions are given, like "Does the duck have a rounded beak?" or "Image a fly on the tip of the duck's wing, up close", or "Rotate the duck 180°", further processes called SCAN, LOOKFOR, PAN, ZOOM, and ROTATE operate on the image (see Kosslyn, 1983, Chapter 7; Kosslyn, 1980, for more details). The names of these processes are self-explanatory and each of them has been modelled as a set of specified procedures in the model that, for instance, SCAN and ROTATE images. These processes are used to explain the results of the mental scanning and mental rotation studies.

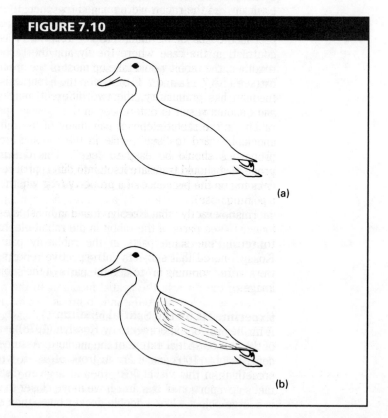

FIGURE 7.10

According to Kosslyn's theory, images are constructed in parts: Someone might first form (a) a skeletal image of a duck and then (b) add a wing-part to this initial skeletal image.

(a)

(b)

Psychological and Neuropsychological Evidence

Kosslyn's work has several important and welcome features. First, by specifying in computational terms the different processes and data structures involved in imagery, he silenced the criticism of vagueness which had long been levelled at imagery theorists. Second, the claims he makes for the properties of imagery are clear. Third, many of these detailed proposals are supported by empirical evidence. Consider some of the evidence for his proposals on limited extent and granularity, the fading of images and the area of high resolution in the spatial medium.

The Image Tracing Task

Kosslyn (1975; 1976; 1980) has used an "image tracing task" to test his proposals on the limited extent of the spatial medium and on granularity. As in the duck example, in these experiments subjects were asked to image an object and then to try to "see" some property of the imaged object (e.g. "Can you 'see' the duck's beak?"). The critical manipulation in the experiment was the context in which the animal was imaged. The "target" animal (e.g. a rabbit) was imaged along with another animal which was either much larger or much smaller than it (i.e. an elephant and a fly, respectively). The rationale was that in the case where the elephant and the rabbit were imaged together, the elephant would take up most of the space and as a result the rabbit would be represented as being much smaller relative to the elephant. In contrast, in the case where the fly and the rabbit were imaged together, the rabbit would take up most of the space relative to the fly (see Fig. 7.11a and 7.11b). Given the hypothesis that the spatial medium has granularity, the two different images of the animal pairs should result in differences in the "visible" properties of the rabbit. In the rabbit-elephant pair many of the rabbit's properties should be hard to "see" while in the rabbit-fly pair most of its properties should be easy to "see". This difficulty in "seeing" properties should translate itself into differential response times in deciding on the presence of a property (e.g. whether the rabbit has a pointed nose).

This is exactly what Kosslyn found in his studies. Subjects take longer to see parts of the rabbit in the rabbit-elephant pair relative to seeing the same parts in the rabbit-fly pair. Furthermore, Kosslyn noted that subjects' introspective reports suggested that they were "zooming in" to see the parts of the subjectively smaller images.

Experiments on the Spatial Medium

A further set of experiments by Kosslyn (1978) examined the idea of the limited spatial extent of the medium. Assume our visual field consists of a 100° visual arc in front of us. If we are looking at something in this visual field, then at a given distance the object takes up a portion of this arc. If we move closer to the object and it is a large object—like a double-decker bus—then eventually it will

FIGURE 7.11

A schematic diagram of how the image of (a) an elephant and a rabbit and (b) a fly and a rabbit might result in the rabbit being imaged at different levels of detail. (Adapted from Ghosts in the mind's machine; Creating and using images in the brain *by Stephen Kosslyn, by permission of the author and the publisher, W.W. Norton & Company Inc. Copyright 1983 by Stephen M. Kosslyn.)*

fill our complete visual arc and may even overflow it. That is, it may stretch beyond our field of view. Kosslyn essentially employs the same idea but in an imagery domain, in order to test the limited extent of the spatial medium. If one assumes that the spatial medium has a limited extent and has a similar visual-image arc then one way of measuring the size of an imaged object is in terms of the arc it subtends. It was predicted that at a certain point an object of a certain size should overflow the medium (see Fig. 7.12). To test this, subjects were asked to close their eyes and to image an object (usually an animal again) far away in the distance. They were then asked to "walk mentally" towards the image until they reached a point where they could see *all* the object at once (i.e. the point just prior to overflow). Finally, they were asked to estimate how far away the animal would be if they were seeing it at that subjective size. If the spatial medium has a limited extent of a constant size then the larger the object the farther away it would seem at the point of overflow. And this is what was found in the results of the experiment. In general, the estimated distance of the point of overflow increases linearly with the size of the imaged object.

Neuropsychological Evidence

As we have seen throughout this book, one strong test of a theory is to see whether it is consistent with neuropsychological evidence from the study of individuals with brain injuries (see, e.g., Chapters 1 and 6). Farah (1984) has carried out a review of imagery deficits following brain injuries and has used the specific processes of Kosslyn's theory to understand them. Farah abstracted the general component processes and structures from the theory; for instance, that there is a process that generates images from long-term memory representations, that there are long-term memory

FIGURE 7.12

Diagram of the relative amounts of the visual arc which are taken up by different-sized animals. (Adapted from Ghosts in the mind's machine; Creating and using images in the brain *by Stephen Kosslyn, by permission of the author and the publisher, W.W. Norton & Company Inc. Copyright 1983 by Stephen M. Kosslyn.)*

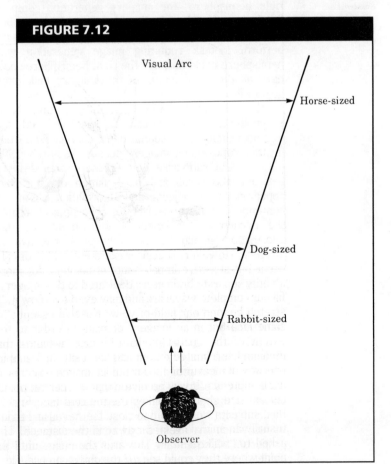

Visual Arc

Horse-sized

Dog-sized

Rabbit-sized

Observer

structures, and a spatial medium. Then, she analysed the various tasks used to test for imagery deficits into these components and attempted to show how different patients had deficiencies in one or more of these components. For example, if there is a deficit in image generation, the patient should not be able to describe the appearance of objects from memory or draw objects from memory. However, the same patient should be able to recognise and draw visually presented objects because these involve component processes other than those used in image generation. Several studies have reported patients with these patterns of behaviour (e.g. Lyman, Kwan & Chao, 1938; Nielsen, 1946).

Moreover, several studies in this line have provided interesting results on the localisation of imagery processes in the cerebral hemispheres (see Farah, 1984; Farah, Peronnet, Gonon, & Giard, 1988; Kosslyn, 1987; Kosslyn, Holtzmann, Farah, & Gazzinga, 1985). For instance, even though it has been generally assumed that imagery is a right-hemisphere function, it seems more likely that, even though many components of imagery are located in the right hemisphere, the imagery generation component is a left-hemisphere function. As Farah et al. (1988) have shown, in a study of a split-brain patient, the disconnected left hemisphere could perform a task requiring image generation when the right hemisphere could not; and the right hemisphere could be shown to have all the components of the imagery task except for image generation.

All of this evidence is important. Not only does it show how psychological theories can be used in and constrained by neuropsychological research but it also has important implications for the propositional–imagery debate. As Farah (1984) has pointed out, in propositionalist terms, there should be no difference between the recall and manipulation of information about the appearances of objects and information about other memory contents (e.g. historical facts or philosophical arguments). Hence, the occurrence of selective impairments to these types of information should be as likely as a selective impairment of imagery. However, specific impairments of historical ability *do not* occur but selective impairments of imagery do; moreover we can identify separate brain areas dedicated to this imagery ability.

Summary

Kosslyn has responded to the first wave of propositionalist criticisms of imagery both theoretically and empirically. Theoretically, he has proposed a theory of imagery which asserts that while images partially involve propositional information, they also involve nonpropositional representations and are represented in a medium with special properties. He has also carried out experiments which have tested and confirmed several of these special properties. The theory has also been extended to account for evidence from neuropsychological studies on imagery impairments.

THE IMAGERY–PROPOSITIONAL DEBATE II

Pylyshyn's Second Wave of Criticisms

Pylyshyn (1981; 1984) introduced a second set of arguments which can be viewed as an attempt to define imagery out of existence or, more precisely, to define imagery out of cognitive science. In concrete terms, Pylyshyn criticises Kosslyn's experiments and echoes Baddeley's (1986) worry mentioned earlier; namely, that subjects in mental scanning experiments are simply doing what they are told to do; they are simulating what it would be like to look at something and scan across it. Their behaviour does not reflect the special properties of the imagery system but simply the instructions used in the experiment. However, Pylyshyn's route to this point is through difficult philosophical terrain about the nature of the mind and of cognitive science as a discipline.

His arguments hinge on the difficult concept of *cognitive penetrability* which is best understood by analogy to distinctions that can be made within the computer. Every computer has hardware, which consists of silicon chips, processors, and wiring, and software made up of the programs which run on this hardware. The hardware is unchanging, unless we open the machine physically and add new components. The software, on the other hand, can be changed in a number of different ways; programs can generate new programs or create data structures that other commands in the program modify. However, software cannot modify the hardware of the computer directly. Pylyshyn argues that the mind has a *functional architecture* like the hardware of the computer which cannot be modified by the higher-level, software-like processes of the mind (i.e. our beliefs, goals, and wishes).

Pylyshyn argues that if images operate in a special medium, they must be part of the functional architecture of the mind (and hence be, in some sense, hard-wired). This, therefore, means that they should not be modifiable by one's high-level beliefs and goals since these beliefs and goals cannot penetrate the functional architecture: In short, images should be *cognitively impenetrable*. Since beliefs and goals are inherently propositional entities, if one shows that images *are* cognitively penetrable then they must be fundamentally the same sort of stuff as propositional representations; and hence be reducible to propositional representations.

Pylyshyn has used these proposals to reinterpret those experiments which seemed to constitute strong evidence for theories of imagery. For example, he points out that close attention must be paid to the instructions in the image-scanning experiments. Recall that in these experiments subjects were instructed to image moving a black dot from one point on an imaged map to another. In a series of experiments Pylyshyn (1984; Bannon, 1981) found, like Kosslyn and his associates, that if subjects were asked to image a real spot moving or really walking from one point to another, the times taken by subjects to "scan" corresponded to the relative distance between points on the map. However, he also found that if subjects were asked to image shifting their gaze as quickly as possible from one point to another, the effects disappeared. Similarly, if subjects were asked to image running (instead of walking), the time taken to complete the task between points was quicker than in the original (walking) experiments. This shows two things: (1) that people did not seem to be scanning an image in a uniform fashion, because these instructions should not have increased the scan rate; and (2) that imagery was clearly under the control of the kind of transformations one expected or believed to occur. In short, it was cognitively penetrable. "To imagine" something means to represent something as if it were real. Thus imagining traversing a space entails imagining being successively at intermediate points—otherwise it would not be traversing that was being imagined.

So, it seems as if subjects are rather better at following the instructions than one would expect and a special representational format is not required to explain the results. The mental rotation studies can be accounted for in the same way. Research which is consistent with this view has been done by Rock (1973), who has shown that it is harder to judge rotation effects in more complex 3-D shapes (see also Hinton's [1979] earlier comments).

Counter-Arguments to the Second Wave

There are several counterpoints to Pylyshyn's second wave of arguments. These replies, like Pylyshyn's, hinge more on analytic points rather than on empirical ones. One counter-argument, proposed by Boden (1988), rejects Pylyshyn's dichotomy of mental representations—into propositional and analogue-as-special-medium representations—as being as too simplistic. She argues that it is more correct to admit a threefold division between propositions, analogue-as-special-medium representations, and simply analogical representations (in a sense which lacks any special medium claims; e.g. see next section on mental models). This means that even though images may be cognitively penetrable (and therefore based on propositions), it does not follow that the imagery *has* to be explained in terms of propositional represent-ations; it could be explained in terms of analogue representations which do not operate in a special medium.

Johnson-Laird (1983) has argued further that Pylyshyn's penetrability argument can be used against him. He points out that a thoroughgoing materialist (like Churchland, 1981) might maintain that Pylyshyn's constructs of beliefs and goals are epiphenomenal because they can be "imagistically penetrated"; that is, the way in which they govern behaviour can be influenced in a rationally explicable way by images. Johnson-Laird (1983, p.152) concludes: "The moral is plain: images and beliefs are both high-level constructs, and it is a mistake to argue that they are epiphenomenal just because they 'penetrate' each other." Johnson-Laird's position on what constitutes a better treatment of these issues will be outlined in the next section.

Summary

Pylyshyn's second wave of arguments against imagery theorists hinge on the notions of cognitive penetrability and functional architecture. He argues that imagery theorists, who posit that imagery involves a special medium, are basically maintaining that imagery is part of the functional architecture of the mind. As such images should be cognitively impenetrable. However, he then shows that images are, in fact, cognitively penetrable and concludes that they must therefore be reducible to propositional representations. The main counter-arguments to this position maintain that: (1) Pylyshyn's simple dichotomy between propositional representations and analogue-as-special-medium representations is unwarranted and therefore his conclusions are unjustified; and (2) that arguments that hinge on penetrability are an inappropriate and misguided treatment of the issues.

MENTAL MODELS AS ANALOGICAL REPRESENTATIONS

There is a third form of representational construct which has cropped up in the psychological literature; these constructs are called *mental models* (Johnson-Laird, 1983; in press). For Johnson-Laird, a mental model is a representation that can be wholly analogical, or partly analogical and partly propositional, which is distinct from but related to an image. However, before we progress, two provisos must be mentioned.

First, the term "mental model" has been used by different theorists in different ways (compare Johnson-Laird, 1983, with Gentner & Stevens, 1983). This is an issue which we return to in Chapter 12, but for the meantime one should note Johnson-Laird's specific representational usage of the term. Second, part of Johnson-Laird's answer to the representational debates we have been reviewing is to define propositional representations differently. He relies on a definition of propositional representations which is closer to that used by philosophers. In philosophy, propositions are generally taken to be (Johnson-Laird, 1983, p.155) "the conscious objects of thought—those entities that we entertain, believe, think, doubt etc., and that are expressed by [natural language] sentences" (see Gale, 1967, for more on the philosophical usage). Thus, in Johnson-Laird's scheme, *a propositional representation is a mental representation of a verbally expressible proposition*. This definitional change may seem a little perverse until one sees how Johnson-Laird uses it to deal with a variety of representational issues.

In particular, Johnson-Laird distinguishes between three types of representational constructs: images, mental models, and propositions. He argues that images and mental models are high-level representations which are essential to an understanding of human cognition. Even though the brain may at base compute images and mental models in some form of propositional code, it is nevertheless important to study the ways in which people use these high-level representations. The reasons why it is important to study such representations can be appreciated by analogy to the use of high-level programming languages in computers.

At their very lowest level of organisation, computers use a programming language called *machine code*, which carries out the basic operations of assigning bits of information to different memory registers and the like. While one can program in this machine code, it is not very "user-friendly" because it is terse and difficult to read (it consists of numbers, dashes, semi-colons etc). To circumvent this problem, a variety of high-level programming languages have been developed (e.g. BASIC, PASCAL, LISP) which are used by programmers. These high-level languages can be translated by the computer into machine code when compiled, but are useful in that they allow the programmer to think about what the computer has to do in a shorter and clearer fashion. Johnson-Laird argues that mental models and images are like high-level programming languages for the brain in the sense that they free human cognition from operating at a machine-code-like, propositional level. So from this perspective, the researcher's concern shifts from proving the existence of a representational format to the goal of understanding how people use different representations to carry out different tasks. As such, Johnson-Laird has mainly looked at how models are used in thinking and reasoning (see Chapter 12), although the ideas can be applied to many aspects of cognition (e.g. language comprehension, consciousness). Consider the more detailed differences between propositions and mental models, and mental models and images.

We have seen that propositions are representations of things which are verbally expressible and hence are close to the form of natural language. Mental models, in contrast, include varying degrees of analogical structure. In some cases, the model may be spatially analogical to the world in that it captures two- or three-dimensional layouts; it may also represent analogically the dynamics of a sequence of events (for other examples see Chapter 12). The essential properties of mental models are that they are analogical, determinate, and concrete (in that they represent specific entities). In contrast, propositions, like linguistic descriptions, are usually indeterminate. That is, for Johnson-Laird, propositions can be taken to describe many different possible states of affairs. For example, the verbal description "The book is on the shelf " is true of the book at the left end of the shelf, the book at the right end of the shelf, the book in the middle of the shelf, the book standing upright on the shelf, the book lying split in two with a half at either end of the shelf, and so on. Propositional representations retain this indeterminacy. Mental models are made determinate through the action of various inference and comprehension processes. So, the mental model for "The book is on the shelf" might represent a specific book as being on the shelf at a particular end, in a particular position. If further sentences contradict this model then it can be revised.

Now, many of these attributes of mental models make them sound like images, so how do the two constructs differ? Johnson-Laird (1983, p.157) assumes that: "images correspond to views of models: as a result either of perception or imagination, they represent the perceptible features of corresponding real-world objects." So, for example, a model of a book on a shelf would represent the relative position of the book with respect to the shelf in an analogical manner that parallels the structure of that state of affairs in the world. An image of a book on a shelf would contain the same information but also involve a view of the book on the shelf from a particular angle (for a fuller treatment of types of mental models the interested reader is referred to Boden [1988, Chapter 6, especially pp.184, 185]; see also Lindsay, 1988, for a similar functional argument for distinguishing representations).

Evidence for the Propositional–Mental Model Distinction

The determinacy differences between propositions and mental models have been examined experimentally by Mani and Johnson-Laird (1982). They reasoned that if subjects were given descriptions which were either determinate or indeterminate they would form a model of the determinate description and would not form a model of the indeterminate description because it is consistent with two models. Later, subjects were given a recognition test and it was found that they tended to recognise falsely sentences that described aspects of the inferred model, even though these aspects were never stated explicitly. The determinate and indeterminate descriptions given to subjects are shown in Table 7.2. Note that the indeterminate descriptions are consistent with two different states of affairs.

In the experimental procedure, subjects heard a description, were shown a diagram of the layout of the objects (see Table 7.2), and were asked to decide whether the diagram was consistent or inconsistent with the description. After this decision task subjects were given an unexpected memory test in which they had to rank four descriptions in terms of their resemblance to the original description. One of these descriptions contained a sentence which should have been inferred if subjects had constructed a mental model, even though it had never been mentioned explicitly: namely, that "The fork is to the left of the cup." The experiments revealed two main findings. First, subjects tended to recognise falsely the inferred description of determinate items; they did not do this for indeterminate items. This was interpreted as indicating that subjects build models of determinate descriptions and hence make the inference that "The fork is to the left of the cup"; but they abandon model construction for indeterminate descriptions because of the multiplicity of models which can be produced. Second, subjects tend to remember the verbatim detail of indeterminate descriptions better than that of determinate descriptions, because having abandoned model construction, they resort to remembering the propositional structure of the descriptions.

TABLE 7.2

Examples of Verbal Descriptions of Spatial Arrays of Objects [a]

Descriptions		Layouts	
Determinate			
The spoon is to the left of the knife.			
The plate is to the right of the knife.	spoon	knife	plate
The fork is in front of the spoon.	fork	cup	
The cup is in front of the knife.			
Indeterminate			
The spoon is to the left of the knife.	spoon	knife	plate
The plate is to the right of the spoon.	fork	cup	
The fork is in front of the spoon.		OR	
The cup is in front of the knife.	spoon	plate	knife
	fork		cup

[a] *The verbal descriptions are determinate and indeterminate as is indicated by the number of different layouts that are consistent with each one, from Mani and Johnson-Laird (1982).*

Summary

Johnson-Laird has argued for a third representational construct—the mental model—that is an analogical representation to be distinguished from propositions and images. However, Johnson-Laird favours a philosophical usage of the term *proposition*; this views it as a representation which is verbally expressible and close to the surface form of natural language. Propositions, in this sense, are indeterminate, while mental models and images are seen as being determinate, analogical, and concrete. Images are mental models viewed from a particular perspective. Johnson-Laird's framework for representations is useful in making predictions about the different types of representations that people are likely to use in different task situations. It has been applied extensively in the area of deductive reasoning (see Chapter 12).

DISTRIBUTED REPRESENTATIONS AND CONNECTIONiSM

In most of this chapter we have concentrated on the traditional symbolic approach to mental representation (see also Chapter 1). The basic view of this approach is that human cognition is centrally dependent on the manipulation of symbolic representations by various rule-like processes. Kosslyn's imagery theory is a prime example of theorising from this viewpoint, in which rule-based processes—like IMAGE and PUT—manipulate various symbols. Even though the symbolic approach has been the dominant one within information-processing psychology (e.g. see all the remaining chapters of the book), some researchers have been concerned about whether this is ultimately the best way to understand human cognition. They have pointed to a number of possible difficulties in the symbolic approach.

First, as we have seen in this chapter, within a symbolic tradition one has to state explicitly how mental contents are represented (whether they be analogical representations or propositions). Moreover, one has to specify how these represent-ations are manipulated by various rules. So even for relatively simple tasks symbolic theories can fast become very complicated. When one moves away from laboratory tasks and looks at everyday tasks (like driving a car), it is sometimes difficult to envision how such a complicated scheme could be at work. People can operate quite efficiently by taking multiple sources of information into account at once. While a symbolic account might be able to account for a task such as driving, many feel that the account would be too inelegant and cumbersome. A second worry about the symbolic approach is that it has tended to avoid the question of how cognitive processes are realised in the brain. Granted, as we saw earlier, it provides evidence for the gross localisation of cognitive processes in the brain, but we are left with no idea of how these symbols are represented and manipulated at the level of a particular neuron (or set of neurons).

In response to these and other issues, in the last few years there has been a growing movement that has attempted to mount a new approach to cognition: the *connectionist approach* (Ballard, 1986; Feldman & Ballard, 1982; Hinton & Anderson, 1981; McClelland, Rumelhart, & the P.D.P. Research Group, 1986; Rumelhart, McClelland, & the P.D.P. Research Group, 1986). As we saw in Chapter 1, connectionists use computational models consisting of networks of neuron-like units. They also have several advantages over their symbolic competitors.

As we shall see, connectionist schemes can represent inform-ation without recourse to symbolic entities like propositions; they are said to represent information sub-symbolically in *distributed representations* (see Smolensky, 1988). Second, without having to use large sets of explicit propositional rules they have the

Two simple pattern associators representing different information. The example assumes that the patterns of activation in the vision units, encoding the sight of (a) a rose or (b) a steak, can be associated with the patterns of activation in olfaction units, encoding the smell of (a) a rose or (b) a steak. The synaptic connections allow the outputs of the vision units to influence the activations of the olfaction units. The synaptic weights shown in the two networks are selected to allow the pattern of activation shown in the vision units to reproduce the pattern of activation in the olfaction units without the need for any olfactory input. (Adapted with the permission of David E. Rumelhart & *James L. McClelland from* Parallel distributed processing: Explorations in the microstructure of cognition, Vol. 1, *published by the M.I.T. Press, 1986 by The Massachusetts Institute of Technology.)*

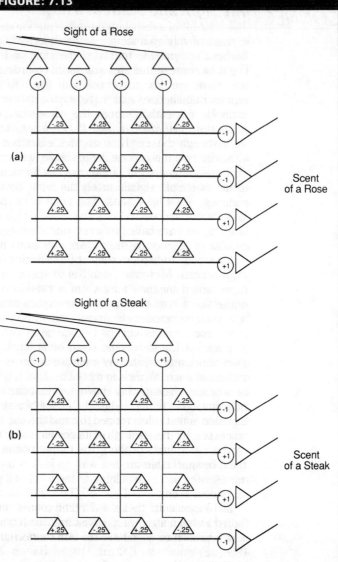

FIGURE: 7.13

Sight of a Rose

(a)

Scent of a Rose

Sight of a Steak

(b)

Scent of a Steak

potential to model complex behaviours (see, e.g., Holyoak & Thagard, 1990; Rumelhart, McClelland, & the PDP Research Group, 1986). Third, in their use of neuron-like processing units they hold out the possibility of theories of cognition that map directly onto detailed aspects of the neurophysiological substrate (but see Smolensky, 1988). It is already clear that connectionist ideas suggest significant answers to many questions we want answered about human cognition. What is not yet clear, is how much of human cognition can be characterised in this way.

Distributed Representation: The Sight and Scent of a Rose

The concept of a distributed representation can be illustrated by an example involving a simple network called a *pattern associator*. Within the symbolic tradition, the sight and the scent of a rose might be represented as some set of co-ordinates (for the image of the rose) or as a proposition (i.e. ROSE). A distributed representation does not have symbols that represent the rose explicitly but rather *stores the connection strengths between units that will allow either the sight or the scent of the rose to be re-created* (see Hinton, McClelland, & Rumelhart, 1986). Consider how this is done in the simple network in Fig. 7.13a.

The sight and scent of the rose can be viewed as being coded in terms of simple signals in certain input cells (i.e. as pluses and minuses, see Fig. 7.13a). The input cells that take signals from vision are called vision units and those which take signals from the smell senses are called olfaction units. Essentially, the network is capable of associating the pattern of activation which arrives at the vision units with that arriving at the olfaction units. The distributed representation of the sight and scent of the rose is thus represented by the "matrix" of activation over the units in the network, without recourse to any explicit symbol for representing the rose. Consider in more detail how this coding of the representation is achieved.

Figure 7.13a shows the vision and olfaction units. The sight of the rose is represented by a particular pattern of activation on the vision units (characterised by $+1$, -1, -1, $+1$), while the pattern of olfactory excitation is shown on the olfaction units (from top to bottom -1, -1, $+1$, $+1$). The effect of a single vision unit on an olfaction unit is determined by multiplying the activation of the vision unit by the strength of its connection to the olfaction unit. So, all the vision units produce the output of the first olfaction unit in the following fashion:

1st Vision unit	$+1 \times -.25$ (1st connecting unit)	$= -.25$
2nd Vision unit	$-1 \times +.25$ (2nd connecting unit)	$= -.25$
3rd Vision unit	$-1 \times +.25$ (3rd connecting unit)	$= -.25$
4th Vision unit	$+1 \times -.25$ (4th connecting unit)	$= -.25$

1st Olfaction unit -1
(by summation)

In cases where the pattern associator does not learn the association, the interconnecting units (which intervene between the vision and olfaction units) can be set so that given the vision input of $+1$, -1, -1, $+1$ the olfaction output -1, -1, $+1$, $+1$ is produced and vice versa (according to the method of combining activation just shown). In this way this pattern associator has represented the association between the sight and scent of the rose in a distributed fashion. We could also represent the sight and smell of another object by a different pattern of activation in the same network. For example, the sight and *scent* of a steak could be characterised by the vision pattern $(-1, +1, -1, +1)$ and the olfactory units $(-1, +1, +1, -1)$; the different pattern of activation for this is shown in Fig. 7.13b. Note the differences in the activation levels in the various interconnecting units in the network.

Distributed Versus Local Representations

Not all connectionist models use distributed representations. They also use representations similar to those used in the symbolic approach, even though the models still use networks of units. Connectionists call the latter *local representations*. The crucial difference between distributed and local representations is sometimes subtle. A *distributed representation* is one in which (Rumelhart, Hinton, & McClelland, 1986, p. 47): "the units represent small feature-like entities [and where] the pattern as a whole is the meaningful unit of analysis." The essential tenet of the distributed scheme is that different items correspond to alternative patterns of activity in the same set of units. A *local representation*, on the other hand, has a one-unit-one-concept representation in which single units represent entire concepts or other large meaningful units.

To be clear about this distinction, consider two networks that deal with the same task domain; one uses a local representation and another uses a distributed representation. These networks represent the mappings between the visual form of a word (i.e. c-a-t) and its meaning (i.e. small, furry, four-legged; see Figs. 7.14a and 7.14b). The network in this case has three layers. A layer for identifying letters of the word (consisting of *grapheme units*, which indicate the letter and its position in the word), a middle layer, and a layer which encodes the semantic units constituting the meaning of the word (see Chapter 8 for further details on such semantic primitives; here we call them *sememe units*).

In the localist version of the model, the middle layer of the network has units which represent one word. So, a particular grapheme string activates this word unit and this activates whatever meaning is associated with it. In short, there is a one-unit-one-concept representation in the middle layer (see Fig. 7.14a). In the distributed version of the network, the grapheme units feed into *word-set units* which in turn feed into the semantic units. A word-set unit is activated whenever the pattern of the grapheme units activate an item in that set. A set could be something like all the three-letter words beginning with CA or all the words ending in AT. So, in this distributed representation, activation goes from the grapheme units to many different word-set units and these in turn send activation to the sememe layer, to indicate uniquely which set of semantic features is associated with this particular configuration of graphemes. This representation is distributed because each word-set unit participates in the rep-

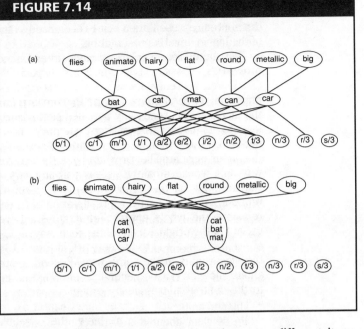

FIGURE 7.14

Three-layered connectionist network. Bottom layer contains units representing particular graphemes in particular positions within a word. Middle layer contains units recognising complete words. Top layer contains units representing semantic features of the meaning of the word. Network (a) uses local representations of words in the middle layer. Network (b) has a middle layer using a more distributed representation. Each unit in the middle layer of network (b) can be activated by the graphemic representation of any one of a whole set of words. The unit then provides input to every semantic feature occurring in the meaning of any words that activate it. Only those word sets containing the word cat are shown in network (b). Notice that the only semantic features receiving input from all these word sets are the semantic features of cat. (Adapted with the permission of D. E. Rumelhart & J. L. McClelland from Parallel distributed processing: Explorations in the microstructure of cognition, Vol. 1. *M.I.T. Press, 1986.*

resentation of many words. Stated another way, different items correspond to alternative patterns of activity in the same set of units (see Fig. 7.14b).

Without wishing to be confusing, it should be noted that research on network representation is relatively new and, as such, the local-distributed representation distinction can often be equivocal. For example, Hinton et al. (1986) admit that semantic networks which use spreading activation (see Chapters 1 and 8) are not very distinguishable from other distributed representations, even though they have units which correspond to single concepts. Similarly, it must be admitted that the word sets in the distributed representation shown are not very feature-like entities but could be categorised as meaningful wholes. However, until more is known about the characteristics of these networks the distinction is heuristically useful.

Distributed Representations and Propositions/Images

The sixty-four million dollar question, which we have been ignoring until now, is "What is the relationship between distributed representations and symbolic representations?" Hinton et al. (1986) argue that the two views do not contradict one another, but rather are complementary to each another. By this they mean that entities which are characterised at higher levels of cognition as, say, propositions may at lower levels be represented in a distributed fashion. They do, however, point out that this complementarity depends on the properties of the lower-level distributed representation being recognised as fundamental aspects of the higher-level representations.

Distributed representations have several, sometimes surprising, properties; consider two which are especially important. First, distributed representations are *content-addressable*. This is an important general characteristic of human memory and refers to the fact that apparently any part of a past occurrence or scene can lead to its later retrieval from memory. I may remember my holiday on the Côte d'Azur on hearing a certain song, when I smell the odour of ratatouille, or when I see the sun reflected in a certain way on a woman's hair. It seems that any part of the memory can reinstate all of the original memory. Similarly, in distributed representations, a partial representation of an entity is sufficient to reinstate the whole entity. For example, if we present a slight variant of the original scent of the rose (say, $-1, -1, +1, 0$ instead of $-1, -1, +1, +1$) to the network in Fig. 7.13a, it will still excite the vision units in the same way. Second, distributed representations allow automatic generalisation. That is, in a manner related to the content-addressability property, patterns which are similar will produce similar responses (see Chapter 5).

In conclusion, one can view the symbolic framework as characterising the macro-structure of cognitive representation (i.e. the broad outlines of symbols and their organisation) while the distributed representations characterise the micro-structure of cognitive representation (see McClelland et al., 1986; Rumelhart et al., 1986). However, the full ramifications of the relationship between the two levels requires substantial elaboration.

Summary

The main problems with the symbolic approach to representation are that (1) its treatments of complex cognition can become cumbersome, and (2) it tends not to be related in a detailed fashion to the neurophysiological substrate of the brain. The advent of connectionism offers a *possible* way of realising this relationship. Connectionist networks can be used to represent entities in a distributed fashion as patterns of activation within the same network. Networks can also represent entities in a localist fashion, where there is a one-to-one-correspondence between concepts and units in the network. Distributed representations can be viewed as being complementary to the representations posited within the symbolic perspective; in the sense that the latter may be viewed as a characterisation of distributed representations at a higher level of abstraction. However, this complementarity is only admissible if the properties of distributed representations are taken as primitives at the higher level. These properties include content-addressability and automatic generalisation.

CONCLUSIONS

Any science is always in a constant state of flux. At any point there are dominant themes which large groups of researchers are involved in investigating. When a dead end is reached or the problems in the area seem to be solved sufficiently, many researchers turn to other issues. The pejorative name for this activity is "bandwagon research". The imagery–propositional debate could be viewed as a prime example of it. For a time in the 1970s and early 1980s it was one of the most hotly researched issues. Now research continues on imagery, but the emphasis has shifted away from attempting to prove that images are a vacuous representational construct. The current consensus could be summarised in two points. First, the whole effort to prove that one format of representation is redundant was a waste of time; the terms of the argument were misplaced, or the issue is not empirically decidable, or both groups of proponents were attempting to answer radically different questions (Anderson, 1988; Baddeley, 1986; Marschark, Richman, Yuille, & Hunt, 1987). Second, there is general agreement that different representational constructs are needed to characterise the richness of human cognition and that imagery should be counted as one of these constructs (see, e.g., Anderson, 1983; Johnson-Laird, 1983). However, even though the debate may have been ill-conceived in itself, it has to be said that it did provoke a clarification of the concept of imagery and led to some creative experimentation. It can also be seen as pushing theorists on to investigate the more practical concerns of the effects of brain injury on imagery ability.

The current interest in connectionism has attracted similar if not more attention than the imagery debate, although this is not to say that it suffers from the same faults. As a concluding comment, it should be noted that we have taken the ecumenical position proposed by Hinton et al. (1986) on the relationship between the symbolic and connectionist representations, in saying that the two are complementary. As we shall see in other areas, not everyone shares this view. In ways which are reminiscent of the propositional–imagery debate, some have taken sides and attempted to argue that one view is redundant or inappropriate. For example, Smolensky's (1988) "proper treatment of connectionism" argues against the complementarity proposed here for some forms of cognition. One of the current interesting issues in cognitive psychology concerns the final resolution of this debate.

FURTHER READING

Several books provide interesting further discussions of the issues raised in this chapter. In particular the following are recommended for further reading.

Boden, M. (1988). *Computer models of the mind*. Cambridge: Cambridge University Press. This book gives an excellent account of various representational and computational modelling issues in modern cognitive psychology. The chapter dealing with mental models is particularly lucid.

Collins, A.M. & Smith, E.E. (1988). *Readings in cognitive science*. San Mateo, Calif.: Morgan Kaufmann. This contains many key articles cited in this chapter on representations and related issues.

Kosslyn, S.M. (1983). *Ghosts in the mind's machine*. New York: Norton. This is a very accessible introduction to his research and theory.

Paivio, A. (1986). *Mental representations*. Oxford: Oxford University Press. This book provides a good treatment of dual-coding theory and the empirical evidence that supports it.

Rumelhart, D.E., McClelland, J.L., & the PDP Research Group (1986). *Parallel distributed processing, Vol.1*. Cambridge, Mass.: M.I.T. Press; and McClelland, J.L., Rumelhart, D.E., & the PDP Research Group (1986). *Parallel distributed processing, Vol.2*. Cambridge, Mass.: M.I.T. Press. The most complete introduction to connectionist treatments of representation can be found in these two volumes.

Chapter Eight

The Organisation of Knowledge

There is a possibly apocryphal tale that in the time of the Ming Emperors the exam for the Chinese civil service was very demanding. Candidates, it is said, were directed to a room containing a chair, a table, and ample writing materials and were asked to write down *all* that they knew. The tale seems a little tall for two reasons. First, we know an awful lot. Second, there are certain things we know which cannot be verbalised easily (e.g. it is not normally possible for us to describe the subtle balancing movements we execute when riding a bicycle).

If you do not agree with this assessment and think that you know little, consider the following very short story:

When Lisa was on her way back from the shop with the balloon, she fell and the balloon floated away.

In understanding this simple sentence we have used a considerable amount of knowledge. Consider all the facts we have taken for granted and the plausible inferences we have made: that Lisa is a girl, that she bought the balloon in the shop, that shops are the sorts of places where balloons can be bought, that Lisa may have cut her knee when she fell, that knees bleed when they are cut, that the balloon was attached to a string, that when she fell she let go of the string, and that the balloon floated up because it was full of a light gas, and so on. When you come to appreciate the extent of the knowledge we use on a daily basis "without even thinking about it," it is astonishing.

INTRODUCTION

This chapter concentrates on the various attempts which have been made to characterise the nature and organisation of this knowledge. In later chapters we look at the ways in which knowledge is used. In Chapter 10 we look at its use in language comprehension. In Chapters 11 and 12, we look at the use of knowledge in higher cognitive processes like problem solving and reasoning. To begin with, however, we need to arm ourselves with two things: a rough idea of exactly what we mean by the term "knowledge" and some of the basic distinctions which are made within this field.

What is Knowledge? Format and Organisation

In general, psychologists have tended to label something as knowledge if it is information that is represented mentally in a particular format and structured or organised in some manner. So, the question—What is knowledge?—is broken down into two further questions: "What format do mental representations take ?" and "How are mental representations organised?"

Essentially, we have dealt with the format question already in Chapter 7. In that chapter, we considered how entities were represented mentally and we elaborated some of the distinctions that can be made between different symbolic codes: That is, between analogue and propositional representations. We also considered the special characteristics of different formats of mental representation; for example, that propositions were abstract, language-like entities whereas analogical representations (like images) had special, analogical properties. Perhaps the most important point to remember in the present chapter is that analogical representations tend to take a back seat when we come to consider the organisation of mental representations (but see Paivio, 1986, on the organisation of imagery). Most of the theories presented in this chapter assume, explicitly or implicitly, that some form of propositional representation is used to represent concepts. There are many reasons for this state of affairs, but two are especially prominent.

First, the over-riding metaphor in concept research is one based on mental chemistry (which can be attributed to British empiricist philosophers, like Locke, 1690). Thus, researchers typically conceive of concepts as atomic units and of combining these basic units in various ways to make more complex, molecule-like structures. Recall that one of the main characteristics of propositions is that they are discrete, atomic entities and therefore they naturally lend themselves to this metaphor. Second, as we pointed out in Chapter 7, propositions can be notated using the predicate calculus which is an ideal language for computational models. Indeed, research on knowledge organisation has largely been inspired and supported by computational modelling.

This chapter reviews attempts to explain how human knowledge is organised. However, not all the researchers in the field have taken the same approach to this issue. There are thus several ways in which the research themes in the area can be segmented (see Fig. 8.1). In most of the recent history of cognitive psychology, one can distinguish between researchers concerned with either simple or complex organisation. By *simple organisation*, we do not mean to suggest that this research deals with trivial issues, but rather that it focuses on how different entities come to be grouped together under a common concept (e.g. why we consider the mongrel next door and the winner of Crufts to be instances of the category dog) and how these categories are related to one another hierarchically (why the categories dog and cat are subordinates of the more general *animal* concept). In contrast, research on *complex organisation*, has concentrated on how large groupings of concepts are structured and used in various complex, cognitive tasks (like the comprehension of the story involving Lisa). Research on simple organisation has tended to investigate *object concepts* (like *dog, bird, chair, furniture*) and has been marked by several theoretical stances; we will call these the defining-attribute, defining- and characteristic-attribute, and prototype views. Research on simple organisation has also examined *relational concepts* (e.g. *hit, make, give*), although to a lesser degree. Under the complex organisation rubric, the predominant emphasis has been on the structure of knowledge about everyday events and the organisation of sequences of these events into plans or other predictive knowledge structures. These knowledge structures are often given a variety of colourful names (e.g. schemata, scripts, frames, MOPS, and TOPS), and we will encounter this menagerie of structures later on.

Although it is useful initially to distinguish between simple and complex organisation, the distinction is only heuristically useful rather than absolute. For example, as can be seen in Fig. 8.1, relational concepts can be considered from both perspectives. The most important point to note is that it is a division of research perspectives, not a real division in the actual subject matter. In fact, as we shall see at the end of this chapter, there is something of a rapprochement between the two research traditions; research on simple organisation seems to indicate that single concepts may depend on complex knowledge structures.

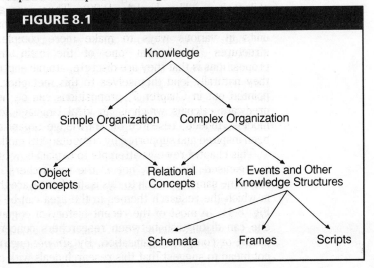

The different distinctions that can be made between the types of knowledge studied in research on the organisation of knowledge.

FIGURE 8.1

Knowledge

Simple Organization   Complex Organization

Object Concepts   Relational Concepts   Events and Other Knowledge Structures

Schemata   Frames   Scripts

Distinguishing Types of Knowledge

Faced with the range, diversity, and individuality of human knowledge, researchers have often attempted to make broad divisions between different types of knowledge. Two major divisions have emerged in the last 20 to 30 years which are helpful in this respect: that between semantic and episodic memory and that between declarative and procedural knowledge. It is wise not to take these as hard and fast distinctions but merely as useful ways of starting to think about knowledge, until a deeper understanding is achieved.

Semantic and Episodic Memory

As we saw in Chapter 6, Tulving (1972; 1983) has argued for a conceptual division in long-term memory between semantic and episodic memory. *Semantic memory* refers our de-contextualised memory for facts about the entities and relations between entities in the world; for instance, that birds have wings and that a canary is a bird. In contrast, *episodic memory* refers to knowledge about episodes and events, to entities that are marked as happening at a particular time. Episodic memory thus has an autobiographical flavour. For instance, the classic example of an episodic memory item would be "my memory of the time last year when I travelled through the Greek Islands." However, there are also less "naturalistic" examples of episodic memories. For example, Tulving argued that all the studies which require subjects to memorise lists of words or other items are essentially stored as episodic memories, because they are marked as occurring at a particular point in time. In much of the concept literature examined in this chapter, researchers have concentrated on semantic memory, by interrogating people about the "factual" relationship of one concept to another (e.g. "Is a canary a bird?"). However, later on, when we consider schema theories, the emphasis is more on episodic structures.

There has been some controversy about how strongly this distinction can be drawn. For example, in Chapter 6 we saw that it is quite helpful in understanding the specific deficits of amnesic patients. However, there is a growing consensus that this distinction is heuristically useful rather than a division between actual distinct types of knowledge. This can easily be appreciated if one considers how both types of memory merge with one another. An episodic memory contains the factual entities of semantic memory (i.e. what an island is, where Greece is). Conversely, usually when we encounter a new word, its meaning is initially contextually recorded in an episodic fashion. For instance, if you first encounter the word "priapistic" in James Joyce's *Ulysses*, it is likely that on encountering it again, you will remember where and when it was first seen. So an inherently semantic entity (i.e. the meaning of a word) can also have episodic characteristics.

Declarative and Procedural Knowledge

In Chapter 6, we also encountered the distinction between *knowing that* and *knowing how* (see Ryle, 1949; and Polanyi, 1967, on tacit knowledge); between declarative and procedural knowledge. I *know how* to ride a bicycle without falling off but I cannot describe to you how I do this. I *know that* a bicycle has wheels, a frame, a carrier, handlebars and a bell. I know how to ride a bicycle because I have some set of *procedures* that allow me to adjust my bodily weight in space in order to stay upright. Unlike declarative knowledge, which I can declare (like the facts about what constitutes a bicycle), procedural knowledge often cannot be stated explicitly.

Even though, in formal computational terms, the same information can be represented either declaratively or procedurally (see, e.g. Holland et al., 1986), the procedural–declarative distinction has proved useful in psychological research. We have already seen (in Chapter 6) that it has been used to understand amnesia. Similarly, Anderson (1983) argues strongly for this distinction to account for aspects of skill learning. Stated simply, he proposes that initially when we learn something it is learned and encoded declaratively, but with practice it becomes "compiled" into a procedural form of knowledge (see Chapter 11).

Summary

Knowledge can be characterised along two important dimensions. First, it can be considered in terms of its representational format (analogue or propositional). Second, we can talk about how the knowledge is organised. In trying to characterise human knowledge, researchers tend to divide into those who examine the structure of single concepts and those concerned with the complex structuring of concepts (in structures called schemata). On a memorial level, Tulving has drawn a distinction between semantic and episodic memory as a way of distinguishing between different types of knowledge. This distinction is heuristically useful. Another distinction is often made between declarative knowledge (which can be expressed or declared) and procedural knowledge (which is knowledge about how to do things and is often difficult to express). Again this is not a hard and fast distinction in a formal sense but it can be useful psychologically.

TRADITIONAL THEORIES OF CONCEPTS

In this and the following two sections we examine several of the theoretical stances that have been taken in the research tradition which has looked at simple organisation. This research has examined the ways in which various objects, encountered in the world, come to be grouped together conceptually. Consider a hypothetical game to explain the phenomena of interest.

The Categorisation Game

Imagine you are put in a room and are asked to record what you are shown, without any external memory aids (like paper, pencils, and computers). After a short wait, during which loud banging noises are heard from without, several attendants parade hundreds of fantastic objects, the likes of which you have never seen before, in front of you. Initially, you might attempt to give them names and memorise what they look like so that when shown them later you could say: "That's the widget I saw yesterday." However, it is likely that as the set of objects increases you would need to organise your conception of them. You may note that, apart from there being individual objects (e.g. the widget I saw yesterday, which I was shown again today), there are several objects which are very alike (the widget I saw last week is the same shape as an object I saw today but they differ in colour). You might therefore decide that rather than giving all these objects different names, it is a good idea to consider them to be *instances* or *members* of a class of things with the same name; so, all objects which are widget-shaped are called widgets irrespective of their colour. In this way, several distinct concepts could be developed (e.g. a widget, a crambag, and a dongle).

You might also go a step further to organise the endless parade of objects. You could invent hierarchies. For instance, you may notice that whereas widgets and crambags are fairly inert and just sit there in the attendants' hands, dongles have certain powers of mobility and sometimes have to be chased around the room by the attendants. So, you decide to invent a new superordinate concept called a widgbag, which distinguishes all inert from all motile things. So, whatever a dongle is, it is certainly not a widgbag.

As children facing the world of objects, we are not really playing this sort of game. We get to interact with the objects we see and our culture and parents have already assigned names and some sort of organisation to them. However, the categorisation game does highlight a very real problem which we face in everyday life, and one of the main functions of concepts: That is, concepts are there to promote *cognitive economy* (Collins & Quillian, 1969). That is, we divide the world into classes of things to decrease the amount of information we must learn, perceive, remember, and recognise. As we shall see in the remainder of this chapter, much of the research has attempted to discover how we organize instances into concepts and relate these concepts to one another.

The Defining-attribute View

In the literature which has examined the nature of concepts, the traditional view owes much to previous work in philosophy and logic. We will call this position the defining-attribute view although it has also been called the classical view of concepts (see Medin & Smith, 1984; Smith & Medin, 1981). This view, based on the work of Gottlob Frege (1952), maintains that a concept can be characterised by a set of *defining attributes*. Frege clarified the distinction between a concept's intension and its extension. The *intension* of a concept consists of the set of attributes which define what it is to be a member of the concept and the *extension* is the set of entities which are members of the concept. So, for example, the intension of the concept *bachelor* might be the set of attributes (*male, unmarried, adult*), whereas the extension of the concept is the complete set of all the bachelors in the world (from the Pope to Mr. Jones next door). Related ideas have appeared at various times in linguistics and psychology (see Clark & Clark, 1977; Glass & Holyoak, 1975; Katz, 1972; Katz & Fodor, 1963; Leech, 1974; Wallace & Atkins, 1960; Weinreich, 1966).

There are two important terminological points to be made at this stage. Throughout this chapter we will use the term "attribute" when discussing the intensions of concepts. However, many other terms are used by individual researchers in the literature, including "property," "semantic marker," and "feature." While some of these terms can have special connotations, in general they can be treated as being interchangeable with the term "attribute." Second, in talking about one of the set of objects in the world that make up a category, we will use the terms "instance" and "member" interchangeably.

The general characteristics of defining-attribute theories of concepts are as follows:

- The meaning of a concept can be captured by a conjunctive list of attributes.
- These attributes are atomic units or primitives which are the basic building blocks of concepts.
- Each of these attributes is singly necessary and all of them are jointly sufficient for something to be identified as an instance of the concept.
- This means that what is and is not a member of the category is clearly defined; so, there are clear-cut boundaries between members and nonmembers of the category.
- All members of the concept are equally representative.
- When concepts are organised in a hierarchy then the defining attributes of a more specific concept (e.g. sparrow) in relation to its more general relative (its superordinate; e.g. bird) includes all the defining attributes of the superordinate.

So, if the defining attributes of the concept *bachelor* are *male, unmarried, adult,* and we are trying to determine if Mr. Jones next door is a bachelor, in order to call him a bachelor it is necessary for him to have each attribute (i.e. *male, unmarried, adult*) and it is sufficient or enough for him to have all these three attributes together; that is, no other attributes enter into determining whether he is an instance of the concept. So, each of the properties is singly necessary and all are jointly sufficient for determining whether Mr. Jones is a member of the concept *bachelor*. This has the implication that what is and is not a *bachelor* is very clear. If Mr. O'Shea is an adult and male but is married then he cannot be considered to be a member of the category bachelor. So, the defining-attribute theory predicts that concepts should divide up individual objects in the world into distinct classes and that the boundaries between categories should be well defined and rigid. Similarly, the theory predicts that all members of the category are equally representative of it. That is, Mr. Jones cannot be considered to be a better example of a bachelor than, say, Mr. Smith, who is also *male, adult*, and *unmarried*. As we shall see, these two predictions are often disconfirmed by people's actual conception of the world.

Finally, consider two other concepts to understand how defining-attribute hierarchies nest one into another. Assume that you have the specific concept *sparrow* (defined as *feathered, animate, two-legged, small, brown*) and its superordinate, *bird* (defined as *feathered, animate, two-legged*). The subordinate concept *sparrow* will contain all the attributes of the superordinate, although it will also have many other attributes (like *brown*), to distinguish it from other subordinate concepts (e.g. *canary*, defined as *feathered, animate, two-legged, small, yellow*). This means that a specific concept will tend to have more attributes in common with its immediate superordinate than with a more distant superordinate. For example, *sparrow* should have more attributes in common with its immediate superordinate, *bird*, than with its more distant superordinate, *animal*.

There is evidence that people can treat concepts in ways which agree with the tenets of the defining-attribute view. Indeed, they expect concepts to adhere to the defining-attribute view (see, e.g., Armstrong, Gleitman, & Gleitman, 1983). In particular, the influential work of Bruner et al. (1956) looked at how people acquire concepts of shapes involving different attributes. In Bruner et al.'s experiments, subjects were shown an array of stimuli (see Fig. 8.2) which had different attributes (e.g. shape, number of shapes, shading of shapes) with different values (e.g. cross/square, one/three, plain/striped). From the experimenter's viewpoint there was a rule which identified certain items in the array as instances of the rule; for example, the rule *three, square, shapes* identifies items 20, 23, 26 as members of it and all other items as nonmembers. In the task, subjects were shown one example of the rule and had to discover the correct rule by asking the experimenter whether other items were instances of the rule.

Bruner et al. identified several different strategies used by subjects in these experiments which could be viewed as possible ways in which people might acquire concepts in everyday life, assuming that the defining-attribute view of concepts was true. However, Bruner et al.'s work was carried out in a domain of fairly artificial categories. Can we expect people to operate according to the defining-attribute view in more natural categories, involving the commonplace objects of everyday life? A means of testing this

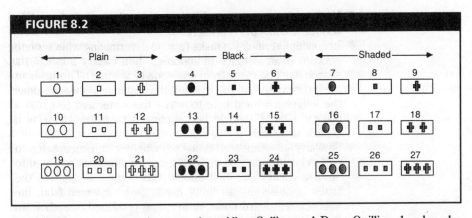

FIGURE 8.2

A sample of the sorts of materials used in Bruner et al.'s (1956) study of concept acquisition.

proposal arose when Allan Collins and Ross Quillian developed a theory and computational model which was a version of the defining-attribute view.

Collins and Quillian's Network Theory and Model

The work of Collins and Quillian (1969; 1970) is one of the prime examples of the burgeoning of cognitive science research. Quillian (1966) had developed a computational model which represented concepts as hierarchical networks (see also Chapter 1). This model was amended with some additional psychological assumptions to characterise the structure of semantic memory: A model of how concepts and their attributes were organised with respect to one another. The basic view of concepts taken in the theory was essentially the defining-attribute view. In detail they proposed that (see Fig. 8.3):

- Concepts are represented as hierarchies of inter-connected concept-nodes (e.g. *animal, bird, canary*).
- Any concept has a number of associated attributes at a given level of the hierarchy (e.g. an *animal* has the attributes *has-skin* and *eats*, whereas a bird has the attributes *has-wings* and *can-fly*).
- Some concept-nodes are superordinates of other nodes (e.g. *bird* is a superordinate of *canary*, and *animal* a superordinate of *bird*); by definition some nodes are therefore subordinates of others (e.g. *canary* is a subordinate of *bird*).
- For reasons of cognitive economy, subordinates *inherit* the attributes of their superordinate concepts; that is, since *animal* and *bird* are superordinates of *canary, canary* inherits their attributes (so a *canary* has the properties *eats, has-skin, has-wings, can-fly, is-yellow, can-sing*).
- Some instances of a concept are excepted from the defining attributes of its superordinates; for example, *ostrich* is excepted from the defining attribute of *can-fly* for the bird category (see Fig. 8.3; this is one of the model's differences from the defining-attribute view).

- Various processes search these hierarchies for information about the concepts represented.
- In concept verification tasks (e.g. in determining whether one concept is an instance of another: "Is a canary a bird?"), a search must be made from one node to another: This leads to the prediction that the greater the distance between nodes the longer it should take to verify the statement (e.g. "Is a canary a bird?" should be responded to faster than "Is a canary an animal?").
- Similarly, if someone is asked whether a concept has a particular property (e.g. "Can a canary sing?" as opposed to "Can a canary fly?"), it should take longer to answer the latter because the attribute needs to be inferred from the superordinate bird node, rather than produced directly from the canary node.

FIGURE 8.3

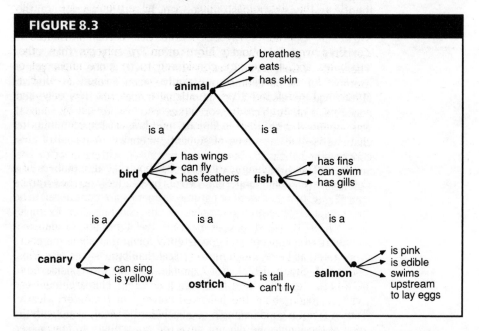

A schematic diagram of the sort of hierarchical, semantic networks proposed by Collins & Quillian (1969).

In the sentence-verification tasks used by Collins and Quillian to test their theory, subjects were asked to say whether simple sentences of two forms were true or false. First, they were asked whether "an INSTANCE was a member of a SUPERORDINATE" (e.g. "Is a canary an animal?" or "Is a canary a fish?"). Second, subjects were asked whether "an INSTANCE had a certain ATTRIBUTE" (e.g. "Can a canary fly?" or "Does a canary have skin?"). In both of these cases Collins and Quillian's predictions were confirmed. In the INSTANCE–SUPERORDINATE case it was found that the greater the distance between the subject and predicate of the sentence in the hierarchy, the longer it took to verify the sentence. And in the INSTANCE–ATTRIBUTE case the place of the attribute in the hierarchy relative to the instance mentioned predicted the time taken to verify the sentence.

Evaluating Defining-attribute Theories

The defining-attribute view and various models which realise it (like Collins and Quillian's) can be challenged in two ways. First, and less seriously, it has been pointed out that the theory fails to capture significant aspects of conceptual behaviour. The second, more serious, criticism is that the central assumption of the view that concepts depend on the conjunction of necessary features is simply wrong.

Prediction Failures of Defining-attribute Theory

First, in the defining-attribute view all attributes are equally important or salient in determining the members of a concept. However, Conrad (1972) discovered that certain attributes of concepts were mentioned more often by subjects than other attributes and, hence, are considered to be more important or salient. For example, the attribute of a salmon *is-pink* is mentioned more often than the attribute *has-fins*. Not only does this suggest that attributes are not given equal weight by subjects but Conrad showed that, in Collins and Quillian's experiments, the fast verifications of some sentences were due to the attribute's salience.

Second, the defining-attribute prediction that all members of a category are equally important or representative was shown to be untrue. Certain members of natural categories are considered to be more typical or better examples of the concept. For example, Rosch (1973) asked people to rate the typicality of different members of a concept and consistently found that some members were rated as being much more typical than others (see also Rips, Shoben, & Smith, 1973). For example, a *robin* was considered to be a better example of a bird than a *canary*. This argument can even be made about the hallowed concept of *bachelor*; clearly, Tarzan is not a good example of a bachelor because, alone with the apes of the jungle, he did not have the opportunity to marry (see Fillmore, 1982; Lakoff, 1982; 1987). The finding that different members of a category differed in terms of their typicality is serious enough, but it was also found that the typicality of members of a concept was a good predictor of the time subjects took to make verification judgements. That is, subjects took longer to verify statements involving less typical members (e.g. "A penguin is a bird") than ones involving more typical members (e.g. "A robin is a bird").

These results do not wholly finish the defining-attribute view. They are still consistent with the proposal that concept membership depends on a conjunction of necessary attributes. However, other lines of research have attacked this central assumption.

Fundamental Problems With the Conjunctive-attribute Assumption

First, it has proven very difficult to determine the defining attributes of many concepts, despite attempts by several generations of linguists, philosophers, and psychologists (for examples of these last see Hampton, 1979; McNamara & Sternberg, 1983). Some, therefore, argue that the whole enterprise of trying to break concepts down into their necessary and sufficient attributes is fundamentally ill-conceived (Fodor, Garrett, Walker, & Parkes, 1980; Wittgenstein, 1958). Some concepts simply do not seem to have defining attributes. Consider Wittgenstein's example of the concept of a *game*. There are clusters of attributes which characterise sets of games (they involve pieces, involve balls, involve one or more players) but hardly any attribute holds in all the members of the concept. Members of the category game, like the faces of the members of a family, bear a *family resemblance* to one another but they do not share a distinct set of necessary and sufficient attributes. Empirical evidence supports this criticism. In terms of the defining-attribute view, people should list the same attributes for all the members of a category (i.e. the defining set). However, people do not do this but tend to mention non-necessary attributes (Conrad, 1972; Rosch & Mervis, 1975).

The assumption that category membership is clear-cut, as it is determined by the set of defining attributes, is undermined by evidence indicating that some categories are fuzzy. That is, even though some highly typical instances are considered by most people to be category members and less typical instances are considered to be nonmembers of the category, between these two extremes people differ on whether an object is a member of the category and are also inconsistent in their judgements. That is, sometimes they think the object is a member of the category and at other times they think it is not. McCloskey and Glucksberg (1978) found evidence for this view. Their subjects were sure about saying that a *chair* was a member of the category furniture and that a *cucumber* was not a member of this category. But they disagreed with one another on whether *book-ends* were a member of the category furniture and differed in their own category judgements from one session to the next (see also Barsalou, 1987, and later sub-section on concept instability).

Third, the predictions made about nested concepts in hierarchies are not wholly confirmed. Contrary to Collins and Quillian's findings, Smith, Shoben, and Rips (1974) showed that in some cases the more distant superordinates can be verified faster than more immediate superordinates. So, when asked "Is a chicken a bird?" and "Is a chicken an animal?", contrary to Collins and Quillian's node-distance prediction, subjects responded faster to the latter than to the former. Hampton (1982) has also produced further disconfirming evidence showing that people do not consider hierarchies of concepts to be transitive (i.e. since "An X is a Y" and "A Y is a Z" is true, "An X is a Z" is also true), even though this is predicted by defining-attribute proposals.

The evidence which was found in response to the Collins and Quillian work led to a re-assessment of the defining-attribute approach to concepts. Several alternative formulations have emerged in the last few years. We shall treat two general classes of these theories. The first class of theories make an attempt to save the defining-attribute view by adding the notion of characteristic attributes. The second class of theories take a more radical line in attempting to replace the defining-attribute view with one which lends a central role to the notion of prototypes.

Summary

The traditional theory of concepts received from philosophy and linguistics views concepts as definable in terms of singly necessary and jointly sufficient attributes. This view thus predicts that (1) such attributes can be found, (2) membership of a category is not a matter of degree but is an all-or-nothing affair, (3) that there are clear boundaries between conceptual categories, and (4) that a subordinate concept should contain all the attributes of its superordinate concept. Collins and Quillian have produced a computational model which realised several of the central predictions of this view. All of these predictions are either highly questionable or have been shown to be untrue of natural categories. Theorists have, therefore, attempted to propose alternative formulations which account for this evidence.

DEFINING- AND CHARACTERISTIC-ATTRIBUTE THEORIES

When long-established theoretical views are challenged, researchers in the field tend to respond in one of several ways. One such response involves a damage-limitation strategy that tries to shore up the traditional view by adding some new assumptions which account for troublesome evidence. This particular strategy has been used in theories that retain the idea that there are defining attributes but add the extra assumption that concepts have *characteristic attributes*. Consider feature-comparison theory (Rips et al., 1973; Smith et al., 1974) as an instance of this class of theories.

Feature-comparison Theory

Feature-comparison theory dispenses with the network proposals of Collins and Quillian and merely assumes that there are two types of attributes which are operated upon by simple comparison processes. It should be noted in passing that using a network model or attribute lists is not really a critical theoretical difference, since the two have been shown to be structurally the same (see Hollan, 1975); both can be used to generate essentially the same empirical predictions. The main points of the theory are:

- A concept is represented by a set of two types of attributes: defining attributes and characteristic attributes.
- *Defining attributes* constitute the core definition of a concept and are those attributes which are shared by all members of it.
- *Characteristic attributes* are those attributes which determine how typical or representative a member of the category is likely to be judged.
- The process of verifying concepts (e.g. A canary is a bird) is carried out in two steps: first, all the attributes (both defining and characteristic) of the mentioned concepts are compared; second, only the defining attributes are compared.
- The second step is applied only if the first stage fails to produce a clear result.

Examples and Evidence

Consider how this theory deals with two different materials: "A robin is a bird" and "An ostrich is a bird." If a subject is asked to determine whether these two sentences are true or false, what we find is that the former is answered more quickly than the latter. In the robin case, all the attributes of the concepts are compared in the first stage and as many of the attributes of *robins* and *birds* match, a quick "yes" answer is given. However, in the ostrich case, the first stage returns a low number of overlapping attributes and, therefore, processing proceeds to the second stage, where only the defining attributes are compared. There are sufficient overlapping attributes in this second stage between the two concepts for a "yes" response to be returned. However, this response will be produced more slowly than in the robin case because two stages of processing are involved. In contrast, sentences like "A cabbage is a bird" can quickly be judged as being false because little or no attribute overlap is found between the two concepts in the initial stage of comparison. Other sentences, like "A bat is a bird," may proceed to the second comparison stage before they are judged as being false, because there is sufficient attribute overlap in the first stage. Subjects may even, when quick responses are demanded, make errors in the bat case and say that the sentence is true, since they do not proceed to the second stage of processing.

With respect to judgements about concepts within hierarchies, Smith et al. (1974) predicted that the speed of verification was a function of the similarity of the subordinate to a superordinate; hence they were able to account for "Is a chicken an animal?" being verified faster than "Is a chicken a bird?" (unlike Collins and Quillian).

This theory thus accounts for some of the objections raised to the defining-attribute view. First, it includes as one of its basic assumptions Conrad's (1972) finding that some attributes are more salient or characteristic of a concept than others. Second, it accounts for the effects of some instances of a concept being viewed as being more typical than others, as reflected in the various defining and characteristic attributes of category members. Third, verification times for positive and negative statements concur with the sorts of performance people show on judgements of subordinates and their relationship to near or distant superordinates.

Evaluating Feature-comparison Theory

While feature-comparison theory accounts adequately for most of the evidence which arose from the criticisms of Collins and Quillian, it has several theoretical and empirical limits. It is limited theoretically in that it is too bound to the particular sentence-verification task in question. It really only deals with the "A something is a some-other-thing" type of sentence. If all of everyday categorisation could be reduced to this task then the theory would be fine, but since it cannot, its generality is highly questionable. Methodologically, it is limited by the failure to distinguish between defining and characteristic attributes in any objective fashion. And again, the old criticism of the defining-attribute approach raises its head; namely, that it is impossible to say what the defining attributes are. In fact, some have argued that there is little evidence that defining attributes exist at all (Rosch & Mervis, 1975; but see McNamara & Sternberg, 1983).

Furthermore, some evidence does not compare favourably with the predictions made by the theory. First, the theory still predicts that members of a category should be clear-cut (as determined by the core of defining attributes), but as we saw earlier there is ample evidence to show that people consider the boundaries between members to be fuzzy.

Second, some evidence for the theory has been shown to be the result of confounding semantic relatedness and the familiarity of the words (McCloskey, 1980). In their experiments, Smith et al. had manipulated the semantic relatedness of concepts in their verification tasks and found their predicted results on reaction times. However, McCloskey has shown that the effects found may reflect the effect of the familiarity of the stimuli used in the verification sentence rather than the proposed manipulation.

More seriously, Loftus (1973) has shown that if the nouns in the sentences are reversed, there are effects on verification speed not predicted by feature-comparison theory. She presented instances and asked subjects to list categories that the instances belonged to and also presented categories and asked for a list of instances. This provided measures of instance-to-category production frequency and of category-to-instance production frequency, respectively. She then measured the reaction times in a verification task in which either the instance preceded the category ("Is a wren a bird?") or the category preceded the instance ("Is a bird a wren?").

According to the feature-comparison model, verification time should be unaffected by this manipulation of noun order. In fact, Loftus discovered that instance-to-category production frequency predicted the reaction time when the instance preceded the category, whereas the category-to-instance production frequency predicted the reaction time when the category preceded the instance (see Collins & Loftus, 1975, for a revised network model of these results).

Other Models and Evidence

Feature-comparison theory is only one of a number of defining- and characteristic-attribute theories. Another variant of this view, identified by Smith and Medin (1981) is based on Miller and Johnson-Laird's (1976) distinction between the "core" of a concept and its "identification procedure." The core of the concept consists of defining attributes and is important in revealing the relations between a given concept and other concepts. That is, the conceptual core of bachelor (*male, unmarried, adult*) is important in revealing why a *bachelor* and a *spinster* (*female, unmarried, adult*) are similar or why the terms "bachelor" and "single male" are considered synonymous. The *identification procedure* is responsive to characteristic attributes and plays a specific role in categorising real-world objects. Thus, the core retains the defining-attribute theory while the identification procedure can account for typicality effects. Armstrong et al. (1983) carried out a study that suggests evidence for this view. They examined concepts that clearly have defining attributes (e.g. *even number, odd number, plane geometry figure*) and found that members of these categories were judged to be more or less typical of the category. For instance, 22 was rated as being more typical of the concept *even number* than was 18, and was also categorised faster. Thus, these concepts seemed to have a conceptual core and yet made use of characteristic attributes in catergorisation tasks. Similarly, McNamara and Sternberg (1983) asked subjects to list the attributes of several different types of nouns (artifacts, natural kinds, and proper names) and to rate the necessity, sufficiency, and importance of each attribute to the word's definition. An inspection of subjects' ratings revealed that they considered some of the words to have defining attributes (i.e. necessary and sufficient attributes) and characteristic attributes. But only half could be defined by the defining attributes produced by subjects. McNamara and Sternberg also showed that these same distinctions were implicated in the real-time processing of the concepts, when they were read as words.

If we assume that concepts have a conceptual core and then other characteristic features, then one would expect there to be linguistic hedges in the language to take this distinction into account. Lakoff (1973; 1982) has argued that such hedges exist and are signalled by terms like "true" and "technically speaking" or "strictly speaking". These terms qualify assertions we might make about category members. For example, if one says "A duck is a true bird" the core definition of the concept bird is being marked explicitly, whereas the sentence "Technically speaking, a penguin is a bird" marks the fact that one knows a penguin is a nonrepresentative example of that category but wishes to include it within the category.

Summary

One response to the failure of the defining-attribute view has been to try to introduce some extra assumptions to account for the troublesome evidence. Feature-comparison theory does just this by positing defining and characteristic attributes and introducing two stages of processing in verification tasks. During the first stage of processing, all the attributes of the to-be-compared objects are compared. An optional second stage compares just the defining attributes, depending on the results of the first stage and task demands. While this theory can account for many of the deficits of Collins and Quillian's theory it still faces some of the fundamental problems of the defining-attribute approach. Feature-comparison theory is only one version of a defining- and characteristic-attribute view; other versions have been proposed and evidence has been found to support these theories.

PROTOTYPE (OR CHARACTERISTIC-ATTRIBUTE) THEORIES

While defining- and characteristic-attribute theories retain something of the traditional defining-attribute view, another set of theories has taken a very different line. These *prototype theories* were specifically proposed to account for the deficits of the defining-attribute view: For example, typicality effects and the fuzziness of concepts. The crucial proposal of the prototype view is that categories are organised around central prototypes. However, different theories conceive of the nature of these prototypes in different ways.

According to one class of prototype theories, the prototype is represented by characteristic attributes. That is, there are no defining attributes but rather only characteristic attributes which have different weights or different degrees of importance within the concept (see, e.g., Hampton, 1979; Posner & Keele, 1968; Rosch, 1978). An object is considered to be a member of the concept if its attributes match those of the prototype's attributes above some threshold. An alternative formulation of this view represents the prototype in terms of the best member (or small set of best members) of the concept (e.g. Brooks, 1978; Hintzman & Ludlum, 1980; Medin & Shaffer, 1978). So, for example, the prototype of the furniture category might be the *chair* exemplar or a set of exemplars (like *chair, table, bed*). Here an object is a member of a category to the extent that it is close to these best examples of the concept. For the purposes of this chapter we will treat both of these sets of theories as prototype theories. However, proponents of both camps often make stronger claims for the differences between them. One essential difference, which may be kept in mind, is that exemplar theories reject the idea that abstractions underlie our concepts and argue that individual entities lie at their heart.

Prototype Theory

Rather than treat all of the variants of the prototype view we will simply represent its main proposals in a general fashion, listing its central assertions:

- Concepts have a prototype structure; the prototype is either a collection of characteristic attributes or the best example (or examples) of the concept.
- There is no delimiting set of necessary and sufficient attributes for determining category membership; although there may be necessary attributes, they are not jointly sufficient; indeed membership often depends on the object possessing some set of characteristic, non-necessary attributes which are considered more typical or representative of the category than others.
- Category boundaries are fuzzy or unclear; what is and is not a member of the category is ill-defined; so some members of the category may slip into other categories (e.g. tomatoes as fruit or vegetables).
- Instances of a concept can be ranged in terms of their typicality; that is, there is a *typicality gradient* which characterises the differential typicality of examples of the concept.
- Category membership is determined by the similarity of an object's attributes to the category's prototype, whether that prototype be represented by characteristic attributes or an exemplar of the category.

Evidence for the Prototype View

There is a considerable corpus of research directed specifically towards testing the prototype view. It includes research on colour categories and on a variety of natural and artificial categories and also deals with proposals about the nature of conceptual hierarchies in human categorisation.

Colour Categories

One of the most striking pieces of evidence for the prototype view has been that gleaned from cross-cultural studies of colour categories. There is a great diversity in the use of colour terms throughout the languages of the world. Some cultures have terms for a wide variety of colours (e.g. in Western Europe we have a huge diversity from magenta to sky-blue to red, and so on), whereas other cultures have very few terms (e.g. the Dani of Papua New Guinea have only two colour terms for things which are dark and bright). Berlin and Kay (1969) suggested that this diversity was only apparent if one distinguished between focal colours and nonfocal colours. In their studies they identified *basic colour terms* using four criteria: (1) the term must be expressed as one morpheme, so something like sky-blue would be ruled out; (2) its meaning cannot be included in that of another term, ruling out scarlet because it includes red; (3) it must not be restricted to a small class of objects, ruling out terms like blond which really only apply to hair and possibly furniture; and (4) it must be a frequently used term, like green, rather than turquoise. Berlin and Kay discovered that all languages draw their basic colour terms from a set of 11. English has words for all of this set; they are black, white, red, green, yellow, blue, brown, purple, pink, orange, and gray.

Using the basic colour terms derived from this analysis they set about examining about 20 different languages in detail, by performing experiments using a set of over 300 colour chips. In these studies, native speakers of the languages in question were asked 2 questions about the colour chips. First, they were asked what chips they would be willing to label using a particular basic colour term. Second, they were asked what chips are the best or most typical examples of a colour term. What they found was that the speakers of different languages agreed in their identification of focal colours; people consistently agreed on the best example of, say, a red or a blue. This, together with the finding that subjects were uncertain about category boundaries, suggested that category membership was judged on the basis of resemblance to focal colours. These and other results were also found for cultures like the Dani with a very limited colour terminology. Rosch (when she was called Heider, 1972; also Rosch, 1975a) showed that the Dani could remember focal colours better than nonfocal colours and that even though they only had two colour terms they could learn names for the focal colours more quickly than they could for nonfocal colours. It should be pointed out that Lucy and Shweder (1979) have shown that some of these memory results need to be questioned because "the colour array previously used to demonstrate the influence of focality on memory was discriminatively biased in favour of focal chips."

Thus, there seems to be a universality in people's categorisation of certain colours and in the structure of colour categories; in particular, it seems that these categories have a prototype structure. However, it is noteworthy that these categories have a strong physiological basis in the nature of the colour vision system. As such colour categories are a special case of a category. It was, therefore, necessary to see whether similar effects were present in categories that lacked such a special basis.

Evidence from Natural and Artificial Categories

Research on both natural categories (i.e. categories of things in the world, like birds and furniture) and artificial categories (e.g. numbers and dot patterns) has also been carried out that provides supportive evidence for detailed aspects of the prototype view. As we saw earlier, some members of categories are considered to be highly representative or highly typical. Subjects will rate the typicality of concept members differentially (Rips et al., 1973; Rosch, 1973). These typicality effects have been shown to have considerable generality; for instance, they have also been found in psychiatric classifications (Cantor, Smith, French, & Mezzich, 1980), in linguistic categories (Lakoff, 1982, talks of degrees of nouniness and verbiness), and in various action concepts (like *to lie* and *to hope*; see Coleman & Kay, 1981; Vaughan, Note 9). Furthermore, the most typical members of a concept have been implicated in several important facets of conceptualisation.

First, the typicality gradient of members of a concept has been shown to be a good predictor of categorisation times. In verification tasks (e.g. "A canary is a bird"), typical members (like *robin*), are verified faster than atypical members (like *ostrich*). This has proven a very robust finding (for reviews see Danks & Glucksberg, 1980; Kintsch, 1980; Smith, 1978; Smith & Medin, 1981). Second, typical members are likely to be mentioned first when subjects are asked to list all the members of a category (Battig & Montague, 1969; Mervis, Catlin & Rosch, 1976). Similarly, Rosch, Simpson, & Miller (1976) found that when subjects were asked to sketch the exemplar of a particular category they were most likely to depict the most typical member. Third, the first members of a concept which children tend to learn are the typical members, as measured by semantic categorisation tasks (Rosch, 1973). Fourth, Rosch (1975b) has found that typical members are more likely to serve as cognitive reference points than are atypical members; for example, people are more likely to say "An ellipse is almost a circle" (where circle is the more typical form and occurs in the reference position of the sentence) than "A circle is almost an ellipse" (where ellipse, the less typical form, occurs in the reference position).

A final important finding which deserves mention is the extent to which estimates of family resemblance correlate highly with typicality. Taking Wittgenstein's term *family resemblance*, Rosch and Mervis (1975) have shown that one can derive a family resemblance score for each member of a category by noting all the attributes that a member has in common with all the other members of the category. Rosch and Mervis found that typical members have high family-resemblance scores and share few (if any) attributes in common with related contrast categories. This is rather direct evidence for the idea that the typicality gradient of a concept's members is a function of the similarity of those members to the prototype of the category.

Levels of Abstraction in Prototype Theory

Collins and Quillian's work posited several levels of generality in characterising the nature of conceptual hierarchies. Since many of their proposals about the levels at which concepts are organised were disconfirmed, the question of the nature of conceptual hierarchies remains to be answered. As an adjunct to prototype theory, Rosch and her associates proposed that conceptual hierarchies had a definite tri-levelled structure for certain reasons; she argued that (see Rosch, Mervis, Gray, Johnson, & Boyes-Braem, 1976):

- People use hierarchies to represent mentally relationships of class inclusion between categories; that is, to include one category within another (e.g. the category of chair within the category for furniture).
- Human conceptual hierarchies have three levels; a super-ordinate level (e.g. weapons, furniture), a basic level (e.g. guns, chair), and a subordinate level of specific concepts (e.g. hand-guns, rifles, kitchen chairs, armchairs).
- The basic level is that level at which concepts have the most "distinctive attributes" and it is the most cognitively economic; that is, the level at which a concept's attributes are *not* shared with other concepts at the same level.
- Categories at the basic level are critical to many cognitive activities; for example, they contain concepts that can be interacted with using similar motor movements, they have the same general shape, and they may be associated with a mental image which represents the whole category.
- The position of the basic level can change as a function of individual differences in expertise and cultural differences.

There is considerable evidence to support this view of conceptual hierarchies. From the Roschian viewpoint, these levels reflect the optimal manner in which one can organise a set of categories. At the top level, the superordinate level, one has general designations for very general categories like furniture. At the lowest level, one ranges specific types of objects (e.g. my favourite armchair, a kitchen chair). In between these two extremes is the basic level, which is critical to our everyday cognitive activities. Whereas we often talk about general categories (that furniture is expensive) and about specific concepts (my new Cadillac), we usually deal with objects at the intermediate, basic level (whether there are enough chairs and desks in the office). It is at the basic level also that there is a maximal, within-category similarity relative to between-category similarity.

The initial idea for a basic level category came from anthropological studies of biological and zoological categories (Berlin, 1972; Berlin, Breedlove, & Raven, 1973; Brown, Kolar, Torrey, Truong-Quang, & Volkman, 1976). Berlin (1972) noted that the classification of plants used by the Tzeltal Indians of Mexico corresponded to the categories at a particular level in the scientific taxonomy of plants. For instance, in the case of trees, the cultures studied by Berlin were more likely to have terms for a genus such as beech than for general, superordinate groupings (e.g. deciduous, coniferous) or for individual species (e.g. silver birch, copper beech). The reason Berlin gave for this basic level was that categories such as "beech" and "birch" were naturally distinctive and coherent groupings; that is, the species they include tend to have common patterns of attributes such as leaf shape, bark colour, and so on. So in some ways the basic level is the best level at which to summarise categories.

Several aspects of the basic level conception were studied by Rosch et al. (1976). They asked people to list all the attributes of items at each of the three levels within a hierarchy (e.g. furniture, chair, easy chair) and discovered that very few attributes were listed for the superordinate categories (like furniture) and many attributes were listed for the categories at the other two levels. However, at the lowest level very similar attributes were listed for different categories (e.g. easy chair, living-room chair). As such, the intermediate-level categories (like chair) are noted by a balance between informativeness (the number of attributes the concept conveys) and economy (a sort of summary of the important attributes which distinguish it from other categories). Informativeness is lacking at the highest level because few attributes are conveyed and economy is missing at the lowest level because too many attributes are conveyed.

Rosch et al. (1976) also found evidence that basic-level categories have special properties not shared by categories at other levels. First, the basic level is the one at which adults spontaneously name objects and is also the one that is usually acquired first by young children. Furthermore, the basic level is the most general level at which people use similar motor movements for interacting with category members; for instance, all chairs can be sat on in roughly the same way and this differs markedly to the way we interact with tables. Category members at the basic level also have fairly similar overall shapes and as such it is not surprising to find that a mental image can reflect the whole category. Finally, objects tend to be recognised more quickly as members of basic-level categories than as members of categories at higher and lower levels.

However, it is important to note that basic-level concepts do not always correspond to intermediate terms (e.g. chair in furniture–chair–armchair). In nonbiological categories (like furniture) the intermediate term tends to correspond to the basic level. However, in biological categories the superordinate term tends to correspond to the basic level (e.g. "bird" in bird–sparrow–song sparrow). This difference is seen as being a function of the amount of experience people have with members of biological categories. That is, one's experience with the instances of a category will lead to differences in one's basic level. So, ornithologists would be more likely to consider sparrow to be the basic level for the bird category because, given their expertise, this is the most distinctive level. Similarly, Berlin's findings with the Tzeltal probably reflects their expertise concerning the differences between trees (see also later section on neuropsychological evidence).

Evaluation of the Prototype View

If we wish to find fault with the prototype view there are three main criticisms which we can make. First, not all concepts have prototype characteristics. Hampton (1981) has examined this question in the case of abstract concepts (like "science," "crime," "a work of art") rather than the concrete concepts which are normally examined. Some of these abstract concepts exhibited a prototype structure but others did not (e.g. "a rule," "a belief," and "an instinct"). The reason for the latter cases seems to lie in the endless flexibility in membership of these categories, in contrast to concrete categories. For instance, it seems impossible to specify the complete set of possible rules or beliefs. Thus there are some limits on the generality of the view.

The prototype view is also incomplete as an account of the sort of knowledge people have about concepts. People seem to know about the relations between attributes, rather than just attributes alone, and this information can be used in categorisation (Malt & Smith, 1983; Walker, 1975). Consider the following case (see also Holland et al., 1986). Imagine going to a strange, Galapagos-like island for the first time, accompanied by a guide. On the journey, one sees a beautiful blue bird fly out of a thicket and the guide indicates that it is called a "warrum." Later in the day, we meet a portly individual fishing and are told that he is a member of the "klaatu" tribe. A day later, wandering without the guide one sees another blue bird, like the first, and considers it to be another warrum; however, on meeting another fat native one does not assume that he is a member of the klaatu tribe. The reason for this is that we know that colour is a particularly diagnostic and invariant attribute of the bird category but physical weight is not a particularly diagnostic attribute of tribal affiliations; in fact, it is known to be a highly variable attribute. Hence, we know that some attributes are more likely to vary than other attributes. The fact that people can make reasonable guesses about the meaning of new terms on the basis of a single exposure to an instance is an important ability that prototype theory is silent about.

Finally, the prototype view does not explain why categories cohere. In recent years, researchers have changed the tack of their questioning. Rather than asking what the structure of concepts like bird and furniture is, they have asked how we come to group objects together in one category rather than in another. Now the traditional answer to this question, in the prototype view and all the other views we have examined, is that some similarity mechanism is responsible for category cohesion. Stated simply, things form themselves into categories because they all have certain attributes in common. However, similarity cannot be the only mechanism because we often form categories which are only tenuously based on shared attributes but which are nevertheless coherent (e.g. see Barsalou's work on ad hoc categories later). Lakoff (1987) mentions one culture which has a category that contains the following disparate objects: women, fire, and dangerous things. Murphy and Medin (1985) point to the biblical categories of clean and unclean animals; clean animals include most fish, grasshoppers, and some locusts whereas unclean animals include camels, ostriches, crocodiles, mice, sharks, and eels. Later on we will see that a number of researchers have recently attempted to explain category cohesiveness.

Summary

The final view taken on concepts can be labelled the prototype view. This is an umbrella term for a whole set of theories which view concepts as being organised around prototypes and expressed as clusters of attributes or some form of exemplar. This view accounts for many of the shortcomings of the other views. It accounts for the evidence of gradients of typicality, of fuzzy boundaries, and of levels of abstraction in both natural and artificial categories. In particular, some exponents of the view have argued that there are three levels of generality at which categories are organised: a superordinate level, a basic level, and a subordinate level. The basic level is viewed as being that level which is most informative and economical. There are some queries about the generality of the prototype view, as it has been found that some abstract concepts do not exhibit prototype structure. More seriously, the view is silent on the knowledge people have about the relations between properties and it cannot adequately account for category cohesiveness, with its similarity mechanism for category formation.

FROM NETWORKS TO SCHEMATA: RELATIONAL CONCEPTS AS SCHEMATA

Thus far, we have merely dealt with "object concepts" (e.g. *cats, dogs, tables, chairs*); surely there is more to our knowledge organisation than this. Well, there is a lot more but it has not received as much attention as research on concepts. In this section, we consider one of the more neglected aspects of knowledge organisation research by examining "relational concepts" (like *hit, bounce, and kiss*); later, we will move on to consider more complex forms of knowledge organisation.

Collins and Quillian's work had an important influence on the expansion of the research program to consider relational as well as object concepts. In 1975, Collins and Loftus proposed a modified network model to deal with the inadequacies of the earlier one. From the perspective of relational concepts, this model was important because it introduced a variety of labelled links between the nodes in the network. Apart from just *is–a* links, as was the case in Collins and Quillian's model, there were also links for relations like *hit* and *kick*. This characteristic of network models became a constant in other examples of the genre (see, e.g. Anderson, 1976; 1983). The Collins and Loftus work connects this research area to mainstream concept research in psychology. However, independent lines of work on relational concepts had already been established in linguistics and computer science, and it was these ideas that informed later psychological work.

Treating Relational Concepts as Propositions

The over-riding concern in the treatment of relational concepts has been with how they should be represented. Initially, propositional representations were used which owed much to the case grammar work of the linguist Charles Fillmore (1968). Several psychologists developed the idea that a relational concept could be represented in the predicate calculus as a predicate taking a number of arguments (see, e.g., Kintsch, 1974; Norman & Rumelhart, 1975). For example:

HIT(Agent, Object, Instrument)
COLLIDE(Object1, Object2)

Here *hit* and *collide* are predicates and the bracketed terms are arguments (see Chapter 7). It was assumed that in understanding a sentence, people encoded the spoken words into this form of mental representation and assigned various object concepts to the arguments. So, for example, the written or spoken sentence:

Karl hit Mark with a copper pipe.

would be represented as

HIT(Karl, Mark, Copper-Pipe)

It was generally assumed that people knew enough about the objects mentioned in the sentence to determine if they could fill the argument slots in the representation. For example, one knew that since Karl is human and animate, he could act as an Agent.

Although this scheme can be used to characterise the representations of relations in sentences, it has been criticised heavily by Johnson-Laird, Herrmann, and Chaffin (1984). They argued, convincingly, that the use of these sorts of propositional representations was not constrained enough to constitute an adequate theory of the meaning of relations. Drawing on the distinction between intensional and extensional aspects of concepts, Johnson-Laird et al. (1984) pointed out that these theories said little about extensional phenomena. Furthermore, since one could cast any theory of meaning in these network representations, they argued that as theories they were massively under-constrained. In Johnson-Laird et al.'s terms they were "only connections."

Semantic Decomposition of Relational Propositions

One partial answer to the Johnson-Laird et al. criticisms is to specify more about the semantic primitives which underlie a particular relation (see, e.g., Gentner, 1975; Miller & Johnson-Laird, 1976; Norman & Rumelhart, 1975). We shall concentrate on one well-known treatment called conceptual dependency theory, proposed by the computer scientist, Roger Schank, of Yale University (Schank, 1972).

Schank proposed that the core meaning of a whole set of action verbs could be captured by 12 to 15 primitive actions. These primitives were called *acts* and the main ones are listed below:

ATRANS: transfer of possession (give, lend, take)
PTRANS: physical transfer from one location to another (move, walk, drive)
MTRANS: transfer of mental information (order, advise)
MBUILD: build memory structures (remember, understand)
ATTEND: receive sensory input (seeing, hearing)
PROPEL: application of force to physical object (push, hit, squeeze)
MOVE: move a body part (wave, lift leg)
INGEST: intake of food or air (breathe, eat)
EXPEL: reverse of ingest (excrete, vomit)

These primitive acts are used in a case-frame fashion to characterise the semantic basis of a whole range of verbs. For example, ATRANS can characterise any verb which involves the transfer of possession:

Actor: person
Act: ATRANS
Object: physical object
Direction TO: person-1
        FROM: person-2

This structure is a form of *schema*. The structure is made up of a series of *variables* (the terms Actor, Act, Object, etc.) and in a specific case certain values are assigned to these variables. So "John gave Mary a necklace" would be represented as:

Actor:	John
Act:	ATRANS
Object:	necklace
Direction TO:	Mary
FROM:	John

A variable, as its name suggests, can take on any of a number of values. Computer scientists often use the term *slot* for variable and *slot filler* for a value; this taps into a spatial metaphor which suggests that slots are like holes in the schema into which specific objects (like necklace) are put.

ATRANS can be used to characterise many relations, such as receive, take, buy, and sell. In a more complicated fashion certain verbs can be characterised by a combination of primitives. For instance, kick involves MOVE and PROPEL, because one moves a body part to impart a force to another object.

Other schemes have been used which are similar to this one, but they all share the characteristic of representing the relational term as a primitive or set of interconnected primitives. As such, this approach is very much an instance of the defining-attribute view that we saw earlier in the object-concept research. As we shall see later, there is evidence which suggests that the defining-attribute view is also inadequate in this area.

Evidence for Semantic Decomposition

In general, in the case of relational representations, empirical testing has tended to be outstripped by theoretical analyses. However, some research has examined whether, in the course of comprehending a sentence, a relation is decomposed into its constituent primitives or not. While some have argued that this *semantic decomposition* does not occur (Fodor, Fodor, & Garrett, 1975; Kintsch, 1974), others have taken an opposing line (Gentner, 1975; 1981). Initially, several studies found that complex sentences, which are assumed to involve more primitives, did not take longer to process than simple sentences or did not differ in memorability (see Carpenter & Just, 1977; Kintsch, 1974). This result seemed to be good evidence for the absence of semantic decomposition. But Gentner (1975; 1981) countered these findings by positing two distinct types of complex sentences. She maintained that "poorly-connected" complex sentences should take less time to process than "well-connected" complex sentences and that previous studies had confounded this difference.

Consider the three main types of materials Gentner (1981) used in her study. First, she distinguished between simple and complex sentences: For instance, "Ida *gave* her tenants a clock" was considered to be simpler than "Ida *mailed* her tenants a clock" or "Ida *sold* her tenants a clock". This was because *give* involves just a transfer of possession, whereas both *mailed* and *sold* involve a transfer of possession and something else; in the case of mailed there are the associated actions of mailing something and sold involves a transfer of goods and of money. However, even though the mailed and sold sentences are both complex, they differ in how well-connected or integrated their elements are. Mailing involves Ida as a principal agent who performs a mail routine which causes a transfer of possession to certain recipients (i.e. her tenants). Selling involves Ida as a principal agent who transfers possession of goods to the tenant recipients, but she is also a recipient for the transfer of money from the tenants acting as principal agents. Gentner, therefore, argues that more connections between Ida and the tenants are elaborated in the selling case than in the mailing case; that the former is more well-connected than the latter. Given these assumed representational differences she predicted that if decomposition occurs then the well-connected sentence should be recalled more accurately than the poorly-connected sentence and the latter should be recalled better than the simple sentence. In essence, all these predictions were confirmed.

Gentner's research provides some support for a defining-attribute theory of relational concepts, but it does not really test the theory's assumptions explicitly. However, work by Coleman and Kay (1981; also Vaughan, Note 9) has shown that primitives should not be treated as defining attributes. Coleman and Kay found that several verbs exhibit typicality effects similar to those observed in object concepts. Coleman and Kay posited that the verb *to lie* (prevaricate) had three semantic components or attributes; in which (1) the statement made is false, (2) the speaker believes the statement is false, and (3) the speaker intends to deceive the hearer. They then made up stories in which they explicitly cancelled some or all of these attributes and asked subjects to judge the degree to which the incident in the story could be regarded as a lie. For example, a story about a railway porter telling a traveller that the train to London leaves from platform 5, when this was not true and the porter was not aware of its falsity, cancels the second two attributes. Using this method they found that different usages were considered to be better or worse examples of a lie. Furthermore, the attributes which made up the representation of the verb were considered to be differentially important in characterising a good example of a lie. These results thus favour a prototype view of relational concepts.

Summary

The main body of research on categorisation has concentrated on object concepts rather than on relational concepts. However, some theoretical and empirical work has been carried out on the latter. Many theories propose that relations can be characterised as sets of relational primitives which take various objects as their arguments in a case-grammar format. Several studies have examined whether relations are decomposed into these primitives during comprehension of sentences. As in the case of object-concept research, there is evidence against a defining-attribute view of relations, which favours a prototype view.

SCHEMATA, FRAMES, AND SCRIPTS

As we said earlier, there is clearly more to human knowledge than attribute-like information about single concepts or relations. At the beginning of this chapter, we showed that even the comprehension of simple sentences, like the one about Lisa returning from the shop, involve the application of a considerable amount of knowledge. It is plausible to assume that this knowledge is organised in a manner which is more complex than class-like or hierarchical groupings of concepts. Concepts are also likely to be related together in many varied ways which reflect the temporal and causal structure of the world. Another line of research, mainly concerned with the comprehension of complex events, has examined this form of organisation and has proposed a variety of mental constructs—most notably the notion of a schema—to account for people's observed behaviour (see also Chapter 9).

Historical Antecedents of Schema Theories

The most commonly used construct to account for complex knowledge organisation is the schema. A *schema* is a structured cluster of concepts; usually, it involves generic knowledge and may be used to represent events, sequences of events, precepts, situations, relations, and even objects. Kant's (1787/1963) philosophical theories originally proposed the idea of schemata as innate structures for organising our perception of the world. In current terms, he was particularly nativistic in his suggestion that innate, a priori structures of the mind allowed us to conceive of time, three-dimensional space, and even geometry (even though many school children might disagree).

In the 1930s, the concept of a schema found its way, via Sir Henry Head's neurophysiology, into the research of Sir Frederic Bartlett at Cambridge University. Bartlett (1932) was struck by the extent to which people's understanding and remembrance of events were shaped by their expectations. He suggested that these expectations were represented mentally in some schematic fashion and he carried out a series of experiments that illustrated the extent to which expectations affected various aspects of cognition. For instance, he gave English subjects a North American Indian folk tale, which had attributions and causal sequences strange to a western mind, and then asked them to recall the stories at various intervals. He found that subjects "reconstructed" the story rather than remembering it verbatim and that they did this in a manner consistent with their western assumptions and expectations (see Table 8.1).

In a developmental context, Piaget (1967; 1970) had also made use of the concept of a schema to understand the changes that occur in children's cognition. However, it was really in the 1970s that the schema concept re-emerged as a dominant interest in cognitive psychology. The concept took on a number of different

---

TABLE 8.1

Part of the Original War of the Ghosts *Story and One Subject's* Subsequent Recall of It (from Bartlett, 1932)

The War of the Ghosts

One night two young men from Edulac went down the river to hunt seals, and while they were there it became foggy and calm. Then they heard war-cries, and they thought: "Maybe this is a war-party." They escaped to the shore, and hid behind a log. Now canoes came up, and they heard the noise of paddles, and saw one canoe coming up to them. There were five men in the canoe, and they said: "What do you think? We wish to take you along. We are going up the river to make war on the people."

. . . one of the young men went but the other returned home . . . [it turns out that the five men in the boat were ghosts and after accompanying them in a fight, the young man returned to his village to tell his tale] . . . and said: "Behold I accompanied the ghosts, and we went to fight. Many of our fellows were killed, and many of those who attacked us were killed. They said I was hit, and I did not feel sick."

He told it all and then he became quiet. When the sun rose he fell down. Something black came out of his mouth. His face became contorted . . . He was dead. (p. 65)

A Subject's Recall of the Story (2 Weeks Later)

There were two ghosts. They were on a river. There was a canoe on the river with five men in it. There occurred a war of ghosts . . . They started the war and several were wounded and some killed. One ghost was wounded but did not feel sick. He went back to the village in the canoe. The next morning he was sick and something black came out of his mouth, and they cried: "He is dead." (p. 76)

---

forms: Schank's (1972; see previous section) primitive acts are one instance of a small schema for organising the concepts predicated by a relation, "story grammars" were proposed by Rumelhart and others to underlie the comprehension of stories (Rumelhart, 1975; Stein and Glenn, 1979; Thorndyke, 1977), and "scripts" were proposed by Schank & Abelson (1977) to account for people's stereotypical knowledge of often-encountered situations. More generally, Rumelhart and Ortony (1977; also Rumelhart, 1980) proposed a general theory of schemata and, in artificial intelligence, Marvin Minsky (1975) suggested similar structures called "frames", which he implicated mainly in visual perception (see Thorndyke & Yekovich, 1980, for a review).

Schemata and Scripts

The concept of a schema is a very loose one in many respects. Because it is an organising structure for knowledge, it tends to take on ostensibly different forms when representing different sorts of knowledge. In general, however, schemata have several common characteristics (see also previous section for specific examples):

- Schemata consist of various relations, variables/slots and values for these variables.
- The relations can take a variety of forms; they can be simple relations like *is-a* and *hit* or *kick*, or they can be more complex "causal" relations (e.g. *enable, cause, prevent, desire*).
- *Variables/slots* contain concepts or other sub-schemata; any concept which fills a slot usually has to satisfy some test (e.g. the argument-slot "Agent" in the relation HIT[Agent, Object, Instrument] requires that the concept which fills it is an animate object).
- *Values* refer to the various specific concepts that fill or instantiate slots.
- Schemata thus encode general or *generic* knowledge which can be applied in many specific situations, if those situations are instances of the schema; for example, the HIT relation just shown could characterise a domestic dispute (e.g. Harry hit the child) or a car crash (e.g. The van hit the lorry).
- Schemata can often leave slots "open" or have associated with them *default concepts* which are assumed if a slot is unfilled; for instance, we are not told what instrument Harry used (in "Harry hit the child"), but we can assume a default value like a hand or a stick was used.

We have illustrated the notion of a schema mainly with respect to the very simple schemata that characterise relations. For more complicated examples of schemata consider Schank and Abelson's (1977) script theory, which attempts to capture the knowledge underlying our comprehension of commonplace events like going to a restaurant.

Schank and Abelson's Script Theory
Schank and Abelson were interested in the sorts of background inferences people make when they comprehend extended texts like the following one:

Ruth and Mark had lunch at a restaurant today. They really enjoyed the meal but were worried about the eventual cost of it. However, after the ice cream, when the bill arrived, they were pleasantly surprised to find that it was very reasonable.

In reading this passage, we infer that the meal (mentioned in the first sentence) was at the restaurant where they had lunch (mentioned in the second sentence), that the meal involved ice-cream and that the bill did not walk up to them but was probably brought by a waiter. To make these sorts of inferences Schank and Abelson argued that we must have schematic structures that predict what would happen next (e.g. that dessert follows the entrée) and fill in those aspects of the event which we leave implicit. The schema they proposed, called a *script*, thus contains the sequence of actions one goes through when carrying out stereotypical events; for example, one would have a script for eating in restaurants, because it is a sequence of actions one has done repeatedly. The script would also encode the sorts of objects and actors one expects to encounter in this context. Their restaurant script had four main divisions: entering, ordering, eating, and leaving. Each of these general parts had sub-actions for what to do: for instance, entering breaks down into walking into the restaurant, looking for a table, deciding where to sit, going to a table, and sitting down (see Table 8.2).

Within this scheme the relations are the various actions, like walking or sitting. The slots in the script contain either roles or other sub-schemata. *Role slots* capture the various "parts" in the script like the waiter, the customers and the cook and are filled by the specific people in the situation (e.g. the tall waiter with the receding hairline). Ordinarily, these roles can only be filled by an object which satisfies the test of being human (e.g. a waiter who is a dog is unexpected and extraordinary). The general components

TABLE 8.2

The Components and Actions of the Restaurant Script Proposed by Schank & Abelson (1977)

Script Name	Component	Specific Action
Eating at a restaurant	Entering	Walk into restaurant
		Look for table
		Decide where to sit
		Go to table
		Sit down
	Ordering	Get menu
		Look at menu
		Choose food
		Waiter arrives
		Give orders to waiter
		Waiter takes order to cook
		Wait, talk
		Cook prepares food
	Eating	Cook gives food to waiter
		Waiter delivers food to customer
		Customer eats
		Talk
	Leaving	Waiter writes bill
		Waiter delivers bill to customer
		Customer examines bill
		Calculate tip
		Leave tip
		Gather belongings
		Pay bill
		Leave restaurant

of the script (e.g. entering, ordering) can also be viewed as slots that contain sub-schemata (pertaining to the various detailed actions of walking, sitting, and so on). In this way, one can see how it is possible to create structures that characterise people's background knowledge about many stereotypical situations.

Evidence for Script Theory

Several studies have investigated the psychological plausibility of scriptal notions (see Abelson, 1981; Bower et al., 1979; Galambos, Abelson, & Black, 1986; Graesser, Gordon, & Sawyer, 1979; Sanford & Garrod, 1981; Walker & Yekovich, 1984). For example, Bower et al. asked subjects to list in order about 20 actions or events which occurred commonly while eating at a restaurant. Even though there are many different types of restaurant one can visit, they found that there was considerable agreement in the lists produced by subjects. When describing the events involved in going to a restaurant, at least 73% of the subjects mentioned sitting down, looking at the menu, ordering, eating, paying the bill, and leaving. In addition, at least 48% included in their descriptions entering the restaurant, giving the reservation name, ordering drinks, discussing the menu, talking, eating a salad or soup, ordering dessert, eating dessert, and leaving a tip. In other words, there are at least 15 events that form part of many people's knowledge of what is involved in having a meal at a restaurant. Other evidence by Galambos and Rips (1982) has shown that when subjects had to make a rapid decision about whether or not an action was part of a script (e.g. determining that "getting to a restaurant" is part of a restaurant script), they answered rapidly when the action is part of the script but take longer when it is not.

Other Evidence for Schemata

There is considerable evidence in several different areas for the operation of schema-like knowledge structures (see, e.g., Alba & Hasher, 1983; Graesser, Woll, Kowalski & Smith, 1980). The strongest evidence comes from studies showing that when people have different expectations about a target event they interpret and recall it in different ways (see, e.g., Anderson & Pichert, 1978; Bransford & Johnson, 1972; and Chapter 9 for more details).

In perception, for example, schemata have also been implicated in freeing up the cognitive system from having to analyse all aspects of a visual scene. When viewing an everyday scene, such as an office or a sitting room, most people have clear expectations about what objects they are likely to see. Since there is no need to spend very long looking at expected objects, this frees up resources for processing more novel and unexpected aspects of any given scene. Friedman (1979) has tested this proposal by presenting subjects with detailed line drawings of six different scenes (from a city, a kitchen, a living room, an office, a kindergarten, and a farm). Each picture contained objects one would expect to see in that particular setting, but a few unexpected objects were also included. Perception was influenced by the extent to which objects conformed to the appropriate frame or schema, with the duration of the first look being almost twice as long for unexpected as for expected objects. The differences between expected and unexpected objects were even more marked on the subsequent recognition-memory test. The subjects rarely noticed missing or partially changed *expected* objects even when only those expected objects that had been looked at were considered. In contrast, deletions or replacements of *unexpected* objects were nearly always detected. As Friedman (1979, p.343) concluded, "The episodic information that is remembered about an event is the difference between that event and its prototypical, frame representation in memory."

Schema Acquisition

In general, schema theorists have not been noted for their concern with the mechanisms of schema acquisition. Many theorists are either silent about how schemata are formed or assume that some type of ill-specified induction is used in which specific experiences are concatenated. This view maintains that on first entering a particular restaurant one somehow learns what to do and muddles through (maybe on the basis of other related knowledge structures such as going to a shop to buy food). On entering another restaurant one notes the similarities between the two episodes and forms an abstraction which excludes the varying characteristics. For example, one might notice that there were waiters in the first restaurant and waiters and waitresses in the second, and therefore form the abstraction that servers can be both male and female. That is, schemata are induced or abstracted from many specific experiences.

This is a fairly loose account and reflects the underdevelopment of theoretical proposals on schema learning. However, at least one serious attempt has been made to elaborate the processes of schema acquisition. Rumelhart and Norman (1981; Rumelhart, 1980) propose that there are three basic ways in which learning can occur in a schema-based system: accretion, tuning, and restructuring. In learning by *accretion*, one simply records a new instance of an existing schema and adds it to one's repertoire. *Tuning* refers to the elaboration and refinement of concepts in the schema through experience. So, for example, one may discover that a new type of object can fill a particular slot and change the tests on possible filler concepts for that slot. *Restructuring* involves the creation of new schemata either by analogy (see Gentner, 1983, Holyoak, 1985; Keane, 1988) or by schema induction (via the repetition of a spatio-temporal configuration of schemata). In the analogy case one takes an existing schema and maps some aspects of it onto a novel situation by changing some of its slot fillers. Unfortunately, there have been few concerted attempts to test these proposals in a direct fashion.

Schank's Dynamic Memory Theory

Many schema theories have tended to be elaborated as abstract statements about the nature of knowledge structures (e.g. Bobrow & Norman, 1975; Minsky, 1975; Rumelhart, 1980; Rumelhart & Ortony, 1977). In contrast, from the initial development of simple relational schemata (Schank, 1972), to the elaboration of script theory (Schank & Abelson, 1977) and the subsequent development of a general, schematic theory of memory (Schank, 1982; 1986), Schank and his associates have repeatedly attempted to apply their theories to specific situations. This research program has been notable in its dependence on computational models but because of its specificity has attracted psychologists to test it experimentally. The influence, however, has not all been one-way. Schank's later work has been inspired, in part, by psychological research indicating limitations in early script theories.

The main problem with script theory is the inflexibility of script structures. Granted, we know a lot about stereotypical situations but we can also deal with the unexpected. We are not thrown when we enter a restaurant which violates the rigid structure of the script. For example, people do not grind to a halt on their first trip to a McDonald's restaurant, where one has to pay for one's food before sitting and eating.

Furthermore, we can act in goal-directed ways in situations where no script could exist. Schank and Abelson had maintained that scripts are only formed from direct personal experience, so few of us should be able to understand bank robbery situations. However, we clearly *can* understand such situations. This means that we must have a more abstract set of structures which allow us to overcome the rigid structure of scripts and to understand the actions and goals of others in situations we have never experienced personally. Schank and Abelson had the concept of a *plan* to capture such abstract structures. Plans contain knowledge about abstract goals which any actor might have (like achieving the goal of satisfying a bodily need). However, the dividing line between scripts and plans has never been clear (see Schank, 1982, Chapter 1).

Psychological evidence has also shown that the script idea was wrong in some respects. Bower et al. (1979) found that subjects confused events that, according to script theory, were stored separately and should not have interfered with one another. For example, recognition confusions were found between stories that called upon distinct but related scripts: visits to the dentist and visits to the doctor. Since scripts had been defined as structures that were specific experiences in specific situations, one clearly could not have a "visit to a health professional" script. In response to these problems, Schank revised script theory in his *dynamic memory theory*.

MOPs , TOPs, and TAUs

In his reorganisation of script theory, Schank (1982) introduced the notion of Memory Organisation Packets (MOPs). These MOPs were made up of generalised clusters of events called *scenes*. Scenes were collections of the high-level components of scripts (i.e. you could have a set of entering scenes for different contexts, like entering the dentist's office or entering a restaurant). However, rather than having a set of components organised together in a script, MOPs organised sets of scenes and added specific contextual information. Consequently, one could have a waiting room scene which contained a set of specific waiting-room events (e.g. waiting at the doctor's, waiting at the dentist's, waiting at the solicitor's). At a higher level, MOPs co-ordinated these scenes together, pointing to the waiting room scene at the doctor's, the consultancy scene at the doctor's, and so on. The introduction of MOPs and scenes makes the system more flexible because the scenes can be combined and recombined in any desired organisation. This thus provides a way of dealing with unexpected orderings of components in new-ish situations. Furthermore, MOPs make central use of the idea that different specific scenes (in doctor visits and dentist visits) are similar and therefore stored in the same place. Evidence from Abbot, Black, and Smith (1984) found support for this type of organisation by showing that various parts of what were formerly called scripts are hierarchically organised. At the top level is the general goal (e.g. eating at a restaurant), at the intermediate level are scenes which denote sets of actions (e.g. entering, leaving, ordering), and at the lowest level there are the actions themselves.

There are also higher levels of organisation above MOPs and scenes. Schank also proposed TOPs, or Thematic Organisation Points, which were less tied to a particular set of situations and could generally apply to the theme of whole sequences of episodes. For example, the theme of *Romeo and Juliet* can be characterised as "Mutual Goal Pursuit against Outside Opposition." Romeo and Juliet, in loving each other, have the "mutual goal" of being together. The "outside opposition" comes from their parents. This theme is identical to that in *West Side Story*, which is a modern equivalent or analogue of *Romeo and Juliet*. Schank argues that since we consider the play and the movie to be thematically similar, we must possess higher-order structures that capture the general character of whole sequences of episodes. From a psychological perspective, Schank viewed TOPs as being implicated centrally in reminding. That is, he proposed that when one was reminded of something (e.g. of *Romeo and Juliet* while watching *West Side Story*), a TOP had been accessed in long-term memory. Schank supposed that this sort of access occurred automatically, but as we shall see this does not appear to be the case.

A similar sort of knowledge structure has been proposed by Dyer (1983): It is called a Thematic Abstraction Unit (TAU). TAUs capture plan-goal patterns reflected in common adages, like "A stitch in time saves nine." In plan-goal terms this suggests that "plans that satisfy a goal are best performed earlier than later, or else a lot more work may have to be done." TAUs raise the interesting idea that adages and proverbs summarise important high-level knowledge structures about the failure of plans and goals (see Kolodner, 1984; Kolodner & Simpson, 1986; Lehnert, Dyer, Johnson, Yang, & Harley, 1983; Wilensky, 1983; for other developments of the work of this Yale group of researchers).

Some psychological research has attempted to test the utility of these constructs more rigorously. Seifert and Black (1983) have shown, using Dyer's TAU structures, that if subjects are given stories that involve a common TAU and are asked to write similar stories, most produce stories which match the hypothesised TAU. They also found that subjects could sort stories reliably according to their TAU pattern. Seifert, McKoon, Abelson, and Ratcliff (1986) have examined the processing of story episodes to see whether thematic structures are activated automatically when processing stories with a related episodic structure. They used a priming technique which looked at whether the verification time for a test sentence from one story was speeded by an immediately preceding test sentence from a thematically similar story. They concluded (Seifert et al., 1986, p.220) that: "during the reading of an episode, thematic information may be encoded so as to lead to activation of similar episodes and formation of connections in memory between episodes, but such encoding is not automatic and depends on subject's strategies and task difficulty."

Finally, Keane (1987; 1988) showed that TOPs could be used to account for the differential frequencies with which subjects retrieved analogous problems in a problem-solving situation (see also Chapter 11). However, the evidence again suggests that reminding is not automatic but only occurs when subjects were specifically searching for an analogous problem (see also Gick & Holyoak, 1980). So all of this research indicates that something like Schank's thematic structures may mediate retrieval from long-term memory, but contrary to his views on reminding these structures are not accessed automatically.

Fundamental Problems with Schema Theories

Schema theory is not without its problems. While it is, and remains, one of the most pervasive proposals about the structure and organisation of knowledge in long-term memory, it has a number of faults which have lead to some disaffection with it.

The Unprincipled Nature of Schema Theories

There is a broad consensus amongst many researchers that schema theories are slightly unprincipled. This stems from the fact that it is often possible to create any particular content for hypothesised knowledge structures in order to account for the pattern of evidence one finds. Schank deals, in part, with this problem in attempting to delimit all the possible structures in long-term memory, but the theory is still underspecified. In proposing that there are distinct types of knowledge structure, one is at least placing some constraint on the nature of the structures proposed, but the problem remains that one has not specified the content of all of these structures. In general, then, schema theories tend to be good at accounting for results in an ad hoc fashion but are not as predictive as one would like them to be.

There are two remedies to this situation. First, one could specify the content of structures which are used, at least for a definable set of situations. That is, if one were using dynamic memory theory, one would specify all the possible scenes which people use, all the MOPs which organise these scenes, and all the TOPs which relate MOPs to one another. Unfortunately, this is probably impossible given the breadth of human knowledge and the possible variability in knowledge structures from one individual to the next. The other option is to be clearer about how these structures come into being. Thus, one could begin to test in a more controlled fashion how different selected experiences might be combined to form hypothetical structures.

The Problem of Inflexibility and Connectionist Schemata

While dynamic memory theory was developed to overcome many of the inflexibilities of script theory, some prominent theorists still consider that the intuitive flexibility of the schematic approach has not been realised in any of the present schemes (see Rumelhart, Smolensky, McClelland, & Hinton, 1986). For example, Rumelhart & Ortony (1977) had proposed that the slots/variables in schemata should have two distinct characteristics. First, as stated earlier, they should test to see whether a certain object is an appropriate filler for the slot or provide a default value. Second, there should be interdependencies among the possible slot fillers. That is, if one slot is filled with a particular value then it should initiate changes in the default values for the other slots in the schema. For example, assume that one has a schema for different rooms that includes slots for the furniture, the small objects found in the room and the usual size of the room. So a kitchen schema would have the following structure and defaults:

Furniture: kitchen table, chairs . . .
Small objects: coffee pot, bread bin . . .
Size: small

Other rooms would have different defaults; for example a bathroom would also be small but would have a toilet, bath, and sink as furniture and toothbrushes as small objects. What Rumelhart and Ortony were suggesting was that, when the small-objects slot is filled with coffee pot, there should be an automatic change in the default value for the furniture slot to kitchen table and chairs. However, this second characteristic of schemata was never realised in the schema theories of the 1970s and 1980s.

Rumelhart et al. proposed to remedy this state of affairs with a connectionist treatment of schemata. In this view, schemata emerge at the moment they are needed from the interaction of large numbers of parallel processing elements all working in concert with one another (for a treatment of connectionist ideas, see Chapters 1 and 7). In this scheme, there is no representational construct which is a schema but only patterns of activation which produce the sorts of effects attributed to schemata in previous research. When inputs are received by a parallel network, certain coalitions of units in the network are activated and others are inhibited. In some cases where coalitions of units tend to work closely together, the more conventional notion of a schema is realised; but where the units are more loosely interconnected the structures are more fluid and less schema-like.

Rumelhart et al. have illustrated the utility of such a scheme by encoding schematic type knowledge in a connectionist network. First, they chose 40 discriptors (e.g. door, small, sink, walls, medium) for 5 types of rooms (e.g. kitchen, bathroom, bedroom). To get the basic data to construct the network they asked subjects to judge whether each descriptor characterised an example of a room type (e.g. a kitchen) that they were asked to imagine. When they built a network that reflected this information, they found that when they kept activation high in the unit standing for the ceiling and then some other unit (e.g. oven), the network settled into a state with high activation in units that corresponded to the typical features of a kitchen (e.g. coffee-pot, cupboard, refrigerator). Similarly, runs starting with other objects resulted in descriptors for other prototypical rooms emerging.

This connectionist work could solve the problem of the unprincipled nature of schema theories in that it promises to specify a means by which schemata acquire their contents. Ironically, it does this without having to specify these schematic contents. However, a lot more needs to be done for it to replace the more explicit symbolic approach of Schank and others.

Summary

An alternative tradition to that looking at single concepts has considered how concepts are related to one another in complex structures called schemata. Schemata are structured clusters of concepts and usually contain generic knowledge about stereotypical situations. Schemata have been used to account for our ability to make inferences in complex situations, to make default assumptions about unmentioned aspects of situations, and to generate predictions about what is likely to occur in the future. There are several specific variants of the schema idea, variously called frames and scripts. Script theory and its successor, dynamic memory theory, have been proposed to characterise people's knowledge of commonplace event sequences such as going to a restaurant.

There is considerable psychological evidence to support many aspects of these theories. Having said this, schema theories have a number of fundamental problems relating to their unconstrained nature and the characterisation the specific content of schematic structures. Others have argued that no current conception of schemata is flexible enough to manifest the behaviour expected of them. Recently, some researchers have proposed that connectionist models can be used to capture the true flexibility of schema-based ideas.

RECENT DIRECTIONS IN CONCEPT RESEARCH: A RAPPROCHEMENT

This chapter has presented research which cleaves into two distinct traditions. Initially, we looked at research on what we called the simple organisation of concepts (examining categories like canary, dog, and cat). This research tradition tends to treat concepts *solely* in terms of attributes and to test its theories in verification or ratings tasks. In contrast, the research tradition which has examined complex organisation (i.e. relations and schemata) has tended to eschew analyses in terms of attributes alone, dealing instead with the diversity of relationships between concepts. It has also tended to use experimental tasks involving more global aspects of cognition: for example, the comprehension of stories and complex situations.

Ideally, one would like to see a unification of these two research streams. Notionally, one could say that the schema tradition is merely looking at concepts at a higher level than the categorisation research, but this is unsatisfactory. It does not tell us, for instance, ' exactly how the variable slots of a schema might relate to a prototype representation of a single concept. However, there are some hints of a rapprochement between the two streams. Recent research is tending towards the view that analyses of concepts that are solely attribute-based cannot account for significant aspects of categorisation without taking into account the complex knowledge people have about concepts (a view previously espoused by Miller & Johnson-Laird, 1976). In this section, we shall look at some of this recent research and indicate some current directions in concept research.

Conceptual Coherence: A Role for Theories?

Traditional concept research has tended to adopt a theory of what concepts might be (e.g. a set of defining attributes) and then to examine concepts which fit the predictions of this view. In contrast, Murphy and Medin (1985) have posited a much broader question, namely, "What makes concepts cohere?" That is, they asked what it is that holds concepts together. *Conceptual coherence* describes groupings of entities that "make sense" to the observer as might be reflected in various measures such as ease of learning or even direct ratings of coherence (Murphy & Medin, 1985; also Medin & Wattenmaker, 1987).

In most of the theories we have reviewed so far, concepts are said to cohere because the members of a category are similar to one another; because they share some attributes and do not share others. However, Murphy and Medin point out that we have categories that could not be formed by such a similarity mechanism. For example, they point out that in the Bible the dietary rules associated with the abominations of Leviticus produce categories of *clean* and *unclean animals*. What is it that makes camels, ostriches, crocodiles, mice, sharks, and eels *unclean* and gazelles, frogs, most fish, grasshoppers, and some locusts *clean*? Murphy and Medin argued that it was not the similarity of members of the concepts that determines the conceptual distinction but some complex explanatory framework or theory for drawing the distinction.

In general, they argued that to explain why concepts cohere it is necessary to include some account of the theories and background knowledge used by people in various situations. In the case of clean and unclean animals, the concepts can be seen as reflecting a correlation between type of habitat, biological structure, and form of locomotion (see Douglas, 1966). Roughly speaking, creatures of the water should have fins and scales and swim; creatures of the land should have four legs or fly with attributed wings. If a creature conforms with this correlation then it is considered clean, but any creature that is not equipped for the right kind of locomotion is considered unclean (e.g. ostriches). Murphy and Medin's (1985, p.290) notion of a *theory* refers to any of a number of mental "explanations" (rather than a complete scientific account): for example, "causal knowledge certainly embodies a theory of certain phenomena; scripts may contain an implicit theory of entailment between mundane events; knowledge of rules embodies a theory of the relations between rule constituents; book-learned, scientific knowledge certainly contains theories." They therefore argue that even though similarity notions are important, they are not sufficient to determine which concepts will be coherent or meaningful.

Rips (1989) has found evidence for this proposal in showing that there is a dissociation between similarity judgements and categorisation. In his study, one group of subjects were asked whether an object five inches in diameter was more likely to be a coin or a pizza. A second group were given the same information and asked to judge the similarity of the object to either the coin or the pizza. Although the object's size was roughly midway between a large coin and a small pizza (as determined by prior norms), subjects in the categorisation group tended to categorise it as a pizza. However, the similarity group judged the object to be more similar to the coin. If categorisation was based on similarity alone, subjects' judgements in both groups should have tallied. The fact that they did not indicates that some other variable was at work. Rips maintained that this variable was knowledge (or a theory) about the variability of the sizes of the objects in question. Coins have a size which is mandated by law, whereas pizzas can vary greatly in size.

Further evidence comes from Medin, Wattenmaker, and Hampson (1987), who have shown that conceptual knowledge seems to drive the application of a family resemblance strategy in concept sorting. Recall that within the prototype view the typicality of a concept member is closely related to the family resemblance score for that instance; that is, the score that reflects the extent to which the instance's attributes are the same as those of other instances of the category. Medin et al. (1987) found that, in a sorting task, subjects persisted in sorting on the basis of a single dimension instead of using many dimensions, which a family resemblance account would predict. Further exploration revealed that subjects abandoned this unidimensional sorting strategy in favour of a strategy which used several dimensions when the item had causally related, correlated properties. That is, when subjects were given conceptual knowledge that made inter-property relationships more salient, family resemblance sorting becomes very common. The moral of this is that correlated-attribute dimensions are really only used in sorting when there is some background knowledge or theory which connects them together.

While this work on the role of theories in concepts is gathering pace, it should be noted that it is not yet wholly clear what theories are. In essence, we need a precise theory of theories, rather than mere indications that it is something which needs to be taken into account. What is interesting, however, is that this work connects the categorisation research tradition to the work on more complex forms of organisation and implicates the latter in the operation of the former.

Conceptual Combination

Thus far we have been concerned with concepts in a fairly straightforward fashion. However, we can also extend our categories of the world by combining existing concepts in novel ways. Thus, we develop concepts like *pet fish*, *fake gun*, and *blue-striped shirt*. These *conceptual combinations* or *complex concepts* raise a whole new set of evidence to be accounted for by concept theories (Osherson & Smith, 1981). Several different types of conceptual combination have been examined in the literature: these include *adjective–noun combinations* (e.g. red fruit, large bird), *adverb–adjective–noun combinations* (e.g. very red fruit, slightly large bird), and *noun–verb combinations* (e.g. birds eat insects). We will concentrate on the most commonly examined of these; namely, adjective–noun combinations (see Hampton, Note 3; 1987; 1988; Jones, 1982b; Osherson & Smith, 1981; 1982; Smith, 1988; Smith & Osherson, 1984; Smith, Osherson, Rips, Albert, & Keane, 1989; Zadeh, 1982).

The phenomena involved in this type of conceptual combination seem to raise problems for both the defining-attribute and the prototype views. First, a simple defining-attribute theory would predict that a combined concept should contain a set of entities that are a conjunction of the members of the sets of two constitutent concepts. Thus, a red apple should refer to objects that are members of the concept set of red things and members of the concept set of apples. However, this is nowhere near a complete account. As Lakoff (1982) indicates, a *fake gun* is not a member of the concept set of *gun*. Second, Osherson and Smith (1981; 1982) pointed out several serious flaws in a prototype explanation of conceptual combination. For instance, they proved formally that the typicality of the member of the conjunction of two concepts could not be a simple function of the two constitutent typicalities. Intuitively, a *guppy fish* is a good example of a pet fish, but a guppy is not typical of the category of *pets* (who are generally warm and furry) nor is it typical of the category of fish (who are generally larger; see Hampton, 1988).

Several models have been proposed to account for conceptual combination and to predict the typicality of members of the combined concept (Cohen & Murphy, 1984; Hampton, Note 3; Murphy & Medin, 1985; Smith & Osherson, 1984; Thagard, 1984). Hampton's (Note 3) model talks of the formation of a composite prototype, by combining various attributes of the constitutent concepts, in an interactive fashion. Hampton (1987; 1988) has produced evidence in favour of this model which shows that the similarity of an object to the composite prototype of the combined concepts determines the typicality and class membership of that object. Murphy and Medin (1985) maintain that conceptual combination is another case where background conceptual knowledge or theories about the concepts in question plays a role. They point out that *ocean drives* are not both *oceans* and *drives* and that *horse races* are not both *horses* and *races*. Some circumstantial evidence for this view has been found by Medin and Shoben (1988).

The work on conceptual combination is an interesting and important extension of the corpus of phenomena that any theory of concepts must explain. What is notable about research in this area is that whereas the defining-attribute view does not seem at all feasible, the two alternative formulations, the defining-attribute and characteristic-attribute and prototype views, have had to work hard to be able to deal with the empirical evidence in this area. It is against this background that views about the role of knowledge or theories in conceptualisation have begun to emerge and question some of the basic proposals of the traditional approaches to categorisation.

Concept Instability

The work on theories is but one of a number of challenges to the standard assumptions in the literature on knowledge organisation. In recent years, researchers—most notably Lawrence Barsalou—

have challenged the assumption that concept representations are static and stable entities. As Barsalou (1989) points out, all work on human knowledge structures (from prototypes to frames) rests on the assumption that:

> . . . knowledge structures are stable: knowledge structures are stored in long-term memory as discrete and relatively static sets of information; they are retrieved intact when relevant to current processing; different members of the population use the same basic structures; and a given individual uses the same structures across contexts . . .

In his argument that concepts are unstable Barsalou (1987; 1989) argues convincingly that this assumption may be unwarranted. To support this argument he points to a host of findings in the literature. First, it has been found that the way people represent a concept changes as a function of the context in which it appears. For example, Anderson and Ortony (1975) have shown that if people are given sentences to memorise like "The man lifted the piano" and "The man tuned the piano," that "something heavy" is a better cue to the former sentence than "something with a nice sound," and vice versa. The most likely explanation of this result is that the representation of the concept's attributes in both sentences is different; the piano has attributes to do with weight in the lifting case and attributes to do with musicality in the tuning case. Barsalou (1982) has researched this finding further and has shown that a subset of the knowledge about a category only becomes active in a given context; he calls this *context-dependent information*. So, for example, when people read "frog" in isolation, "eaten by humans" typically remains inactive in memory. However, "eaten by humans" becomes active when reading about frogs in a French restaurant. Thus, concepts are unstable to the extent that different information is incorporated into the representation of a concept in different situations.

Instability has been found in the graded structure of category exemplars (see Barsalou, 1985; 1989). As we saw earlier (in the treatment of prototype theory), a category's graded structure is simply the ordering of its exemplars from most to least typical. For instance, in the *bird* category American subjects order the following instances as decreasing in typicality from *robin* to *pigeon* to *parrot* to *ostrich*. Instability shows itself here in the rearrangement of this ordering as a function of the population, the individual, or the context (see Barsalou, 1989). For example, even though Americans consider a robin to be more typical than a swan, they treat a swan as being more typical than a robin when they are asked to take the viewpoint of the average Chinese citizen.

Barsalou (1983) has also shown that some categories are not well established in memory but seem to be formed on-the-fly. These so-called *ad hoc categories* are constructed by people to achieve certain goals. For example, if you wanted to sell off your unwanted possessions you might construct a category of "things to sell at a garage sale." Barsalou has shown that the associations between instances of these concepts and the concept itself are not well established in memory but can be constructed if required.

So how can these views be squared with the research we have reviewed in this chapter? Barsalou's account is reminiscent of some of the defining-and characteristic-attribute theories we met earlier in this chapter. He posits that concepts have a conceptual core of context-independent information that gives rise to the more stable aspects of conceptualisation. As well as this core information, there is also context-dependent information activated by the current context and recent context-dependent information activated in recent contexts.

So in Barsalou's (1989) view a person possesses a tremendous amount of loosely organised knowledge for a category in long-term memory. Even though much of this knowledge may be shared with other members of the population because of the different subsets of knowledge that can become active in a given context (as a function of context dependence or recent experiences), more often than not conceptualisation will give the appearance of instability rather than stability. Barsalou's contribution is an important antidote to the view that everybody conceives of things in the same way. However, it remains to be seen whether a theory of the sort proposed by him can account for the extensive evidence on conceptualisation in the literature.

Neurological Evidence on Concepts

Throughout this chapter we have concentrated on attempts to understand the nature of the "normal" knowledge organisation. However, in the last 20 years a parallel research stream has examined the impairments of knowledge that arise after neurological damage. Many interesting findings have emerged from this literature, three of which we will outline briefly.

First, people with a variety of neurological illnesses develop specific impairments of their semantic memory. When the cognitive systems involved in reading and speaking remain intact, there is evidence that the storage of knowledge or access to it, or both, can be disrupted. For example, Schwartz, Marin, and Saffran (1979; Schwartz, Saffran, & Marin, 1980) studied a patient, called WLP, suffering from a severe dementing disease. WLP's ability to read was intact but her comprehension was poor. For example, when she was asked to indicate which one of a set of words a picture represented (using basic level words, like "spoon," "apple," "cigarette"), she was poor at selecting the correct word for the picture. Furthermore, when she chose the wrong word, she tended to choose one that was related semantically to the correct choice. So, for example, for a picture of a fork she chose the word "spoon" and for a picture of a brush she chose "comb."

A second noteworthy finding is the way in which knowledge about superordinate concepts seems to be less susceptible to damage than more subordinate information (Warrington, 1975). Warrington (see also Coughlan & Warrington, 1981) studied a patient called EM, also with a dementing illness, using a forced-choice decision task; that is, the patient was given a question like "Is cabbage an animal, a plant, or an inanimate object?" or "Is cabbage green, brown, or grey?" and had to choose one of the options. It was discovered that EM was only wrong in 2% of cases on the former type of question but was wrong 28% of the time on the latter type of question. This showed that more subordinate attribute information about the cabbage concept was lost, even though the superordinate classification of a cabbage as a plant was retained (although see Rapp & Caramazza, 1989, for a recent challenge of this finding). Similar evidence has been found by Martin & Fedio (1983) in the naming errors made by Alzheimer's patients. These patients tend to give superordinates when they name objects wrongly. So, for example, asparagus is named as a vegetable and a pelican as a bird.

A third, and perhaps most surprising, finding from the neurological literature is evidence that patients have deficits in their knowledge of specific categories of objects. For example, Dennis (1976) has reported a patient who had difficulties only with the category "body parts." Warrington and Shallice (1984) have studied patients with similar deficits following damage to the medial temporal lobes, arising from herpes simplex encephalitis. These patients were very good at identifying inanimate objects by either verbal description or picture but were considerably poorer on objects that were living things or foods. More specifically, Hart, Berndt, and Caramazza (1985) have reported a patient, MD, with a deficit specific to the naming and categorisation of fruits and vegetables.

How are we to understand these findings in the light of the previous theories of concepts? Shallice (1988) suggests that the salience of superordinate information indicates that the Roschian basic level is less important than previously thought. In terms of specific psychological models he suggests that these results favour later network models (e.g. Collins & Loftus, 1975) and distributed memory schemes (McClelland & Rumelhart, 1985). Distributed memory models operate in such a way that the patterns of activation encoded by superordinate information tends to be less disrupted than patterns of activation representing exemplars (Shallice, 1988). The explanation of category-specific deficits by Shallice and others (Allport, Note 1) should have interesting implications for mainstream concept research. Essentially, they propose that different parts of a distributed memory may encode different aspects of a concept. So, one subsystem may encode function information (what you do with a spade), another subsystem might encode sensory information (the visible attributes of a spade), another knowledge about where the object is found (spades are usually in garden sheds). If any of the pathways between these subsystems or the subsystems themselves are disrupted, then observed difficulties in categorisation ensue. This notion of distinctly different types of information making up a concept is most reminiscent of the view espoused by Barsalou on concept instability.

Summary

Several important research strands have emerged in the last few years which suggest that it may be possible to marry the two research traditions that have examined either simple or complex knowledge organisation. Work on conceptual coherence has shown that theory-like knowledge about the relationships of concepts to one another has a role to play. Other research on conceptual combination has highlighted some difficulties in extending existing theories and has widened the corpus of evidence to be considered. Research on concept instability has emphasised some of the variability that exists in concepts across individuals and populations. Finally, work from cognitive neuropsychology has added some constraints to the range of models that might suitably be applied to the understanding of conceptualisation.

CONCLUSIONS

The organisation of knowledge is one of the oldest and most researched areas in cognitive psychology. As such, it should act as a barometer of the state of the discipline. Has progress been made? Well, it is clear that research is not standing still. Researchers have used everything in the cognitive science cupboard (from empirical tests to formal tests and computational models) to challenge each other's and often their own theories (note how Medin moves from one opposing camp to another). And clearly certain theoretical views are being modified by the evidence found or in some cases wholly defeated. For instance, straight defining-attribute views have had their day, even though it has been the dominant view of conceptualisation for most of the intellectual history of Western Europe.

It is hard to draw clear lines between the other views and to say that one is better than another. Since both the defining- and characteristic-attribute and the prototype approaches really consist of confederacies of many specific theories, arbitrating between the approaches is very difficult. One view will succeed in one area and another in another area, and the overall evaluation of scientific theories in some quantified sense is very difficult. However, some progress has been made and, more importantly, the conditions for progress seem good. That is, the area does not seem to be hindered by unfruitful wrangles about basic philosophical positions like those that can be pointed to in other areas (e.g. the imagery–propositional debate reviewed in Chapter 7).

What is required, however, is more bridging work to be done on connecting the two distinct research traditions: Those which have looked at simple and complex organisation. Ideally, what we should have is some (hopefully simple) unified mechanism which can account for people's formation of categories, hierarchies, and other more complex forms of schematic organisation. Many are currently looking to connectionism as a possible source of such a mechanism, but we are by no means in the closing stages of this particular contest.

FURTHER READING

Hampton, J. (1990). *Concepts*. London: Lawrence Erlbaum Associates Ltd. This book provides a detailed review of the recent concept research.

Schank, R.C. & Abelson, R.P. (1977). *Scripts, plans, goals, and understanding*. Hillsdale, N.J.: Lawrence Erlbaum Associates Inc.

Schank, R.C. (1982). *Dynamic memory*. Cambridge: Cambridge University Press.

Schank, R.C. (1986). *Explanation patterns*. Hillsdale, N.J.: Lawrence Erlbaum Associates Inc. All of Schank's books are very readable and interesting. They constitute a good account of an attempt to push the explicit schema view to its limits.

Smith, E.E. & Medin, D. (1981). *Categories and concepts*. Cambridge, Mass.: Harvard University Press. The treatment of theories of categorisation presented here is, by necessity, somewhat simplified. This book provides a fuller treatment even though some time has passed since it was written.

Chapter Nine

LANGUAGE PROCESSING: LISTENING AND READING

This chapter is concerned with language processing. In particular, we will be concerned with the processes involved in listening to speech and in reading. For many purposes, it may not make much difference whether a message is presented to our ears or to our eyes. For example, we can understand the sentence, "You have done exceptionally well in your cognitive psychology examination," regardless of whether we hear it or read it. The important similarities between listening and reading mean that there are good reasons for dealing with both processes in the same chapter.

INTRODUCTION

Despite the similarities, listening to speech and reading differ in a number of significant ways. One important difference is that in reading each word can be seen as a whole, whereas a spoken word is spread out in time. A more important difference between listening to speech and reading is that speech generally provides a much more ambiguous and unclear signal than does printed text. When words were spliced out of spoken sentences and presented on their own, they were recognised only approximately half the time (Lieberman, 1963). Anyone who has studied a foreign language at school will remember the initial shock at being totally unable to understand the extremely rapid and apparently un-interrupted flow of speech produced by a native speaker of that language.

The fact that listening to speech and reading are quite different in some ways can be demonstrated most easily by considering children and brain-damaged patients. Young children often have good comprehension of spoken language, but struggle to read even simple stories. As we will see later in this chapter, there are some adult brain-damaged patients who can understand spoken language but cannot read properly, and there are others who can read perfectly well but cannot understand the spoken word.

The basic structure of the chapter is as follows. Those processes which are specific to listening to speech are dealt with first, followed by a consideration of processes which are specific to reading. After that, the language comprehension processes which are common to listening and reading are discussed. That is the general structure of the chapter, but the alert reader may spot the occasional deviation from this structure. These deviations occur in the interests of providing a coherent account.

LISTENING TO SPEECH

Initial Stages of Speech Perception

There is substantial evidence that the accurate perception of speech is a more complex achievement than might be imagined. Although we generally perceive speech as consisting of a series of separate sounds, the reality is quite different. Analysis of speech by means of a spectrograph (which provides a visual record of sound patterns) reveals that speech consists of a continuously changing pattern of sound with relatively few periods of silence (Potter, Kopp, & Green, 1947). It also reveals that the sound pattern for a particular speech component such as a phoneme (= an identifiable unit of sound) is not invariant; rather, it is affected by the sound or sounds preceding it. As Darwin (1990) points out, additional variability in the speech signal is introduced in rapid speech by the problem of moving the articulators quickly enough to produce all of the appropriate sounds.

Speech perception appears to differ from other kinds of auditory perception in a number of ways. For example, there is a definite left-hemisphere advantage for perception of speech that does not extend to other auditory stimuli. Speech perception also exhibits what is known as 'categorical perception': Listeners generally show superior ability to discriminate between a pair of sounds belonging to different phonetic categories (e.g. 'ba' and 'pa') than a pair of sounds belonging to the same category (Repp, 1984, provides a review). For example, the Japanese language does not distinguish between [l] and [r]; since these sounds belong to the same category for Japanese listeners, it is no surprise that they find it extremely difficult to discriminate between them. This is very different to the case with ordinary sounds, where discrimination between pairs of sounds is superior to the ability to label them as belonging to separate categories.

The major differences between speech perception and auditory perception in general led Mattingly and Liberman (1988) to argue that speech perception involves a special module or cognitive processor functioning independently of other modules (the notion of a 'module' is discussed in Chapter 1). We would agree with Mattingly and Liberman that some of the mechanisms involved in speech perception are probably different from those required for auditory perception in general. It is also possible that our knowledge of how speech is produced by the vocal tract may influence speech perception. However, even if speech perception does possess some special features, the evidence so far does not justify the assumption that there is a specialised module for speech perception.

Word Recognition
Interactive Models

How are spoken words recognised and understood? One view (e.g. Forster, 1979) is that processing proceeds in a serial or sequential fashion, with language comprehension involving analysis of the spoken input at several different levels in turn. An alternative interactive-model approach favoured by Marslen-Wilson and Tyler (1980) and by others is based on the assumption that the processing system is more flexibly structured. According to interactive models, various knowledge sources (e.g. lexical, syntactic, semantic) interact and combine with each other in complex ways to produce an efficient analysis of spoken language. Thus, a crucial distinction between serial and interactive models is that the former models assume that spoken language is processed in a relatively fixed and invariant series of processing stages, whereas the latter models are based on the assumption that the different processing activities involved in recognition and comprehension can occur at the same time.

Some of the points raised so far can be clarified if we consider the specific version of an interactive model proposed by Marslen-Wilson and Tyler (1980). According to their cohort model:

- Early in the auditory presentation of a word, those words known to the listener which conform to the sound sequence that has been heard so far become active; this collection of potential candidates for the presented word is the "word-initial cohort."
- Words belonging to this cohort are then eliminated either because they cease to match further information from the input word as this becomes available or because they are inconsistent with the semantic or other context.
- Processing of the auditory word needs to continue only until the information available from the context and from the word itself is sufficient to eliminate all but one of the words in the word-initial cohort.

Marslen-Wilson and Tyler (1980) tested some of these theoretical notions in a word-monitoring task, in which subjects had to identify pre-specified target words presented within spoken sentences. The sentences were normal sentences, syntactic sentences (i.e. grammatically correct but meaningless), or random sentences (i.e. unrelated words), and the target looked for was a member of a given category, a word that rhymed with a given word, or a word that was identical to a given word. The measure of interest was the speed with which the target could be detected.

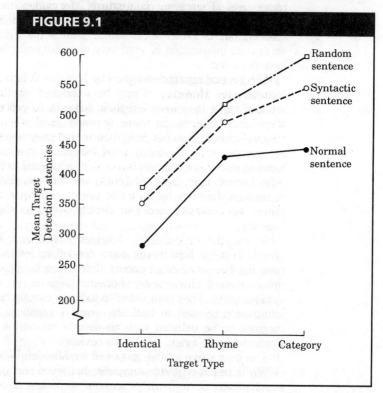

FIGURE 9.1

Detection latencies for word targets presented in sentences. Adapted from Marslen-Wilson & Tyler (1980).

The interactive model predicts that sensory information from the target word and contextual information from the rest of the sentence are both used at the same time in word recognition. In contrast, serial models predict that sensory information is extracted prior to the use of contextual information. In general terms, the results conformed much more closely to the predictions of an interactive model than of a serial model. As can be seen in Fig. 9.1, complete sensory analysis of the longer words was not needed provided that there was adequate contextual information. This fits in much better with the predictions of interactive models than of serial ones. It was only necessary to listen to the entire word when the sentence context contained no useful syntactic or semantic information (i.e. the random word order condition).

Further support for the interactive approach comes from a consideration of the great speed of word recognition in the normal sentence context. In that context, subjects initiated their responses approximately 200msec. after the onset of the target word when it was identical to the given word. This figure should be compared against the mean spoken duration of the target words used in this study, which was 369msec. The first 200msec. of a word typically correspond to the first two phonemes of a word, and there are usually numerous English words consistent with those two phonemes. Therefore, contextual information must be used extremely early in processing. This is assumed by interactive models, but is rather inconsistent with serial models in which contextual information is used only after several other processes have occurred.

The general approach adopted by Marslen-Wilson and Tyler is a valuable one. However, it may be wondered whether the rather artificial tasks they used led their subjects to process speech in ways quite different to those normally used when listening for comprehension. Another limitation is that they investigated word recognition under relatively good listening conditions. When the listening conditions are less favourable, additional factors come into play. For example, Bard, Shillcock, and Altmann (1988) found that in such conditions subjects made use of *subsequent* (rather than preceding) context in order to identify words to which they were listening.

At the theoretical level, Marslen-Wilson and Tyler did not specify in detail how words were divided up for the purposes of reducing the word-initial cohort. For example, processing might proceed on a phoneme-by-phoneme basis or on a syllable-by-syllable basis. They also failed to indicate exactly how contextual information is used to facilitate word recognition. These issues continue to be debated with no definite resolution in sight (see Frauenfelder & Tyler, 1987, for a review).

The interactive model proposed by Marslen-Wilson and Tyler (1980) is based on the assumption that word recognition involves simultaneous *bottom-up processes* stemming directly from the spoken word and *top-down processes* based on the listener's expectations formed from contextual information. Other research has shed additional light on each of these processes. Some of the relevant findings are now discussed.

So far as bottom-up processes are concerned, spoken language consists of a series of sounds or phonemes. These phonemes incorporate various features. Among the features for phonemes are the following: the consonantal feature (i.e. the presence or absence of a consonant-like quality); the place of articulation; and voicing (the larynx vibrates for a voiced but not for a voiceless phoneme). The value of a feature approach to spoken language was demonstrated in a classic study by Miller and Nicely (1955). They gave their subjects the task of recognising consonants which were presented auditorily against a background of noise. The key finding was that the most frequently confused consonants were those that differed from each other on the basis of only one feature.

Convincing evidence that word recognition does not always depend entirely on bottom-up processes, but that top-down processes based on context can also be involved, was obtained by Warren and Warren (1970). They investigated what is known as the *phonemic restoration effect*. Twenty people were presented with a recording of the following sentence:

The state governors met with their respective legi*latures convening in the capital city.

The asterisk indicates a 0.12sec. portion of the recorded sentence that had been removed and replaced with the sound of a cough. Warren and Warren found that all but one of their subjects claimed that there was no missing sound, and the remaining subject identified the wrong sound as missing.

Warren and Warren then modified the basic experimental technique slightly in order to provide an even more striking demonstration of the ways in which top-down processing based on stored knowledge can affect perception. Their subjects were presented with one of the following sentences; the asterisk again indicates a deleted portion of the sentence:

- It was found that the *eel was on the axle.
- It was found that the *eel was on the shoe.
- It was found that the *eel was on the table.
- It was found that the *eel was on the orange.

The perception of the crucial element in the sentence (i.e. "*eel") was much affected by sentence context. Subjects listening to the first sentence tended to hear "wheel," those listening to the second sentence heard "heel," whereas those exposed to the third and fourth sentences heard "meal" and "peel," respectively. In this case, all of the subjects heard the same speech sound (i.e. "*eel"), so that the bottom-up processes were the same. All that differed was the contextual information which was available.

Interactive models are attractive because they describe a very efficient way in which word recognition may occur. The efficiency stems from the fact that all relevant sources of information are used at the same time to provide rapid word identification. In contrast, serial models will often produce rather inefficient and slow performance. However, word recognition is only one aspect of sentence comprehension, and it remains to be seen whether interactive models can be applied successfully to larger units of spoken speech.

Lip-reading

Many people (especially those who are hard of hearing) are aware that they make some use of lip-reading in order to understand what someone is saying to them. However, this seems to happen to a far greater extent than is generally believed among those whose hearing is entirely normal. A few years ago, McGurk and MacDonald (1976) provided a striking demonstration of the importance of lip-reading. They prepared a videotape of someone repeating "ba" over and over again, but then changed the sound channel so that there was a voice saying "ga" repeatedly in synchronisation with the lip movements. Subjects reported that they heard "da" rather than either "ga" or "ba," which represents almost literally a blending of the visual and the auditory information.

The reason why visual information from lip movements is used to make sense of speech sounds is presumably because the information conveyed by the speech sounds is often inadequate (cf. Lieberman, 1963). Much is now known about the ways in which visual information provided by the speaker is used in speech perception, and the interested reader should consult Dodd and Campbell (1986). Of course, there are circumstances (e.g. listening to the radio) in which no relevant visual information is available. We can usually follow what is said on the radio because broadcasters are trained to articulate clearly.

Cognitive Neuropsychology of Word Processing

An apparently simple task is to repeat a spoken word immediately after you have heard it. However, there are many brain-damaged patients who experience difficulties with this task, despite the fact that audiometric testing reveals that they are not deaf. Detailed analysis of these patients has suggested that there are actually a number of somewhat different processes which can be used to permit repetition of a spoken word.

Information from such patients was used by Ellis and Young (1988) to propose a model of the processing of spoken words (see Fig. 9.2). In essence, the model consists of five components:

- The *auditory analysis system* is used to extract phonemes or other sounds from the speech wave.
- The *auditory input lexicon* contains information about spoken words known to the listener, but does not contain information about their meaning. The purpose of the auditory input lexicon is to recognise familiar words via the activation of the appropriate word units.
- The meanings of words are stored within the *semantic system*, about which relatively little is known (cf. semantic memory, which is discussed in Chapter 6).
- The *speech output lexicon* serves to provide the spoken forms of words.
- Speech sounds themselves are available at the *phoneme level*.
- These components can be used in various combinations, so that there are three different routes between hearing a spoken word and saying it.

FIGURE 9.2

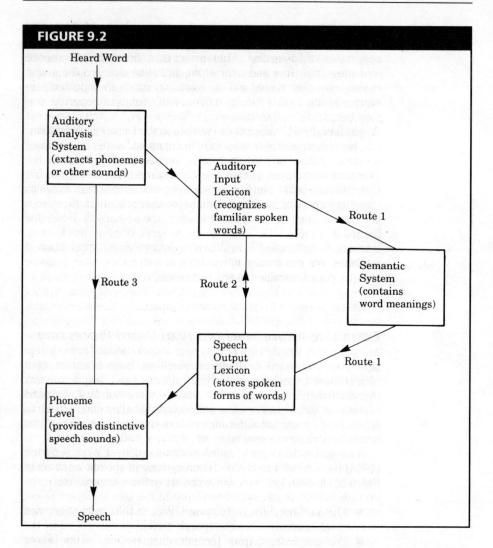

Processing and repetition of spoken words. Adapted from Ellis & Young (1988).

It will be noticed in Fig. 9.2 that there is a bidirectional arrow linking the auditory input lexicon and the semantic system. We saw earlier that Marslen-Wilson and Tyler (1980) found evidence that word recognition is affected by the semantic context in which a word is presented, and the arrow going from the semantic system to the auditory input lexicon acknowledges this.

The most striking feature of the model proposed by Ellis and Young (1988) is the notion that saying a spoken word can be achieved using three different routes. It is this feature of their model to which we will devote the most attention.

Route 1

This route makes use of the auditory input lexicon, the semantic system, and the speech output lexicon. It represents the normal way in which familiar words are identified and comprehended by those with no brain damage. If a brain-damaged patient could use only this route, then one would expect that familiar words could be said correctly. However, there would be severe problems with saying unfamiliar words and nonwords, because they do not have entries in the auditory input lexicon, and therefore require use of Route 3.

McCarthy and Warrington (1984) described a patient (ORF) who fits the bill reasonably well. ORF repeated words much more accurately than nonwords (85% versus 39%, respectively), indicating that Route 3 was severely impaired. However, the fact that he made a fair number of errors in repeating words suggests that there was also some impairment to other parts of the system.

Route 2

If a patient could use Route 2 (and possibly Route 3), but Route 1 was severely impaired, one would expect that he or she would be able to repeat familiar words but would often find it difficult to understand what the words meant. Patients suffering from a condition known as "word-meaning deafness" seem to fit this description. Ellis (1984) has reprinted the case of a young woman suffering from word-meaning deafness which was originally reported by Bramwell (1897). She could understand written sentences reasonably well, and she could say sentences that were spoken to her, and even write them down to dictation. However, she found it extremely difficult to understand things that were said to her. Intriguingly, when she was asked, "Do you like to come to Edinburgh?", she failed to understand the question. When she wrote the question down, however, it finally made sense to her.

Two additional cases of word-meaning deafness were reported by Kohn and Friedman (1986). Their symptoms resembled those of Bramwell's (1897) patient, but were rather less severe. While the precise nature of the impairment producing this condition is not known for certain, Ellis and Young (1988, p.155) have suggested that it may represent "a complete or partial disconnection of the auditory input lexicon from the semantic system." This seems reasonable, since the ability of patients with word-meaning deafness to understand written words implies that the semantic system is relatively intact, and their ability to write to dictation implies that the auditory input lexicon is not impaired. If there were a problem of communication between the auditory input lexicon and the semantic system, the main consequence would be a difficulty in understanding spoken words, and that is precisely what is involved in word-meaning deafness.

Route 3

If a patient were to use only Route 3, then one would expect heard words and nonwords to be repeated reasonably accurately, but there would be very poor comprehension of the words. There do not appear to be any reported cases indicating precisely this pattern. However, McCarthy and Warrington (1984) reported on a patient, ART, who seemed to make use of Route 3. This patient had rather poor spontaneous speech, but he was consistently good at repeating spoken words regardless of whether they were common or rare. He was actually worse at repeating a word when it was preceded by an appropriate semantic context, suggesting that he could not take advantage of the semantic system to facilitate word recognition. However, the failure to investigate ART's ability to repeat nonwords, which should theoretically have been good, means that it is difficult to identify the precise nature of his impairment.

Deep Dysphasia
Some brain-damaged patients have been found to make semantic errors when they are asked to repeat spoken words, i.e. they say words which are related in meaning to the words they are supposed to be saying. These patients have sometimes been termed "deep dysphasics." One of the most interesting cases was reported by Michel and Andreewsky (1983). Their patient made numerous semantic errors when repeating spoken words, but not when reading aloud. He was unable to repeat nonwords, suggesting that he could not make use of Route 3. Presumably such a patient has a number of different impairments, so that none of the three routes between heard words and speech is intact. Route 1 is the route most commonly employed, but some impairment in or near the semantic system makes this route rather fallible.

Summary
There has been relatively little research on auditory word recognition and comprehension in brain-damaged patients. As a result, it would be premature to draw any sweeping conclusions on the basis of the cognitive neuropsychological evidence. However, it has been established that there are different patterns of impairment in the ability to repeat and to understand spoken words. This encourages the belief that there are a number of separate components involved, and that there is more than one route between hearing a word and then saying it. Fig. 9.2 represents a possible set of components and their interactions. However, its validity will become clear only after considerable further research.

Cognitive neuropsychological research in this area has emphasised the differences between listening to speech and reading. For example, patients with word-meaning deafness can often understand written sentences reasonably well, but cannot make sense of the same sentences when spoken to them. This indicates strongly that rather different theories are needed to explain what happens when linguistic material is presented to our ears and to our eyes.

Summary

There are several processes involved in listening to and making sense of spoken language. Speech perception makes use of many of the processes normally involved in auditory perception, but it differs in a number of important ways (e.g. categorical perception). Since the information contained in spoken words tends to be somewhat ambiguous, and the sound pattern for any given phoneme is not invariant, the comprehension of speech often involves making use of top-down processes based on relevant contextual information. In addition, even listeners with normal hearing tend to rely surprisingly heavily on lip-reading in order to make sense of what is being said to them.

Some of the complexities of speech processing can be seen if we consider attempts by brain-damaged patients to say a word which has just been spoken to them. Detailed analyses of the errors made by these patients indicate that there are probably three different processing routes between auditory input and subsequent speaking of the word.

BASIC READING PROCESSES

Reading is an apparently straightforward and effortless activity for most adults. However, observation of young children struggling to make sense of simple stories provides some indication of the true complexity of the skills involved. As we shall see shortly, reading requires several different perceptual and other cognitive processes, as well as a good knowledge of language and of grammar.

Why is it important to investigate the skills involved in reading? Skilled reading is of great value in contemporary society, and adults who fail to develop effective reading skills are at a great disadvantage. There are thus considerable practical benefits to be gained from discovering enough about the processes involved in reading to be able to sort out the reading problems of poor readers.

Some of the processes involved in reading are concerned with identifying and extracting meaning from individual words. Other processes operate at the level of the phrase or sentence, and still other processes deal with the overall organisation or thematic structure of an entire story or book.

Eye Movements in Reading

There are several different ways in which we could attempt to obtain evidence about some of the basic processes involved in reading. One method is to set up a computer so that a text is presented word by word to the subject, with the subject pressing a button every time he or she wants to see the next word. It is hoped that use of this method will be informative about the length of time required to process different words within a sentence. However, this method is highly artificial, and there must be grave doubts as to whether findings obtained with its use actually tell us much about normal reading. In contrast, the study of eye movements made during reading provides a relatively unobtrusive way of collecting information about the processes occurring while reading under natural conditions.

We have the impression that our eyes move smoothly across the page while reading, but this impression is quite mistaken. In fact, we make a series of rapid eye movements known as *saccades*, which are separated by fixations which typically last for approximately 200 to 250msecs. Readers generally fixate about halfway between the beginning and the middle of a word. Approximately 10% or 15% of saccades are regressions, i.e. the eye moves back over the text. The length of each saccade is influenced by a variety of factors (e.g. the complexity of the text), but it is typically approximately 8 letters or spaces. Information is extracted from the text only during each fixation, and not during the intervening saccades. Indeed, even a bright flash of light is generally not perceived if it is presented entirely within a saccade (Latour, 1962).

One of the main issues in eye-movement research is that of establishing the amount of text from which useful information is obtained on each fixation. One would expect such information to be relatively limited in terms of the number of words of the text involved because of basic characteristics of the human visual system. There is a small area of high acuity in the centre of the retina known as the *fovea* (see Chapter 4), and visual perception is much less precise outside foveal vision. The limitations on intake of information from text have been established by using the 'moving window' technique (see Rayner & Pollatsek, 1987). In essence, most of the text is mutilated except for an experimenter-defined area or window surrounding the reader's point of fixation. Every time the reader moves his or her eyes, different parts of the text are mutilated so as to permit normal reading within the window region. The effects of different-sized windows on reading performance can be compared.

An alternative method of assessing how much text can be processed in a single fixation is the boundary technique. With this technique, the entire text is displayed, but a critical word or letter is altered during a saccade. Evidence about the amount of text being processed can be obtained by varying the distance between the altered word or letter and the point of fixation.

Any reader interested in the finer details of studies using the moving window or boundary techniques should consult Rayner and Pollatsek (1987). Here we will focus on the main conclusions that have been reached. *The perceptual span* (= effective field of view) is affected to some extent by the difficulty of the text, the size of print, and so on, but it is relatively small under all conditions. In general, it extends no more than approximately 3 or 4 letters to the left of fixation and 15 letters to the right. This asymmetry presumably occurs because the most informative text lies to the right of the fixation point. The form of the asymmetry is clearly learned. Readers of Hebrew, which is read from right to left, show the opposite asymmetry (Pollatsek, Bolozky, Well, & Rayner, 1981).

We have discussed the size of the perceptual span in terms of the number of letters it contains. However, there is increasing evidence that matters are more complex than that. For example, the left boundary of the perceptual span is generally defined by the beginning of the fixated word (Rayner, Well, & Pollatsek, 1980), whereas the right boundary is defined mainly in terms of the number of letters (Rayner, Well, Pollatsek, & Bertera, 1982). On the basis of this, and other evidence, Rayner and Pollatsek (1987) tentatively put forward the following viewpoint:

- Three different spans can be distinguished.
- The first is *total perceptual span*, which consists of the total area from which useful information is extracted on a fixation.
- The second is *letter identification span*, which is the area from which information about letters is obtained.
- The third is *word identification span*, which is the area from which information relevant to word-identification processes is obtained.
- The total perceptual span is probably the longest of these three spans, and the word identification span is the shortest.

The size of the perceptual span means that parafoveal information (= information from outside the high acuity foveal region) is used in reading. The relevance of parafoveal information is also shown by the fact that the length of the fixation on a word is shorter if that word was previously presented in the parafoveal part of the perceptual span than when it was not. What information is extracted at the parafoveal level? Rayner, Balota, and Pollatsek (1986) addressed this issue. They discovered that the fixation time on a word (e.g. tune) was reduced when a visually similar string of letters (e.g. turc) had just been presented to parafoveal vision. However, presenting a semantically similar word (e.g. song) to the parafovea had no effect on subsequent fixation time. These findings suggest that information about letters is extracted at the parafoveal level. This information seems to concern the identity of the letters (i.e. the fact that a 't' and a 'u' were presented) rather than their visual shapes. There is a reduction of fixation time on a word even when none of the visual shapes of the letters match those presented at a parafoveal level (e.g. cHaNgE presented to the parafovea and ChAnGe presented to the fixation point; see Rayner, McConkie, & Zola, 1980). The fixation time on a word in a sentence is determined by numerous factors. Of particular interest to cognitive psychologists are the ways in which meaning influences fixation times. One way in which meaning has an effect on fixation time is via the context provided by the earlier part of the sentence. A word that is highly predictable on the basis of contextual information is fixated for less time than a relatively unpredictable word (Balota, Pollatsek, & Rayner, 1985). Another influence of meaning on fixation time is to be found in the fact that the last critical word in clauses and sentences is fixated for longer than the same word presented in the middle of a clause or sentence (Rayner & Pollatsek, 1987). This probably occurs because of the need to integrate information within the clause or sentence.

Another way in which meaning affects eye movements is when a sentence is deliberately designed to mislead the reader. For example, Carpenter and Daneman (1981) included the following two sentences in a passage describing a fishing contest:

Tomorrow was the annual, one-day fishing contest and fishermen would invade the place. Some of the best bass guitarists in the country would come to this spot.

What typically happened was that the reader fixated an abnormally long time on the word 'guitarists', which is the word disambiguating the previous word 'bass'. This lengthened fixation time was necessitated by the need to resolve the discrepancy between the anticipated and actual meanings of 'bass'.

As we shall see later in the chapter, there has been much interest in the inferences which readers draw while they are reading a text. Most of the relevant research has tested for inference drawing by memory tests, and this poses the problem of deciding whether the inferences were drawn at the time of reading or whether they were drawn only at the time of testing. Evidence that inferences are drawn during reading was obtained in a study discussed by Rayner and Pollatsek (1987). They found that the fixation time on a target word (e.g. knife) was less when the word 'knife' rather than 'weapon' had been referred to earlier. However, if the reference to 'weapon' included enough additional information to permit the inference that the weapon was a knife, then the subsequent fixation time on the word 'knife' was no longer than when the actual word 'knife' had been mentioned. This suggests that the inference was drawn *before* the target word 'knife' was presented.

We have seen that the fixation time on a word is affected by the amount of semantic processing that is required in order to understand that word in its sentential context. Beck and Carpenter (1986) have extrapolated from this to propose the *immediacy assumption*:

- The reader completes the cognitive processes needed to understand each word in a sentence, and to integrate its meaning with the earlier words in the sentence, immediately upon encountering it.

Although it is true that there is a considerable amount of semantic processing of words when they are initially fixated, the immediacy assumption is too sweeping. Some words are fixated more than once, and there are fairly frequent regressions of eye movements to earlier parts of the text. These phenomena should not occur on a strict interpretation of the immediacy assumption.

Word Recognition

Common sense may suggest that the recognition of a word on the printed page involves two successive stages: the first stage consists of identifying the individual letters in the word, and the second stage consists of the identification of the word. The notion that letter identification must be complete before word identification can begin appears to be wrong, however. For example, consider the phenomenon of the "word superiority effect," which was first demonstrated by Reicher (1969). In essence, a letter string is presented very briefly, and followed by a pattern mask usually consisting of letter fragments. The subject's task is to decide which of two letters was presented in a particular position (e.g. the third letter). Performance is better when the letter string forms a word than when it does not: This is the word superiority effect.

On the face of it, the word superiority effect indicates that information about the word presented can facilitate identification of the letters of that word. However, since words obviously differ from nonwords in a number of different ways, it is necessary to specify more precisely why words have this advantage. It has been found (e.g. Marmurek & Briscoe, 1982) that there is still a word superiority effect even when the nonword strings have spelling patterns which are as familiar as those of words. This suggests that the advantage of words is due to the fact that they are stored in memory as familiar forms.

The most influential account of word recognition and of the word superiority effect is the interactive activation model of McClelland and Rumelhart (1981). However, it should be emphasised that their model is only designed to account for word recognition in four-letter words written in capital letters, even though many of the principles incorporated in the model have more general applicability. Some of the major theoretical assumptions made by McClelland and Rumelhart (1981) are as follows:

- There are recognition units at three levels: the feature level at the bottom; the letter level in the middle; and the word level at the top.
- The features in individual letters are identified at the feature level; when a feature is detected (e.g. vertical line at the right-hand side of a letter), activation is sent to all of the letter units containing that feature (e.g. H, M, N) and inhibition is sent to all other letter units.
- Letters are identified at the letter level; when a letter in a particular position within a word is identified, activation is sent to the word level for all four-letter word units containing that letter in that position, and inhibition is sent to all other word units.
- Words are recognised at the word level; activated word units increase the level of activation in the letter-level units for the letters forming that word (e.g. activation of the word SEAT would increase activation for the four letters "S", "E", "A",

and "T" at the letter level) and inhibit activity of all other letter units.
- At each level in the system, activation of one particular unit leads to suppression or inhibition of competing units.

This interactive activation model may seem very complicated, but the basic ideas contained in it are reasonably straightforward. McClelland and Rumelhart (1981) argued that bottom-up and top-down processes are both involved in letter identification and word recognition. The bottom-up processes stemming directly from the written word proceed from the feature level through the letter level to the word level by means of activation and inhibition. Top-down processing is involved in the activation and inhibition processes going from the word level to the letter level.

The word superiority effect occurs because of the top-down influences of the word level on the letter level. Suppose the word SEAT is presented, and the subjects are asked whether the third letter is an "A" or an "N". If the word unit for SEAT is activated at the word level, then this will increase the activation of the letter "A" at the letter level, and inhibit the activation of the letter "N". This beneficial top-down effect of word level activation and inhibition on letter identification is much greater for words than for nonword letter strings.

The interactive activation model provides an interesting example of how a connectionist processing system (see Chapter 1) can be applied to visual word recognition. The basic notion of an interactive system can be extended to cover other aspects of language processing, and that is exactly what McClelland (1987) proposed. He identified several different levels of language processing (e.g. semantic level; syntactic level; word-sense level; word level; letter level; phoneme level), and argued that these different levels all have interactive links with other components of the system. An interactive system is clearly more flexible in its functioning than a system in which processing proceeds in an invariant serial fashion from one language process to the next, and McClelland made a good case for preferring the interactive approach.

In spite of the general plausibility of the interactive approach, there are some limitations with the model put forward by McClelland and Rumelhart (1981). High-frequency or common words are more readily recognised than low-frequency or rare words, and this can be explained by assuming either that stronger connections are formed between the letter units and the word units of high-frequency words or that high-frequency words have a higher resting level of activation. However, it follows from this viewpoint that there should be a larger word superiority effect for high-frequency words than for low-frequency words, because there would be more top-down activation from the word level to the letter level. In fact, the size of the word superiority effect is the same with high-and low-frequency words (Gunther, Gfoerer, &

Weiss, 1984), and this is in apparent conflict with what might be expected from the interactive activation model.

Routes from Print to Sound

Suppose you were asked to read out the following list of words and nonwords:

CAT   FOG   COMB   PINT   MANTINESS   FASS

You would probably find it a simple task, but it actually involves some hidden complexities. For example, how do you know that the "b" in "comb" is silent, and that "pint" does not rhyme with "hint" or with "mint"? Presumably you have specific information stored in long-term memory about how to pronounce these words. However, this cannot explain how you are able to pronounce nonwords such as "mantiness" and "fass," because you do not have any stored information about their pronunciation. Accordingly, a rather different strategy must be used with these nonwords. One possibility is that they are pronounced by analogy with real words (e.g. "fass" is pronounced to rhyme with "mass"). Another possibility is that rules governing the translation of letter strings into sounds are used to generate a pronunciation for nonwords. These alternative strategies are discussed in some detail by Patterson and Coltheart (1987).

The notion that there is more than one way in which readers can decide on the appropriate pronunciation of words and nonwords goes back a long way. Teachers and educationalists have often drawn a distinction between two methods of reading:

- The look-and-say method, which is based on identifying words by their visual appearance;
- The phonic method, which involves sounding out the letters of a word (e.g. c-a-t) in order to work out its pronunciation.

Skilled adult readers can usually identify words correctly "by sight", and so only rarely need to resort to sounding them out in order to understand them. Young children, however, are familiar with the spoken versions of many words that they are unfamiliar with in their written form. Therefore, saying words aloud or to themselves is the only way in which children can recognise many words.

The description of the reading of individual words which has been offered so far is an oversimplified one. The study of adult patients whose reading skills have been impaired as a result of brain damage suggests that there are several rather different reading disorders, depending on which part or parts of the cognitive system involved in reading are damaged. Some of the major findings from the cognitive neuropsychological approach are discussed in the following section.

Cognitive Neuropsychology

Some of the processes and structures involved in reading are shown in Fig. 9.3. Ellis and Young (1988) identified these components on the basis of the study of acquired dyslexias (i.e. impairments of reading produced by brain damage in adults who were previously skilled readers). Only selected aspects of the cognitive neuropsychological account of reading will be presented here; the reader interested in knowing the whole story is referred to Ellis and Young (1988).

The most important message of Fig. 9.3 is the notion that there are three different routes between the printed word and speech. All three routes start with the visual analysis system, which has the functions of identifying and grouping letters in printed words. The simplest way of enabling the reader to make sense of Fig. 9.3 is by considering each of these routes in turn.

Route 1

Route 1 differs from the other routes between the printed word and speech in making use of the process of grapheme-phoneme conversion. This process may well involve working out pronunciations for unfamiliar words and nonwords in a piecemeal fashion by translating letters or letter groups into phonemes by the application of rules. However, not everyone has agreed with this view. Kay and Marcel (1981) argued that unfamiliar words and nonwords are actually pronounced by analogy with familiar words. In support of that argument, they discovered that the pronunciations of nonwords by normal readers were sometimes altered to rhyme with real words which had just been presented. The similarities and differences between these two theoretical approaches are discussed by Patterson and Coltheart (1987).

If a brain-damaged patient could use only Route 1 when pronouncing words and nonwords, what would one expect to find in their pronunciation performance? In essence, the use of grapheme-phoneme conversion rules should permit accurate pronunciation of words having regular spelling-sound correspondences but not of irregular words. If an irregular word such as "pint" has grapheme-phoneme conversion rules applied to it, it should be pronounced to rhyme with "hint". Finally, the grapheme-phoneme conversion rules can be used to provide pronunciations of nonwords.

The patients who adhere most closely to exclusive use of Route 1 were labelled as surface dyslexics by Marshall and Newcombe (1973). The surface dyslexic JC was able to read 67 out of 130 regular words correctly, but he was successful with only 41 out of 130 irregular words. Similar, but more striking, findings were reported by Bub, Cancelliere, and Kertesz (1985). Their patient MP read nonwords well, and had a reading accuracy of over 90% with common and rare regular words. In contrast, while common words were read with an accuracy of approximately 80%, only 40% of rare irregular words were read accurately.

The evidence from surface dyslexics such as JC and MP indicates that they have a strong, but not exclusive, reliance on

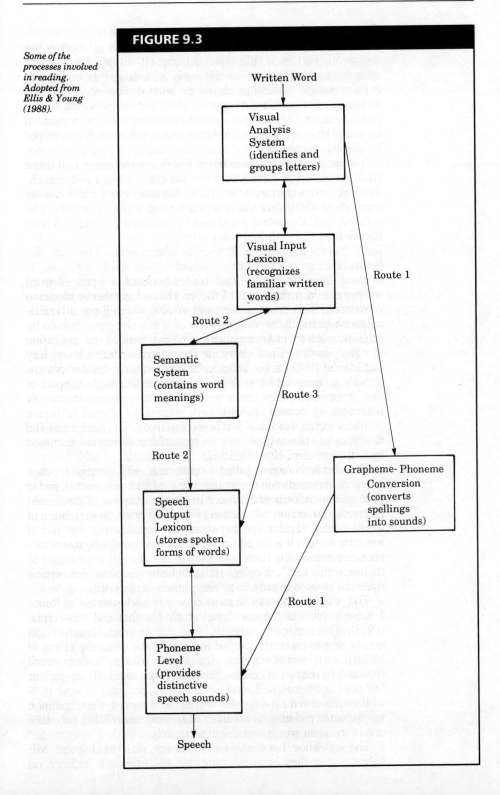

FIGURE 9.3

Some of the processes involved in reading. Adopted from Ellis & Young (1988).

Written Word

Visual Analysis System (identifies and groups letters)

Visual Input Lexicon (recognizes familiar written words)

Route 1

Route 2

Semantic System (contains word meanings)

Route 3

Route 2

Speech Output Lexicon (stores spoken forms of words)

Grapheme- Phoneme Conversion (converts spellings into sounds)

Route 1

Phoneme Level (provides distinctive speech sounds)

Speech

Route 1. If all words were read by means of grapheme-phoneme conversion, then most (or all) irregular words would be mispronounced, and this simply does not happen. Presumably surface dyslexics can make some use of routes in reading other than Route 1, even though these other routes are severely impaired.

Finally, it should be noted that surface dyslexics vary considerably in the nature of the impairment which led them to adopt the strategy of grapheme-phoneme conversion. For example, JC had no problem with understanding words that he pronounced correctly, whereas MP frequently failed to understand words she could pronounce. The fact that the syndrome category of "surface dyslexia" camouflages important differences among patients suggests that it might usefully be abandoned.

Route 2

Route 2 is the route generally used by adult readers. The basic idea is that representations of thousands of familiar words are stored in a visual input lexicon. Visual presentation of a word leads to activation in the visual input lexicon. This is followed by obtaining its meaning from the semantic system, after which the word can be spoken (see Fig. 9.3).

How could we identify patients who use Route 2 but not Route 1? Their intact visual input lexicon means that they should experience little or no difficulty in pronouncing familiar words. However, their inability to use grapheme-phoneme conversion should mean that they find it very difficult to pronounce relatively unfamiliar words and nonwords.

Phonological dyslexics fit this predicted pattern rather well. The first case of phonological dyslexia reported in a systematic fashion was the patient RG (Beauvois & Derousne, 1979). In one experiment with 40 words and 40 nonwords, RG successfully read 100% of the real words but only 10% of the nonwords. Similar findings with patient AM were reported by Patterson (1982). AM had problems in reading function words (e.g. with, if, yet), but was very successful in reading content words (nouns, verbs, and adjectives). In contrast, he managed to read correctly only 8% of a list of nonwords.

Deep dyslexia is more severe and mysterious than phonological dyslexia. Deep dyslexics resemble phonological dyslexics in finding it very difficult to read unfamiliar words and nonwords, which indicates that they cannot use grapheme-phoneme conversion effectively. In addition, deep dyslexics make several other kinds of error. Of particular theoretical interest is the semantic error, in which a word related in meaning to the printed word is read instead of the printed word itself. Examples are reading "costs" as "money" and "city" as "town".

Probably the most persuasive account of deep dyslexia is that it occurs when patients cannot use Route 1 or Route 3, but can make use of the semantic system. Semantic errors can then be explained by arguing either that the semantic system, unaided by grapheme-phoneme conversion, is intrinsically error-prone, or that deep dyslexics have some impairment of the semantic system.

There is evidence that deep dyslexics vary in terms of the problems they have with analysing meaning. More specifically, some deep dyslexics experience difficulties in moving from the printed word to its meaning in the semantic system, whereas others access the appropriate meanings of printed words, but cannot move accurately from the semantic system to the speech output lexicon. These have been labelled "input" and "output" deep dyslexia, respectively, by Shallice and Warrington (1980).

In fairness to the uninitiated reader, it should be pointed out that there has been considerable theoretical controversy concerning the proper interpretation of the reading deficits found in deep dyslexics. Coltheart (1983b) argued in favour of the right-hemisphere hypothesis, according to which deep dyslexics make use of a visual input lexicon in the right hemisphere followed by the speech output lexicon in the left hemisphere. This heavy reliance on the right hemisphere produces severe reading problems, because in most normals the processes and structures best suited to reading are located in the left hemisphere.

There are some similarities among the reading difficulties of deep dyslexics, those of patients who have lost the use of the whole of their left hemispheres, and those of split-brain patients whose two hemispheres have been separated surgically (Coltheart, 1983b). Nevertheless, it is reasonably clear that the reading skills of the right hemispheres of split-brain patients are markedly inferior to those of most deep dyslexics. Indeed, some experts (e.g. Gazzaniga, 1983) have argued that most split-brain patients possess minimal or nonexistent right-hemisphere language skills. It is thus unlikely that deep dyslexia can be accounted for by the right-hemisphere hypothesis. The implications of accepting the right-hemisphere hypothesis would be quite serious. As Ellis and Young (1988, p.217) pointed out, "If what we see in deep dyslexia is the performance of a secondary, and possibly inessential, right-hemisphere reading system, then we are unlikely to be able to draw any conclusions from deep dyslexia about the nature of the normal, dominant (left-hemisphere) reading system."

Route 3

Route 3 resembles Route 2 in that the visual input lexicon and the speech output lexicon are involved in the reading process. However, the semantic system is bypassed in Route 3, so that printed words which are pronounced are not understood. Other-wise, the expectations about reading performance for users of Route 3 are the same as those for users of Route 2: Familiar regular and irregular words should be pronounced correctly, whereas most unfamiliar words and nonwords should not (see Fig. 9.3).

Schwartz, Saffran, and Marin (1980) reported the case of WLP, a 62-year-old woman suffering from senile dementia. She showed a reasonable ability to read familiar words whether they were regular or irregular, but she often indicated that even words she pronounced correctly meant nothing to her. She was totally unable to relate the written name of animals to pictures of them, despite the fact that she was quite good at reading animal names aloud. While these findings are consistent with the view that WLP was bypassing the semantic system when reading words, they are by no means definitive. It is possible that processing occurred in WLP's semantic system but that she was unable to use such processing to facilitate performance on the tasks she was given.

Summary

Eye movements provide useful information about some of the basic processes involved in reading. Fixation on the text alternates with rapid eye movements known as *saccades*. Information is only extracted from text during the fixation periods, and is usually obtained not only from the word actually fixated but also from one or more words to the right of the fixation point. Such information seems to relate largely to the letters in the nonfixated word or words. Most (but not necessarily all) of the semantic processing of each word occurs during the time that it is initially fixated. As a consequence, the better the word fits into the sentential context, the lower its fixation time.

It seems natural to assume that word recognition occurs after the identification of its constituent letters has been completed. In fact, there is strong evidence from the word superiority effect and other phenomena indicating that information about the word can influence letter identification. According to McClelland and Rumelhart's (1981) interactive activation model, letter identification is influenced by both bottom-up or stimulus-driven processes and by top-down processes.

The greatest success achieved by cognitive neuropsychologists studying reading has been to provide evidence supporting the view that there are several different components or modules involved in the reading process. Our focus has been on the *different* routes in reading, with a consequent de-emphasis on those components which are *common* to all of the routes. However, there is evidence not discussed here that some patients have suffered damage to the visual analysis system, or to the visual input lexicon, or to the speech output lexicon (see Ellis & Young, 1988, for details).

What are the weaknesses of the cognitive neuropsychological approach to reading? First, it has proved rather difficult to interpret many of the findings obtained. Despite much research, it is not really very clear how many routes there are between print and sound, and the three-route model presented here may well need revision in the future. Part of the problem is that brain damage often has the inconvenient property of affecting more than one component of reading. This makes it harder to make sense of the data. Second, there are great areas of ignorance concerning the functioning of the components shown in Fig. 9.3. For example, very little is known about the semantic system in terms of the precise information about words which it contains.

DISCOURSE COMPREHENSION AND MEMORY

This section of the chapter is concerned mainly with text comprehension and memory. However, it should be borne in mind that nearly all of the theories discussed have equal relevance to speech comprehension. If many of the structures and processes used in text comprehension are also used in speech comprehension, then we would expect that individuals with good reading skills should also have good listening skills, whereas poor readers should also tend to be poor listeners. The evidence indicates that there is, indeed, a very close relationship between text comprehension and speech comprehension (e.g. Daneman & Carpenter, 1980).

How do we understand a story or book that we are reading, or someone's conversation? It is clear that numerous different processes are involved. Some of the basic processes in reading and listening to speech have already been discussed, but the reader or listener also needs to take account of grammatical and semantic considerations when attempting to comprehend text or speech. For example, a knowledge of grammar enables us to appreciate the great difference in meaning between "The man bit the dog" and "The dog bit the man." There is a discussion of grammar in the following section.

At the semantic level, it is crucially important for information in the text to be related to information that we already have stored in long-term memory. If that did not happen, then everything we read would seem to be completely novel and bewildering; indeed, reading in the accepted sense would be impossible. Numerous theorists have attempted to describe how previous knowledge and experience are brought to bear on the processes involved in reading and comprehension, and we will shortly consider these theories.

What is perhaps less obvious is that there is a reasonably close relationship between text comprehension and memory. The results of the comprehension process will frequently be stored in long-term memory, so that recall of a text will tend to reflect the ways in which the text was interpreted. It should be noted, however, that text recall is influenced by processes operating at the time of recall as well as by the earlier comprehension processes, and so it does not always provide an accurate reflection of text comprehension. Suppose, for example, that you were asked to recall a story you read several years ago. Under such circumstances, your recall would almost certainly include only a small fraction of the information that was comprehended at the time of reading, and you would use your general knowledge to fill in the gaps.

One might argue that language processing proceeds in an orderly serial fashion, starting with the meaning of individual words, progressing through considerations of word order and syntax, and concluding with an overall understanding of each sentence. In fact, it is probable that the various processes involved interact with each other in complex ways. McClelland (1987) has put forward an interactive model of language processing based on the assumption that bottom-up or stimulus-driven and top-down or conceptually driven processes are both involved in language comprehension. That means that we cannot argue that the syntax of a sentence is processed either before or after the overall meaning of the sentence; rather, syntax and meaning are usually considered at the same time.

Grammar

An infinite number of utterances is possible in any language, but these utterances are nevertheless systematic and organised in various ways. Linguists such as Chomsky (1957; 1965) have attempted to produce a set of rules that will simultaneously take account of the productivity and the regularity of language. Such a set of rules is commonly referred to as a grammar. Ideally, a grammar should be able to generate all of the permissible sentences in a given language, while at the same time rejecting all of the unacceptable sentences. For example, as Harris (1990) pointed out, our knowledge of grammar allows us to be confident that "Matthew is likely to leave" is grammatically correct, whereas the rather similar sentence, "Matthew is probable to leave" is not.

Chomsky's (1957; 1965) attempts to wrestle with these problems culminated in his transformational grammar. As with many other linguistic systems, this grammar distinguished between the syntax, the phonology, and the semantics of language. Syntax is concerned with the rules specifying what strings of words are structurally and propositionally well formed. Phonology deals with rules for moving from the phrases forming a sentence to the appropriate sounds. Finally, semantics refers to the rules that determine how meaning is assigned to well-formed sentences.

A further important distinction emphasised by Chomsky was that between the surface and the deep structure of a sentence. The surface structure involves a hierarchical division of a sentence into units usually known as phrases. A surface analysis can be used to clarify certain ambiguities. For the ambiguous sentence "They are cooking apples," there are two possible surface-structure representations. In one of these representations, "cooking" is part of the same phrase as "apples," and in the other "cooking" is part of the verb. However, such analyses do not serve to resolve ambiguities in other sentences. In the sentence, "Visiting relatives can be boring," "visiting" modifies "relatives" irrespective of whether the meaning is that it is sometimes tedious to go to see relatives, or that relatives who come on a visit can be boring. The two meanings of this and other sentences are distinguished in the deep structure. Whereas the surface structure involves the actual phrases used in a sentence, deep structure refers to the phrases in an underlying hypothetical word string. According to Chomsky (1965), the deep structure reflects the meaning of a sentence more directly than does the surface structure. Different deep structures can be changed into the same surface structure by means of transformation rules that specify how surface structures are to be derived from deep structures.

The value of postulating a deep structure in addition to a surface structure can be seen if we consider the following two sentences: "The man wrote the book" and "The book was written by the man." The meaning of those two sentences is obviously very similar, but the surface-structure representations of the sentences do not reflect that fact. In contrast, the similarity of meaning is made manifest in the deep-structure representations.

In recent years, Chomsky has developed his theoretical views on grammar. For example, Chomsky (1982) proposed a Government and Binding Theory in which the rules of syntax (= grammatical arrangement of words) were more abstract than in previous theories, and were potentially applicable to languages other than English. His views have been very influential over the years, but they have various limitations from the perspective of cognitive psychology. For example, Chomsky has primarily been concerned with linguistic competence, i.e. the abstract knowledge that people possess about a language, rather than with linguistic performance. Cognitive psychologists are interested in the mistakes people make when using language, but Chomsky's lack of interest in linguistic performance means that his theoretical ideas are of little value in this connection. It is appropriate, therefore, for us to turn now to a consideration of the use of grammatical information in linguistic performance.

When we listen to or read a sentence, one of the tasks we perform is that of parsing, which involves working out its grammatical structure. Evidence that we parse while we are listening to, or reading, a sentence rather than waiting until the end of the sentence has been obtained in several studies. A popular approach has been to use so-called garden-path sentences, in which the initial attempt at parsing is likely to be wrong. Examples taken from a study by Kramer and Stevens (reported in Rumelhart, 1977) are as follows: "The old man the boats"; "The steel ships are transporting is expensive." Kramer and Stevens asked their subjects to read these, and other, sentences out loud. They noticed that pauses in reading tended to occur at the point where the original parsing proved unworkable (i.e. between "man" and "boats" in the first sentence, and between "transporting" and "is expensive" in the second sentence). Similar difficulties associated with inaccurate parsing of garden-path sentences can be demonstrated when sentences are listened to rather than read.

The role of the clause (= distinct part of a sentence including a subject and a predicate) boundary in parsing was shown by Caplan (1972). Subjects heard a sentence followed by a probe word, and had to decide as rapidly as possible whether the probe word had appeared in the sentence. A certain amount of ingenuity produced pairs of sentences in which the only significant difference was whether or not the probe word occurred in the last clause of the sentence. As an illustration, consider the following sentences that were both probed with the word "oil":

1. Now that artists are working fewer hours oil prints are rare.
2. Now that artists are working in oil prints are rare.

In the first sentence, "oil" is part of the last clause, whereas it is part of the first clause in the second sentence. The key result was that the probe word was recognised more rapidly if it occurred in the last clause, presumably because information in the last clause had just been processed.

Not surprisingly, parsing and comprehension of sentences are greatly influenced by their semantic content or meaning. Schlesinger (1968) discovered that the first of the following sentences was more readily understood than the second:

1. This is the hole that the rat which our cat whom the dog bit made caught.
2. This is the boy that the man whom the lady whom our friend saw knows hit.

The reason why the first sentence is easier to comprehend is presumably because of what we know about the typical behaviour of rats, cats, and dogs. Intriguingly, careful reading of the first sentence will indicate that it actually states that the rat caught the hole, and that the hole was made by the cat! This is an example of our knowledge of the world influencing the comprehension process more than parsing per se.

Recently, there have been attempts to spell out in more detail the processes involved in parsing. For example, words such as "because" or "which" are often found at the beginning of clauses, and "a" and "the" tend to occur at the start of a noun phrase. Listeners and readers both take advantage of this information when parsing sentences. A full account of the strategies used in the parsing processes is provided by Pullman (1987).

In spite of the importance of parsing in the comprehension of discourse, it has usually been found in memory tests that there is extremely poor retention of grammatical structure or syntax. This was shown by Sachs (1967), who presented short passages to her subjects. After the passage was over, a test sentence was presented. Subjects had to decide whether it was the same as one of the sentences in the passage. Changes in meaning were usually spotted. However, changes in syntax which preserved meaning (e.g. changing from the active to the passive voice) were poorly detected, even when the corresponding sentence had been presented only a few seconds previously.

A more dramatic demonstration that it is the meaning of spoken sentences which is remembered was provided by Johnson-Laird and Stevenson (1970). They presented short passages including a sentence such as: "John liked the painting and bought it from the duchess." On a recognition-memory test shortly thereafter, subjects very often mistakenly claimed that they had heard the following sentence: "The painting pleased John and the duchess sold it to him." Despite the substantial differences in wording between the two sentences, the fact that they are very similar in meaning confused the subjects.

Although it would be tempting to conclude that it is always the gist of spoken sentences that we remember and not the wording, this would be an over-simplification. Keenan, MacWhinney, and Mayhew (1977) pointed out that nearly all of the sentences used in laboratory studies have no personal significance for the listener. They discovered that there was good retention of the exact wording of sentences having personal relevance (e.g. "Do you always put your foot in your mouth?").

Inferences

Perhaps the simplest illustration of the crucial role played by stored knowledge in the comprehension of text is provided by considering the process of inference or filling in of gaps. Some of the processes involved in drawing inferences were considered in Chapter 8. Bransford (1979) and others have put forward the following notion:

- Comprehension typically requires our active involvement in order to supply information which is not explicitly contained in the text or speech.

Some idea of how readily we make inferences can be formed if you try your hand at understanding what is going on in the following story taken from Rumelhart and Ortony (1977):

1. Mary heard the ice cream van coming.
2. She remembered the pocket money.
3. She rushed into the house.

You probably made various assumptions or inferences while reading the story, perhaps including the following: Mary wanted to buy some ice cream; buying ice cream costs money; Mary had some pocket money in the house; and Mary had only a limited amount of time to get hold of some money before the ice cream man arrived. The important point to note is that none of these assumptions is explicitly stated in the three sentences that were presented. It is so natural for us to draw inferences in order to facilitate understanding that we are by no means always aware that we are doing so.

We are especially likely to attempt to draw inferences if a sentence does not appear to fit the current context. When that happens, we tend to generate backward inferences in order to locate an earlier context that is appropriate. Thorndyke (1976) investigated backward inferencing in a study on story memory. In one story, the sentence "The hamburger chain owner was afraid his love for french fries would ruin his marriage", was followed a few sentences later by the final sentence "The hamburger chain owner decided to join weight-watchers in order to save his marriage." In connecting these sentences, it is appropriate to infer that the hamburger chain owner was fat and his wife did not like obesity, but it is inappropriate to infer that the hamburger chain owner's wife did not like french fries.

Thorndyke (1976) tested to see whether subjects had been more likely to draw the appropriate than the inappropriate inferences by using a recognition-memory test on which subjects had to decide whether various sentences had been presented in the story. Actual story sentences were correctly recognised 85% of the time, appropriate inferences were incorrectly recognised as having been presented 58% of the time, but only 6% of the subjects falsely recognised inappropriate inferences. These findings indicate that the appropriate inferences were drawn, but do not show definitely that they were drawn at the actual time the story was comprehended. However, the use of more sensitive techniques has shown that many inferences are drawn as part of the comprehension process (e.g. McKoon & Ratcliff, 1981).

There are other circumstances in which inferences must be drawn. If the literal meaning of a sentence seems appropriate to the context, then that is assumed to be the intended meaning. However, if the literal meaning does not seem to be appropriate, then the listener goes beyond the literal meaning to discover the conversationally implied meaning. If a wife says to her husband "Would you mind opening the window, dear?", he is asking for trouble if he only takes account of the literal meaning of the question, and responds "yes" or "no." Other cases in which the literal meaning is not the intended meaning include such rhetorical devices as irony, sarcasm, and understatement.

Clark and Lucy (1975) discovered that statements with both literal and intended meanings were nearly always interpreted in terms of their intended meaning. However, they also found evidence that the literal meaning was worked out. The sentences "I'll be very happy if you make the circle blue" and "I'll be very sad unless you make the circle blue" both have the same intended meaning, and yet the latter sentence took much longer to comprehend. Since negative sentences typically take longer to understand than positive sentences, this result is probably due to a difference in the literal meanings of the two sentences, with "unless" having the inherent negative meaning "if not."

One of the most common circumstances in which inferences tend to be drawn is when a statement strongly implies something that is not explicitly stated. Such statements are said to contain a *pragmatic* implication. This can be contrasted with a *logical* implication, in which some information is necessarily implied by an utterance. The distinction can be clarified by one or two examples. The statement "Juliet forced Willie to rob the bank" logically implies that "Willie robbed the bank." In contrast, the statement "The dangerous fugitive was able to leave the country" only pragmatically implies that "The fugitive left the country." Pragmatic implication was also involved in ex-President Nixon's statement "And I just feel that I have to be in a position to be clean and to be forthcoming." This implies that Nixon is, in fact, clean and forthcoming, but is also compatible with the statement "I am not actually clean and forthcoming."

Strong evidence that people do typically make the predicted inferences from sentences containing pragmatic implications was obtained by Brewer (1974). He presented sentences such as "The angry rioter threw a rock at the window" (implying that the rock went through the window) and "Dennis the Menace sat in Santa's chair and asked for an elephant" (implying that Dennis the Menace sat on Santa's lap). In a subsequent test of cued recall, subjects recalled the pragmatic implications of the sentences more frequently than the sentences they had actually heard.

Are pragmatic inferences made at the time of comprehension and storage, or are they constructed at retrieval? Most of the available evidence suggests that they are usually made during the process of comprehension. Monaco (Note 8) discovered that telling subjects before presenting a passage that they would receive a multiple-choice retention test led them to draw fewer inferences from the passage than they did when told they would be given an essay test. These instructions could have affected inference drawing at either input or retrieval. However, the same instructions had no differential effect on inference drawing when given *only after* the passage had been presented, presumably because they could not influence passage comprehension.

The ability to make inferences obviously requires appropriate knowledge about the world. Several theorists have argued that much of the knowledge about the world is stored in the form of organised packets of knowledge which have variously been variously termed "schemata," "scripts" and "frames." It is to such matters that we now turn.

Schemata, Scripts, and Frames
Definitions
As we saw in Chapter 8, the term "schema" is used to refer to well-integrated chunks of knowledge about the world, about events, about people, and about actions. Scripts and frames are relatively specific kinds of schemata. Scripts deal with knowledge about events and sequences of events. Thus, for example, Schank and Abelson (1977) referred to a restaurant script, which contains information about the usual sequence of events involved in going to

a restaurant to have a meal. In contrast, frames deal with knowledge about the properties of objects and locations.

The crucial function of all of these different kinds of schemata is that they allow us to form *expectations*. In a restaurant, for example, we expect to be shown to a table, to be given a menu by the waiter or waitress, to order the food and drink, and so on. If any of these expectations are violated, then we usually take appropriate action. For example, if no menu is forthcoming, we try to catch the eye of the waiter or waitress. Since our expectations are generally confirmed, schemata help to make the world a more predictable place than it would otherwise be.

Rumelhart and Norman (1983) identified several characteristics of schemata. First, schemata vary enormously in the kinds of information they contain, ranging from the very simple to the very complex. Second, schemata are often organised in a hierarchical fashion. For example, we have a restaurant schema or script, but also probably more specific schemata relating to the kinds of food and drink that one would expect to see on the menu of that particular type of restaurant. Third, schemata operate in a top-down or conceptually driven fashion to facilitate interpretation of the world about us. These top-down processes may interact in quite complex ways with bottom-up or stimulus-driven processes stemming from environmental stimuli to provide an adequate interpretation of our environment.

Fourth, as we saw in Chapter 8, schemata have slots, some of which have fixed values and others of which have optional values. For example, the restaurant schema has sitting at a table and eating food as fixed values, but the people present at the meal, the number of courses, the type of food, and so on, all have optional values. Most importantly, slots often have *default values*, which means that plausible guesses or inferences are made if the relevant information is not explicitly supplied. Thus, we might well assume that people having a meal in a restaurant receive a bill and pay it even if we are not told so in unambiguous terms.

Comprehension
Interesting evidence that schemata can influence the process of comprehension was obtained by Bransford and Johnson (1972). What they did was to present a passage in which it was very difficult for people who had it read to them to work out which schemata were relevant. This is the passage they used (Bransford & Johnson, 1972, p.722):

> The procedure is quite simple. First you arrange items into different groups. Of course one pile may be sufficient depending on how much there is to do. If you have to go somewhere else due to lack of facilities that is the next step; otherwise, you are pretty well set. It is important not to overdo things. That is, it is better to do too few things at once than too many. In the short run this may not seem important but complications can easily arise. A mistake can be

expensive as well. At first, the whole procedure will seem complicated. Soon, however, it will become just another facet of life. It is difficult to foresee any end to the necessity for this task in the immediate future, but then, one never can tell. After the procedure is completed one arranges the materials into their appropriate places. Eventually, they will be used once more and the whole cycle will then have to be repeated. However, that is part of life.

It was mentioned in Chapter 8 that Bartlett (1932) was perhaps the first psychologist to argue persuasively that schemata play an important role in memory. In essence, he argued that memory is affected not only by the presented information but also by the subject's store of relevant prior knowledge or schemata. He had the ingenious idea of asking subjects to learn stories that produced a conflict between what was presented in them and the prior knowledge possessed by the subjects. If, for example, people read a story taken from a culture different from their own, then prior knowledge might produce distortions in the remembered version of the story, rendering it more conventional and acceptable from the standpoint of their own cultural background.

As we saw in Chapter 8, Bartlett's findings supported his predictions. In particular, a substantial proportion of the recall errors were in the direction of making the story read more like a conventional English story. He used the term "rationalisation" to refer to this type of error.

Bartlett's classic work was well received at the time. Indeed, he is one of only three British psychologists to be knighted (the others are the notorious Sir Cyril Burt and the obscure Sir Godfrey Thomson). However, his influence declined in the 1950s and 1960s, and it is only in recent years that the true value of his research has once again been recognised. Despite the impact he has had on contemporary thinking, there are various deficiencies in Bartlett's work. One problem is that he did not give very specific instructions to his subjects (he stated (Bartlett, 1932, p.78): "I thought it best, for the purposes of these experiments, to try to influence the subjects' procedure as little as possible"). As a consequence, it is possible that some of the distortions observed by Bartlett were due to conscious guessing rather than pure memorial malfunctioning. There is some force in this criticism, because instructions stressing the need for accurate recall have been found to eliminate almost half of the errors usually obtained (Gauld & Stephenson, 1967).

Another problem is that Bartlett assumed that memorial distortions occurred largely as a result of schema-driven processes operating at the time of retrieval. As we have already seen in the study by Bransford and Johnson (1972), schemata often influence comprehension processes rather than retrieval processes. However, it is certainly true that schemata do sometimes influence the retrieval of information from long-term memory. Anderson and Pichert (1978) asked subjects to read a story from the perspective of either a burglar or of someone interested in buying a home. After they had recalled the story, they were asked to shift to the alternative perspective and then to recall the story again. On the second recall, subjects recalled more information that was important only to the second perspective or schema than they had done on the first recall (see Fig. 9.4).

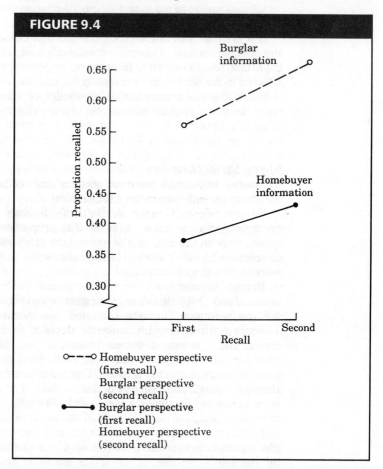

FIGURE 9.4

Recall as a function of perspective at the time of retrieval. Based on data in Anderson & Pichert (1978).

Burglar information

Homebuyer information

o— —o Homebuyer perspective
(first recall)
Burglar perspective
(second recall)

●——● Burglar perspective
(first recall)
Homebuyer perspective
(second recall)

These findings of Anderson and Pichert (1978) confirm the notion of schema-driven retrieval. Further support comes from the subjects' introspective reports, such as the following (Anderson & Pichert, 1978, p.10):

When he gave me the homebuyer perspective, I remembered the end of the story, you know, about the leak in the roof. The first time through I knew there was an ending, but I couldn't remember what it was. But it just popped into my mind when I thought about the story from the homebuyer perspective.

Evaluation of Schema Theory

It is probable that schema theory is on the right lines. That is to say, our organised knowledge of the world is used in a systematic fashion to facilitate text comprehension and recall. However, it has proved rather difficult to identify the characteristics of schemata with any precision. More importantly, most versions of schema theory are sadly lacking in testability. If some predicted effect of a schema on performance fails to occur, it is always possible to explain the data away by arguing that the subjects did not actually possess the relevant schema, or that an inappropriate schema was used. If we are trying to explain text comprehension and memory in terms of the activation of certain schemata, then we really need to have independent evidence of the existence of those schemata in order to avoid circular arguments. Such evidence is generally lacking, however.

Story Structure

If someone asks us to tell them about a story or book which we have read recently, there are certain fairly obvious characteristics of our reply. Typically, we refer to the major events and themes of the story and leave out virtually all of the minor details. In other words, our description of the story is highly selective, and is determined by its meaning. Indeed, imagine the questioner's reaction if we simply recalled a random selection of sentences taken from the story!

Gomulicki (1956) provided a straightforward demonstration of the selective way in which stories are comprehended and remembered. One group of subjects wrote a precis (abstract or summary) of a story which was visible in front of them, and a second group of subjects recalled the story from memory. A third group of subjects who were given the precis and the recalls found it extremely difficult to tell which were which. This indicates that story memory resembles a precis in focusing on important information and ignoring what is relatively unimportant.

There have been various attempts to consider in some detail how readers discriminate between what is important and what is unimportant in stories. One of the most influential of these attempts is considered next.

Story Processing

Kintsch and van Dijk (1978) and van Dijk and Kintsch (1983) have attempted to provide an account of the processes involved in story processing. According to Kintsch and van Dijk (1978), the text of a story is processed so as to extract its propositions (i.e. assertions which may be true or false). These propositions are entered into a short-term working buffer of limited capacity resembling the working memory system discussed in Chapter 5. When this buffer contains a number of propositions, the reader attempts to link them together in a coherent fashion. The probability of subsequent recall of propositions depends in general on the length of time they spend in the working buffer.

The notion that propositions play an important role in text comprehension and memory was shown by Kintsch and Keenan (1973). They manipulated the number of propositions in sentences and paragraphs, but equated the number of words. An example of a sentence with four propositions is "Romulus, the legendary founder of Rome, took the women of the Sabine by force," whereas the following sentence contains eight propositions: "Cleopatra's downfall lay in her foolish trust of the fickle political figures of the Roman world." The reading time increased by approximately one second for each additional proposition.

Some propositions stay in the working buffer longer than others, and a crucial part of the theory put forward by Kintsch and van Dijk (1978) concerns the factors determining length of stay in the buffer. Those propositions (e.g. thematically relevant ones) which are well connected to other propositions are likely to be retained in the buffer, since they are likely to be important in the context of the story. Recently mentioned propositions are also likely to be chosen to remain in the buffer, because they are likely to be of relevance to the propositions which follow immediately after them in the story.

One of the implications of the theory proposed by Kintsch and van Dijk (1978) is that propositions which are of central importance in the story (e.g. those relating to the main theme) are likely to be especially well recalled. The reason for this is that such propositions are likely to spend a disproportionate amount of time in the working buffer, and time in the buffer determines long-term memory. It has been found many times (e.g. Thorndyke, 1977) that thematic information is better remembered than nonthematic information.

Van Dijk and Kintsch (1983) considered further the issue of how stories are processed, and in particular how readers arrive at an understanding of the gist of a story (or *macrostructure* as they call it). They argued that readers are continuously using their general knowledge in an attempt to work out the central theme of the text they are reading. These attempts are represented in the form of *macropropositions* or general propositions, which are used to construct the overall macrostructure of the text.

They obtained some evidence that readers initially make elaborative inferences in order to fill in gaps in the information presented in the text, followed by reductive inferences which reduce the text to its essential macrostructure. When subjects were asked to prepare text summaries, they first of all produced summaries containing several elaborations and additions to the original test. On the second attempt at preparing a summary, however, the elaborations tended to disappear, together with most of the relatively unimportant information from the text, leaving only the macrostructure.

Evaluation

It is somewhat difficult to evaluate the theoretical contributions of Kintsch and van Dijk. Part of the problem is that there are considerable individual differences in the kinds of knowledge which subjects bring to bear on a text, and so the way in which the working buffer is used and the macrostructure formed from a text will vary considerably from one reader to another. In other words, it is not possible to predict precisely how the comprehension process will operate for any particular individual. However, their theory is in good general agreement with the data, and it is probable that macropropositions are constructed in approximately the ways specified by van Dijk and Kintsch (1983).

Summary

Language comprehension typically occurs very rapidly, and does not await the end of each phrase or sentence. In a sense, we understand more than is presented, because it would usually be extremely tedious to present every single piece of relevant information to the reader or to the listener. The missing information is filled in by the use of inferences, and our ability to use inferences stems from the numerous schemata or packets of organized knowledge which we have stored in long-term memory. In our memory for discourse, we often find it difficult to distinguish between information that was actually presented and the inferences we drew.

TEACHING READING SKILLS

Much is now known of the several component skills involved in reading (e.g. word recognition; use of relevant schemata). This knowledge is increasingly being applied to the practical task of teaching reading skills. A useful first step is to compare skilled and unskilled readers in order to identify those component skills in which poor readers are especially deficient. The teaching process can then focus on those particular skills.

Word Recognition

Young children starting to read generally have great problems with word recognition. Traditionally, there has been much controversy concerning which of two approaches to teaching word-recognition skills is preferable:

- The look-and-say or whole-word strategy, in which children learn to associate the shapes of words with their pronunciations;
- The phonic method, in which children learn the sounds of letters, and so work out the pronunciations of words on a letter-by-letter basis.

The evidence was reviewed by Anderson, Hiebert, Scott, and Wilkinson (1985), who concluded that the phonic method generally produces better results. They went further, and identified the best way of using the phonic method (Anderson et al., 1985, p.118):

> Phonics is more likely to be useful when children hear the sounds associated with most letters both in isolation and in words, and when they are taught to blend together the sounds of letters to identify words. In addition, encouraging children to think of other words they know with similar spellings, when they encounter words they cannot readily identify, may help them develop the adult strategy of decoding unknown words by analogy with ones that are known.

It used to be argued that what was crucial for children's future reading success was the accuracy with which they could pronounce words. However, there is recent evidence suggesting that matters are more complicated than that. Lesgold, Resnick, and Hammon (1985) discovered that the *speed* with which young children pronounced words was more predictive than *accuracy* of pronunciation of later reading comprehension ability. Why should pronunciation speed be so important? The most plausible reason is based on the notion that speed of pronunciation reflects the extent to which word recognition has become automatic. If word-recognition skills are automatic, then all of the attentional processes can be used for comprehension purposes.

How can the necessary word-recognition skills be taught? Beck and Roth (in research discussed by Beck and Carpenter, 1986) have had some success with a training programme in which children were given a huge amount of practice in identifying and making use of sub-word units (e.g. letter clusters; syllables). The training increased both the speed and accuracy of word recognition; most encouragingly, it also led to enhanced comprehension.

Of course, word-recognition skills are a more important factor in determining the overall reading skills of children than of adults. Nevertheless, there is some evidence that they are of relevance with respect to adult reading ability. In a study on adults, Perfetti (1985) discovered that skilled readers could pronounce words faster than less skilled readers. If adults do not complete mastery of the simple skills involved in reading (such as word recognition), then this may interfere with the ability to perform the more complex skills of comprehension.

Comprehension

The number of words whose meanings one knows (i.e. one's vocabulary) correlates highly with both reading ability and with I.Q. If one takes the view that vocabulary is generally learned in a rote fashion by learning to associate new words with their definitions, then these correlations are surprisingly high. However, a more accurate view is almost certainly that most vocabulary is learned by using contextual information to draw plausible inferences about the meaning of an unknown word. For example, suppose you read the following sentence (taken from Sternberg, 1985): "At dawn, the *blen* arose on the horizon and shone brightly." Even though you have never encountered the word *blen* before, it is reasonably clear from the context that it is a synonym of the word *sun*.

It follows from this viewpoint that the kinds of active processing and inference drawing which characterise vocabulary acquisition are also used in reading comprehension. This accounts for the close link between vocabulary and reading skill. It also follows that attempts to increase poor readers' vocabularies would have a much greater impact on their reading comprehension if they involved the development of inferential skills than if they simply involved the learning of word definitions. That is exactly what has been found. Teaching poor readers to use new words in different contexts and to link related words together led to better reasoning with those words than was found with simple learning of word definitions (McKeon, Beck, Omanson, & Pople, 1985). In addition, the context-based method of teaching produced a much greater improvement in overall text comprehension.

We saw earlier that many texts have an underlying structure which includes a main theme. A failure to identify this underlying structure may be an important ingredient in deficient reading skills. Striking evidence that this is so was obtained by Palincsar and Brown (1984). They trained children to think about the structure of the texts they were reading, and to ask questions about each text in order to pinpoint the main theme. This training was remarkably effective: The children initially had very poor reading comprehension, but by the end of training their comprehension was well above average for their age group.

There is considerable evidence that relevant knowledge in the form of schemata plays a very important part in the comprehension process. Indeed, we saw earlier in the study by Bransford and Johnson (1972) on the text "Washing clothes" that it can be extremely difficult to understand a passage adequately if the appropriate schema or schemata cannot be brought to bear on it. The impact of relevant knowledge on comprehension was shown by Pearson, Hansen, and Gordon (1979). Two groups of seven-year-old children whose reading skill was the same, but who differed in their knowledge of spiders, were asked to read a text about spiders. The two groups were comparable in their ability to answer questions about the main points contained in the text, but the more knowledgeable group was much better at drawing appropriate inferences from the text.

Summary and Evaluation

The development of several very different successful training programmes has strengthened the view that there are numerous different components involved in fluent reading. By and large, there has been a good measure of agreement between the components of reading which appear to be important under laboratory conditions, and those which have been found to be important in training programmes. However, a note of caution needs to be injected here. Most of the more successful training programmes have been developed only recently. As a consequence, it is rather difficult at the moment to evaluate the long-term value of these programmes.

SUMMARY

Language processing usually appears to be relatively straight-forward. In fact, however, there are numerous processes involved in comprehending speech and text. Many of these processes normally work rather rapidly and at the same time in order to allow the efficient understanding which generally characterises adult language processing.

One of the major problems with listening to speech is that the auditory signal is usually somewhat unclear and ambiguous. As a consequence, identifying the words which are being spoken tends to involve reliance on the sentence context. In addition, we make much more use than we usually imagine of the visual information conveyed by the speaker's lip movements.

The investigation by cognitive neuropsychologists of brain-damaged patients who experience difficulties in repeating spoken words has revealed some of the complexities involved in word recognition. More specifically, there is evidence suggesting that the task of saying a spoken word can be achieved in at least three different ways.

Analysis of eye movements has been used to reveal some of the processes involved in reading. We make a series of eye movements known as saccades during reading, but all of the information about the text is extracted during the fixation periods which generally last for about 200 to 250msecs. The fixation time on a word tends to be shorter when the word is highly predictable in the context of the sentence in which it appears.

The processing of text and of speech is primarily concerned with the extraction of meaning, although grammatical features obviously play an important part in the comprehension process. Studies of memory for text and for speech typically indicate that we remember mainly the gist of what we have seen or heard, but there are some exceptions to this (e.g. memory for sentences having personal significance).

Research within cognitive neuropsychology has revealed that there are probably three routes between seeing a word on the page and saying it. The main evidence for this is that brain-damaged patients who cannot say printed words normally differ considerably in the nature of their performance decrement.

Studies of reading have pointed to numerous processes involved in text comprehension. First, numerous inferences are usually drawn from the text, although this typically happens below the level of conscious awareness. Second, relevant past knowledge in the form of schemata, scripts, and frames is used to guide the interpretation of the text. Third, the comprehension process may involve identifying the propositions in a text, and organising them hierarchically in terms of their importance within the text.

The fact that we now have considerable knowledge about the structures and processes involved in reading has encouraged many researchers to develop training programmes to facilitate the learning of reading skills. These training programmes differ in terms of the specific aspect or aspects of reading which they address. Some programmes are designed to increase the speed and accuracy of word recognition, whereas others deal with the comprehension process itself (e.g. vocabulary growth; identification of text structure; increased background knowledge). Nearly all of these programmes have been reasonably successful, which indicates clearly that reading does not involve a single skill but rather a set of somewhat distinct skills.

FURTHER READING

Allport, D.A., MacKay, D.G., Prinz, W., & Marshall, J.C. (Eds.) (1987). *Language perception and production: shared mechanisms in listening, reading, and writing*. London: Academic Press. There is much useful information in this book, but the uninitiated reader may find it tough going.

Ellis, A.W. & Beattie, G. (1986). *The psychology of language and communication*. London: Lawrence Erlbaum Associates Ltd. This is a readable account of the psychological processes involved in language.

Ellis, A.W. & Young, A.W. (1988). *Human cognitive neuropsychology*. London: Lawrence Erlbaum Associates Ltd. Chapters 6, 8, and 9 contain a wealth of fascinating information about the impairments to reading and listening to speech shown by brain-damaged patients.

Garnham, A. (1985). *Psycholinguistics: Central topics*. London: Methuen. This book provides much more extensive coverage of the role of grammar in language processing than we have been able to include here.

Greene, J. (1986). *Language understanding: A cognitive approach*. Milton Keynes: Open University Press. This book provides broad and readable coverage of many of the topics discussed in this chapter. It deals with the artificial intelligence approach to language comprehension in much more detail than we have here.

Just, M.A. & Carpenter, P.A. (1987). *The psychology of reading and language comprehension*. Newton, Mass.: Allyn & Bacon. This book gives a very good overview of the contemporary scene.

Chapter Ten

LANGUAGE PRODUCTION: SPEECH AND WRITING

We know rather more about language comprehension than we do about language production. Why should this be so? It is fairly easy to exercise experimental control over material to be comprehended, whereas it is much more difficult to constrain an individual's production of language. A further problem in accounting for language production is that one really needs more than simply a theory of language. Language production is basically a goal-directed activity. People speak and write in order to influence other people, to impart information, to express concern, to be friendly, and so on.

INTRODUCTION

The two major topics considered within this chapter are speech production and writing, which are the two main forms of language production. Somewhat more is known about speech production than about writing. Part of the reason for this may be that nearly everyone spends more time talking than writing. It is thus of more practical use to understand the processes underlying talking than those involved in writing. However, writing is clearly an important skill in contemporary Western society, and this fact justifies its inclusion in this chapter.

This chapter and the previous one are both concerned with the processes involved in language. An issue which is obviously of importance is the relationship between language and thought. This issue is considered towards the end of this chapter, following our coverage of language production.

SPEECH PRODUCTION

Speech as Communication

For most people (unless there is something seriously wrong with them), speech nearly always occurs as conversation in a social context. We speak because we want to communicate with other people. If that communication is to be successful, then there has to be adherence to certain conventions. Grice (1967) argued that the key to successful communication lies in the Co-operative Principle, according to which both speakers and listeners must attempt to be co-operative.

In addition to the Co-operative Principle, Grice proposed a total of four maxims that the speaker should heed: quantity; quality; relation; and manner. According to the maxim of quantity, the speaker should be as informative as necessary, but not more so. According to the maxim of quality, the speaker should be truthful. The maxim of relation requires the speaker to say things which are relevant to the conversation, and the maxim of manner exhorts the speaker to make his contribution easy to understand.

Some evidence that speakers do, indeed, heed the maxim of quantity was obtained by Olson (1970). He pointed out that what needs to be said depends on the context. For example, it is not possible to account for what someone says simply by focusing on what the speaker wishes to describe (often called the referent). It is also necessary to know the objects from which the referent needs to be differentiated. It is sufficient to say "The boy is good at football" if the other players in a football game are all men, but not if the other players are also boys. In the latter case, it is necessary to be more specific (e.g. "The boy with red hair is good at football").

In applying the maxim of quantity, the speaker also has to take account of what has been called the "common ground" (Clark & Carlson, 1981). The "common ground" between two people consists of their mutual suppositions, beliefs, and knowledge. It will typically increase as two people interact more with each other. The way in which the "common ground" influences speakers can be seen if we consider a concrete example. If a speaker and his or her listener have several friends in common, then it may be reasonable for the speaker to say "Willie bought Tom's old Beetle." However, if the listener does not know who Tom is, and only knows Willie as Dr. Smith, then the speaker will typically convey the information in a rather different fashion: "Dr. Smith bought the orange car parked outside your office." The key point is that the process of language production often involves deciding on the factual information to be expressed, and then deciding exactly how this information should be expressed in the light of factors such as the environmental context and the available knowledge of the listener.

The power of these influences can be observed if you overhear a conversation between two friends on a bus or train. Since you lack the common ground which they share, it can sometimes be amazingly difficult to make much sense of what they are saying to each other.

Processes in Speech Production

One of the skills we tend to take for granted is that of speech production. Even young children are usually adept at talking in a reasonably sensible and grammatical way. Despite the prevalence in our society of people who can talk fluently, speech is actually a rather complex activity which involves a number of different skills. These include the ability to think of what one wants to say, to select the appropriate words to express it, to organise those words in a grammatical fashion, and to turn the sentences one wants to say into actual speech.

How can we attempt to come to grips with the processes involved in speech production? The answer in a nutshell is to take the advice of Polonius in Shakespeare's *Hamlet*: "By indirections find directions out." What that means in the present context is that in order to discover how people normally produce fluent speech, we need to focus on those occasions when errors creep into spoken language. As Dell (1986, p.284) pointed out, "The inner workings of a highly complex system are often revealed by the way in which the system breaks down."

It is generally supposed that there are several different mechanisms or components involved in speech production, e.g. those involved in deciding on the content of what is to be said; the exact words to use; and so on. If one assumes that each component can malfunction separately, then it should be possible to observe a large variety of different kinds of error in speech production. To anticipate a little, it has been shown that speech production can go wrong for several different reasons, and that it is possible to make theoretical sense of the findings by assuming that speech production involves a number of components in combination.

Two related theoretical frameworks for considering speech production will be considered first. The errors in speech production caused by temporary malfunctioning of one or more of these components in normal individuals will then be considered. This will be followed by an analysis of errors caused by permanent malfunctioning of speech-production components in brain-damaged patients. The errors made by normals and by brain-damaged patients will be related to the theoretical frameworks discussed initially.

Garrett's Theoretical Approach

Garrett (1976; 1984) has proposed a theory of speech production which involves a series of processing stages. At the most general level, his theory claims that there is a substantial amount of pre-production planning with speech. In other words, the speaker engages in fairly detailed planning of an utterance before beginning to speak. As we will see a little later, there is considerable evidence that the mind usually operates in advance of the mouth, even if you can think of one or two exceptions!

According to Garrett, there are four levels or stages involved in the planning of speech:

1. The first stage is the *message level*; this is the level at which the gist or overall meaning of what is to be said is worked out.
2. The second stage is the *functional level*; at this level, the outlines of the subsequent utterance are produced. These outlines have grammatical structure or syntax. In other words, it is decided at this level where the subject and object nouns will appear in the sentence, which nouns will have adjectives associated with them, and so on. The meanings to be expressed by these nouns, adjectives, and other parts of speech are calculated, but the specific words themselves are not chosen at the functional level.
3. The third stage is the *positional level*; this is the point at which the rather abstract representations of the earlier levels are fleshed out in a more concrete fashion to produce a sequence of sounds or phonemes. There are basically two separate stages involved here. The first stage involves selecting the basic forms or root morphemes (= the basic units of meaning) of the words to be spoken (e.g. the words "loves," "loving," and "loved" would all be represented by "love"). The second stage involves adding the appropriate inflections (e.g. "-s," "-ing," and "-ed") to the root morphemes.
4. The fourth stage is the *articulatory/phonetic level*, which is the final stage of speech production. As its name implies, this is the stage at which what the speaker intends to say is turned into a form ready for overt speech.

All of this probably sounds rather complicated, but some of the reasons for the complexities of Garrett's theory will be discussed shortly. For the present, it is interesting to note that the order of the processes in speech production is somewhat like the processes involved in comprehension, except that the processes are in approximately the opposite order. Thus, for example, the goal of comprehension is to understand the meaning of a message, whereas with speech production the meaning of the message is the starting point.

It is also worth noting that speech production can deviate from the systematic level-by-level progression described by Garrett. People listen to themselves talking. If they realise that they are not expressing themselves properly, then they will often stop in mid-sentence and have a second attempt to get it right. The role played by such feedback in correcting speech production is not dealt with explicitly in Garrett's (1976; 1984) model.

Dell's Theoretical Approach

Dell (1986) proposed a theory of speech production which resembles that of Garrett in some ways. Both theorists agree that the planning of speech proceeds through a number of different levels or stages, and there is some agreement on the characteristics of the various levels. According to Dell, there are four separate levels:

- The *semantic level* is the highest level and is concerned with the meaning of what is to be said; it is not considered in detail within the theory.
- The *syntactic level* is the second highest level and is concerned with the grammatical structure of the words in the utterance that is being planned.
- The *morphological level* is the third level and is concerned with the morphemes or basic units of meaning in the sentence being planned
- The *phonological level* is the lowest level and is concerned with the phonemes or basic units of sound in the planned sentence.
- A representation is formed at each of these four levels.
- Processing during planning of speech occurs concurrently at all four levels, but at any given moment processing will typically be more advanced at the higher levels than at the lower levels.

Dell (1986) discussed the relationship between some of his levels of speech production and those of Garrett (1976). He argued that Garrett's (1976) distinction between the functional and positional levels resembles his distinction between the syntactic level on the one hand and the morphological and phonological levels on the other hand. There are *categorical rules* at each of these four levels. These rules set constraints on the categories of items and on the combinations of categories which are and are not acceptable in constructing the representations. The rules at each level define categories which are appropriate to that level. Thus, for example, the categorical rules at the syntactic level specify the syntactic categories (e.g. noun, verb, adjective) of items within the sentence.

In addition to the categorical rules, there is a *lexicon* (= dictionary), which is in the form of a network. This lexicon contains nodes for concepts, words, morphemes, and phonemes. When a node is activated, it sends activation to all of the nodes which are connected to it (see Chapter 1 for a discussion of activation in semantic networks). Finally, *insertion rules* select the items for inclusion in the representation at each level according to the following criterion: The most highly activated node belonging to the appropriate category is chosen. For example, if the categorical rules at the syntactic level dictate that a verb is required at a particular point within the syntactic representation, then that verb whose node is most activated will be selected. After an item has been selected, its activation level immediately reduces to zero. This prevents it from being selected repeatedly.

Why do speech errors occur, according to the theory? At the simplest level, errors occur because some of the time an incorrect item will have a higher activation level than the correct item. Spreading activation means that numerous nodes are all activated at the same time, and this increases the likelihood of errors being made in speech.

What kinds of errors are predicted by the theory? First, errors should belong to the appropriate category (e.g. an incorrect noun replacing the correct noun). This is predicted because of the operation of the categorical rules. Most errors do belong to the appropriate category (Dell, 1986). Second, many errors should be anticipation errors, in which an item is spoken earlier in the sentence than is appropriate (e.g. "The sky is in the sky"). This happens because all of the items in the sentence will tend to become activated during the planning for speech. Third, anticipation errors should often turn into exchange errors, in which two items within a sentence are swapped (e.g. "I must write a wife to my letter"). Remember that the activation level of a selected item immediately reduces to zero. Therefore, once "wife" has been selected too early in the representation, it is unlikely to compete successfully to be selected in its correct place in the sentence. This allows a previously unselected and highly activated item such as "letter" to appear in the wrong place. As we shall see shortly, many speech errors are of the exchange variety. Fourth, anticipation and exchange errors generally involve items moving only a short distance within the sentence. In general terms, those items relevant to the part of the sentence which is under current consideration will tend to be more highly activated than those items relevant to more distant parts of the sentence. Fifth, it is predicted that speech errors should tend to consist of actual words or morphemes (this is known as the lexical bias effect). This is because activation at the word and morpheme levels affects processing at the lower levels. This effect was demonstrated experimentally by Baars, Motley, and MacKay (1975). Word pairs were presented briefly, and the subjects had to say both words as rapidly as possible. The error rate was twice as great when the word pair could be re-formed to create two new words (e.g. "lewd rip" can be turned into "rude lip") than when it could not (e.g. "Luke risk" turns into "ruke lisk"). Sixth, the notion that the various levels of processing involved in speech planning interact with each other in a flexible fashion means that it is possible for a speech error to be multiply determined. Dell (1986) quoted the example of someone saying "Let's stop" instead of "Let's start." The error is certainly semantic, but it could also be regarded as phonological, since the substitute word shares a common sound with the appropriate word. Detailed investigation of such word-substitution errors reveals that the two words concerned (i.e. the spoken word and the intended word) tend to be more similar in sound than would be expected by chance alone (e.g. Harley, 1984).

On the face of it, it seems somewhat strange that the human speech-production system has been designed in such a way that it is error-prone. If, for example, activation did not spread so widely through the lexicon, then perhaps there would be fewer speech errors. Dell addressed this issue, and argued that there are positive virtues associated with our flexible speech-production system. This flexibility permits the production of novel sentences, and prevents our utterances from becoming too stereotyped. The small cost that needs to be paid for flexibility is the relatively infrequent occurrence of slips of the tongue.

Dell's (1986) spreading-activation theory is clearly related to Garrett's (1976; 1984) earlier theory. The single most important difference is that Dell provides a considerably more detailed account of the mechanisms responsible for speech errors. As a consequence, his theory generates far more specific predictions about the kinds of speech errors to be expected than does Garrett's. Another attractive feature of Dell's theory is that its emphasis on spreading activation provides links between speech production and other cognitive activities (e.g. word recognition: McClelland & Rumelhart, 1981).

Speech Errors in Normals

Most of our knowledge about speech errors in normal individuals is based on collections of errors (e.g. Garrett, 1975; Stemberger, 1982). The errors in these collections consist of those that were personally heard by the researchers concerned. This procedure clearly carries problems with it: For example, there may be systematic biases because some kinds of error are more readily detectable than others. This means that one needs to be sceptical about the percentage figures for the different kinds of speech errors, but it is less clear that there are any major problems about the main categories of speech errors which have been identified. The existence of some types of speech errors has been confirmed by experimentation in which techniques have been used to create errors in the laboratory (see Dell, 1986).

The "Tip-of-the-Tongue" Phenomenon

We have all had the experience of having a concept or idea in mind, but searching in vain for the right word to describe it. This frustrating state of affairs has been called the "tip-of-the-tongue" state, and was first investigated systematically by Brown and McNeill (1966). They stated that a subject in this state: "would appear to be in a mild torment, something like the brink of a sneeze, and if he found the word his relief was considerable."

The experimental approach adopted by Brown and McNeill involved reading out dictionary definitions of rare words, and asking their subjects to identify the words defined. Thus, for example, the correct answer to the definition "A navigational instrument used in measuring angular distances, especially the altitude of the sun, moon and stars at sea" is "sextant". If the subjects were unable to come up with the right word, but felt that the answer was on the tip of their tongue, then they tried to guess the initial letter, the number of syllables, and so on, of the missing word. It was clear that those in the tip-of-the-tongue state often had access to many of the features of the word they were trying to recall. For example, subjects in that state were correct 57% of the time when guessing the word's initial letter.

The relevance of the tip-of-the-tongue state to Garrett's (1976; 1984) model is that it indicates that Garrett was right to draw a distinction between having an abstract idea (as in the message level representation) and having the appropriate words to express it (as in the positional level). In other words, the individual in the tip-of-the-tongue state has a very precise abstract concept in mind but just cannot locate the word required to express it.

Word-exchange Errors

Word-exchange errors are those in which two words in a sentence switch places (e.g. "I must let the house out of the cat"). These errors, as in the example just given, nearly always involve two words belonging to the same part of speech (e.g. both nouns or both verbs). These word-exchange errors presumably occur during the functional level on Garrett's (1984) theory, at the time at which the positioning of nouns, verbs, and so on, within the sentence is being decided. According to Dell (1986), word-exchange errors occur at the syntactic level, and depend upon patterns of activation.

The simple fact that words from the later parts of a sentence sometimes intrude into the earlier part of a spoken sentence suggests that Garrett (1984) and Dell (1986) were correct in assuming that there is pre-production planning of what is to be said. How far does this planning extend? Garrett (1976) found in a collection of 97 word-exchange errors that 85% of them involved words within the same clause (i.e. a part of a sentence centred on a verb). This suggests that at least some speech planning occurs on a clause-by-clause basis. According to Dell's theory, patterns of activation lead to the expectation that word-exchange error would involve words which are reasonably close to each other within the sentence.

Morpheme-exchange Errors

Morpheme-exchange errors are of particular interest to cognitive psychologists trying to understand speech production. These errors involve switching the roots of two words while leaving their inflections in place (e.g. "He has already trunked two packs"). According to Garrett (1984), morpheme-exchange errors occur during the positional level stage of speech production. The basic forms or root morphemes of words and their inflections are dealt with rather separately at the positional level of analysis. One plausible consequence is the existence of morpheme-exchange errors.

It will be remembered that Garrett (1984) argued that the roots or basic forms of words are worked out *before* the inflections are added. Some evidence for this ordering can be obtained by considering the details of pronunciation in morpheme-exchange errors. Smyth, Morris, Levy, and Ellis (1987) pointed out that inflections are generally altered so as to fit in with the new word roots they find themselves linked with. For example, the "s" sound in the phrase "the forks of a prong" is pronounced in a way which is appropriate within the word "forks", but this is different to the "s" sound in the original word "prongs".

Morpheme-exchange errors are readily predictable from Dell's (1986) spreading-activation theory. In essence, they occur during the construction of the morphological representation. When planning the sentence, "He has already packed two trunks," the morpheme "trunk" will be highly activated because it is part of the planned utterance. If its activation exceeds that of "pack" when the middle of the morphological representation is reached, then a speech error will be made at that point. Since the activation of "trunk" then falls to zero, it will usually not compete successfully with "pack" at the end of the sentence, and so a morpheme-exchange error will result.

Spoonerisms

One of the best-known errors of spoken language is the Spoonerism, in which the initial letter or letters of two or more words are switched. The Rev. W.A. Spooner, after whom the Spoonerism is named, is credited with several memorable examples. These include: "You have hissed all my mystery lectures"; and "The Lord is a shoving leopard to his flock." It should perhaps be pointed out that there is a strong suspicion that many of the Rev. Spooner's gems were not produced spontaneously, but rather were the result of much painstaking work.

Garrett (1976) reported that 93% of the Spoonerisms in his collection involved a switching of letters between two words belonging to the same clause. This strengthens the notion that the clause is an important unit in speech production. Spoonerisms presumably arise at the positional level of speech production, during the stage at which the sounds of the root morphemes are being worked out.

In Dell's (1986) theory, Spoonerisms occur at the phonological level during the formation of the phonological representation. The detailed reasons for their existence correspond closely to the reasons for the existence of morpheme-exchange errors.

Hesitations and Pauses

Hesitations and pauses are not exactly speech errors. Nevertheless, they can be informative about some of the processes involved in speech production, in part because pauses and hesitations in speech are made use of by speakers in order to enable them to plan ahead (see Butterworth, 1980, for a detailed review). However, matters are complicated by the fact that speech pauses are sometimes related to the speaker's task, or to his or her emotional and motivational states, rather than to speech planning. Despite these complications, it has been found that pauses in spontaneous speech typically occur more often at grammatical junctures than anywhere else. Boomer (1965) discovered that such pauses last longer on average than those at other locations (1.03sec. versus 0.75sec., respectively). Pauses that coincide with phrase boundaries tend to be filled with sounds such as "um," "er," or "ah," whereas those occurring within a phrase tend to be silent (Maclay & Osgood, 1959).

The data on pauses are consistent with evidence discussed already in suggesting that much language planning and production occurs clause by clause. Maclay and Osgood (1959) investigated the repetitions which occur in speech. They found that speakers tend to repeat or correct an entire clause (e.g. "Turn on the stove—the heater switch").

Speech Errors in Patients

Garrett (1976; 1984) argued that there are various conceptually distinct processes involved in speech production. If that is indeed the case, then presumably brain-damaged patients with impaired speech will vary in the specific process or processes which are disrupted. It might, for example, be possible to identify some patients with particular problems at the message level, others with problems at the functional level, and so on. Of course, many patients have widespread brain damage, so that most or even all of the speech-production processes may be impaired. However, some patients have more circumscribed brain damage, and investigations of their speech impairments are of particular value.

Anomia

Many brain-damaged patients who cannot speak normally suffer from what is known as *anomia*. This involves problems with retrieving and saying words, and can greatly reduce the ability of the patient to communicate effectively. Ellis and Young (1988) have argued convincingly that the precise nature of the problem in anomic patients varies considerably. More specifically, anomia is sometimes associated with a semantic impairment, and sometimes not. In those cases where there is a semantic impairment, this would indicate the existence of a problem between the message and the functional levels in terms of Garrett's (1976; 1984) theoretical approach.

A case of anomia in which a semantic impairment appeared to be mainly responsible was reported by Howard and Orchard-Lisle (1984). The patient, JCU, had good object recognition and reasonable comprehension. However, she was very poor at naming the objects shown in pictures unless she was given the first phoneme or sound as a cue. If the cue was the first phoneme of a word closely related to the object shown in the picture, then JCU would often be misled into producing the wrong answer. This wrong answer she accepted as correct 76% of the time. In contrast, if she produced a name that was quite different in meaning to the object depicted, then she rejected it 86% of the time. The implication is that JCU had some access to semantic information, but the information was often insufficient to specify precisely what it was she was looking at.

A very different case of anomia was investigated by Kay and Ellis (1987). Their patient, EST, had very good comprehension. He did not have the semantic impairment shown by JCU, and so outperformed JCU on the tasks just described. Indeed, his performance on a range of tasks was so good that it appeared that he had no significant impairment to his semantic system. Despite this, he had a very definite anomia, as can be seen from this attempt to describe a picture (Kay & Ellis, 1987):

Er . . . two children, one girl one male . . . the . . . the girl, they're in a . . . and their, their mother was behind them in in, they're in the kitchen . . . the boy is trying to get . . . a . . . er, a part of a cooking . . . jar . . . He's standing on . . . the lad, the boy is standing on a . . . standing on a . . . standing on a . . . I'm calling it a seat, I can't . . . I forget what it's, what the name of it is . . . It is er a higher, it's a seat, standing on that, 'e's standing on that . . . this boy is standing on this, seat . . . getting some of this er stuff to . . . biscuit to eat. As he is doing that, the post, it's not a post, it's the, seat, is falling down, is falling over . . .

Close inspection of EST's speech indicates that it is reasonably grammatical, and that his greatest problem lies in finding words other than those in very common usage. In terms of Garrett's (1976; 1984) theory, his problem can be placed between the functional and positional levels. More specifically, two major possibilities suggest themselves as to why most words cannot be found by EST:

- Information about them is no longer contained in the store which makes the spoken forms of words available;
- The information is still there, but for some reason is inaccessible.

The evidence tends to favour the second alternative. EST is better at repeating spoken words he never uses in his spontaneous speech than he is at repeating spoken nonwords, indicating that at least some residual information about most words is still present in his memory system.

What are we to make of EST's anomia? Kay and Ellis (1987) have come up with the ingenious solution that his condition resembles in greatly magnified form that of the rest of us when in the "tip-of-the-tongue" state. The difference, of course, is that it is mostly rather uncommon words which cause us problems with finding and saying the word corresponding to a concept that we have, whereas with EST the problem is present with all but the most common words.

Syntactic Problems: Agrammatism

Suppose for the sake of argument that there are some patients who can formulate ideas clearly at the message level, but who are severely impaired in forming appropriate grammatical or syntactic outlines at the functional level. The speech of such patients might contain many meaningfully related words, but would lack the normal structure. The lack of appropriate grammatical structure seems to reveal itself mainly by the omission of inflections and function words from their speech. There is also inappropriate ordering of the words within a sentence, but this tends to be more the case for comprehension than for speech. For example, the words in the following two phrases are the same, but the different ordering of the words makes a substantial difference to the meaning: "Dog bites man" and "Man bites dog." Patients who exhibit grammatical problems have been discovered, and are sometimes referred to by the rather vague term of "agrammatic aphasia."

Saffran, Schwartz, and Marin (1980a; 1980b) investigated patients suffering from grammatical impairments. For example, one patient was asked to describe a picture of a woman kissing a man, and produced the following: "The kiss . . . the lady kissed . . . the lady is . . . the lady and the man and the lady . . . kissing." In addition, Saffran et al. found that agrammatic aphasics had great difficulty in putting the two nouns in the correct order when asked to describe pictures containing two living creatures in interaction.

The majority of patients who produce numerous grammatical errors in speaking also have problems in making use of grammatical information in comprehension. It is currently uncertain whether there are separate syntactic modules involved in comprehension and production, or whether there is a single syntactic module involved in both input and output (Ellis, personal communication).

Summary

The main reason for speaking is for the purpose of communicating with other people. This goal can only be achieved if speakers and listeners both try to be co-operative (the Co-operative Principle). While speech production generally appears fairly effortless, there is a considerable amount of evidence to support the view that most speakers engage in detailed planning before they start to speak.

The analysis of errors in speaking can provide insights into the processes involved in speech production. Normal individuals make various errors when they are speaking. Some of these errors merely reflect a lack of knowledge of grammar or vocabulary, and are therefore of rather little theoretical interest. However, there are other kinds of speech errors (e.g. the "tip-of-the-tongue" phenomenon; word-exchange errors) which are quite revealing about the various stages of pre-planning of speech. Each of these stages is fallible, and it is for this reason that several very different kinds of speech errors are made.

Many of the most common kinds of speech error can be accounted for within a theoretical approach which assumes that a spreading-activation retrieval mechanism is involved in speech production. According to this approach, speech errors occur whenever an incorrect item belonging to the appropriate category (e.g. noun; verb) is more strongly activated than the correct item. Dell (1986) proposed a theory of this type, and argued that an advantage of spreading-activation theories is that they can potentially account for the production of novel sentences.

Cognitive neuropsychology offers considerable potential for identifying the processes involved in speech production. So far, however, research in this area has produced a somewhat complex and puzzling picture. It is probably fair to say that the available evidence is consistent with the type of theory of speech production proposed by Garrett (1976; 1984), and extended by Dell (1986), but that much more research needs to be done before that theoretical approach can be evaluated properly by cognitive neuropsychologists.

WRITING

Theoretical Considerations

One of the most thorough theoretical approaches to writing was proposed by Hayes and Flower (1980). They proposed that writing consists of three main processes: PLANNING, TRANSLATING, and REVIEWING. Within each of these processes, various sub-processes can be identified. Thus, the PLANNING process makes use of three sub-processes: *generating, organising*, and *goal-setting*. In general terms, the PLANNING process uses information from the task environment and from long-term memory in order to set goals.

Collins and Gentner (1980) have been rather more specific about some of the goals in writing. They argued that there are at least four general objectives: making the text comprehensible; making it enticing; making it persuasive; and making it remember-able. As you have undoubtedly discovered to your cost, writers differ enormously in terms of the importance which they attach to each of these objectives!

When the goals have been established, a writing plan is formulated to produce written text conforming to those goals. More specifically, the *generation* process retrieves information from long-term memory, and each item of information that is retrieved is used as a cue to retrieve the next item of information. In this way, a retrieval chain is created, which continues to grow until an irrelevant item of information is retrieved. The organising process selects the most relevant information retrieved by the generation process, and organises it into a coherent writing plan. The *goal-setting* process stores away useful rules (e.g. "Keep it simple") for subsequent use by the *editing* process.

The TRANSLATING process operates in the service of the

overall writing plan to produce language that conforms in meaning to information retrieved from the writer's long-term memory. This process is needed, because information in long-term memory may often be stored in a rather abstract propositional form rather than directly as language. Finally, the REVIEWING process consists of the two sub-processes of *reading* and *editing*. Its function is basically to improve the quality of the text produced by the TRANSLATING process. These improvements can be quite varied, ranging from corrections of spelling and grammar to changes in the text to make it conform better to the writing plan.

Hayes and Flower (1980) assumed that the order in which these processes and sub-processes are used is quite flexible. However, the natural sequence is clearly PLANNING, then TRANSLATING, and finally REVIEWING. This orderly progression can be altered, however, because both the *editing* and *generating* processes can interrupt other processes. It is assumed that the editing process is used whenever deficiencies in the text are detected. Of course, individual differences also affect the ordering of the processes. Some writers prefer to produce a rapid first draft before reviewing the text, whereas others edit frequently as they write and attempt to produce a perfect first draft.

The main evidence that Hayes and Flower put forward to support their proposed theoretical account of writing was based on protocol analysis. The essence of a protocol analysis approach to writing is that writers attempt to verbalise their mental activities during writing tasks. A tape recording is made of these verbalisations, and then a verbatim transcript is prepared. In addition, all of the notes which the writer has made during the writing task are studied. Hayes and Flower made particular use of a writer who seemed to be especially aware of his ongoing writing processes. He produced one page of completed text, together with 14 pages based on thinking aloud and 5 pages of notes.

It appeared from his protocol analysis that he had started with the *generating* process, followed by the *organising* process, and then the TRANSLATING process. Analysis of what he wrote confirmed this impression, since there was a definite progression over time from unorganised fragments to more structured items, and then to complete sentences. The mean length of the retrieval chain was 6.4 ideas during the generating stage, against only 2.0 thereafter. Finally, as expected, the flow of processing was frequently interrupted by the editing and generating processes.

There are various potential problems with protocol analysis. It is likely that providing a verbal protocol affects the composition and writing processes, perhaps because the writer thinks more analytically than he or she usually would. It is also possible that the task of providing a protocol makes the composition process more difficult than usual, especially for those writers who find composing text a rather difficult task under normal circumstances. The discussion of introspection in Chapter 1 deals with some additional problems with protocols.

Hayes and Flower (1986) developed some of the theoretical views of their earlier study. They put more emphasis on the notion that writing is goal directed. Evidence for this emerged clearly from protocol analysis. For example, someone who was asked to write about the role of women for a hostile audience focused very much on what he was trying to achieve: "I'm not really trying to persuade these people of anything. I'm simply being descriptive . . . I'm saying, 'This is the way the world is.'"

The goals involved in writing tend to be hierarchically organised. Many writers make notes before they start writing, including the major points they want to make and more minor points associated with the major ones. The writer who said that he was being descriptive analysed his writing goals as follows: "I think what I really want is to present maybe one [point] with a lot of illustrations."

Hayes and Flower (1986) continued to propose three main processes involved in writing. However, they changed the names of some of those processes. Thus, whereas Hayes and Flower (1980) distinguished between planning, translating, and reviewing, Hayes and Flower (1986) identified planning, sentence generation, and revising as the key processes. The essence of what was proposed by Hayes and Flower (1986) was as follows:

- The planning process involves producing ideas and organising them into a writing plan which will satisfy the goals the writer is seeking to achieve.
- The sentence generation process involves turning the writing plan into the actual writing of sentences.
- The revision process involves evaluating what has been written. This process can operate at a relatively specific level (i.e. individual words or phrases) or at a more general level (e.g. the structural coherence of the writing).
- The natural sequence is planning, sentence generation, and revision, but these processes generally do not happen in a strictly serial fashion. In other words, it is rarely the case that all of the planning is done before any of the sentence generation and revision.

Planning

Writing plans obviously depend heavily on the knowledge which the writer possesses about the topic in question. However, it would be ludicrous to argue that the quality of a writing plan is influenced only by the writer's topic knowledge. Experts are often notoriously bad at organising their ideas into a form which is comprehensible, in part because their expertise distances them from the problems in understanding experienced by the nonexpert.

According to Hayes and Flower (1986), strategic knowledge plays a major role in the construction of a writing plan. Strategic knowledge is knowledge about ways of organising the goals and sub-goals of writing so as to construct a coherent writing plan.

Perhaps the simplest way of illustrating what is meant by strategic knowledge is to consider what happens when such knowledge is absent. Scardamalia and Bereiter (1987) have studied writing in children. They discovered that children relied heavily on an associative search of memory during the planning stage. The information thus retrieved was then used in a knowledge-telling strategy. This strategy involves simply writing down everything that the child knows about a topic without any real planning or attempt to organise the information for the reader's benefit. As all academics discover when reading students' essays, the knowledge-telling strategy often persists in adulthood!

Scardamalia and Bereiter found that skilled writers continued to use the knowledge-telling strategy, but that they could also employ a knowledge-transforming strategy. This strategy involves actively considering problems with the planning process (e.g. "Can I express the main idea more simply?") and making use of a directed search of long-term memory to resolve these problems.

Hayes and Flower (1986) have found that good writers use strategic knowledge in a very flexible way. The structure of the writing plan often changes considerably during the writing period as new ideas occur to the writer, or dissatisfaction grows with the original plan. Hayes and Flower make the interesting suggestion that writers who are afflicted by writer's block tend to adhere rigidly to their original writing plan. If it becomes obvious that the plan is inadequate, then the writing process grinds to a halt.

Not surprisingly, producing an outline of what one intends to write tends to improve the quality of the finished product (Kellogg, 1990). It appears that an outline serves the function of reducing attentional overload during the planning stage (Kellogg, 1988). It also reduces the need to keep swapping between the planning, translating, and reviewing processes.

Adults possessing either a lot of knowledge or relatively little on a topic were compared by Hayes and Flower (1986). The experts produced more goals and sub-goals, and so constructed a more complex overall writing plan. However, the greatest difference between the experts and the novices was in terms of plan integration: The various goals of the experts were much more interconnected.

Sentence Generation

The gap between the writing plan and the actual writing of sentences is usually large. Kaufer, Hayes, and Flower (1986) compared the outlines which writers produced with the essays they wrote subsequently. Even for those writers who produced the longest outlines, the essay was approximately eight times longer than the outline. In some ways, the process going on here is the opposite of that involved in comprehension. Van Dijk and Kintsch (1983) argued that comprehension involves extracting the macro-structure from the micropropositions, and sentence generation could be regarded as generating micropropositions from the macrostructural plans.

The technique of asking writers to think aloud permitted Kaufer et al. to gain some insight into the process of sentence generation. Here is a typical verbal protocol of a writer engaged in writing, with dashes being inserted at those points where there was a pause of at least two seconds:

The best thing about it is (1) ___ what? (2) Something about using my mind (3) ___ it allows me the opportunity to (4) ___ uh ___ I want to write something about my ideas (5) ___ to put ideas into action (6) ___ or ___ to develop my ideas into (7) ___ what? (8) ___ into a meaningful form? (9) Oh, Bleh! ___ say it allows me (10) ___ to use (11) ___ Na ___ allows me ___ scratch that. The best thing about it is that it allows me to use (12) ___ my mind and ideas in a productive way (13).

In this above protocol, fragments 12 and 13 formed the written sentence, and the earlier fragments 1, 4, 6, 7, 9, and 11 were attempts to produce parts of the sentence.

Kaufer et al. (1986) compared the sentence-generation styles of expert and average writers. Both groups accepted approximately 75% of the sentence parts they verbalised, and those sentence parts that were changed were nearly always those which had just been produced. The most interesting difference between the two groups was in terms of the length of the average sentence part which was proposed: It was 11.2 words for the expert writer compared with 7.3 words for the average writers. The implication is that good writers make use of larger units or "building blocks" in writing than do others.

Revision

Expert writers differ from nonexpert writers in terms of both the amount of time spent revising what they have written and in terms of how they approach the task of revision. Since increased expertise usually means that less time is needed to perform a task, it is perhaps surprising that expert writers typically spend *longer* than nonexpert writers in revision. Matters become clearer, however, when one considers differences between the two groups in how they perceive the revision process. Expert writers tend to focus on the coherence and structure of the arguments expressed, whereas nonexpert writers focus on individual words and phrases. It is a much more complex and time-consuming task to modify the hierarchical structure of a text than to change individual words.

Faigley and Witte (1983) compared the revisions made by writers at different levels of skill. They discovered that 34% of the revisions of experienced adult writers involved a change of meaning, against 25% of the revisions of experienced college writers, and only 12% of the revisions of inexperienced college writers. These differences probably occur because experienced writers are more concerned with the broad issues of coherence and meaning than are inexperienced ones.

Further evidence on differences in revision processes between expert and nonexpert writers was obtained by Hayes, Flower,

Schriver, Stratman, and Carey (1985). They discovered that expert writers detected approximately 60% more problems in a text than did nonexperts. Of the problems that were detected, the expert writers correctly identified the nature of the problem in 74% of the cases, against only 42% for the nonexpert writers. Rather surprisingly, both groups of writers often re-wrote sections of the text without working out what was deficient in the original.

One of the greatest problems in revision is to alter the text in such a way that it becomes more comprehensible to the intended reader or readers. This is a particularly acute problem in writing a textbook such as this, where the readers are likely to vary considerably in their previous knowledge of the topics being discussed. An interesting way of teaching writers to be more alert to the reader's needs was used by Schriver (1984). Students read an imperfect text, and tried to predict the comprehension problems that a reader would have with it. Then the students read a reader's verbal protocol which was produced while he or she was struggling to understand that text. After the students had been given a number of texts and the accompanying reader's protocols, they became better at predicting the kinds of problems readers would have with new texts.

Evaluation

Hayes and Flower (1980; 1986) have greatly advanced our understanding of the processes involved in writing. However, it is a complex matter to identify all of these processes, since they often proceed below the level of conscious awareness. The greatest weakness of protocol analysis, upon which Hayes and Flower rely heavily, is precisely that it can provide information only about those processes of which there is conscious awareness. This criticism may well apply more to some aspects of their theorising than to others. For example, writers may often use a partially organised writing plan without being able to verbalise it, whereas they may generally have a clear idea of what they are trying to achieve during the revision process. Future research needs to consider more fully the problems of elucidating those problems which are not revealed by protocol analysis.

One of the most valuable aspects of the approach taken by Hayes and Flower (1986) is their comparison of more and less skilled writers. This facilitates the identification of the specific strategies involved in skilled writing. It is also useful in terms of producing practical advice for those who find it difficult to develop adequate writing skills.

On the negative side, there are some doubts as to whether the three processes of planning, sentence generation, and revision can be neatly separated from each other. In particular, planning and sentence generation are often almost inextricably bound up with each other. A further criticism was raised by Kellogg (1990), who argued that writing is more of a social act than is proposed by Hayes and Flower (1986). According to Kellogg, "Instead of focusing on the cognitive processes of an individual, the social approach studies the writer as an agent in a literate community of discourse."

Writing Problems: Cognitive Neuropsychology

Several brain-damaged patients who have particular problems with spelling and with writing have been studied over the years (Ellis & Young, 1988). The focus here will be on two of the major issues in this area. First, there has been a certain amount of controversy about the role played by inner speech in the writing process, and about whether or not it is necessary. Second, there have been suggestions that the processes involved in spelling and writing can vary. The notion of different "routes" to the writing of words is considered in the light of the relevant cognitive neuropsychological evidence. It should be emphasised that cognitive neuropsychologists have focused on only certain limited aspects of writing, especially those concerned with the spelling of individual words. Some reasons for the circumscribed nature of the cognitive neuropsychological approach are discussed in Chapter 14.

Inner Speech and Writing

It has often been assumed (e.g. Luria, 1970) that writing depends heavily on inner speech, and that one says words to oneself before writing them down. This makes intuitive sense, because we often have the impression that inner speech is accompanying the writing process. In addition, many of the spelling mistakes made in writing (e.g. "akshun" instead of "action") are consistent with the notion that spellings are sometimes based almost entirely on knowledge of the sound of the word.

These considerations certainly suggest that inner speech is sometimes involved in writing. However, the interesting issue theoretically is whether inner speech is necessary for writing or whether it is an "optional extra." Perhaps the most direct way of tackling this issue is to consider brain-damaged patients who appear to have little or no inner speech, and see whether any of them are able to write in a reasonably normal fashion. Precisely this has been done in a number of studies in recent years, and we now turn to the relevant evidence.

Levine, Calvanio, and Popovics (1982) reported on the case of EB, who was an engineer in his mid-fifties who had had a stroke. This stroke had virtually removed any ability to produce overt speech, but his comprehension of speech and of written text was very good. Of most immediate interest, his inner speech appeared to be practically nonexistent. In one task, he was given a target picture and four further pictures. His task was to decide which of the four pictures had a name which rhymed with the name of the target picture. He was able to work out the names and spellings of most of the pictures, but could not use the sounds of the picture names to perform the task accurately. In another task, he could not match spoken and written nonwords, presumably because he was unable to make use of inner speech.

Despite his apparent lack of inner speech, EB's writing skills were largely intact. He sometimes experienced problems with grammatical structure in his writing, but the quality of his written language can be seen very clearly in this account (Levine et al., 1982) of his first memories after his stroke:

> Gradually after what seemed days and days, got back enough strength to pull myself up and sit if I held on. I tilted off to the right and had a hard time maintaining my balance. The nurse and doctor and an orderly helped me up then . . . I got to another part of the hospital where there were two doctors asking me questions I couldn't answer.

It should be noted that the findings from EB are unusually clear. The great majority of aphasic patients are severely impaired in both writing and speaking, and so lack the marked discrepancy between writing and speaking skills shown by EB. Some problems with an undue reliance on the data from individual patients are discussed in Chapter 14.

Further evidence that some brain-damaged patients do not rely on inner speech when engaged in writing comes from the study of patients suffering from what has been termed "neologistic jargonaphasia." Their speech is full of nonwords which sound similar to the intended words (e.g. "skut" instead of "scout"; "orstrum" instead of "saucepan"). These errors do not seem to be due to problems of articulation, because patients with neologistic jargonaphasia can often pronounce correctly common multi-syllabled words.

If neologistic jargonaphasics relied on inner speech while writing, it would be expected that the kinds of errors present in their pronunciation of words would affect their spelling of the same words. The patient RD (Ellis, Miller, & Sin, 1983) was shown various pictures, and called an elephant an "enelust," a screwdriver a "kistro," and a penguin a "senstenz." Despite these substantial mispronunciations, his spellings of all of these names were completely accurate. In spite of the clarity of the findings from RD, it has not been established that the superiority of writing over speech which he displayed is generally true of neologistic jargonaphasics (Ellis, personal communication).

In sum, there are patients (e.g. EB) whose writing skills are reasonably intact, but who do not appear to use inner speech at all. Other patients (e.g. RD) can write many words accurately in spite of the fact that they cannot pronounce them properly. It seems necessary on the basis of such evidence to conclude that spelling and writing do not necessarily depend on inner speech at all. Despite this, it is entirely possible that inner speech is often used during writing by normal individuals. We now turn to a more detailed consideration of the various ways in which we spell words that we hear.

Routes to Spelling

A sketch-map of current thinking on how heard words are spelled is shown in Fig. 10.1, which is adapted from Ellis and Young (1988). The main points to be noted are as follows:

- There are several different routes between hearing a word and spelling it.
- The spelling of known or familiar words involves use of the *graphemic output lexicon* (a store containing information about the written forms of familiar words). Heard words can gain access to the graphemic output lexicon either through the *semantic system* (which stores word meanings), or through the *speech output lexicon* (which provides information about the spoken forms of words). Both routes are often used at the same time in normal individuals. This serves the function of minimising the number of errors in writing.
- The spelling of unknown words or nonwords cannot involve

Components for a model for the spelling of heard words. Adapted from Ellis & Young (1988).

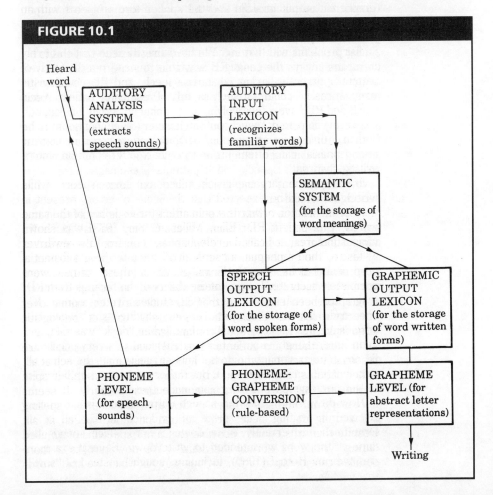

FIGURE 10.1

Heard word

AUDITORY ANALYSIS SYSTEM (extracts speech sounds)

AUDITORY INPUT LEXICON (recognizes familiar words)

SEMANTIC SYSTEM (for the storage of word meanings)

SPEECH OUTPUT LEXICON (for the storage of word spoken forms)

GRAPHEMIC OUTPUT LEXICON (for the storage of word written forms)

PHONEME LEVEL (for speech sounds)

PHONEME-GRAPHEME CONVERSION (rule-based)

GRAPHEME LEVEL (for abstract letter representations)

Writing

use of the graphemic output lexicon, because no information about them is available in the lexicon. What happens instead is that spellings are constructed from the spoken or phonemic forms of words by means of *phoneme-grapheme conversion*, which capitalises on the regularities in the language. The irregularities of the English language mean that this route will often produce plausible but incorrect spellings of irregular words (e.g. "yacht" might be spelled as "yot").

This theoretical model makes several assumptions about the different components or modules which can be involved in spelling. In order to evaluate its adequacy, it will be useful to consider some of the evidence relating to each of the major assumptions incorporated in the model. Much greater detail on all of this is provided by Ellis and Young (1988).

How do we know that there are separate graphemic output and speech output lexicons? If information about the written forms (graphemic output lexicon) and the spoken forms (speech output lexicon) of words were stored in the same lexicon, then presumably patients who had problems with speaking would have similar problems with writing. We have already seen that this is by no means always the case. EB was able to write reasonably well despite apparently having no inner speech, and RD could write many words he could not say properly. Presumably patients such as EB and RD have a relatively intact graphemic output lexicon, but a severely impaired speech output lexicon (or connections to or from it). In contrast to EB and RD, the more common pattern among brain-damaged patients is to have a greater problem with writing than with speech. Such patients presumably have more severe impairment of the graphemic output lexicon than of the speech output lexicon.

How do we know that the semantic system is involved in the writing process? If, for some reason, only partial semantic information about a heard word was passed on from the semantic system to the graphemic output lexicon, then we would expect a word similar in meaning to be written down in place of the actual word. Precisely this has been observed in so-called "deep dysgraphics". Bub and Kertesz (1982) studied a young woman, JC, who made numerous semantic errors, writing "sun" when the word "sky" was spoken, writing "chair" when "desk" was said, and so on. Interestingly enough, her reading aloud was very good, and did not contain semantic errors. This suggests that the semantic system itself was not damaged, but rather the connection between the semantic system and the graphemic output lexicon.

How do we know that the speech output lexicon is sometimes involved in writing? One piece of evidence is that all of us sometimes inadvertently write down a word which sounds the same as the word we intended to write down. Several examples are given by Hotopf (1980), including "sought" instead of "sort", "their" instead of "there," and "scene" instead of "seen". The fact that actual words are nearly always written down suggests the involvement of the speech output lexicon. If the sounds of words were being used to produce spellings by means of phoneme-grapheme correspondence, then we would expect there to be numerous non-words produced (e.g. "sawt" instead of "sort" and "thair" instead of "there").

More evidence of the involvement of the speech output lexicon in spelling is available in the case of patient PR, who was studied by Shallice (1981). He (PR rather than Shallice!) had made a good recovery from a stroke, and his spelling and writing generally were quite good. However, those spelling mistakes he made often involved producing words which resembled the correct word in sound (e.g. "caught" instead of "quart" and "thumb" instead of "plum"). As we shall see shortly, this patient made little or no use of phoneme-grapheme correspondence, so that we can be reasonably confident that these spelling errors stemmed from the speech output lexicon.

How do we know that phoneme-grapheme conversion is sometimes involved in writing? As has already been pointed out, words that we do not know at all do not have entries in either the graphemic output lexicon or the speech output lexicon. As a consequence, we can only hazard a guess at their appropriate spelling by using some other strategy such as phoneme-grapheme conversion, in which rules are used to translate sound into spelling. Children often seem to use phoneme-grapheme conversion, producing misspellings which sound like the word in question (e.g. "skool" instead of "school").

If a patient relied largely on phoneme-grapheme conversion in spelling, what pattern of performance would we expect to see? Apart from producing misspellings sounding like the relevant word, such a patient would have some success in generating spellings of nonwords, and would be more accurate at spelling regular words (i.e. those words where the spelling can be worked out from the sound) than at spelling irregular words. All of these features characterised the spelling of a patient, TP, who was studied by Hatfield and Patterson (1983). For example, she wrote "flud" instead of "flood" and "neffue" instead of "nephew." However, she did not rely totally on phoneme-grapheme correspondence. The fact that she could spell some irregular words correctly (e.g. "sign" and "cough") indicates that she could still make limited use of the graphemic output lexicon.

What would we expect to find if a patient could make practically no use of phoneme-grapheme correspondence, but the other components or modules involved in spelling were reasonably intact? He or she would be able to spell known words accurately, because their spellings would be accessible in the graphemic output lexicon. However, there would be great problems with unfamiliar words and nonwords, because they are spelled by normal individuals via phoneme-grapheme correspondence.

A patient fitting this description rather well was PR, who was mentioned earlier. When he was tested, he had good comprehension of speech, fluent speech production, and reasonable reading skills. He wrote over 90% of common words correctly to dictation, and was only slightly worse in his spelling of relatively uncommon words. However, he was extremely poor at producing appropriate spellings for nonwords, succeeding less than 20% of the time. On the rare occasions that he did spell a nonword accurately, he often reported that he had used a real word to assist him in the task.

Summary

Writing is a skilled activity which involves a number of different processes or stages. According to Hayes and Flower (1986), the key processes are those of planning, sentence generation, and revising. Expert writers differ from nonexperts in that their writing plans are much more integrated, the average sentence parts which they produce are much longer, and their revision of written text focuses more on the coherence and structure of the arguments expressed. The approach adopted by Hayes and Flower relies heavily on protocol analysis, and this suffers from the limitation of providing information only about those processes of which there is conscious awareness.

The study of spelling and writing by cognitive neuropsychologists has demonstrated very clearly that there are various different ways in which writers can decide on the appropriate spellings of words. There are thus several different modules or components which are (or can be) involved in the writing process. Ellis and Young's (1988) model (which resembles the earlier proposals of other theorists) definitely appears to be on the right lines. At the very least, there is substantial justification for the components or modules which they have identified. It is possible, however, that the inter-relationships among the components may be more complex than is suggested by them.

The major limitation of the cognitive neuropsychological approach to spelling and writing is that it tells us rather little about several of the major issues. This can be seen clearly if we compare the cognitive neuropsychological approach with that adopted by Hayes and Flower (1986). Cognitive neuropsychology deals with some of the processes involved in sentence generation, but is almost silent on the processes involved in planning and revision. In other words, cognitive neuropsychology provides us with a very detailed and accurate picture of a small fraction of the processes involved in writing.

SPEAKING AND WRITING COMPARED

We have now considered the processes involved in speaking and in writing in both normals and in brain-damaged patients. Since speech and writing are both forms of language production which express our knowledge of people and the world, it seems commonsensical to assume that there are important similarities between them. However, some of the evidence considered already in this chapter has suggested that rather different processes are involved in these two major modes of language production.

It would be a major undertaking to compare speaking and writing in a thorough fashion. What is more feasible (and what is done here) is to attempt to consider some of the main similarities and dissimilarities between speaking and writing. This is done by considering the evidence obtained from brain-damaged patients and from normal individuals.

As we saw in the last section of the chapter, cognitive neuropsychologists have demonstrated conclusively that some of the processes involved in speaking and in writing are (or can be) different from each other. Some brain-damaged patients have writing skills which are largely intact despite an almost total inability to speak and a lack of inner speech. Others can speak fluently but find writing extremely difficult. Apart from these extreme cases, there are other patients whose patterns of errors in speaking and in writing differ so much that it is hard to believe that a single system could underlie both speaking and writing.

It is important to remember that cognitive neuropsychologists have focused very largely on only certain aspects of speaking and writing. More specifically, it has been shown that there are separate lexicons containing information about the spellings and spoken forms of words. However, it could still be the case that speaking and writing share several processes. For example, the knowledge that a normal individual possesses about a topic is presumably equally useful whether that knowledge is communicated by speaking or by writing.

Studies of brain-damaged patients by cognitive neuropsychologists have tended to emphasise differences between speaking and writing. In contrast, many studies of normal individuals have led to the discovery of important similarities. A comparison of Garrett's (1976; 1984) model of speech production with the theory of writing proposed by Hayes and Flower (1980; 1986) suggests the existence of some similarities. For example, there is an initial attempt to decide on the overall meaning which is to be communicated by speaking or by writing. At this stage, the actual words to be spoken or written are not considered. This is followed by the production of language, which in both cases often proceeds on a clause-by-clause basis.

Despite such similarities, it is a fact that people can speak approximately five or six times faster than they can write. It might be thought that this rate differential would have important implications for linguistic production. However, it actually appears that the mode of response output sometimes has surprisingly little impact on language production. Gould (1978) compared the adequacy of dictated and written letters. He discovered that people became as competent at dictating letters as at writing them after less than one day's practice at dictation. In spite of that, many of those involved in this study reported that they did not feel confident about dictation, perhaps because of the lack of a readily available external record of what they had said up to that point.

In view of the much greater speed with which sentences can be spoken than written, one might anticipate that dictating would be much faster than writing among those whose dictating skills have been acquired over a number of years. Once again, the differences were modest. Dictation rarely becomes much more than 35% faster than writing (Gould, 1979).

Gould (1980) divided the time taken to dictate and to write letters into various component times. His subjects were video-taped while composing letters, and the generating, reviewing, accessing, editing, and planning times were calculated. Planning, which was assumed to occur during pauses not obviously devoted to other processes, accounted for a greater proportion of the total time than any other process. Of particular interest, planning time represented approximately two-thirds of composition time for both dictated and written letters.

Even if the quality of the finished product is comparable within different response modes, it is still possible that some people excel at writing, others at speaking, and still others at dictating. Gould (1978) compared the quality of letter writing across these three response modes. He discovered that there were generally high inter-correlations. Important for language production are the internal mechanisms responsible for composition. Composition is the fundamental skill, and the method of composition is of lesser significance.

In sum, speaking and writing resemble each other in that the same knowledge base and the same (or similar) planning skills can be used in both forms of language production. However, there are separate lexicons containing information about the spoken and the written forms of words. It is for this reason that some brain-damaged patients can speak well although their spelling and writing is poor, and there are other patients who can write accurately but can hardly speak at all. In a nutshell, it is during the initial planning stage that the processes involved in speaking and writing are most similar, with dissimilarities becoming increasingly apparent as processing moves towards the end product of the spoken or written word.

LANGUAGE AND THOUGHT

The major language processes we have been concerned within this and the previous chapter (i.e. listening to speech; reading; speech production; and writing) raise the issue of the relationship between language and thought. For example, speaking and writing are both activities in which thought about what one wants to say or write is translated into language. It is therefore relevant at this point to consider various views on the relationship between language and thought.

The best-known theory about the inter-relationship of language and thought was put forward by Benjamin Lee Whorf (1956). He was a fire prevention officer for an insurance company who spent his spare time working in linguistics. According to his hypothesis of linguistic relativity, language determines or strongly influences thinking. To begin with, there are significant differences among the world's languages. The Hanuxoo people in the Philippines have 92 names for different varieties of rice, the Eskimoes have dozens of words to describe different snow and ice conditions, and there are hundreds of camel-related words in Arabic. It is possible, but unlikely, that these differences influence thought. A more plausible explanation is that different environmental conditions affect the things that people think about and their linguistic usage.

It is extremely difficult to submit the Whorfian hypothesis to direct experimental test. In order to do so, it is useful to follow Miller and McNeill (1969) in distinguishing between three somewhat different versions of the Whorfian hypothesis. These three versions are consistent with Whorf's (1956) general theoretical position, but they vary in the strength of the predictions incorporated in them. According to the strong hypothesis, language determines thinking. The weak hypothesis states that language affects perception. Finally, the weakest hypothesis claims only that language affects memory, i.e. information that is easily encoded linguistically will be better remembered than information that is less readily encoded. In practice, it is the weakest hypothesis that has been tested most frequently, and it is to such research that we now turn.

There has been a fair amount of research concerned with possible cultural differences in memory for colours. For example, Lenneberg and Roberts (1956) discovered that Zuni speakers made more errors than English speakers did in recognising yellows and oranges. The relevance of this finding is that there is only one word in the Zuni language to refer to yellows and oranges. While the findings of Lenneberg and Roberts suggested that language affects memory, later studies brought this conclusion into doubt. Heider (1972) made use of the fact that there are 11 basic colour words in English, and that each of these words has one generally agreed upon best colour, known as a focal colour. The typical finding is that English speakers find it easier to remember focal than nonfocal colours, and Heider wondered whether the same would be true of the Dani. The Dani are a Stone-Age agricultural people living in Indonesian New Guinea, and their language has only two basic colour terms: "mola" for bright, warm hues, and "mili" for dark, cold hues. In spite of the substantial linguistic differences between English speakers and the Dani, both groups of people showed better recognition memory for focal colours.

The basic finding from the research of Heider and that of other researchers is that the similarities between cultures regarding which colours are remembered most easily are far more pronounced than the dissimilarities. This is in spite of the fact that there are considerable differences from one language to the next in the terms available to describe colours. The natural interpretation of this finding is that language does not dictate the way in which colours are perceived and remembered. Indeed, the evidence is more consistent with the notion that thought affects language. Numerous languages have words for the same 11 focal colours, and it appears from work on the physiology of colour vision (DeValois & Jacobs, 1968) that these colours are processed specially by the visual system.

It may be too sweeping to conclude that language has no effect on thought. At the very least, each language may affect certain habits of thought, even if it does not restrict cognitive functioning to a major extent. Ervin-Tripp (1964) investigated the thinking of Japanese-American bilinguals. When these subjects were given sentence-completion or word-association tests, their performance resembled that of Japanese monolinguals when they responded in Japanese, but it was like that of American monolinguals when they responded in English.

Is the structure of language influenced by thought? Thinking certainly begins at an earlier developmental stage than language in the human child, and it seems reasonable to follow Piaget (1967) in arguing that language in the young child builds on the cognitive abilities which have developed during the pre-language sensori-motor period. According to this viewpoint, language is shaped, at least in part, by the thoughts it must communicate. It seems intuitively plausible to assume that language is the servant of thought rather than its master. For example, some of the evidence cited by Whorf (1956) in support of his hypothesis of linguistic relativity seems more consistent with the opposite point of view, that thought influences language. The fact that Eskimoes have many words to describe snow and Arabs have several terms to refer to camels suggests that language users develop highly differentiated terms to describe aspects of their environment as and when such differentiation is relevant to their life experiences.

Renewed interest in the relationship between language and thought was stimulated by Fodor (1983). According to him, there is a module or cognitive processor dedicated to language processing. As may be remembered from our discussion of modules in Chapter 1, one of the defining characteristics of modules is that they involve informational encapsulation, i.e. each module functions independently of other modules. One of the implications is that the process of language comprehension is not influenced by nonlinguistic information (e.g. thoughts). As a consequence, it would be expected that language comprehension should proceed in an entirely bottom-up or stimulus-driven fashion. In fact, there is strong evidence that top-down processes can affect some of the processes involved in the comprehension of speech (see Chapter 9).

Fodor's theoretical position is probably too extreme. However, there are grounds for arguing that many aspects of language processing are relatively separate from nonlinguistic processes.

The cognitive neuropsychological evidence discussed in this chapter and the previous one indicates that there are processing components devoted to specific aspects of language processing at both the comprehension and the production levels. Furthermore, as Harris (1990) pointed out, "Language processing has to be largely independent of other cognitive activities. For, if it were not, we would hear only what we expected to hear and read only what we expected to read."

SUMMARY

Speaking and writing are the two main forms of language production. The fact that those who speak well generally also write well, whereas those who speak poorly tend to write poorly, suggests that speaking and writing share common processes. However, cognitive neuropsychological evidence from brain-damaged patients has demonstrated that some of the processes involved in speaking and writing are quite different. There are some patients who can speak adequately but have immense problems with writing, and there are other patients who can write but not speak.

Speech production is best regarded as a form of communication. In order for that communication to be effective, there are certain rules which need to be heeded. For example, speakers should take account of the "common ground," which consists of the attitudes, knowledge, and so on which are shared by speakers and their listeners.

One of the key characteristics of speech is that there is typically a substantial amount of pre-production planning. In other words, a speaker's mind is generally on what will be said in a second or two rather than on what they are currently saying. Garrett has identified a total of four different levels or stages involved in this planning for speech. Evidence supporting his theoretical model has come from two major sources: the speech errors made by normal individuals, and the patterns of speech impairment shown by brain-damaged patients. A related theory of speech production has been proposed by Dell (1986). It makes use of a spreading-activation retrieval mechanism to account with reasonable success for the main categories of slips of the tongue.

The speech of normal individuals is usually reasonably accurate, but various problems do occur from time to time. These include the tip-of-the-tongue state, word-exchange errors, morpheme-exchange errors, Spoonerisms, and hesitations and pauses. The existence of so many different kinds of speech error supports Garrett's view that there are several stages of speech planning, all of which are fallible. The same message comes from research on brain-damaged patients, who have impairments ranging from anomia (inability to find and say words) to agrammatism (grammatically unstructured speech).

Writing resembles speaking in that there appear to be a number of different stages involved. According to Hayes and Flower (1986), the major stages in writing are planning, sentence generation, and revising. In general, the stages occur one after the other in the order: planning, sentence generation, and finally revising; but the writing process often deviates from this tidy ordering. Planning involves the generating of ideas which will satisfy the writing goals, and arranging them into a coherent structure. Sentence generation involves turning the results of the planning stage into actual sentences. Expert writers typically generate larger sentence parts than less expert ones. Revising involves identifying deficiencies in what has been written. Expert writers tend to focus on the coherence of the text in their revising, whereas nonexpert writers focus more on individual words and phrases.

Writers often feel that they say words and parts of sentences to themselves before writing them down. While that may be so, cognitive neuropsychologists have discovered that some patients who lack any inner speech can nevertheless write in a perfectly adequate fashion. This demonstrates that writing does not necessarily depend on inner speech. Cognitive neuropsychologists have also found that spelling and writing can occur in a number of different ways, depending on such factors as whether it is a familiar or an unfamiliar word which must be written. Cognitive neuropsychologists have been successful in identifying various components or modules involved in writing, but they have so far focused on the detailed mechanisms of spelling rather than on broader issues of how ideas are organised into a writing plan.

Research on the relationship between language and thought has indicated that language has few or no constraining influences on thought. It is more likely that thought processes influence the structure of language. Fodor (1983) argued that there is a module specifically dedicated to language processing. Cognitive neuropsychological and other evidence certainly suggests that there are processing components used solely for language processing, but Fodor's position seems too extreme.

FURTHER READING

Dell, G.S. (1986). A spreading-activation theory of retrieval in sentence production.*Psychological Review*, *93*, 283–321. This article illustrates contemporary thinking on the mechanisms involved in speech production.

Ellis, A.W. & Young, A.W. (1988). *Human cognitive neuropsychology*. London: Lawrence Erlbaum Associates Ltd. Chapters 5 and 7 give detailed accounts of brain-damaged patients who have problems with spoken and written language, respectively.

Hayes, J.R. & Flower, L.S. (1986). Writing research and the writer. *American Psychologist*, *41*, 1106–1113. This article provides a very readable and up-to-date account of theory and research on writing.

Patterson, K.E. (1988). Disorders of spelling. In G. Denes, C.

Semenza, P. Bisiacchi, & E. Andreewsky (Eds.), *Perspectives in cognitive neuropsychology*. London: Lawrence Erlbaum Associates Ltd. An excellent analysis of spelling from the cognitive neuropsychological perspective is presented in this chapter.

Chapter Eleven

THE USE OF KNOWLEDGE IN PROBLEM SOLVING

Walking and talking are fairly amazing abilities, but humanity really starts to get streets ahead of the rest of the animal kingdom when thinking is added. We start this chapter by considering a sample of the sorts of things to which we apply the term "thinking".

INTRODUCTION

First, consider a fragment of Molly Bloom's sleepy thoughts from James Joyce's *Ulysses* (1922/1960, pp. 871–872), about Mrs. Riordan:

> . . . God help the world if all the women in the world were her sort down on bathing-suits and low-necks of course nobody wanted her to wear I suppose she was pious because no man would look at her twice I hope I'll never be like her a wonder she didn't want us to cover our faces but she was a well-educated woman certainly and her gabby talk about Mr. Riordan here and Mr. Riordan there I suppose he was glad to get shut of her . . .

Next, a person (S) answering an experimenter's (E) question about regulating the thermostat on a home-heating system (Kempton, 1986, p.83):

> E: Let's say you're in the house and you're cold . . . Let's say it's a cold day, you feel cold, you want to do something about it.
> S: Oh, what I might do is, I might turn the thing up high to get out, to get a lot of air out fast, then after a little while turn it off or turn it down.
> E: Un-huh.
> S: So there are also, you know, these issues about, um, the rate at which the thing produces heat, the higher the setting is, the

> more heat that's produced per unit of time, so if you're cold,
> you want to get warm fast, um, so you turn it up high.

Finally, a protocol of one of the authors adding 457 and 638 aloud.

> Eight and seven is fifteen and then you carry one so, one and three
> is four and five is nine, and six and four is ten, so the final number is
> . . . one, nought, nine, five; one thousand and ninety-five.

These three instances of thinking behaviour are useful in illustrating several general aspects of thinking. First, all the pieces involve individuals being *conscious* of their thoughts. Clearly, any definition of thinking must include the idea that it involves conscious awareness. However, we are not aware of all of our thought processes. Rather, we only tend to be conscious of the products of thinking processes. For example, we are conscious of taking eight and seven to add together and of the product of adding them, fifteen, but the processes that produce this result are not open to introspection because they are unconscious. Indeed, it is not always possible for us to report our conscious thoughts accurately. Joyce does a good job of reconstructing the character of idle, associative thought in Molly Bloom's internal monologue, but if we interrupted her and asked her to tell us her thoughts from the previous five minutes, little of it would be recalled accurately. Similarly, in psychological experiments subjects' retrospective recollections of their conscious thoughts are often unreliable. In fact, even introspective evidence taken as the thoughts are being produced is only reliable under some conditions (see Ericsson & Simon, 1980; 1984; for more details see the section in Chapter 1 on introspection).

Second, thinking can vary in the extent to which it is directed (Gilhooly, 1988). At one end of the scale it can be relatively undirected and at the other extreme it can be sharply directed towards a specific goal. Molly Bloom's piece is more undirected relative to the other pieces. On the point of slipping into a dream, she is just letting one thought slide into another. If she has any goal it is a very general and loose one (e.g. reflect on the day's happenings). In the other two pieces, the goal is much clearer and more well-defined. In the addition example, a specific answer must be provided which is known to be either right or wrong (i.e. the goal is clearly defined and can be evaluated easily). As we shall see, most of the research on thinking has been concerned with fairly well-defined, goal-driven situations and, hence, these situations will be the main focus of this and the next chapter (see Gilhooly, 1988, for an exploration of undirected thinking).

Third, the amount and nature of the knowledge used in different thinking tasks can vary enormously. For example, the knowledge required in the addition case is circumscribed. It mainly hinges on knowing how to add any number between one and ten and the rule that you carry numbers above ten from one column to the next (see Anderson, 1983, for a production system model of this behaviour). On the other hand, Molly Bloom is using a vast amount of knowledge about the mores of old widows, what she herself will be like when old, the irony of those who criticise what they cannot indulge, in and much more besides. Technically, situations that require little knowledge are called *knowledge-poor* whereas those requiring more knowledge are termed *knowledge-intensive*. Knowledge-intensive situations are much harder to characterise because of the extent of the knowledge and the variety of ways in which it can be applied. For this very reason, much of the initial success in thinking research has come from examining knowledge-poor situations.

Summary and Overview

One of the important properties of thought is its conscious character. However, it should be remembered that we tend to be conscious of the products of thinking rather than the thinking processes themselves. Furthermore, even these conscious products may not be recalled accurately by many people. Thinking tasks vary in the extent to which they are directed. Thinking episodes also differ in terms of the amount of knowledge used; they may be knowledge-poor or knowledge-intensive. Most of the research on thinking looks at directed thinking in knowledge-poor situations involving specific goals.

In this book we have made a broad division between several main types of thinking: problem solving, reasoning, and decision making. These divisions exist more in the minds of theorists than they do in the psychological phenomena. Many everyday thinking situations may involve complex mixtures of problem solving, reasoning, and decision making. However, the subject matter is made more tractable by introducing these divisions. In this chapter we will concentrate on thinking as problem solving. In the next chapter we will turn to reasoning and decision making.

The present chapter is structured along historical lines: We begin with a review of early problem-solving research before turning to a treatment of the information processing theories of problem solving that emerged in the late 1950s and early 1960s. We then follow the subsequent development of these theories in studies of expertise and research on analogies and mental models of the world. We also consider how these information processing theories have tried to account for the findings of early research. Finally, we conclude the chapter with a general evaluation of progress in problem-solving research.

EARLY RESEARCH: THE GESTALT SCHOOL

At the beginning of this century, adherents of the Gestalt school of psychology extended their theories of perception to the area of problem solving. These researchers were particularly creative in performing experimental tests of their theories and produced a large corpus of evidence. During the behaviourist period much of this research was re-interpreted in behaviourist terms (see, e.g., Maltzman, 1955), even though the basic experimental paradigms remained essentially unchanged. During much of the 1950s and 1960s this type of problem-solving research became more of a background activity, although it was researched actively again in the 1970s and 1980s (see, e.g., Ohlsson, 1984a; Raaheim, 1974; Weisberg & Suls, 1973).

Gestalt Research on Problem Solving in Animals

The work of the Gestalt school of psychology had its origins in problem-solving research on animals. Early associationist and behaviourist psychologists had characterised problem solving as the result of either trial-and-error or the reproduction of previously learned responses (e.g. Hull, 1930, 1931; Maltzman, 1955; Thorndike, 1911). Thorndike's famous experiments on cats were taken as strong evidence for this view.

FIGURE 11.1

A Necker Cube which illustrates the perceptual restructuring in which the corner marked by the "Y" alternates between being at the back or the front of the figure.

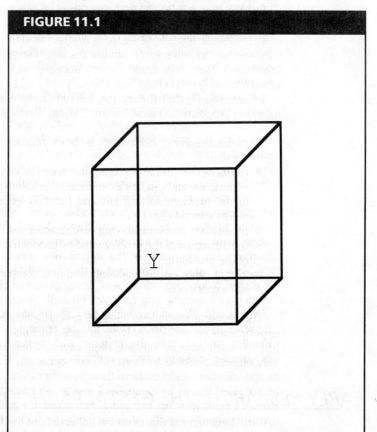

Thorndike had placed hungry cats in closed cages where they could see a dish of food outside the cages. The cage doors could be opened when a pole inside the cage was hit. Initially, the animals thrashed about and clawed the sides of the cage. Inevitably, at some point, the cat hit the pole inside the cage and opened the door. On repeated trials, when the cat was placed in the cage again, similar energetic behaviour ensued but gradually the animal seemed to learn that hitting the pole opened the cage. So, eventually, when placed in the cage it went to the pole, hit it, and escaped. Thus it was surmised that new problems were initially solved by trial-and-error behaviour and then accidental solutions were amalgamated into responses that were reproduced when the appropriate stimulus was presented.

One of the founders of the Gestalt school, Wolfgang Kohler, disagreed with this formulation and believed that there was more to animal problem solving than trial-and-error and reproductive responses. The Gestalt psychologists had been fairly successful in showing that perception was something more than mere associations (see Chapter 2), and felt that the same ideas could be applied to problem solving. In the perception of the Necker cube, an illusion shown in Fig. 11.1, the corner marked "Y" sometimes appears to be at the front of the figure and other times at the back of it. In Gestalt terms, the figure is restructured to be perceived in one way or the other. In a similar fashion, Gestalt psychologists maintained that one could have "insight" into the problem's structure and "restructure" a problem in order to solve it.

In general, Gestalt theory can be summarised in terms of the following propositions (see Ohlsson, 1984a; Wertheimer, 1954):

- problem-solving behaviour is both reproductive and productive;
- reproductive problem solving involves the re-use of previous experience and can hinder successful problem solving (e.g. as in the problem-solving set and functional-fixedness experiments which follow);
- productive problem solving is characterised by insight into the structure of the problem and by productive restructurings of the problem;
- insight often occurs suddenly and is accompanied by an "ah-ha" experience.

The classical example of Gestalt research was Kohler's (1927) experiments on problem solving in apes. In Kohler's studies apes had to reach bananas outside their cages, when sticks were the only objects available to them. On one occasion, Kohler observed an ape take two sticks and join them together to reach the bananas; he heralded this as an example of insight. In contemporary terms, Kohler's point was that the animal had acted in a goal-directed way; it was trying to solve the problem using the sticks. He also pointed out that even though the ape had used the sticks initially in a trial-

and-error manner, it was only after sitting quietly for a time that the animal produced the insightful solution. Kohler's evidence was not cast-iron because the previous experiences of this once-wild ape were not known. Later, Birch (1945) was to find little evidence of this sort of "insightful" problem solving in apes that were raised in captivity. However, such research set the agenda for later Gestalt psychologists to extend their analyses to human problem solving.

Restructuring, Insight, Functional Fixedness, and Set

Restructuring and Insight

One of the better-known Gestalt problems (one which is quite close to the ape studies) is Maier's (1931) "two-string" or "pendulum" problem. In the original version of the problem, human subjects were brought into a room which had two strings hanging from the ceiling and a number of other objects (e.g. poles, pliers, extension cords). They were then asked to tie the two strings together that were hanging from the ceiling. However, they soon found out that when they took hold of one string and went to grab hold of the other, it was too far away for them to reach. Subjects produced several different types of solutions to this problem but the most "insightful" and infrequently produced solution was the pendulum solution. This involved taking a pair of pliers and tying them to one of the strings and swinging them. So, while holding one string, it was possible to catch the other on its up-swing and tie the two together. Maier demonstrated a striking example of "problem restructuring" by first allowing subjects to get to a point where they were stuck and then (apparently accidentally) brushing off the string to set it swinging. Soon after this was done subjects tended

The objects presented to subjects in the candle problem (adapted from Weisberg, 1980, with the permission of the author).

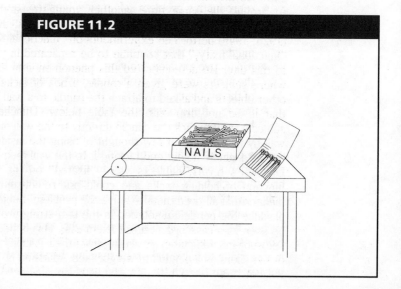

FIGURE 11.2

NAILS

FIGURE 11.3

(a) The nine—dot problem and (b) its solution.

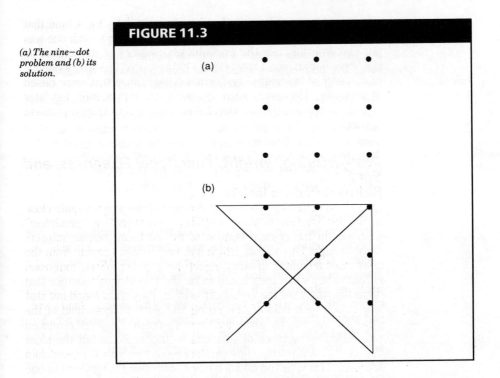

to produce the pendulum solution, even though few reported noticing the experimenter brush against the string. According to Maier, this subtle hint resulted in a reorganisation or restructuring of the problem so that the solution emerged.

Functional Fixedness and Fixity
At around the same time, another young researcher was also expanding Gestalt theory. During his twenties, Karl Duncker (1926; 1945) performed experiments on "functional fixedness," or "functional fixity," that continue to be replicated in various guises to this day. He demonstrated this phenomenon in an experiment where subjects were given a candle, a box of tacks, and several other objects and asked to attach the candle to a wall by a table, so that it did not drip onto the table below. Duncker found that subjects tried to tack the candle directly to the wall or glue it to the wall by melting it, but few thought of using the inside of the tack-box as a candle holder and tacking it to the wall (see Fig. 11.2). In Duncker's terms, subjects were "fixated" on the box's normal function of holding tacks and could not re-conceptualise it in a manner that allowed them to solve the problem. Subjects' failure to produce the pendulum solution in the two-string problem can also be seen as a case of functional fixedness. This is because one can see subjects' difficulties as arising from their inability to reconceive of the pliers as a pendulum weight (see Adamson & Taylor, 1954; Keane, 1989).

Another famous problem from the Gestalt school is Scheerer's (1963) nine-dot problem. As can be seen in Fig. 11.3, the problem involves nine dots organised in a three-by-three matrix. In order to solve the problem one must draw four continuous straight lines, connecting all the dots, without lifting the pencil from the paper. The correct solution is also shown in Fig. 11.3 (although see Adams, 1979, for several wild but valid alternatives). Most people cannot solve the problem because, Scheerer maintained, they assume that the lines must stay within the square formed by the dots. In Gestalt terms, subjects had "fixated" on the shape of the dots and could not solve the problem for this reason. In a later section, we shall see that this is not the whole truth.

Problem-solving Set

A final set of experiments produced by the Gestalt school that deserve mention are the water-jug experiments of Luchins and Luchins (1959; Luchins, 1942). Viewed as another case of the general notion of fixation, the Luchins demonstrated the idea of *problem-solving set*. In a typical water-jug problem you have to imagine that you are given an eight-pint jug full of water, and a five-pint jug and three-pint jug that are empty (represented as 8-8, 5-0, 3-0, where the first figure indicates the size of the jug and the second the amount of water in that jug). Your task is to pour the water from one jug to another until you end up with four pints in the eight-pint jug and four pints in the five-pint jug (i.e. 8-4, 5-4, 3-0). Even though this problem looks fairly straightforward it can take some time to solve (Table 11.1 shows one possible solution.)

In order to demonstrate problem-solving set Luchins and Luchins typically had two groups in their experiments: a set and a

TABLE 11.1

Shortest Set of Moves to Solution in the Luchins' Water-jug Problem (8–8, 5–0, 3–0)

	Jar 1	Jar 2	Jar 3
Initial State	8-8	5-0	3-0
Intermediate States	8-3	5-5	3-0
	8-3	5-2	3-3
	8-6	5-2	3-0
	8-6	5-0	3-2
	8-1	5-5	3-2
	8-1	5-4	3-3
Goal State	8-4	5-4	3-0

control condition. The set condition received a series of problems that could be solved using the same solution method, but the control group received problems which had to be solved using different methods. Then, both groups were given a test problem that could be solved using either a very simple method or the more complex method that the set condition subjects had been applying to all the previous problems. Not surprisingly, the control group tended to use the simple method but the set group opted for the more complex method. In fact, they did not "see" the simpler method until it was pointed out to them. The set group had, in Gestalt terms, been fixated on the more complex method.

Evaluating Gestalt Problem-solving Theory and Its Legacy

In general, the Gestalt assault on associationist views involved a pincer movement. First, Gestalt psychologists tried to show that problem solving was something more than the "mere" reproduction of learned responses; it also involved insight and restructuring. For instance, recall Maier's demonstration of the effects of the "swing" hint on the solution of the two-string problem. Second, they showed that the direct use of past experience often led to failure rather than success in problem solving; that is, when people routinely used a previous method, or assumed that an object was to be used in its habitual way, they were often led astray. This has been demonstrated repeatedly in the research on functional fixedness and problem-solving set.

A salient aspect of the theory is its dependence on the perceptual metaphor carried over from the Gestalt theory of perception. This metaphor underlies the theory's attractiveness and its weakness. The concepts of "insight" and "restructuring" are attractive because they are easily understood, especially when they are accompanied by perceptual demonstrations, and convey something of the mysterious dynamism of human creativity. As theoretical constructs they are radically under-specified; the conditions under which, say, insight or restructuring will occur are unclear and the theory is not clear about what insight involves. However, the Gestalt work is not a total waste. In many ways the spirit of Gestalt research, with its emphasis on the goal-directed and nonassociationistic nature of thinking, informed the information processing approach which followed some decades later (see, e.g., Newell, 1980; Ohlsson, 1984a). The school also left a large corpus of experimental materials (in the form of problems) and evidence that had to be re-interpreted by any later theory. The legacy of the school was, therefore, substantial.

Summary

In the early part of this century, the Gestalt school of psychologists argued in opposition to associationist psychologists that thinking in both animals and man involved a productive component. Using a perceptual metaphor—involving terms like *insight, restructuring,* and *fixation*—they showed that there were dynamic aspects to human thinking that went beyond mere reproductive thought. Even though the heyday of the school has passed, its legacy of experimental evidence and materials continues to play an important part in modern information processing theories.

NEWELL AND SIMON'S INFORMATION PROCESSING THEORY

The problem-solving research of Allen Newell and Herb Simon, of Carnegie-Mellon University, has contributed enormously to the formation of the information processing framework. In the late 1950s, they produced the first computational models of psychological phenomena and made milestone discoveries in cognitive psychology and artificial intelligence. Their problem-space theory of problem solving, recounted in their 1972 magnum opus entitled *Human problem solving*, remains at the centre of current problem-solving research. In fact, many of the remaining areas reviewed in this chapter are elaborations or extensions of Newell and Simon's basic views.

Problem-space Theory

It is very natural to think of problems as being solved through the exploration of different paths to a solution. This is literally the case if we are trying to find our way through a labyrinth. We start at a definite point outside the maze and then progress through it to the centre. On our way, we meet junctions where we have the choice of turning left or right, going straight on or turning back. Each of these alternative paths may branch again and again so that, in the maze as a whole, there are hundreds of alternative paths (only some of which will lead to the centre). Different strategies can be used to find one's way through a labyrinth (e.g. mark one's past path, initially always take the left turn). Umberto Eco's (1984) novel *The Name of the rose* gives a vivid description of just such a problem-solving exercise in the deadly labyrinth of a monastery library. Such strategies reduce the number of alternative paths one has to consider in getting through the maze.

Newell and Simon have used parallels to these basic ideas to characterise the solution processes in many different problems. They suggested that the objective structure of a problem can be characterised as a set of states, beginning from an initial state (e.g. standing outside the maze) and ending with a goal state (e.g. being at the centre of the maze). Just as in the labyrinth, actions can be performed or "operators applied" (e.g. turn left, turn right). The application of these operators results in a move from one state to another. In any given state there may be several different operators that apply (e.g. turn left, turn right, go back) and each of these will generate numerous alternative states. Thus, there is a whole space of possible states and paths through this space (only some of which will lead to the goal state). This is a way of describing the *abstract structure of problems* in themselves.

Newell and Simon take the further step of proposing that when people solve problems they pass through correlative "knowledge states" in their heads. They begin at an initial knowledge state and "search" through a space of alternatives states until they reach a goal knowledge state. Moves from one knowledge state to the next are achieved by the application of "mental operators." Since a given problem may have a large number of alternative paths, people use strategies (or heuristic methods) in order to move from the initial state to the goal state efficiently. Thus, subjects' conception of a problem (i.e. the nature of the initial state) and the knowledge they bring to it (the operators and strategies available to them) make important contributions to the observed problem-solving behaviour. In summary, the theory is as follows (see Newell & Simon, 1972; Simon, 1978):

- People's problem-solving behaviour can be viewed as the production of knowledge states by the application of mental operators, moving from an initial state to a goal state.
- Operators encode legal moves that can be made and restrictions that explicitly disallow a move if certain conditions hold.
- For any given problem there are a large number of alternative paths from an initial state to a goal state; the total set of such states, as generated by the legal operators, is called the basic problem space.
- However, people use their knowledge and various heuristic methods (like means-end analysis; see next section for details) to search through this problem space and to find a short route from the initial state to the goal state.
- All of these processes occur within the limits of a particular cognitive system; that is, there may be working memory limitations and limitations on the speed with which information can be stored and retrieved from long-term memory.

This theory pins down in explicit representational terms the various hypothetical knowledge states and processes that are used in solving many different problems. Most of Newell and Simon's work has been accompanied by computational models that usually take the form of production systems (see Chapter 1). In these models, the various knowledge states are held in a working memory and long-term memory consists of a set of productions or operators that modify these states. Their earliest and now-famous model was called the *General Problem Solver* (G.P.S.; see Newell, Shaw, & Simon, 1958; 1960). However, let us consider a typical problem to which the theory has been applied.

FIGURE 11.4a

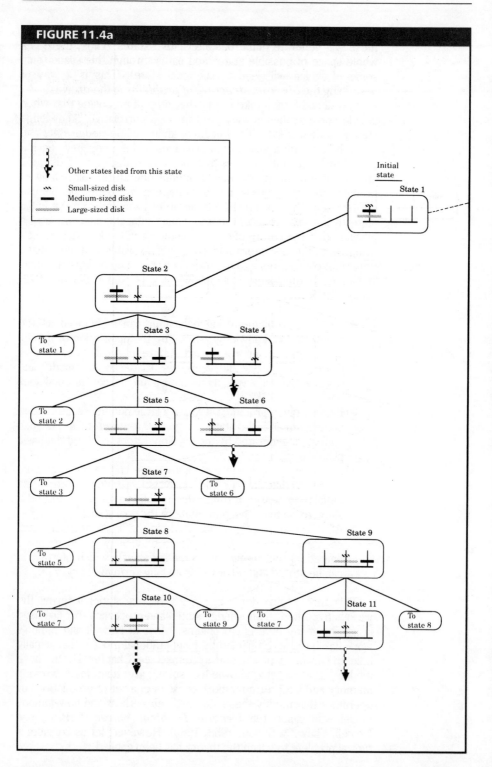

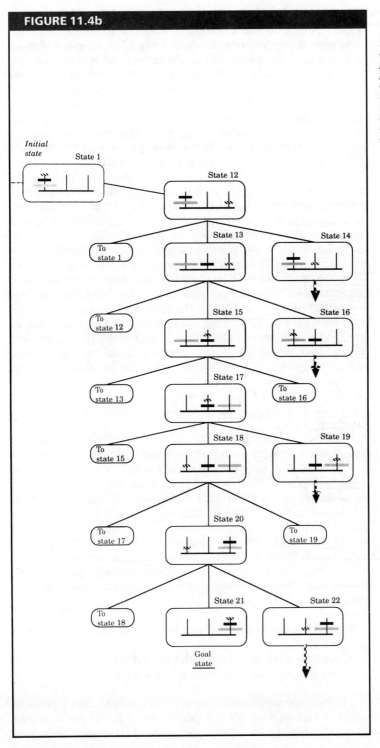

FIGURE 11.4b

Figures 11.4 a and 11.4b show a diagram of a portion of the problem space of alternative states that intervenes between the initial state and goal state of the Tower of Hanoi problem.

The Example of the Tower of Hanoi Puzzle

In the "Tower of Hanoi" problem, subjects are presented with three vertical pegs in a row, the first of which has a number of disks piled on it in order of size; that is, the largest disk is at the bottom, the next largest on top of it, and so on to the smallest at the top (see Fig. 11.4). The goal of the problem is to have all the disks piled in the same order on the last peg. However, disks can only be moved in certain ways. Only one disk can be moved at a time and a larger disk cannot be placed on top of a smaller disk. The standard version of the problem uses three disks. Figure 11.4 shows some of the legal states that make up the structure of the problem.

The state described in the problem statement, where all of the disks are stacked on the first peg, is the *initial knowledge state* and the *goal knowledge state* consists of all the disks stacked on the last peg, in order of size. Subjects can use *mental operators* that move disks from one peg to another, with the operator restriction that no move places a larger disk on a smaller disk. This gives rise to varying numbers of alternative states at each stage. From the initial state, if one applies the move operation, two alternative new states are possible; moving the small disk from the first peg to either the second or the third peg (i.e. states 2 and 12 respectively in Fig. 11.4). Each of these intermediate states can, in turn, give rise to several alternatives (see Fig. 11.4). The number of these alternative states, between the initial and goal state, increases rapidly, so when people solve the problem, they use strategies that reduce the number of states they have to pass through to reach the goal. Newell and Simon (1972) described several such strategies, which they called *heuristic methods* or *heuristics*.

Heuristic methods are to be contrasted with algorithms. An *algorithm* is a method or rule that will definitely solve a problem, if it is applied. For example, one could use a "check-every-state algorithm" to solve the Tower of Hanoi problem; one could start at the beginning and systematically check every alternative state until the goal state is encountered. This method might take a long time but, eventually, it would solve the problem. *Heuristic methods* are rules-of-thumb that do not guarantee a solution to the problem, but if they do succeed, they will save a lot of time and effort.

One of the most important heuristic methods proposed by Newell and Simon was means-end analysis. Means-end analysis consists of the following steps:

- note the difference between the current state and the goal state;
- create a sub-goal to reduce this difference;
- select an operator that will solve this sub-goal.

To illustrate means-end analysis, let us assume that a problem solver is one step off solving the Tower of Hanoi problem (see state 20 in Fig. 11.4). At this point, one of three possible moves could be made, but only one of these moves will solve the problem. Means-end analysis proposes that one first notes the difference between the current state and the goal state; that is, the small disk is on the first peg instead of being on the third peg. Second, establish the sub-goal of reducing this difference; create the new sub-goal of moving the small disk from the first to the third peg. Third, select an operator that solves this sub-goal and apply it. So, the small disk will be moved to the third peg and the problem solved. In this way means-end analysis can be applied from the initial state of the problem. This method reduces the number of alternative states one has to consider and, yet depending on the nature of the problem, may not guarantee a solution in every case where is it applied.

Goal/Sub-goal Structures in Problem Solving

Means-end analysis generates various sub-goals to be solved on the way to the main goal. This suggests that if a subject can structure a problem into appropriate sub-goals—sub-goals like "attempt to get the largest disk onto the third peg"—then problem-solving performance should improve. One possible source of such sub-goal structures should be prior experience on related problems.

Several researchers have tested this prediction (Egan & Greeno, 1974; Luger, 1976). For instance, Egan and Greeno gave different groups of subjects complex five- and six-disk versions of the Tower of Hanoi. Experimental groups received prior experience on three-disk and four-disk problems, whereas controls did not. Egan and Greeno found that subjects with prior experience on the easier problems, which instilled an appropriate goal structure, showed some benefits. Furthermore, the error profiles (as measured by any deviation from the minimal solution path for each problem) indicated that subjects performed better as they neared important goals/sub-goals and, conversely, tended to experience more difficulty when they were far from an important goal.

Learning Different Strategies

Egan and Greeno's work illustrates the effects that experience can have on subjects' ability to solve the problem. Egan and Greeno's subjects adopted the strategy of partitioning a complex problem into several simpler sub-problems and then solving each of these in turn. Anzai and Simon (1979) examined other strategies adopted by a single subject in four successive attempts to solve a five-disk version of the Tower of Hanoi.

On each of the four attempts the subject used a different strategy, becoming progressively more efficient at solving the problem. Initially, the subject seemed to explore the problem space without much planning of moves. Search at this stage seemed to be guided by avoidance of certain states rather than moves towards definite goal/sub-goal states. Anzai and Simon argued that the subject was using general *domain-independent strategies*.

These strategies included a *loop-avoidance strategy* to avoid returning to previously visited states and an heuristic strategy that preferred shorter sequences of moves to achieve a goal to longer sequences. These general strategies allowed the subject to learn better sequences of moves and these sequences were carried forward to be used in later attempts to solve the problem. Anzai and Simon developed an adaptive production system model (see Chapter 1) that learned in the same manner. This model could create new productions that were used in solving the problem on a later attempt. From Anzai and Simon's research, the general course of learning in these situations hinges on the initial use of general, domain-independent heuristics which then allow one to learn domain-dependent or domain-specific heuristics (see also Anderson's theory in a later section).

Understanding Isomorphic Problems

Intuitively, the way in which one understands a problem should have an important effect on whether one subsequently solves it. This intuition has been borne out by a variety of findings which show that even though, in terms of a problem state analysis, two problems may be isomorphic (i.e. they have the same structure), slight differences in the way they are presented have significant effects on subjects' ability to solve them. Furthermore, problem space theory is specific enough to allow one to pinpoint what it is about subjects' understanding of the problem that causes these effects.

Several studies of this type have been performed on variants of the Tower of Hanoi (see Hayes & Simon, 1974; 1977; Simon & Hayes, 1976). In one study, Simon and Hayes (1976) used problem isomorphs about a tea ceremony involving three different people (corresponding to the three pegs) carrying out three ritual tasks for one another (like the three disks) in differing orders of importance (like disks of different sizes).

In other studies, Hayes and Simon used isomorphs to the Tower of Hanoi that involved monsters and globes. In the basic monster-globe problem there are three monsters of different sizes (small, medium, and large), each holding different-sized globes (small, medium, and large). The small monster is holding the large globe; the medium-sized monster the small globe, and the large monster the medium-sized globe. The goal is to achieve a state in which each monster is holding a globe proportionate to his size (e.g. the small monster holding the smallest globe). However, monster etiquette demands that (1) only one globe is transferred at a time, (2) if a monster is holding two globes, only the larger of the two is transferred, and (3) a globe may not be transferred to a monster who is holding a larger globe. This monster-globe problem is a move problem that corresponds to the Tower of Hanoi problem with three disks (three globes) distributed over three pegs (three monsters).

Simon and Hayes also had a *change* version of the monster-globe problem with the same monsters and globes but one had to

FIGURE 11.5

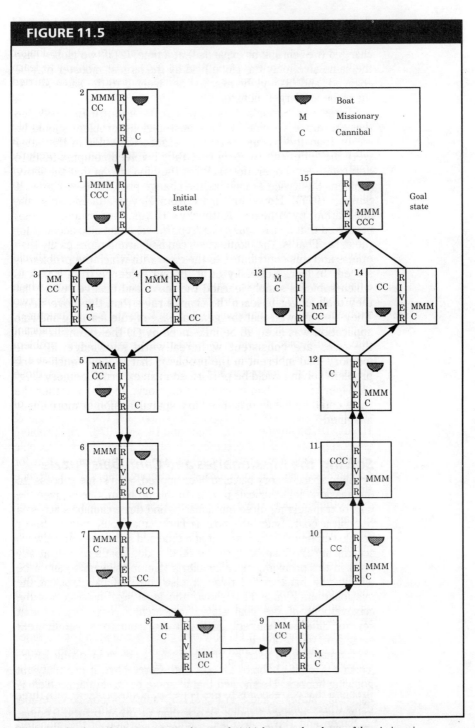

The shortest legal search space intervening between the initial state and goal state of the missionaries–cannibals problem.

shrink and expand the globes held by the monsters rather than moving them; the rules were that (1) only one globe may be changed (i.e. shrunk or expanded) at a time, (2) if two globes have the same size, only the globe held by the largest monster may be changed, and (3) a globe may not be changed to the same size as the globe of a larger monster.

Hayes and Simon's *rule application hypothesis* predicted that the move version of the monster-globe problem should be easier than the change version, because the rules in the latter were more difficult to apply (i.e. they involved complex tests to determine legal operations). What they found was that the move problem was twice as easy as the change problem (see Hayes & Simon, 1977). However, apart from Hayes and Simon's rule application hypothesis, Kotovsky, Hayes, and Simon (1985) proposed that a *rule learning hypothesis* could also account for the data. That is, that some rules can be learned more easily than others and this contributes to the ease with which the problem is solved. In fact, Kotovsky et al. Found evidence from a task in which subjects simply learned the move and change rules, that they took longer to learn the change rules than the move rules. They also showed that the general ease of rule learning and rule application was likely to be influenced by (1) the extent to which the rules are consistent with real-world knowledge, (2) the memory load inherent in the problem; that is, how much of the problem solving could be performed in an external memory (e.g. on paper) rather than in working memory, and (3) whether the rules could be easily organised in a spatial fashion or more easily imagined.

Solving the Missionaries and Cannibals Puzzle

Problem space theory has also been applied, with some success, to the missionaries-cannibals puzzle. In this problem, one is given the task of transferring three missionaries and three cannibals across a river in a boat. Since the boat is fairly small, only two or fewer people can be taken across in it at a time and someone must always accompany the boat back to the other side. Furthermore, at any point in the problem, more cannibals than missionaries cannot be left on one bank of the river or else the cannibals will eat the missionaries. Figure 11.5 shows the legal search space for the achievement of the goal state. Researchers have argued that several different heuristic methods are used to solve different variants of this problem.

Thomas (1974) used a variant of this problem involving J.R.R. Tolkien's (1966) hobbits and orcs; the orcs have a proclivity for gobbling hobbits. He showed that at some points in the problem— especially states 5 and 8 in Fig. 11.5—subjects took considerably longer and produced more errors than at other points. Thomas maintained that the difficulties experienced at these states had different cognitive sources. In the case of the 5 state, the difficulty lies in the many alternative moves that can be made at this point; five in total. Only two of these are illegal and of the remaining three legal moves only one is really helpful. In the case of state 8, subjects are misled because they need to move away from the goal state in order to get closer to it. As can be seen in Fig. 11.5, in going from state 8 to state 9, one enters a state which seems further away than closer to the goal. Subjects typically think that they have reached a blind alley and start to backtrack.

Thomas also suggested that subjects made three or four major planning decisions in solving the problem, and having made each of these decisions carried out whole blocks of moves with increasing speed. Then, at the beginning of each planned sequence of moves, there would be a long pause before the next decision was made. Thomas' statistical analysis of the distributions of subjects' times-to-move supported this hypothesis.

Other researchers have looked at more complex versions of the problem and noted strategic changes in subjects' behaviour. Simon and Reed (1976) investigated a version of the missionaries-cannibals problem, involving five missionaries and five cannibals. This problem is more complex in the number of legal states, but it can be solved in 11 moves. However, subjects take 30 moves, on average, to solve the problem. Simon and Reed suggested that there were three main strategies used in solving the problem. Initially, subjects adopted a *balancing strategy* whereby they simply tried to ensure that equal numbers of missionaries and cannibals remained on each side of the river. This strategy avoids illegal moves, resulting in more cannibals than missionaries on either side of the river. At a certain point, subjects become more oriented towards the goal state and adopt a *means-end strategy*. This strategy is manifested by a tendency to move more people to the goal-side of the river. Finally, subjects use a simple anti-looping heuristic to avoid moves that reverse the immediately-preceding move.

Simon and Reed maintained that the key to efficient solution of the problem rested on a *strategy shift* from the balancing strategy to the means-end strategy. The problem with the balancing strategy is that it leads one into blind-alley states in the problem. Thus, they predicted that any manipulation that increased the probability of strategy shift would result in improved performance on solving the problem.

In an experiment designed to test this prediction, a control group of subjects received the problem to solve with no hints and an experimental group was given, as a hint, a sub-goal to achieve on the way to solving the problem. This hint suggested that subjects should work to reach a state where three cannibals were on the goal-side of the river on their own without a boat. Since this sub-goal involves a state where there are unequal numbers of missionaries and cannibals on either side of the river, it was expected that this sub-goal should discourage the use of the balancing strategy early on. This prediction was confirmed. Subjects in the experimental group tended to shift strategies after about four moves, whereas those in the control group only shifted after about 15 moves.

Problem Space Models of Water-Jug Problems

We saw earlier that water-jug problems were intensively investigated by Gestalt researchers. Clearly, these problems are very amenable to a treatment in terms of problem space theory. In the 8-8, 5-0 and 3-0 problem we encountered earlier (see Table 11.1), the initial state consists of the largest jug being full of water and the other two empty. The goal state has four pints of water in the largest and middle-sized jugs, and nothing in the smallest. The operators consist of pouring various amounts of water from one jug to another and the operator restrictions are that the water cannot be added to or flung away while solving the problem. In their problem space model of these problems, Atwood and Polson (1976) were particularly interested in 2 problems: one involving jugs of 8, 5 and 3 units and one involving jugs of 24, 21, and 3 units. In both cases, the largest jug is filled and the other jugs are empty and the goal is to distribute the largest jug's contents evenly between the largest and middle jug. Both problems are isomorphic in the number of moves one needs to consider to solve the problem.

Atwood and Polson (1976) supplemented a state-space analysis of these problems with a full process model for explaining subjects' behaviour on water-jug problems. They specified the various heuristic methods used by subjects and included assumptions about the limitations on human information processing (i.e. working memory limitations). Their model contained the following proposals:

- In planning moves, subjects only look ahead to a depth of one move.
- Moves are evaluated using a means-end analysis method, where subjects look at the difference between the actual and goal quantities in the two largest jugs and see which of the next alternative states will bring them closer to the goal state.
- Subjects also tend to avoid moves that return them to immediately preceding states (an anti-looping heuristic).
- There are limitations on the number of possible alternative moves that can be stored in working memory.
- This limitation can be somewhat alleviated by transferring information into long-term memory.

This model's predictions about the points of difficulty in solving water-jug problems were examined in several experiments by Atwood and Polson (1976). One main prediction made is that the 8-8, 5-0, 5-0 problem should be harder than the 24-24, 21-0, 3-0, because the latter could be solved simply by applying the means-end heuristic whereas the former required a violation of this heuristic. Their results showed that the mean number of moves to solve either problem confirmed this prediction.

Atwood, Masson, and Polson (1980) tested the proposal that subjects only planned one move ahead to avoid overloading working memory. They assumed that any reduction of the memory load should have the effect of freeing up the problem solver for more long-term planning. To achieve this manipulation they provided subjects with information about all the different moves available from any state in the problem. One group of subjects received even more information in the form of a record of the previous states they had visited. However, although Atwood et al. discovered that the more information subjects received the fewer the number of moves they needed to consider in solving the problem, they did not find the big "planning improvement" they expected. It seems that when the information load is lifted subjects do not use the extra capacity to plan ahead but rather become more efficient at avoiding states that lead them back to the initial state of the problem.

However, this sort of basic model has been shown to be very useful. Jeffries, Polson, Razran, and Atwood (1977) and Polson and Jeffries (1982) have extended it to apply to versions of the missionaries-cannibals and Tower of Hanoi problems. So the model combines predictive specificity with some generality in its applicability.

Evaluation: Well- and ill-Defined Problems

Perhaps the truest evaluation one can make of problem space theory is that it is very successful *as far as it goes*. The theory has produced analyses that can be modelled computationally and, empirically, it makes strong predictions. However, it has really only worked for a narrow class of puzzle-like problems and its extension to more complex, real-world problems is a moot point. Consider some of the salient differences between the two problem types.

First, puzzle problems are unfamiliar problems about which we have little knowledge. Many of the problems encountered in everyday life require considerable amounts of knowledge. Second, the knowledge required to solve puzzle problems is present in the statement of the problem. In everyday life all the information required to solve problems is often not present. In fact, much of the difficulty of everyday problems may hinge on finding the relevant information required to solve the problem. If one has to buy a house, one needs to know all about mortgages and current houses on sale and finding this information is a significant part of solving the problem. Third, the requirements in puzzle problems are relatively unambiguous; the start state and goal state are clearly specified and what can and cannot be done in the problems is known (i.e. the legal moves). In everyday problems, the real difficulty may lie in specifying the nature of the goal state. For instance, doing a masters or doctoral thesis is essentially a matter of specifying where one wants to end up.

In short, problem space theory has concentrated on *well-defined* as opposed to *ill-defined* problems (Reitman, 1965; Simon, 1973; 1978). In *well-defined problems* the operators, initial state, and goal state are well-specified and subjects tend to have little *specific knowledge* about the problem. The relevant knowledge they do have is *general-purpose* or *domain-independent heuristic knowledge*. For example, the means-end analysis heuristic can be applied in a wide range of different situations and domains. These heuristic methods are generally applicable but they are not always very efficient. Hence, in artificial intelligence they are often called *universal, weak methods*.

In contrast, *ill-defined problems* can be under-specified in many ways and require the use of substantial amounts of *domain-specific knowledge*. The initial state of an ill-defined problem may be uncertain; what is and is not part of the initial state may be unclear from the situation. If someone locks their keys inside their car, it is clear that the car and the keys locked in it are part of the initial state but coat hangers, brooms, the police, and owners of cars of a same make are also potentially part of the initial state too. Second, the operators and operator restrictions may have to be discovered and/or created. One may have to dredge one's memory for suitable operators (e.g. using a coat hanger in a certain way, forcing a back window, finding a route into the car through the boot). Finally, the goal state may need definition. On the face of it, getting into the car is a reasonable goal state, but smashing a window to do this does not seem like a good solution; so one may want to define the goal further to stipulate that one should get into the car without doing much damage. But what constitutes "much damage"? Ill-definition and knowledge go hand in hand because ill-defined problems are usually made more well-defined through the application of knowledge.

In conclusion, problem space theory has the potential to provide a framework for characterising ill-defined problems, but a lot more work needs to be done to extend it to these problems. However, in the next section, we will deal with some research that has attempted to do this.

Summary

One of the most successful theories of cognition that has emerged from the information processing revolution is Newell and Simon's (1972) problem space theory. At base, it characterises problem solving as a constrained and guided search through a space of alternative possibilities. This search is guided by various heuristic methods or rules of thumb that co-ordinate the application of various operators used for transforming one state into another. This theory has been used to predict problem-solving behaviour in puzzle problems, like the Tower of Hanoi, the missionaries-cannibals problem, and water-jug problems. Computational models have been constructed for many of these problems and they demonstrate close parallels to subjects' behaviour. The strength of this approach has been its predictive success; its weakness is manifested in the narrow range of problem situations to which it has been applied. However, as we shall see later, this is a "limitation in practice" rather than a "limitation in principle."

EXPERTS AND NOVICES: KNOWLEDGE-INTENSIVE PROBLEM SOLVING

One of the main distinctions between puzzle-like, well-defined problems and more everyday, ill-defined problems is the amount and specificity of the knowledge brought to the problem situation. The nature of this knowledge has been examined in studies of expertise. Someone who has, for example, just begun to learn physics lacks a considerable amount of knowledge relative to another person, of equivalent intellectual abilities, who has studied the subject for several years. These differences in knowledge result in behavioural differences between learners or *novices* and *experts*. In this section, we will consider some of the evidence of such differences and the theoretical explanations of them. Part of the definition of the term "expertise" is that it means being good at something in a particular area or domain (e.g. chess, physics, psychology). As we shall see, many of the domains studied in this research area have enormous practical significance and represent a major move in cognitive psychology towards research that is concerned with everyday, realistic situations (i.e. ecologically valid research).

The Skills of Chess Masters

The game of chess was one of the first domains in which novice-expert differences were studied. From a theoretical point of view it is very interesting because it can be analysed easily in problem space terms and also involves the use of large amounts of problem-specific knowledge.

Combinatorial Explosions in Chess

In terms of a state-space analysis, the initial state of a chess game consists of all the pieces on the board in their starting positions and the goal state is to checkmate one's opponent. From any state the different alternative moves can be specified. For instance, from the initial state the legal moves are clear: One can move any of the pawns or either of the knights. However, the sheer number of alternatives that need to be considered quickly gets out of hand. For each possible move, the opponent can make one of a large number of replies; each of these replies can be countered with many more moves, and so on. In computational terms, one faces a "combinatorial explosion" of possibilities. That is, the number of alternative paths increase exponentially. Early chess-playing computer programs tried to search through a considerable number of alternatives and to evaluate each alternative. For example, Newell and Simon (1972) report a program called MANIAC, developed at Los Alamos in the 1950s, that explored nearly 1,000,000 moves at each turn. This merely reflected the consideration of alternative moves to a depth of four turns (an initial move, an opponent's reply, a reply to this move, and the opponent's counter move). However, even with this brute force computation, it did not play very good chess and occasionally made serious mistakes. Since people cannot do this sort of brute force computation with any speed, something else seemed to underlie the expertise of chess masters. But, what might this something else be?

DeGroot's Chess Studies

Some initial answers to this question were provided by DeGroot (1965; 1966), even though, at first, his results thicken the sense of mystery surrounding chess expertise. DeGroot compared the performance of five grand masters and five expert players on choosing a move from a particular board position. He asked his subjects to think aloud and then determined the number and type of different moves they had considered. One of his most striking findings was that grand masters did not consider more alternative moves than expert players, that they did not search any deeper than expert players and, yet, took slightly less time to make a move. Furthermore, independent raters judged the final moves produced by the masters to be better than those produced by expert players.

Also, in contrast to chess programs, the human players manifested a paradoxical mix of laziness and efficiency. They tended to consider only around 30 alternative moves and about 4 alternative first moves. At most, they searched to a depth of 6 turns although frequently they searched a lot less. Wagner and Scurrah (1971) examined this behaviour in further detail and found that chess players used a *progressive deepening strategy*. That is, initially a small number of alternative first moves are checked. These are then returned to repeatedly and explored to a greater depth each time that they are re-examined.

Wherein, then, lies the difference in expertise between grand masters and experts and humans and computers? The initial explanation for the former, proposed by DeGroot, was that the difference lay in the knowledge of different board positions stored in long-term memory. It is well-known that chess players study previous games and can recall their own games in detail. Therefore, it was proposed that good chess players recognise previous board positions and remember good moves to make from these positions. This use of prior knowledge excludes any need to entertain irrelevant moves and a host of alternatives. DeGroot argued that if chess players had stored previous board positions in some schematic fashion (see Chapter 8) then this knowledge should be reflected in tasks that measured memory.

He therefore gave subjects brief presentations of board positions from actual games (i.e. for five seconds) and asked them to reconstruct the positions after the board had been taken away. The main finding was that chess masters could recall the positions very accurately (91% correct), whereas less expert players made many more errors (41% correct). It was thus clear that chess masters could recognise and encode the various configurations of pieces using their prior knowledge in a manner which was only poorly-approximated by less expert players. This explanation is substantiated by DeGroot's other finding that when the pieces were randomly arranged on the board (i.e. were not arranged in a familiar configuration), both groups of players did equally badly. That is, neither group had the knowledge available to encode the configurations because they were unfamiliar.

Chunking in Chess

DeGroot's results were later followed up by Simon and his associates (Chase & Simon, 1973a; 1973b; Simon & Barenfeld, 1969; Simon & Gilmartin, 1973). Chase and Simon elaborated the notion that, in the memory task, players were "chunking" the board (see Miller, 1956; and Chapters 4 and 5); that is, that they broke board positions down into seven or so familiar units and held these in their short-term memory temporarily while doing the task. The essential difference in the behaviour of masters and other players was in terms of the size of the chunk that they could encode. That is, the seven chunks of the masters contained considerably more than the seven chunks of the poorer players. In their studies, they provided evidence for this proposal by using a modified version of DeGroot's task.

Chase and Simon asked subjects to reconstruct a board position on a second chess board, while the first board was still in view. They then recorded the number and type of pieces subjects placed on the second board after a glance at the first board. The chunking hypothesis predicts that only a few pieces should be placed after each glance and that they should form some coherent whole. In each of the three players studied, they found that the average number of pieces taken at a glance was small in number (i.e. about three) and was similar in content. However, better players were more rapid in their encodings, as indicated by their significantly shorter glances. Simon and Chase estimated from their studies that there were also systematic differences in the number of pieces encoded in a chunk as a function of expertise. The strongest player encoded about 2.5 pieces per chunk, whereas the weakest player encoded only 1.9 pieces per chunk. So the evidence indicated that expert players can recognise chunks of a board position more quickly and can encode more information in these chunks than can novice players.

A Cognitive Model of Chess Knowledge

Simon and Gilmartin (1973) modelled some of these effects computationally in a model called the Memory-Aided Pattern Perceiver (MAPP). This program contained a large number of different board patterns and encoded a "presented" board configuration into its short-term memory by recognising various chunks of the total configuration. To support the proposal that it was knowledge that led to the differences between masters and less expert players, Simon and Gilmartin had one version of the program with more patterns than another version (1114 patterns versus 894 patterns). They then ran the two different versions on board reconstruction tasks and found that the version with fewer patterns performed the poorest. On the basis of these results and the relationship between the model's performance and that of human subjects, Simon and Gilmartin estimated that master level performance could be achieved by a long-term memory with between 10,000 and 100,000 patterns.

Is Board-Position Knowledge All There Is to Chess Expertise?

The view, originally espoused by DeGroot, that chess expertise relies on knowledge of board positions is not the whole truth. Granted, performance differences seem to reflect differences in the numbers of board patterns known by players (e.g. see MAPP), but some evidence has shown that there is more to chess expertise than just board-position knowledge.

There also appears to be problem-specific, heuristic knowledge for evaluating moves and sequences of moves that is quite independent of board-position knowledge (see Charness, 1981; Holding, 1985). Holding and Reynolds (1982) presented players (rated as being of high or low ability) with random board positions for eight seconds and asked them to recall the positions later. As in the DeGroot-type studies the finding was that all subjects, irrespective of their ability, were poor at recalling the positions. However, when subjects were asked to evaluate the strength of the position and decide on the next best move to make, from the same random board positions, the high-ability players produced better quality moves. This result suggests that, even though the subjects had no specific schemata for these board positions, they had other knowledge that allowed them to generate and evaluate potential moves from that position.

Physics Expertise

Anyone who has studied physics will recall (possibly with dread) problems like the following one:

A block of mass M is dropped from a height x onto a spring of force constant K. Neglecting friction, what is the maximum distance the spring will be compressed?

The solution of physics problems depends on the selection of appropriate principles from the physics domain and the derivation of a solution through the application of these principles. So, in solving such problems, a problem solver must analyse the problem, construct some cognitive representation of it and then strategically apply relevant principles to solve it. The simplest view of novice-expert differences in physics is that, as was maintained in chess skill, novices lack a large repertoire of relevant schemata for solving problems. In the physics case, novices lack the schemata that link problem situations to principles. In the absence of such knowledge they fall back on more domain-independent heuristic knowledge similar to that used in puzzle problems (like means-end analysis).

Evidence of Novice–Expert Differences in Physics

In physics problem solving, it has been proposed that experts build more complete representations of the problem than novices because of the extra knowledge they have available (Heller & Reif, 1984; Larkin, 1983; 1985). This is supported by Chi, Feltovich, and Glaser's (1981; Chi, Glaser, & Rees, 1983) finding that if experts and novices are asked to sort problems into related groups, the resultant behaviour is quite different. Novices tended to group problems together that have the same *surface features*. That is, novices grouped two problems together if they used pulleys or ramps; they were led by the keywords and the objects in the problem. However, experts classified problems in terms of their *deep structure*. That is, they grouped problems together that could be solved by the same principles, even though these problems "looked" different and involved different objects.

Furthermore, Chi et al. discovered that even though experts solved the problems four times faster than novices, they spent more time than novices analysing and understanding the problems. Unlike the novices, who waded into the problem immediately applying equations, the experts elaborated the representation of the problem by selecting the appropriate principles that applied in the situation. In essence, this amounts to the complex categorisation of the problem situation with respect to their available knowledge.

Strategic differences have also been found between experts and novices. Experts tend to *work forwards* to a solution whereas novices tend to *work backwards* (Larkin, McDermott, Simon, & Simon, 1980). After spending some time analysing the problem, experts apply the principles they have selected to the given quantities in the problems, in order to generate the unknown quantities they need to solve the problem. This is, thus, a planned working-forward strategy. It is both efficient and powerful and relies heavily on domain-specific knowledge about the problem. Novices, in contrast, have an impoverished repertoire of available principles. Typically, they take the goal (e.g. what is the maximum distance the spring will be compressed?) and find a principle that contains the desired quantity and usually no more than one other unknown quantity. They then try to find this new unknown quantity and hence work backwards to the givens of the problem statement.

Computational Models of Physics Skills

Several computational models of physics problem solving have been produced (Lambert, in press; Larkin, 1979; Priest, 1986). Most of these models are conventional symbolic models, like production systems (see Chapter 1). However, recently Lambert (in press) has produced an interesting *hybrid model* which mixes connectionist and production system ideas. Lambert noted that physics expertise seems partly a matter of knowing about many different previous problems and partly a strategic component (e.g. forward reasoning). He therefore proposed a connectionist model to deal with the memory aspect and a production system model to handle the strategic aspects.

In Lambert's model, long-term memory is a distributed memory for previous problem situations (see Chapters 1 and 7). This memory has input units that are divided into three types: data units, final goal units, and sub-goal units. The *data units* can encode different sorts of symbols in problem statements (e.g. the explicitly mentioned objects and variables), wheras the *final goal units* encode the required quantity to be found in the problem. With these two sets of units, problems can be encoded in the distributed memory. The knowledge the memory builds up with the successive solution of problems is an association between a particular set of problem statements (including their goals) and a set of useful sub-goals. Consider how the whole system, combining the connectionist memory and the production system, operates.

When running on a problem the model goes through four stages. First, the problem to be solved is encoded by both the distributed memory system and the production system. The former encodes the problem statement in terms of activations to the appropriate data and final goal units (it should be noted that no encoding of sub-goals occurs). The production system encodes the problem as a structured representation in its working memory. Second, the encoded problem is processed by the distributed memory until it settles into a stable state, at which point one or more of the units in the sub-goal set may become activated above a threshold. Third, the production system then comes into play and uses its sets of inference rules on the problem representation and the sub-goals generated by the distributed memory. These inference rules are thus used to reach the goals of the problem using forward inference. If this forward inference fails then the system starts backward inference. Fourth, if a solution is learned in the third stage then the sub-goals that were found to be useful are used along with the problem statement and goal to put the network through a learning cycle that encodes the association between these three entities. So, in the future, if the same or a similar problem is encountered the network will produce a certain set of suitable sub-goals to be adopted. Lambert has shown that the system, when trained, can produce solutions that closely correspond to those generated by human experts.

Computer Programming Skills

A third strand of expert–novice research has examined computer programming skills. In recent years, as the information revolution has spurred apace, many people have had to learn to program computers. Two unassailable facts have emerged from this experience. First, programming takes time and second, programmers frequently make mistakes. These facts have raised fundamental questions about the cognitive demands of computer programming and, more importantly for the future, about what features of programming languages make them cognitively difficult to use efficiently (see, e.g., Anderson, Boyle, & Reiser, 1985;

Eisenstadt, Rajan, & Keane, in press; Kahney, 1989; Kahney & Eisenstadt, 1982; Soloway & Spohrer, 1989).

Plans in Programming

Research on computer programming has been influenced by theories of knowledge organisation, especially by the work of Schank and his associates (Schank, 1982; Schank & Abelson, 1977; see Chapter 8). In particular, Elliot Soloway and his associates at Yale University maintain that expert programmers develop script-like plans that are stereotypical chunks of code; for example, one might have an "averaging plan"; that is, one knows that an average is a sum divided by a count. When programmers write a program they plan at an abstract level how these chunks will be co-ordinated and sequenced in the program, in order to make it carry out the required task (see Erlich & Soloway, 1984). The plans are seen as being "natural" in the sense that programmers possess them before they learn computer programming.

The close proximity of this position to work on schema theories of comprehension has led to similar predictions being made for programming skills. For example, when skilled readers encounter stories in which certain actions are left unstated but implicit, they can easily infer these actions. Similarly, if expert programmers are given a program with some missing statements, they can easily fill in the missing plan-part of it (Soloway & Erlich, 1984). Novice programmers are not half as adequate at filling in the same blanks. Results from this "fill-in-the-blank" task indicate that skilled programmers select appropriate plans from memory and adapt them to the local requirements of a specific programming task.

A second prediction from schema research is that programmers' plans should be interfered with by existing planning knowledge from everyday life. Bower et al. (1979) have shown that when stories violated the stereotypical sequences dictated by a script structure their contents were re-ordered by subjects in recall (see Chapter 8). Similarly, Soloway, Bonar, and Erlich (1983) found that programmers show a tendency to put program statements in the order that their everyday knowledge dictates, even when this ordering leads to bugs in their programs. For example, the process/read loop construct in PASCAL is a major source of bugs because it mismatches the normal course of events in the real world; in the real world we get an object (read it), and then do something with it (process it), but in the PASCAL loop world items are processed first and then read.

Recently, Gilmore and Green (1988) have argued against the view that programming plans are necessarily natural and general. They had skilled programmers in two languages—PASCAL and BASIC—carry out plan-related and plan-unrelated tasks. They also used a manipulation that highlighted the plan structure of the programs presented to subjects. They reasoned that if plans were being used then highlighting the structure of these plans should facilitate subjects in a plan-related task. This prediction was confirmed in the PASCAL case. However, no similar facilitation was found in BASIC. They interpreted the results to indicate that the content of programming plans do not generalise across languages, even though they admitted that BASIC programmers may use other plans. In particular, they maintained that plans may in some sense emerge from notational aspects of the programming language in question. Hence, the notation of PASCAL makes it easier to form plans within that language (see Davies, in press a).

A synthesis of these apparently opposing views has been proposed by Davies (in press a; in press b). He suggests that natural plans may exist but that it may be more difficult to express these plans in one language than in another. Davies reasons that one factor that might have an impact on this ability to apply natural plans to different target languages may be the extent of novices' training in program design. He points out that the PASCAL programmers in the Gilmore and Green study were more likely to have design experience, thus accounting for the results found. He therefore performed a similar study looking at novice BASIC programmers with or without design experience. Contrary to the Gilmore and Green study he found that BASIC programmers *could* benefit from the cues to plan structures in programs but only when they had received prior training in design. Thus, in Davies' view there are three components to take into account in characterising programming expertise: structures in the problem domain (i.e. natural plans), structures in the particular programming language domain (to do with the notation of the language), and a mapping between the former and the latter. Education in program design is seen as providing the basis for this mapping.

On Becoming an Expert: Acquiring Expertise

Throughout this section we have reviewed some of the differences that have been found between novices and experts in several different problem-solving domains. What we have not broached is how these differences come about; how novices become experts. In general terms, the acquisition of cognitive skills consists of moving from having a little knowledge to having a lot more knowledge. In particular, the picture is somewhat more complicated; it is more like moving from having a little domain-independent knowledge to having a lot of domain-specific knowledge. This, as we shall see, is one of the central tenets of John Anderson's theory of skill acquisition.

Anderson's Theory of Skill Acquisition

Anderson's (1982; 1983; 1987a) theory of skill learning has been applied to several different domains including geometry (Anderson, Greeno, Kline, & Neves, 1981), computer programming (Anderson & Reiser, 1985; Pirolli & Anderson, 1985), and computer text-editing (Singley & Anderson, in press). His cognitive architecture —called ACT* (*Adaptive Control of Thought*; pronounced act-star)—includes these skill learning processes as some of its central principles (see Chapter 1 on cognitive architectures).

ACT* has three main processing components. First, there is a *declarative memory*, that is a semantic network of interconnected concepts that have different activation strengths (see Chapters 1 and 8). Second, there is a *procedural memory*, that is, basically, a production system. Finally, there is a *working memory* that contains currently active information. In essence, the working memory is not so much a separate component as that part of declarative knowledge, permanent or temporary, that is in an active state (see Fig. 11.6). *Encoding processes* result in information being placed in working memory and *performance processes* change commands in working memory into behaviour. Information can be *stored* and *retrieved* from declarative memory by a number of methods. When the rules or productions in the production memory *match* the contents of working memory they are fired or *executed*. But production memory can also be applied to itself by *application processes*. That is, new productions can be learned by examining existing productions.

As we shall see later, a large part of skill learning consists of changing declarative knowledge into procedural knowledge and then modifying this procedural knowledge via application processes. Clearly, the declarative-procedural knowledge distinction is a central pillar of the theory (see Chapter 8 here). Recall that, typically, declarative knowledge is knowledge that can be reported and is not tied to the situation in which it can be used. Procedural knowledge is applied automatically, often cannot be reported, and is specifically tuned to be applied in specific situations.

Stated broadly, Anderson sees skill acquisition as a move from the use of declarative knowledge to procedures that can be applied

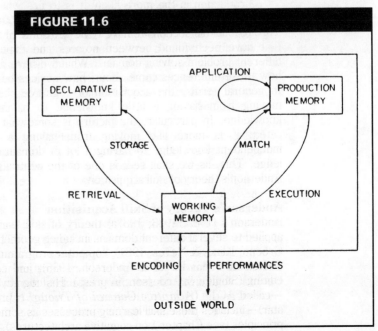

FIGURE 11.6

A schematic diagram of the major structural components and their interlinking processes in Anderson's (1983) ACT production system (reproduced with the permission of the publishers from Architecture of Cognition *by J.R. Anderson, Cambridge, Mass.: Harvard University Press. Copyright © 1983 by the President and Fellows of Harvard College. All rights reserved.)*

APPLICATION

DECLARATIVE MEMORY

PRODUCTION MEMORY

STORAGE

MATCH

RETRIEVAL

EXECUTION

WORKING MEMORY

ENCODING   PERFORMANCES

OUTSIDE WORLD

quickly and automatically in specific situations. Skill learning can thus be viewed as passing through three stages, from a *declarative stage* to a *procedural stage* to a *tuning stage*. In detail, the theory is as follows:

- During the initial *declarative stage* a learner of a new domain will rely on any available declarative knowledge and will use this in conjunction with domain-independent, weak methods to solve problems (e.g. hill climbing, means-end analysis).
- The *procedural stage* may occur even after one instance of solving a problem declaratively; in this stage successful sequences of activity, produced by the application of weak methods to declarative knowledge, are *compiled* into new domain-specific productions.
- This *knowledge compilation* takes two distinct forms: practice proceduralisation and composition.
- *Proceduralisation* takes place when a particular piece of declarative knowledge is used repeatedly in the context of a particular sub-goal; it results in a new production rule being created which has the declarative information as a pattern (its IF-part) and the executed action as its action (its THEN-part).
- *Composition* is a learning mechanism that cuts out unnecessary productions from a sequence of productions.
- In the *procedure tuning stage*, existing procedural knowledge is either strengthened, generalised, or discriminated.
- Productions are *strengthened* in their activation value every time they are used successfully, and the stronger a production is the more likely it is to fire when it competes with other productions; productions are *generalised* when part of their condition or "IF" patterns are replaced by variables; when a production cannot be executed for some reason or an impasse is reached discrimination occurs, whereby one production's activation is weakened relative to other productions with similar conditions that are more successful.

Anderson's stages of skill acquisition show a plausible fit to human behaviour. The *declarative stage*, for example, corresponds to the behaviour we see in novices when they attempt to solve maths or programming problems from a textbook, purely on the basis of declarative knowledge they have acquired in instruction. In the procedural stage, after someone has succeeded in solving a problem, they will typically solve the same or similar problems much faster in the future. In terms of ACT*, this is seen as being the result of having developed a set of productions that are carried out when a particular problem situation is encountered. Declarative information describing aspects of the problem has been encoded as the IF-part of these new production rules in production memory (i.e. proceduralisation occurs). Note that on a first attempt to solve a problem, learners will typically follow many false paths and use wrong strategies, but if they are asked to solve the same problem again, they will generally have learned to ignore these false paths and produce the correct solution sequences (in ACT*'s terms, compilation has occurred). *Production tuning* is reflected in the behavioural changes that result from the effects of practice where, even though little new knowledge is being acquired, we get faster and faster at carrying out the skill (in this case through the strengthening of relevant productions).

Summary

One of the standard features of human cognitive performance is that people get better at doing things with experience. They become experts and manifest what is broadly termed expertise. Recently, various attempts have been made to extend mainstream cognitive theories of problem solving (i.e. problem space formulations) and memory (semantic memory and schema theories) to the understanding of human expertise. Striking differences in the amount and kinds of knowledge possessed by experts and novices have been demonstrated in this research, covering domains such as chess playing, physics problem solving, and computer programming. The practical significance of this work cannot be undervalued. There are well-elaborated and often computationally modelled theories of acquisition in these areas. J.R. Anderson has produced a general theory of skill acquisition, as part of his ACT* cognitive architecture, that can be applied to skill learning in a variety of different domains of expertise.

ANALOGIES, MODELS, AND INSIGHT REVISITED

The novice–expert research is but one area in which researchers have tried to understand the knowledge that problem solvers bring to problem situations. Other distinct strands of research have examined alternative ways in which knowledge is accessed and used. As we pointed out earlier, the amount of knowledge a subject brings to a problem is a rough indicator of the extent to which that problem is ill-defined. So all of the research reviewed in this and the previous section can be viewed as an attempt to elucidate ill-defined problem-solving situations.

Creativity and Analogical Problem Solving

Most of the research on the use of expertise deals with how people solve relatively familiar problems. Thus, theories of expertise are concerned mainly with the direct application of schematic knowledge. But people can also solve unfamiliar or novel problems. Sometimes we can produce creative solutions when we have no directly applicable knowledge about the problem situation. How do we manage this?

Much of the research on creativity in psychology has tended to be descriptive rather than explanatory (but for some recent exceptions see Johnson-Laird, 1988b; Sternberg, 1988). The classic example of this descriptive approach is Wallas's (1926) classification of the broad stages of the creative process into:

- *preparation*, where the problem under consideration is formulated and preliminary attempts are made to solve it;
- *incubation*, where the problem is left aside to work on other tasks;
- *illumination*, in which the solution comes to the problem solver as a sudden insight; and
- *verification*, in which the problem solver makes sure that the solution really works.

The problem with analyses such as these, however, is that they are too general and descriptive. They say little about the specific cognitive processes underlying the creative act. There have, though, been some attempts to explain creativity.

Some have proposed that we use prior experiences which are not *directly* applicable but are *indirectly* applicable, by analogy. For example, Koestler's (1964) famous work on the act of creation examined accounts of creativity in disparate domains—including literature, the arts, and science—and proposed that creativity often results from the juxtaposition of two sets of very different ideas. The anecdotal reports of various creative individuals suggest

---

TABLE 11.2

The Solar System/Atom Analogy

Base Domain *Solar System*	*Target Domain* *Atom*
The sun attracts the planets.	The nucleus attracts the electrons.
The sun is larger than the planets.	The nucleus is larger than the electrons.
The planets revolve around the sun.	*The electrons revolve around the nucleus.*
The planets revolve around the sun because of the attraction and weight difference.	*The electrons revolve around the nucleus because of the attraction and weight difference.*
The planet Earth has life on it.	No transfer.

Note: Table shows those parts of the base and target domains that match and those that need to be transferred to the target (italic type). Adapted from Genther, 1983.

that deep analogies form the basis of solutions to unfamiliar problems. For example, in his early conception of the structure of the atom, Rutherford is reputed to have used a solar system analogy, viewing the electrons as revolving around the nucleus in the same way that the planets revolve around the sun (see Gentner, 1980; 1983; and Table 11.2). Similarly, Einstein performed thought experiments based on analogies about riding on a light beam and travelling in elevators.

Various theorists have characterised this analogical thinking as being the result of processes that map the conceptual structure of one set of ideas (called a base domain) into another set of ideas (called a target domain); technically, this is called an *analogical mapping* from a base domain (e.g. the solar system) to a target domain (e.g. the atom) (see Gentner, 1980; 1983; Holyoak, 1985; Keane, 1985a; 1988). Analogical mapping is characterised as follows:

- Certain aspects of the base and target domains are *matched*; for example, one notices that there are objects in the solar system that attract each other and objects in the atom that attract each other (see Table 11.2).
- Certain aspects of the base (usually relations, like *revolves around*) are transferred into the target domain; for instance, relations about the planets revolving around the sun are *transferred* into the atom domain to create some new conceptual structure there (i.e. that the electrons revolve around the nucleus).
- When knowledge is transferred from one domain to another there is a tendency for coherent, integrated pieces of knowledge rather than fragmentary pieces to be transferred (see Gentner's, 1983, *systematicity principle*); so, the integrated knowledge that attraction and weight difference *cause* the planets to revolve around the sun is transferred before nonintegrated information about the earth having life on it (see Table 11.2).
- Sometimes knowledge is transferred because it is viewed as being pragmatically important or goal-relevant in some respect (see Holyoak, 1985; Keane, 1985a).

Gick and Holyoak (1980; 1983) have studied this phenomenon of analogical mapping in problem-solving situations. They gave subjects analogous stories to Duncker's (1945) "radiation problem." The radiation problem involves a doctor's attempt to destroy a malignant tumour using rays. The doctor needs to use high-intensity rays to destroy the tumour but these high-intensity rays will destroy the healthy tissue surrounding the tumour. If the doctor uses low-intensity rays then the healthy tissue will be saved but the tumour will remain unaffected too. This dilemma can be solved by a "convergence solution," which proposes that the doctor send low-intensity rays from a number of different directions so that they converge on the tumour, summing to a high intensity to destroy it. However, only about 10% of subjects produce this solution if they are given the problem on its own.

Gick and Holyoak (1980) gave subjects a story about a general attacking a fortress. The general was prevented from using his whole army to take the fortress because the roads leading to it were mined to explode if large groups of men pass over them. He, therefore, divided his army up into small groups of men and sent them along different roads to the fortress so that they converged on it. When subjects were given this analogous story to memorise and later asked if they could use it to solve the radiation problem the rates of convergence solutions rose to about 80%. This was, thus, strong evidence that people could use the analogous story to solve the problem.

In terms of analogical mapping, in this situation subjects are *matching* various aspects of the initial situation of the problem with those of the story. That is, they may notice that the general's inability to use his whole army corresponds to the doctor's inability to use high-intensity rays. Then, having made some further correspondences, they can *transfer* the knowledge that splitting the army up and sending it from different directions can be applied to the rays and so generate the solution to the problem. What gets transferred from one domain to another is a coherent bundle of knowledge; all the causally relevant knowledge about what actions will solve the problem. In short, subjects take the solution part of the story (about how the general solves his problem) and transfer it to construct a solution for the radiation problem.

Gick and Holyoak also found interesting evidence about subjects' failure to notice the analogous story. If subjects were not directed explicitly to use the story, they often failed to notice that it was relevant to the problem. This suggested that stories like the general story that were superficially dissimilar or semantically remote were not recalled in an automatic fashion from memory when the problem was presented. Keane (1987; see also Holyoak & Koh, 1987) tested this prediction by presenting subjects with either a semantically close story-analogue (about a surgeon using rays on a cancer) or a semantically remote analogue (namely, the general story). Subjects received the story during a weekly lecture and some days later were asked to take part in an experiment on problem solving. As expected, it was found that many subjects spontaneously retrieved the close analogue (88%), but very few retrieved the remote analogue (12%). Keane also found that a story which was mid-way between these two extremes (about a general using rays to destroy a missile) produced intermediate rates of retrieval; he modelled these effects using Schank's (1982) theory of reminding and, specifically, the notion of "thematic organisation points" (see Chapter 8). These results support the intuition that one reason why acts of creativity, involving remote analogies, are fairly rare is that most people have difficulties retrieving potentially relevant experiences from memory.

The role of analogy in problem solving has been demonstrated in many domains: for example, in computer programming (Anderson & Reiser, 1985; Conway & Kahney, 1986; Keane, Kahney, & Brayshaw, 1989), in the missionaries-cannibals problem (Luger & Bauer, 1978; Reed, Ernst & Banerji, 1974) and in solving electric circuit problems (Gentner & Gentner, 1983). Many of the experiments on analogy have also been modelled computationally using either conventional, symbolic programs (Falkenhainer, Forbus, & Gentner, 1986; Keane & Brayshaw, 1988) or connectionist schemes (Holyoak & Thagard, 1989; 1990). However, even given the extent of this empirical and computational research, much more detailed tests of analogical processes need to be carried out. For example, Keane (1985a) has shown that if subjects are given simply the solution-part of the story (about the army converging on the fortress), they still produce high rates of convergence solutions by analogy. Most current theories see matching as an important precursor to the formation of transfers, yet this research indicates that successful transfer can occur with little or no matching.

Re-interpreting Insight Problems

Like the problem space work on the water-jug problems, analogy research is interesting in the extent to which it harks back to earlier Gestalt work. This re-conception of things past has been another theme of recent problem-solving research, as proponents of information processing psychology have attempted to reinterpret early Gestalt theory (see, e.g., Keane, 1985b; 1989; Newell, 1980; Ohlsson, 1984a; 1985; Sternberg & Davidson, 1983; Weisberg, 1980; Weisberg & Alba, 1981; Weisberg & Suls, 1973).

Recent Research on the Nine-dot Problem

Weisberg and Alba (1981) re-examined the nine-dot problem (see Fig. 11.3). In Scheerer's (1963) original paper on the nine-dot problem, he had argued that subjects failed to solve the problem because they assumed that the lines drawn had to stay within the square shape formed by the dots; they were "fixated" on the Gestalt of the nine dots. To test this, Weisberg and Alba gave subjects a hint that they could draw lines outside the square. However, with this hint, only 20% solved the problem. They therefore concluded that fixation on the square of dots was not the only factor responsible for subjects' failures. In further experiments, Weisberg and Alba used simpler versions of the problem (a four-dot task) and explored the use of specific hints (e.g. drawing some of the lines that lead to the solution). From these experiments they concluded that in order to solve the problem subjects required highly problem-specific knowledge. In their eyes, this undercut the Gestalt concepts of "insight" and "fixation," which they argued were of dubious explanatory value. However, several opponents have countered this point (see Dominowski, 1981; Ellen, 1982; Lung & Dominowski, 1985).

A Problem-space View of Insight and Restructuring

Several other theorists have made a backward glance at Gestalt research. Ohlsson (1984a; 1984b; 1985) has re-assessed the basic constructs of the Gestalt tradition in terms of Newell and Simon's theory. Ohlsson points to the definition of insight as "understanding the solution to the problem," as being of central importance, and underscores the Gestalt definition of "restructuring" as a process that "changes the possibilities for action inherent in a particular situation". He then recasts both of these definitions in problem space terms.

One of the basic proposals of problem space theory is that people are limited-capacity processors. In planning the solutions to problems there is therefore a limit to what has been called "mental look-ahead." Recall, for example, that one of the basic assumptions in Atwood and Polson's model of the water-jug problems was that subjects only "looked" one move ahead. Ohlsson thus maintained that insight occurs when a knowledge state is reached that "brings the goal state within the horizon of mental look-ahead". In other words, problem solvers have insights when they reach a knowledge state from which a plan of moves that will take them to the goal state is apparent.

Ohlsson explains restructuring as the re-description of a particular knowledge state in the subject's representation of the problem. This re-description allows other operators to be used (changing the possibilities for action inherent in the situation) because the potential applicability of an operator depends on the content of the current knowledge state. For example, if someone had the knowledge state and operator shown in Table 11.3:

TABLE 11.3

Knowledge State	Operator
	IF
There is something that is noisy	There is something that is noisy
This something is a canary	This something is a *bird*
One's goal is to have peace and quiet	One's goal is to have peace and quiet
	THEN
	shoo that something away

A Knowledge state that will not match the IF-part of the Operator.

then the operator will not apply because "the something is a canary" and "the something is a bird" conditions do not match. Ohlsson, therefore, proposes that for every knowledge state there is a "description space" that contains all the alternative descriptions of a single knowledge state that can be generated on the basis of one's knowledge. So, for example, the knowledge state just mentioned could be re-described as:

New Knowledge State
There is something that is noisy
This something is a canary
This something is a bird
One's goal is to have peace and quiet

using the knowledge that a canary is a subordinate of the concept bird (see Chapter 8). When this change is made to the knowledge state the shoo-away operator becomes applicable and the problem can be solved.

Similar ideas have been used by Keane (1985b; 1989) to account for the results of functional fixedness phenomena in the two-string problem, although there one also needs to include ideas about how concepts are represented in a problem-solving context. That is, when people are faced with the two-string problem they represent the objects in terms of their usual uses. That is, they represent the strings as long, thin, and flexible (but not swingable) and the pliers as being used for electrical tasks (but not as a heavy object). The essence of fixedness is the failure of the subject to re-describe the problem situation so that these objects are conceived of as having different properties, the sorts of properties that will solve the problem.

Several Different Types of Insight

Apart from theoretical re-interpretations of Gestalt research, some have argued in a more empirical vein, that there are several distinct types of insight (Sternberg, 1987; Sternberg & Davidson, 1982; 1983). Sternberg argues that there are at least three distinct forms of insight. First, in some task situations a critical insight depends on *selective encoding*. That is, in comprehending the problem one must distinguish between the relevant and irrelevant aspects of the problem. Once you have selected the key pieces of information the problem is effectively solved. For example, in any legal case there are many facts that can be used to mount a prosecution or a defence. However, an insightful lawyer will know which ones to select and relate to particular principles of law. Alternatively, an insight may hinge on *selective combination*; that is, on the insightful combination of apparently unrelated pieces of information into a more coherent whole. That is, the lawyer must know how the relevant facts of the case fit together. Finally, one may have insights based on *selective comparison*, where the "trick" is to relate the current information to other information acquired in the past. This would include the use of analogy (see earlier section). For example, a good lawyer might relate the current case to a previously encountered precedent.

Sternberg and Davidson (1982; 1983) examined these three types of insight in problems like the following ones:

- If you have black socks and brown socks in your drawers mixed in the ratio of 4 to 5, how many socks will you have to

take out to make sure of having a pair of socks of the same colour?
- Suppose you and I have the same amount of money. How much must I give you so that you have 10 dollars more than I?
- Water lilies double in area every 24 hours. At the beginning of the summer there is one water lily on a lake. It takes 60 days for the lake to become covered with water lilies. On what day is the lake half-covered?

The first of these problems was predicted to require selective encoding, the second selective combination, and the third both selective encoding and selective combination. The answers, if you have not yet worked them out, are "3," "5 dollars," and "the 59th day," respectively. On looking at subjects' protocols for 12 problems of this sort, Sternberg and Davidson found that selective combination was the most common strategy used. From these and other studies, they concluded that subjects use these three different types of insight in solving problems and that there are individual differences between subjects in their tendency to use one type of insight rather than another.

The main criticism one might have of the Sternberg and Davidson work is that the three categories of insight are merely high-level re-descriptions of processes examined in other problem-solving research. For example, selective encoding is reminiscent of the sort of behaviour exhibited by expert physicists in physics problem solving. Similarly, selective comparison is effectively analogical problem solving. Perhaps the work's most important finding is that, irrespective of one's basic store of knowledge, different individuals may have a predisposition to employ one or more of these strategies in problem-solving situations.

Mental Models of the World

The research on analogy and insight problems sticks closely to a sample of laboratory-type problems. Happily, another line of research has investigated more everyday problem situations in which people used their own "naive theories" or "mental models" to understand the world (see Brewer, 1987; Gentner & Stevens, 1983; Gilhooly, 1987; Norman, 1983; Rips, 1986). These *mental models* are theoretical constructs used to account for a variety of aspects of behaviour in novel problem-solving situations. The term mental models has been used in many different ways, but several common properties in these conceptions have emerged:

- mental models constitute a person's causal understanding of a physical system and are used to understand and make predictions about that system's behaviour;
- they are incomplete, unstable, and may even be partly *ad hoc;*
- these models can be run, in the sense that they can simulate

the behaviour of a physical system and may be accompanied by visual imagery;
- they are unscientific; people maintain "superstitious" behaviour patterns even though they are known to be unnecessary, because they may cost little physical effort and save mental effort.

An important point about mental representations may be made here with reference to Chapter 7. It may be remembered that in considering mental representation we classified mental models (as proposed by Johnson-Laird, 1983) as being a specific type of analogical representation; a representational construct that reflected the structure of states of affairs in the world. This conception is *not* the same as the Gentner and Stevens conception of *mental models* (see Chapters 7 and 12 for further discussion). The Gentner and Stevens mental models are characterised typically in propositional terms (even though they may be accompanied by mental imagery) and as such are not a special representational format but rather a theoretical construct concerned with the way in which propositional knowledge is organised. So, like most research on problem solving, mental models assume that propositional representations are of primary importance.

Mental Models of Home Heating

Kempton's (1986) work is an example of the use of mental models that brings the idea home to us. Kempton proposed that when people regulated their thermostats to heat their houses they were usually using one of two models of how a heating system works: a "feedback model" or a "valve model."

The *feedback model* proposes that the thermostat turns the furnace on and off according to room temperature. So, when the room is too cold, the thermostat turns the furnace on and when the room is warm enough, it turns the furnace off. The temperature at which the furnace is turned on is determined by the setting on the dial on the wall. This model posits that the furnace runs at a constant rate and so the only way that the thermostat can control the amount of heat in a room is by the length of time that the furnace is on. If the dial is adjusted upward only a little bit, the furnace will run a short time and turn off; if it is adjusted upward a large amount, the furnace must run longer to bring the house to that temperature. Left at one setting the thermostat will switch the furnace off and on as necessary to maintain the temperature on the dial setting.

The valve model sees the thermostat as controlling the rate at which the furnace generates heat, rather than having a feedback function. That is, the furnace runs at variable rates depending on the setting on the dial. So, to maintain a constant temperature in a house or a room the setting is adjusted so that the amount of heat coming in balances the amount being lost. In this model, the thermostat has no specific role as a regulator of heat; indeed, in one sense, it is the person adjusting the thermostat that acts as the regulator. Several other common physical devices operate in a similar manner and may, in some cases, be the analogical basis for the valve model as it is applied to heating. For example, the more you turn the tap on, the more water comes out.

Both of these models make different predictions about how heating systems work and about how energy can be saved in the home. However, even though they are elaborate and intriguing, neither of them is technically accurate. For example, the valve model predicts that more fuel is consumed at higher settings than at lower settings. This prediction is correct but for the wrong reasons; the higher fuel consumption is not the result of the valve opening wider but is due to higher internal temperatures in the house resulting in greater heat loss through walls, windows, and ceilings. Hence, people using the valve model tend to readjust their thermostats more frequently and be more efficient energy users. In contrast, the feedback model can, under certain circumstances lead to fuel wastage. People with the feedback model tend to leave their thermostat settings at a set, often high, level for long periods of time; they assume that the thermostat will turn the heating off when the required temperature is reached. This often leads to heating being left on more than is necessary. In an ecologically conscious world, the importance of these findings are enormous. Kempton estimates that if people had an appropriate and accurate model of home heating then the saving for all U.S. households in a single year could be in the region of $5 billion.

The home heating example illustrates nicely some of the properties of mental models. First, it should be clear how they are predictive, in that they suggest different ways in which physical mechanisms operate. Second, they can be run in a way that is easy to imagine; for example, someone with the valve model could easily imagine a signal going from the dial on the wall to the furnace valve, opening it wider and wider and stoking the flames of the boiler. Third, people may have multiple models to deal with different aspects of the same system; Kempton identified two different models but admitted that many people may have a mixture of both. Burstein (1986) has cited similar evidence of the use of multiple models in the learning of the BASIC programming language. Fourth, it follows from much of the foregoing that mental models are often inherently unscientific, in the sense that they are not tested carefully and vetted by their users. Finally, the use of multiple models is only one way in which mental model analyses of behaviour become more complex. Models can undergo sudden changes depending on the knowledge used to construct them and an individual's conception of the task situation. We must also entertain the possibility that they include *ad hoc* rationalisations to account for actions that have been taken.

Naive Models of Motion
Similar evidence for the use of such models has been found in studies of people's naive theories of the motion of objects (see

Caramazza, McCloskey, & Green, 1981; McCloskey, 1983). These models are fairly consistent across individuals and can be applied in many different situations; however, they are strikingly inconsistent with the fundamental principles of classical physics (interestingly enough, they parallel early pre-Newtonian physics). McCloskey and his colleagues examined these naive theories or mental models by looking at subjects' answers to problems like the following one (see Fig. 11.7):

The correct response (a) and incorrect responses (b–d) for the airplane problem (reproduced with the permission of Michael McCloskey from Mental models, *edited by D. Gentner & A. Stevens, © 1983 by Lawrence Erlbaum Associates, Inc.)*

In the diagram, an airplane is flying along at a constant speed. The plane is also flying at a constant altitude, so that the flight path is parallel to the ground. The arrow shows the direction in which the plane is flying. When the plane is in the position shown in the diagram a large metal ball is dropped from the plane. The plane continues flying at the same speed in the same direction and at the same altitude. Draw the path the ball will follow from the time it is dropped until it hits the ground. Ignore wind or air resistance. Also show as well as you can the position of the plane at the moment that the ball hits the ground.

FIGURE 11.7

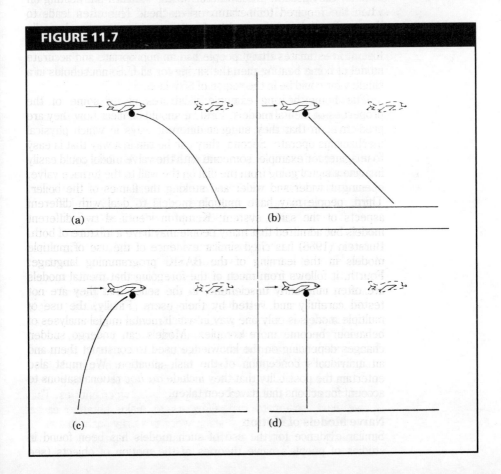

Only one of the diagrams in Fig. 11.7 is correct (the first). That is, when the ball is dropped it will ascribe a parabolic arc and the airplane will be above the ball when it hits the ground. Physics explains this by characterising the total velocity of the ball as consisting of two independent velocities: a horizontal and a vertical velocity. Before the ball is dropped, it has a horizontal velocity equal to that of the plane and a vertical velocity of zero. After the ball is released, it undergoes a constant vertical acceleration due to gravity, and thus acquires a constantly increasing vertical velocity. The ball's horizontal velocity, however, does not change. That is, it continues to move horizontally at the same speed as the plane. It is the combination of the constant horizontal velocity and the continually increasing vertical velocity that produces a parabolic arc. Finally, it should be clear that because the horizontal velocity of the ball and plane are equal the former hits the ground directly beneath the latter.

However, few subjects think about the problem in this way. Only 40% of subjects drew diagrams with parabolic arcs and not all of these place the plane above the ball as the ball hits the ground. The remaining 60% produced the other variants shown in Fig. 11.7. McCloskey (1983) characterises these responses as being the result of a simple model of motion which he calls impetus theory. In deference to classical physics, *impetus theory* proposes that: (1) the act of setting an object in motion imparts to the object an internal force or "impetus" that serves to maintain the motion; (2) a moving object's impetus gradually dissipates. It is this sort of mental model that is useful in predicting the motions of objects, in a gross fashion, in everyday life. However, it is not true and leads to anomalous predictions in many contexts.

Theoretical Issues Surrounding Mental Models as Schemata

Theoretically, there has been much confusion about the exact nature of mental models (see Brewer, 1987; Johnson-Laird, in press; Norman, 1983; Rips, 1986) and how they differ from other propositional representations like *schemata* (see Chapter 8 for a review). Brewer (1987) provides one of the clearer "clarifications" of the latter issue. We have seen that schemata (i.e. abstract knowledge structures about a specific domain) can in specific situations become *instantiated*. For example, one's general script for restaurants can be instantiated in one way in MacDonalds but in a different way when dining at the Ritz. Brewer maintains that both of these conceptions, schemata and instantiated schemata, are distinct from mental models. He points out that there are novel situations for which we have no domain-specific schemata, but are still comprehensible because we have schemata about the general spatial, causal, and intentional contingencies between entities. That is, we have schemata that allow us to make putative causal connections between things which were not previously known to be causally connected. In these cases, we construct specific knowledge representations called mental models (which are, if you like, instantiations of these very general schemata). It could also be argued that we often find analogy implicated in the construction of mental models because it is another source of such causal or spatial patterns.

Summary
Beyond the research on novice–expert differences, several other strands of problem-solving research have examined more ill-defined problems that involve varying amounts of prior knowledge. Research on analogical problem solving has looked at the conditions under which people recall and draw analogies in several different domains. Other attempts to re-interpret early Gestalt research have hinged on specifying how problem-specific knowledge is brought to bear in problem solving. Finally, mental models research has shown that people's understanding of complex mechanisms and physical phenomena can be characterised as incomplete, explanatory theories that are used to generate predictions and explanations in different situations.

EVALUATIONS OF PROBLEM-SOLVING RESEARCH

Problem-solving research is one of the most important testbeds for the cognitive science approach. We have seen that the area is marked by traditional empirical testing combined with the construction of computational models. It is, therefore, important to assess the success of the approach and to account for what has been learned. This evaluation is organised around four major questions. First, we consider the state of the productive versus reproductive thinking controversy. Second, we assess the ecological validity of research and the completeness of its coverage. Then we deal with the centrality of knowledge in problem solving. Finally, we consider some theoretical issues surrounding problem space theory.

Is Problem Solving Productive or Reproductive?
We began this chapter with a consideration of the Gestalt claim that human problem solving was dynamic and productive rather than passive and reproductive. In one sense, this question has never disappeared. The initial work of Newell and Simon (1972) can be viewed as a search for a set of general, problem-solving strategies that people use in the absence of specific knowledge about a problem. In the studies of chess expertise, we encountered the contrast between productive, evaluative knowledge and a repro-ductive memory for board patterns. The results of the research we have reviewed suggests that human problem solving is both productive *and* reproductive. However, we think that a new sense of the term "reproductive" has emerged that resists the "mere" prefix.

First, even though universal, weak methods (like means-end analysis) are interesting and productive, the core of human problem solving seems to rely on the use of specific heuristic knowledge about particular situations. Even though this is strictly speaking "reproduced knowledge," it is not "mere reproduced knowledge" because of the amazing variety of this knowledge, the complexity of the mechanisms used to acquire it, and the flexibility of the ways in which it is used (see, e.g., Anderson's account of skill acquisition). Second, various psychological processes, like analogy, introduce an extra twist to the use of prior experience. They show that past experience is not necessarily applied in a humdrum and reproductive fashion. Rather we have the ability to change and mould our prior experience selectively, in purely conceptual ways, in order to make it applicable in new and unexpected situations.

Is Problem-solving Research Ecologically Valid?

Earlier we encountered the criticism that problem-solving research was not ecologically valid because it only considered well-defined, puzzle-like problems. This is certainly true to some extent, but in the late 1970s and 1980s several attempts have been made to redress this imbalance.

We have seen that the expert–novice work widens the scope of the research in a way that is likely to be important to the improvement of teaching methods and the design of better computer programming languages. Other expert–novice research we have not reviewed is also applied to everyday tasks in specialist domains. For example, Lesgold and his associates (Lesgold, Rubinson, Feltovich, Glaser, Klopfer, & Wang, 1988; see also Lesgold, 1988) have examined expertise in the reading of X-rays among radiologists and Glaser, Lesgold, and Lejoie (in press) have studied expertise in electronics technicians. This work has taken cognitive psychology out into the world and, indeed, has led some to argue that the everyday world is the most important context in which to test cognitive theories (see Anderson, 1987b). Furthermore, mental models research has also been directed at everyday contexts, as we saw in the home heating example.

There are, however, two caveats that we must bear in mind when making such an assessment. First, we must be aware that the domains in which problem-solving research have been carried out are only a small sample of the total set of domains in which people solve problems. Much more work needs to be done on other domains. Second, the sample of domains is somewhat biased. Ohlsson (1983) has pointed out that most problem-solving research has concentrated on what he calls *technical knowledge domains* (e.g. physics, chess) rather than *natural knowledge domains* (e.g. the mundane mutations of everyday life). Technical knowledge domains may have a peculiar character that is quite distinct from natural knowledge domains.

Is Knowledge the Key?

It should be clear by now that the lynch-pin of our current understanding of problem solving rests on a consideration of the *role of knowledge*. Throughout this chapter we have seen that the essential task carried out by researchers has been to capture the different types of knowledge required by people to solve problems. Indeed, if we abstract away from this research it is clear that problem-solving methods can be classified in terms of the amount and specificity of their domain knowledge (see Carbonell, 1986, and Fig. 11.8).

- In knowledge-poor situations where we have little useful past experience, the only useful methods we can use are universal, weak methods (e.g. means-end analysis).
- A problem may be relatively familiar but we may lack specific plans to solve it, in which case general plans may be applied; these plans will break the problem down into sub-problems, in a divide-and-conquer fashion, even though these sub-problems will not suggest immediate solutions.
- With more familiar problems we may have various specific plans or schemata about how to solve them (e.g. the expert physicist); here, we can instantiate such plans and solve any sub-problems that arise with other instantiated schemata.
- Finally, if problem solvers have no specific or general plans, they may choose a specific past experience (e.g. a specific previously encountered problem) and apply it by analogy to solve the problem they face.

Problem solving may involve the following: (a) instantiating specific plans, (b) using analogical transformation to a known solution of a similar problem, (c) applying general plans to reduce the problem, (d) applying weak methods to search heuristically for a possible solution, or (e) using a combination of these approaches (reprinted with the permission of Jamie G. Carbonell from Machine learning: An artificial intelligence approach, Vol 2, *edited by Michalski, Carbonell, & Mitchell, © by Morgan Kaufmann, Publishers, San Mateo, Calif., 1986.*

These four situations lay out the main ways in which researchers have proposed that different types of knowledge are used. Clearly, we would not want to maintain that the application of these approaches is mutually exclusive; people may use a combination of all four at different points in solving a particular problem. The key

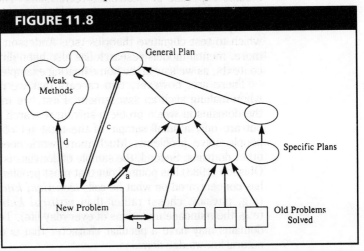

FIGURE 11.8

General Plan

Weak Methods

Specific Plans

New Problem

Old Problems Solved

point, however, is that different methods of problem solving can be distinguished by the amount and types of knowledge they use.

Are Problem-solving Theories Too Powerful?

It may seem ironic to say that a theory is too powerful, that it can account for too much, but it can be a real flaw in cognitive science theories. Many of the methods and formalisms developed in artificial intelligence can be used to carry out any task that can be specified symbolically. They can be applied to almost any domain. However, when we import these ideas into cognitive psychology and use them as central parts of our theories, it is necessary to constrain them. A psychological account must generate predictions that are testable and, more importantly, falsifiable. If a theory can model any task, even tasks that people clearly cannot do, then it can account for any piece of evidence found (albeit often in an ad hoc fashion).

In particular, this concern can be voiced about theories that rely heavily on production systems. IF–THEN rules and production system models are very powerful techniques for characterising cognitive processes. If they are applied loosely one can always make up a set of productions that will carry out a certain cognitive task (even though this may require considerable ingenuity). In recent years, to avoid this criticism, researchers have tried to constrain such ideas using the notion of a cognitive architecture (see Anderson, 1983; Newell, 1989; Chapters 1 and 14).

Cognitive architectures are attempts at unified theories; that is, theories that will naturally make predictions about many diverse aspects of cognition (from language to problem solving and even perception). While many of the current architectures are some way off this goal, and some think it a questionable enterprise (see Gardner, 1985; Holyoak, 1983), the general direction does place further constraints on problem-solving theories. So much so, that it is no longer sufficient to say that such-and-such a set of rules are used in solving certain problems, without being explicit about the whole cognitive system that makes solving that problem possible. For example, one must specify the nature of working memory, long-term memory, and the way in which knowledge is organised; the basic learning mechanism for skill and knowledge acquisition and the specific knowledge employed in various situations.

The antidote to this state of affairs, some would maintain, is the use of connectionist models, which learn their "knowledge" from training rather than from some explicit formulation on the part of the theorist. This looks attractive from a distance, but these theorists make many assumptions about the nature of input and output units and the structure of a network that suggest that even this is not a solution to all known ills. Furthermore, as we have seen in Anderson's work and Newell's SOAR architecture (in press; Laird et al., 1987; Rosenbloom & Newell, 1986) that adaptive production systems models can also learn too.

FURTHER READING

Chi, M.T.H., Glaser, R., & Farr, M. (Eds.) (1988). *The nature of expertise*. Hillsdale, N.J.: Lawrence Erlbaum Associates Inc. This book provides a recent collection of research on expert–novice differences.

Gentner, D. & Stevens, A. (Eds.) (1983). *Mental models*. Hillsdale, N.J.: Lawrence Erlbaum Associates Inc. This book has a good selection of papers on mental models research.

Gilhooly, K.J. (1988) *Thinking: Directed, undirected, and creative* (2nd Ed.). London: Academic Press. This provides more detail on some of the research covered here and explores other areas too.

Gilhooly, K.J., Keane, M.T.G., Logie, R., & Erdos, G. (Eds.) (1990a; 1990b). *Lines of thinking: Reflections on the psychology of thought. Vols. 1 & 2*. Chichester: John Wiley. These two volumes provide an up-to-date review of many areas of thinking research and contain chapters by leading researchers in the field.

Keane, M.T. (1988). *Analogical problem solving*. Chichester: Ellis Horwood (New York: Wiley). This book reviews research on analogy and outlines experiments on the various stages of analogical thinking.

Newell, A. & Simon, H.A. (1972). *Human problem solving*. Englewood Cliffs, N.J.: Prentice-Hall. This is not an easy book to read but it is *the* presentation of problem space theory.

Newell, A. (1989). *Unified theories of cognition*. Harvard: Harvard University Press. This book considers the nature of a unified theory of cognition and shows how SOAR attempts to deal with this challenge.

Soloway, E. & Spohrer, J. (Eds.) (1989). *Studying the novice programmer*. Hillsdale, N.J.: Lawrence Erlbaum Associates Inc. This work contains a collection of the major articles on the subject of programming expertise.

Sternberg, R.J. & Smith, E.E. (Eds.) (1988). *The psychology of thinking*. Cambridge: Cambridge University Press. This book is an interesting collection of chapters on different aspects of thinking, some of which are not considered here.

Chapter Twelve

REASONING AND DECISION MAKING

his chapter covers the two other main areas of research, aside from problem solving, that have emerged on the topic of thinking, namely, reasoning and decision making. Reasoning and decision making are central intellectual abilities in our cognitive repertoire. As Johnson-Laird & Byrne (1990) point out, deductive reasoning is necessary:

> in order to formulate plans; to evaluate alternative actions; to determine the consequences of assumptions and hypotheses; to interpret and formulate instructions, rules and general principles; to pursue arguments and negotiations; to weigh evidence and to assess data; to decide between competing theories; and to solve problems. A world without deduction would be a world without science, technology, laws, social conventions and culture.

Similarly, in everyday life we often have to decide between several alternative courses of action. Some decisions are easy (e.g. whether to have the cheesecake or the ice cream for dessert), but others are more difficult; for example, deciding between taking up a job or continuing at university. In the latter case, there is uncertainty about what will follow from one course of action (e.g. will staying at university be likely to lead to a better job?). Thus, an important part of decision making consists of determining the probability of certain outcomes and assessing alternatives relative to one another. These are issues we will return to later in the chapter.

INTRODUCTION

The major division in this chapter is between research on reasoning and research on decision making. This division has more to do with the research groupings of cognitive psychologists than fundamental differences in the mechanisms responsible for both types of behaviour. Later, we will discuss some of the connecting threads that can be drawn between the two areas.

Deductive reasoning research makes central use of logical systems—especially the propositional calculus—to characterise the abstract structure of reasoning problems. Hence, initially, we will consider the logic of deduction in some detail before considering psychological research. Any student who does not know something about logic already will find this treatment difficult because it *is* difficult. However, a little extra effort on this section will pay enormous dividends when we come to consider psychological research on reasoning.

The treatment here of the psychology of reasoning is organised around the three main theoretical perspectives in the area: abstract-rule theories, concrete-rule theories, and model theories. Many of these theories have been proposed to explain particular sorts of reasoning. For example, abstract-rule theories have, on the whole, been applied to propositional reasoning (i.e. reasoning involving the use of *and, or, not, if . . . then*). Thus, each theoretical perspective is presented along with evidence from those tasks with which it has mainly been concerned. We will also indicate, however, whether they can deal with other phenomena. Finally, we will attempt to gather these sections together in a general section that evaluates the corpus of reasoning research.

In decision making research we will consider some of the major findings and evaluate this approach. Before the curtain closes on this chapter, we will broach the vexed question of how we are to relate all of these diverse thinking phenomena together; how problem solving, reasoning, and decision making might be gathered together under the common umbrella term of "thinking."

Deduction and Induction

The division between deductive and inductive reasoning, made in philosophy and logic, has been carried over into psychology. When people carry out deductive reasoning they usually determine what conclusion, if any, *necessarily* follows when certain statements or premises are assumed to be true. In inductive reasoning, people make a generalised conclusion from premises that describe particular instances (see examples in Chapter 1).

The distinction between deduction and induction can be more formally specified using the notion of *semantic information* (Johnson-Laird, Note 5). A proposition is said to be high in semantic information the more possible situations it eliminates from consideration (see Bar-Hillel & Carnap, 1964; Johnson-Laird, 1983; Chapter 2). For example, the assertion "It is freezing but there is no fog" excludes more situations than "It is freezing," because the former rules out all those freezing situations in which fog is present, whereas the latter leaves the possibility open. When a deductive inference is made there will be no increase in semantic information. However, an inductive inference will, more often than not, lead to an increase in semantic information.

Even though the deductive–inductive distinction is often used to organise and draw distinctions between reasoning tasks, we shall not stick steadfastly to it here because some tasks involve a mixture of both. Furthermore, at the end of the day, an adequate theory of reasoning should account for both types in a unified fashion.

The Use of Logic in Reasoning Research

Newell and Simon's problem space theory uses the notion of an idealised problem space to characterise the abstract structure of a problem, quite independently of any psychological proposals (see Chapter 11). In reasoning research, some logics—usually the propositional calculus —have been used in a similar manner. That is, they are used to characterise the abstract structure of reasoning problems and to determine categories of responses (i.e. incorrect and correct answers). So this sub-section *must* be understood if one is to make sense of large portions of reasoning research.

In mathematical systems we use symbols to stand for things (e.g. let *h1* be the height of the Empire State building and *h2* be the height of Nelson's Column) and then apply mathematical operators to these symbols to manipulate them in various ways (the combined height of both buildings should be *h1 plus h2*, where *plus* is the operator used). In an analogous way, logical systems use symbols to stand for sentences and apply logical operators to them to reach conclusions. So, in the propositional calculus, we might use P to stand for the verbally expressible proposition "it is raining" and Q to stand for "Mary gets wet," and then use the logical operator *if . . . then* to relate these two propositions: *if P then Q*. Perhaps the most difficult idea to keep in mind about logic is that even though logical operators use the same words as we use in every day life (like *or, and, if . . . then*) in logic these terms have very different meanings. The logical meaning of the conditional (i.e. *if . . . then*) is well specified and differs markedly from everyday conceptions of the words "If . . . then." In the next sub-section, we attempt to explain how logicians specify the semantics of these operators.

Truth Tables and the "Meaning" of Logical Operators

The propositional calculus has a small number of logical operators: *not, and, or, if . . . then, if and only if*. In the logics with which we are concerned, propositions can only have one of two truth-values; that is, they are either true or false. For instance, if P stands for "it is raining," then P is either true (in which case it is raining) or P is false (it is not raining). The calculus does not admit any intervening uncertainty (where it is not really raining but is so misty you could almost call it raining).

Logicians use a system of *truth tables* to lay out the possibilities for a proposition (i.e. whether it is true or false) and to specify the effects of a logical operator on that proposition. For example, a single proposition P can be either true or false. In truth tables, this is notated by putting P as a heading and showing the two values of it, as follows:

$$P$$
$$T$$
$$F$$

If we want to indicate the effects of *not* on P, then we get the following truth table:

P	$not\ P$
T	F
F	T

This new column shows the effects of *not* on P, when P is true or false. So, when P is true the result of negating P will make that proposition false and when P is false it will make P true. This truth table defines the "meaning" of *not*.

TABLE 12.1

Truth Tables for the Conditional and the Biconditional

		Conditional	Biconditional
P	Q	If P then Q	if and only if P then Q
T	T	T	T
T	F	F	F
F	T	T	F
F	F	T	T

Consider the more complicated case of the conditional, which unlike negation involves two propositions (P, Q): *if P then Q*. On their own P and Q can each be true or false, but when they are combined there are four possible states of affairs (see Table 12.1): both P and Q can be true, P can be true when Q is false and vice versa, and both can be false.

Now consider what happens when *if . . . then* is applied to these propositions. First, where P and Q are true then clearly *if P then Q* is true. For example, the assertion "If it is raining, Ronan gets wet" is true when we know that it is the case that "it is raining" and "Ronan is wet." Second, if we are told "If it is raining, Ronan gets wet" and it is raining (P is true) but Ronan is not wet (Q is false), then clearly the assertion is false.

The next two cases are somewhat trickier. Assume we are told "If it is raining, Ronan gets wet" and it turns out that it is not raining (P is false) and Ronan still gets wet (Q is true), then, psychologically, one may feel uncertain whether the assertion is true or false. However, *if P then Q* is still true logically because something else may have made Ronan wet—someone may have thrown a bucket of water over him. Hence, *if P then Q* is considered by logicians to be true when *P* is false and *Q* is true. Finally, when *P* and *Q* are false—when "it is not raining" and "Ronan does not get wet"—the assertion is also true. So, when *P* is false and *Q* is false, *if P then Q* is considered to be true.

Logicians distinguish this treatment of *if . . . then* (called material implication in logic) from *if and only if*, the *biconditional* (or in logic *material equivalence*). The biconditional (notated as ⟷) has a similar truth table to the conditional except for the *P* is false and *Q* is true case; it characterises this case as making the assertion false. The reason for this is that the biconditional rules out other states of affairs (like the bucket of water); that is, P ⟷ Q is read as "if and only if *P* is true, then *Q* is true."

As we shall see later, it is often the case that people do not conform to the logical interpretation of the conditional in their reasoning. However, the importance of the logical analysis is that reasoning problems in natural language can be re-stated and classified using the propositional calculus and it gives us a criterion for determining whether a certain conclusion is valid or invalid, correct or in error.

Valid and Invalid Inferences

Initially, we talked about propositions being manipulated in some way by logical operators. Typically, a number of propositions related together by a given logical operator (e.g. *If P or R then Q*) is called a premise. There are a variety of rules of inference specified by logic that can be used to evaluate and draw logically valid conclusions from these premises. Consider some inference rules used on premises involving the conditional *if . . . then*. Depending on the premises one is given there are two valid inferences that can be made involving conditionals: *modus ponens* and *modus tollens*. An argument of the modus ponens form is as follows (it may help to write the truth table in Table 12.1 on a separate piece of paper, in order to follow the following discussion):

Valid: Modus Ponens

Premises

If it is raining, then Ronan gets wet	*If P then Q,*
It is raining.	*P,*

Conclusion

Therefore, Ronan gets wet.	*Therefore, Q*

So, if one is given the conditional about it raining and Ronan getting wet, and then is told that it is raining, one can validly conclude that "Ronan gets wet." This conclusion can be understood with respect to the truth table shown because there is only one line in the truth table where *P* is true and *if P then Q* is true, and this is the one where *Q* is true too (see Table 12.1).

It is important to remember that *logical validity* is purely formal and is not affected by whether propositions are really true (i.e. in the world). So, even premises and conclusions we know to be patently ridiculous can be logically valid:

Valid: Modus Ponens

Premises
If she is a woman, then she is   *If P then Q,*
Aristotle

She is a woman.   *P,*

Conclusion
Therefore, she is Aristotle.   *Therefore, Q*

The modus ponens form is very obvious and many people find it easy to accept when the content is sensible. The other valid inference that can be made from a conditional, known as *modus tollens*, is not as intuitively obvious. This rule states that, if we are given the proposition *If P then Q* and the fact that *Q* is false, then we can infer that *P* is false. Thus, the following argument is valid:

Valid: Modus Tollens

Premises
If it is raining, then Ronan gets   *If P then Q,*
wet

Ronan is not wet.   *not Q*

Conclusion
Therefore, it is not raining.   *Therefore, not P*

Again, this argument is consistent with the truth table (in Table 12.1). The line where *If P then Q* is true and *Q* is false, is that one in which *P* is false.

Modus ponens and modus tollens are the two valid inferences one can draw from simple conditional arguments. There are two other possible inferences that can be drawn but they are invalid (even though people often think them plausible). They are called the "affirmation of the consequent" and the "denial of the antecedent."

In the *affirmation of the consequent* one is told that *if P then Q* is true and *Q* is true, for instance:

Invalid: Affirmation of the Consequent

Premises

If it is raining, then Ronan gets wet	*If P then Q,*
Ronan is wet.	*Q,*

Conclusion

Therefore, it is raining.	*Therefore, P*

One can see where this form gets its name, because the consequent of the conditional premise (i.e. *Q*) has been affirmed. But why is it considered invalid? Well, if the truth table is examined for lines where *If P then Q* is true and *Q* is true, one can see that there are two lines that meet this description. On one of these lines, *P* is true and on the other *P* is false. This means that the most we can conclude is that "no conclusion can be made." So, a conclusion that asserts that *P* is true is considered invalid.

A similar explanation can be made for the other invalid form, the *denial of the antecedent*; for example:

Invalid: Denial of the Antecedent

Premises

If it is raining, then Ronan gets wet	*If P then Q,*
It is not raining.	*not P,*

Conclusion

Therefore, Ronan does not get wet.	*Therefore, not Q*

TABLE 12.2

Valid and Invalid Inferences for the Conditional

Valid	*Modus Ponens*	If P then Q, Q, Therefore, P
	Modus Tollens	If P then Q not-Q Therefore, not-P
Invalid	*Affirmation of Consequent*	If P then Q, Q, Therefore, P
	Denial of the Antecedent	If P then Q, not-P Therefore, not-Q

Here one has denied the antecedent of the conditional (i.e. the *P*). There are two lines in the truth table where *If P then Q* is true and *P* is false. In one of these *Q* is false and in the other *Q* is true. Therefore, again, no firm conclusion can be made. So, to conclude that *not-Q* is the case is invalid (all of these forms are summarised in Table 12.2). If you think that these two invalid forms yield plausible conclusions, you are not alone.

People frequently make the valid modus ponens inference but considerably fewer subjects make the valid modus tollens inference. Furthermore, well over 50% of subjects regularly make the fallacious denial of the antecedent and affirmation of the consequent inferences (see Evans, 1982; Chapter 8). As we will see, this evidence must be accounted for by any adequate theory of deductive reasoning.

ABSTRACT-RULE THEORIES OF PROPOSITIONAL REASONING

Setting the Agenda

Deductive reasoning is one of the oldest research areas in psychology. The agenda was, therefore, set some time ago and the question at the top of the list is: Are human beings rational? A long philosophical tradition has answered this question with a resounding "yes" and has supported this answer with the argument that the laws of logic are the laws of thought (Boole, 1854; Mill, 1843). This basic idea from philosophy has found its way, albeit in increasingly sophisticated forms, into psychology. The most immediate problem for this view is the evidence which shows that people do not always make valid inferences; that they do not always behave in accordance with the laws of logic. However, several convincing arguments have been made to account for these deviations.

Mary Henle (1962) has argued that people make invalid inferences because they misunderstand or misrepresent the reasoning task; after this initial misunderstanding the reasoning itself is logical. More recently, this basic position has been elaborated in several psychological theories and modelled computationally (see, e.g., Braine, 1978; Johnson-Laird, 1975; Osherson, 1975; Rips, 1983). Here, we will call these theories *abstract-rule theories*, because they propose that humans reason using a set of very abstract, logic-like rules that can be applied to any domain of knowledge (e.g. rules like modus ponens). Abstract rule theories are also called *syntactic theories*; because their rules are so general, they do not take the content of the premises into account but merely manipulate these contents in a syntactic fashion. These abstract-rule theories, which effectively constitute a *mental logic*, have been applied most successfully to propositional reasoning (e.g. Braine, 1978; Rips, 1983). Propositional reasoning is a very important and central form of human reasoning; it involves reasoning about hypothetical states of affairs, taking into account the conjunction or disjunction of multiple events. In short, it is central to the sorts of planning we carry out in everyday life. As an illustrative example of these theories we will deal with Martin Braine's natural deduction theory.

Braine's Natural Deduction Theory

Braine's (1978) theory maintains that deductive reasoning is mediated by basic, abstract rules or schemata (see Chapter 8). The premises of an argument are comprehended and encoded into abstract schemata/rules from which inferences can be drawn. In summary, the theory is as follows (Braine, 1978; Braine & Rumain, 1983; Braine, Reiser, & Rumain, 1984; Rumain, Connell, & Braine, 1984):

- natural language premises are encoded by a comprehension mechanism and the resulting representation is related to abstract, reasoning schemata;
- these schemata are considered to be elementary and are used to draw valid conclusions (e.g. a modus ponens rule);
- there are strategies that co-ordinate a chain of inferences, selecting the schema that is to be applied at each point in the reasoning process;
- if this reasoning process does not deliver a straightforward conclusion then a set of nonlogical or quasi-logical rules determine the response made (see, e.g. evidence of biases in later sections);
- if a subject draws invalid conclusions or makes errors they may be of three types: comprehension errors, heuristic inadequacy errors, or processing errors;
- *comprehension errors* occur when the premises or conclusion are misconstrued in some fashion
- *heuristic inadequacy errors* occur when the conclusion to a reasoning problem fails to be reached because the strategies for co-ordinating numerous sets of reasoning schemata are inadequate; stated simply, the problem is too difficult;
- *processing errors* may result from lapses of attention, a failure to hold relevant information in working memory and slips in the application of schemata.

Making the Valid Inferences with Abstract Rules

The general picture that Braine's theory gives us of humans is that they are natural logicians who are slightly fallible at the edges. People have a set of abstract, logic-like schemata that they apply to solve deductive reasoning problems and would always reason validly except for extraneous influences; influences from the comprehension of premises or the inherent limitations of working memory. Consider the theory's account of how a conclusion is drawn for the following premises:

If I get hungry, then I will go for a walk,	*If P then Q*
If I go for a walk, I will feel much better,	*If Q then R*
I am hungry	*P*

Most abstract-rule theories, including Braine's, have a reasoning schema that corresponds to the modus ponens rule; theorists assume that since people find this inference so easy, there must be an appropriate mental rule to deal with it. A conclusion to this argument can be derived by the repeated application of this modus ponens rule. First, the rule is applied to the first premise (If I get hungry then I will go for a walk) and third premise (I am hungry) to produce the intermediate conclusion of "I will go for a walk"; then the rule is applied again to the second premise "If I go for a walk, I will feel much better" and the intermediate conclusion "I will go for a walk" to produce the final conclusion "I will feel much better" (see Byrne, 1989a, for explicit tests of these chains of inferences). So, various rules are applied to a set of premises until a conclusion is derived.

The existence of a modus ponens rule accounts nicely for why people find this argument so easy, but why do they find the other valid form, modus tollens, so hard? In natural deduction theory, modus tollens is a harder inference to make because no single schema can be applied to it. Rather, several different rules have to be applied in order to reach a conclusion. In general, the longer the derivation needed to reach a conclusion the more likely that errors will occur or no conclusion will be reached (due to factors like increasing memory load and heuristic inadequacy).

Accounting for Invalid Inferences with Abstract Rules

The rules of natural deduction theories typically correspond to the valid inferences, so when people make errors or fallacious inferences, like the invalid denial of the antecedent and affirmation of the consequent inferences, they are seen as being due largely to comprehension errors. Specifically, they are seen as being the result of certain conversational assumptions that people make in everyday life. These assumptions result in a re-interpretation of the premises in a manner that changes their cognitive representation. The system still applies its logically valid rules but as the input to the rules is erroneous, the output is often erroneous too.

Consider the detailed explanation for why people make the fallacious denial of the antecedent inference:

Invalid: Denial of the Antecedent

Premises

If it is raining, then Ronan gets wet	*If P then Q,*
It is not raining.	*not P,*

Conclusion

Therefore, Ronan does not get wet.	*Therefore, not Q*

Rumain et al. (1984) maintained that the conditional premise of this argument, *If P then Q*, was re-interpreted as *If not-P then not-Q*. As Geis and Zwicky (1971) have pointed out, the statement "if you mow the lawn I will give you five dollars" invites the inference "If you don't mow the lawn, I won't give you five dollars." If one starts with this as the conditional premise then by the application of the modus ponens rule one reaches the conclusion *not-Q*; for example:

Premises

If it is not raining, then Ronan does not get wet	*If not P then not Q,*
It is not raining.	*not P,*

Conclusion

Therefore, Ronan does not get wet.	*Therefore, not Q*

So, valid schemata are still being applied, but to re-interpreted premises. A similar explanation can be made for the affirmation of the consequent fallacy:

Invalid: Affirmation of the Consequent

Premises

If it is raining, then Ronan gets wet	*If P then Q,*
Ronan is wet.	*Q,*

Conclusion

Therefore, it is raining.	*Therefore, P*

This fallacy is made because subjects re-interpret the premises to accept the invited inference *if Q then P*. Thus, the premise "If it is raining, then she will get wet" is cast as "If she gets wet then it has been raining." Thus, the argument is assumed to be dealt with in the following form:

If it is raining, then Ronan gets   *If Q then P,*
wet

Ronan is wet.   *Q,*

Therefore, it is raining.   *Therefore, P*

P is made as the conclusion, by the application of the modus ponens rule again. This switch is said to occur because of Grice's (1975) *co-operative principle*. This principle maintains essentially that people tell each other exactly what they think each other needs to know. For example, if a speaker says "If it is raining, then she will get wet" the hearer will assume, in the context of the conversation, that rain is the only likely event that will lead to her getting wet. The hearer assumes that no other alternative *P*s will play a role. Thus, in terms of natural deduction theory, the invalid inference is made because during comprehension people make a reasonable assumption that modifies the premises. Having made this comprehension error, reasoning proceeds normally through the application of the various reasoning schemata.

In conclusion, the empirical point to be made is that the theory can account for the main results found in propositional reasoning research. Theoretically, the abstract-rule approach is attractive in the elegance and specificity of its rules. Typically, only a few abstract rules are proposed to account for all of reasoning behaviour; for instance, there are 16 rule schemata in a recent version of natural deduction theory (see Braine et al., 1984).

Other Evidence on Propositional Reasoning

There is considerable evidence from an extensive corpus of research for the proposals of natural deduction theory. For example, Braine et al. (1984) examined several predictions from the theory in a series of experiments. In one experiment, subjects were given a simple reasoning task about the presence or absence of letters on an imaginary blackboard (from Osherson, 1975). So, on being given a problem like:

If there is a T, there is an L,
There is a T
? There is an L ?

Subjects were asked to evaluate whether the provided conclusion was true. These problems were designed to be soluble in a single step by one of the 16 schemata proposed by the theory. The confirmed prediction was that reasoning on these problems should be essentially error-free (the materials were designed to rule out other sources of error). The results of reasoning on these problems were used to derive difficulty measures that were then used to predict behaviour on problems that involved short chains of reasoning (on the assumption that the difficulty measures for single rules would be additive in more complex tasks). A variety of measures were used to determine problem difficulty, including difficulty ratings, times taken to solve a problem, and the number of errors made. Braine et al. found high correlations between the difficulty measures of problems and the number of predicted inferences, from the repertoire of schemata, required to solve the problems.

Rips (1983) has used a slightly different set of schemata (see Johnson-Laird & Byrne, 1990; Chapter 2, for a summary of rules in the different theories) to make similar predictions. Rips' production system model, which is similar to Newell and Simon's models, has rules that break down the premises into simpler components and inference rules that are applied to these simpler components to produce conclusions. These simpler components constitute sub-goals that are matched against the abstract inference rules. This analysis also allows predictions to be made about what will be recalled from working memory after someone has read or carried out a reasoning sequence. This prediction is made by virtue of the assumption that embedded sub-goals will be less likely to be recalled than main goals or sub-goals (see Marcus, 1982).

Finally, several researchers have tested the proposal that fallacious inferences—like the denial of the antecedent and the affirmation of the consequent—are due to conversational assumptions made during comprehension (see, e.g., Rumain et al., 1983). For example, in the case of the affirmation of the consequent, the conversational assumption invites the inference *If Q then P* from *If P then Q*, that rules out any alternative antecedent states of affairs. This assumption can be undone by providing alternative antecedents to the conditional (Markovits, 1984; 1985; Rumain et al., 1983). For example, the following argument explicitly indicates *alternative antecedents* to the consequent:

If it is raining then she will get wet,	*If P then Q,*
If it is snowing then she will get wet,	*If R then Q,*
She got wet,	*Q,*
Therefore, ?	*Therefore, ?*

It is quite clear from this argument that people would be more likely to produce the correct answer (i.e. no conclusion can be made) than the fallacious *P* conclusion they usually make in the affirmation of the consequent. This is exactly what has been found in these studies; that is, subjects avoid making the fallacious inferences. In short, when the extraneous effects of comprehension processes are excluded the fallacies were suppressed and correct, valid reasoning is observed. Braine et al. (1983) took this as evidence that there could not be rules for invalid inferences of the denial of the antecedent and the affirmation of the consequent.

Evaluation of Abstract-rule Theories

The abstract-rule approach is very attractive in its promise to account for all of propositional reasoning behaviour with recourse to a limited set of reasoning rules. There are two main criticisms that can be made of these theories.

In the first place, abstract-rule theories achieve their elegance at the price of a considerable under-specification of the accompanying comprehension component. That is, the core reasoning system is well-specified and makes predictions about what inferences people should and should not make. However, when deviations from these predictions occur they often have to be accounted for with recourse to a comprehension component that is considerably less specified (or some other processing difficulty). In fact, Rips' (1983) theory has no specified comprehension component. As long as a comprehension component is under-specified the theory is incomplete. Rumain et al. (1983; Rumain & Braine, 1983) are an exception to this in that they have attempted to pin down the comprehension mechanisms that are responsible for the production of fallacious conclusions.

However, there is other evidence that undermines the rationale adopted by Braine et al. in these studies. Byrne (1989b) has found, using a similar paradigm to Rumain et al., that the provision of extra information can suppress the *valid* inferences as well as the invalid inferences. As we saw earlier, Braine and his colleagues had shown that the frequencies of invalid inferences were reduced when an alternative antecedent was given (i.e. If it is raining she gets wet, If it is snowing then she gets wet). Byrne replicated this effect but also showed that the provision of an additional antecedent had the effect of reducing the frequency of valid modus ponens and modus tollens inferences (see Table 12.3).

TABLE 12.3

Percentages of Inferences Made as a Function of the Type of Contextual Information Given (Byrne, 1989b)

	Modus Ponens	Modus Tollens	Denial of Antecedent	Affirmation of Consequent
Simple Arguments	96	92	46	71
Alternative Arguments	96	96	4	13
Additional Arguments	38	33	63	54

That is, when subjects were given the following sort of materials:

If she has an essay to write then she will study late in the library,	*If P then Q,*
If the library stays open then she will study late in the library,	*If R then Q,*
She has an essay to write	*P,*
Therefore, ?	*Therefore, ?*

which contained the additional requirement of the "library staying open," people did not typically make the modus ponens inference to conclude that "she will study late in the library" (i.e. *Q*). Rumain et al. had argued that since alternative antecedents reduced the frequency of invalid inferences there are no mental inference rules corresponding to these inferences. However, if we apply the same line of argument to Byrne's results, we would have to conclude that the results indicate that no mental inference rules exist for the valid inferences.

The final problem for abstract-rule theories is one of generality. Propositional reasoning is only one of many different reasoning tasks that people can perform (we will meet some others later). There is no single abstract-rule scheme that has been applied to all of these tasks. So it remains to be proven whether these or similar ideas can account, in a complete manner, for the many different forms of reasoning. This and other issues will be returned to later when we evaluate all three theories.

Summary

Abstract-rule theories assume that people have a set of rules, akin to those of the propositional calculus, that they apply to premises in order to make valid deductive inferences. When people make fallacious inferences that contradict this view, they are seen as being the result of misconstruals of the premises during comprehension or other processing difficulties (like working memory limitations). These theories have been applied mainly to propositional reasoning and have been tested extensively and shown to be in accordance with the data. However, experiments designed to support their proposals, that comprehension processes produce invalid inferences, have been shown to be inconclusive because similar effects can be shown for valid inferences. There is also some doubt about the generality of the view.

CONCRETE-RULE THEORIES OF WASON'S SELECTION TASK

Moving on to the second main theoretical approach to reasoning, this section is concerned mainly with a hypothetico-deductive reasoning task—called Wason's selection task—that has been studied extensively in reasoning research (see Wason, 1966; Evans, 1982; 1989; for reviews). One of the main findings that has emerged from studies of this task is that subjects' performance is affected if the task is presented with different sorts of materials: That is, whether the materials involve abstract or concrete content. Abstract-rule theories predict no performance differences, assuming extraneous factors are held constant (e.g. comprehension errors), between problems stated in abstract or concrete form. For example, the reasoning system should deal with "If there is an M then there is a P" using the same rules as it does for "If she stays up late then she will oversleep in the morning" (i.e. both are parsed in an *If P then Q* form).

So, the effects of concrete (or thematic or realistic) materials on the Wason selection task have led some theorists to conclude that people reason using concrete rules rather than abstract ones. That is, in a manner similar to the distinction we encountered in Chapter 11 on problem solving, the proposal is that people use domain-specific rules rather than general, domain-independent rules. After we have introduced the task and considered some of the different accounts that have been advanced to explain it, we will elaborate one of the concrete-rule views of it; namely, Cheng and Holyoak's pragmatic reasoning schema theory.

Examples of the abstract and concrete (postal) versions of Wason's selection task, with an indication of how the different cards/ envelopes are labelled for the classification of subjects' choices in experiments.

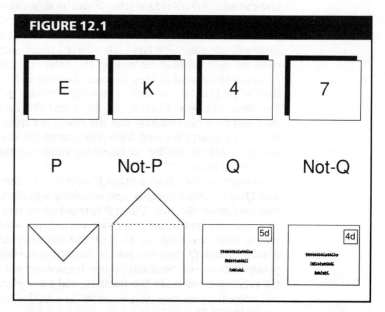

FIGURE 12.1

Wason's Selection Task
The Task
The selection task, first proposed by Wason (1966), looks like a fairly innocuous puzzle but hides a multitude of difficulties. In its original form subjects are shown four cards face down with letters or numbers on each of them (see Fig. 12.1). They are told that each of these cards has a letter on one side and a number on the other side and that their task is to name the cards that *need* to be turned over in order to test the following rule:

If there is a vowel on one side of a card, then there is an even number on the other side of the card

As one can choose to turn over any of the four cards, there are four possible choices one can make in this problem. But subjects are asked to turn over only those cards that need to be turned over. The correct answer is to turn over just two cards, the E-card and the 7-card. However, few subjects spontaneously pick these cards on this abstract version of the task. To understand why this is the correct answer, first consider why the 4-card and K-card choices are wrong (have the truth table for *if . . . then* handy).

In logical formalism, the rule in the selection task can be expressed by the conditional *if P then Q*; *P* here is the statement that "there is a vowel on one side of the card" and *Q* is "there is an even number on the other side of the card." This also means that each of the cards can be re-expressed as follows: the E-card is *P*, the K-card is *not-P*, the 4-card is *Q* and the 7-card is *not-Q* (see Fig. 12.1). It is not a good idea to pick the *Q* card (i.e. 4) because, as you can see from the truth table in Table 12.1, when *Q* is true and the rule *if P then Q* is true, *P* can be either true or false. This means that no matter what is on the other side of the 4-card (a vowel or a consonant) the rule will be true. Thus, turning over this card will tell you very little. Of course, many subjects who turn over the *Q* card may be making the fallacious affirmation of the consequent inference; they assume the rule *If P then Q* is true, they know *Q* to be true and so they can conclude that *P* must be on the other side (see Table 12.2). So, if *not-P* is on the other side, they feel they can conclude that the rule is not true. The same sort of reasoning may account for turning over the K-card, except in this case one is making an inference similar to the denial of the antecedent fallacy.

In contrast, the choices of the E-card (i.e. *P*) and the 7-card (i.e. *not-Q*) are correct because one is making logically valid inferences that may falsify the rule. When *P* is true and we turn over the card, then what we find on the other side will indicate whether the rule is true or false (see Table 12.1). If *Q* is on the other side then the rule is true, if *not-Q* then the rule is false (this is similar to a modus ponens inference). Similarly, if one turns over *not-Q* then a *P* on the other side will make the rule false and a *not-P* on the other side will make the rule true (this is similar to a modus tollens inference; see Table 12.1).

The difficulty of reasoning in this problem should be apparent. What is typically found in abstract versions of the task (i.e. ones involving vowels and consonants) is that very few subjects make the correct choices. In Johnson-Laird and Wason's (1970) study, only 5 subjects out of 128 chose the *P* and *not-Q* cards alone. The overwhelming majority of subjects chose either the *P* and *Q* cards (59 out of 128) or the *P* card alone (42 out of 128). However, as we shall see, variants of the task involving more concrete materials lead to very different behaviour.

Developing Explanations of the Task

Several attempts have been made to explain behaviour on this task (we will review only some of these accounts; see also Cosmides, 1989; Evans, 1989; Margolis, 1987). Initially, it was considered that subjects' behaviour was the result of an attempt to verify the rule rather than falsify it. That is, subjects turn over the *P*-card to see if there is a *Q* (i.e. an even number) on the other side and the *Q*-card to see if there is a *P* (i.e. a vowel) on the other side. If one wanted to falsify the rule the only choices that could make the rule false would be the *P*-card to see if there is *not-Q* on the other side (i.e. a consonant) and *not-Q* to see if there is *P* (i.e. a vowel) on the other side of it. Wason and Johnson-Laird (1972) favoured this explanation and argued that subjects' responses were a function of the extent to which they had insight into the need to falsify rather than verify the rule.

Another account proposed by Evans (1984; Evans & Lynch, 1973; Wason & Evans, 1975) sees subjects' behaviour as the result of a nonlogical matching bias. That is, subjects simply select those cards showing the symbols that are mentioned in the rule. So, when subjects are given another variant of the rule (i.e. "If there is a B on one side, there is not a 3 on the other side"), they choose the B and the 3 card because these are the ones referred to in the rule (corresponding to the *P* and *not-Q* cases); resulting in a high rate of correct answers. Evans (1983) found interesting evidence about the conditions affecting such biases in a conditional truth table task. Matching bias seems to be dependent on the way in which the "negative cards" are presented. That is, the negative cards, *not-P* and *not-Q*, can be presented as "explicit negatives" (e.g. *not-P* can be presented as the "there is not a vowel" or "not an A") or as "implicit negatives" (e.g. *not-P* presented as "there is a consonant" or "K"). Evans found that the use of explicit negatives reduced the matching bias tendency and facilitated subjects' performance on the task.

The most heavily researched effect on performance in the selection task is the change in subjects' performance when they are given concrete or realistic content in the task (see Bracewell & Hidi, 1984; Gilhooly & Falconer, 1974; Wason & Shapiro, 1971). For example, Johnson-Laird, Legrenzi, and Sonino-Legrenzi (1972) used a concrete materials version of the task based on sorting letters. They asked subjects to imagine that they worked in the Post Office and had to discover whether the following rules had been violated given letters of different types:

If a letter is sealed, then it has a 5d. stamp on it

The envelopes provided were either sealed or unsealed and had a 4d. or a 5d. stamp on the side that was showing (see Fig. 12.1). Again, subjects had to make the minimum number of choices needed to determine whether the rule was true. Johnson-Laird et al. also used an abstract version of the task involving an abstract rule (i.e. "If there is a D on one side, then there is a 5 on the other side"). They found that, of the 24 subjects who attempted the tasks, 22 produced the correct choices on the concrete version and only 2 were successful on the abstract version.

These results turn out not to be as straightforward as they first seemed: Manktelow and Evans (1979) found no facilitation for other concrete, realistic materials (such as "If I eat haddock then I drink gin"). After further research (e.g. Griggs, 1983; Griggs & Cox, 1982; Reich & Ruth, 1982), a *memory-cueing hypothesis* was proposed which maintained that subjects required specific prior experience before performance could be facilitated (see Griggs, 1983; Griggs & Cox, 1982; Manktelow & Evans, 1979; Reich & Ruth, 1982).

This memory-cueing account is a special case of the concrete-rule view, and explains these results as being due to the availability of prior experience with counter-examples to the rule. That is, people must have encountered instances where the rule was not the case; for example, where there was "a sealed letter without a 5d. stamp on it". It is this specific knowledge that prompts them to make the correct choice of the *P* and *not-Q* cards. This interpretation of the results was supported by Griggs and Cox's (1982) finding that when this postal rule lapsed, the facilitating effects of the concrete materials disappeared in young adults who had no experience with the old rule. However, Griggs and Cox still found the facilitating effect for a drinking-age rule that was enforced in Florida (i.e. If a person is drinking beer then that person must be over 19 years of age) amongst Florida students.

However, the memory-cueing hypothesis was thrown into question by other results. D'Andrade had found (reported in Rumelhart, 1980; replicated by Griggs & Cox, 1983) that subjects could also solve tasks that involved concrete content for which they could not have had direct experience. He used a concrete version of the task in which subjects had to imagine they were Sears' store managers responsible for checking sales receipts in Sears. The rule subjects had to test was "If a purchase exceeds $30, then the receipt must be approved by the department manager." They were then shown four receipts: one for $15, one for $45, one signed and one not signed. Even without direct experience of this situation, subjects made the correct choices about 70% of the time.

There are two main ways in which concrete-rule theories have been modified to deal with these results. First, it has been argued that subjects do not have to have direct experience of the situation but that, for instance in the Sear's shopping case, they could use analogous prior experience (see Griggs, 1983; Chapter 11 on analogy). However, this option has never been fully elaborated and tested specifically. The second strategy has been to reconceive of the nature of concrete rules. As we have seen, the memory-cueing variant of the concrete-rule theory assumes that the rules reflect specific knowledge about the situation. A more recent theory has suggested that concrete rules are specific to classes of situations (e.g. permission situations). It is this pragmatic reasoning schema theory (Cheng & Holyoak, 1985) to which we now turn.

Pragmatic Reasoning Schemata

Cheng and Holyoak (1985; Cheng, Holyoak, Nisbett, & Oliver, 1986) have argued that the effects found in the concrete versions of the selection task can be explained by the rules that are concrete in the sense of being sensitive to particular classes of situations. They call these rules *pragmatic reasoning schemata* because they are sensitive to the pragmatics of the situation (see Chapters 8 and 9 for accounts of schemata). One class of such situations examined by Cheng and Holyoak are permission situations. These occur regularly in everyday life; for example, in order to gain permission to enter a university one must satisfy the precondition of achieving a certain exam result. The schemata for such situations are "highly abstract rule systems, in as much as they potentially apply to a wide range of content domains"; however, unlike abstract rules "they are constrained by particular inferential goals and event relationships of certain broad types" (see Holland et al., 1986).

Pragmatic schema theory proposes that:

- People have rules that are concrete to the extent that they are sensitive to the situation in which people find themselves.
- Two sorts of context-specific rules—permission schemata and obligation schemata—have been explored.
- The rules in the permission schemata take the form "If one is to do X, then one must satisfy precondition Y"; if one is given a rule to test that elicits a permission situation then the appropriate rule from this schema is applied (its logic is like the conditional in Table 12.1).
- Obligation schemata have also been elaborated for situations in which one is obliged to do something; the rules in the schema take the form "If situation A arises then action C must be done."
- In this theory, errors are seen as being due to two sources; (i) errors may arise if situations cannot be mapped easily into pragmatic schemata, and (ii) errors can be due to the inferences generated by schemata, since the rules in the schema do not always conform with those sanctioned by propositional logic.

Evidence for Pragmatic Schemata

In one experiment designed to test the theory, Cheng and Holyoak looked at a version of the selection task manipulating concrete experience and a rationale for the task. Subjects in Hong Kong and Michigan were given a version of the Johnson-Laird et al. postal problem and another variant about checking passengers' forms at an airport. The latter involved the testing of the following rule:

If the form says 'ENTERING' on one side, then the other side includes cholera among the list of diseases.

Again, each problem had the appropriate *P*, *Q*, *not-P* and *not-Q* cases. Neither group of subjects should have had direct experience of the airport problem, but the Hong Kong subjects were expected to be familiar with the postal rule. So, the memory-cueing hypothesis would predict that, on the airport problem, subjects in both Hong Kong and Michigan should be equivalent. However, Hong Kong subjects should do better than Michigan subjects on the postal version because of their prior experience.

Cheng and Holyoak also had a manipulation that included the provision of a rationale for half the subjects on both the postal and airport tasks. The stated rationale for the postal task was that a sealed envelope indicated first-class mail, for which the Post Office received more revenue; the rationale for the airport task was that a cholera inoculation was required to protect the entering passengers from the disease. Cheng and Holyoak predicted that this rationale would cue the permission schema for the task because it casts the problem as a situation in which some action/precondition must be carried out before another action is permitted. For example, the higher postage must be paid (precondition Y), before a letter can be mailed first class (action X). As the pattern of inferences suggested by the permission schema correspond closely to the logical treatment of *if . . . then*, they predicted that the provision of the rationale would facilitate performance on the task. That is, all subjects should improve on both versions of the task (accepting that there may be a ceiling effect for the Hong Kong group on the postal task with the rationale).

The percentage of subjects who solved Wason's selection task correctly in each condition as a function of provision of a rationale (reproduced from Cheng & Holyoak, 1985, with the permission of the authors and the publishers of Cognitive psychology, 1985 *by Academic Press, Inc.).*

FIGURE 12.2

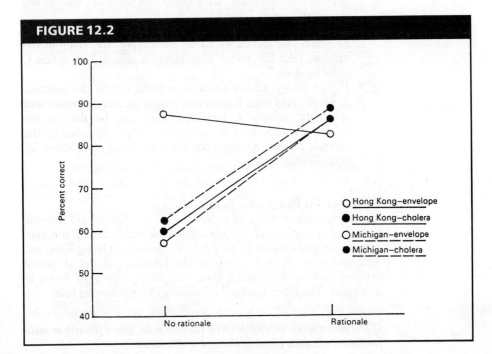

Legend:
○ Hong Kong–envelope
● Hong Kong–cholera
○ Michigan–envelope
● Michigan–cholera

Figure 12.2 indicates the results from the experiment. They show that the memory-cueing hypothesis has some validity but is clearly not the whole story. The Hong Kong subjects did do better on the postal task with no rationale relative to the comparable Michigan group. However, all subjects produced uniformly high rates of correct responses when the rationale was provided, in a fashion that contrasts with performance without the rationale (when experience was not available).

In their second experiment, Cheng and Holyoak found a potentially more important result. They demonstrated an improvement in performance for abstract materials when the selection task was presented as an abstract description of a permission situation (i.e. If one is to take action A, then one must satisfy precondition P). Subjects in the abstract-permission version fared better (61% correct) than those in the usual version of the abstract task (19%). This is a significant finding because (Jackson & Griggs, in press): "such facilitation had never been observed for any other abstract versions of the standard selection task."

Cheng et al. (1986) also pitted their theory against abstract-rule theories in a series of training studies. These results indicate that if people are trained on standard logic they do not improve as well in their performance on the selection task, relative to training on rules that correspond to pragmatic schemata.

Problems with Concrete-rule Theories

In general, pragmatic schema theory is an interesting addition to the theoretical corpus of research on the selection task. It has been used to generate new and interesting predictions about the underlying basis of subjects' performance on the task and some of these predictions have been confirmed. However, the main theoretical criticism that can be made is that it is not complete enough in its proposals.

Unlike the abstract-rule theories we have examined, it does not generate any predictions for reasoning involving all of the logical connectives; the theory says nothing about *and* and *or*. This means that it is silent about the difficulty or ease of reasoning on more complex premises involving these connectives. Second, even in the cases towards which it is directed (i.e. conditionals) the theory is less than complete. For instance, it is not clear about what people are doing when they are not using pragmatic schemata. Cheng and Holyoak say that some responses may be due to non-logical biases, but they do not elaborate a full account. Furthermore, the theory says little about wider issues like comprehension and the effects of processing limitations. It posits a set of plausible content-specific rules for reasoning that are well-specified; however, the processes that parse natural language into these rules are unspecified. This means that many of the theory's predictions about when pragmatic schemata will be used in specific contexts (e.g. the provision of a rationale) are too open to *ad hoc* interpretations.

More serious than the theoretical objections, some recent empirical evidence challenges one of Cheng and Holyoak's central findings. Recall that Evans (1983) had shown that subjects made less errors on a closely related task when they were given explicit negatives as opposed to implicit negatives (see earlier). Jackson and Griggs (in press) have pointed out that the condition in which subjects got the abstract-permission version of the selection task made use of explicit negatives. However, in the comparable condition that received the standard abstract version of the task, subjects received the negative cards with both implicit and explicit negatives (e.g. the *not-P* card has "B (not A)" on it). Jackson and Griggs, therefore, argued that the observed facilitation may not be due to the permission schema, but may rather be due in part to the way in which the negative cards were presented. When Jackson and Griggs replicated Cheng and Holyoak's experiment using implicit negatives in the abstract-permission and standard abstract versions of the task, the observed facilitation in the former condition disappeared. This finding was replicated twice. Jackson and Griggs concluded, after several other experiments, that the facilitation found by Cheng and Holyoak cannot be attributed to an abstract permission schema but is due to other factors (e.g. the provision of explicit negatives and a context). This research does not conclusively defeat the predictions of the pragmatic schema theory; more work needs to be done to determine the exact locus of the facilitating effect found in the abstract-permission version of the selection task. However, it does raise some important empirical questions which need to be answered.

Summary

Several different types of concrete-rule theory have been proposed to explain the effects of concrete materials on Wason's selection task. Some have argued that these effects are best accounted for by the recall and use of specific prior experiences. Cheng and Holyoak have recently argued that people use relatively abstract, but context-specific, schemata in solving the selection task. They call these pragmatic reasoning schemata (they involve permission and obligation schemata). Several studies have been carried out to test pragmatic schema theory and much confirming evidence has been found. Cheng and Holyoak have also found that performance on the task can be facilitated by the provision of an abstract statement of the permission schema. However, recently Jackson and Griggs have shown that this facilitation can be attributed to other factors.

THE MODEL THEORY OF SYLLOGISTIC REASONING

We have seen that the abstract- and concrete-rule theories of reasoning have been found most wanting in their treatment of comprehension processes. In general they assume that a natural language sentence is parsed into a mental representation against which various reasoning rules are matched. In underplaying the comprehension component, these theories omit many interesting phenomena that could have an impact on people's reasoning.

For example, when we read a story we add additional information from our general knowledge; for a simple sentence like "The lieutenant bandaged the soldier's arm" we add the information, from our sex-stereotypes, that both actors are male. Natural language can often be ambiguous in the information it conveys. Words are often imprecise and, depending on what assumptions we make, many different conceptions of a verbally described situation can be created. Consider two alternative conceptions for the situation described in the following problem:

A bear set out from his house one day and marched south for five miles, then turned east for three miles and then north for five miles. How far was he from his house? (Hint: The bear is white)

The answer is that he was back at his house because it was situated exactly on the north pole. One conception of the description has the bear marching along a flat plane. Yet, the same description is perfectly consistent with the alternative conception described in the solution; given an alternative assumption that the bear is travelling on a curved hemisphere. You can understand the solution because you can revise your model of the situation. Clearly, these aspects of comprehension have some impact on reasoning too. To an abstract-rule theorist these are extraneous influences that may misguide valid reasoning, as determined by the rules of a mental logic. However, the theory of reasoning based on mental models (Johnson-Laird, 1983) has embraced these phenomena and given them a central role in the reasoning process (see Chapter 7 for the representational issues associated with this theory). Model theories of reasoning come in several different forms. Several researchers have used models based on representational variants of Euler circles (Erickson, 1974; Guyote & Sternberg, 1981) and Venn diagrams (Newell, 1981). We will concentrate on a more general scheme proposed by Johnson-Laird that characterises models as having the same structure as the situations they represent (Johnson-Laird, 1983; Johnson-Laird & Byrne, 1990).

Stated simply, the model theory maintains that people reason by constructing a representation or model of the state of affairs described in the premises, based on the meanings of the premises and general knowledge; next, if it is at all possible, they formulate a novel conclusion based on the model, and if there are no alternative models of the premises that refute the conclusion they may draw it as a valid inference (Johnson-Laird & Byrne, 1990). The basic idea can be illustrated easily in simple spatial problems used by Johnson-Laird and his colleagues (see Byrne & Johnson-Laird, 1989; Erlich & Johnson-Laird, 1982; Mani & Johnson-Laird, 1982).

Consider the representation or model one might build from the following set of premises, given the instructions to imagine the state of affairs described in them:

The lamp is on the right of the pad
The book is on the left of the pad
The clock is in front of the book
The vase is in front of the lamp

Spatially, these objects can be viewed as being arranged in the following manner:

book   pad   lamp
clock   vase

So, one could make the novel inference from this model that "the clock is to the left of the vase." A novel inference or conclusion is any new statement that was not explicitly stated in the premises (so many more could be made). If we try to refute this conclusion then we need to discover another layout or model of the objects that is consistent with the description in the premises, but is not consistent with the conclusion of "the clock is on the left of the vase." In fact, there is no such model.

But consider the following premises:

The lamp is on the right of the pad
The book is on the left of the lamp
The clock is in front of the book
The vase is in front of the pad

This is consistent with two distinct models (see Byrne & Johnson-Laird, 1989):

book pad lamp   pad   book lamp
clock vase   vase clock

In this case, the conclusion that we might make from the first model, that "the clock is to the left of the vase," is inconsistent with an alternative model of the premises in which "the clock is to the right of the vase." Thus, in this case, one would have to admit that "there is no valid conclusion" to be made about the relationship of the vase and the clock on their own.

The theory has been applied to the primary domains of deduction; to propositional inferences (including the selection task), to spatial inferences, and to inferences based on quantifiers (e.g. some, all, none). We will concentrate our exposition of the theory on how it fares on syllogistic reasoning tasks.

The Model Theory

The model theory makes the following proposals (see Johnson-Laird, 1983; Johnson-Laird & Byrne, 1990):

- Deductive reasoning involves three stages of thought: the comprehension of premises resulting in the formation of a model (or set of models); the formulation of a novel conclusion based on the models that have been constructed; and the elimination of the possibility that there are alternative models of the premises that show the putative conclusion to be false.
- In *comprehending the premises*, various semantic procedures are used to construct models; the models are specific (i.e. they do not contain variables but specific mental tokens) and structurally analogous (they parallel states of affairs in the world; see Chapter 7); the mental tokens that make up models may be in visual images or they may be inaccessible to consciousness.
- *Conclusion-forming procedures* interrogate models to formulate a novel conclusion that is not explicitly stated in the premises.
- *Revision procedures* search for counter-examples or alternative models of the premises in which the putative conclusion is false; if there is no such model then the conclusion is valid, if a model is found that falsifies the conclusion then the ideal reasoner should attempt to discover whether there is any conclusion that is true in all the constructed models; if it is uncertain whether there is an alternative model to the conclusion then the conclusion can only be drawn tentatively.
- *Errors* occur because people have a limited working memory; thus, the more models they have to construct to solve a reasoning problem the harder the problem becomes; errors should take the form of conclusions made from initial models that have not been rigorously evaluated.

We have already seen, in a rough fashion, how this theory is applied to spatial reasoning. In the next section, we consider how it has been applied to syllogistic reasoning (see Johnson-Laird & Bara, 1984; Johnson-Laird & Byrne, 1989).

Syllogistic Reasoning

The Nature of Syllogisms

Technically, a syllogism is any argument that consists of two premises and a conclusion. However, most experimental studies have looked at Aristotle's *categorical syllogisms*; for example:

All animals are mortal,	All B are A
All men are animals,	All C are B
Therefore, all men are mortal.	Therefore, all C are A

The conclusion drawn here is considered to be valid. Instead of just using the *universal quantifier* (i.e. all), syllogisms can also be constructed using the *particular quantifier* (i.e. some) and *negatives* (i.e. not). This means that premises can occur in one of four "moods", that are conventionally designated by the mnemonics A, I, E, and O:

All A are B	(A; universal affirmative premise)
Some A are B	(I; particular affirmative premise)
No A are B	(E; universal negative premise)
Some A are not B	(O; particular negative premise)

The arrangements of terms in the premises, setting aside their moods, make up the *four figures of the syllogism*:

A–B	B–A	A–B	B–A
B–C	C–B	C–B	B–C

It should be appreciated immediately that the number of possible syllogisms is quite large. In fact, there are 64 possible logical forms for the premises of a syllogism (4 moods for each premise × 4 figures). Twenty-seven of these premise pairs yield valid conclusions interrelating the end terms, provided that one bears in mind that a conclusion may take the form A–C or C–A.

As in the case of propositional reasoning, in the earliest studies of syllogisms (e.g. Wilkins, 1928) it was found that people often make errors or invalid conclusions and their performance is affected by whether the content is abstract or concrete (for a fuller treatment of the structure of the syllogism and evidence, see Gilhooly, 1988; Chapter 5).

Previous Explanations of Syllogistic Reasoning

One of the earliest explanations of performance on syllogistic tasks maintained that people were operating on the basis of a nonlogical bias, called the "atmosphere effect" (Woodworth & Sells, 1935). The *atmosphere hypothesis* claimed that people failed to act in accordance with logical principles because their conclusions were affected by the atmosphere of the premises. Stated succinctly, it maintained:

- That a negative premise creates a negative atmosphere, even when the other premise is affirmative, resulting in a negative conclusion being made.
- That a particular premise creates a particular atmosphere, even when the other premise is universal, resulting in a particular conclusion being made.
- Since the effect appears to be stronger for valid than invalid conclusions, there also appears to be a contribution from some inferential mechanism.

However, as Johnson-Laird and Steedman (1978) have pointed out, the most damning evidence against the hypothesis is that people often respond with the wholly unpredicted conclusion of "no valid conclusion follows." They even make this response when the atmosphere hypothesis predicts a valid conclusion, for example:

Some B are A
No C are B
_____
Some A are not C

Only 10% of subjects produce this valid conclusion, whereas 60% maintain that there is no valid conclusion.

Apart from negative results, there are also alternative explanations of many of the atmosphere findings. Chapman & Chapman's (1959) *conversion hypothesis*, maintained that invalid conclusions are accepted because the premises are misinterpreted. Specifically, Chapman and Chapman argued that subjects commonly misinterpret universal affirmative propositions to mean that the converse is also true (e.g. "All As are Bs" is taken to mean "All Bs are As"). Similarly, particular negative premises are converted too (e.g. "Some As are not Bs" is taken to mean "Some Bs are not As"). Some of the clearest support for the conversion hypothesis was obtained by Ceraso and Provitera (1971). They showed that when the premises were stated less ambiguously (e.g. "All As are Bs" was stated as "All As are Bs, but some Bs are not As"), there was a substantial improvement in performance.

The problem with accounts like the atmosphere and conversion hypotheses is that they walk a very thin line between being "explanations of performance" and "descriptions of performance." If they are only descriptions of performance, then we are still left with the need to explain why subjects indulge in this behaviour. For example, what is it that causes subjects to convert? Newstead (1990) has recently addressed this issue and evaluated all of the various proposals about conversion effects. His conclusion is that the best account, with the strongest predictive value, is one based on Johnson-Laird's model theory. So, perhaps it is time to consider how this is applied to syllogistic reasoning in detail.

The Model Theory of Syllogistic Reasoning

We have already seen how the model theory proposes a three-stage process of deductive reasoning: comprehend the premises and construct a model, form a putative conclusion from that model, and then attempt to refute this conclusion with alternative models of the premises. Consider first how this is applied to syllogistic reasoning.

Building Models from the Premises

Johnson-Laird (1983; Johnson-Laird & Bara, 1984; Johnson-Laird & Byrne, 1989; 1990) propose that during comprehension people try to build an integrated model of the premises, as we saw earlier in the spatial reasoning case. So given a premise like:

| (1) Some of the artists are beekeepers | Some of the A are B |

it is proposed that people construct a model of the following type:

| artist | = | beekeeper |
| 0artist | | 0beekeeper |

Clearly, several points need to be made about this model and the notation. Johnson-Laird maintains that people construct models that are specific and analogous to the structure of the world (see Chapter 7 for more details). In comprehending singly quantified premises like the one just shown, this suggestion has two immediate implications. First, as we said in the statement of the theory, the model contains "mental tokens" that represent specific individuals; it does not contain variables. That is, it does not contain a single symbol that stands for all artists (e.g. ∀ artist, that is used in the predicate calculus). Rather, it is proposed that people represent all artists by an arbitrary number of individuals (in this case two); in fact, the model could have assumed more than two and taken the following form:

artist	=	beekeeper
artist	=	beekeeper
0artist		0beekeeper

One function of the "0artist" notation is to indicate that an artist who is not a beekeeper, may or may not exist. Second, the model represents the state of affairs of there being "some artists who are beekeepers" by relating these mental tokens to one another (this is notated by the "=" sign). Note that this notation indicates that there may or may not be an artist who is not a beekeeper (in the third line); that is, only a few or some artists are beekeepers. This captures the logically-correct interpretation of "some." In the logic of quantification, "some" means some and possibly all. So, if we ask you for some of your crisps and you agree to our request, under the logical meaning of some we could eat the whole bag (without any logical qualms).

Syllogisms have two premises, so we need to consider what happens when a second premise, like the following, is added:

| (2) All of the beekeepers are chemists | All of the B are C |

On its own this premise can be represented by the following model:

beekeeper = chemist

beekeeper = chemist

0chemist

This indicates that all those individuals who are beekeepers are chemists, although there may be other chemists who are not beekeepers. Comprehension must combine two premises in a single model by adding the information from subsequent premises to the model of earlier ones. So:

(1) Some of the artists are   Some of the A are B
    beekeepers

(2) All of the beekeepers are   All of the B are C
    chemists

can be combined in the following model:

artist   =   beekeeper   =   chemist

0artist   0beekeeper =   chemist

0chemist

What has happened here should be clear. We have simply taken the model of the first premise and related the beekeepers in it to new tokens added for chemists, in accordance with the universal quantifier in the second premise.

Forming a Conclusion from the Model
In forming a conclusion from the model, a set of procedures scan the model and describe a novel conclusion that can be made. In syllogisms the task is to relate the first and third terms, so we might state the conclusion as:

(3) Some of the artists are   Some of the A are C
    chemists

This is consistent with the model because there may be other artists (see 0artist) who are not chemists.

Searching for Alternative Models of the Premises
Just as in the case of the spatial descriptions, premises can be consistent with many different models. So, in order to determine whether one's conclusion is valid, it is necessary to see if there are any other models, consistent with the premises, in which the putative conclusion is untrue. In this problem there is no alternative model to the one shown that refutes the conclusion. However, in

other problems there may be alternative models in which the initial conclusion is not true. Consider the premises:

(4) All of the artists are   All of the A are B
    beekeepers

(5) Some of the beekeepers are   Some of the B are C
    chemists

These can be represented by the model:

artist	=	beekeeper	=	chemist
artist	=	beekeeper		0chemist
		0beekeeper		

The model suggests the following conclusion:

(6) Some of the artists are   Some of the A are C
    chemists

But here there is another model that is consistent with the premises in which the conclusion is not the case, namely,

artist	=	beekeeper		
artist	=	beekeeper		0chemist
		0beekeeper	=	chemist

In this model, none of the artists are related to the chemists. There is no conclusion that is true in both models, so the best we can say is that there is no valid conclusion.

As a final point, one may be wondering how negative premises are represented in these models. Recently, Johnson-Laird and Byrne (1990) have characterised negation by using explicitly propositional-like tags in their models. So, for example, the premise

(7) None of the artists is a   None of the A is a B
    beekeeper

can be represented by the explicit model:

artist	=	¬ beekeeper
artist	=	¬ beekeeper
¬ artist	=	beekeeper
¬ artist	=	beekeeper

Stated succinctly, this model shows that any given artist you might pick is not a beekeeper and any given beekeeper you choose is not an artist. The three dots notation allows for other sorts of individual, yet to be made explicit. Reasoners may not represent all of this information in their model, as we will in the next sub-section. The model also illustrates the mixture of analogical and propositional representation used in the theory. As we shall see in the next section, there is evidence to suggest that conceptual tags for negation are used by people in their models (see Johnson-Laird & Byrne, 1989; 1990).

Evidence for the Model Theory

According to Johnson-Laird and Bara (1984), errors can arise in the conclusions made by subjects as a function of difficulties at any of the three stages of reasoning. We will, however, concentrate on the predictions they make about influences on the third stage (searching for alternative models), as it is a general prediction of the theory that has been found in many types of deductive reasoning.

Different problems can require different numbers of models in order to determine a valid conclusion. The first problem we examined [i.e. (1), (2), and (3)] admitted a valid conclusion from a single model. However, the second problem [i.e. (4), (5), and (6)], required two models to be constructed before one could conclude that "There is no valid conclusion relating the two terms." As people have a limited working memory, problems that require more models to be constructed will be more difficult because of information overload. This prediction has been confirmed by numerous experiments (e.g. Johnson-Laird & Bara, 1984; Johnson-Laird & Byrne, 1990) in which subjects received different syllogisms that required one model or more than one model to be constructed. Moreover, they also argued that subjects' erroneous conclusions should be ones that followed if one or more of the possible models of the premises were neglected. This is what they found; namely, that subjects' errors were the sorts of conclusions that one would expect subjects to make from initial models that had not been rigorously tested by searching for other alternative models.

More recently, Johnson-Laird & Byrne (1989) have investigated the use of "only" in syllogistic reasoning (e.g. Only criminals are psychopaths). *Only* is interesting because logically "All the psychopaths are criminals" is equivalent to "Only the criminals are psychopaths". However, they predicted that people's mental representation of *only* would be more complex than *all* because it makes negative relations between the sets of individuals salient. That is, with "Only criminals are psychopaths," one grasps immediately that some criminals are psychopaths and that anyone who is not a criminal is not a psychopath. However, in the case of "All psychopaths are criminals," one grasps that this is the case and that there may be criminals who are not psychopaths, but the latter is less obvious than in the "only" case. Hence, Johnson-Laird and Byrne propose that reasoners construct a model of the following sort for the only premise:

criminal   =   psychopath

criminal   =   psychopath

0 criminal   =   ¬ psychopath

¬ criminal   =   ¬ psychopath

¬ criminal   =   ¬ psychopath

Assuming this representational difference between "all" and "only," Johnson-Laird and Byrne (1989) predicted that premises of syllogisms involving *only* would be harder than one using *all*. This prediction was confirmed in their study and they also showed that inferences that required reasoners to consider explicit negatives were easier from only than from all.

Further research by Johnson-Laird, Byrne, and Tabossi (1989) has extended the theory to multiply-quantified assertions. A singly-quantified assertion is one like "All of the beekeepers are chemists," whereas a multiply-quantified assertion is one like "*None* of the beekeepers is taller than *any* of the chemists." Inferences based on premises containing multiply-quantified relations cannot be dealt with using other model representations, like Euler circles or Venn diagrams. Again, these experiments show that inferences that require the construction of one model are considerably easier for subjects than those requiring more than one model. These results have the extra theoretical significance lent by the absence of any existing psychological theory based on abstract rules to handle these assertions. Indeed, Johnson-Laird and Byrne (1990) argue convincingly that likely extensions of current abstract-rule theories could not account for the results of their experiments.

Evaluation of Model Theory

Around 1983, there was considerable excitement about the term "mental models." Two books appeared in that year bearing it as their title. Both works reflected new theoretical directions for the characterisation of problem solving (see Gentner & Stevens, 1983; Chapter 11) and reasoning (Johnson-Laird, 1983). As is always the case, new developments first tend to be hailed, sometimes amid considerable conceptual confusion, and then are followed by a rising chorus of criticism. In the case of the Gentner and Steven's mental models, it came to be realised that these ideas were more of an empirical addition to cognitive psychology than a radically different theoretical direction. Johnson-Laird's mental models have been more difficult to discount, partly because of his comprehensive treatment of the topic; he argued that mental models were central to a wide variety of psychological phenomena and drew in research from several of the cognitive sciences to bolster his arguments. It has thus taken some time for the dust to settle (indeed it may still be happening) and to evaluate the novelty and significance of the contribution.

What *is* clear is that, in the last few years, the theory has drawn a lot of fire (see Ford, 1985; Goldman, 1986; Rips, 1984; 1986). These criticisms have been both theoretical and empirical. Theoretically, many have said that Johnson-Laird's original conception of a mental model was unclear and that the procedures for constructing and manipulating models were opaque. Johnson-Laird and Byrne (1990) maintain that since the theory has been specified computationally, this criticism must arise from a poor exposition of it. This seems partially true, but it is also the case that the extension of the theory to new areas was not at all obvious. However, there is a sense in which this criticism is now obviated as the theory has been extended to the main areas of deductive reasoning (see Johnson-Laird & Byrne, 1990).

The other main theoretical criticism, from abstract-rule theorists (Goldman, 1986; Rips, 1984; 1986), is that there is essentially no difference between mental models and abstract rules of inference. It is clear that at some level of abstraction, any two theories can be said to be the same (e.g. they both involve domain-independent rules) but these sorts of identities are superficial and do not capture essential differences. The essential difference seems to be this; if one took both theories and applied them to the same tasks and noted the rules or procedures that would have to be used to deal with these tasks, then the nature of these rules in both theories would be very different. In an abstract-rule theory, one would have rules, like modus ponens, that resemble the rules of the propositional calculus. In contrast, the rules of a model theory would not resemble the rules of the propositional calculus but would instead be procedures for constructing models, for searching for alternative models, and for reading off conclusions. Many problem-solving theories are considered to be different even if they apply the same rules in different strategic ways. Given that the abstract-rule and model accounts use radically different rules, it is hard to escape the conclusion that they are different.

Of course, at a certain point, the determination of theoretical differences becomes academic if the two theories lead to different empirical predictions. This is certainly the case but empirical criticisms have been made here too. These criticisms grant that the model theory may account for behaviour in categorical syllogisms and some forms of spatial reasoning, but argue that it cannot account for many other reasoning phenomena. This is connected to the lack-of-clarity objection, in that commentators have difficulties imagining extensions of the theory to new areas. In particular, critics have pointed to the area of propositional reasoning (Braine et al., 1984; Evans, 1987; Rips, 1986; earlier section). This is a "hasn't-done-it-yet" rather than a "can't-do-it-at-all" criticism and can therefore be answered.

Johnson-Laird and Byrne (1990; Johnson-Laird, Byrne, & Schaeken, Note 6) report on a model theory of propositional reasoning that accounts for the selection task. In this theory they propose that a conditional premise like "If there is a circle then there is a triangle" is represented explicitly by the following three models:

O   △

¬O   △

¬O   ¬△

In this notation, each line represents a new model. However, Johnson-Laird and Byrne argue that people avoid representing the conditional in this fully explicit and fleshed-out manner but rather represent it minimally as follows:

[O]   △

. . .

where the three dots indicate that the representation can be fleshed out if needs be and the square brackets indicate that the circle has been represented exhaustively in the models. When someone is given a second premise—"There is a circle"—they make the modus ponens inference that "there is a triangle" by noting that the only model they have represented, where there is a circle, is one in which there is also a triangle. Since they know that the circle is represented exhaustively (indicated by the square brackets), they know that there is no need to flesh out their representation in terms of other models to find a case where there is a circle with something else (see Table 12.2). However, in the more difficult modus tollens inference, where subjects are given the extra premise "There is not a triangle," subjects must flesh out their representation to include all three models to find the model in which there is not a triangle (i.e. ¬△). If they do this they will conclude that there is not a circle (i.e. ¬O). However, as in other models research, the more models one has to consider the harder the task becomes, and hence if people do not make these other models explicit they will fail to make the correct inference. This is just a hint of how the model theory accounts for the basic finding that modus ponens is easier than modus tollens; for more novel predictions and results see Johnson-Laird and Byrne (1990; Chapter 3).

Johnson-Laird and Byrne (1990) seem to have respectable answers to many of the criticisms of model theory. However, we would like to add another "hasn't-done-it-yet" criticism to the rest. One of the central points made by Johnson-Laird (1983) was that general knowledge played an important role in the construction of models. In the polar-bear problem, it is one's general knowledge that adds the plausible assumption that the bear is walking on a flat plane. The model theory has explored the multiple-model aspect of the polar-bear problem, but it has said little about the impact of such assumptions based on general knowledge. The issue has already arisen in reasoning research too. Byrne's (1989b) model account for the effects of alternative and additional information in propositional reasoning rests on the assumption that general knowledge plays a role. General knowledge may also play an important role in the search for counter-examples. One of the golden rules learned from Newell and Simon's research is that people use various rules of thumb or prior experience to reduce the search space of alternatives. The addition of detailed mechanisms that specify the role of general knowledge may also constitute an important clarification of the basic differences between abstract-rule theories, concrete-rule theories, and model theories (see Brewer, 1987, for one possible direction).

Summary

A third alternative to the abstract-rule and concrete-rule theories is the model theory. This argues that reasoning occurs in three stages: first, the premises are comprehended and a model of them constructed; second, one draws a putative conclusion from this model; third, one attempts to find alternative models of the premises in which this conclusion is not the case. This theory has been applied to many different areas of reasoning, but has dealt most notably with syllogistic reasoning. The repeated finding that is predicted by the theory in this area is that the more models that subjects have to construct in order to reach a valid conclusion, the greater the likelihood that they will tend to make errors. Furthermore, the character of these errors reflects early conclusions made from initial models that have not been evaluated sufficiently.

EVALUATIONS OF REASONING RESEARCH

In general, we have stuck fairly close to our chosen structure of pairing each theory with its best area in our treatment of reasoning research. Later, we will consider the broader canvas of reasoning as an instance of thinking. For the present, we will consider two central questions that must be part of any assessment of reasoning. The first is the question we began with, the item at the top of the agenda: Are humans rational? The second question, which is partly contingent on the first, concerns which of the theories reviewed can be considered to be the most adequate.

Are We Rational?

The simple definition of rationality is that one acts in accordance with the laws of logic. However, modern logic consists of a vast number of logical systems, of which the propositional calculus is just one. So it seems a little arbitrary to pick this one and call it the laws of logic (e.g. see Cohen, 1981, for a detailed argument concerning this point). It is, therefore, more reasonable to ask whether there is any sense in which people attempt to operate in accordance with a rational principle; whether they will try to deduce valid conclusions from the premises of an argument.

In fact, most theorists argue that people *do* operate in accordance with some rational principle. The most extreme anti-rationalist stance one can find is a biases approach to reasoning (see Evans, 1989). Recall, for example, the evidence from the selection task on the matching bias, in which subjects simply respond to superficial features of the task situation. However, even bias theorists do not postulate that people operate in this fashion all the time (see Evans, 1984). It could be argued, though, that a concrete-rule theorist, who does not admit the abstract rules of a natural deduction theory, has a fundamentally anti-rationality view of human reasoning. From this perspective, people are always operating in accordance with their prior experience and, as such, may perform in a reasonable but not a rational fashion.

The abstract-rule and model theories are committed to the view that people are rational. Abstract-rule theories assert this in their identification of people's mental logic with the axioms of propositional logic. People are swayed from this rationality by re-interpreting information during comprehension and by the vagaries of their information processing systems (e.g. working memory limitations). Johnson-Laird and Byrne (1990) also believe that people are rational; but rational in principle rather than in practice. Given sufficient time, the motivation, and a light working memory load they will produce valid conclusions; that is, conclusions that are true in all the possible models of the premises. People are able to make valid deductions and can sometimes know that they have made a valid deduction. In both of these theories, Chomsky's competence–performance distinction is useful (see Chapter 9). Both of these theories suggest that people have the basic competence to be rational, but that they err in the execution or performance of this rationality. Thus, the burden of theoretical opinion seems to lie with the view that people can be rational.

Assessing Competing Theories

A complete evaluation of all the theories we have reviewed so far is beyond the scope of this chapter. However, we will make an assessment within certain constraints. First, we will only look at empirical evidence rather than considering more complex factors like theoretical completeness. Second, we will only consider the theories in the light of the three main topics of reasoning research we have reviewed: propositional reasoning, the selection task, and syllogistic reasoning. So any conclusions we make about the relative merits of competing theories must be taken within the context of these constraints.

The concrete-rule view comes off as being the least adequate. From a psychological perspective, it has not been applied explicitly with any rigour to syllogistic reasoning or to propositional reasoning. Furthermore, its performance on the selection task is a little spotty. Memory-cueing accounts and pragmatic schemata can account for some, but not all, of the evidence. In abstract materials they have recourse to biases accounts or to an abstract-rule account lurking in the background. On a broad front, then, this approach begins to look like a pastiche of theories rather than a coherent, unified view of the basis of human reasoning abilities.

The abstract-rule theory has been applied most successfully to propositional reasoning. It can generate precise predictions about subjects' judgements of validity (Braine et al., 1984; Osherson, 1974; 1975; Rips, 1983), about the reaction times of subjects on tasks (Braine et al., 1984), and about inter-subject differences on problems (Rips & Conrad, 1983). Indications have also been given about how it might be applied to classical syllogisms (Braine & Rumain, 1983; Osherson, 1976) involving singly-quantified assertions. The results of research on the selection task is more embarrassing. The variety of ways in which different concrete versions of the task (e.g. different contexts and materials) can have radical effects on subjects' behaviour can only be accounted for by added assumptions on the effects of comprehension and other factors, which have not been forthcoming.

When we take recent research into account, the model theory scores fairly high on generality. Within syllogistic reasoning it has been extended from singly-quantified premises to multiply-quantified ones (see Johnson-Laird et al., 1989). It has also been applied to non-standard quantifiers like "only" (see Johnson-Laird & Byrne, 1989). Within propositional reasoning, Byrne (1989a; 1989b) has explained the results of experiments on the suppression of valid inferences and reasoning with conditional sequences in terms of a model theory. Johnson-Laird and Byrne (1990; Johnson-Laird et al., Note 6) have also produced a model account of propositional reasoning. Finally, Johnson-Laird and Byrne (1990) have produced an account of the selection task. Furthermore, much of the evidence from Johnson-Laird and Byrne's recent research supports the model theory and rejects the abstract-rule theory. They have been carrying out competitive tests of the two theories, in these various topic areas, and their data consistently shows that abstract-rule accounts produce predictions that are not met by the data.

The evaluation of competing theories is a very difficult business (see Thagard, 1989). However, within the constraints of the current review, the weight of the evidence points at present towards some form of model theory of reasoning.

Summary

There is some consensus among theories of reasoning that, above and beyond the vagaries of the human information processing system, people are rational in principle. If we consider the evidence from each of the three areas of reasoning we have reviewed— propositional reasoning, the selection task, and syllogistic reasoning —each of the three main groups of theories can be evaluated. At present, the model theory fares better than the abstract-rule theory and both of these fare better than concrete-rule accounts.

DECISION MAKING

Normative Theories of Decision Making

One of the noteworthy aspects of thinking research is the distinctive role that idealised, normative, or formal theories play in guiding investigations. For example, in problem-solving research we saw how Newell and Simon used problem space graphs to plot the abstract structure of problems independently of psychological considerations (see Chapter 11). Then they developed psychological theories that assumed this structure and made extra assumptions about the nature of search strategies (like means-ends analysis) and other processing limitations. Similarly, in deductive-reasoning research, we saw that various logics could be used as idealised theories about the structure of reasoning problems and that psychological theories of reasoning could be, to a greater or lesser extent, based on these ideas. These idealised, normative theories are often useful for three main reasons. First, they allow researchers to characterise the structure of problems in some objective, agreed-upon fashion. Second, they indicate what researchers may consider to be correct or incorrect answers, good or bad strategies, and valid or invalid conclusions. Third, they may provide the basis for a psychological theory (e.g. abstract-rule theories of reasoning).

Decision-making research, which has concerned itself largely with statistical judgements, has taken a similar route. The psychological research on judgements of utility and intuitive statistics has been led by theories of optimal decision making and statistics developed by philosophers and economists (e.g. Coombs, Dawes, & Tversky, 1970; Edwards, 1954). These normative theories describe how one should go about determining the best possible course of action, given one's knowledge about the world and what one wants. They describe, given certain strong assumptions, how one can make optimal decisions.

Psychologically, an individual may have many emotional factors and conflicting beliefs to take into account when making a judgement about taking one alternative rather than another, but a normative theory characterises the choice in a formulaic fashion; for example (see Fischhoff, 1988):

$$\sum_{i=1}^{n} P_i W_i = P_1 W_1 + P_2 W_2 + \ldots + P_n W_n$$

In this formula the expected worth of a particular action is formalised in terms of the probability (P) and worth of the possible consequences of the action (W). For example, if a student is choosing between going to one university or another they may consider the different consequences of either alternative; the attractiveness of the university town for living $(P_1 W_1)$, its closeness to family and friends $(P_2 W_2)$, the reputation of the university $(P_3 W_3)$, probability of getting a job from the course in question (P_4W_4), and so on. Each of these consequences can be assigned a probability of their occurring (P) and an evaluation of their worth if obtained (W). Presumably, the best choice would be that one in which the highly-probable consequences are good, and they are many in number.

Such models try to find formal and rigorous means for decision making, but may have little to do with psychological processes. Much of the research in decision making has attempted to isolate the deviations that people make from such principles. As such, it is often characterised under the general heading of *bias research* (see, e.g., Evans, 1989). In this section we will concentrate on research that has been done on statistical judgements. Statistical theories (like Bayesian probability theory) characterise the mathematically correct judgements to make in many different decision-making situations; however, people often reach different conclusions.

Biases in Statistical Judgements

One important statistical theory that has been used in a normative fashion in decision-making research is Bayesian probability theory. Again, as in the section on logic, if one wishes to understand decision-making research it is necessary to have some idea about statistical theories. In the next sub-section we have tried to provide a gentle introduction to the basics of Bayes' Theorem.

Bayes' Theorem

Much of the research we will review is based on the Bayesian approach to hypothesis testing and, in particular, on Bayes' theorem: a rule for changing one's beliefs in the probability (represented by P) of a hypothesis (represented by H) in the light of new evidence (represented by E).

$$P(H/E) \ = \ \frac{P(E/H) \times P(H)}{P(E)}$$

where

$$P(E) = P(E/H) \times P(H) + P(E/Ha) \times P(Ha)$$

The top formula can be read as follows; the new or *posteriori* probability for the truth of an hypothesis in the light of new evidence [i.e. P(H/E)] is given by the probability of H being correct given a piece of evidence [i.e. P(E/H)] multiplied by the *prior* probability of the hypothesis being correct [i.e. P(H)], all over the probability that the evidence will occur [i.e. P(E)]. The probability that the evidence will occur, P(E), is computed from P(H/E) multiplied by P(H), plus the probability of the alternative hypothesis, Ha, being correct given the evidence [i.e. P(E/Ha)] multiplied by the prior probability of the alternative hypothesis being correct [i.e. P(Ha)]. Consider how this is applied to a probability problem adapted from Edwards (1968):

> Assume there are two bags, each of which are filled with 100 poker chips. One of the bags, the red bag, contains 70 red chips and 30 blue chips and the other, the blue bag, contains 70 blue chips and 30 red chips. The bags are unmarked, so the only way to tell which is which is by sampling the chips from each. Assume that one of the bags is chosen at random and a red chip is drawn from it. How likely is it to be the red bag on the basis of this single piece of evidence?

The hypothesis, H, here is "the selected bag is the red bag" and the alternative hypothesis, Ha, is that "the selected bag is the blue bag." The *prior probability* of each of these being the case is 0.5 because there are two bags, so there is a 50–50 chance that it is one or the other; so:

$$P(H) \quad = \quad 0.5$$

$$P(Ha) \quad = \quad 0.5$$

If one assumes that the red bag has been selected, then the probability that a red chip is chosen from it is 0.7, because 70 of the 100 chips in the bag are red; the probability of drawing the red chip from the blue bag is 0.3 because only 30 of the 100 chips in it are red. So:

$$P(E/H) \quad = \quad 0.7$$

$$P(E/Ha) \quad = \quad 0.3$$

These values can be used to compute the lower line of the theorem:

$$P(E) \quad = \quad P(E/H) \times P(H) + P(E/Ha) \times P(Ha)$$

$$= \quad (0.7) \times (0.5) + (0.3) \times (0.5)$$

$$= \quad 0.35 + 0.15$$

$$= \quad 0.50$$

This is all one needs to establish the *posterior probability* of the bag being the red bag, on the basis of the evidence of the red chip:

$$P(H/E) = \frac{P(E/H) \times P(H)}{P(E)} = \frac{(0.7) \times (0.5)}{0.5} = 0.7$$

So, the probability that we have chosen the red bag on the basis of this one piece of evidence is 0.7, as opposed to 0.5 in advance of the selection. In Edwards' experiments, perhaps unsurprisingly, subjects did not wholly agree with the probabilities generated by the theorem. Their judgements of the change in probability were more *conservative*. For example, they considered the probability of the red bag hypothesis being true as being 0.6 rather than 0.7. However, as we shall see, this is just one of many different deviations subjects make from the theorem.

Ignoring Base Rates

It should be clear from this treatment of Bayes' theorem that the contribution of prior probabilities is very important. In the bags task, subjects can be viewed as taking these *base rates* into account in their probability judgements. However, it has been shown that there are cases when subjects neglect base rates. Tversky and Kahneman (1980) found such results in subjects' answers to the following problem:

> A taxi-cab was involved in a hit-and-run accident one night. Two cab companies, the Green and the Blue, operate in the city. You are given the following data: (a) 85% of the cabs in the city are Green, and 15% are Blue, and (b) in court a witness identified the cab as a Blue cab.
>
> However, the court tested the witness's ability to identify cabs under appropriate visibility conditions. When presented with a series of cabs, half of which were Blue and half of which were Green, the witness made the correct identifications in 80% of the cases, and was wrong in 20% of cases.
>
> What was the probability that the cab involved in the accident was Blue rather than Green? . . . . . . per cent.

If one takes into account the base rate information, Bayes' theorem results in a probability of 0.41% or a 41% likelihood that the taxi-cab was Green. However, most subjects ignored this information and, concentrating on the witness's information, maintained that there was an 80% likelihood that the taxi was Blue rather than Green. This radical overestimate of the posterior probability of the hypothesis is as striking as it is modifiable.

Tversky and Kahneman also demonstrated some alternative conditions under which people take base rate information into account. They changed the (a) part of problem to be (1980):

> Although the two companies are roughly equal in size, 85% of cab accidents in the city involve Green cabs, and 15% involve Blue cabs.

In this version of the problem, a clear *causal* relation is drawn between the accident record of a cab company and the likelihood of there being an accident. In the original version of the problem, the population difference for the two cab companies is given no causal significance. So, in this new problem the base rate information was predicted to be of more significance and to play a greater part in subjects' assessments; this result was confirmed, with most subjects producing estimates of a 60% likelihood. So, the suggestion is that base rates may be ignored but various factors, like the presence of a causal relation, can reverse this behaviour.

The Availability Heuristic

Judgements of probabilities can also be swayed by other factors. Tversky and Kahneman (1974) have shown that in a variety of different situations people will tend to adopt an availability heuristic, rather than act in concert with probability theory. When people are asked to assess the frequency of a class or the plausibility of a particular consequence, they base their judgement on the availability of instances or scenarios. For example, people often base their assessment of the risk of a heart attack in middle-aged people by determining how many occurrences of such an event have happened to people they know. Similarly, the judgement of the probability of certain consequences occurring when an action is carried out will often hinge on how easy certain consequences are to imagine.

For example, Tversky and Kahneman (1974) asked subjects the following question:

> If a word of three letters or more is sampled at random from an English text, is it more likely that the word starts with "r" or has "r" as its third letter?

Tversky and Kahneman found that most subjects report that a word beginning with "r" was more likely to be picked out at random than a word with "r" in its third position. In reality the reverse is the case. Words beginning with "r" can be retrieved more readily from memory (i.e. are more available) than words with "r" as their third letter. As a result subjects make the wrong judgement about the relative frequency of the two classes of words.

In this case availability is based on the effectiveness of the search set in the problem. Availability can also be based on frequency of occurrence; that is, one tends to recall those things that have been encountered most frequently in the past. When it is based on frequency it can often lead to effective judgements. However, availability can also be affected by the relative salience of instances; that is, happenings or objects that have been encountered recently or have become salient for some reason can be temporarily more available. If you are a U.S. citizen trying to decide where to go on holiday and there is a sudden rash of terrorist incidents in Europe against U.S. citizens, it is highly likely that you will be swayed into taking a holiday in the U.S. (even though the probability of getting killed, in, say, Florida may be comparable to Europe or higher). Lichenstein, Slovic, Fischhoff, Layman, and Coombes (1978) have shown how causes of death that have more publicity (e.g. murder) are judged more likely than causes that have less publicity (e.g. suicide), contrary to the true state of affairs.

The Representativeness Heuristic

Tversky and Kahneman and their associates have also investigated a representativeness heuristic. The representativeness heuristic tends to be used in situations where people are asked to judge the probability that an object or event A belongs to a class or process B. So, if someone is given a description of an individual and asked to guess the probability that this individual has a certain occupation, it is typically found that they judge probabilities in terms of the similarity of the individual to their stereotype for that occupation. So, given a description (Tversky & Kahneman, 1974) of Steve as:

> . . . very shy and withdrawn, invariably helpful, but with little interest in people, or in the world of reality. A meek tidy soul, he has a need for order and structure and a passion for detail . . .

and the task of determining the probability that he is a farmer, pilot, doctor, or librarian, many people will choose librarian as a high probability job for Steve: This is because he is a good match to the stereotype for this occupation (it should be clear that these predictions are closely related to Rosch's theory of concepts; see Chapter 8).

Evaluation of Decision-Making Research

Decision-making research is of enormous practical importance (for a good overview see Kahneman, Slovic, & Tversky, 1982). There are many everyday situations in which people have to make important decisions about the probability of future events. In many of these situations, a reliance on intuitive statistics can be badly misleading (e.g. in the selection of sample sizes for experiments).

However, despite this success, the theory really needs to be better specified. If one examines the "heuristics" mentioned it is clear that they are not heuristics in the same sense as, say, means-end analysis (see Chapter 11). The availability heuristic is really a general description for a collection of different specific rules (e.g. search efficiency, frequency, recency). In contrast, the means-end analysis heuristic is a single well-specified rule.

One way of overcoming this problem is to assimilate this research to other conceptual frameworks, like problem space theory (Newell & Simon, 1972), Anderson's (1983) cognitive architecture, or one or other of the reasoning theories. As we will see in the next section, it looks as if some researchers are starting to do this. For example, many availability effects can be dealt with by Anderson's spreading activation mechanism (see Chapter 1).

Summary

Normative theories of statistics and probability have been used to show that people are biased in their intuitive notions of statistics. In particular, Tversky and Kahneman have shown that several general tendencies underlie decision making in many different contexts: Two instances of these tendencies are the availability heuristic and the representativeness heuristic. The availability heuristic refers to the tendency to use the availability of instances or scenarios in assessments of the frequency of a class or plausibility of a happening. The representativeness heuristic makes use of the similarity of a target item to a representative instance of a class in making judgements about the probability that an object or event belongs to another class or process. Considerable research has been carried out on these biases and they are of great practical importance. However, theoretically, these hypotheses need to be specified more clearly.

WHAT IS THINKING?

Many undergraduates approach the chapters on thinking in an introductory text with avid interest and leave them with a strong sense of disappointment. The refrain is usually, "Is that all there is to it?" This reaction may be, in part, due to the demystification that often follows a scientific treatment of a topic, but there may also be reasonable grounds for it. Two points deserve mention.

First, the coverage of thinking topics from problem solving to reasoning and decision making seems limited in some sense. There are other topics that we have not covered but we have given a representative sample of research from the field. For example, Gilhooly (1988) goes into greater depth on less directed types of thinking, like daydreaming. It is clear that thinking research has attempted to deal with the most tractable cases of thinking, with those tasks that can be studied in the laboratory with some degree of control. This has resulted in some selectivity that can be a source of discontent.

However, the second point is probably more important. There is a strong sense in which thinking research has failed to capture the dynamic qualities of everyday thought. We think that this is a result of the often-lamented, fragmentary nature of the field. As researchers have tried to come to grips with the phenomena of thinking. They have carved them up into bite-sized chunks and undone a wholistic conception of a set of processes working together. We have said a number of times that many of the divisions in the field are created by researchers rather than inherent in the phenomena. In everyday life we use a rich mix of deductive and inductive reasoning and problem-solving strategies. The one shades imperceptibly into the other. Therefore, the big question we need to answer is as follows: Is a unified theory of thinking possible?

Is a Unified Theory Possible?

Even though we have not yet got a unified theory of thinking, we feel that one is feasible: One need only consider the various commonalities between the ostensibly fragmented theories at present.

Practically every theory we have reviewed in the last couple of chapters assumes that people have a limited working memory and a long-term memory containing a set of rules that manipulate representations to carry out thought processes. First, working memory is not only mentioned by theorists but often plays a central role in their predictions. For example, in the water-jug problems, Atwood and Polson make it a core limitation on processing, and the model theory of reasoning derives its predictions regarding the effects of multiple models on performance from the same limitation. Second, most theories assume that the basic process of thinking involves the manipulation of representations using rules of different specificity. For example, in some problem-solving tasks (like the puzzle problems), in propositional reasoning and syllogistic reasoning, and in decision making it has been argued that people use domain-independent, general heuristics. The basic argument between these theorists (if we wish to set them in opposition) concerns the exact nature of these rules and the representations they operate on. We have seen that other theories have elaborated more domain-specific rules to account for expertise and skill acquisition and some forms of reasoning.

In a sense, then, the diversity is more apparent than actual. Researchers agree on the memory components of the system and the means by which processes are carried out. What needs to be done is to coalesce these agreements into a general theory that will deal with the variety of phenomena. The development of cognitive architectures is clearly one attempt to do this and their progress deserves to be followed closely in the coming years.

FURTHER READING

Baron, J. (1988). *Thinking and deciding*. Cambridge: Cambridge University Press. This work provides a good introduction to many of the central issues in decision-making research.

Evans, J.St.B.T. (1989). *Bias in human reasoning*. London: Lawrence Erlbaum Associates Ltd. This recent book reviews research on biases in deductive reasoning and decision making.

Gilhooly, K. (1988). *Thinking: Directed, undirected and creative* (2nd ed.). London: Academic Press. This book provides more detail on some of the research covered here and also other research not considered here.

Gilhooly, K.J., Keane, M.T., Logie, R., & Erdos, G. (1990a; 1990b). *Lines of thinking, Vols.1 & 2*. Chichester: John Wiley. These two volumes contain chapters written by leading researchers on recent developments in many areas of thinking.

Johnson-Laird, P.N. (1983). *Mental models*. Cambridge: Cambridge University Press. This book explores the wider implications of the mental models view.

Johnson-Laird, P.N. & Byrne, R.M.J. (1990). *Deduction*. London: Lawrence Erlbaum Associates Ltd. This work provides the most up-to-date statement of recent developments and extensions of the model theory.

Kahneman, D., Slovic, P., & Tversky, A. (1982). *Judgement under uncertainty*. Cambridge: Cambridge University Press. This book is a good source text for a wide range of papers on decision making.

Chapter Thirteen

COGNITION, EMOTION, AND CLINICAL PSYCHOLOGY

Much of contemporary cognitive psychology has developed from the information-processing approach proposed by Broadbent (1958). This approach has tended to be dominated by the computer analogy or metaphor, and has led to an emphasis on stages of information processing such as encoding, storage, and retrieval. One of the limitations of this approach is that it does not readily lend itself to an examination of the relationship between cognition and emotion. Indeed, Eysenck (1984, p.5) bemoaned the failure of cognitive psychologists to take emotion seriously into account:

> Philosophers of yesteryear used to distinguish between cognition, conation (or motivation), and affect (emotion). Cognitive psychologists have the choice of attempting to keep the motivational and emotional states of their subjects constant (so that these factors can be ignored), or of systematically manipulating both motivation and emotion in order to observe their effects on cognition. With very few exceptions, cognitive psychologists have made the former choice.

Matters have not changed enormously in the years since then. However, there has been a definite increase in the interest which cognitive psychologists have shown in the area of cognition and emotion. The goal of this chapter is to provide coverage of some of the main issues and current research in this area.

INTRODUCTION

Before proceeding, it is desirable to consider some definitions. The term "affect" is a very broad one, and has often been used to cover a wide variety of experiences such as emotions, moods, and preferences. The term "emotion" tends to be used to refer to relatively brief but intense experiences, whereas the term "mood" or "state" is used to describe less intense but more prolonged experiences.

The so-called affective mood disorders are of great relevance to this chapter. These mood disorders include clinical anxiety and clinical depression. Clinical anxiety can be sub-categorised into agoraphobia, social phobia, panic disorder, generalised anxiety disorder, obsessive compulsive disorder, and so on. However, our main focus will be on generalised anxiety disorder, in which the patient experiences anxiety across a wide range of situations. In similar fashion, clinical depression can be sub-categorised. Two of the most influential distinctions are those between unipolar and bipolar depression (Depue & Monroe, 1979), and between endogenous (= originating from within) and nonendogenous depression (Fowles & Gersh, 1979), but sub-categories within clinical depression will not generally be considered in the research to be discussed.

As we will see later in the chapter, several differences in cognitive functioning have been discovered between patients with mood disorders and normal individuals. This raises the exciting possibility that some understanding of the nature of mood disorders, and of the factors responsible for their development, can be obtained by studying the cognitive system of anxious and depressed patients. At present, there is a slightly odd situation; considerable use is made of cognitive therapy for mood-disordered patients (e.g. Beck, 1976; Meichenbaum, 1977), despite the fact that relatively little is known for certain about the functioning (or malfunctioning) of the cognitive system in such patients. For malfunctioning) of the cognitive system in such patients. For anyone interested in the practical applications of cognitive psychology, there may well be more scope here than anywhere else.

DOES AFFECT REQUIRE COGNITION?

Suppose that a stimulus is presented to an individual, as a result of which the individual's affective response to that stimulus changes in a systematic way. Is it essential for the stimulus to be processed cognitively by that individual in order for the changed affective response to occur? This issue is of theoretical importance. If affective responses to all stimuli depend on cognitive processing, it follows that theories of emotion should have a distinctly cognitive flavour about them. In contrast, if cognitive processing is not necessary in the development of affective responses to stimuli, then a specifically cognitive approach to emotion may be less necessary.

There is a genuine controversy here, because there have been major disagreements about the answer to the question posed in the previous paragraph. Zajonc (1980; 1984) has consistently argued that the affective evaluation of stimuli is a very basic process which can occur independently of cognitive processes. In the words of Zajonc (1984, p.117), "affect and cognition are separate and partially independent systems and . . . although they ordinarily function conjointly, affect could be generated without a prior cognitive process." In contrast, Lazarus (1982, p.1021) claimed that some cognitive processing is an essential prerequisite for an affective reaction to a stimulus to occur: "Cognitive appraisal (of meaning or significance) underlies and is an integral feature of all emotional states."

Zajonc's (1980) Theoretical Position

Since this controversy was started by Zajonc (1980), it is probably appropriate to start with a consideration of his point of view. According to him, we frequently make affective judgements about people and objects even though we have processed very little information about them. For example, we may meet someone very briefly, and be left with a positive or negative feeling about that person despite not remembering any detailed information about them (e.g. hair colour; eye colour; and so on).

At the empirical level, Zajonc discussed several studies which he claimed provided support for his theoretical position. In these studies, it was found that stimuli (e.g. melodies, pictures), if presented either very briefly at a subliminal level or while the subject was involved in another task, could not subsequently be recognised. In spite of the absence of any recollection of having seen or heard the stimuli before, subjects were still more likely to choose previously presented stimuli than equivalent new stimuli when asked to select the ones they preferred. In other words, there was a positive affective reaction to the previously presented stimuli (as assessed by the preference judgements), but there was no evidence of cognitive processing (as assessed by recognition-memory performance). This phenomenon has been described as the "mere exposure" effect (e.g. Seamon, March, & Brody, 1984).

The notion that such findings indicate that affect can occur in the absence of prior cognitive processing has been criticised on various counts by several theorists including Lazarus (1982). One limitation of such studies is that they do not have much obvious relevance to ordinary emotional states. The subjects were only required to make superficial preference judgements to relatively meaningless stimuli having little relevance to their personal lives, and so no more than minimal affect is likely to have been involved. Another major problem with these studies is that the conclusion that the stimuli had not been processed cognitively was based on a failure of recognition memory. This conclusion may make sense if one equates cognition with consciousness, but very few cognitive psychologists would be willing to do that. The data by no means rule out the possibility that there was extensive pre-conscious processing involving automatic and other processes. As we saw in

Chapter 2, there is evidence from other experiments that suggests the existence of subliminal perception.

Lazarus's (1982) Theoretical Position

Lazarus (e.g. Lazarus, 1982; Lazarus, Kanner, & Folkman, 1980) has argued for many years that *cognitive appraisal* plays a crucial role in emotional experience. Cognitive appraisal can be sub-divided into three more specific forms of appraisal:

- *primary appraisal*, in which an environmental situation is regarded as being positive, stressful, or irrelevant to well-being;
- *secondary appraisal*, in which account is taken of the resources which the individual can call on to cope with the situation;
- *reappraisal*, in which the stimulus situation and the coping strategies are monitored, with the primary and secondary appraisals being modified if necessary.

The importance of cognitive appraisal in determining emotional experience has been shown in several studies by Lazarus and his associates (see Lazarus, 1966, for a review). The basic approach involved presenting an anxiety-evoking film under various conditions. One film showed a Stone-age ritual in which adolescent boys had their penises deeply cut, and another film showed various workshop accidents. The most dramatic of these accidents involved a board caught in a circular saw which rammed with tremendous force through the midsection of a worker, who dies writhing on the floor. Cognitive appraisal was manipulated by varying the accompanying soundtrack, and then comparing the stress experienced against a control condition in which there was no sound track. Denial was produced by indicating that the subincision film did not show a painful operation, or that those involved in the safety film were actors. Intellectualisation was produced in the subincision film by considering matters from the perspective of an anthropologist viewing strange native customs, and was produced in the workshop film by telling the viewer to consider the situation in an objective fashion. Various psycho-physiological measures of arousal or stress (e.g. heart rate; galvanic skin response) were taken continuously during the viewing of the film.

The major finding of the various studies was that denial and intellectualisation both produced substantial reductions in stress as indexed by the psychophysiological measures. In other words, manipulating an individual's cognitive appraisal when confronted by a stressful event can have a significant effect on physiological stress reactions.

In essence, Lazarus (1982) generalised from his experimental findings, and proposed that cognitive appraisal invariably precedes any affective reaction. However, he was careful to point out that cognitive appraisal does not have to involve a conscious process.

The weakness in his theoretical position, as is pointed out by Zajonc (1984), is that very often the notion that pre-conscious cognitive processes determine affective reactions is no more than an article of faith. That is to say, we generally have little direct evidence of either the existence or of the nature of such cognitive processes. However, the literature on subliminal perception (see Chapter 2) suggests that there are probably important pre-conscious cognitive processes.

Summary

Zajonc (1980) provided some evidence that affective responses can occur in the absence of any conscious awareness of cognitive processing, and even Lazarus (1982) does not dispute that this is possible. There is also agreement that cognition and emotion have reciprocal influences on each other. Furthermore, it is not contentious to assume that these reciprocal influences can be rather complex.

Zajonc (1984, p.122) pinpointed the area of controversy: "It is a critical question for cognitive theory and for theories of emotion to determine just what is the minimal information process that is required for emotion. Can untransformed, pure sensory input directly generate emotional reactions?" Unfortunately, as we have seen, the available empirical evidence does not really permit us to provide a convincing answer to the question. However, it is revealing that Lazarus made use of studies involving genuine emotional reactions to meaningful stimuli to support his argument that cognition always precedes affect, whereas Zajonc (1980) relied heavily on studies involving marginally emotional reactions to relatively meaningless stimuli to confirm his view that cognition does not necessarily precede affect. There is no doubt that Lazarus's studies have far more direct relevance to everyday emotional experiences than do those of Zajonc. This provides grounds for assuming (albeit tentatively) that emotional experience is generally preceded by cognitive processes, even if that is not invariably the case.

EMOTION, LEARNING, AND MEMORY

Repression

Freud (1915; 1943) consistently emphasised the importance of emotional factors in affecting memory. In particular, he argued that very threatening or anxiety-provoking material would be unable to gain access to conscious awareness, and he used the term *repression* to refer to this phenomenon. According to Freud (1915, p.86), "The essence of repression lies simply in the function of rejecting and keeping something out of consciousness." This is a very general definition, and it should be noted that Freud actually attached somewhat different meanings to the concept of "repression" at different times (Madison, 1956). For example, he sometimes used it to refer to the inhibition of the capacity for emotional experience. According to this definition, repression can occur even when there is conscious awareness of ideas, provided that these ideas are lacking their emotional content.

Freud's ideas emerged as a result of his clinical experiences. The repression which he claimed to observe mostly involved traumatic events which had happened to his patients. In spite of the fact that there are obvious ethical reasons why it is totally out of the question to produce repression in the clinical sense under laboratory conditions, there have been numerous attempts to study repression at an experimental level. Such attempts have usually involved creating anxiety in order to produce forgetting (repression), followed by removal of the anxiety in order to show that the repressed information is still stored ("return of the repressed"). In practical terms, anxiety has usually been produced by providing failure feedback to subjects performing a task, and anxiety has then been reduced either by reassuring the subjects that the failure feedback was not genuine or by providing success feedback on the task previously associated with failure.

Apparent evidence of repression and the return of the repressed has been obtained in several studies (see Eysenck, 1977, and Holmes, 1974, for reviews). However, the interpretation of the findings is controversial. It is possible that people show poor recall after a failure experience simply because they are thinking about their failure rather than devoting all of their attention to the recall test. D'Zurilla (1965) found that subjects exposed to failure feedback did, indeed, report more thoughts that were quite irrelevant to the subsequent task of recall than did subjects not exposed to failure feedback.

Holmes (1972) investigated this hypothesis further. Subjects were presented with a list of words. Subsequently, they received a personality test incorporating the same words, and were given ego-threatening, ego-enhancing, or neutral feedback. Holmes discovered that ego-enhancing feedback reduced recall to the same extent as ego-threatening feedback. There is no reason at all for supposing that ego enhancement produced repression. It is more likely that, as Holmes suggested, both ego enhancement and ego threat caused a relative lack of attention to the immediately following recall test.

In sum, it has not been possible to obtain convincing evidence of repression under laboratory conditions. The main reason is that even the apparently favourable findings are open to a variety of interpretations that have nothing to do with repression. However, there is reasonable evidence for the related phenomenon of *perceptual defence*, which was discussed in Chapter 3. This phenomenon refers to the finding that visual stimuli of an emotionally disturbing character need to be presented for longer durations than neutral stimuli for them to be recognised. Perceptual defence is of importance in its own right, but in terms of its relevance to repression it is hard to disagree with Brewin's

(1988, p.28) assessment: "The raising of a perceptual threshold is still a long way from the complete absence of a memory for a traumatic event."

Bower's Network Theory of Affect

Bower and his associates (e.g. Bower, 1981; Bower & Cohen, 1982; Gilligan & Bower, 1984) have proposed what they term a network theory of affect, aspects of which are shown in Fig. 13.1. This theory has been very influential, and is well worth considering in some detail. Gilligan and Bower (1984) have put forward the most comprehensive statement of network theory, and so the description of the theory will be based on their account. The theory makes six theoretical assumptions:

Bower's (1981) semantic network theory. The circles represent modes or units within the network.

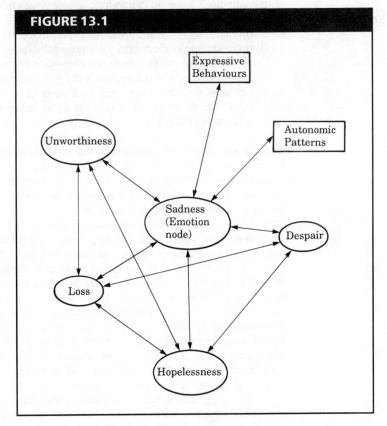

FIGURE 13.1

- emotions can be regarded as units or nodes in a semantic network, with numerous connections to related ideas, to physiological systems, to events, and to muscular and expressive patterns;
- emotional material is stored in the semantic network in the form of propositions or assertions;

- thought occurs via the activation of nodes within the semantic network;
- nodes can be activated either by external or by internal stimuli;
- activation from an activated node spreads in a selective fashion to related nodes;
- "consciousness" consists of a network of nodes which is activated above some threshold value.

These assumptions lead to four hypotheses:

Hypothesis 1 (mood-state-dependent recall): recall memory is best when the mood at recall matches that at the time of learning.

Hypothesis 2 (thought congruity): an individual's free associations, interpretations, thoughts, and judgements tend to be thematically congruent with his or her mood state.

Hypothesis 3 (mood congruity): emotionally toned information is learned best when there is correspondence between its affective value and the learner's current mood state.

Hypothesis 4 (mood intensity): increases in intensity of mood cause increases in the activation of associated nodes in the associative network.

How exactly do the six theoretical assumptions relate to the four hypotheses? So far as mood-state-dependent recall is concerned, associations are formed at the time of learning between the activated nodes representing the to-be-remembered items and the emotion node or nodes activated because of the subject's mood state. At the time of recall, the mood state at that time leads to activation of the appropriate emotion node. Activation then spreads from that emotion node to the various nodes associated with it. If there is a match between the mood state at learning and at recall, then this increases activation of the nodes of to-be-remembered items, and enhances recall. However, the associative links between the to-be-remembered stimulus material and the relevant emotion node are likely to be relatively weak. As a consequence, mood-state-dependent effects are likely to be much greater when the memory test is a difficult one offering few retrieval cues (e.g. free recall) than when the memory test provides strong retrieval cues (e.g. recognition memory).

It should be noted that mood-state-dependent effects are also predicted by other theories. For example, according to Tulving's (1979) encoding specificity principle, the success of recall or recognition depends on the extent to which the information available at the time of retrieval matches the information stored in memory (see Chapter 5 for details). If information about the mood state at the time of learning is stored in memory, then being in the same mood state at the time of retrieval obviously increases this matching of information. Theoretically, this should increase both recall and recognition.

Thought congruity occurs for two reasons. First, the current mood state leads to activation of the corresponding emotion node. Second, activation spreads from that emotion node to other, associatively related nodes, which will tend to contain information that is emotionally congruent with the activated emotion node.

Mood congruity occurs when people in a good mood remember emotionally positive stimulus material better than those in a bad mood, whereas the opposite is true for emotionally negative stimulus material. According to Gilligan and Bower (1984), mood congruity depends on the fact that emotionally loaded information tends to be associated more strongly with its congruent emotion node than with any other emotion node. Thus, for example, those nodes containing information about anxiety-provoking events and experiences are associatively linked to the emotion node for anxiety. To-be-remembered stimulus material which is congruent with the current mood state links up with this associative network of similar information, and this leads to extensive or elaborative encoding of the to-be-remembered material. As we saw in Chapter 5, elaborate encoding is generally associated with superior long-term memory.

It seems reasonable to assume that the effects described here would simply become stronger as the intensity of the current mood increases. The reason for assuming this is that the spread of activation from the activated emotion node to other related nodes would increase in line with the intensity with which that emotion was experienced. However, it is possible that a very sad mood leads to a focus on internal information relating to failure, fatigue, and so on. This may inhibit processing of all kinds of external stimuli, whether or not they are congruent with the sad mood state.

Mood States

The most difficult issue so far as testing Bower's network theory is concerned is to decide how to make sure that the subjects are in the appropriate mood state. In a very general sense, one can either attempt to induce the required mood state under laboratory conditions, or one can make use of naturally occurring mood states (e.g. in patients with mood disorders). As we will see shortly, both approaches have their problems and limitations.

The most popular mood-induction approach is based on the procedure introduced by Velten (1968). What happens is that subjects read a set of sentences which are designed to induce increasingly intense feelings of either elation or depression. Subjects exposed to this procedure typically report that their mood has altered in the predicted direction, but it is possible that they are simply responding in the way they believe the experimenter expects of them. A further problem is that this mood-induction procedure typically produces a blend of several different mood states rather than just the desired one (Polivy, 1981).

Bower (e.g. Bower, Gilligan, & Monteiro, 1981; Bower & Mayer, 1985) has used hypnosis combined with self-generated imagery. The subjects are hypnotised at the beginning of the experiment. When in the hypnotic state, they are asked to think of images of a past happy or sad emotional experience, using those images to produce the appropriate mood state. This approach appears to produce relatively strong and long-lasting moods, but it suffers from some disadvantages. It is necessary to use subjects who score highly on tests of hypnotic susceptibility, and it may be unwise to generalise from them to people who are low in hypnotic susceptibility.

Some researchers have made use of naturally occurring mood states. A particularly interesting way of doing this is to study manic-depressive patients. These patients have very large mood swings between great excitement or mania and great sadness or depression. The strength of their mood states and the fact that their memory can be tested either in the same mood as at learning or in the opposite mood are two good reasons for studying such patients.

Experimental Findings

There is some experimental support for all four hypotheses proposed by Gilligan and Bower (1984). The strongest support has been for mood congruity, i.e. learning is best when the subject's mood matches the emotional tone of the to-be-learned material. However, as the review by Blaney (1986) indicates, there have been several failures to obtain mood-state-dependent recall, thought congruity, mood congruity, and mood intensity.

Experimental studies designed to test for mood-state-dependent recall have typically made use of either one or two learning lists of words. Learning occurs in one mood state (e.g. happy or sad), and recall occurs in the same mood state or in a different one. When two lists are presented (e.g. Bower, Monteiro, & Gilligan, 1978; Schare, Lisman, & Spear, 1984), one list is learned in one mood and the other list is learned in a different mood. Subsequently subjects are put back into one of these two moods, and asked to recall only the list learned first. The prediction from the mood-state-dependent hypothesis is that recall should be higher when the mood state at the time of recall is the same as that at the time of learning.

Schare et al. (1984) and Bower et al. (1978) obtained mood-state-dependent recall with the two-list design but not with the one-list design. It is possible to explain this in terms of interference. If subjects were attempting to recall the first list with the mood appropriate to the second list, then they might think of some of the words from the second list, and this would interfere with the task of recalling first-list words, thus producing a stronger effect. Although this sounds plausible, some researchers (e.g. Wetzler, 1985) have been unable to replicate the mood-state-dependent recall effect with either the one-list or the two-list design.

Thought congruity has been investigated in various ways. One popular method is to present subjects with a list of pleasant and unpleasant words prior to mood induction, and then to test for recall after mood induction. The prediction is that pleasant words will be recalled better after pleasant mood induction than after unpleasant mood induction, with the opposite being the case for unpleasant words. Another common method is to ask subjects to recall autobiographical memories following mood induction. Pleasant moods should increase the number of pleasant memories recalled, and perhaps the speed with which they are recalled, and unpleasant moods should do the same for unpleasant memories.

Thought congruity has been shown in a number of studies using both of the methods just described (see Blaney, 1986, for a review). One of the more interesting studies was reported by Clark and Teasdale (1982). They tested depressed patients on two occasions close in time, with the depth of the depression being more severe on one occasion than on the other. More depressing or unhappy memories and fewer happy memories were recalled on the more depressed occasion, with the opposite being the case on the less depressed occasion. As they pointed out, these findings are consistent with the notion of a vicious circle in depressed patients: Depressed mood state leads to recall of depressing memories, and the recall of depressing memories exacerbates the depressed mood state.

As already indicated, there is perhaps more experimental support for mood congruity than for any of the other hypotheses put forward by Gilligan and Bower (1984). The usual procedure in studies of mood congruity is that a mood is induced, followed by the learning of a list or the reading of a story containing emotionally toned material. There is then a memory test for the list or the story after the subject's mood state has returned to normal. Mood congruity is demonstrated by finding that recall is best when the affective value of the to-be-learned material matches the subject's mood state at the time of learning.

Bower et al. (1981, Exp. 1) investigated mood congruity. Subjects who had been hypnotised to feel happy or sad read a story about two college men, Jack and Andre. Jack is very depressed and glum, whereas Andre is very happy. On a subsequent memory test, subjects tended to recall more information about the character whose emotional state was similar to, or congruent with, their own when reading the story (see Fig. 13. 2). Bower et al. also found that the subjects reported identifying with the story character whose mood resembled their own while they were reading the story.

Although there are several experimental demonstrations of mood congruity, some doubts about their value have been raised by Perrig and Perrig (1988, Exp. 1). They instructed their subjects to behave as if they were depressed or happy, but they made no attempt to induce any mood state. This was followed by a word list containing positive, negative, and neutral words, which had to be

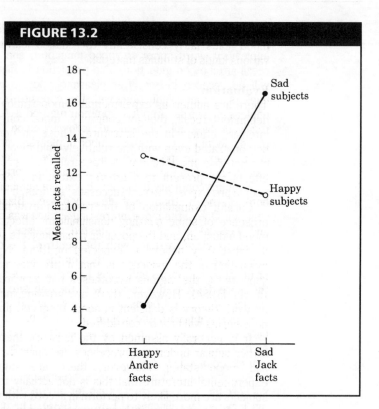

FIGURE 13.2

Recall of happy and sad facts by happy and sad subjects. Based on data in Bower, Gilligan, and Monteiro (1981, Exp.1).

recalled. Those subjects who indicated an awareness of mood-congruity effects produced results very similar to those obtained by Bower et al. (1981, Exp. 1), whereas those subjects who did not showed no evidence of selective learning.

One interpretation of Perrig and Perrig's findings is that the subjects were simply behaving in the way they thought the experimenter wanted them to behave. It might even be that the mood-congruity effects obtained in mood-induction studies merely reflect a desire on the part of subjects to do what is expected of them. An alternative (and more plausible) interpretation is the one offered by Perrig and Perrig (1988, p.102): "Mood may be a sufficient but not a necessary condition to produce the mood-congruity effect of selective learning." In other words, mood-congruity effects can be produced *either* by means of genuine mood induction *or* by means of mood simulation. If mood-congruity effects can occur in two different ways, then researchers need to pay more attention to the difficult task of distinguishing between genuine mood effects and simulated mood effects.

There has been relatively little work concerned with the mood-intensity hypothesis. Such research as there is tends to support this hypothesis with positive moods but not with negative moods. The notion that very sad moods lead to reduced processing of all kinds of external stimuli has been investigated by Ellis (e.g. Ellis,

Thomas, McFarland, & Lane, 1985). He has found that depressed mood leads fairly consistently to reduced learning and recall of various kinds of stimulus material.

Evaluation

There are numerous experimental demonstrations of mood-state-dependent recall, thought congruity, mood congruity, and mood intensity effects in the literature. These phenomena have been demonstrated even with the relatively mild mood inductions which characterise most laboratory research. It is probable that these effects are present to a greater extent in everyday life, where people are exposed to real successes, failures, and tragedies.

Careful examination of the research evidence points to the presence of some puzzling nonsignificant effects, problems with mood induction, and the possibility that subjects sometimes simply do what they believe is expected of them. Nevertheless, our evaluation of the evidence is that it provides reasonably strong support for the various hypotheses put forward by Gilligan and Bower (1984). However, there are growing indications that the network theory is deficient in some respects, and some of these deficiencies will now be considered.

It is generally assumed by the network theory of affect that rather similar underlying processes are operative in happy and in sad mood states. However, there are suggestions in the experimental literature that this is not actually the case, and that subjects are more likely to perform in accord with the predictions of network theory when in happy moods than in sad moods. Happy moods typically facilitate the learning and the recall of affectively positive material while inhibiting the learning and recall of affectively negative material. However, sad moods have often been found to reduce the learning and recall of affectively positive material without enhancing the learning and recall of negative material.

A rather striking disconfirmation of Bower's semantic network theory of affect was reported by Williams and Broadbent (1986). They investigated the retrieval of autobiographical memories to positive and negative cue words by people who had recently attempted suicide by overdose and by normal controls. The suicide attempters were slower to retrieve personal memories to the positive cue words, but somewhat surprisingly the two groups did not differ in their performance with the negative cue words.

What is going on here? While Bower (1981) and Gilligan and Bower (1984) predict that a sad mood will always lead to increased learning and memory for affectively negative material, this seems somewhat dubious from a commonsensical point of view. Presumably anyone who is in a sad mood will be motivated to improve his or her mood, and focusing on associations which are congruent with the sad mood is hardly likely to achieve that objective. What may well be happening is that a negative or sad mood activates negative assocations in the relatively automatic way specified by these researchers, but that efforts are then made to counteract the resultant negative effects by actively attempting to focus on noncongruent or positive associations (Fiske & Taylor, 1984).

One of the somewhat unusual characteristics of the network theory of affect is the extent to which emotions are treated as being rather similar to semantic concepts and ideas. Thus, semantic concepts and emotions are both represented as nodes within the same semantic network. It is highly probable that this is an over-simplified view. For example, emotional states or moods can be experienced in several different intensities ranging from the very strong to the very weak, which is not the case with semantic concepts. Since moods typically change relatively slowly over time, it is reasonable to assume that activated emotion nodes tend to remain activated for some time. In contrast, semantic concepts are usually activated for only relatively short periods of time.

Mood Disorders and Memory

The relationship between emotion and memory can also be investigated by studying patients suffering from mood disorders. Such studies are of theoretical interest, but tend not to provide direct tests of Bower's network theory of affect. The reason in a nutshell is that the hypotheses proposed by Gilligan and Bower (1984) can only be tested by manipulating the subjects' mood states at the time of learning and at the time of the memory test. Most anxious patients will be anxious both at learning and at retrieval, and depressed patients will be depressed at learning and at test. If such patients show especially good recall for stimulus material matching their mood, it is not clear whether this occurs because of a matching between mood and material at the time of learning (i.e. mood congruity) or because of a matching between mood and material at the time of the memory test (i.e. thought congruity).

Depression

Research on memory in depressed patients has been much influenced by the theoretical views of Beck and the findings of Rogers, Kuiper, and Kirker (1977). Beck (1976) argued that depressed patients possess various cognitive schemata (i.e. organised packets of knowledge) concerned with the self. For example, they allegedly have negative schemata involving themes such as personal deficiency, worthlessness, self-blame, guilt, rejection, and deprivation. Schemata are discussed in Chapter 8. Rogers et al. discovered that asking subjects to make self-reference judgements (i.e. describes you?) about words led to much higher levels of subsequent word recall than other processing tasks such as semantic judgements (i.e. means the same as?). According to them, performance is high in the self-reference condition (especially when the self-referent judgements are affirmative) because of the existence of a self-schema which provides a rich network of associations.

If we combine Beck's views with the data of Rogers et al., it is possible to derive predictions concerning memory in depressed patients. Depressed patients given a self-referent task should recall relatively more negative words relevant to their negative self-schemata than should normal controls; this is known as negative recall bias. However, if this negative recall bias depends on the operation of negative self-schemata, then it should not be obtained with other judgement tasks.

The findings have generally supported these predictions. Derry and Kuiper (1981) compared the recall of depressed patients, nondepressed patients, and normal controls for adjectives which had received self-referent, semantic, or structured (i.e. big letters?) judgements. The negative self-schemata of depressed patients should be involved primarily on the self-referent task with those negative adjectives which were rated affirmatively, i.e. felt to be self-referent. Accordingly, depressed patients should show a negative recall bias for these adjectives. The results were in line with this prediction, and the groups did not differ in recall following semantic or structured judgements.

Proportions of recalled words that were negative in content in each condition for depressed patients and normal controls. Data are corrected for the total number of items presented in each condition and come from Bradley and Mathews (1983).

Rather similar findings were reported by Bradley and Mathews (1983). They presented depressed patients and normal controls with positive and negative adjectives. Subjects had to make self-referent judgements on some of the adjectives, whereas for others they had to decide either whether the adjective applied to a familiar

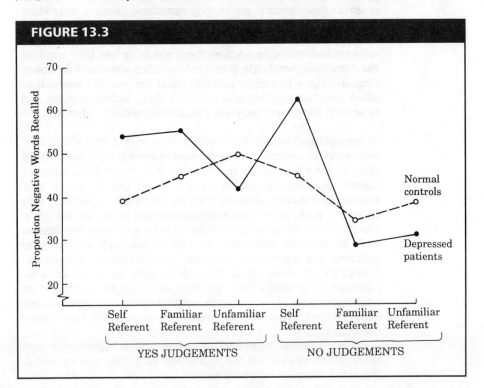

FIGURE 13.3

person or to an unfamiliar person. It was expected that the depressed patients would show a negative recall bias only in the self-referent condition. Despite some variability in the data, this was the result obtained (see Fig. 13.3).

If depressed patients learn and/or recall negative information about themselves to a greater extent than normals, this would presumably tend to increase their depressed mood state. In turn, an increase in depressed mood state could lead to a greater negative recall bias, thus creating a vicious cycle. In other words, the negative recall bias shown by depressed patients is of theoretical and clinical significance because it could play a part in maintaining their clinically depressed state. More will be said about the interpretation of these findings later in the chapter.

Anxiety

According to Beck and Clark (1988, p.26), anxious patients resemble depressed patients in possessing negative schemata. In the case of anxious patients, these schemata involve "perceived physical or psychological threat to one's personal domain as well as an exaggerated sense of vulnerability." It would seem reasonable to predict that anxious patients would also resemble depressed patients in showing a negative recall bias. In fact, most of the evidence resolutely fails to confirm this prediction. For example, Mogg, Mathews, and Weinman (1987) presented a mixture of positive, threatening negative (e.g. humiliated), and nonthreatening negative (e.g. bored) adjectives to patients with generalised anxiety disorder and to normal controls. For some of the words the subjects had to decide whether the word described them, and for the remaining words they decided whether the word described Angela Rippon (a well-known television performer). Subsequent recall and recognition tests indicated that anxious patients had relatively poorer memory for threatening material than did the control subjects.

Mogg (1988) reported five further experiments in which patients with generalised anxiety disorder failed to exhibit a negative recall bias. In a sixth experiment, they did show a significant negative memory bias when a recall test was used, but failed to do so with a recognition-memory test. Why is there so little evidence of a negative recall bias in anxious patients? According to Mathews, Mogg, May, and Eysenck (1989), the reason may be that anxious patients have learned the strategy of voluntary avoidance of elaborative or extensive processing of threat-related information, presumably because it is very unpleasant to focus on such information. It follows from this reasoning that it might be possible to demonstrate a negative memory bias in anxious patients provided that the memory test selected was unaffected by learning strategies.

Mathews et al. (1989) made use of the distinction between explicit and implicit memory that was discussed in Chapter 6. Explicit memory can be assessed by free recall, by cued recall, or by recognition, and performance on tests of explicit memory is affected by the strategic processes involved in elaboration of the stimulus material. In contrast, implicit memory can be assessed by means of a word-completion test, and is largely or entirely unaffected by strategic processes. Subjects given a word-completion test are simply asked to complete word stems (e.g. SEC) by writing down the first word which comes to mind (e.g. SECRET). Some subjects have previously been presented with words fitting the word stems, and their greater tendency than control subjects to produce these words on the word-completion test provides a measure of implicit memory.

Mathews et al. presented patients with generalised anxiety disorder and normal controls with threat-related words and nonthreatening words. They instructed their subjects to imagine themselves in a scene involving themselves and the referent of each word. They were then given a cued recall task to assess explicit memory and a word-completion task to assess implicit memory.

The key results are shown in Fig. 13.4. As had previously been found by Mogg et al. (1987) and by Mogg (1988), the anxious patients did not show a negative recall bias in explicit memory. However, they did show a negative bias in implicit memory. These findings suggest that there is greater activation of the internal representations of threatening words in anxious patients than in normal controls (thus producing effects on implicit memory), but that this greater activation is counteracted in explicit memory by attempts to avoid elaborate processing of the threatening words.

These findings may shed some light on the problems experienced by anxious patients. It has been argued (e.g. Foa & Kozak, 1986) that anxiety is often reduced by actively considering threatening information, and looking for additional, reassuring information that will reduce the subjective threat. The combination of repeated activation of threatening representations in memory and curtailed elaborative processing may play a part in maintaining the clinically anxious state precisely because it reduces the probability of restructuring long-term memory in that way.

As we saw earlier, Beck and Clark (1988) assumed that anxious patients possess negative schemata relating to physical and/or psychological threat. If this is the case, then such schemata might influence the way in which ambiguous stimuli are interpreted and remembered. More specifically, if an ambiguous stimulus can be interpreted in either a threatening or a neutral fashion, then anxious patients might tend to favour the threatening interpretation more than would be the case with normal controls (see Chapter 9 for a discussion of comprehension processes).

The evidence broadly supports the notion that anxious patients differ from normal controls in their interpretation of, and memory for, ambiguous stimuli. For example, Mathews, Richards, and Eysenck (1989) asked patients with generalised anxiety disorder and normal controls to write down the spelling of auditorily

Explicit memory (cued recall) and implicit memory (word completion) for patients with generalised anxiety disorder and normal controls. Data from Mathews, May, Mogg, and Eysenck (1989).

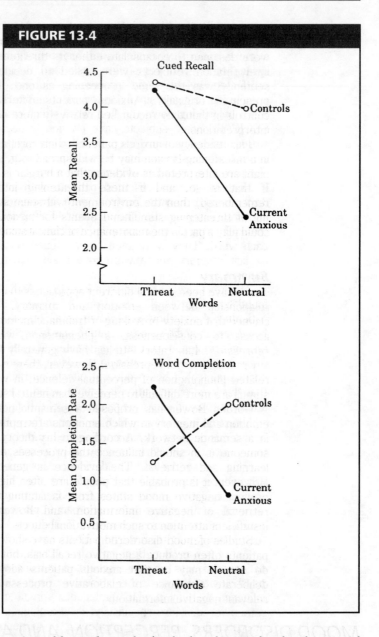

FIGURE 13.4

presented homophones having both a threat-related and a neutral interpretation (e.g. die, dye; guilt, gilt). The percentages of threat-related homophone spellings were significantly higher in the anxious patient group than in the control group.

Memory for ambiguous sentences was examined by Eysenck, Mogg, Richards, and Mathews (Note 2). They presented ambiguous sentences (e.g. "The two men watched as the chest was opened") which could be interpreted in either a threatening or a nonthreatening fashion. Reworded versions of each ambiguous sentence were used on a subsequent recognition-memory test, and were designed to encapsulate either its threatening or its neutral interpretation. Subjects were asked to decide whether each sentence was the same in meaning as one of the sentences presented originally. Anxious patients differed from normal controls in that they recognised relatively more of the threatening interpretations.

This tendency of anxious patients to interpret ambiguous stimuli in a threatening fashion may be widespread (e.g. strange noises at night are interpreted as evidence that a burglar is trying to get in). If that is so, and if these threatening interpretations are remembered, then the environment will seem subjectively to be full of threatening stimuli and events for anxious patients. This could play a part in the maintenance of clinical anxiety.

Summary

There have been several different approaches to understanding the relationship between emotion and memory. Sigmund Freud claimed that anxiety-provoking or traumatic memories were denied access to consciousness, a phenomenon which he termed *repression*. Laboratory studies have generally failed to provide any real support for repression. However, there is evidence for the related phenomenon of perceptual defence, in which threatening stimuli are more difficult to perceive than neutral stimuli.

Gordon Bower has proposed a semantic network theory of emotion and memory in which emotions are represented as nodes in a semantic network. According to his theory, the mood that someone is in should influence the processes occurring at both learning and retrieval. The evidence is generally supportive. However, it is probable that people are often highly motivated to prevent negative mood states from facilitating the learning and retrieval of negative information, and Bower's theory pays insufficient attention to such motivational effects.

Studies of mood-disordered patients have shown that depressed patients often produce a negative recall bias, but anxious patients do not. It may be that anxious patients adopt a strategy of deliberate avoidance of elaborative processing of personally relevant negative information.

MOOD DISORDERS, PERCEPTION, AND ATTENTION

Anxiety

It has often been assumed (e.g. Beck & Emery, 1985; Eysenck, 1982; 1988) that many of the major effects of anxiety on cognitive functioning involve attentional processes. One possible reason for this is that the anxious individual feels vulnerable and is very concerned about possible dangers. As a consequence, he or she scans the environment in a vigilant fashion looking for signs of danger. In the words of Beck and Emery (1985, p.31), individuals suffering from generalised anxiety disorder can be regarded as "hypersensitive alarm systems." Major characteristics of attention are discussed in Chapter 4.

There are several different ways in which anxiety might affect attentional processes:

- There is the *content* of the information to which attention is directed. If anxious patients are sensitive to danger, then it is entirely possible that they are more likely than normal individuals to attend to threat-related stimuli.
- There is attentional control or *distractibility*; the sensitivity to danger of anxious individuals may mean that they find it difficult to avoid attending to task-irrelevant stimuli, and are thus highly distractible.
- There is *attentional selectivity*; this refers to the extent to which attention is narrowly or broadly focused.
- There is the available *capacity* of the attentional system.

Attentional Content
Common sense indicates that anxious individuals are more likely than nonanxious individuals to attend to, and to process, threat-related stimuli (e.g. obscene words; words relating to social or physical threat). However, it turns out that reality is more complicated than common sense would have one believe. Individuals high and low in trait anxiety (i.e. a personality dimension referring to individual differences in susceptibility to anxiety) have not generally been found to differ in their processing of threatening stimuli (see Eysenck, MacLeod, & Mathews, 1987, for a review).

These nonsignificant findings may simply mean that individuals varying in anxiety level do not differ in their processing of threat-related stimuli. However, there is a more interesting possibility. Suppose for the sake of argument that those high and low in anxiety differ in terms of a *selective* bias. If a threat-related and a neutral stimulus are presented together, then individuals high in anxiety will selectively attend to the threat-related stimulus, whereas those low in anxiety will selectively attend to the neutral stimulus. This hypothesis could account for the nonsignificant findings in most of the published research, in which one stimulus was presented at a time. In such circumstances, selective allocation of processing resources was not possible.

This selective bias hypothesis was first tested in an experiment reported in Eysenck et al. (1987). They discovered that normals high in anxiety showed a selective bias in favour of processing threatening stimuli. The selective bias hypothesis has also been tested a number of times with anxious patients with a diagnosis of generalised anxiety disorder. For example, MacLeod, Mathews, and Tata (1986) used a task in which two words were presented visually at the same time, and the upper word had to be read aloud. On some trials a dot replaced one of the words, and the subjects were asked to respond as rapidly as possible to the dot. The speed of response to the dot was used as a measure of attentional allocation. On critical trials, one threatening and one neutral word were presented, and one of them was replaced by a dot.

The results are shown in Fig. 13.5. The anxious patients showed attentional bias towards threatening words (a mixture of social threat, e.g. "humiliated," and physical threat, e.g. "crippled"). In contrast, the normal controls showed a slight bias away from threat. These findings are consistent with the views of Beck and Emery (1985, p.31) based on their clinical experience: "An anxious patient will be hypersensitive to any aspects of a situation that are potentially harmful, but will not respond to its benign or positive aspects."

Mean detection latencies to the probe as a function of the area of the screen where the probe was presented and as a function of groups (anxious patients vs. normal controls). Data from MacLeod, Mathews, and Tata (1986).

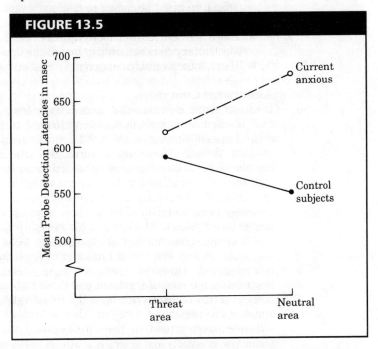

FIGURE 13.5

Mathews and MacLeod (1986) obtained evidence that the selective processing bias in anxious patients occurred even in the absence of conscious awareness. Unattended threatening stimuli had a greater disruptive effect on performance than did unattended neutral stimuli, and this was so despite the fact that the anxious patients exhibited no awareness that the threatening stimuli had been presented. The performance of normal controls was affected comparably by threatening and neutral stimuli.

Distractibility
It has often been assumed that anxious individuals are more distractible than nonanxious ones. For example, Korchin (1964) concluded as follows on the basis of his clinical observations: "The

anxious patient is unable to concentrate, hyper-responsive, and hyper-distractible." This distractibility may well extend to both external and internal stimuli, but it is obviously difficult to assess the impact of internal stimuli (e.g. worries, self-concerns) on task performance.

Most studies concerned with the effects of anxiety on distractibility have compared performance of a task in the presence or absence of task-irrelevant or distracting stimuli. Distractibility is assessed by the extent to which performance deteriorates in the presence of the task-irrelevant stimuli. There have been several such studies comparing normal individuals high and low in trait anxiety, and the typical finding has been that those high in trait anxiety are significantly more distractible than those low in trait anxiety (see Eysenck, 1982, for a review).

Mathews, May, Mogg, and Eysenck (Note 7) investigated distractibility in clinically anxious patients with a diagnosis of generalised anxiety disorder. In contrast to previous studies which had used only neutral distracting stimuli, they made use of neutral and threat-related distracting stimuli. They discovered that anxious patients were more distractible than normal controls. In addition, they found that this enhanced distractibility of anxious patients was more marked with threat-related distractors than with neutral ones. These findings suggest that the anxious have a rather general tendency to be distracted by task-irrelevant stimuli. In addition, they also have a more specific tendency to have their attention captured by threat-related task-irrelevant stimuli.

Attentional Selectivity

Easterbrook (1959, p.193) argued that the range of environmental cues used (i.e. the breadth of attention) reduces as anxiety or arousal increases, which "will reduce the proportion of irrelevant cues employed, and so improve performance. When all irrelevant cues have been excluded, however, . . . further reduction in the number of cues employed can only affect relevant cues, and proficiency will fall."

Easterbrook's (1959) hypothesis has often been tested by making use of a paradigm in which a primary (or central) task and a secondary (or less important) task are performed at the same time. For example, Bacon (1974) made use of a pursuit rotor tracking task (i.e. manually following a moving target) and an auditory signal-detection task which were given at the same time. Some of the subjects were told that the tracking task was more important (and thus the primary task), whereas the detection task was less important (and thus the secondary task). The expectation is that the reduced range of cue utilisation in heightened anxiety should have a more adverse effect on performance of the secondary than of the primary task. Eysenck (1982) reviewed ten experiments designed to test this hypothesis, using normal groups high and low in trait anxiety. The modal findings were that the two groups did not differ in performance of the primary task, but that the group high in trait anxiety performed at a significantly inferior level to the group low in trait anxiety on the secondary task. These findings are consistent with Easterbrook's hypothesis.

Unfortunately, there do not seem to be any studies looking directly at attentional selectivity in anxious patients. In view of the encouraging results from studies of normals high and low in anxiety, it seems likely that patients with generalised anxiety disorder would display greater attentional selectivity than normal controls.

Attentional Capacity

Eysenck (1979b; 1988) argued that individuals high in trait anxiety, especially when also high in state anxiety (i.e. in an anxious mood), have less working memory or attentional capacity available for task performance than those low in trait anxiety. He suggested as a reason for this that worry, self-concern, and other task-irrelevant cognitive activities make use of some of the available limited capacity. The most straightforward prediction from this hypothesis is that any adverse effects of anxiety on task performance should be greater on tasks making substantial demands on the capacity of attention or working memory. Several studies have supported this prediction (e.g. Calvo, 1985; Eysenck, 1985).

There do not appear to be any studies of attentional or working memory capacity in anxious patients. However, it is of interest in this connection that Beck and Emery (1985) arrived at a rather similar theoretical position to Eysenck (1979b) on the basis of therapeutic sessions with patients suffering from anxiety disorders. According to them (Beck & Emery, 1985, p.31), "Because the patient 'uses up' a large part of his cognitive capacity by scanning for threatening stimuli, the amount available for attending to other demands is severely restricted."

Theoretical Analysis

Why do anxious patients exhibit the attentional style described here, which reflects a very *active engagement* with the external environment? Part of the answer probably lies in the fact that anxious patients are very concerned about potential environmental dangers and also wish to minimise uncertainty about possible future events. Constant scanning of the environment combined with selective allocation of processing resources to threatening and threat-related stimuli occur as a consequence. It is possible, as Beck and Emery suggested, that the reduced attentional or processing capacity for task performance shown by anxious individuals occurs because some of the available attentional capacity is diverted to scanning the environment. It is less clear how attentional selectivity fits in, but there is as yet no definitive evidence that anxious patients show increased attentional selectivity.

Depression

Attentional Content

As we saw earlier, MacLeod et al. (1986) discovered that anxious patients selectively allocated processing resources to threatening stimuli when threatening and neutral words were presented visually at the same time. They went further, and considered the performance of depressed patients on the same task. They found that depressed patients did not show any tendency to attend to either threatening or neutral words. Therefore, it appears that there is a selective processing bias in anxious patients but not in depressed patients.

Distractibility

Anxiety is usually associated with high distractibility and poor attentional control, but the same does not appear to be the case with depression. Indeed, there have even been reports of distracting stimuli leading to improvements in performance of a central task! For example, Foulds (1952) discovered that a distracting task (repeating back digits spoken by the experimenter) increased performance speed on the Porteus Maze Test for depressed patients. However, the distracting task led to more errors on the maze task, so that it is unclear whether distraction actually improved overall performance effectiveness. Campbell (1957) obtained very similar findings, and also found that repeating digits did not speed up the performance of normal controls. Shapiro, Campbell, Harris, and Dewsberry (1958) also obtained evidence of a beneficial effect of distraction on the performance of depressed patients.

In sum, there is very little evidence that depressed patients are more distractible than normals, and they may even be less distractible. It is not known why this should be the case. However, it may occur because demanding tasks reduce the frequency of distracting thoughts.

Attentional Selectivity

Anxious individuals tend to display greater attentional selectivity than nonanxious ones, but the only study known to the authors which investigated attentional selectivity in depressed patients found that they exhibited less attentional selectivity than normals. Hemsley and Zawada (1976) presented their subjects with a series of digits, some of which were spoken in a male voice and the others in a female voice. Normals had better digit recall when they were instructed which set of digits to recall before (rather than after) the digits have been presented. In contrast, depressed patients were unaffected by the timing of the recall instructions, presumably because of their inability to focus attention selectively.

Attentional Capacity

As we have seen, there is plentiful evidence to support Eysenck's hypothesis that anxious individuals have lower attentional or working memory capacity than nonanxious ones. A very similar hypothesis has been proposed for depression by Ellis and Ashbrook (1987). They argued that depression produces a reduction in the capacity available as a consequence of extra-task processing (e.g. negative thoughts about the self), and through other task-irrelevant processing. The most obvious prediction from this theoretical position is that depressed patients should be at a greater disadvantage to normal controls on complex tasks with high processing demands than on simple tasks with much smaller demands.

There are no convincing studies of Ellis and Ashbrook's hypothesis with depressed patients. However, studies using depressed mood induction have provided some support. For example, Ellis et al. (1985) found that induction of a depressed mood state reduced recall when the learning task required high effort, but not when it did not.

Theoretical Analysis

The attentional style of depressed patients appears to reflect a *passive disengagement* from the external environment. If attention is likened to a beam of light, then depressed patients seem to have a broad, weak beam which is relatively unresponsive to changes in the environment. These characteristics are shown by the apparent lack of distractibility and selectivity shown by depressed patients, coupled with their failure to allocate processing resources selectively to threatening stimuli.

Why do depressed patients have this lack of involvement in the external environment? There are probably several factors involved. Beck and Clark (1988) have discussed a "cognitive triad" in depressed patients consisting of a negative view of the self, the world, and the future. It is not surprising that individuals having such a negative set of views should regard the environment as an uninteresting source of information.

At the risk of severe over-simplification, one might argue that depressed patients have a greater bias towards attending to internal rather than external sources of information than anxious individuals. This may relate to the extremely interesting findings of Finlay-Jones and Brown (1981). They found that depression tended to follow losses (e.g. bereavement), whereas anxiety tended to follow danger events. It may thus be that depressed patients focus on the past, particularly on losses that have occurred, whereas anxious patients focus on the present and the future, particularly on potential dangers.

Summary

Anxious individuals differ from nonanxious individuals in several aspects of attentional functioning. More specifically, they attend more to threat-related stimuli, they are more distractible, they have greater attentional selectivity, and they have reduced attentional capacity. Most of these differences occur because anxious individuals have an active engagement with the environment which involves scanning for possible signs of danger. Depressed individuals exhibit a very different pattern of attentional functioning. They appear to be little affected attentionally by the content of stimuli, they are not especially distractible, and they do not show attentional selectivity. This pattern may occur because depressed individuals show passive disengagement with the environment; their attentional focus is on internal concerns.

COGNITION IN MOOD DISORDERS: THE CAUSALITY ISSUE

We have seen that anxious patients and depressed patients differ from normal controls with respect to several aspects of cognitive functioning. These findings are of interest, but leave an extremely important theoretical issue unclear. In essence, there are two major possible explanations for the fact that patients with a mood disorder have non-normal cognitive performance on various tasks. The first possibility is that the non-normal cognitive functioning occurs simply as a consequence of the patients' current mood state. The second possibility is that the cognitive differences between patients and normal controls reflect stable characteristics associated with a cognitive vulnerability factor. In other words, those normal individuals with a cognitive system functioning in a similar way to that of clinical patients may be more likely than other normal individuals subsequently to develop a mood disorder. If so, the functioning of the cognitive system may be a contributory factor in mood disorders.

What we are concerned with here is basically the causality issue. At the risk of over-simplification, the non-normal cognitive functioning found in anxious and in depressed patients may occur because the mood disorder causes the altered cognitive functioning, or the altered cognitive functioning may play a role in causing the mood disorder. Why is the causality issue so important? The reason is that we need to understand exactly why and how people develop mood disorders in order to improve the measures that are taken to prevent mood disorders developing and in order to improve forms of treatment. Only those aspects of cognitive functioning which form part of a cognitive vulnerability factor are of relevance to the development of mood disorders. It is crucial, therefore, to be able to identify those aspects as accurately as possible.

Prospective Studies

On the face of it, the obvious way of attempting to resolve the causality issue is to carry out what is known as a prospective study. What would be involved will be described in the case of clinical anxiety, but exactly the same approach could be adopted with clinical depression. The study would involve assessing the cognitive performance of normal individuals who subsequently develop clinical anxiety, and then comparing it against that of current patients and normals who do not subsequently develop clinical anxiety. The patterns of results that might be obtained are shown in Fig. 13.6.

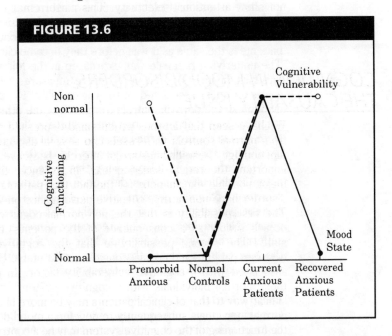

FIGURE 13.6

Patterns of cognitive performance which would be obtained if there were a cognitive vulnerability factor or if non-normal cognitive functioning reflects clinically anxious mood state.

If the two normal groups did not differ in their cognitive functioning, then cognitive functioning would not be predictive of clinical anxiety, and it could reasonably be concluded that non-normal cognitive functioning was neither a precipitant nor a cause of that mood disorder. In contrast, if those normals who subsequently developed clinical anxiety resembled current clinically anxious patients in their cognitive functioning more than did those normals who did not subsequently develop clinical anxiety, then that would strengthen the argument that non-normal cognitive functioning plays a part in the development of that mood disorder.

There are practical problems associated with prospective studies. Very large numbers of subjects need to be tested in order to ensure that there are a reasonable number of normal subjects who subsequently develop a mood disorder, and such a study obviously has to be longitudinal. As a consequence, prospective studies are nearly always both expensive and time-consuming. Another potential problem concerns the interpretation of the results. If the time interval between testing and the onset of clinical anxiety is very short, then evidence of non-normal cognitive functioning in normals who develop clinical anxiety may simply reflect the first signs of the mood disorder itself.

Studies with Recovered Patients

In view mainly of the practical problems associated with prospective studies, there have been numerous attempts to employ an alternative approach based on the use of recovered patients. The approach will be described with respect to anxiety, but is equally applicable to depression. This approach requires extensive cognitive assessment of three groups of subjects: currently anxious patients; recovered anxious patients; and normal controls. It is assumed that the cognitive functioning of recovered anxious patients is the same as it was before they became clinically anxious. The underlying rationale was expressed in the following terms by Eysenck (in press): "Those cognitive measures reflecting stable characteristics associated with vulnerability to anxiety should distinguish the normal controls from both of the other two groups, whereas those cognitive measures which reflect current mood state should distinguish the currently anxious group from the other two." These possibilities are shown in Fig. 13.6.

What are the problems with this research strategy? One potential difficulty concerns the notion of "recovery". If allegedly recovered patients perform cognitively in the same fashion as current patients, it is always possible to argue that this simply means that they have not really recovered. Another problem is that suffering from clinical anxiety may have a semi-permanent effect on the cognitive system, so that it never returns to the state that it was in prior to the onset of the clinical anxiety.

Depression

One of the ways in which depressed patients differ from normal controls is in terms of a negative recall bias. As we saw earlier in the chapter, depressed patients show a relative tendency to recall more negative information encoded in relation to themselves. In order to decide whether this negative recall bias forms part of a vulnerability factor, Bradley and Mathews (1988) and Teasdale and Dent (1987) considered the recall performance of recovered depressed patients. Bradley and Mathews discovered that recovered depressed patients resembled normal controls in recalling more positive than negative self-referent items. This suggests that the negative recall bias is simply a reflection of depressed mood, and thus is no longer found when there is recovery from clinical depression. In contrast, Teasdale and Dent found that recovered depressed individuals recalled fewer positive adjectives than normal controls, with both groups having comparable recall of negative adjectives. This appears to suggest that the negative recall bias may form part of a vulnerability factor, but the recovered depressed group was slightly more depressed than the normal controls in the week before testing. It is thus possible that differences in depressed mood state played at least some part in producing the group differences in recall. On balance, the available evidence does not lend much support to the notion that a vulnerability factor is involved.

According to Beck (1976), depressed patients have negative schemata about themselves, about the world, and about the future. Several studies have considered whether these negative cognitions merely reflect depressed mood state or whether they might be a cognitive vulnerability factor. Lewinsohn, Steinmetz, Larson, and Franklin (1981) carried out a prospective study in which negative attitudes and cognitions were assessed by questionnaire. Their findings (Lewinsohn et al., 1981, p.218) indicated that these attitudes and cognitions were consequences of being in a depressed state:

> Prior to becoming depressed, . . . future depressives did not subscribe to irrational beliefs, they did not have lower expectancies for positive outcomes or higher expectancies for negative outcomes, they did not attribute success experiences to external causes and failure experiences to internal causes, nor did they perceive themselves as having less control over the events of their lives . . . People who are vulnerable to depression are not characterised by stable patterns of negative cognitions.

Rather similar findings were obtained by Wilkinson and Blackburn (1981) with recovered depressed patients. They administered various questionnaires designed to assess negative cognitions to depressed patients, recovered mixed psychiatric patients, and normal controls, as well as to recovered depressed patients. The results of their study were summarised in the following way by Wilkinson and Blackburn (1981, pp.289–290): "Depressed patients did not show any cognitive distortions after recovery, their scores, on all measures, being equivalent to those of normal and recovered other subjects. Hence, cognitive distortions would appear to be specific to the illness phase of depression and not to depression-prone individuals."

Segal and Shaw (1986) have reviewed the evidence on negative cognitions in recovered depressed patients. The findings vary somewhat from study to study, but there is general agreement that those individuals who have recovered from clinical depression have fewer and less intense negative cognitions than current depressed patients. However, there is some dispute as to whether the negative cognitions of recovered patients have improved to the level of normal controls.

What are we to make of the experimental studies which have attempted to clarify the causality issue? Miller and Morley (1986, p.97) were obviously correct to conclude that "the evidence that depressive ways of thinking predispose people to become depressed is not at all strong." However, a stronger negative conclusion is warranted only if one assumes that self-report questionnaires provide a reasonable assessment of the functioning of the cognitive system. There are various reasons for rejecting that assumption. First, self-report measures often provide distorted information because of attempts at self-justification. Second, there is increasing evidence that the information about themselves to which people can gain conscious access is far more restricted than used to be believed (an issue which is discussed in Chapter 1). Third, it seems likely that it would be relatively automatic and over-learned processes which would form part of a vulnerability factor, whereas the more controlled processes can change substantially over time. Controlled processes of which there is conscious awareness have been investigated in most studies, and so little or nothing is known about whether any automatic or pre-attentive processes might be involved in a cognitive vulnerability factor.

Anxiety

Eysenck and Mathews have carried out several studies to investigate whether differences in cognitive functioning between anxious patients and normal controls reflect a cognitive vulnerability factor or anxious mood state. What is common to all of these studies is that three groups of subjects have been compared: current patients with generalised anxiety disorder; recovered anxious patients who had received a diagnosis of generalised anxiety disorder, but who had been recovered for at least six months prior to testing; and normal controls. Some of the relevant studies have already been discussed in this chapter, but without reference to the recovered anxious group.

Memory

It will be remembered that anxious patients differ from normal controls in that they exhibit relatively greater implicit memory for threatening words, but the groups do not differ in explicit memory (Mathews et al., 1989). Data were also collected from a group of recovered anxious patients. They performed equivalently to the other two groups in explicit memory. On the test of implicit memory (word-completion test), the performance of the recovered anxious patients was intermediate between that of the currently anxious patients and the normal controls. This provides tentative support for the view that the negative bias effect in implicit memory shown by anxious patients reflects a mixture of a vulnerability factor and a consequence of anxious mood state.

The effects of anxiety on interpretation of, and memory for, ambiguous stimuli have been examined in recovered anxious patients. Mathews et al. (1989) investigated the interpretation of homophones, and found that 85.4% of homophone spellings by anxious patients were threat-related, compared to 69.9% by normal controls. The recovered anxious subjects had 77.1% threat-related homophones spellings, which is almost exactly intermediate between the other two groups. Eysenck et al. (Note 2) found that currently anxious patients recognised relatively more of the threatening interpretations of ambiguous sentences than normals on a memory test, and that the recovered anxious group closely resembled the normals. Overall, then, it appears that the tendency of anxious patients to perceive and to remember the threatening interpretations of ambiguous stimuli is largely a reflection of anxious mood state rather than forming part of a vulnerability factor.

In sum, the findings from studies of memory are somewhat inconclusive. There is suggestive evidence that a cognitive vulnerability factor may be involved (especially so far as the negative bias in implicit memory is concerned), but it is clear that the various memory effects found in currently anxious patients owe much to their anxious mood state. The findings are generally consistent with the view that it is relatively automatic processes (such as those involved in implicit memory) that are most likely to be involved in a cognitive vulnerability factor.

Attention

The clearest evidence on the causality issue as it relates to the effects of anxiety on attentional processes was reported by Mathews et al. (Note 7). It will be remembered that they found that anxious patients were more distractible than normal controls, and that this increased distractibility was more marked with threat-related distractors than with neutral distractors. The findings for recovered anxious patients were relatively straightforward: They resembled control subjects when neutral distractors were used, but showed significantly greater distractibility than controls when threatening distractors were used.

These findings may have major theoretical significance. They indicate that the tendency for attention to be captured by emotionally threatening stimuli forms part of a cognitive vulnerability factor. It is certainly plausible that individuals who find it difficult to avoid processing mildly threatening environmental stimuli should be vulnerable to generalised anxiety disorder, and it is exciting to discover that at least one aspect of attentional functioning may play a causal role in the development of clinical anxiety.

Summary

Discovering that there are differences in cognitive performance between mood-disordered patients and normal controls leaves open the causality issue. In essence, it could be the case that altered cognitive performance plays a role in causing the mood disorder (indicating a cognitive vulnerability factor), or it may be that altered cognitive performance simply reflects the current mood state. Some clarification of this issue is possible by studying individuals who have recovered from clinical mood disorder.

So far as clinical depression is concerned, there is rather little evidence of a cognitive vulnerability factor which predisposes to depression. However, most of the cognitive measures which have been used are so limited that no firm conclusions can be drawn at present. So far as clinical anxiety is concerned, there is some support for the notion that high distractibility to threat-related stimuli forms part of a cognitive vulnerability factor. Some aspects of non-normal memory functioning in currently anxious patients may involve a mixture of a vulnerability factor and current mood state.

SUMMARY

Despite the importance of the relationship between cognition and emotion, most cognitive psychologists have not considered emotional factors at all in their research and theorising. However, there are signs of growing interest in this area, and some headway has been made in recent years.

One of the major issues which has been addressed is whether it is possible for an affective or emotional reaction to a stimulus to occur in the absence of any cognitive processing of that stimulus. In other words, does affect require cognition? It has been shown that affective responses can occur without any conscious awareness of cognitive processing, but this by no means rules out the possibility of pre-conscious cognitive processing. It is difficult to investigate pre-conscious processing, but it seems likely that such processing generally precedes any affective reaction in those cases where there is no conscious awareness of cognitive processing. After the early stages of cognitive processing, there are usually mutual influences of cognition on affect and of affect on cognition.

There has been much interest in emotional effects on memory. Freud, with his notion of "repression" or motivated forgetting of anxiety-provoking events, put forward one of the earliest theories. There are various ethical and methodological obstacles in the way of providing an adequate experimental test of repression theory under laboratory conditions. However, such experiments as have been carried out have consistently failed to produce any convincing evidence of repression.

More recent research on emotion and memory has been heavily influenced by Bower's semantic network theory of affect. The major predictions of this theory (e.g. mood-state-dependent recall; mood congruity) have been confirmed several times, so the theory appears to be on the right lines. However, there are some fairly obvious deficiencies with the theory. First, emotions are surely much more than simply nodes in a semantic network. Second, the theory seems to provide too passive a view of the ways in which individuals in negative emotional states react. Being in a negative emotional state generally leads individuals to take steps to improve their mood. However, Bower's theory lacks a motivational component, and so cannot account for such behaviour.

Investigations of cognitive functioning in patients with the mood disorders of anxiety and depression have revealed that these patients differ from normal individuals in several aspects of cognitive performance. These cognitive differences have encouraged the view that any adequate account of the mood disorders will have an important cognitive dimension. The most difficult issue is to decide whether non-normal cognitive functioning plays a part in the development of the mood disorders, or whether non-normal cognitive functioning merely reflects the mood states of patients with mood disorders. Most research with depression has favoured the latter explanation, but this may be due to the rather limited range of cognitive processes which have been examined. The findings with clinical anxiety are more complex. There are indications that some aspects of non-normal cognitive functioning in anxious patients may form part of a cognitive vulnerability factor (e.g. attentional capture by threatening stimuli), whereas others (e.g. interpretation of ambiguity) may reflect anxious mood state.

FURTHER READING

Blaney, P.H. (1986). Affect and memory: A review. *Psychological Bulletin, 99*, 229–246. This article provides a very thorough and well-argued analysis of recent research on emotion and memory.

Brewin, C.R. (1988). *Cognitive foundations of clinical psychology*. London: Lawrence Erlbaum Associates Ltd. This is an excellent book. It provides an up-to-date account of most of the issues discussed in this chapter.

Eysenck, M.W. (in press). *Anxiety: The cognitive perspective*. London: Lawrence Erlbaum Associates Ltd. Much of this book deals with cognitive functioning in patients with generalised anxiety disorder.

Williams, J.M.G., Watts, F.N., MacLeod, C., & Mathews, A. (1987). *Cognitive psychology and emotional disorders*. Chichester: Wiley. This book is of particular interest because of the numerous comparisons which are drawn between the cognitive performance of anxious and depressed patients.

Chapter Fourteen

COGNITIVE PSYCHOLOGY: PRESENT AND FUTURE

Contemporary research and theory in cognitive psychology have been dealt with at some length in the previous chapters of this book. We have seen that cognitive psychologists have made considerable theoretical and empirical headway in making sense of human cognition. Some of this progress is negative, in the sense that we now know that certain theoretical approaches that seemed promising at one time are actually dead ends. Of course, eliminating erroneous approaches is not the same as discovering the correct approach, but the history of science reveals that it is usually an important step along the way.

Most of the emphasis in this book has been on specific theories and bodies of research. In contrast, the primary aim of this chapter is to provide a more global perspective on the current state of cognitive psychology. More specifically, this chapter reflects one of the main themes of Chapter 1, which was that cognitive psychology can usefully be regarded as consisting of three main perspectives: experimental cognitive psychology; cognitive neuropsychology; and cognitive science. Each of these perspectives to cognitive psychology will be evaluated in turn. To anticipate a little, it will be concluded that each view has different strengths and weaknesses, and that all are needed to provide converging evidence on cognitive functioning.

EXPERIMENTAL COGNITIVE PSYCHOLOGY

The recent dramatic increase in the impact of cognitive neuropsychology and of cognitive science on cognitive psychology has led many people to de-emphasise the contribution made by the more traditional experimental cognitive approach. In fact, both cognitive neuropsychology and cognitive science owe much to experimental cognitive psychology. Cognitive neuropsychology became a significant discipline approximately 20 years after cognitive psychology. It was only after cognitive psychologists had developed reasonable accounts of normal human cognition that the performance of brain-damaged patients could be understood. Similarly, the computational modelling activities of cognitive scientists are often informed importantly by pre-computational psychological theories.

One of the most striking successes of experimental cognitive psychology has been the way its approach has influenced several areas of psychology. For example, social and developmental psychology have both become decidedly more "cognitive" in recent years. The influence of cognitive psychology on some aspects of clinical psychology was demonstrated in Chapter 13. Most of the paradigms used to study attention, comprehension, and memory in mood-disordered patients were developed in the research laboratories of experimental cognitive psychologists.

Experimental cognitive psychology has led psychology from the barren wilderness of behaviourism into a discipline which has developed some of the empirical and theoretical tools needed to provide a realistic account of the complexities of human cognition. However, experimental cognitive psychology has had its critics. In order to present a fair evaluation, it is necessary to consider some of the criticisms that have been made of it.

One of the most obvious weaknesses of experimental cognitive psychology is the reluctance to take individual differences seriously. The typical research strategy is to use analysis of variance to assess statistically the effects of various experimental manipulations on cognitive performance, but to relegate individual differences to the error term (but see Sternberg, 1985, as one important exception). In effect, cognitive psychologists who adopt this strategy seem to be assuming implicitly that individual differences are unimportant and do not interact with any of the experimental manipulations.

The reality is quite different. For example, Bowers (1973) considered 11 studies in which the percentages of the variance accounted for by individual differences, by situational factors, and by their interaction could be assessed. On average, individual differences accounted for 11.27% of the variance, the situation for 10.17%, and the interaction between individual differences and situation for 20.77%. In the light of such evidence, it seems rather perverse to ignore individual differences altogether!

A second problem with experimental cognitive psychology was expressed forcefully by Newell (1973). He argued that cognitive psychology tends to be phenomenon-driven, in the sense that the discovery of a new phenomenon (e.g. the visual icon) leads to a tremendous volume of research directed at exploring all of its ramifications. According to Newell, our investigation of a phenomenon often proceeds on the basis of binary oppositions. Thus, for example, we ask of a phenomenon, "Does it depend on serial or parallel processing?" or "Does it depend on top-down or bottom-up processing?"

Newell (1973, pp.288–289) claimed that this entire approach is rather futile:

> As I examine the fate of our [binary] oppositions, looking at those already in existence as a guide to how they fare and shape the course of science, it seems to me that clarity is never achieved. Matters simply become muddier and muddier as we go down through time. Thus, far from providing the rungs of a ladder by which psychology climbs to clarity, this form of conceptual structure leads to an ever increasing pile of issues, which we weary of or become diverted from, but never really settle.

It can be argued against Newell that it is perfectly reasonable to postulate binary oppositions in order to get the theoretical show on the road. Relatively few cognitive psychologists are beguiled into remaining at that simplistic level of analysis for very long. However, one of the implications of Newell's argument is indisputable. The emphasis within experimental cognitive psychology has been on relatively specific theories which are applicable to only a narrow range of cognitive tasks. What has been lacking is an overarching theoretical architecture (see Chapter 1). Common structures, representations, or processes may underlie performance in a great range of tasks, and such an architecture would fulfil the function of clarifying the inter-relationships among different components of the cognitive system. In its absence, experimental cognitive psychology has lacked integration at the theoretical level.

A further criticism of experimental cognitive psychology is that it is removed from everyday events and concerns. In other words, it is claimed that experimental cognitive psychology lacks ecological validity: that is, direct relevance to cognition and behaviour under naturalistic conditions. The extent of this problem was spelled out in an amusing fashion by Claxton (1980, p.13), who noted that much of cognitive psychology does not:

> . . . deal with whole people but with a very special and bizarre— almost Frankensteinian—preparation, which consists of a brain attached to two eyes, two ears, and two index fingers. This preparation is only to be found inside small, gloomy cubicles, outside which red lights burn to warn ordinary people away . . . It does not feel hungry or tired or inquisitive; it does not think extraneous thoughts or try to understand what is going on. It is, in short, a computer, made in the image of the larger electronic organism that sends it stimuli and records its responses.

Claxton was obviously caricaturing experimental cognitive psychology. Nevertheless, many psychologists would be prepared to admit that there is at least a grain of truth in what he has to say. Many laboratory studies are also artificial in another way. In everyday life, cognitive processes usually occur in the service of some higher purpose or goal, whereas they function as ends in themselves in the laboratory. Consider a standard laboratory task on semantic memory (see Chapter 8), in which people decide on the answers to questions such as "Can canaries fly?" In the laboratory, such questions are answered readily, with no thought being given to any ulterior motives that the questioner might have. A rather different reaction would be forthcoming if the same question were asked in the context of a casual conversation. As Claxton (1980, p.11) pointed out, "If someone asks me 'Can canaries fly?' in the pub I will suspect either that he is an idiot or that he is about to tell me a joke."

The criticism that experimental cognitive psychology lacks ecological validity has lost some of its force in recent years. There are several examples in this book of the increased willingness of cognitive psychologists to move closer to "real life." For example, as we saw in Chapter 2, researchers in perception have become more and more interested in perceptual processing of the human face, which is a highly significant stimulus in everyday life. In Chapter 4 there is a discussion of attentional and automatic processes in connection with the "real world" phenomenon of absent-mindedness. Much of Chapter 9 is concerned with the important everyday activity of reading and Chapter 11 touches on the problems people have to solve in everyday contexts.

Although many experimental cognitive psychologists are aware that much of their research is somewhat lacking in ecological validity, they are quite rightly sceptical of a wholesale abandonment of experimental rigour and control in favour of a totally naturalistic approach. There are so many variables influencing behaviour in the real world, and it is so difficult to manipulate them systematically, that it can become almost impossible to assess the relative importance of each variable in determining behaviour. It is no easy matter to obtain the required combination of experimental rigour and ecological validity, but some of the more successful endeavours in that direction have been discussed throughout this book.

A final criticism of experimental cognitive psychology, and one that is related to the issue of ecological validity, concerns what Reitman (1970) referred to as the "decoupling" problem. If a researcher wants to explore some facet of, say, human memory, then an attempt is usually made to decouple the memory system from other cognitive systems, and to minimise the impact of motivational and emotional factors on performance. Even if it is possible to study the memory system in isolation, it is manifestly obvious that the memory system usually operates in interaction with other functional systems. Accordingly, the more successful we are in examining part of the cognitive system in isolation, the less our data are likely to tell us about cognition in everyday life. For example, there are bi-directional influences of emotional states on cognition and of cognition on emotional states (see Chapter 13). As a consequence, the usual strategy of ignoring emotional factors cannot be recommended if we want to extrapolate from the circumscribed emotional states studied in the laboratory to the very different states often found in everyday life.

COGNITIVE NEUROPSYCHOLOGY

The cognitive neuropsychological approach has become much more influential within cognitive psychology in recent years. It has been applied to several areas, including perception, attention, memory, and language. However, as was probably apparent from our treatment of these topics, cognitive neuropsychologists have carried out far more research on language than on the other topics, and the least on attention.

Why has language functioning received a quite disproportionate amount of research effort? For one reason, this is simply part and parcel of the generally increased interest in language by cognitive psychologists. In addition, however, it seems that language lends itself especially well to the cognitive neuropsychological approach. The comprehension and production of language involve a number of different skills (i.e. those of reading, listening, writing, and speaking), each of which has various modules or cognitive processes associated with it. In a nutshell, the investigation of brain-damaged patients by cognitive neuropsychologists has proved particularly successful in the identification of some of the modules involved in cognitive functioning, and the evidence so far suggests that there may be more modules involved in language processing than in many other cognitive activities.

At the other extreme, there are a number of important cognitive activities which probably are relatively resistant to a modular approach. Temple (1990) has argued that creative thought and organisational planning are two cognitive activities which may not be amenable to modular fractionation, and there may well be others.

While the study of language may be regarded as the "jewel in the crown" of cognitive neuropsychology, there are nevertheless significant limitations apparent in the research which has been carried out. There has been a substantial amount of work on the reading and spelling of individual words by brain-damaged patients, but rather little on larger units of language. Many important language processes are involved in reading and spelling single words, but equally there are important additional factors (e.g. contextual influences; structural themes) which are only of relevance to larger units of language (see Chapters 9 and 10).

As well as the limitations of cognitive neuropsychology at the empirical level, there are further limitations at the theoretical level. This can be seen if we consider language processing a little further. The available neuropsychological evidence (Ellis & Young, 1988) indicates that speaking and writing differ in that there are separate lexicons which contain information about the spoken and written forms of words, but they are similar in that they share the same semantic system. According to Ellis and Young (1988, p.223), "the semantic system is the (grossly underspecified) component in which word meanings are represented." The semantic system presumably plays some part (albeit rather modest) in planning the meaning of what is to be said (Garrett's, 1984, message level) and in the planning process in writing (Hayes & Flower, 1986). These planning activities are of fundamental importance to speaking and to writing, but so far cognitive neuropsychology has not been able to provide anything approximating an adequate theoretical account of how they occur.

Why has cognitive neuropsychology been so uninformative about the planning processes involved in speaking and writing? Cognitive neuropsychology has been largely concerned with the identification of modules. Most of the modules identified by cognitive neuropsychologists are relatively peripheral (i.e. they are parts of the cognitive system which are close to either the input or the output of information), whereas planning processes occur at a relatively central level within the processing system. In other words, cognitive neuropsychology seems rather poorly equipped to provide detailed theoretical treatments of important cognitive functions which are central and nonmodular.

In fairness to cognitive neuropsychologists, it should be pointed out that traditional cognitive psychology suffers from the same problems. There are good reasons for this. Central cognitive functions occur some time after the stimulus input has taken place, and can thus be difficult to manipulate effectively. They are also somewhat removed from response output, and so behavioural measures often provide a rather indirect reflection of their functioning. As a consequence, it will probably always be more difficult to pinpoint central than peripheral processes.

Cognitive neuropsychologists traditionally studied groups of patients who allegedly suffered from the same syndrome or set of symptoms. However, as Ellis (1990) pointed out, "The trend in cognitive neuropsychology has been to carry out intensive investigations of single cases." This emphasis on single cases is quite different from standard research in cognitive psychology, where the norm is to compare the performance of reasonably large groups of subjects.

The issue of the relative usefulness of single cases and groups of brain-damaged patients in cognitive neuropsychological research is both important and controversial. One extreme position was advocated by Caramazza and McCloskey (1988, p.519): "Valid inferences about the structure of normal cognitive systems from patterns of impaired performance are only possible for single-patient studies." In contrast, Caplan (1988, pp.546–547) argued as follows: "Group studies . . . are a legitimate and potentially useful tool in using pathological cases to infer both aspects of normal cognitive functions and the neural basis for such functions."

Our view is that it is appropriate to carry out group studies when theory and research in an area are undeveloped. However, the balance of advantage shifts towards single-case studies when relatively detailed theories are available. Why should this be so? In the early days of cognitive neuropsychological research, there was a natural interest in establishing the typical patterns of cognitive impairment produced by different forms of brain damage. This involves considering association of symptoms (i.e. symptoms which tend to be found together). The discovery that two symptoms occur in a single patient is very limited evidence, because there could be unusual features of the brain damage suffered by that patient. Furthermore, in the absence of adequate theories, it would be extremely difficult to decide which individual patients were providing theoretically significant data.

When (as is now the case) fairly detailed theories have been constructed, then the potential value of single-case studies increases considerably. For example, as Newcombe and Marshall (1988, p.561) argued persuasively, "When a theory that is plausible on other grounds predicts a dissociation, one may accept just one actual case of empirical dissociation as adequate proof and dismiss on the grounds of anatomical contiguity all other cases of association." To illustrate this point, they referred to the rather unusual patient studied by Campbell and Butterworth (1985). This patient was an undergraduate girl with an I.Q. of 123 who could read unusual words such as "placebo" or "idyll" with ease, but who experienced great difficulty in reading even simple nonwords like "bant". In spite of the rare nature of her reading impairment, this single patient is of great theoretical significance because of the relevance of her reading performance to triple-route reading models (see Chapter 9). Someone who could make use of the internal lexicon but not of grapheme-phoneme conversion should theoretically be able to read words but not nonwords, and that is precisely what was found in this case.

In spite of the usefulness of single-case studies, there are some problems with interpreting the data from individual patients. First, we generally do not know how well a brain-damaged patient would have been able to perform any given cognitive task prior to brain damage. If his or her brain-damaged performance is, say, one standard deviation below the mean of normal individuals, it is not possible to tell whether or not brain damage has produced any impairment. Second, the cognitive system of the brain-damaged patient could differ qualitatively from that of most normal people prior to brain damage. If that were the case, then no general conclusions about normal human cognition can be drawn from that patient's performance. Third, the patient may have responded to brain damage by developing compensatory strategies which obscure the direct effects of brain damage on the cognitive system.

In essence, the limitations of the single-case study stem from the fact that we often have insufficient evidence to provide a definitive interpretation of the patient's cognitive performance. It might seem that group studies provide a useful way of obtaining additional evidence. However, there are considerable problems associated with forming groups of patients, all of whom allegedly suffer from the same neuropsychological syndrome. In view of the enormous differences in the nature of the brain damage from one patient to the next, it is probably unrealistic to assume that homogenous groups of brain-damaged patients can be formed, and so categorisation in terms of syndromes is hazardous. As a consequence, we agree with the conclusion drawn by Newcombe and Marshall (1988, p.552): "In the absence of specific valid arguments to the contrary, it is safer to map data from individual patients directly onto structural models of cognitive functioning, rather than to do so via the intermediate step of grouping patients into syndromes."

An approach which is generally superior to the group-study method is simply to carry out a number of single-case studies. If a theoretically crucial dissociation is found in a single patient, then (as we have seen) there are various possible ways of interpreting the data. However, if the same dissociation is obtained in a number of individual patients, then it is less likely (although not impossible) that all of the patients had qualitatively unusual cognitive systems prior to brain damage or that they have all made use of similar compensatory strategies.

COGNITIVE SCIENCE

For most of this book we have concentrated on one dimension of the cognitive science perspective: that is, the cross-disciplinary interaction between artificial intelligence and experimental cognitive psychology (for other interactions see Gardner, 1985). In this final chapter we will, therefore, concentrate on evaluating the specific contribution of this brand of cognitive science.

Many different opinions have been offered about the success (or otherwise) of the cognitive science approach. Some have merely sneered at practitioners in this area, dismissing them as an "artificial intelligentsia" whose activities have no tangible relationship to actual human behaviour. Others have been markedly more enthusiastic, none more so than Allport (1980, p.31): "The advent of Artificial Intelligence is the single most important development in the history of psychology." However, it should be noted that it is really too early to make any sweeping conclusions about the usefulness of the approach. As Boden (1988, p.260) has pointed out, "The space of computational possibilities has hardly been entered, never mind fully explored or satisfactorily mapped . . . It is too early, therefore, to predict the success of the computational approach in general."

With this caveat in mind, we will do what we can to consider the balance sheet for cognitive science. There are various major items on the credit side of the balance. The computational modelling of psychological theories enforces a strong test of their adequacy. Many theories from traditional cognitive psychology have been found to be inadequate because crucial aspects of the human information-processing system were not spelled out or could not be spelled out computationally. For example, Marr (1982) discovered that previous theoretical assumptions about feature detectors in visual perception were over-simplified when he began to construct programs to specify precisely how feature extraction might occur (see Chapter 2). The intellectual discipline associated with the requirement to specify every process in detail often gives the cognitive scientist a significant advantage over traditional cognitive psychologists.

A second advantage of the cognitive science approach is that, in theoretical terms, it tends to be very advanced. As a consequence, cognitive scientists have been more disposed than other cognitive psychologists to address fundamental or high-level theoretical issues concerning the forms of representation and the processes to be found in the human information-processing system. As we saw in Chapter 1, cognitive scientists have proposed computer models based on semantic networks, production systems, and connectionist networks. All of these modelling techniques can be applied to a wide range of topic areas within cognitive psychology. For example, connectionist networks have been used in theories of perception, learning, memory, and reading (see Chapters 5 and 9). Indeed, we have seen that some of these computational models have been proposed as general, cognitive architectures that can be applied to the understanding of all cognitive functioning (see, e.g., Anderson, Note 1; Newell, 1989; Rumelhart, McClelland, & the PDP Research Group, 1986). Such widely applicable theoretical notions have emerged less frequently from the work of traditional cognitive psychologists and cognitive neuropsychologists.

On the debit side, it has often been argued that the entire cognitive science approach is misguided since there are fundamental differences between the functioning of computers and that of the human information-processing system. Some cognitive scientists subscribe to the view that if a computer can be programmed to behave like a human then it is intelligent in the same way that a human is. So a program which enabled a computer to behave as if it understood Chinese would be able to understand Chinese in the same way a person does. This position is often called the "Strong A.I. Position" and can be traced back to one of the founders of computational science, Alan Turing. The so-called "Turing Test" essentially proposed that if one could not distinguish the behaviour of a computer from that of a human, on the same task, then the machine was intelligent like the human (see Turing, 1950).

Searle (1989) has countered this view clearly and forcefully. He admitted that cognitive scientists have been reasonably successful in using computer programs to simulate aspects of human cognitive performance, but claimed that they cannot duplicate human cognition; that is, crucial ingredients of human cognition are missing in the computer simulation. Searle supports this position by means of the so-called Chinese room thought experiment.

Imagine that there was a person locked in a room which contains several baskets full of Chinese symbols. This person does not understand Chinese at all, but is provided with a rule book in English which indicates how the Chinese symbols are to be manipulated. Thus, for example (Searle, 1989, p.32), one rule might be: "Take a squiggle-squiggle sign out of basket number one and put it next to a squoggle-squoggle sign from basket number two." The person armed with these rules might be able to answer questions in Chinese by passing the appropriate Chinese symbols out of the room. Indeed, the answers might be indistinguishable from those of a native Chinese person. However, this excellent level of performance would be achieved without the person involved having any understanding of Chinese. By analogy, even computers that have been programmed to respond in the same way as people are simulating human cognition but not duplicating it: The computer has no understanding of what it is doing or why. The computer program manipulates symbols in a purely syntactic manner; it does not know what the meaning of these symbols are in the same way that we do. Searle argues that human brains differ crucially from computers precisely because they do manifest a high degree of understanding; they know what the symbols they manipulate mean; they are semantic rather than syntactic systems.

In one sense, you either agree with Searle or disagree with him. The issue is not empirically decidable, it is more a matter of what you accept as reasonable assumptions to make about the nature of artificial and human intelligence. However, Searle's position signals an important point to keep in mind about computer models. Namely, that models of human cognitive functioning are *only* models. There is no guarantee that a given computational model of a specific behaviour *really* captures the way in which humans do that behaviour. The same specific behaviour can be modelled by many different models. For example, the behaviour of drivers in the United Kingdom could be characterised by a model involving the following rule: "Drive in such a way that the steering wheel is nearest to the centre line of the road." A computer model incorporating that rule might simulate the driving behaviour of British people, but another model using a rule about driving on the left-hand side of the road would produce the same behaviour.

There are other differences between human cognitive functioning and computer functioning. There is still a gap between the ways in which brains and computers compute. As Churchland (1989, p.100) pointed out: "The brain seems to be a computer with a radically different style. For example, the brain changes as it learns, it appears to store and process information in the same places . . . Most obviously, the brain is a parallel machine, in which many interactions occur at the same time in many different channels." Connectionist models with their parallel distributed processing and modifiable connections resemble human brain functioning rather better than traditional, symbolic models in a number of important respects. However, as we saw in Chapter 1, even connectionist models capture only some aspects of brain functioning.

There are further differences between brain and computer functioning. Human cognition is influenced by several potentially conflicting motivational and emotional factors, many of which may be operative at the same time. This state of affairs can be contrasted (Boden, 1988, p.262) with the "single-minded nature of virtually all current computer programs." It is possible in the future that the complexity of human purposes can be captured by more powerful computer programs, but the feasibility of such programs remains an article of faith for the moment.

One other major limitation of cognitive science will be considered. As Norman (1980) pointed out, human functioning can be regarded as dependent on an interplay of a cognitive system (which he called the Pure Cognitive System) and a biological system (which he termed the Regulatory System). Much of the activity of the Pure Cognitive System is determined by the various needs of the Regulatory System, including the need for survival, for food and water, and for protection of oneself and one's family. Cognitive science, in common with most of the rest of cognitive psychology, focuses on the Pure Cognitive System and virtually ignores the key role played by the Regulatory System.

In one sense, all these commentators have identified various ways in which the analogy between computer functioning and human cognitive functioning breaks down. This may or may not pose serious problems. In spite of the fact that virtually all analogies or metaphors break down at some point, there are numerous examples in the history of science (e.g. Rutherford's planetary model of the atom) where analogies or metaphors have proved very useful in advancing theoretical understanding. What is certainly the case is that the computer provides a more plausible metaphor for brain functioning than do most earlier metaphors (e.g. the brain has been likened to a catapult and to a mill). At least the computer metaphor has the advantage that the computer more closely approximates the complexity of the human brain than do the catapult and the mill. The computer metaphor has the additional advantage over previous metaphors that computers can be used in very flexible ways. As a consequence, the "fit" between brain and computer functioning has improved considerably in recent years, and may be relied on to improve still further in the future.

SUMMARY

The three major approaches within cognitive psychology (i.e. experimental cognitive psychology; cognitive neuropsychology; cognitive science) were evaluated. Experimental cognitive psychology has been very successful both in its own right and in its influence on the development of both cognitive neuropsychology and cognitive science. Its limitations include some lack of ecological validity, the failure to develop overarching theoretical systems or architectures, and the relative neglect of individual differences.

Cognitive neuropsychology has proved particularly successful in identifying several of the modules or cognitive components involved in cognition. This is especially true of cognitive neuropsychological studies of language in brain-damaged patients. On the negative side, cognitive neuropsychologists have as yet failed to shed much light on such aspects of language as the planning processes involved in speaking and writing. It seems that cognitive neuropsychology is better suited to an analysis of relatively peripheral modules than more central (and possibly nonmodular) cognitive functions.

Cognitive science has been influential in the development of important new theoretical approaches and cognitive architectures (e.g. connectionism). It has also served the useful function of requiring theorists to be very precise in their theoretical accounts of cognition. In its computational emphasis it has also provided the best available means for modelling cognitive processes. On the debit side, it should always be remembered that the human computer analogy is only an analogy. Like all analogies the correspondences between the two domains break down at a certain point.

In view of the varied strengths and weaknesses of the three major perspectives to cognitive psychology, there are strong grounds for arguing that all three approaches are required. If all three approaches converge on an agreed theory in a particular area of cognitive psychology, then we can be more confident that the theory is approximately correct than if a theory emerges out of only one of three approaches. Divided we fall, united we stand!

FURTHER READING

Boden, M. A. (1988). *Computer models of mind*. Cambridge: Cambridge University Press. A fair-minded and readable evaluation of the cognitive science approach.

Caramazza, A. & McCloskey, M. (1988). The case for single-patient studies. *Cognitive Neuropsychology, 5*, 517–528. A strong indictment of group studies in cognitive neuropsychology is presented, and the current trend towards the study of individual patients is supported by powerful arguments.

Searle, J. (1989). *Minds, brains, and science*. Harmondsworth: Penguin. This is refreshingly readable, but many of the ideas in it need to be taken with a pinch of salt.

Temple, C. M. (1990). Developments and applications of cognitive neuropsychology. In M.W. Eysenck (Ed.), *International review of cognitive psychology*. Chichester: Wiley. This chapter contains an excellent discussion of some of the achievements and limitations of the cognitive neuropsychological approach.

REFERENCES

Abbot, V., Black, J.B., & Smith, E.E. (1985). The representation of scripts in memory. *Journal of Memory and Language, 24*, 179–199.

Abelson, R.P. (1981). Psychological status of the script concept. *American Psychologist, 36*, 715–729.

Adams, D. (1979). *The hitch-hiker's guide to the galaxy.* London: Pan.

Adams, J.L. (1979). *Conceptual blockbusting: A guide to better ideas* (2nd Edition). New York: W.W. Norton.

Adamson, R.E. & Taylor, D.W. (1954). Functional fixedness as related to elapsed time and set. *Journal of Experimental Psychology, 47*, 221–226.

Alba, J.W. & Hasher, L. (1983). Is memory schematic? *Psychological Bulletin, 93*, 203–231.

Allport, D.A. (1980). Attention and performance. In G. Claxton (Ed.), *Cognitive psychology: New directions.* London: Routledge & Kegan Paul.

Allport, D.A. (1985). Distributed memory, modular systems and dysphasia. In H. Bouma & D.G. Bouwhuis (Eds.), *Attention & performance X: Control of language processes.* Hillsdale, N.J.: Lawrence Erlbaum Associates Inc.

Allport, D.A., Antonis, B., & Reynolds, P. (1972). On the division of attention: A disproof of the single channel hypothesis. *Quarterly Journal of Experimental Psychology, 24*, 225–235.

Allport, D.A., MacKay, D.G., Prinz, W., & Marshall, J.C. (Eds.) (1987). *Language perception and production: Shared mechanisms in listening, reading, and writing.* London: Academic Press.

Anderson, J.R. (1976). *Language, memory and thought.* Hillsdale, N.J.: Lawrence Erlbaum Associates Inc.

Anderson, J.R. (1978). Arguments concerning representations from mental imagery. *Psychological Review, 85*, 249–277.

Anderson, J.R. (1982). Acquisition of cognitive skill. *Psychological Review, 89*, 396–406.

Anderson, J.R. (1983). *The architecture of cognition.* Harvard: Harvard University Press.

Anderson, J.R. (1987a). Skill acquisition: Compilation of weak-method problem solutions. *Psychological Review, 94*, 192–210.

Anderson, J.R. (1987b). Methodologies for studying human knowledge. *Behavioural & Brain Sciences, 10*, 467–505.

Anderson, J.R. (1988). The place of cognitive architectures in a rational analysis. *Tenth Annual Conference of the Cognitive Science Society.* Hillsdale, N.J.: Lawrence Erlbaum Associates Inc.

Anderson, J.R., Boyle, C.F., & Reiser, B.J. (1985). Intelligent tutoring systems. *Science, 228*, 456–462.

Anderson, J.R., Greeno, J.G., Kline, P.J., & Neves, D.M. (1981). Acquisition of problem solving skill. In J.R. Anderson (Ed.), *Cognitive skills and their acquisition.* Hillsdale, N.J.: Lawrence Erlbaum Associates Inc.

Anderson, J.R. & Reiser, B.J. (1985). The LISP tutor. *Byte, 10*, 159–175.

Anderson, R.C., Hiebert, E.H., Scott, J.A., & Wilkinson, I.A.G. (1985). *Becoming a nation of readers: The report of the Commission on Reading.* Washington, D.C.: U.S. Department of Education, National Institute of Education.

Anderson, R.C. & Ortony, A. (1975). On putting apples in bottles: A problem of polysemy. *Cognitive Psychology, 7*, 167–180.

Anderson, R.C. & Pichert, J.W. (1978). Recall of previously unrecallable information following a shift in perspective. *Journal of Verbal Learning and Verbal Behaviour, 17*, 1–12.

Anzai, Y. & Simon, H.A. (1979). The theory of learning by doing. *Psychological Review, 86*, 124–180.

Arbib, M.A. (1987). Many levels: More than one is algorithmic. *Behavioural and Brain Sciences, 10*, 478–479.

Armstrong, S.L., Gleitman, L.R. & Gleitman, H. (1983). What some concepts might not be. *Cognition, 13*, 263–308.

Atkinson, R.C. & Shiffrin, R.M. (1968). Human memory: A proposed system and its control processes. In K.W. Spence & J.T. Spence (Eds.), *The psychology of learning and motivation, Vol. 2.* London: Academic Press.

Atkinson, R.C. & Shiffrin, R.M. (1971). The control of short-term memory. *Scientific American, 225,* 82–90.

Atwood, M.E., Masson, M.E., & Polson, P.G. (1980). Further exploration with a process model for water jug problems. *Memory & Cognition, 8,* 182–192.

Atwood, M.E. & Polson, P.G. (1976). A process model for water jug problems. *Cognitive Psychology, 8,* 191–216.

Baars, B.J. (1986). *The cognitive revolution in psychology.* New York: Guilford Press.

Baars, B.J., Motley, M.T., & MacKay, D.G. (1975). Output editing for lexical status from artificially elicited slips of the tongue. *Journal of Verbal Learning and Verbal Behaviour, 14,* 382–391.

Bacon, S.J. (1974). Arousal and the range of cue utilisation. *Journal of Experimental Psychology, 102,* 81–87.

Baddeley, A.D. (1979). Working memory and reading. In P.A. Kolers, M.E. Wrolstad, & H. Bouma (Eds.), *Processing of visible language.* New York: Plenum.

Baddeley, A.D. (1982). Domains of recollection. *Psychological Review, 89,* 708–729.

Baddeley, A.D. (1984). Neuropsychological evidence and the semantic/episodic distinction. *Behavioural and Brain Sciences, 7,* 238–239.

Baddeley, A.D. (1986). *Working memory.* Oxford: Oxford University Press.

Baddeley, A.D., Grant, S., Wight, E., & Thomson, N. (1975). Imagery and visual working memory. In P.M.A. Rabbitt & S. Dornic (Eds.), *Attention and performance, Vol V.* London: Academic Press.

Baddeley, A.D. & Hitch, G. (1974). Working memory. In G.H. Bower (Ed.), *The psychology of learning and motivation, Vol. 8.* London: Academic Press.

Baddeley, A.D. & Lewis, V.J. (1981). Inner active processes in reading: The inner voice, the inner ear and the inner eye. In A.M. Lesgold and C.A. Perfetti (Eds.), *Interactive processes in reading.* Hillsdale, N.J.: Lawrence Erlbaum Associates Inc.

Baddeley, A.D. & Lieberman, K. (1980). Spatial working memory. In R. Nickerson (Ed.), *Attention and performance, Vol. 8.* Hillsdale, N.J.: Lawrence Erlbaum Associates Inc.

Baddeley, A.D., Thomson, N., & Buchanan, M. (1975). Word length and the structure of short-term memory. *Journal of Verbal Learning and Verbal Behaviour, 14,* 575–589.

Baddeley, A.D. & Warrington, E.K. (1970). Amnesia and the distinction between long- and short-term memory. *Journal of Verbal Learning and Verbal Behaviour, 9,* 176–189.

Baddeley, A.D. & Wilson, B. (1985). Phonological coding and short-term memory in patients without speech. *Journal of Memory and Language, 24,* 490–502.

Bahrick, H.P. (1970). Two-phase model for prompted recall. *Psychological Review, 77,* 215–222.

Ballard, D.H. (1986). Cortical connections and parallel processing. *Behavioural and Brain Sciences, 9(1),* 67–120.

Balota, D.A., Pollatsek, A., & Rayner, K. (1985). The interaction of contextual constraints and parafoveal visual information in reading. *Cognitive Psychology, 17,* 364–390.

Bannon, L.J. (1981). *An investigation of image scanning: Theoretical claims and empirical evidence.* Unpublished PhD Diss., University of Western Ontario, Canada.

Bard, E.G., Shillcock, R.C., & Altmann, G.T.M. (1988). The recognition of words after their acoustic offsets in spontaneous speech: Effects of subsequent context. *Perception and Psychophysics, 29,* 191–211.

Bar-Hillel, Y. & Carnap, R. (1964). An outline of a theory of semantic information. In Y. Bar-Hillel, *Language and information.* Reading, Mass.: Addison-Wesley.

Baron, J. (1988). *Thinking and deciding.* Cambridge: Cambridge University Press.

Barsalou, L.W. (1982). Context-independent and context-dependent information in concepts. *Memory and Cognition, 10,* 82–93.

Barsalou, L.W. (1983). Ad hoc categories. *Memory and Cognition, 11,* 211–227.

Barsalou, L.W. (1985). Ideals, central tendency, and frequency of instantiation as determinants of graded structure in categories. *Journal of Experimental Psychology: Learning, Memory and Cognition, 11,* 629–654.

Barsalou, L.W. (1987). The instability of graded structure: Implications for the nature of concepts. In U. Neisser (Eds.), *Concepts and conceptual development: Ecological and intellectual factors in categorisation.* Cambridge: Cambridge University Press.

Barsalou, L.W. (1989). Intra-concept similarity and its implications for inter-concept similarity. In S.

Vosniadou & A. Ortony (Eds.), *Similarity and analogy*. Cambridge: Cambridge University Press.

Bartlett, F.C. (1932). *Remembering: A study in experimental and social psychology*. Cambridge: Cambridge University Press.

Bartley, S.H. (1969). *Principles of perception*. London: Harper & Row.

Basso, A., Spinnler, H., Vallar, G., & Zanobio, E. (1982). Left hemisphere damage and selective impairment of auditory short-term memory: A case study. *Neuropsychologia, 20*, 263–274.

Battig, W.F. & Montague, W.E. (1969). Category norms for verbal items in 56 categories. *Journal of Experimental Psychology Monograph, 80*, 1–46.

Beales, S.A. & Parkin, A.J. (1984). Context and facial memory: The influence of different processing strategies. *Human Learning, 3*, 257–264.

Beatty, W.W., Salmon, D.P., Bernstein, N., Martone, M., Lyon, L., & Butters, N. (1987). Procedural learning in a patient with amnesia due to hypoxia. *Brain and Cognition, 6*, 386–402.

Beauvois, M.-F. & Derousne, J. (1979). Phonological alexia: Three dissociations. *Journal of Neurology, Neurosurgery and Psychiatry, 42*, 1115–1124.

Beck, A.T. (1976). *Cognitive theory and the emotional disorders*. New York: International Universities Press.

Beck, A.T. & Clark, D.A. (1988). Anxiety and depression: An information processing perspective. *Anxiety Research, 1*, 23–36.

Beck, A.T. & Emery, G. (1985). *Anxiety disorders and phobias: A cognitive perspective*. New York: Basic Books.

Beck, I.L. & Carpenter, P.A. (1986). Cognitive approaches to understanding reading. *American Psychologist, 41*, 1088–1105.

Benson, D.F. & Greenberg, J.P. (1969). Visual form agnosia: A specific defect in visual discrimination. *Archives of Neurology, 20*, 82–89.

Berlin, B. (1972). Speculations on the growth of ethnobiological nomenclature. *Language in Society, 1*, 51–86.

Berlin, B., Breedlove, D.E., & Raven, P.H. (1973). General principles of classification and nomenclature in folk biology. *American Anthropologist, 75*, 214–242.

Berlin, B. & Kay, P. (1969). *Basic colour terms: Their universality and evolution*. Berkeley, Calif.: University of California Press.

Berlyne, D.E. (1960). *Conflict, arousal, and curiosity*. London: McGraw-Hill.

Birch, H.G. (1945). The relationship of previous experience to insightful problem solving. *Journal of Comparative Psychology, 38*, 267–383.

Blaney, P.H. (1986). Affect and memory: A review. *Psychological Bulletin, 99*, 229–246.

Bobrow, D.G. & Norman, D.A. (1975). Some principles of memory schemata. In D.G. Bobrow & A. Collins.(Eds), *Representation and understanding: Essays in cognitive science*. New York: Academic Press.

Boden, M. (1988). *Computer models of mind*. Cambridge: Cambridge Univeristy Press.

Boles, D.B. (1983). Dissociated imagibility, concreteness, and familiarity in lateralised word recognition. *Memory and Cognition, 11*, 511–519.

Boole, G. (1854). *An investigation of the laws of thought on which are founded the mathematical theories of logic and probabilities*. London.

Boomer, D. (1965). Hesitation and grammatical encoding. *Language and Speech, 8*, 145–158.

Bower, G.H. (1970). Imagery as a relational organiser in associative learning. *Journal of Verbal Learning and Verbal Behaviour, 9*, 529–533.

Bower, G.H. (1972). Mental imagery and associative learning. In L. Gregg (Ed.), *Cognition in learning and memory*. New York: Wiley.

Bower, G.H. (1981). Mood and memory. *American Psychologist, 36*, 129–148.

Bower, G. H., Black, J.B., & Turner, T.J. (1979). Scripts in memory for text. *Cognitive Psychology, 11*, 177–220.

Bower, G.H. & Cohen, P.R. (1982). Emotional influences in memory and thinking: Data and theory. In M.S. Clark & S.T. Fiske (Eds.), *Affect and cognition: The 17th Annual Carnegie Symposium on Cognition*. Hillsdale, N.J.: Lawrence Erlbaum Associates Inc.

Bower, G.H., Gilligan, S.G., & Monteiro, K.P. (1981). Selectivity of learning caused by affective states. *Journal of Experimental Psychology: General, 110*, 451–473.

Bower, G.H. & Mayer, J.D. (1985). Failure to replicate mood-dependent retrieval. *Bulletin of the Psychonomic Society, 23*, 39–42.

Bower, G.H., Monteiro, K.P., & Gilligan, S.G. (1978). Emotional mood as a context for learning and recall. *Journal of Verbal Learning and Verbal Behaviour, 17*, 573–585.

Bower, G.H. & Winzenz, D. (1969). Group structure, coding and memory for digit series. *Journal of Experimental Psychology Monograph, 80* (No. 2, Pt. 2), 1–17.

Bowers, K.S. (1973). Situationism in psychology: An analysis and critique. *Psychological Review, 80*, 307–336.

Bracewell, R.J. & Hidi, S.E. (1974). The solution of an inferential problem as a function of stimulus materials. *Quarterly Journal of Experimental Psychology, 26*, 480–488.

Bradley, B. & Mathews, A. (1983). Negative self-schemata in clinical depression. *British Journal of Clinical Psychology, 22*, 173–181.

Bradley, B. & Mathews, A. (1988). Memory bias in recovered clinical depressives. *Cognition and Emotion, 2*, 235–245.

Braine, M.D.S. (1978). On the relationship between the natural logic of reasoning and standard logic. *Psychological Review, 85*, 1–21.

Braine, M.D.S., Reiser, B.J., & Rumain, B. (1984). Some empirical justification for a theory of natural propositional logic. In G.H. Bower (Ed.), *The psychology of learning and motivation, 18*. New York: Academic Press.

Braine, M.D.S. & Rumain, B. (1983). Logical reasoning. In J.H. Flavell & E.M. Markman (Eds.), *Handbook of child psychology, Vol. 3: Cognitive development*. (4th Edition). New York: Wiley.

Bramwell, B. (1897). Illustrative cases of aphasia. *The Lancet, 1*, 1256–1259.

Bransford, J.D. (1979). *Human cognition: Learning, understanding and remembering*. Belmont, Calif.: Wadsworth.

Bransford, J.D., Franks, J.J., Morris, C.D., & Stein, B.S. (1979). Some general constraints on learning and memory research. In L.S. Cermak and F.I.M. Craik (Eds.), *Levels of processing in human memory*. Hillsdale, N.J.: Lawrence Erlbaum Associates Inc.

Bransford, J.D. & Johnson, M.K. (1972). Contextual prerequisites for understanding: Some investigations of comprehension and recall. *Journal of Verbal Learning and Verbal Behaviour, 11*, 717–726.

Brewer, W.F. (1974). The problem of meaning and the interrelations of the higher mental processes. In R. Shaw & J.D. Bransford (Eds.), *Perceiving, acting, and knowing*. Hillsdale, N.J.: Lawrence Erlbaum Associates Inc.

Brewer, W.F. (1987) Schemas versus mental models in human memory. In P.E. Morris (Ed.), *Modelling cognition*. Chichester: Wiley.

Brewin, C.R. (1988). *Cognitive foundations of clinical psychology*. London: Lawrence Erlbaum Associates Ltd.

Broadbent, D.E. (1958). *Perception and communication*. Oxford: Pergamon.

Broadbent, D.E. (1971). *Decision and stress*. London: Academic Press.

Broadbent, D.E. (1982). Task combination and selective intake of information. *Acta Psychologica, 50*, 253–290.

Brooks, L. (1978). Non-analytic concept formation and memory for instances. In E. Rosch & B.B. Lloyd (Eds.), *Cognition and categorisation*. Hillsdale, N.J.: Lawrence Erlbaum Associates Inc.

Brown, C.H., Kolar, J., Torrey, B.J., Truong-Quang, T., & Volkman, P. (1976). Some general principles of biological and non-biological folk classification. *American Ethologist, 3*, 73–85.

Brown, R., & McNeill, D. (1966). The "tip of the tongue" phenomenon. *Journal of Verbal Learning and Verbal Behaviour, 5*, 325–337.

Bruce, V. (1988). *Recognising faces*. London: Lawrence Erlbaum Associates Ltd.

Bruce, V. & Green, P. (1985). *Visual perception: Physiology, psychology, and ecology*. London: Lawrence Erlbaum Associates Ltd.

Bruce, V. & Young, A. (1986). Understanding face recognition. *British Journal of Psychology, 77*, 305–327.

Bruner, J.S. (1957). On perceptual readiness. *Psychological Review, 64*, 123–152.

Bruner, J.S., Goodnow, J.J., & Austin, G.A. (1956). *A study of thinking*. New York: Wiley.

Bruner, J.S. & Postman, L. (1949). On the perception of incongruity: A paradigm. *Journal of*

Personality, 18, 206–223.

Bub, D., Black, S., Howell, J., & Kertesz, A. (1987). Speech output processes and reading. In M. Coltheart, G. Sartori, & R. Job (Eds.), *The cognitive neuropsychology of language.* London: Lawrence Erlbaum Associates Ltd.

Bub, D., Cancelliere, A., & Kertesz, A. (1985). Whole-word and analytic translation of spelling to sound in a nonsemantic reader. In K.E. Patterson, J.C. Marshall, and M. Coltheart (Eds.), *Surface dyslexia: Neuropsychological and cognitive studies of phonological reading.* London: Lawrence Erlbaum Associates Ltd.

Bub, D. & Kertesz, A. (1982). Deep agraphia. *Brain and Language, 17,* 146–165.

Burns, B., Shepp, B.E., McDonough, D., & Wiener-Ehrlich, W. (1978). The relation between stimulus analysability and perceived dimensional structure. In G.H. Bower (Ed.), *The psychology of learning and motivation, Vol. 12.* London: Academic Press.

Burstein, M.H. (1986). Analogical learning with multiple models. In T.M. Mitchell, J.G. Carbonell, & R.S. Michalski (Eds.), *Machine learning: A guide to current research.* Lancaster: Kluwer Academic Publishers.

Butler, B.E. (1974). The limits of selective attention in tachistoscopic recognition. *Canadian Journal of Psychology, 28,* 199–213.

Butters, N. & Cermak, L.S. (1980). *Alcoholic Korsakoff's Syndrome: An information-processing approach.* London: Academic Press.

Butterworth, B. (1980). Evidence from pauses. In B. Butterworth (Ed.), *Language production, Vol. 1.* London: Academic Press.

Byrne, R.M.J. (1989a). Everyday reasoning with conditional sequences. *Quarterly Journal of Experimental Psychology, 41A,* 141–166.

Byrne, R.M.J. (1989b). Suppressing valid inferences with conditionals. *Cognition, 31,* 61–83.

Byrne, R.M.J. & Johnson-Laird, P.N. (1989). Spatial reasoning. *Journal of Memory and Language, 28,* 564–575.

Byrne, R.M.J. & Johnson-Laird, P.N. (1990). Models and deductive reasoning. In K.J. Gilhooly, M.T. Keane, R. Logie & G. Erdos (Eds), *Lines of thinking: Reflections on the psychology of thought Vol. 1.* Chichester: John Wiley.

Calvo, M. (1985). Effort, aversive representations and performance in test anxiety. *Personality and Individual Differences, 6,* 563–571.

Campbell, D. (1957). *A study of some sensory-motor functions in psychiatric patients.* Unpublished Ph.D. thesis, University of London.

Campbell, R. & Butterworth, B. (1985). Phonological dyslexia and dysgraphia in a highly literate subject: A developmental case with associated deficits of phonemic processing and awareness. *Quarterly Journal of Experimental Psychology, 37A,* 435–475.

Campion, J. & Latto, R. (1985). Apperceptive agnosia due to carbon poisoning: An interpretation based on critical band masking from disseminated lesions. *Behavioural Brain Research, 15,* 227–240.

Cantor, N., Smith, E.E., French, R.D., & Mezzich, J. (1980). Psychiatric diagnosis as prototype categorisation. *Journal of Abnormal Psychology, 89,* 181–193.

Caplan, D. (1972). Clause boundaries and recognition latencies for words in sentences. *Perception and Psychophysics, 12,* 73–76.

Caplan, D. (1988). On the role of group studies in neuropsychological and pathopsychological research. *Cognitive Neuropsychology, 5,* 535–548.

Caramazza, A. (1984). The logic of neuropsychological research and the problem of patient classification in aphasia. *Brain and Language, 21,* 9–20.

Caramazza, A. & McCloskey, M. (1988). The case for single-patient studies. *Cognitive Neuropsychology, 5,* 517–528.

Caramazza, A., McCloskey, M., & Green, B. (1981). Naive beliefs in "sophisticated" subjects: Misconceptions about trajectories of objects. *Cognition, 9,* 117–123.

Carbonell, J.G. (1986). Derivational analogy: A theory of reconstructive problem solving and expertise acquisition. In R.S. Michalski, J.G. Carbonell, & T.M. Mitchell (Eds.), *Machine learning II: An artificial intelligence approach.* Los Altos, Calif: Kaufmann.

Carpenter, P.A. & Daneman, M. (1981). Lexical retrieval and error recovery in reading: A model based on eye fixations. *Journal of Verbal Learning and Verbal Behavior, 20,* 137–160.

Carpenter, P.A. & Just, M.A. (1977). Reading comprehension as eyes see it. In M.A. Just & P.A. Carpenter (Eds.), *Cognitive processes in comprehension*. Hillsdale, N.J.: Lawrence Erlbaum Associates Inc.

Ceraso, J. & Provitera, A. (1971). Sources of error in syllogistic reasoning. *Cognitive Psychology, 2*, 400–410.

Cermak, L.S. (1979). Amnesic patients' level of processing. In L.S. Cermak & F.I.M. Cermak (Eds.), *Levels of processing in human memory*. Hillsdale, N.J.: Lawrence Erlbaum Associates Inc.

Cermak, L.S., Lewis, R., Butters, N., & Goodglass, H. (1973). Role of verbal mediation in performance of motor tasks by Korsakoff patients. *Perceptual and Motor Skills, 37*, 259–262.

Cermak, L.S. & O'Connor, U. (1983). The anterograde and retrograde ability of a patient with encephalitis. *Neuropsychologia, 23*, 615–622.

Cermak, L.S., Talbot, N., Chandler, K., & Wolbarst, L.R. (1985). The perceptual priming phenomenon in amnesia. *Neuropsychologia, 23*, 615–622.

Chalmers, A.F. (1982). *What is this thing called science?* Milton Keynes: Open University Press.

Chapman, J.L. & Chapman, J.P. (1959). Atmosphere re-examined. *Journal of Experimental Psychology, 58*, 220–226.

Charness, N. (1981). Ageing and skilled problem solving. *Journal of Experimental Psychology: General, 110*, 21–38.

Chase, W.G. & Simon, H.A. (1973a). Perception in chess. *Cognitive Psychology, 4*, 55–81.

Chase, W.G. & Simon, H.A. (1973b). The mind's eye in chess. In W.G. Chase (Ed.), *Visual information processing*. London: Academic Press.

Cheesman, J. & Merikle, P.M. (1984). Priming with and without awareness. *Perception and Psychophysics, 36*, 387–395.

Cheesman, J. & Merikle, P.M. (1985). Word recognition and consciousness. In D. Besner, T.G. Waller, & G.E. MacKinnon (Eds.), *Reading research: Advances in theory and in practice*. New York: Academic Press.

Cheng, P.W. (1985). Restructuring versus automaticity: Alternative accounts of skill acquisition. *Psychological Review, 92*, 414–423.

Cheng, P. & Holyoak, K.J. (1985). Pragmatic reasoning schemas. *Cognitive Psychology, 17*, 391–416.

Cheng, P., Holyoak, K.J., Nisbett, R.E., & Oliver, L.M. (1986). Pragmatic versus syntactic approaches to training deductive reasoning. *Cognitive Psychology, 18*, 293–328.

Cherry, E.C. (1953). Some experiments on the recognition of speech with one and two ears. *Journal of the Acoustical Society of America, 25*, 975–979.

Chi, M.T.H., Feltovich, P.J., & Glaser, R. (1981). Categorisation and representation of physics problems by experts and novices. *Cognitive Science, 5*, 121–152.

Chi, M.T.H., Glaser, R., & Farr, M. (1988). *The nature of expertise*. Hillsdale, N.J.: Lawrence Erlbaum Associates Inc.

Chi, M.T.H., Glaser, R., & Rees, E. (1983). Expertise in problem solving. In R.J. Sternberg (Ed.), *Advances in the psychology of human intelligence, Vol. 2*. Hillsdale, N.J.: Lawrence Erlbaum Associates Inc.

Chomsky, N. (1957). *Syntactic structures*. The Hague: Mouton.

Chomsky, N. (1959). Review of Skinner's "verbal behaviour". *Language, 35*, 26–58.

Chomsky, N. (1965). *Aspects of the theory of syntax*. Cambridge, Mass.: M.I.T. Press.

Chomsky, N. (1982). *Some concepts and consequences of the theory of government and binding*. Cambridge, Mass.: M.I.T. Press.

Churchland, P.M. (1981). Eliminative materialism and the propositional attitudes. *Journal of Philosophy, 78*, 67–90.

Churchland, P.S. (1989). From Descartes to neural networks. *Scientific American*, July, 100.

Clarapede, E. (1911). Recognition of moiite. *Archives de Psychologie, 11*, 75–90.

Clark, D.M. & Teasdale, J.D. (1982). Diurnal variation in clinical depression and accessibility of memories of positive and negative experiences. *Journal of Abnormal Psychology, 91*, 87–95.

Clark, H.H. & Carlson, T.B. (1981). Context for comprehension. In J. Long & A. Baddeley (Eds.), *Attention and performance, Vol. IX*. Hillsdale, N.J.: Lawrence Erlbaum Associates Inc.

Clark, H.H., & Chase, W.G. (1972). On the process of comparing sentences against pictures. *Cognitive Psychology, 3*, 472–517.

Clark, H.H. & Clark, E.V. (1977). *Psychology and language*. New York: Harcourt Brace.

Clark, H.H. & Lucy, P. (1975). Understanding what is meant from what is said: A study in conversationally conveyed requests. *Journal of Verbal Learning and Verbal Behaviour, 14*, 56–72.

Claxton, G. (1980). Cognitive psychology: A suitable case for what sort of treatment? In G. Claxton (Ed.), *Cognitive psychology: New directions*. London: Routledge & Kegan Paul.

Clocksin, W.F. & Mellish, C.S. (1981). *Programming in Prolog*. Berlin: Springer-Verlag.

Cohen, B. & Murphy, G.L. (1984). Models of concepts. *Cognitive Science, 8*, 27–58.

Cohen, G. (1983). *The psychology of cognition*. (2nd Ed.) London: Academic Press.

Cohen, G., Eysenck, M.W., & LeVoi, M.E. (1986). *Memory: A cognitive approach*. Milton Keynes: Open University Press.

Cohen, L.J. (1981). Can human irrationality be experimentally demonstrated? *Behavioural and Brain Sciences, 4*, 317–331.

Cohen, N.J. (1984). Preserved learning capacity in amnesia: Evidence for multiple memory systems. In L.R. Squire & N. Butters (Eds.), *Neuropsychology of memory*. New York: Guilford Press.

Cohen, N.J. & Squire, L.R. (1980). Preserved learning and retention of pattern-analyzing skill in amnesia using perceptual learning. *Cortex, 17*, 273–278.

Coleman, L. & Kay, P. (1981). Prototype semantics. *Language, 57*, 26–44.

Collins, A.M. & Gentner, D. (1980). A framework for a cognitive theory of writing. In L.W. Gregg & E.R. Sternberg (Eds.), *Cognitive processes in writing*. Hillsdale, N. J.: Lawrence Erlbaum Associates Inc.

Collins, A.M. & Loftus, E.F. (1975). A spreading-activation theory of semantic processing. *Psychological Review, 82*, 407–428.

Collins, A.M. & Quillian, M.R. (1969). Retrieval time from semantic memory. *Journal of Verbal Learning and Verbal Behaviour, 8*, 240–248.

Collins, A.M. & Quillian, M.R. (1970). Does category size affect categorisation time? *Journal of Verbal Learning and Verbal Behaviour, 9*, 432–438.

Collins, A.M. & Smith, E.E. (1988). *Readings in cognitive science*. San Mateo, Calif.: Morgan Kaufmann.

Coltheart, M. (1983a). Ecological necessity of iconic memory. *Behavioural and Brain Sciences, 6*, 17–18.

Coltheart, M. (1983b). The right hemisphere and disorders of reading. In A.W. Young (Ed.), *Functions of the right cerebral hemisphere*. London: Academic Press.

Coltheart, M., Patterson, K., & Marshall, J.C. (Eds.) (1980). *Deep dyslexia*. London: Routledge & Kegan Paul.

Conrad, C. (1972). Cognitive economy in semantic memory. *Journal of Experimental Psychology, 92*, 148–154.

Conway, M. & Kahney, H. (1986). Transfer of learning in acquiring the concept of recursion. In J. Hallam & C. Mellish (Eds.), *Advances in artificial intelligence*. Chichester: Wiley.

Coombs, C.H., Dawes, R.M. & Tversky, A. (1970). *Mathematical psychology*. Englewood Cliffs, N.J.: Prentice Hall.

Cooper, L.A. (1975). Mental rotation of random two-dimensional shapes. *Cognitive Psychology, 7*, 20–43.

Cooper, L.A. & Podgory, P. (1976). Mental transformations and visual comparison processes. *Journal of Experimental Psychology: Human Perception and Performance, 2*, 503–514.

Cooper, L.A. & Shepard, R.N. (1973). Chronometric studies of the rotation of mental images. In W.G. Chase (Ed.), *Visual information processing*. New York: Academic Press.

Corkin, S. (1968). Acquisition of motor skill after bilateral medial temporal-lobe excision. *Neuropsychologia, 6*, 255–265.

Cornoldi, C. & Paivio, A. (1982). Imagery value and its effects on verbal memory: A review. *Archivio de Psicologia Neurologia e Psichiatria, 2*, 171–192.

Cosmides, L. (1989). The logic of social exchange: Has natural selection shaped how humans reason? *Cognition, 31*, 187–276.

Coughlan, A.K. & Warrington, E.K. (1978). Word-comprehension and word-retrieval in patients with localised cerebral lesions. *Brain, 101*, 163–185.

Coughlan, A.K. & Warrington, E.K. (1981) The impairment of verbal semantic memory: A single case study. *Journal of Neurology, Neurosurgery and Psychiatry, 50*, 1110–1116.

Craik, F.I.M. (1973). A "levels of analysis" view of memory. In P. Pliner, L. Krames, & T.M. Alloway (Eds.), *Communication and affect: Language and thought.* London: Academic Press.

Craik, F.I.M. & Lockhart, R.S. (1972). Levels of processing: A framework for memory research. *Journal of Verbal Learning and Verbal Behaviour, 11*, 671–684.

Craik, F.I.M. & Tulving, E. (1975). Depth of processing and the retention of words in episodic memory. *Journal of Experimental Psychology: General, 104*, 268–294.

Crick, F. (1989). *What mad pursuit?* New York: Basic Books.

Crick, F. & Asanuma, C. (1986). Certain aspects of the anatomy and physiology of the cerebral cortex. In J. L. McClelland, D.E. Rumelhart, & the PDP Research Group (Eds.), *Parallel distributed processing, Volume 2, Psychological and biological models.* Cambridge, Mass.: M.I.T. Press.

Crovitz, H.F., Harvey, M.T., & McClanahan, S. (1981). Hidden memory: A rapid method for the study of amnesia using perceptual learning. *Cortex, 17*, 273–278.

Daneman, M. & Carpenter, P.A. (1980). Individual differences in working memory and reading. *Journal of Verbal Learning and Verbal Behaviour, 19*, 450–466.

Danks, J.H. & Glucksberg, S. (1980). Experimental psycholinguistics. *Annual Review of Psychology, 31*, 391–417.

Darwin, C.J., Turvey, M.T., & Crowder, R.G. (1972). An auditory analogue of the Sperling partial report procedure: Evidence for brief auditory storage. *Cognitive Psychology, 3*, 255–267.

Darwin, C.J. (1990). Speech perception. In M.W. Eysenck (Ed.), *The Blackwell dictionary of cognitive psychology.* Oxford: Blackwell.

Davies, S.P. (In press a). The nature and development of programming plans. *International Journal of Man-Machine Studies.*

Davies, S.P. (In press b). Plans, goals and selection rules in the comprehension of computer programs. *Behaviour and Information Technology.*

Day, R.H. (1980). Visual illusions. In M.A. Jeeves (Ed.), *Psychology survey, No. 3.* London: Allen & Unwin.

DeGroot, A.D. (1965). *Thought and choice in chess.* The Hague: Mouton.

DeGroot, A.D. (1966). Perception and memory versus thought. In B. Kleinmuntz (Ed.), *Problem solving.* New York: Wiley.

Dell, G.S. (1986). A spreading-activation theory of retrieval in sentence production. *Psychological Review, 93*, 283–321.

Dennis, M. (1976). Dissociated naming and locating of body parts after left anterior lobe resection: An experimental case study. *Brain and Language, 3*, 147–163.

Depue, R.A. & Monroe, S.M. (1979). The unipolar-bipolar distinction in the depressive disorders. *Psychological Bulletin, 85*, 1001–1029.

DeRenzi, E. (1986). Current issues in prosopagnosia. In H.D. Ellis, M.A. Jeeves, F. Newcombe, & A. Young (Eds.), *Aspects of face processing.* Dordrecht: Martinus Nijhoff.

Derry, P.A. & Kuiper, N.A. (1981). Schematic processing and self-reference in clinical depression. *Journal of Abnormal Psychology, 90*, 286–297.

de Saussure, F. (1960). *Course in general linguistics.* London: Peter Owen.

Deutsch, J.A. & Deutsch, D. (1963). Attention: Some theoretical considerations. *Psychological Review, 70*, 80–90.

DeValois, R.L. & Jacobs, F.H. (1968). Primate colour vision. *Science, 162*, 533–540.

Dixon, N.F. (1981). *Preconscious processing.* Chichester: Wiley.

Dodd, B. & Campbell, R. (1986). *Hearing by eye: The psychology of lip reading.* London: Lawrence Erlbaum Associates Ltd.

Dominowski, R.L. (1981). Comment on "an examination of the alleged role of 'fixation' in the solution of several insight problems" by Weisberg & Alba. *Journal of Experimental Psychology: General, 110*, 199–203.

Donders, F.C. (1868). Over de snelheid van psychische processen. *Onderzoekingen gedaan in het Psyiologish Laboratorium der Utrechtsche Hoogeschool: Tweede Reeks, II*, 92–120.

Douglas, M. (1966). *Purity and danger.* London: Routledge & Kegan Paul.

Duncan, J. (1979). Divided attention: The whole is more than the sum of its parts. *Journal of Experimental Psychology: Human Perception, 5*, 216–228.

Duncker, K. (1926). A qualitative (experimental and theoretical) study of productive thinking (solving of comprehensible problems). *Journal of Genetic Psychology, 68,* 97–116.

Duncker, K. (1945). On problem solving. *Psychological Monographs, 58* (Whole No. 270).

Dyer, M.G. (1983). *In-depth understanding: A model of integrated processing for narrative comprehension.* Cambridge, Mass.: M.I.T. Press.

D'Zurilla, T. (1965). Recall efficiency and mediating cognitive events in "experimental repression". *Journal of Personality and Social Psychology, 3,* 253–256.

Easterbrook, J. A. (1959). The effect of emotion on cue utilisation and the organisation of behaviour. *Psychological Review, 66,* 183–201.

Eco, U. (1984). *The name of the rose.* London: Picador.

Edwards, W. (1954). The theory of decision making. *Psychological Bulletin, 51,* 380–417.

Edwards, W. (1968). Conservatism in human information processing. In B. Kleinmuntz (Ed.), *Formal representations of human judgement.* New York: Wiley.

Egan, D.W. & Greeno, J.G. (1974). Theories of rule induction: Knowledge acquired in concept learning, serial pattern learning and problem solving. In W.G. Gregg (Ed.), *Knowledge and cognition.* Hillsdale, N.J.: Lawrence Erlbaum Associates Inc.

Egly, R. & Homa, D. (1984). Sensitization of the visual field. *Journal of Experimental Psychology: Human Perception and Performance, 10,* 778–793.

Eisenstadt, M. (1988). *Intensive prolog.* Milton Keynes, England: The Open University Press.

Eisenstadt, M., Rajan, T., & Keane, M.T. (in press). *Novice programming environments.* London: Lawrence Erlbaum Associates Ltd.

Ellen, P. (1982). Direction, past experience and hints in creative problem solving: A reply to Weisberg & Alba. *Journal of Experimental Psychology: General, 111,* 316–325.

Ellis, A.W. (1984). Introduction to Bramwell's (1897) case of word meaning deafness. *Cognitive Neuropsychology, 1,* 245–258.

Ellis, A.W. (1987). Intimations of modularity, or, the modularity of mind: Doing cognitive neuro-psychology without syndromes. In M. Coltheart, G. Sartori, and R. Job (Eds.), *The cognitive neuropsychology of language.* London: Lawrence Erlbaum Associates Ltd.

Ellis, A.W. (1990). Cognitive neuropsychology. In M.W. Eysenck (Ed.), *Blackwell's dictionary of cognitive psychology.* Oxford: Blackwell.

Ellis, A.W. & Beattie, G. (1986). *The psychology of language and communication.* London: Lawrence Erlbaum Associates Ltd.

Ellis, A.W., Miller, D., & Sin, G. (1983). Wernicke's aphasia and normal language processing: A case study in cognitive neuropsychology. *Cognition, 15,* 111–144.

Ellis, A.W. & Young, A.W. (1988). *Human cognitive neuropsychology.* London: Lawrence Erlbaum Associates Ltd.

Ellis, H.C. & Ashbrook, P.W. (1987). Resource allocation model of the effects of depressed mood states on memory. In K. Fiedler & J. Forgas (Eds.), *Affect, cognition, and social behaviour.* Toronto: Hogrefe.

Ellis, H.C., Thomas, R.L., McFarland, A.D., & Lane, J.W. (1985). Emotional mood states and retrieval in episodic memory. *Journal of Experimental Psychology: Learning, Memory, and Cognition, 10,* 470–482.

Erdelyi, M.H. (1974). A new look at the new look: Perceptual defence and vigilance. *Psychological Review, 81,* 1–24.

Erickson, J.R. (1974). A set analysis theory of behaviour in formal syllogistic reasoning tasks. In R. Solso (Ed.), *Loyola symposium: Vol. 2.* Hillsdale, N.J.: Lawrence Erlbaum Associates Inc.

Ericsson, K.A. & Simon, H.A. (1980). Verbal reports as data. *Psychological Review, 87,* 215–251.

Ericsson, K.A. & Simon, H.A. (1984). *Protocol analysis.* Cambridge, Mass.: M.I.T. Press.

Erlich, K. & Johnson-Laird, P.N. (1982). Spatial descriptions and referential continuity. *Journal of Verbal Learning and Verbal Behaviour, 21,* 296–306.

Erlich, K. & Soloway, E. (1984). An empirical investigation of tacit plan knowledge in programming. In J.C. Thomas & M.L. Schneider (Eds.), *Human factors in computing systems.* Norwood, N.J.: Ablex.

Ervin-Tripp, S. (1964). An analysis of the interaction of language, topic and listener. *American Anthropologist, 66,* 94–100.

Evans, J.St.B.T. (1982). *The psychology of deductive reasoning.* London: Routledge & Kegan Paul.

Evans, J.St.B.T. (1983). Linguistic determinants of bias in conditional reasoning. *Quarterly Journal of Experimental Psychology, 35A*, 635–644.

Evans, J.St.B.T. (1984). Heuristic and analytic processes in reasoning. *British Journal of Psychology, 75*, 451–458.

Evans, J.St.B.T. (1987). Reasoning. In H. Beloff & A.M. Coleman (Eds.), *Psychological survey, 6*, 74–93.

Evans, J.St.B.T. (1989). *Bias in human reasoning*. London: Lawrence Erlbaum Associates Ltd.

Evans, J.St.B.T., & Lynch, L.S. (1973). Matching bias in the selection task. *British Journal of Psychology, 64*, 391–397.

Eysenck, M.W. (1972). *Conditions modifying memory: The von Restorff and "release" effects*. Unpublished Ph.D. thesis, University of London.

Eysenck, M.W. (1977). *Human memory: Theory, research, and individual differences*. Oxford: Pergamon.

Eysenck, M.W. (1978). Verbal remembering. In B. M. Foss (Ed.), *Psychology survey, No. 1*. London: Allen & Unwin.

Eysenck, M.W. (1979a). Depth, elaboration, and distinctiveness. In L. S. Cermak & F. I. M. Craik (Eds.), *Levels of processing in human memory*. Hillsdale, N. J.: Lawrence Erlbaum Associates Inc.

Eysenck, M.W. (1979b). Anxiety, learning, and memory: A reconceptualisation. *Journal of Research in Personality, 13*, 363–385.

Eysenck, M.W. (1982). *Attention and arousal: Cognition and performance*. Berlin: Springer.

Eysenck, M.W. (1984). *A handbook of cognitive psychology*. London: Lawrence Erlbaum Associates Ltd.

Eysenck, M.W. (1985). Anxiety and cognitive-task performance. *Personality and Individual Differences, 6*, 579–586.

Eysenck, M.W. (1988). Anxiety and attention. *Anxiety Research, 1*, 9–15.

Eysenck, M.W. (in press). *Anxiety: The cognitive perspective*. London: Lawrence Erlbaum Associates Ltd.

Eysenck, M.W. & Eysenck, M.C. (1980). Effects of processing depth, distinctiveness, and word frequency on retention. *British Journal of Psychology, 71*, 263–274.

Eysenck, M.W., MacLeod, C., & Mathews, A. (1987). Cognitive functioning and anxiety. *Psychological Research, 49*, 189–195.

Faigley, L. & Witte, S. (1983). Analysing revision. *College Composition and Communication, 32*, 400–414.

Falkenhainer, B., Forbus, K.D., & Gentner, D. (1986). Structure-mapping engine. *Proceedings of the Annual Conference of the American Association for Artificial Intelligence*. Philadelphia: AAAI.

Fancher, R.E. (1979). *Pioneers of psychology*. New York: Norton & Co.

Farah, M.J. (1984). The neurological basis of mental imagery: A componential analysis. *Cognition, 18*, 245–272.

Farah, M.J., Hammond, K.M., Levine, D.N, & Calvanio, R. (1988). Visual and spatial mental imagery: Dissociable systems of representation. *Cognitive Psychology, 20*, 439–462.

Farah, M.J., Peronnet, F., Gonon, M.A., & Giard, M.H. (1988). Electrophysiological evidence for a shared representational medium for visual images and visual percepts. *Journal of Experimental Psychology: General, 117*, 248–257.

Feldman, J.A. & Ballard, D.H. (1982). Connectionist models and their properties. *Cognitive Science, 6*, 205–254.

Feyerabend, P. (1975). *Against method: Outline of an anarchist theory of knowledge*. London: New Left Books.

Fillmore, C.J. (1968). The case for case. In E. Bach & R.T. Harms (Eds.), *Universals of linguistic theory*. New York: Holt, Rinehart, & Winston.

Fillmore, C.J. (1982). Frame semantics. In linguistic society of Korea (Eds.), *Linguistics in the morning calm*. Seoul: Hanshin.

Finlay-Jones, R. A. & Brown, G.W. (1981). Types of stressful life events and the onset of anxiety and depressive disorders. *Psychological Medicine, 11*, 803–815.

Fischhoff, B. (1988). Judgement and decision making. In R.J. Sternberg & E.E. Smith (Eds.), *The psychology of human thought*. Cambridge: Cambridge University Press.

Fiske, S.T. & Taylor, S.E. (1984). *Social cognition*. Reading, Mass.: Addison-Wesley.

Foa, E.B. & Kozak, M.J. (1986). Emotional processing of fear: Exposure to corrective information. *Psychological Bulletin, 99*, 20–35.

Fodor, J.A. (1983). *The modularity of mind*. Cambridge, Mass.: M.I.T. Press.

Fodor, J.D., Fodor, J.A., & Garrett, M.F. (1975). The psychological unreality of semantic representations. *Linguistic Inquiry, 4*, 515–531.

Fodor, J.A., Garrett, M.F., Walker, E.C.T., & Parkes, C.H. (1980). Against definitions. *Cognition, 8*, 263–367.

Ford, M. (1985). Review of mental models. *Language, 61*, 897–903.

Forster, K. (1979). Levels of processing and the structure of the language processor. In W.E. Cooper & E.C.T. Walker (Eds.), *Sentence processing: Psycholinguistic studies presented to Merrill Garrett*. Hillsdale, N.J.: Lawrence Erlbaum Associates Inc.

Foulds, G.A. (1952). Temperament differences in maze performance. Part II. The effect of distraction and electroconvulsive therapy on psychiatric retardation. *British Journal of Psychology, 43*, 33–41.

Fowles, D. & Gersh, F. (1979). Neurotic depression: The endogenous–neurotic distinction. In R. Depue (Ed.), *The psychobiology of the depressive disorders: Implications of the effects of stress*. New York: Academic Press.

Franks, J.J. & Bransford, J.D. (1971). Abstraction of visual patterns. *Journal of Experimental Psychology, 90*, 65–74.

Frauenfelder, U.H. & Tyler, L.K. (1987). The process of spoken word recognition: An introduction. *Cognition, 25*, 1–20.

Frege, G. (1952). On sense and reference. In P. Geach & M. Black (Eds.), *Translations from the philosophical writings of Gottlob Frege*. Oxford: Basil Blackwell.

Freud, S. (1915). Repression. In Freud's *Collected Papers, Vol. IV*. London: Hogarth.

Freud, S. (1943). *A general introduction to psychoanalysis*. New York: Garden City.

Friedman, A. (1979). Framing pictures: The role of knowledge in automatised encoding and memory for gist. *Journal of Experimental Psychology: General, 108*, 316–355.

Frisby, J.P. (1986). The computational approach to vision. In I. Roth & J.P. Frisby, *Perception and representation: A cognitive approach*. Milton Keynes: Open University Press.

Gabrieli, J.D.E., Cohen, N.J., & Corkin, S. (1983). The acquisition of lexical and semantic knowledge in amnesia. *Society for Neuroscience Abstracts, 9*, 238.

Galambos, J.A., Abelson, R.P, & Black, J.B. (1986) *Knowledge structures*. Hillsdale, N.J.: Lawrence Erlbaum Associates Inc.

Galambos, J.A. & Rips, L.J. (1982). Memory for routines. *Journal of Verbal Learning and Verbal Behaviour, 21*, 260–281.

Gale, R.M. (1967). Propositions, judgements, statements and sentences. In P. Edwards (Ed.), *The encyclopedia of philosophy*. New York: Macmillan.

Galton, F. (1883). *Inquiries into human development and its development*. London: Macmillan.

Gardiner, J.M. (1988). Functional aspects of recollective experience. *Memory and Cognition, 16*, 309–313.

Gardner, H. (1985). *The mind's new science*. New York: Basic Books.

Garner, W.R. (1974). *The processing of information and structure*. Potomac, Maryland.: Lawrence Erlbaum Associates Inc.

Garnham, A. (1985). *Psycholinguistics: Some central topics*. London: Methuen.

Garrett, M.F. (1976). Syntactic processes in sentence production. In R.J. Wales & E. Walker (Eds.), *New approaches to language mechanisms*. Amsterdam: North Holland.

Garrett, M.F. (1984). The organisation of processing structures for language production: Applications to aphasic speech. In D. Caplan, A.R. Lecours, & A. Smith (Eds.), *Biological perspectives on language*. Cambridge, Mass.: M.I.T. Press.

Gauld, A. & Stephenson, G.M. (1967). Some experiments relating to Bartlett's theory of remembering. *British Journal of Psychology, 58*, 39–50.

Gazzaniga, M.S. (1983). Right hemisphere language following brain bisection: A 20 year perspective. *American Psychologist, 38*, 525–537.

Geis, M. & Zwicky, A.M. (1971). On invited inferences. *Linguistic Inquiry, 2*, 561–566.

Gentner, D. (1975). Evidence for the psychological reality of semantic components: The verbs of possession. In D.A. Norman & D.E. Rumelhart (Eds.), *Explorations in cognition*. San Francisco: Freeman.

Gentner, D. (1980). *The structure of analogical models in science*. B.B.N. Technical Report No. 4454.

Gentner, D. (1981). Verb structures in memory for sentences: Evidence for componential representation. *Cognitive Psychology, 13*, 56–83.

Gentner, D. (1983). Structure-mapping: A theoretical framework for analogy. *Cognitive Science, 7*, 155–170.

Gentner, D. & Gentner, D.R. (1983). Flowing waters and teeming crowds: Mental models of electricity. In D. Gentner & A.L. Stevens (Eds.), *Mental models*. Hillsdale, NJ: Lawrence Erlbaum Associates Inc.

Gentner, D. & Stevens, A.L. (1983). *Mental models*. Hillsdale, N.J.: Lawrence Erlbaum Associates Inc.

Ghiseli, B. (1952). *The creative process*. New York: Mentor.

Gibson, E.J. (1969). *Principles of perceptual learning and development*. New York: Appleton-Century-Crofts.

Gibson, E.J., Shapiro, F., & Yonas, A. (1968). *Confusion matrices of graphic patterns obtained with a latency measure. The analysis of reading skill: A program of basic and applied research* (Final report project No. 5-1213). Cornell University.

Gibson, J.J. (1966). *The senses considered as perceptual systems*. Boston: Houghton Mifflin.

Gibson, J.J. (1979). *The ecological approach to visual perception*. Boston: Houghton Mifflin.

Gick, M.L. & Holyoak, K.J. (1980). Analogical problem solving. *Cognitive Psychology, 12*, 306–355.

Gick, M.L., & Holyoak, K.J. (1983). Schema induction in analogical transfer. *Cognitive Psychology, 15*, 1–38.

Gilhooly, K.J. (1987). Mental modelling: A framework for the study of thinking. In D.N. Perkins, J. Lochhead, & J.C. Bishop (Eds.), *Thinking*. Hillsdale, N.J.: Lawrence Erlbaum Associates Inc.

Gilhooly, K.J. (1988). *Thinking: Directed, undirected, and creative* (2nd Edn.). London: Academic Press.

Gilhooly, K.J. & Falconer, W. (1974). Concrete and abstract terms and relations in testing a rule. *Quarterly Journal of Experimental Psychology, 26*, 355–359.

Gilhooly, K., Keane, M.T., Logie, R., & Erdos, G. (Eds.) (1990a). *Lines of thinking: Reflections on the psychology of thought. Vol. 1*. Chichester: John Wiley.

Gilhooly, K., Keane, M.T., Logie, R., & Erdos, G. (Eds.) (1990b). *Lines of thinking: Reflections on the psychology of thought. Vol. 2*. Chichester: John Wiley.

Gilligan, S.G. & Bower, G.H. (1984). Cognitive consequences of emotional arousal. In C. Izard, J. Kagen, and R. Zajonc (Eds.), *Emotions, cognition, and behaviour*. New York: Cambridge University Press.

Gilmore, D.J. & Green, T.R.G. (1988). Programming plans and programming expertise. *Quarterly Journal of Experimental Psychology, 40A*, 423–442.

Glanzer, M. & Cunitz, A. R. (1966). Two storage mechanisms in free recall. *Journal of Verbal Learning and Verbal Behaviour, 5*, 351–360.

Glaser, R., Lesgold, A., & Lejoie, S. (in press). Toward a cognitive theory for the measurement of achievement. In J. Glover (Ed.), *The influence of psychology on testing and measurement*. Hillsdale, N.J.: Lawrence Erlbaum Associates Inc.

Glass, A.L. & Holyoak, K.J. (1975). Alternative conceptions of semantic memory. *Cognition, 3*, 313–339.

Glisky, E.L., Schachter, D.L., & Tulving, E. (1986). Computer learning by memory-impaired patients: Acquisition and retention of complex knowledge. *Neuropsychologia, 24*, 313–328.

Godden, D.R. & Baddeley, A.D. (1975). Context–dependent memory in two natural environments: On land and under water. *British Journal of Psychology, 66*, 325–331.

Godden, D. & Baddeley, A.D. (1980). When does context influence recognition memory? *British Journal of Psychology, 71*, 99–104.

Goldman, A.I. (1986). *Epistemology and cognition*. Cambridge, Mass.: Harvard University Press.

Gomulicki, B.R. (1956). Recall as an abstractive process. *Acta Psychologica, 12*, 77–94.

Goodman, K.S. (1967). Reading: A psycholinguistic guessing game. *Journal of the Reading Specialist, 6*, 126–135.

Gould, J.D. (1978). An experimental study of writing, dictating and speaking. In J. Requin (Ed.), *Attention and performance, Vol. VII*. Hillsdale, N.J.: Lawrence Erlbaum Associates Inc.

Gould, J.D. (1979). *Writing and speaking letters and messages*. IBM Research Report, RC-7528.

Gould, J.D. (1980). Experiments on composing letters: Some facts, some myths, and some observations. In L.W. Gregg and E.R. Sternberg (Eds.), *Cognitive processes in writing*. Hillsdale, N.J.: Lawrence Erlbaum Associates Inc.

Graesser, A.C., Gordon, S.E., & Sawyer, J.D. (1979). Recognition memory for typical and atypical actions: Tests of a script pointer + tag hypothesis. *Journal of Verbal Learning and Verbal Behaviour, 18,* 319–332.

Graesser, A.C., Woll, S.B., Kowalski, D.J., & Smith, D.A. (1980). Memory for typical and atypical actions in scripted activities. *Journal of Experimental Psychology: Human Learning and Memory, 6,* 503–515.

Graf, P. & Schachter, D.L. (1985). Implicit and explicit memory for new associations in normal and amnesic subjects. *Journal of Experimental Psychology: Learning, Memory, and Cognition, 11,* 501–518.

Graf, P., Squire, L.R., & Mandler, G. (1984). The information that amnesic patients do not forget. *Journal of Experimental Psychology: Learning, Memory, and Cognition, 10,* 164–178.

Gray, J.A. & Wedderburn, A.A. (1960). Grouping strategies with simultaneous stimuli. *Quarterly Journal of Experimental Psychology, 12,* 180–184.

Greene, J. (1986). *Language understanding: A cognitive approach*. Milton Keynes: Open University Press.

Gregg, V.H. (1976). Word frequency, recognition and recall. In J. Brown (Ed.), *Recall and recognition*. New York: Wiley.

Gregory, R.L. (1970). *The intelligent eye*. New York: McGraw-Hill.

Gregory, R.L. (1972). Seeing as thinking. *Times Literary Supplement*, June 23.

Gregory, R.L. (1980). Perceptions as hypotheses. *Philosophical Transactions of the Royal Society of London, Series B, 290,* 181–197.

Grice, H.P. (1967). Logic and conversation. In P. Cole & J. L. Morgan (Eds.), *Studies in syntax, Vol. III*. New York: Seminar Press.

Grice, H.P. (1975). Logic and conversation. In P. Cole & J.L. Morgan (Eds.), *Syntax and semantics, III: Speech acts*. New York: Seminar Press.

Griggs, R.A. (1983). The role of problem content in the selection task and THOG problem. In J.St.B.T. Evans (Ed.), *Thinking and reasoning: Psychological approaches*. London: Routledge & Kegan Paul.

Griggs, R.A. & Cox, J.R. (1982). The elusive thematic–material effect in Wason's selection task. *British Journal of Psychology, 73,* 407–420.

Griggs, R.A. & Cox, J.R. (1983). The effects of problem content and negation on Wason's selection task. *Quarterly Journal of Experimental Psychology, 35A,* 519–533.

Gunther, H., Gfoerer, S., & Weiss, L. (1984). Inflection, frequency, and the word superiority effect. *Psychological Research, 46,* 261–281.

Guyote, M.J. & Sternberg, R.J. (1981). A transitive-chain theory of syllogistic reasoning. *Cognitive Psychology, 13,* 461–524.

Haber, R.N. (1983). The impending demise of the icon: A critique of the concept of iconic storage in visual information processing. *Behavioural and Brain Sciences, 6,* 1–11.

Hampson, P. J. (1989). Aspects of attention and cognitive science. *The Irish Journal of Psychology, 10,* 261–275.

Hampton, J.A. (1979). Polymorphous concepts in semantic memory. *Journal of Verbal Learning and Verbal Behaviour, 18,* 441–461.

Hampton, J.A. (1981). An investigation of the nature of abstract concepts. *Memory and Cognition, 9,* 149–156.

Hampton, J.A. (1982). A demonstration of intransitivity in natural categories. *Cognition, 12,* 151–164.

Hampton, J.A. (1987). Inheritance of attributes in natural concept conjunctions. *Memory and Cognition, 15,* 55–71.

Hampton, J.A. (1988). Overextension of conjunctive concepts. *Journal of Experimental Psychology: Language, Memory and Cognition, 14,* 12–32.

Hampton, J.A. (1990). *Concepts*. London: Lawrence Erlbaum Associates Ltd.

Hardy, G.R. & Legge, D. (1968). Cross-modal induction of changes in sensory thresholds. *Quarterly Journal of Experimental Psychology, 20*, 20–29.

Harley, T. (1984). A critique of top-down independent levels models of speech production: Evidence from non-plan-internal speech errors. *Cognitive Science, 8*, 191–219.

Harris, M. (1990). Language and thought. In M. W. Eysenck (Ed.), *The Blackwell dictionary of cognitive psychology*. Oxford: Blackwell.

Hart, J., Berndt, R.S., & Caramazza, A. (1985). Category-specific naming deficit following cerebral infarction. *Nature, 316*, 439–440.

Hasemer, T. & Domingue, J.D. (1989). *Common lisp programming for artificial intelligence.* Wokingham: Addison-Wesley.

Hatfield, F.M. & Patterson, K.E. (1983). Phonological spelling. *Quarterly Journal of Experimental Psychology, 35A*, 451–468.

Hayes, J.R. & Flower, L.S. (1980). Identifying the organisation of writing processes. In L.W. Gregg & F.R. Steinberg (Eds.), *Cognitive processes in writing*. Hillsdale, N. J.: Lawrence Erlbaum Associates Inc.

Hayes, J.R. & Flower, L.S. (1986). Writing research and the writer. *American Psychologist, 41*, 1106–1113.

Hayes, J.R., Flower, L.S., Schriver, K., Stratman, J., & Carey, L. (1985). *Cognitive processes in revision* (Technical Report No. 12). Pittsburgh, PA: Carnegie Mellon University.

Hayes, J.R. & Simon, H.A. (1974). Understanding written problem instructions. In R.L. Gregg (Ed.), *Knowledge and cognition*. Hillsdale, N.J.: Lawrence Erlbaum Associates Inc.

Hayes, J.R. & Simon, H.A. (1977). Psychological differences among problem isomorphs. In N.J. Castellan, D.B. Pisoni, & G.R. Potts (Eds.), *Cognitive theory: Vol. 2*. Hillsdale, N.J.: Lawrence Erlbaum Associates Inc.

Hayes, P.J. (1985). Some problems and non-problems in representational theory. In R.J. Brachman & H.J. Levesque (Eds.), *Readings in knowledge representation*. Los Altos, Calif.: Morgan Kaufmann.

Hebb, D.O. (1949). *The organisation of behaviour*. New York: Wiley.

Heider, E. (1972). Universals in colour naming and memory. *Journal of Experimental Psychology, 93*, 10–20.

Heller, J. & Reif, F. (1984). Prescribing effective human problem solving: Problem description in physics. *Cognition & Instruction, 2*, 191–203.

Hemsley, D.R. & Zawada, S.L. (1976). "Filtering" and the cognitive deficit in schizophrenia. *British Journal of Psychiatry, 128*, 456–461.

Henle, M. (1962). On the relation between logic and thinking. *Psychological Review, 69*, 366–378.

Hinton, G.E. (1979). Some demonstrations of the effects of structural descriptions in mental imagery. *Cognitive Science, 3*, 231–251.

Hinton, G.E. & Anderson, J.A. (1981). *Parallel models of associative memory*. Hillsdale, N. J.: Lawrence Erlbaum Associates Inc.

Hinton, G.E., McClelland, J.L., & Rumelhart, D.E. (1986). Distributed representations. In D.E. Rumelhart, J.L. McClelland, & the PDP Research Group (Eds.), *Parallel distributed processing: Vol. 1. Foundations*. Cambridge, Mass.: M.I.T. Press.

Hintzman, D.L. (1986). "Schema abstraction" in a multiple-trace memory model. *Psychological Review, 93*, 411–428.

Hintzman, D.L. & Ludlam, G. (1980). Differential forgetting of prototypes and old instances: Simulation by an exemplar-based classification model. *Memory and Cognition, 8*, 378–382.

Hirst, W., Spelke, E.S., Reaves, C.C., Caharack, G., & Neisser, U. (1980). Dividing attention without alternation or automaticity. *Journal of Experimental Psychology: General, 109*, 98–117.

Hitch, G.J. (1978). The role of short-term working memory in mental arithmetic. *Cognitive Psychology, 10*, 302–323.

Hitch, G.J. & Baddeley, A.D. (1976). Verbal reasoning and working memory. *Quarterly Journal of Experimental Psychology, 28*, 603–621.

Holding, D.H. (1985). *The psychology of chess*. Hillsdale, N.J.: Lawrence Erlbaum Associates Inc.

Holding, D.H., & Reynolds, J.R. (1982). Recall or evaluation of chess positions as determinants of chess skill. *Memory and Cognition, 10*, 237–242.

Holender, D. (1986). Semantic activation without conscious activation in dichotic listening, parafoveal vision, and visual masking: A survey and appraisal. *Behavioral and Brain Sciences, 9*, 1–33.

Hollan, J.D. (1975). Features and semantic memory: Set-theoretic or network model. *Psychological Review, 82,* 154–155.

Holland, J.H., Holyoak, K.J., Nisbett, R.E., & Thagard, P. (1986). *Induction: Processes in inference, learning and discovery.* Cambridge, Mass.: M.I.T. Press.

Holmes, D.S. (1972). Repression or interference? A further investigation. *Journal of Personality and Social Psychology, 22,* 163–170.

Holmes, D.S. (1974). Investigations of repression: Differential recall of material experimentally or naturally associated with ego threat. *Psychological Bulletin, 81,* 632–653.

Holyoak, K.J. (1983). Toward a unitary theory of mind (Review of J.R. Anderson's Architecture of Cognition). *Science, 222,* 499–500.

Holyoak, K.J. (1985). The pragmatics of analogical transfer. *The Psychology of Learning and Motivation, 19,* 59–87.

Holyoak, K.J. & Koh, K. (1987). Surface and structural similarity in analogical transfer. *Memory and Cognition, 15,* 332–340.

Holyoak, K.J. & Thagard, P. (1989). Analogical mapping by constraint satisfaction. *Cognitive Science, 13,* 295–355.

Holyoak, K.J. & Thagard, P. (1990). A constraint satisfaction approach to analogical mapping and retrieval. In K.J. Gilhooly, M.T. Keane, R. Logie & G. Erdos (Eds), *Lines of thinking: Reflections on the psychology of thought: Vol. 1.* Chichester: John Wiley.

Horton, D.L. & Mills, C.B. (1984). Human learning and memory. *Annual Review of Psychology, 35,* 361–394.

Hotopf, W.H.N. (1980). Slips of the pen. In U. Frith (Ed.), *Cognitive processes in spelling.* London: Academic Press.

Howard, D. & Orchard-Lisle, V. (1984). On the origin of semantic errors in naming: Evidence from the case of a global aphasic. *Cognitive Neuropsychology, 1,* 163–190.

Howie, D. (1952). Perceptual defence. *Psychological Review, 59,* 308–315.

Hubel, D.H. & Wiesel, T.N. (1962). Receptive fields, binocular interaction and functional architecture in the cat's visual cortex. *Journal of Physiology, 160,* 106–154.

Hull, C.L. (1930). Knowledge and purpose as habit mechanisms. *Psychological Review, 37,* 511–525.

Hull, C.L. (1931). Goal attraction and directing ideas conceived as habit phenomena. *Psychological Review, 38,* 487–506.

Humphreys, G.W. (1981). On varying the span of visual attention: Evidence for two nodes of spatial attention. *Quarterly Journal of Experimental Psychology, 33A,* 1–15.

Humphreys, G.W. & Bruce, V. (1989). *Visual cognition: Computational, experimental and neuropsychological perspectives.* London: Lawrence Erlbaum Associates Ltd.

Humphreys, G.W. & Riddoch, M.J. (1984). Routes to object constancy: Implications from neurological impairments of object constancy. *Quarterly Journal of Experimental Psychology, 36A,* 385–415.

Humphreys, G.W. & Riddoch, M.J. (1985). Author's corrections to "Routes to object constancy". *Quarterly Journal of Experimental Psychology, 37A,* 493–495.

Humphreys, G.W. & Riddoch, M.J. (1987). *To see but not to see: A case study of visual agnosia.* London: Lawrence Erlbaum Associates Ltd.

Humphreys, G.W., Riddoch, M.J., & Quinlan, P.T. (1985). Interactive processes in perceptual organization: Evidence from visual agnosia. In M.I. Posner & O.S.M. Marin (Eds.) *Attention and performance, Vol XI.* Hillside, N.J.: Lawrence Erlbaum Associates Inc.

Huppert, F.A. & Piercy, M. (1976). Recognition memory in amnesic patients: Effect of temporal context and familiarity of material. *Cortex, 4,* 3–20.

Huppert, F.A. & Piercy, M. (1978). The role of trace strength in recency and frequency judgements by amnesic and control subjects. *Quarterly Journal of Experimental Psychology, 30,* 346–354.

Hyde, T.S. & Jenkins, J.J. (1973). Recall for words as a function of semantic, graphic, and syntactic orienting tasks. *Journal of Verbal Learning and Verbal Behaviour, 12,* 471–480.

Ittelson, W.H. & Cantril, H. (1954). *Perception: A transactional approach.* New York: Doubleday.

Jackson, S.L. & Griggs, R.A. (1990). The elusive pragmatic reasoning schemas effect. *Quarterly Journal of Experimental Psychology, 42A,* 353–373.

Jacoby, L.L. & Dallas, M. (1981). On the relationship between autobiographical memory and perceptual learning. *Journal of Experimental Psychology: General, 110,* 306–340.

James, W. (1890). *Principles of psychology.* New York: Holt.

Jeffries, R., Polson, P., Razran, L., & Atwood, M.E. (1977). A process model for missionaries–cannibals and other river-crossing problems. *Cognitive Psychology*, *9*, 412–440.

Johnson-Laird, P.N. (1975). Models of deduction. In R.J. Falmagne (Ed.), *Reasoning: Representation and process in children and adults*. Hillsdale, N.J.: Lawrence Erlbaum Associates Inc.

Johnson-Laird, P.N. (1977). Procedural semantics. *Cognition*, *5*, 189–214.

Johnson-Laird, P.N. (1983). *Mental models*. Cambridge: Cambridge University Press.

Johnson-Laird, P.N. (1988a). *The computer and the mind*. Cambridge, Mass.: Harvard University Press.

Johnson-Laird, P.N. (1988b). Freedom and constraint in creativity. In R.J. Sternberg (Ed.), *The nature of creativity*. Cambridge: Cambridge University Press.

Johnson-Laird, P.N. (in press). Mental models. In M. Posner (Ed.), *Foundations of cognitive science*. Cambridge, Mass.: M.I.T. Press.

Johnson-Laird, P.N. & Bara, B.G. (1984). Syllogistic inference. *Cognition*, *16*, 1–61.

Johnson-Laird, P.N. & Byrne, R.M.J. (1989). Only reasoning. *Journal of Memory and Language*, *28*, 313–330.

Johnson-Laird, P.N., & Byrne, R.M.J. (1990). *Deduction*. London: Lawrence Erlbaum Associates Ltd.

Johnson-Laird, P.N., Byrne, R.M.J., & Tabossi, P. (1989). Reasoning by model: The case of multiple quantification. *Psychological Review*, *96*, 658–673.

Johnson-Laird, P.N., Herrmann, D.J., & Chaffin, R. (1984). Only connections: A critique of semantic networks. *Psychological Bulletin*, *96*, (2), 292–315.

Johnson-Laird, P.N., Legrenzi, P., & Sonino-Legrenzi, M. (1972). Reasoning and a sense of reality. *British Journal of Psychology*, *63*, 395–400.

Johnson-Laird, P.N. & Steedman, M.J. (1978). The psychology of syllogisms. *Cognitive Psychology*, *10*, 64–99.

Johnson-Laird, P.N. & Stevenson, R. (1970). Memory for syntax. *Nature*, *227*, 412.

Johnson-Laird, P.N. & Wason, P.C (1970). A theoretical analysis of insight into a reasoning task. *Cognitive Psychology*, *1*, 134–148.

Johnston, W.A. & Dark, V.J. (1985). Dissociable domains of selective processing. In M.I. Posner and O.S.M. Marin (Eds.), *Mechanisms of attention: Attention and performance, Vol. XI*. Hillsdale, N.J.: Lawrence Erlbaum Associates Inc.

Johnston, W.A. & Dark, V.J. (1986). Selective attention. *Annual Review of Psychology*, *37*, 43–75.

Johnston, W.A. & Heinz, S.P. (1978). Flexibility and capacity demands of attention. *Journal of Experimental Psychology: General*, *107*, 420–435.

Johnston, W.A. & Heinz, S.P. (1979). Depth of non-target processing in an attention task. *Journal of Experimental Psychology*, *5*, 168–175.

Johnston, W.A. & Wilson, J. (1980). Perceptual processing of non-targets in an attention task. *Memory & Cognition*, *8*, 372–377.

Jones, G.V. (1978). Recognition failure and dual mechanisms in recall. *Psychological Review*, *85*, 464–469.

Jones, G.V. (1982a). Tests of the dual-mechanism theory of recall. *Acta Psychologica*, *50*, 61–72.

Jones, G.V. (1982b). Stacks not fuzzy sets: An ordinal basis for prototype theory of concepts. *Cognition*, *12*, 281–290.

Jones, G.V. (1987). Independence and exclusivity among psychological processes: Implications for the structure of recall. *Psychological Review*, *94*, 229–235.

Jonides, J., Naveh-Benjamin, M., & Palmer, J. (1985). Assessing automaticity. *Acta Psychologica*, *60*, 157–171.

Joyce, J. (1922/1960). *Ulysses*. London: Bodley Head.

Just, M.A. & Carpenter, P.A. (1987). *The psychology of reading and language comprehension*. Newton, Mass.: Allyn & Bacon.

Kahneman, D. & Henik, A. (1979). Perceptual organization and attention. In M. Kubovy & J.R. Pomerantz (Eds.) *Perceptual organization*. Hillsdale, N.J.: Lawrence Erlbaum Associates Inc.

Kahneman, D., Slovic, P., & Tversky, A. (1982). *Judgement under uncertainty: Heuristics and biases*. Cambridge: Cambridge University Press.

Kahneman, D. & Treisman, A. (1984). Changing views of attention and automaticity. In R. Parasuraman & D.R. Davies (Eds.), *Varieties of attention*. London: Academic Press.

Kahney, H. (1989). What do novice programmers know about recursion? In E. Soloway & J.C. Spohrer (Eds.), *Studying the novice programmer*. Hillsdale, N.J.: Lawrence Erlbaum Associates Inc.

Kahney, H. & Eisenstadt, M. (1982). Programmers' mental models of their programming tasks. *Proceedings of the Fourth Annual Conference of the Cognitive Science Society*. Ann Arbor, Michigan.

Kant, E. (1963). *Critique of pure reason* (2nd Edition). London: Macmillan (Original work published 1787).

Katz, J.J. (1972). *Semantic theory*. New York: Harper & Row.

Katz, J.J. & Fodor, J.A. (1963). The structure of a semantic theory. *Language, 39*, 170–210.

Kaufer, D., Hayes, J.R., & Flower, L.S. (1986). Composing written sentences. *Research in the Teaching of English, 20*, 121–140.

Kay, J. & Ellis, A.W. (1987). A cognitive neuropsychological case study of anomia: Implications for psychological models of word retrieval. *Brain, 110*, 613–629.

Kay, J. & Marcel, T. (1981). One process not two in reading aloud: Lexical analogies do the work of nonlexical rules. *Quarterly Journal of Experimental Psychology, 33A*, 397–413.

Keane, M. (1985a). On drawing analogies when solving problems: A theory and test of solution generation in an analogical problem solving task. *British Journal of Psychology, 76*, 449–458.

Keane, M. (1985b). Restructuring revised: A theoretical note on Ohlsson's mechanism of restructuring. *Scandinavian Journal of Psychology, 26*, 363–365.

Keane, M.T. (1987). On retrieving analogues when solving problems. *Quarterly Journal of Experimental Psychology, 39A* , 29–41.

Keane, M.T. (1988). *Analogical problem solving*. Chichester: Ellis Horwood (New York: Wiley).

Keane, M.T. (1989). Modelling "insight" in practical construction problems. *Irish Journal of Psychology, 11*, 201–215.

Keane, M.T., & Brayshaw, M. (1988). The incremental analogical machine: A computational model of analogy. In D. Sleeman (Ed.), *European working session on machine learning*. London: Pitman.

Keane, M.T., Kahney, H., & Brayshaw, M. (1989). Simulating analogical mapping difficulties in recursion problems. *Proceedings of Annual Conference of the Society for the Study of Artificial Intelligence and Simulation of Behaviour*. London: Pitman.

Keenan, J.M., MacWhinney, B., & Mayhew, D. (1977). Pragmatics in memory: A study of natural conversation. *Journal of Verbal Learning and Verbal Behaviour, 16*, 549–560.

Kellogg, R.T. (1988). Attentional overload and writing performance: Effects of rough draft and outline strategies. *Journal of Experimental Psychology: Learning, Memory, and Cognition, 14*, 355–365.

Kellogg, R.T. (1990). Writing. In M.W. Eysenck (Ed.), *The Blackwell dictionary of cognitive psychology*. Oxford: Blackwell.

Kempton, W. (1986). Two theories used of home heat control. *Cognitive Science, 10*, 75–91.

Kinchla, R.A. & Wolf, J.M. (1979). The order of visual processing: "Top-down", "bottom-up", or "middle-out". *Perception and Psychophysics, 25*, 225–231.

Kintsch, W. (1974). *The representation of meaning in memory*. Hillsdale, N.J.: Lawrence Erlbaum Associates Inc.

Kintsch, W. (1980). Semantic memory: A tutorial. In R.S. Nickerson (Ed.), *Attention and performance, Vol. VIII*. Hillsdale, N.J.: Lawrence Erlbaum Associates Inc.

Kintsch, W. & Keenan, J. (1973). Reading rate and retention as a function of the number of propositions in the base structure of sentences. *Cognitive Psychology, 5*, 257–274.

Kintsch, W. & van Dijk, T.A. (1978). Toward a model of text comprehension and production. *Psychological Review, 85*, 363–394.

Koestler, A. (1964). *The act of creation*. London: Picador.

Kohler, W. (1927). *The mentality of apes* (2nd Edn.). New York: Harcourt Brace.

Kohn, S.E. & Friedman, R.B. (1986). Word-meaning deafness: A phonological–semantic dissociation. *Cognitive Neuropsychology, 3*, 291–308.

Kolers, P.A. (1972). *Aspects of motion perception*. New York: Pergamon.

Kolers, P.A. & Palef, S.R. (1976). Knowing not. *Memory and Cognition, 4*, 553–558.

Kolodner, J.L. (1984). *Retrieval and organizational strategies in conceptual memory*. Hillsdale, N.J.: Lawrence Erlbaum Associates Inc.

Kolodner, J.L. & Simpson, R. (1986). Using experience as a guide for problem solving. In T.M. Mitchell, J.G. Carbonell, & R.S. Michalski (Eds.), *Machine learning: A guide to current research.* Lancaster: Kluwer Academic Publishers.

Korchin, S. (1964). Anxiety and cognition. In C. Scheeser (Ed.), *Cognition: Theory, research, promise.* New York: Harper & Row.

Korsakoff, S.S. (1889). Über eine besondere Form psychischer Störung, kombiniert mit multiplen Neuritis. *Archiv für Psychiatrie und Nervenkrankheiten, 21,* 669–704.

Kosslyn, S.M. (1975). Information representation in visual images. *Cognitive Psychology, 7,* 341–370.

Kosslyn, S.M.(1976). Can imagery be distinguished form other forms of internal representation?: Evidence from studies of information retrieval time. *Memory and Cognition, 4,* 291–297.

Kosslyn, S.M.(1978). Measuring the visual angle of the mind's eye. *Cognitive Psychology, 10,* 356–389.

Kosslyn, S.M. (1980). *Image and mind.* Cambridge, Mass.: Harvard University Press.

Kosslyn, S.M. (1981). The medium and the message in mental imagery: A theory. *Psychological Review, 88,* 44–66.

Kosslyn, S.M. (1983). *Ghosts in the mind's machine: Creating and using images in the brain.* New York: Norton.

Kosslyn, S.M. (1987). Seeing and imagining in the cerebral hemispheres: A computational approach. *Psychological Review, 94,* 148–175.

Kosslyn, S.M., Ball, T.M., & Reiser, B.J.(1978). Visual images preserve metric spatial information: Evidence from studies of image scanning. *Journal of Experimental Psychology: Human Perception and Performance, 4,* 47–60.

Kosslyn, S.M., Holtzman, J.D., Farah, F., & Gazzinga, M.S. (1985). A computational analysis of mental image generation: Evidence from functional dissociations in split-brain patients. *Journal of Experimental Psychology: General, 114,* 311–341.

Kosslyn, S.M. & Shwartz, S.P. (1977). A simulation of visual imagery. *Cognitive Science, 1,* 265–295.

Kotovsky, K., Hayes, J.R., & Simon, H.A. (1985). Why are some problems hard?: Evidence from the Tower of Hanoi. *Cognitive Psychology, 17,* 248–294.

Kuhn, T.S. (1970). *The structure of scientific revolutions.* Chicago: Chicago University Press.

Kuhn, T.S. (1977). *The essential tension: Selected studies in scientific tradition and change.* Chicago: Chicago University Press.

LaBerge, D. (1983). Spatial extent of attention to letters and words. *Journal of Experimental Psychology: Human Perception and Performance, 9,* 371–379.

Lachman, R., Lachman, J.L., & Butterfield, E.C. (1979). *Cognitive psychology and information processing.* Hillsdale, N.J.: Lawrence Erlbaum Associates Inc.

Laird, J.E., Newell, A., & Rosenbloom, P. (1987). SOAR: An architecture for general intelligence. *Artificial Intelligence, 33,* 1–64.

Lakoff, G. (1973). Hedges: A study of meaning criteria and the logic of fuzzy concepts. *Journal of Philosophical Logic, 2,* 458–508.

Lakoff, G. (1982). *Categories and cognitive models.* Berkeley Cognitive Science Report No. 2, November.

Lakoff, G. (1987). *Women, fire, and dangerous things.* Chicago: Chicago University Press.

Lambert, K. (in press). A hybrid model of learning to solve physics problems. *European Journal of Cognitive Psychology.*

Larkin, J.H. (1979). Information processing models and science instructions. In J. Lochhead & J. Clement (Eds.), *Cognitive process instructions.* Philadelphia, Pa: Franklin Institute Press.

Larkin, J.H. (1983). The role of problem representation in physics. In D. Gentner & A.L. Stevens (Eds.), *Mental models.* Hillsdale, N.J.: Lawrence Erlbaum Associates Inc.

Larkin, J.H. (1985). Understanding problem representations and skill in physics. In S.F. Chipman, J.W. Segal, & R. Glaser (Eds.), *Thinking and learning skills: Vol. 2; Research and open questions.* Hillsdale, N.J.: Lawrence Erlbaum Associates Inc.

Larkin, J.H., McDermott, J., Simon, D., & Simon, H.A. (1980). Expert and novice performance in solving physics problems. *Science, 208,* 1335–1342.

Latour, P. L. (1962). Visual threshold during eye movements. *Vision Research, 2,* 261–262.

Lazarus, R.S. (1966). *Psychological stress and the coping process.* New York: McGraw-Hill.

Lazarus, R.S. (1982). Thoughts on the relations between emotion and cognition. *American Psychologist, 37*, 1019–1024.

Lazarus, R.S., Kanner, A.D., & Folkman, S. (1980). Emotions: A cognitive-phenomenological analysis. In R. Plutchik & H. Kellerman (Eds.), *Emotion: Theory, research, and experience: Vol. 1*. New York: Academic Press.

Leech, G. (1974). *Semantics*. Harmondsworth: Penguin.

Lehnert, W.G., Dyer, M.G., Johnson, P.N., Yang, C.J., & Harley, S. (1983). BORIS: An experiment in in-depth understanding of narratives. *Artificial Intelligence, 20*, 15–62.

Lenneberg, E.H. & Roberts, J.M. (1956). *The language of experience memoir 13*. Indiana: University of Indiana, Publications in Anthropology and Linguistics.

Lesgold, A.M (1988). Problem solving. In R.J. Sternberg & E.E. Smith (Eds.), *The psychology of human thought*. Cambridge: Cambridge University Press.

Lesgold, A., Resnick, L.B., & Hammon, K. (1985). Learning to read: A longitudinal study of word skill development in two curricula. In G. Waller & E. MacKinnon (Eds.), *Reading research: Advances in theory and practice: Vol. 4*. New York: Academic Press.

Lesgold, A.M., Rubinson, H., Feltovich, P., Glaser, R., Klopfer, D., & Wang, Y. (1988). Expertise in a complex skill: Diagnosing X-ray pictures. In M.T.H. Chi, R. Glaser & M. Farr (Eds.), *The nature of expertise*. Hillsdale, N.J.: Lawrence Erlbaum Associates Inc.

Levine, D.N., Calvanio, R., & Popovics, A. (1982). Language in the absence of inner speech. *Word, 15*, 19–44.

Levy, B.A. (1978). Speech analysis during sentence processing: Reading and listening. *Visible Language, 12*, 81–101.

Lewinsohn, P.M., Steinmetz, J.L., Larson, D.W., & Franklin, Y. (1981). Depression related cognitions: Antecedents or consequences. *Journal of Abnormal Psychology, 90*, 213–219.

Lhermitte, F. & Signoret, J.L. (1972). Analyse neuropsychologique et différenciation des syndromes amnésiques. *Revue Neurologique, 126*, 86–94.

Libet, B. (1973). Electrical stimulation of cortex in humans and conscious sensory aspects. In A. Iggo (Ed.), *Handbook of sensory physiology: Vol. 2*. New York: Springer.

Lichenstein, S., Slovic, P., Fischhoff, B., Layman, M., & Coombes, B. (1978). Judged frequency of lethal events. *Journal of Experimental Psychology: Human Learning and Memory, 4*, 551–578.

Lieberman, P. (1963). Some effects of semantic and grammatical context on the production and perception of speech. *Language and Speech, 6*, 172–187.

Lindsay, R.K. (1988). Images and inference. *Cognition, 29*, 229–250.

Locke, J. (1690). *Essay on human understanding*. Oxford: Clarendon Press (1924)

Loftus, E.F. (1973). Category, dominance, instance dominance, and categorisation time. *Journal of Experimental Psychology, 97*, 70–74.

Loftus, E.F. & Loftus, G.R. (1980). On the permanence of stored information in the human brain. *American Psychologist, 35*, 409–420.

Logan, G.D. (1988). Toward an instance theory of automatisation. *Psychological Review, 95*, 492–527.

Logie, R. & Baddeley, A.D. (1990). Imagery and working memory. In P.J. Hampson, D.F. Marks, & J.T.E. Richardson (Eds.), *Imagery: Current developments*. London: Routledge.

Luchins, A.S. (1942). Mechanisation in problem solving. The effect of Einstellung. *Psychological Monographs, 54*, (248).

Luchins, A.S. & Luchins, E.H. (1959). *Rigidity of behaviour*. Eugene, Oregon: University of Oregon Press.

Lucy, J. & Scheweder, R. (1979). Whorf and his critics: Linguistic and nonlinguistic influences on colour memory. *American Anthropologist, 81*, 581–615.

Luger, G.F. (1976). The use of the state space to record the behavioural effects of sub-problems and symmetries in the Tower of Hanoi problem. *International Journal of Man-Machine Studies, 8*, 411–421.

Luger, G.F. & Bauer, M.A. (1978). Transfer effects in isomorphic problem situations. *Acta Psychologica, 34*, 121–131.

Lung, C.T. & Dominowski, R.L. (1985). Effects of strategy instructions and practice on nine-dot problem solving. *Journal of Experimental Psychology: Learning, Memory and Cognition, 11*, 804–811.

Lupker, S.J. (1979). On the nature of perceptual information during letter perception. *Perception and Psychophysics, 25*, 303–312.

Luria, A.R. (1970). *Traumatic aphasia*. The Hague: Mouton.

Lyman, R.S., Kwan, S.T., & Chao, W.H. (1938). Left occipito-parietal brain tumour with observations on alexia and agraphia in Chinese and English. *Chinese Medical Journal, 54*, 491–516.

Maclay, H. & Osgood, C.E. (1959). Hesitation phenomena in spontaneous English speech. *Word, 15*, 19–44.

McAndrews, M.P., Glisky, E.L., & Schachter, D.L. (1987). When priming persists: Long-lasting implicit memory for a single episode in amnesic patients. *Neuropsychologia, 25*, 497–506.

McCarthy, R. & Warrington, E.K. (1984). A two-route model of speech production. *Brain, 107*, 463–485.

McClelland, J.L. (1981). Retrieving general and specific information from stored knowledge of specifics. *Proceedings of the Third Annual Meeting of the Cognitive Science Society*, 170–172.

McClelland, J.L. (1987). The case for interactionism in language processing. In M. Coltheart (Ed.), *Attention and performance, XII*. London: Lawrence Erlbaum Associates Ltd.

McClelland, J.L., & Rumelhart, D.E. (1981). An interactive activation model of context effects in letter perception. Part 1. An account of basic findings. *Psychological Review, 88*, 375–407.

McClelland, J.L. & Rumelhart, D.E. (1985). Distributed memory and the representation of general and specific information. *Journal of Experimental Psychology: General, 114*, 159–188.

McClelland, J.L. & Rumelhart, D.E. (1986a). A distributed model of human learning and memory. In D.E. Rumelhart, J.L. McClelland, & the PDP Research Group (Eds.), *Parallel distributed processing: Vol. 2, Psychological and biological models*. Cambridge, Mass.: M.I.T. Press.

McClelland, J.L., & Rumelhart, D.E. (1986b). Amnesia and distributed memory. In D.E. Rumelhart, J.L. McClelland, & the PDP Research Group (Eds.), *Parallel distributed processing: Vol. 2, Psychological and Biological Models*. Cambridge, Mass.: M.I.T. Press.

McClelland, J.L., Rumelhart, D.E., & Hinton, G.E. (1986). The appeal of parallel distributed processing. In D.E. Rumelhart, J.L. McClelland and the PDP Research Group (Eds.) *Parallel distributed processing, Vol. 1, Foundations*. Cambridge, Mass.: MIT Press.

McClelland, J.L., Rumelhart, D.E., & the PDP Research Group (Eds.) (1986). *Parallel distributed processing: Vol. 2, Psychological and biological models*. Cambridge, Mass.: M.I.T. Press.

McCloskey, M. (1980). The stimulus familiarity problem in semantic memory research. *Journal of Verbal Learning and Verbal Behaviour, 19*, 485–504.

McCloskey, M. (1983). Intuitive physics. *Scientific American, 24*, 122–130.

McCloskey, M.E. & Glucksberg, S. (1978). Natural categories: Well-defined or fuzzy sets. *Memory and Cognition, 6*, 462–472.

McCulloch, W.S. & Pitts, W. (1943). A logical calculus of the idea immanent in nervous activity. *Bulletin of Mathematical Biophysics, 5*, 115–133.

McGurk, H. & MacDonald, J. (1976). Hearing lips and seeing voices. *Nature, 264*, 746–748.

McKenna, P. & Warrington, E.K. (1980). Testing for nominal dysphasia. *Journal of Neurology, Neurosurgery, and Psychiatry, 43*, 781–788.

McKeon, M.G., Beck, I.L., Omanson, R.C., & Pople, M.T. (1985). Some effects of the nature and frequency of vocabulary instruction on the knowledge and use of words. *Reading Research Quarterly, 20*, 522–535.

McKoon, G. & Ratcliff, R. (1981). The comprehension processes and memory structures involved in instrumental inference. *Journal of Verbal Learning and Verbal Behaviour, 20*, 671–682.

MacLeod, C., Mathews, A., & Tata, P. (1986). Attentional bias in emotional disorders. *Journal of Abnormal Psychology, 95*, 15–20.

McLeod, P. (1977). A dual-task response modality effect: Support for multiprocessor models of attention. *Quarterly Journal of Experimental Psychology, 29*, 651–667.

McNamara, T.P. & Sternberg, R.J. (1983). Mental models of word meaning. *Journal of Verbal Learning and Verbal Behaviour, 22*, 449–474.

Madison, P. (1956). Freud's repression concept: A survey and attempted clarification. *International Journal of Psychoanalysis, 37*, 75–81.

Magee, B. (1973). *Popper*. London: Fontana.

Maier, N.R.F. (1931). Reasoning in humans II: The solution of a problem and its appearance in consciousness. *Journal of Comparative Psychology, 12,* 181–194.

Malone, D.R., Morris, H.H., Kay, M.C., & Levin, H.S. (1982). Prosopagnosia: A double dissociation between the recognition of familiar and unfamiliar faces. *Journal of Neurology, Neurosurgery, and Psychiatry, 45,* 820–822.

Malt, B.C. & Smith, E.E. (1983). Correlated properties in natural categories. *Journal of Verbal Learning and Verbal Behaviour, 23,* 250–269.

Maltzman, I (1955). Thinking: From a behaviouristic point of view. *Psychological Review, 62,* 275–286.

Mandler, G. (1967). Organisation and memory. In K. W. Spence & J.T. Spence (Eds.), *The psychology of learning and motivation: Advances in research and theory: Vol. 1.* London: Academic Press.

Mandler, G. (1980). Recognising: The judgment of previous occurrence. *Psychological Review, 87,* 252–271.

Mandler, G. & Boeck, W. (1974). Retrieval processes in recognition. *Memory and Cognition, 2,* 613–615.

Mandler, G., Pearlstone, A., & Koopmans, H.S. (1969). Effects of organisation and semantic similarity on recall and recognition. *Journal of Verbal Learning and Verbal Behaviour, 8,* 410–423.

Mandler, J.M. & Mandler, G. (1964). *Thinking: From Association to gestalt.* New York: Wiley.

Mani, K. & Johnson-Laird, P.N. (1982). The mental representation of spatial descriptions. *Memory and Cognition, 10,* 181–187.

Manktelow, K.I., & Evans, J.St.B.T. (1979). Facilitation of reasoning by realism: Effect or noneffect? *British Journal of Psychology, 70,* 477–488.

Marcel, A.J. (1983). Conscious and unconscious perception: Experiments on visual masking and word recognition. *Cognitive Psychology, 15,* 197–237.

Marcel, A.J. (1986) Peer commentary on Holender's "Semantic activation without conscious activation in dichotic listening, parafoveal vision, and visual masking: A survey and appraisal". *Behavioral and Brain Sciences, 9,* 40.

Marcus, S.L. (1982). Recall of logical argument lines. *Journal of Verbal Learning and Verbal Behaviour, 21,* 549–562.

Margolis, H. (1987). *Patterns, thinking, and cognition: A theory of judgement.* Chicago, Illinois: The University of Chicago Press.

Markovits, H. (1984). Awareness of the "possible" as a mediator of formal thinking in conditional reasoning problems. *British Journal of Psychology, 75,* 367–376.

Markovits, H. (1985). Incorrect conditional reasoning among adults: Competence or performance? *British Journal of Psychology, 76,* 241–247.

Marmurek, H.H.C. & Briscoe, G. (1982). Orthographic and lexical processing of visual letter strings. *Canadian Journal of Psychology, 36,* 368–387.

Marr, D. (1976). Early processing of visual information. *Philosophical Transactions of the Royal Society (London), B275,* 483–524.

Marr, D. (1982). *Vision: A computational investigation into the human representation and processing of visual information.* San Francisco: W.H. Freeman.

Marr, D. & Nishihara, K. (1978). Representation and recognition of the spatial organisation of three-dimensional shapes. *Philosophical Transactions of the Royal Society (London), B200,* 269–294.

Marr, D. & Poggio, T. (1976). Co-operative computation of stereo disparity. *Science, 194,* 283–287.

Marschark, M., Richman, C.L., Yuille, J.C., & Hunt, R.R. (1987). The role of imagery in memory: On shared and distinctive information. *Psychological Bulletin, 102,* 28–41.

Marshall, J.C. & Newcombe, F. (1973). Patterns of paralexia: A psycholinguistic approach. *Journal of Psycholinguistic Research, 2,* 175–199.

Marslen-Wilson, W. & Tyler, L.K. (1980). The temporal structure of spoken language understanding. *Cognition, 8,* 1–71.

Martin, A. & Fedio, P. (1983). Word production and comprehension in Alzheimer's disease: The breakdown of semantic knowledge. *Brain and Language, 19,* 121–141.

Martone, M., Butters, N., Payne, M., Becker, J. T., & Sax, D.S. (1984). Dissociations between skill learning and verbal recognition in amnesia and dementia. *Archives of Neurology, 41,* 965–970.

Mathews, A. & MacLeod, C. (1986). Discrimination of threat cues without awareness in anxiety states. *Journal of Abnormal Psychology, 95,* 131–138.

Mathews, A., Mogg, K., May, J., & Eysenck, M. W. (1989). Implicit and explicit memory biases in anxiety. *Journal of Abnormal Psychology*, *98*, 236–240.

Mathews, A., Richards, A., & Eysenck, M.W. (1989). The interpretation of homophones related to threat in anxiety states. *Journal of Abnormal Psychology*, *98*, 31–34.

Mattingly, I.G. & Liberman, A. M. (1988). Specialised perceiving systems for speech and other biologically significant sounds. In G. W. Edelman, W.E. Gall, and W.M. Cowan (Eds.), *Functions of the auditory system*. New York: Wiley.

Mayes, A.R., Meudell, P.R., & Pickering, A. (1985). Is organic amnesia caused by a selective deficit in remembering contextual information? *Cortex*, *21*, 167–202.

Medin, D.L. & Shaffer, M.M. (1978). Context theory of classification learning. *Psychological Review*, *85*, 207–238.

Medin, D.L. & Shoben, E.J. (1988). Context and structure in conceptual combination. *Cognitive Psychology*, *20*, 158–190.

Medin, D.L. & Smith, E.E. (1984). Concepts and concept formation. *Annual Review of Psychology*, *35*, 113–138.

Medin, D.L. & Wattenmaker, W.D. (1987). Category cohesiveness, theories, and cognitive archaeology. In U. Neisser (Ed.), *Concepts and conceptual development: Ecological and intellectual factors in categorisation*. Cambridge: Cambridge University Press.

Medin, D.L., Wattenmaker, W.D., & Hampson, S.E. (1987). Family resemblance, conceptual cohesiveness, and category construction. *Cognitive Psychology*, *19*, 242–279.

Meichenbaum, D. (1977). *Cognitive-behaviour modification: An integrative approach*. New York: Plenum.

Mervis, C.B., Catlin, J., & Rosch, E. (1976). Relationships among goodness-of-example, category norms, and word frequency. *Bulletin of the Psychonomic Society*, *7*, 283–284.

Meudell, P.R. & Mayes, A.R. (1981). The Claparède phenomenon: A further example in amnesics, a demonstration of a similar effect in normal people with attenuated memory, and a reinterpretation. *Current Psychological Research*, *1*, 75–88.

Meyer, D.E., & Schvaneveldt, R.W. (1971). Facilitation in recognising pairs of words: Evidence of a dependence between retrieval operations. *Journal of Experimental Psychology*, *90*, 227–234.

Michel, F. & Andreewsky, E. (1983). Deep dysphasia: An analogue of deep dyslexia in the auditory modality. *Brain and Language*, *18*, 212–223.

Mill, J.S. (1843). *A system of logic*. London: Longman.

Miller, E. & Morley, S. (1986). *Investigating abnormal behaviour*. London: Lawrence Erlbaum Associates Ltd.

Miller, G.A. (1956). The magic number seven, plus or minus two: Some limits on our capacity for processing information. *Psychological Review*, *63*, 81–93.

Miller, G.A. & Johnson-Laird, P.N. (1976). *Language and perception*. Cambridge: Cambridge University Press.

Miller, G.A. & McNeill, D. (1969). Psycholinguistics. In G. Lindzey & E. Aronson (Eds.), *The handbook of social psychology, Vol. III*. Reading, Mass.: Addison-Wesley.

Miller, G.A., & Nicely, P. (1955). An analysis of perceptual confusions among some English consonants. *Journal of the Acoustical Society of America*, *27*, 338–352.

Minsky, M. (1975). A framework for representing knowledge. In P.H. Winston (Ed.), *The psychology of computer vision*. New York: McGraw-Hill.

Minsky, M. & Papert, S. (1969). *Perceptrons*. Cambridge, Mass.: M.I.T. Press.

Minsky, M. & Papert, S. (1988). *Perceptrons* (2nd Edition). Cambridge, Mass.: M.I.T. Press.

Mitroff, I. (1974). *The subjective side of science*. Amsterdam: Elsevier.

Mogg, K. (1988). *Processing of emotional information in clinical anxiety states*. Unpublished Ph.D. thesis, University of London.

Mogg, K., Mathews, A., & Weinman, J. (1987). Memory bias in clinical anxiety. *Journal of Abnormal Psychology*, *96*, 94–98.

Moray, N. (1959). Attention in dichotic listening: Affective cues and the influence of instructions. *Quarterly Journal of Experimental Psychology*, *11*, 56–60.

Moray, N. (1969). *Attention: Selective processes in vision and hearing*. London: Hutchinson.

Morris, C.D., Bransford, J.D., & Franks, J.J. (1977). Levels of processing versus transfer appropriate processing. *Journal of Verbal Learning and Verbal Behaviour, 16*, 519–533.

Morton, J. (1969). Interaction of information in word recognition. *Psychological Review, 76*, 165–178.

Morton, J. (1979). Facilitation in word recognition: Experiments causing change in the logogen model. In P.A. Kolers, M. Wrolstead, & H. Bouma (Eds.), *Processing of visible language, Vol. 1*. New York: Plenum Press.

Morton, J. (1984). Brain-based and non-brain-based models of language. In D. Caplan, A.R. Lecours, & A. Smith (Eds.), *Biological perspectives on language*. Cambridge, Mass.: M.I.T. Press.

Moscovitch, M. (1984). The sufficient conditions for demonstrating preserved memory in amnesia: A task analysis approach. In L.R. Squire & N. Butters (Eds.), *Neuropsychology of memory*. New York: Guilford.

Moscovitch, M. (1985). Memory from infancy to old age: Implications for theories of normal and pathological memory. *Annals of the New York Academcy of Science, 444*, 78–96.

Murphy, G.L. & Medin, D.L. (1985). The role of theories in conceptual coherence. *Psychological Review, 92*, 289–316.

Mynatt, C.R., Doherty, M.E., & Tweney, R.D. (1977). Confirmation bias in a simulated research environment. *Quarterly Journal of Experimental Psychology, 29*, 85–95.

Navon, D. (1977). Forest before trees: The precedence of global features in visual perception. *Cognitive Psychology, 9*, 353–383.

Neisser, U. (1964). Visual search. *Scientific American, 210*, 94–102.

Neisser, U. (1967). *Cognitive psychology*. New York: Appleton-Century-Crofts.

Neisser, U. (1976). *Cognition and Reality*. San Francisco: W.H. Freeman.

Nelson, T.O., & Vining, S.K. (1978). Effect of semantic versus structural processing on long-term retention. *Journal of Experimental Psychology: Human Learning and Memory, 4*, 198–209.

Newcombe, F. & Marshall, J.C. (1988). Idealisation meets psychometrics: The case for the right groups and the right individuals. *Cognitive Neuropsychology, 5*, 549–564.

Newell, A. (1973). You can't play 20 questions with nature and win. In W.G. Chase (Ed.), *Visual information processing*. New York: Academic Press.

Newell, A. (1980). Duncker on thinking: An inquiry into progress in cognition. C.M.U. Tech. Rept., CMU-CS-80-151, and to appear in S. Koch & D. Leary (Eds.), *A century of psychology as science: Retrospections and Assessments*. New York: McGraw-Hill.

Newell, A. (1981). Reasoning, problem solving, and decision processes. In R.S. Nickerson (Ed.), *Attention and performance, Vol VIII*. Hillsdale, N.J.: Lawrence Erlbaum Associates Inc.

Newell, A. (1982). The knowledge level. *Artificial Intelligence, 18*, 87–127.

Newell, A. (1989). *Unified theories of cognition*. Harvard: Harvard University Press.

Newell, A., Shaw, J.C., & Simon, H.A. (1958). Elements of a theory of human problem solving. *Psychological Review, 65*, 151–166.

Newell, A., Shaw, J.C., & Simon, H.A. (1960). Report on a general problem solving program for a computer. In *Information processing: Proceedings of the International Conference on Information Processing*. Paris: U.N.E.S.C.O.

Newell, A. & Simon, H.A. (1972). *Human problem solving*. Englewood Cliffs, N.J.: Prentice Hall.

Newstead, S.E. (1990). Conversion in syllogistic reasoning. In K.J. Gilhooly, M.T. Keane, R. Logie, & G. Erdos (Eds), *Lines of thinking: Reflections on the psychology of thought. Vol. 1*. Chichester: John Wiley.

Nielsen, J.M. (1946). *Agnosia, apraxia, aphasia: Their value in cerebral localisation*. New York: Paul B. Hoeber.

Nisbett, R.E. & Wilson, T.D. (1977). Telling more than we can know: Verbal reports on mental processes. *Psychological Review, 84*, 231–259.

Norman, D.A. (1980). Twelve issues for cognitive science. *Cognitive Science, 4*, 1–32.

Norman, D.A. (1981). Categorisation of action slips. *Psychological Review, 88*, 1–15.

Norman, D.A. (1983). Some observations on mental models. In D. Gentner & A.L. Stevens (Eds.), *Mental models*. Hillsdale, N.J.: Lawrence Erlbaum Associates Inc.

Norman, D.A., & Bobrow, D.G. (1975). On data-limited and resource-limited processes. *Cognitive Psychology, 7*, 44–64.

Norman, D.A. & Rumelhart, D.E. (1975). *Explorations in cognition*. San Francisco: Freeman.

Norman, D.A. & Shallice, T. (1980). *Attention to action: Willed and automatic control of behaviour* (CHIP Report 99). San Diego, Calif.: University of California, San Diego.

Ohlsson, S. (1983). On natural and technical knowledge domains. *Scandinavian Journal of Psychology, 25,* 89–91.

Ohlsson, S. (1984a). Restructuring revisited I: Summary and critique of Gestalt theory of problem solving. *Scandinavian Journal of Psychology, 25,* 65–76.

Ohlsson, S. (1984b). Restructuring revisited II: An information processing theory of restructuring and insight. *Scandinavian Journal of Psychology, 25,* 117–129.

Ohlsson, S. (1985). Retrieval processes in restructuring: Answer to Keane. *Scandinavian Journal of Psychology, 26,* 366–368.

Olson, D.R. (1970). Language and thought: Aspects of a cognitive theory of semantics. *Psychological Review, 77,* 257–273.

Osherson, D.N. (1974) *Logical abilities in children, Vol. 2.* Hillsdale, N.J.: Lawrence Erlbaum Associates Inc.

Osherson, D.N. (1975). *Logical abilities in children, Vol. 3.* Hillsdale, N.J.: Lawrence Erlbaum Associates Inc.

Osherson, D.N. (1976). *Logical abilities in children, Vol. 4.* Hillsdale, N.J.: Lawrence Erlbaum Associates Inc.

Osherson, D.N. & Smith, E.E. (1981). On the adequacy of prototype theory as a theory of concepts. *Cognition, 9,* 35–58.

Osherson, D.N. & Smith, E.E. (1982). Gradedness and conceptual conjunction. *Cognition, 12,* 299–318.

Paivio, A. (1971). *Imagery and verbal processes.* New York: Holt, Rinehart, & Winston (reprinted by Lawrence Erlbaum Associates Inc. in 1979).

Paivio, A. (1975). Coding distinctions and repetition effects in memory. In G.H. Bower (Ed.), *The psychology of learning and motivation, Vol. 9.* New York: Academic Press.

Paivio, A. (1979). Psychological processes in the comprehension of metaphor. In A. Ortony (Ed.), *Metaphor and thought.* New York: Cambridge University Press.

Paivio, A. (1983). The empirical case for dual coding. In J.C. Yuille (Ed.), *Imagery, memory and cognition: Essays in honour of Allan Paivio.* Hillsdale, N.J.: Lawrence Erlbaum Associates Inc.

Paivio, A. (1986). *Mental representations: A dual coding approach.* Oxford: Oxford University Press.

Paivio, A. & Csapo, K. (1973). Picture superiority in free recall: Imagery or dual coding? *Cognitive Psychology, 5,* 176–206.

Paivio, A. & te Linde, J. (1982). Imagery, memory, and brain. *Canadian Journal of Psychology, 36,* 243–272.

Paivio, A., Yuille, J.C., & Madigan, S.A. (1968). Concreteness, imagery, and meaningfulness values for 925 nouns. *Journal of Experimental Psychology Monographs, 78* (1, Pt. 2).

Palincsar, A.S. & Brown, A.L. (1984). Reciprocal teaching of comprehension-fostering and comprehension-monitoring activities. *Cognition and Instruction, 1,* 117–175.

Palmer, S.E. (1975). The effects of contextual scenes on the identification of objects. *Memory and Cognition, 3,* 519–526.

Palmer, S.E. & Kimchi, R. (1986). The information processing approach to cognition. In T. Knapp & L.C. Robertson (Eds.), *Approaches to cognition: Contrasts and controversies.* Hillsdale, N.J.: Lawrence Erlbaum Associates Inc.

Parkin, A.J. (1982). Residual learning capacity in organic amnesia. *Cortex, 18,* 417–440.

Parkin, A.J. (1984). Amnesic syndrome: A lesion-specific disorder? *Cortex, 20,* 497–508.

Parkin, A.J. (1987). *Memory and amnesia.* Oxford: Blackwell.

Parkin, A.J. (1990). Recent advances in the neuropsychology of memory. In J. Hunter & J. Weinman (Eds.), *Mechanisms of memory: Clinical and neurochemical contributions.* London: Harwood.

Parkin, A.J. & Leng, N. (1987). Comparative studies of human amnesia: Methodological and theoretical issues. In H.J. Markowitsch (Ed.), *Information processing by the brain.* Toronto: Huber.

Patterson, K.E. (1982). The relation between reading and phonological coding: Further neuropsychological observations. In A.W. Ellis (Ed.), *Normality and pathology in cognitive functions.* London: Academic Press.

Patterson, K.E. (1988). Disorders of spelling. In G. Denes, C. Semenza, P. Bisiacchi, & E. Andreewsky

(Eds.), *Perspectives in cognitive neuropsychology*. London: Lawrence Erlbaum Associates Ltd.

Patterson, K.E. & Coltheart, V. (1987). Phonological processes in reading: A tutorial review. In M. Coltheart (Ed.), *Attention and performance, Vol. XII*. London: Lawrence Erlbaum Associates Ltd.

Pearson, P.D., Hansen, J., & Gordon, G. (1979). The effect of background knowledge on young children's comprehension of explicit and implicit information. *Journal of Reading Behaviour, 11*, 201–210.

Penfield, W. (1969). Consciousness, memory, and man's conditioned reflexes. In K. Pribram (Ed.), *On the biology of learning*. New York: Harcourt, Brace, & World.

Perfetti, C.A. (1985). *Reading ability*. Oxford: Oxford University Press.

Perrig, W.J. & Perrig, P. (1988). Mood and memory: Mood-congruity effects in absence of mood. *Memory and Cognition, 16*, 102–109.

Piaget, J. (1967). *The child's conception of the world*. Totowa, N.J.: Littlefield, Adams.

Piaget, J. (1970). Piaget's theory. In J. Mussen (Ed.), *Carmichael's manual of child psychology, Vol. 1*. New York: Basic Books.

Pinker, S. (1984). Visual cognition: An introduction. *Cognition, 18*, 1–63.

Pirolli, P.L. & Anderson, J.R. (1985). The role of learning from examples in the acquisition of recursive programming skill. *Canadian Journal of Psychology, 39*, 240–272.

Polanyi, M. (1967). *The tacit dimension*. London: Routledge & Kegan Paul.

Polivy, J. (1981). On the induction of emotion in the laboratory: Discrete moods or multiple affect states? *Journal of Personality and Social Psychology, 41*, 803–817.

Pollatsek, A., Bolozky, S., Well, A.D., & Rayner, K. (1981). Asymmetries in the perceptual span for Israeli readers. *Brain and Language, 14*, 174–180.

Polson, P. & Jeffries, R. (1982). Problem solving as search and understanding. In Sternberg, R.J. (Ed.), *Advances in the psychology of human intelligence, Vol. 1*. Hillsdale, N.J.: Lawrence Erlbaum Associates Inc.

Poltrock, S.E., Lansman, M., & Hunt, E. (1982). Automatic and controlled attention processes in auditory target detection. *Journal of Experimental Psychology: Human Perception and Performance, 8*, 37–45.

Popper, K.R. (1968). *The logic of scientific discovery*. London: Hutchinson.

Popper, K.R. (1969). *Conjectures and refutations*. London: Routledge & Kegan Paul.

Popper, K.R. (1972). *Objective knowledge*. Oxford: Oxford University Press.

Posner, M.I. & Keele, S.W. (1968). On the genesis of abstract ideas. *Journal of Experimental Psychology, 77*, 353–363.

Potter, R., Kopp, G., & Green, H. (1947). *Visible speech*. New York: Van Nostrand Reinhold.

Priest, A.G. (1986). Inference strategies in physics problem-solving. In A.G. Cohn & J.R. Thomas (Eds.), *Artificial intelligence and its applications*. Chichester: Wiley.

Pritchard, R.M. (1961). Stabilised images on the retina. *Scientific American, 204*, 72–78.

Pullman, S.G. (1987). Computational models of parsing. In A.W. Ellis (Ed.), *Progress in the psychology of language, Vol. 3*. London: Lawrence Erlbaum Associates Ltd.

Putnam, B. (1979). Hypnosis and distortions in eyewitness memory. *International Journal of Clinical and Experimental Hypnosis, 27*, 437–448.

Pylyshyn, Z. (1973). What the mind's eye tells the mind's brain. *Psychological Bulletin, 80*, 1–24.

Pylyshyn, Z. (1979). Imagery theory: Not mysterious — just wrong. *Behavioural and Brain Sciences, 2*, 561–563.

Pylyshyn, Z. (1981). The imagery debate: Analogue media versus tacit knowledge. *Psychological Review, 88*, 16–45.

Pylyshyn, Z. (1984). *Computation and cognition*. Cambridge, Mass.: M.I.T. Press.

Quillian, M.R. (1966). *Semantic memory*. Unpublished PhD Diss., Carnegie Institute of Technology, Pittsburgh, Pa.

Raaheim, K.J. (1974). *Problem solving and intelligence*. Bergen: Universitetforlaget.

Rabinowitz, J.C., Mandler, G., & Patterson, K.E. (1977). Determinants of recognition and recall: Accessibility and generation. *Journal of Experimental Psychology: General, 106*, 302–329.

Rapp, B.C. & Caramazza, A. (1989). General to specific access in word meaning: A claim re-examined. *Cognitive Neuropsychology, 6*, 251–272.

Rayner, K., Balota, D.A., & Pollatsek, A. (1986). Against parafoveal semantic preprocessing during eye fixations in reading. *Canadian Journal of Psychology, 40,* 473–483.

Rayner, K., McConkie, G.W., & Zola, D. (1980). Integrating information across eye movements. *Cognitive Psychology, 12,* 206–226.

Rayner, K. & Pollatsek, A. (1987). Eye movements in reading: A tutorial review. In M. Coltheart (Ed.), *Attention and performance, Vol. XII.* London: Lawrence Erlbaum Associates Ltd.

Rayner, K., Well, A.D., & Pollatsek, A. (1980). Asymmetry of the effective visual field in reading. *Perception and Psychophysics, 27,* 537–544.

Rayner, K., Well, A.D., Pollatsek, A., & Bertera, J.H. (1982). The availability of useful information to the right of fixation in reading. *Perception and Psychophysics, 31,* 537–550.

Reason, J.T. (1979). Actions not as planned. In G. Underwood & R. Stevens (Eds.), *Aspects of consciousness.* London: Academic Press.

Reason, J.T. & Mycielska, K. (1982). *Absent minded? The psychology of mental lapses and everyday errors.* Englewood Cliffs, N.J.: Prentice-Hall.

Reed, S.K., Ernst, G.W., & Banerji, R. (1974). The role of analogy in transfer between similar problem states. *Cognitive Psychology, 6,* 436–450.

Reich, S.S. & Ruth, P. (1982). Wason's selection task: Verification, falsification, and matching. *British Journal of Psychology, 73,* 395–405.

Reicher, G.M. (1969). Perceptual recognition as a function of meaningfulness of stimulus material. *Journal of Experimental Psychology, 81,* 274–280.

Reitman, J.S. (1974). Without surreptitious rehearsal, information in short-term memory decays. *Journal of Verbal Learning and Verbal Behaviour, 13,* 365–377.

Reitman, W. (1965). *Cognition and thought.* New York: Wiley.

Reitman, W. (1970). What does it take to remember? In D.A. Norman (Ed.), *Models of human memory.* London: Academic Press.

Repp, B.H. (1984). Categorical perception: Issues, methods and findings. In N.J. Lass (Ed.), *Speech and language: Advances in basic research and practice, Vol. 10.* New York: Academic Press.

Richardson, J.T.E. (1980). *Mental imagery and human memory.* London: Macmillan.

Riddoch, M.J. & Humphreys, G.W. (1987). Visual object processing in optic aphasia: A case of semantic access agnosia. *Cognitive Neuropsychology, 4,* 131–185.

Rips, L.J. (1983). Cognitive processes in propositional reasoning. *Psychological Review, 90,* 38–71.

Rips, L.J. (1984). Reasoning as a central intellective ability. In R.J. Sternberg (Ed.), *Advances in the study of intelligence.* Hillsdale, N.J.: Lawrence Erlbaum Associates Inc.

Rips, L.J. (1986). Mental muddles. In M. Brand & R.M. Harnish (Eds.), *Problems in the representation of knowledge and belief.* Tucson, Arizona: University of Arizona Press.

Rips, L.J. (1989). Similarity, typicality, and categorisation. In A. Ortony & S. Vosniadou (Eds.), *Similarity and analogy.* Cambridge: Cambridge University Press.

Rips, L.J. & Conrad, F.J. (1983). Individual differences in deduction. *Cognition and Brain Theory, 6,* 259–285.

Rips, L.J., Shoben, E.J., & Smith, E.E. (1973). Semantic distance and the verification of semantic relations. *Journal of Verbal Learning and Verbal Behaviour, 12,* 1–20.

Rock, I. (1973). *Orientation and form.* New York: Academic Press.

Roediger, H.L. (1980). Memory metaphors in cognitive psychology. *Memory and Cognition, 8,* 231–246.

Roediger, H.L., & Blaxton, T.A. (1987). Retrieval modes produce dissociations in memory for surface information. In D.S. Gorfein & R.R. Hoffman (Eds.), *Memory and cognitive processes: The Ebbinghaus Centennial Conference.* Hillsdale, N. J.: Lawrence Erlbaum Associates Inc.

Rogers, T.B., Kuiper, N., & Kirker, W. (1977). Self reference and the encoding of personal information. *Journal of Personality and Social Psychology, 35,* 677–688.

Rosch, E. (1973). Natural categories. *Cognitive Psychology, 4,* 328–350.

Rosch, E. (1975a). The nature of mental codes for colour categories. *Journal of Experimental Psychology: General, 104,* 192–233.

Rosch, E. (1975b). Cognitive reference points. *Cognitive Psychology, 7,* 532–547.

Rosch, E. (1978). Principles of categorisation. In E. Rosch & B.B. Lloyd (Eds.), *Cognition and categorisation.* Hillsdale, N.J.: Lawrence Erlbaum Associates Inc.

Rosch, E & Mervis, C.B. (1975). Family resemblances: Studies in the internal structure of categories. *Cognitive Psychology, 7,* 573–605.

Rosch, E, Mervis, C.B., Gray, W.D., Johnson, D.M., & Boyes-Braem, P. (1976). Basic objects in natural categories. *Cognitive Psychology, 8*, 382–439.

Rosch, E., Simpson, C., & Miller, R.S. (1976). Structural bases of typicality effects. *Journal of Experimental Psychology: Human Perception and Performance, 2*, 491–502.

Rosenblatt, F. (1959). Two theorems of statistical separability in the perceptron. In *Mechanisation of thought processes: Proceedings of a symposium held at the National Physical Laboratory, November 1958. Vol.1.* London: H.M. Stationery Office.

Rosenbloom, P. & Newell, A. (1986). The chunking of goal hierarchies: A generalised model of practice. In R.S. Michalski, J.G. Carbonell, & J.M. Mitchell (Eds.), *Machine learning II: An artificial intelligence approach.* Los Altos, Calif.: Kaufman.

Roth, I. (1986). An introduction to object perception. In I. Roth & J.P. Frisby, *Perception and representation: A cognitive approach.* Milton Keynes: Open University Press.

Rumain, B., Connell, J., & Braine, M.D.S. (1984). Conversational comprehension processes are responsible for reasoning fallacies in children as well as adults: IF is not the biconditional. *Developmental Psychology, 19*, 471–481.

Rumelhart, D.E. (1975). Notes on a schema for stories. In D.G. Bobrow & A. Collins (Eds.), *Representation and understanding: Studies in cognitive science.* New York: Academic Press.

Rumelhart, D.E. (1977). *Introduction to human information processing.* Chichester: Wiley.

Rumelhart, D.E. (1980). Schemata: The basic building blocks of cognition. In R. Spiro, B. Bruce, & W. Brewer (Eds.), *Theoretical issues in reading comprehension.* Hillsdale, N.J.: Lawrence Erlbaum Associates Inc.

Rumelhart, D.E., Hinton, G.E., & McClelland, J.L. (1986). A general framework for parallel distributed processing. In D.E. Rumelhart, J.L. McClelland, & the PDP Research Group (Eds.), *Parallel distributed processing: Vol. 1, Foundations.* Cambridge, Mass.: M.I.T. Press.

Rumelhart, D.E., McClelland, J.L., & the PDP Research Group (Eds.) (1986). *Parallel distributed processing: Vol. 1, Foundations.* Cambridge, Mass.: M.I.T. Press.

Rumelhart, D.E. & Norman, D.A. (1981). Analogical processes in learning. In J.R. Anderson (Ed.), *Cognitive skills and their acquisition.* Hillsdale, N.J.: Lawrence Erlbaum Associates Inc.

Rumelhart, D.E. & Norman, D.A. (1983). Representation in memory. In R.C. Atkinson, R.J. Herrnstein, B. Lindzey, & R.D. Luce (Eds.), *Handbook of experimental psychology.* Chichester: Wiley.

Rumelhart, D.E. & Ortony, A. (1977). The representation of knowledge in memory. In R.C. Anderson, R.J. Spiro, & W.E. Montague (Eds.), *Schooling and the acquisition of knowledge.* Hillsdale, N.J.: Lawrence Erlbaum Associates Inc.

Rumelhart, D.E., Smolensky, P., McClelland, J.L., & Hinton, G.E. (1986). Schemata and sequential thought processes in PDP models. In J.L. McClelland, D.E. Rumelhart, & the PDP Research Group (Eds.) (1986). *Parallel distributed processing: Vol. 2, Psychological and biological models.* Cambridge, Mass.: M.I.T. Press.

Rundus, D. & Atkinson, R.C. (1970). Rehearsal processes in free recall, a procedure for direct observation. *Journal of Verbal Learning and Verbal Behaviour, 9*, 99–105.

Rylander, G. (1939). Personality changes after operations on the frontal lobes. *Acta Psychologica,* Supplement No. 30.

Ryle, G. (1949). *The concept of mind.* London: Hutchinson.

Sachs, J.S. (1967). Recognition memory for syntactic and semantic aspects of connected discourse. *Perception and Psychophysics, 2*, 437–442.

Saffran, E.M., Schwartz, M.F., & Marin, O.S.M. (1980a). Evidence from aphasia: Isolating the components of a production model. In B. Butterworth (Ed.), *Language production, Vol. 1.* London: Academic Press.

Saffran, E.M., Schwartz, M.F., & Marin, O.S.M. (1980b). The word order problem in agrammatism. II. Production. *Brain and Language, 10*, 249–262.

Sanford, A.J. & Garrod, S.C. (1981). *Understanding written language.* New York: Wiley.

Scardamalia, M. & Bereiter, C. (1987). Written composition. In M. Wittrock (Ed.), *Third handbook of research on teaching.* New York: Macmillan.

Schacter, D.L. (1983). Amnesia observed: Remembering and forgetting in a natural environment. *Journal of Abnormal Psychology, 92*, 236–242.

Schachter, D.L. (1987). Implicit memory: History and current status. *Journal of Experimental*

Psychology: Learning, Memory, and Cognition, 13, 501–518.

Schachter, D.L. & Graf, P. (1986). Preserved learning in amnesic patients: Perspectives from research on direct priming. *Journal of Clinical and Experimental Neuropsychology, 8*, 727–743.

Schachter, D.L., Harbluk, J.L., & McLachlan, D.R. (1984). Retrieval without recollection: An experimental study of source amnesia. *Journal of Verbal Learning and Verbal Behaviour, 23*, 593–611.

Schank, R.C. (1972). Conceptual dependency: A theory of natural language understanding. *Cognitive Psychology, 3*, 552–631.

Schank, R.C. (1982). *Dynamic memory*. Cambridge: Cambridge University Press.

Schank, R.C. (1986). *Explanation patterns*. Hillsdale, N.J.: Lawrence Erlbaum Associates Inc.

Schank, R.C. & Abelson, R.P. (1977). *Scripts, plans, goals and understanding*. Hillsdale, N.J.: Lawrence Erlbaum Associates Inc.

Schare, M.L., Lisman, S.A., & Spear, N.E. (1984). The effects of mood variation on state-dependent retention. *Cognitive Therapy and Research, 8*, 387–408.

Scheerer, M. (1963). Problem-solving. *Scientific American, 208*, (4), 118–128.

Schlesinger, I.M. (1968). *Sentence structure and the reading process*. The Hague: Mouton.

Schneider, W. & Fisk, A.D. (1982). Concurrent automatic and controlled visual search: Can processing occur without resource cost? *Journal of Experimental Psychology: Learning, Memory, and Cognition, 8*, 261–278.

Schneider, W. & Fisk, A.D. (1984). Automatic category search and its transfer. *Journal of Experimental Psychology: Learning, Memory, and Cognition, 10*, 1–15.

Schneider, W. & Shiffrin, R.M. (1977). Controlled and automatic human information processing: 1. Detection, search, and attention. *Psychological Review, 84*, 1–66.

Schneider, W. & Shiffrin, R.M. (1985). Categorisation (restructuring) and automatisation: Two separable factors. *Psychological Review, 92*, 424–428.

Schriver, K. (1984). *Revised computer documentation for comprehension: Ten lessons in protocol-aided revision* (Tech. Rep. No. 14). Pittsburgh, Penn.: Carnegie Mellon University, Communication Design Centre.

Schwartz, M.F., Marin, O.S.M., & Saffran, E.M. (1979). Dissociation of language function in dementia: A case study. *Brain and Language, 7*, 277–306.

Schwartz, M.F., Saffran, E.M., & Marin, O.S.M. (1980). Fractionating the reading process in dementia: Evidence for word-specific print-to-sound associations. In M. Coltheart, K.E. Patterson, & J.C. Marshall (Eds.), *Deep dyslexia*. London: Routledge.

Scoville, W.B. & Milner, B. (1957). Loss of recent memory after bilateral hippocampal lesions. *Journal of Neurology, Neurosurgery, and Psychiatry, 20*, 11–21.

Seamon, J.G., March, R.L., & Brody, N. (1984). Critical importance of exposure duration for affective discrimination of stimuli that are not recognised. *Journal of Experimental Psychology: Learning, Memory, and Cognition, 10*, 465–469.

Searle, J. (1989). *Minds, brains, and science*. Harmondsworth: Penguin.

Segal, S.J. & Fusella, V. (1970). Influence of imaged pictures and sounds on detection of visual and auditory signals. *Journal of Experimental Psychology, 83*, 458–464.

Segal, Z.V. & Shaw, B.F. (1986). Cognition in depression: A reappraisal of Coyne and Gotlib's critique. *Cognitive Therapy and Research, 10*, 671–694.

Seifert, C.M. & Black, J.B. (1983). Thematic connections between episodes. *Proceedings of the Fifth Annual Conference of the Cognitive Science Society*. Rochester, New York: Cognitive Science Society.

Seifert, C.M., McKoon, G., Abelson, R.P., & Ratcliff, R. (1986). Memory connections between thematically similar episodes. *Journal of Experimental Psychology: Learning, Memory, and Cognition, 12*, 220–231.

Sejnowski, T.J. & Rosenberg, C.R. (1987). Parallel networks that learn to pronounce English text. *Complex Systems, 1*, 145–168.

Shaffer, L.H. (1975). Multiple attention in continuous verbal tasks. In P.M.A. Rabbitt and S. Dornic (Eds.), *Attention and performance, Vol. V*. London: Academic Press.

Shallice, T. (1979). Case study approach in neuropsychological research. *Journal of Clinical Neuropsychology, 1*, 183–211.

Shallice, T. (1981). Phonological agraphia and the lexical route in writing. *Brain, 104,* 413–429.

Shallice, T. (1982). Specific impairments of planning. *Philosophical Transactions of the Royal Society of London, B 298,* 199–209.

Shallice, T. (1988). *From neuropsychology to mental structure.* Cambridge: Cambridge University Press.

Shallice, T. & Butterworth, B. (1977). Short-term memory impairment and spontaneous speech. *Neuropsychologia, 15,* 729–735.

Shallice, T. & Warrington, E.K. (1970). Independent functioning of verbal memory stores: A neuropsychological study. *Quarterly Journal of Experimental Psychology, 22,* 261–273.

Shallice, T. & Warrington, E.K. (1974). The dissociation between long-term retention of meaningful sounds and verbal material. *Neuropsychologia, 12,* 553–555.

Shallice, T. & Warrington, E.K. (1980). Single and multiple component central dyslexic syndromes. In M. Coltheart, K.E. Patterson, & J. C. Marshall (Eds.), *Deep dyslexia.* London: Routledge & Kegan Paul.

Shannon, C.E., & Weaver, W. (1949). *The mathematical theory of communication.* Urbana, Il.: University of Illinois Press.

Shapiro, M.B., Campbell, D., Harris, A., & Dewsberry, J.P. (1958). Effects of E.C.T. upon psychomotor speed and the "distraction effect" in depressed psychiatric patients. *Journal of Mental Science, 104,* 681–695.

Shepard, R.N. (1978). The mental image. *The American Psychologist, 33,* 125–137.

Shepard, R.N. & Metzler, J. (1971). Mental rotation of three-dimensional objects. *Science, 191,* 701–703.

Shepp, B.E., Burns, B., & McDonough, D. (1980). The relation of stimulus structure to perceptual and cognitive development: Further tests of a separability hypothesis. In F. Wilkering, J. Becker, & T. Trabasso (Eds.), *The integration of information by children.* Hillsdale, N.J.: Lawrence Erlbaum Associates Inc.

Shiffrin, R.M., Dumais, S.T., & Schneider, W. (1981). Characteristics of automatism. In J. Long and A. Baddeley (Eds.), *Attention and performance, Vol IX.* Hillsdale, N.J.: Lawrence Erlbaum Associates Inc.

Shiffrin, R.M. & Schneider, W. (1977). Controlled and automatic human information processing: II. Perceptual learning, automatic attending, and a general theory. *Psychological Review, 84,* 127–190.

Shinamura, A.P. & Squire, L.R. (1986). Memory and metamemory: A study of the feeling-of-knowing phenomenon in amnesic patients. *Journal of Experimental Psychology: Learning, Memory, and Cognition, 12,* 452–460.

Simon, H.A. (1973). The structure of ill-structured problems. *Artificial Intelligence, 4,* 181–201.

Simon, H.A. (1974). How big is a chunk? *Science, 183,* 482–488.

Simon, H.A. (1978). Information-processing theory of human problem solving. In W.K. Estes (Ed.), *Handbook of learning and cognitive processes: Vol. 5.* Hillsdale, N.J.: Lawrence Erlbaum Associates Inc.

Simon, H.A. (1980). Cognitive science: The newest science of the artificial. *Cognitive Science, 4,* 33–46.

Simon, H.A. & Barenfeld, M. (1969). Information processing analysis of perceptual processes in problem solving. *Psychological Review, 76,* 473–483.

Simon, H.A. & Gilmartin, K. (1973). A simulation of memory for chess positions. *Cognitive Psychology, 5,* 29–46.

Simon, H.A. & Hayes, J.R. (1976). The understanding process: Problem isomorphs. *Cognitive Psychology, 8,* 165–190.

Simon, H.A. & Reed, S.K. (1976). Modelling strategy shifts on a problem solving task. *Cognitive Psychology, 8,* 86–97.

Singley, M.K. & Anderson, J.R. (in press). The transfer of text editing skill. *International Journal of Man-Machine Studies.*

Skinner, B.F. (1971). *Beyond freedom and dignity.* London: Pelican Books.

Smith, E.E. (1978). Theories of semantic memory. In W.K. Estes (Ed.), *Handbook of learning and cognitive processes: Vol. 6.* Hillsdale, N.J.: Lawrence Erlbaum Associates Inc.

Smith, E.E. (1988). Concepts and thought. In R.J. Sternberg & E.E. Smith (Eds.), *The psychology of human thought.* Cambridge: Cambridge University Press.

Smith, E.E. & Medin, D.L. (1981). *Categories and concepts.* Harvard: Harvard University Press.

Smith, E.E. & Osherson, D.N. (1984). Conceptual combination with prototype concepts. *Cognitive Science, 8,* 337–361.

Smith, E.E., Osherson, D.N., Rips, L.J., Albert, K., & Keane, M. (1989). Combining prototypes: A modification model. *Cognitive Science, 12,* 485–528.

Smith, E.E., Shoben, E.J., & Rips, L.J. (1974). Structure and process in semantic memory: A featural model for semantic decisions. *Psychological Review, 81,* 214–241.

Smolensky, P. (1988). On the proper treatment of connectionism. *Behavioural and Brain Sciences, 11,* 1–74.

Smyth, M.M., Morris, P.E., Levy, P., & Ellis, A.W. (1987). *Cognition in action.* London: Lawrence Erlbaum Associates Ltd.

Soloway, E., Bonar, J., & Erlich, K. (1983). Cognitive strategies and looping constructs: An empirical study. *Communications of the A.C.M., 26,* 853–860.

Soloway, E. & Erlich, K. (1984). Empirical studies of programming knowledge. *I.E.E.E. Transactions of Software Engineering, 5,* 595–609.

Soloway, E. & Spohrer, J. (1989). *Studying the novice programmer.* Hillsdale, N.J.: Lawrence Erlbaum Associates Inc.

Solso, R.L. (1974). Theories of retrieval. In R.L. Solso (Ed.), *Theories in cognitive psychology.* Potomac, Maryland: Lawrence Erlbaum Associates Inc.

Spelke, E.S., Hirst, W.C., & Neisser, U. (1976). Skills of divided attention. *Cognition, 4,* 215–230.

Sperling, G. (1960). The information available in brief visual presentations. *Psychological Monographs, 74* (Whole No. 498), 1–29.

Spoehr, K.T. & Lehmkuhle, S.W. (1982). *Visual information processing.* San Francisco: W.H. Freeman.

Squire, L.R. (1987). *Memory and brain.* Oxford: Oxford University Press.

Squire, L.R. & Cohen, N.J. (1984). Human memory and amnesia. In J. McGaugh, G. Lynch, & N. Weinberger (Eds.), *Proceedings of the Conference on the Neurobiology of Learning and Memory.* New York: Guilford Press.

Steele, G.L. (1984). *Common Lisp.* Bedford, Mass.: Digital Press.

Stein, N.L. & Glenn, C.G. (1979). An analysis of story comprehension in elementary school children. In R. Freedle (Ed.), *Multidisciplinary perspectives in discourse comprehension.* Norwood, N.J.: Ablex.

Stemberger, J.P. (1982). The nature of segments in the lexicon: Evidence from speech errors. *Lingua, 56,* 235–259.

Sternberg, R.J. (1985). *Beyond I.Q.: A triarchic theory of human intelligence.* Cambridge: Cambridge University Press.

Sternberg, R.J. (1987). Coping with novelty and human intelligence. In P.Morris (Ed.), *Modelling cognition.* Chichester: Wiley.

Sternberg, R.J. (1988). *The nature of creativity.* Cambridge: Cambridge University Press.

Sternberg, R.J. & Davidson, J.E. (1982). Componential analysis and componential theory. *Behavioural and Brain Sciences, 53,* 352–353.

Sternberg, R.J. & Davidson, J.E. (1983). Insight in the gifted. *Educational Psychologist, 18,* 51–57.

Sternberg, R.J. & Smith, E.E. (1988). *The psychology of thinking.* Cambridge: Cambridge University Press.

Stroop, J.R. (1935). Studies of interference in serial verbal reactions. *Journal of Experimental Psychology, 18,* 643–662.

Teasdale, J.D. & Dent, J. (1987). Cognitive vulnerability to depression: An investigation of two hypotheses. *British Journal of Clinical Psychology, 26,* 113–126.

Temple, C. (1990). Developments and applications of cognitive neuropsychology. In M.W. Eysenck (Ed.), *International review of cognitive psychology.* Chichester: Wiley.

Tenebaum, J.M., Witkin, A.P., & Wandell, B.A. (1983). Review of "Vision: A computational investigation into the human representation and processing of visual information" by D. Marr. *Contemporary Psychology, 28,* 583–584.

Teuber, H.-L., Milner, B., & Vaughan, H.G. (1968). Persistent anterograde amnesia after stab wound of the basal brain. *Neuropsychologia, 6*, 267–282.

Thagard, P. (1984). Conceptual combination and scientific discovery. In P. Asquith & P. Kitcher (Eds.), *P.S.A. Vol.1*. East Lansing, Missouri: Philosophy of Science Association.

Thagard, P. (1989). Explanatory coherence. *Behavioural and Brain Sciences, 12*, 435–502.

Thomas, J.C. (1974). An analysis of behaviour in the hobbits–orcs problem. *Cognitive Psychology, 6*, 257–269.

Thomson, D.M. & Tulving, E. (1970). Associative encoding and retrieval: Weak and strong cues. *Journal of Experimental Psychology, 86*, 255–262.

Thorndike, E.L. (1911). *Animal intelligence*. New York: Macmillan.

Thorndyke, P.W. (1976). The role of inferences in discourse comprehension. *Journal of Verbal Learning and Verbal Behaviour, 15*, 437–446.

Thorndyke, P.W. (1977). Cognitive structures in comprehension and memory of narrative discourse. *Cognitive Psychology, 9*, 77–110.

Thorndyke, P.W. & Yekovich, F.R. (1980). A critique of schema-based theories of human memory. *Poetics, 9*, 23–49.

Tolkien, J.R.R. (1966). *The hobbit* (3rd Ed.). London: Allen & Unwin.

Tolman, E.C. (1932). *Purposive behaviour in animals and men*. New York: Appleton-Century-Crofts.

Treisman, A.M. (1964). Verbal cues, language, and meaning in selective attention. *American Journal of Psychology, 77*, 206–219.

Treisman, A.M. (1988). Features and objects: The 14th Bartlett Memorial Lecture. *Quarterly Journal of Experimental Psychology, 40A*, 201–237.

Treisman, A.M. & Davies, A. (1973). Divided attention to ear and eye. In S. Kornblum (Ed.), *Attention and performance: Vol. IV*. London: Academic Press.

Treisman, A.M. & Geffen, G. (1967). Selective attention: Perception or response? *Quarterly Journal of Experimental Psychology, 19*, 1–18.

Treisman, A.M. & Gelade, G. (1980). A feature-integration theory of attention. *Cognitive Psychology, 12*, 97–136.

Treisman, A.M. & Riley, J.G.A. (1969). Is selective attention selective perception or selective response: A further test. *Journal of Experimental Psychology, 79*, 27–34.

Treisman, A.M. & Schmidt, H. (1982). Illusory conjunctions in the perception of objects. *Cognitive Psychology, 14*, 107–141.

Tulving, E. (1972). Episodic and semantic memory. In E. Tulving & W. Donaldson (Eds.), *Organisation of memory*. London: Academic Press.

Tulving, E. (1974). Cue-dependent forgetting. *American Scientist, 62*, 74–82.

Tulving, E. (1979). Relation between encoding specificity and levels of processing. In L.S. Cermak and F.I.M. Craik (Eds.), *Levels of processing in human memory*. Hillsdale, N.J.: Lawrence Erlbaum Associates Inc.

Tulving, E. (1982). Synergistic ecphory in recall and recognition. *Canadian Journal of Psychology, 36*, 130–147.

Tulving, E. (1983). *Elements of episodic memory*. Oxford: Oxford University Press.

Tulving, E. (1989). Memory: Performance, knowledge, and experience. *The European Journal of Cognitive Psychology, 1*, 3–26.

Tulving, E. & Thomson, D.M. (1971). Retrieval processes in recognition memory: Effects of associative context. *Journal of Experimental Psychology, 87*, 116–124.

Tulving, E. & Thomson, D.M. (1973). Encoding specificity and retrieval processes in episodic memory. *Psychological Review, 80*, 353–373.

Tulving, E., Mandler, G., & Baumal, R. (1964). Interaction of two sources of information in tachistoscopic word recognition. *Canadian Journal of Psychology, 18*, 62–71.

Turing, A. (1950). Computing machinery and intelligence. *Mind, 59*, 433–460.

Tversky, A. (1977). Features of similarity. *Psychological Review, 84*, 327–352.

Tversky, A. & Kahneman, D. (1974). Judgement under uncertainty: Heuristics and biases. *Science, 125*, 1124–1131.

Tversky, A. & Kahneman, D. (1980). Causal schemas in judgements under uncertainty. In M. Fishbein (Ed.), *Progress in social psychology*. Hillsdale, N.J.: Lawrence Erlbaum Associates Inc.

Ullman, S. (1980). Against direct perception. *Behavioural and Brain Sciences, 3*, 373–415.

Underwood, G. (1974). Moray vs. the rest: The effects of extended shadowing practice. *Quarterly Journal of Experimental Psychology, 26*, 368–372.

Underwood, G. (1977). Contextual facilitation from attended and unattended messages. *Journal of Verbal Learning and Verbal Behaviour, 16*, 99–106.

Vallar, G. & Baddeley, A. (1984). Phonological short-term store, phonological processing, and sentence comprehension: A neuropsychological case study. *Cognitive Neuropsychology, 1*, 121–141.

Van Dijk, T.A. & Kintsch, W. (1983). *Strategies of discourse comprehension*. London: Academic Press.

Vaughn, J. (1984). *Distance of attention switch affects R.T. only for some stimuli*. Presented at Annual Meeting of the Psychonomic Society, San Antonio.

Velten, E. (1968). A laboratory task for induction of mood states. *Behaviour Research and Therapy, 6*, 473–482.

Von Restorff, H. (1933). Über die Wirkung von Bereichsbildungen im Spurenfeld. In W. Köhler & H. von Restorff, Analyse von Vorgängen im Spurenfeld, I. *Psychologische Forschung, 18*, 299–342.

Von Senden, M. (1932). *Space and sight: The perception of space and shape in the congenitally blind before and after operation* (translated by P. Heath). London: Methuen.

Von Wright, J.M., Anderson, K., & Stenman, U. (1975). Generalisation of conditioned G.S.R.s in dichotic listening. In P.M.A. Rabbitt & S. Dornic (Eds.), *Attention and performance: Vol. V*. London: Academic Press.

Wagner, D.A. & Scurrah, M.J. (1971). Some characteristics of human problem solving in chess. *Cognitive Psychology, 2*, 451–478.

Walker, C.H. & Yekovich, F.R. (1984). Script-based inferences: Effects of text and knowledge variables on recognition memory. *Journal of Verbal Learning and Verbal Behaviour, 23*, 357–370.

Walker, J.H. (1975). Real-world variability, reasonableness judgements, and memory representations for concepts. *Journal of Verbal Learning and Verbal Behaviour, 14*, 241–252.

Wallace, A.F.C & Atkins, J.R. (1960). The meaning of kinship terms. *American Anthropologist, 62*, 58–80.

Wallas, G. (1926). *The art of thought*. London: Cape.

Warren, R.M. & Warren, R.P. (1970). Auditory illusions and confusions. *Scientific American, 223*, 30–36.

Warrington, E.K. (1975). The selective impairment of semantic memory. *Quarterly Journal of Experimental Psychology, 27*, 635–657.

Warrington, E.K. & Shallice, T. (1972). Neuropsychological evidence of visual storage in short-term memory tasks. *Quarterly Journal of Experimental Psychology, 24*, 30–40.

Warrington, E.K. & Shallice, T. (1984). Category-specific semantic impairments. *Brain, 107*, 829–853.

Warrington, E.K. & Taylor, A.M. (1978). Two categorical stages of object recognition. *Perception, 7*, 695–705.

Wason, P.C. (1966). Reasoning. In B.M. Foss (Ed.), *New horizons in psychology*. Harmondsworth: Penguin.

Wason, P.C. & Evans, J.St.B.T. (1975). Dual processes in reasoning? *Cognition, 3*, 141–154.

Wason, P.C. & Johnson-Laird, P.N. (1972). *The psychology of reasoning: Structure and content*. Cambridge, Mass.: Harvard University Press.

Wason, P.C. & Shapiro, D. (1971). Natural and contrived experience in a reasoning problem. *Quarterly Journal of Experimental Psychology, 23*, 63–71.

Watkins, M.J. (1973). When is recall spectacularly higher than recognition? *Journal of Experimental Psychology, 102*, 161–163.

Watkins, M.J. & Gardiner, J.M. (1979). An appreciation of generate–recognise theory of recall. *Journal of Verbal Learning and Verbal Behaviour, 18*, 687–704.

Waugh, N.C. & Norman, D. (1965). Primary memory. *Psychological Review, 72*, 89–104.

Weinreich, U. (1966). Explorations in semantic theory. In T. Seboek (Ed.), *Current trends in linguistics: Vol. 3*. The Hague: Mouton.

Weisberg, R.W. (1980). *Memory, thought and behaviour*. Oxford: Oxford University Press.

Weisberg, R.W. & Alba, J.W. (1981). An examination of the alleged role of "fixation" in the solution of several insight problems. *Journal of Experimental Psychology: General, 110*, 169–192.

Weisberg, R.W. & Suls, J. (1973). An information-processing model of Duncker's candle problem. *Cognitive Psychology, 4*, 255–276.

Weiskrantz, L. (1980). Varieties of residual experience. *Quarterly Journal of Experimental Psychology, 32*, 365–386.

Weiskrantz, L. (1985). Issues and theories in the study of the amnesic syndrome. In N.M. Weinberger, J.L. McGaugh, & G. Lynch (Eds.), *Memory systems of the brain*. New York: Guilford Press.

Weiskrantz, L. (1986). *Blindsight: A case study and its implications*. Oxford: Oxford University Press.

Weiskrantz, L. (1990). Blindsight. In M.W. Eysenck (Ed.), *The Blackwell dictionary of cognitive psychology*. Oxford: Blackwell.

Weisstein, N. & Harris, C.S. (1974). Visual detection of line segments: An object-superiority effect. *Science, 186*, 752–755.

Wertheimer, M. (1958). *Productive thinking* (2nd Edition). New York: Harper & Row.

Wetzler, S. (1985). Mood state-dependent retrieval: A failure to replicate. *Psychological Reports, 56*, 759–765.

Whorf, B.L. (1956). *Language, thought, and reality*. Cambridge, Mass.: M.I.T. Press.

Wickelgren, W.A. (1968). Sparing of short-term memory in an amnesic patient: Implications for strength theory of memory. *Neuropsychologia, 6*, 235–244.

Wickens, C.D. (1984). Processing resources in attention. In R. Parasuraman & D.R. Davies (Eds.), *Varieties of attention*. London: Academic Press.

Wilensky, R. (1983). *Planning and understanding: A computational approach to human reasoning*. Massachusetts: Addison-Wesley.

Wilkins, M.C. (1928). The effect of changed material on the ability to do formal syllogistic reasoning. *Archives of Psychology, 16*, no. 102.

Wilkinson, D.A. & Carlen, P.L. (1982). Chronic organic brain syndromes associated with alcoholism: Neuropsychological and other aspects. In Y. Israel et al. (Eds.), *Research advances in alcohol and drug problems: Vol. 6*. New York: Plenum.

Wilkinson, I.M. & Blackburn, J.M. (1981). Cognitive style in depressed and recovered depressed patients. *British Journal of Clinical Psychology, 20*, 283–292.

Williams, J.M.G. & Broadbent, K. (1986). Autobiographical memory in suicide attempters. *Journal of Abnormal Psychology, 95*, 144–149.

Williams, J.M.G., Watts, F.N., MacLeod, C., & Mathews, A. (1987). *Cognitive psychology and emotional disorders*. Chichester: Wiley.

Winston, P.H. & Horn, K. (1988). *LISP* (3rd Edn.). London: Addison-Wesley.

Wiseman, S. & Tulving, E. (1976). Encoding specificity: Relations between recall superiority and recognition failure. *Journal of Experimental Psychology: Human Learning and Memory, 2*, 349–361.

Wittgenstein, L. (1958). *Philosophical investigations* (2nd Edn.). Oxford: Blackwell.

Woodworth, R.S. & Sells, S.B. (1935). An atmosphere effect in formal syllogistic reasoning. *Journal of Experimental Psychology, 18*, 451–460.

Yates, F.A. (1966). *The art of memory*. London: Routledge & Kegan Paul.

Young, A.W. & Ellis, H.D. (1988). Childhood prosopagnosia. *Brain and Cognition, 9*, 16–47.

Young, A.W., Hay, D.C., & Ellis, A.W. (1985). The faces that launched a thousand slips: Everyday difficulties and errors in recognising people. *British Journal of Psychology, 76*, 495–523.

Young, A.W., McWeeny, K.H., Ellis, A.W., & Hay, D.C. (1986a). Naming and categorisation latencies for faces and written names. *Quarterly Journal of Experimental Psychology, 38A*, 297–318.

Young, A.W., McWeeny, K.H., Hay, D.C., & Ellis, A.W. (1986b). Access to identity-specific semantic codes from familiar faces. *Quarterly Journal of Experimental Psychology, 38A*, 587–603.

Zadeh, L.(1982). A note on prototype theory and fuzzy sets. *Cognition, 12*, 291–297.

Zajonc, R.B. (1980). Feeling and thinking: Preferences need no inferences. *American Psychologist, 35*, 151–175.

Zajonc, R.B. (1984). On the primacy of affect. *American Psychologist, 39*, 117–123.

Zola-Morgan, S., Cohen, N.J., & Squire, L.R. (1983). Recall of remote episodic memory in amnesia. *Neuropsychologia, 21*, 487–500.

REFERENCE NOTES

1. Anderson, J.R. (1988). *A theory of the origins of human knowledge.* Unpublished manuscript. Department of Psychology, Carnegie-Mellon University.
2. Eysenck, M.W., Mogg, K., Richards, A., & Mathews, A. *Interpretation of ambiguity related to threat in anxiety.* Submitted manuscript.
3. Hampton, J.A. (1983) *A composite prototype model of conceptual conjunction.* Unpublished manuscript. The City University, London.
4. Hintzman, D.L. (1983). *"Schema abstraction" in a multiple-trace memory model.* Paper presented at the Conference on the Priority of the Specific. Elora, Ontario, June 1983.
5. Johnson-Laird, P.N. (1988). *Semantic information: A framework for induction.* Mimeo, MRC Applied Psychology Unit, Cambridge.
6. Johnson-Laird, P.N., Byrne, R.M.J., Schaeken, W. (1989). *Reasoning by model: The case of propositional reasoning.* Mimeo, MRC Applied Psychology Unit, Cambridge.
7. Mathews, A., May, J., Mogg, K., & Eysenck, M.W. (Submitted). *Attentional bias in anxiety: Selective search or defective filtering?*
8. Monaco, G.E. (1976). *Construction as a storage phenomenon.* Unpublished M. A. thesis, Kansas State University.
9. Vaughan, J.T. (1985). *Hoping and commanding: Prototype semantics demonstrated.* Unpublished B.A. thesis, Dept. of Psychology, Trinity College, Dublin, Ireland.

AUTHOR INDEX

SUBJECT INDEX